# The Psychology of Religion and Spirituality for Clinicians

# The Psychology of Religion and Spirituality for Clinicians

## Using Research in Your Practice

Edited by
JAMIE D. ATEN, KARI A. O'GRADY,
AND EVERETT L. WORTHINGTON, JR.

Routledge
Taylor & Francis Group
New York London

Routledge
Taylor & Francis Group
711 Third Avenue
New York, NY 10017

Routledge
Taylor & Francis Group
27 Church Road
Hove, East Sussex BN3 2FA



International Standard Book Number: 978-0-415-87343-7 (Hardback)



**Library of Congress Cataloging-in-Publication Data**

The psychology of religion and spirituality for clinicians : using research in your practice / [edited by] Jamie D. Aten, Kari A. O'Grady, Everett L. Worthington, Jr.
p. cm.
Includes bibliographical references and index.
ISBN 978-0-415-87343-7 (hardback)
1. Spirituality--Psychological aspects. 2. Psychology and religion. 3. Psychology--Religious aspects. I. Aten, Jamie D. II. O'Grady, Kari A., 1969- III. Worthington, Everett L., 1946-

BF51.P78 2011
200.1'9--dc23 2011023048

**Visit the Taylor & Francis Web site at**
**http://www.taylorandfrancis.com**

**and the Routledge Web site at**
**http://www.routledgementalhealth.com**

*To Dr. Michele C. Boyer—my graduate school major professor and mentor—thank you for encouraging me to pursue my interest in the psychology of religion during a time when the topic was still less than popular. I am grateful to have had the opportunity to be your student and opportunity to continue to learn from you. Thank you for all the time and energy you invested in my training and for doing so for all those that passed through the doors of the department at Indiana State University under your leadership.*

**Jamie D. Aten**

*To Dr. P. Scott Richards, who first introduced me to the psychology of religion and spirituality and mentored me throughout most of my graduate studies. Thank you for training me how to research and integrate the psychology of religion and spirituality into practice. I am grateful for your thoughtful guidance and for your example of outstanding scholarship. Your pioneering efforts helped move the field forward and shape it into what it is today.*

**Kari A. O'Grady**

*To the many pioneers who, early on, applied the scientific findings in the psychology of religion and spirituality into clinical practice. Among those, Allen Bergin, Ed Shafranske, Siang-Yang Tan, Larry Beutler, Len Sperry, Jon Carlson, Bill Miller, and Mark McMinn exemplify that frontier spirit.*

**Everett L. Worthington, Jr.**

# *Contents*

# *Editors*

**Jamie D. Aten, PhD (Indiana State University),** is currently the Dr. Arthur P. Rech and Mrs. Jean May Rech Associate Professor of Psychology and the Co-Director of the Humanitarian Disaster Institute at Wheaton College. He also maintains a small clinical private practice. He has published numerous journal articles on the psychology of religion and spirituality. He is the coeditor of three books, including *Spirituality and the Therapeutic Process* (APA, 2009), *Culture and the Therapeutic Process* (Routledge, 2009), and *Spiritually Oriented Interventions for Counseling and Psychotherapy* (APA, 2011). He has received more than $1 million in external funding over the last 5 years for his work on the psychology of religion and disasters. He served as the newsletter editor for Division 36 (Psychology of Religion) of the American Psychological Association and has been awarded the Margaret Gorman Early Career Award by the division. He has also been appointed to the Faith-Based Learning Collaborative for decreasing health disparities sponsored by the Substance Abuse and Mental Health Services Administration.

**Kari A. O'Grady, PhD (Brigham Young University),** is currently an assistant professor at Loyola University Maryland, primarily affiliated with the Council for the Accreditation of Counseling and Related Educational Programs (CACREP)-accredited doctoral program in pastoral counseling. She serves on the multicultural research committee and as acting director of the certificate in spirituality and trauma program. She served as the American Psychological Association Division 36's first student representative and currently is the chair of the Division 36 early career professional task force. She is the coauthor of several publications and presentations on the topics of spirituality, psychotherapy, and multiculturalism, including treating the religiously committed client (*Psychologists' Desk Reference, 2nd ed.* [Oxford University Press, 2004]), theistic psychotherapy and god image (*The God Image Handbook: Research, Theory, and Practice* [Haworth Press, 2007]), spirituality and therapeutic process case study (*Spirituality and the Therapeutic Process: A Guide for Mental Health Professionals* [APA, 2009]), and inspiration ("The Role of Inspiration in the Helping Professions," *Psychology* *of Religion and Spirituality*, 2010]). Her doctoral dissertation examined scientists' and health professionals' beliefs and experiences regarding inspiration in research and practice. She also maintains a small faith-based private clinical practice.

**Everett L. Worthington, Jr., PhD (University of Missouri–Columbia),** is a professor of psychology at the Virginia Commonwealth University (since 1978), where he primarily works with the American Psychological Association-accredited program in counseling psychology and secondarily with three other programs—social, developmental, and health psychology programs. He has served as director of training of counseling psychology and as chair of the Department of Psychology. He was the 2010 Past President for Division 36 of the American Psychological Association (Psychology of Religion). He has authored or coauthored more than 20 books and edited or coedited 4 scholarly volumes and several special issues of journals. He also has published more than 250 refereed articles and chapters. In 2003, he won the Virginia Sexton Mentoring Award from Division 36 APA, and he has won the top awards in both the American Association of Christian Counseling and the Christian Association for Psychological Studies. He has helped numerous people conduct research on forgiveness in his past role (1998–2005) as the executive director of A Campaign for Forgiveness Research. In 2009, he won Virginia Commonwealth University's top award, the University Award for Excellence (in research, teaching, and service). He is a licensed clinical psychologist in Virginia, where he has maintained an active license since 1982.

# *Contributors*

**Jonathan M. Adler**
Franklin W. Olin College of Engineering
Needham, Massachusetts

**Jeremy D. Bartz**
Primary Care Integration Program
Veterans Affairs Caribbean Healthcare System
Ponce, Puerto Rico

**Don E. Davis**
Georgia State University
Atlanta, Georgia

**Edward B. Davis**
Rosemead School of Psychology
Biola University
La Mirada, California

**Alethea Desrosiers**
Teachers College
Columbia University
New York, New York

**Michele Dillon**
Department of Sociology
University of New Hampshire
Durham, New Hampshire

**Aubrey L. Garnter**
Department of Psychology
Virginia Commonwealth University
Richmond, Virginia

**Chelsea L. Greer**
Department of Psychology
Virginia Commonwealth University
Richmond, Virginia

**Todd W. Greer**
School of Global Leadership and Entrepreneurship
Regent University
Virginia Beach, Virginia

**Peter C. Hill**
Department of Psychology
Rosemead School of Psychology
Biola University
La Mirada, California

**Joshua N. Hook**
Department of Psychology
University of North Texas
Denton, Texas

**Stephanie A. Hooker**
Department of Psychology
University of Colorado Denver
Denver, Colorado

**David J. Jennings, II**
Department of Psychology
Virginia Commonwealth University
Richmond, Virginia

**Whitney Keltner**
Department of Psychology
Luther College
Decorah, Iowa

**Elizabeth J. Krumrei**
Social Science Division
Pepperdine University
Malibu, California

**Kevin S. Masters**
Department of Psychology
University of Colorado Denver
Denver, Colorado

**Andrea J. Miller**
Department of Psychology and Sociology
Georgia Southwestern State University
Americus, Georgia

**Glendon L. Moriarty**
School of Psychology and Counseling
Regent University
Virginia Beach, Virginia

**Aaron B. Murray-Swank**
Veterans Affairs Medical Center
Washington, District of Columbia
and
Department of Psychiatry and Behavioral Sciences
Howard University School of Medicine
Washington, District of Columbia

**Nichole A. Murray-Swank**
Pastoral Counseling Department
Loyola University
Baltimore, Maryland

**Crystal L. Park**
Department of Psychology
University of Connecticut
Storrs, Connecticut

**David H. Rosmarin**
Department of Psychiatry
McLean Hospital/Harvard Medical School
Belmont, Massachusetts

**Steven J. Sandage**
Bethel University
St. Paul, Minnesota

**Jeanne M. Slattery**
Department of Psychology
Clarion University
Clarion, Pennsylvania

**Evonne Smith**
Department of Psychology
Rosemead School of Psychology
Biola University
La Mirada, California

**Loren Toussaint**
Department of Psychology
Luther College
Decorah, Iowa

**Daryl R. Van Tongeren**
Department of Psychology
Virginia Commonwealth University
Richmond, Virginia

**Jon R. Webb**
Department of Psychology
East Tennessee State University
Johnson City, Tennessee

**Marsha I. Wiggins**
University of Colorado Denver
(retired)
Denver, Colorado

**Paul Wink**
Department of Psychology
Wellesley College
Wellesley, Massachusetts

# 1

# *The Psychology of Religion and Spirituality for Clinicians*

## An Introduction

Jamie D. Aten, Kari A. O'Grady, and
Everett L. Worthington, Jr.

Perhaps you have a number of clients who are explicitly religious. Perhaps these clients even want you to deal with religious issues. Or maybe you have a number of clients who report not being religious, but they keep bringing up spiritual themes. Even if you are religious or spiritual in your personal orientation, you might find it daunting to deal with these overtly religious clients, or clients exploring spiritual issues, who might have many different beliefs, values, and practices from your own. You might think of turning to a good book on the psychology of religion and spirituality to supplement your knowledge and equip you to deal with religious issues you are not informed or certain about. But, as you heft the books or peruse an online store, you think, "It's just too much information. I can't process all of this. And any way, most of it is very, well, scientific. It isn't directly related to my clinical practice and applied issues."

In this book, we try to save you time and heartache in finding, digesting, and applying relevant issues from the psychology of religion and spirituality for your clinical practice. We asked experts on topics of the psychology of religion and spirituality to digest the information for you. Instead of wading through a tome of scientifically worded studies or summaries of studies, you can read through the chapters of this book with relative ease. Moreover, the authors have thought through many clinical issues and provide practical applications of these issues by illustrating them with case examples. You can obtain the equivalent of many hours of training and reading in this single volume, written accessibly to enable you to immediately apply the information to your practice. Users of this volume can be assured that the lessons learned are grounded strongly in solid research.

## A BIT OF HISTORICAL CONTEXT THAT POINTS TO THE NEED FOR THIS BOOK

### Personal Histories of the Editors

Each of the editors of this volume completed their graduate education in psychology at distinct times related to the psychology of religion and spirituality under the larger historical umbrella of psychology. Worthington completed graduate study during a period when religion was talked about only rarely, and if addressed, it often was done so negatively. Aten finished during a period when religion began to gain acceptance in the larger field of psychology by broadening the discussion to include spirituality. O'Grady ended her graduate studies during a period when religion and spirituality truly began to boom.

Overall, a lot has changed in the last 30 years. Religion and spirituality are no longer on the *fringe* or considered *taboo* within the larger field of psychology. In fact, research on the psychology of religion and spirituality has surged, and according to many influential voices in the field, religion and spirituality represent one of the five major forces in modern psychology (e.g., Standard, Sandhu, & Painter, 2000).

### Psychology of Religion (and Spirituality): Past, Present, and Future

For those versed in the history of psychology of religion and spirituality, this recent wellspring in interest and growth comes as no surprise. Although often overlooked, some of the earliest contributions to the field of psychology grew out of religious movements, religious orders, or religious experiences. For example, in 1902, William James (1961), one of the ancestors of psychology, penned the classic *The Varieties of Religious Experience*. James recognized the important role that faith played in many people's lives and brought a scientific lens to studying religious phenomena. During the early 1900s, the Emmanuel Movement also spread across the United States. This movement consisted of collaborations between medicine and the church, with the goal of providing medical and religious education and counseling. What started as a project to address poverty in the greater Boston area turned into a national movement that attempted to unite the best that psychology and piety had to offer at the time, with the hope of providing holistic treatment for the entire person (Caplan, 1998).

Over the next 100 years, many others would follow in the steps of such pioneering thinkers and clinicians. For instance, influential clinical figures, such as former Freudian analyst Carl Jung (1938) and Holocaust survivor and psychiatrist Victor Frankl (1962), made significant contributions that added to the psychology of religion. Yet, on the whole, matters of faith often were depicted in a negative light, as religion was thought by some to be the root of most negative mental health issues. Freud played a major role in ushering in this negative view of religion, beginning with a series of lectures at Clark University that helped to give birth to psychoanalysis in the United States, and within that early message of psychoanalysis, a disdain for religion was spread. This negative conceptualization of religion and mental health would continue and appear almost unquestioned by most clinicians for decades (Blazer, 1998). For instance, other advocates outside of psychoanalysis, such as behaviorist B. F. Skinner and rational emotive behavioral therapist Albert Ellis (Brown & Srebalus, 1996), eventually would emerge who continued to carry the torch that Freud had lit, fueled with a depressing view of religion that would last through the 1970s and into the 1980s.

Despite the apparent historic lack of acceptance of religion within applied psychology (e.g., clinical psychology, counseling psychology) through the 1980s, the psychology of religion movement had been embraced early on primarily by personality and social psychologists. This is not to minimize integral contributions from developmentalists, cognitive psychologists, or health researchers. Applied researchers also have contributed to the psychology of religion, but on the whole, it was the experimental side of psychology that laid the vast majority of the foundation for the psychology of religion. Major contributions by past experimental psychologists like Gordon Allport (1950) to present-day personality psychologists like Robert Emmons (2003) have played a major role in the evolution and sustainability of this subspecialty.

Still, even during periods when most of psychology seemed to be resisting the study of religion (and its inclusion as a psychological subdiscipline), discussions about how religion and spirituality might be integrated into psychotherapy were occurring. For example, during the late 1930s and early 1940s, individuals like Rollo May and organizations like the American Association of Marital and Family Therapists opened the dialogue on existential issues and encouraged conversations between secular therapists and pastoral counselors (Worthington, 2010).

During the 1950s, former seminary student turned psychologist Carl Rogers (1951) began to question the notion that psychotherapy was a value-free endeavor. According to Rogers, psychotherapy was a phenomenological experience, and he advocated for a value-neutral approach. Despite the overall resistance to religion and spirituality held by the larger field of psychology, the writings of Rodgers further ushered in the pastoral counseling movement and sparked interest among religious clinicians to delve more deeply into the psychological sciences. Moreover, during this period, several new professional organizations like the Christian Association for Psychological Studies were formed. Likewise, special interest groups and divisions of the American Counseling Association and American Psychological Association devoted to religious issues also were founded (Vande Kemp, 1996).

In the 1960s and 1970s, an increasing number of both mental health professionals and clients were beginning to more strongly voice a need for religion to be addressed in psychotherapy. As a result, several religious doctoral programs began emerging, most from a Christian faith tradition (e.g., Fuller Theological Seminary, Rosemead School of Psychology). These programs were interested in exploring how faith and psychology might be integrated into the therapeutic process (Aten & Leach, 2008). Likewise, interest increased in Eastern religious experiences, which also began to take a foothold in small pockets of clinicians throughout the country as the countercultural revolution continued to grow in influence in the United States.

During the early 1980s, the negative zeitgeist assumptions about religion started to be revisited and questioned within the larger field of psychology. For example, researcher and clinician Allen Bergin (1980) began to revisit early studies on the negativity of religion on mental health outcomes. He found numerous methodological problems and biases, which had upheld the unfavorable view of religion for years if not decades. During this period, several additional reviews of the literature were written that provided further support and exploration of the role of religion within the context of mental health (e.g., Worthington, 1989; for a history, see Worthington, 2010).

### The Tipping Point

In many ways, during the 1990s, the psychology of religion appears to have reached a tipping point, and the popularity and acceptance of religion within psychology began to spread. Stanton Jones's (1994) prospectus of a model for incorporating religion into psychotherapy, which appeared in the *American Psychologist*, played a major role in bringing conversations that had largely taken place outside of mainstream psychology directly to mainstream psychology. Likewise, during the 1990s, Edward Shafranske (1996) published *Religion and the Clinical Practice of Psychology*, giving the American Psychological Association their first book on matters of faith and setting the stage for numerous books on religion and spirituality to follow. More than any decade before, a clear upswing in religious books, articles, professional organizations, and graduate programs emerged (Worthington et al., 2008). What had been largely talked, researched, and written about in experimental circles now was gaining momentum in applied circles as well.

The late 1990s and early 2000s were marked by an even greater openness to religion, which was furthered by an increased interest in spirituality and its relationship to religion. Moreover, over the course of these two decades, more and more applied psychologists began contributing to the psychology of religion field—now the psychology of religion and spirituality field. Likewise, increasing collaboration between applied and experimental psychologists emerged and continued until today. These are just a few of the major events that helped to set the stage for the infusing of what primarily had been an experimental endeavor into a clinical endeavor. Now, onto the present, and onto the need for this book.

### The Need for This Book

Despite the merging interests of applied and experimental psychologists, a gap appears to exist between the psychology of religion and spirituality research and the clinical application of this research to practice. The psychology of religion and spirituality has a fruitful history that has led to a vast body of empirical research. The past two decades also have been rich with clinical advances in understanding how to work with religion and spirituality in counseling and psychotherapy. Yet, in many ways, it almost feels as though these advances have been emerging in parallel rather than in unison, with the psychology of religion on one plane and the spirituality of counseling on the other plane. It is our hope that this book will begin to bridge the gap between the psychology of religion and spirituality research and clinical practice, thus helping readers learn to use research in their practice.

## OVERVIEW AND GOALS FOR THIS BOOK

Each subsequent chapter aims to provide readers with a functional understanding of the psychology of religion and spirituality empirical literature, while at the same time outlining clinical implications, assessments, and strategies for counseling and psychotherapy. Having taught psychology of religion courses and spirituality in counseling courses, the authors have heard students voice their struggle with trying to connect the psychology of religion and spirituality research with clinical practice. We also have heard this concern voiced many times by practicing and experienced mental health professionals and academic researchers.

To accomplish these goals, we have pulled together a talented team of respected scholar–clinicians who are able to speak to the empirical particulars and clinical nuances of major psychology of religion and spirituality topics (e.g., religious coping) equally. We have asked each author to bridge research and clinical practice. As a result, each chapter is empirically grounded and clinically rich. The authors have drawn out clinical implications embedded in traditional psychology of religion and spirituality research. Furthermore, each chapter addresses clinical assessment and clinical strategies along with diverse religious and spiritual clinical examples and case studies.

Whether you are a student or seasoned professional, you will benefit from reading this book. Psychology of religion and spirituality students who want to prepare for dealing with religion and spirituality as a multicultural issue can do so quickly without great intrusion into their busy schedule. Overworked professors who teach counseling and psychotherapy courses and want to include religious and spiritual issues within those courses can update their knowledge quickly and rely on the knowledge and timeliness of the summaries and applications provided by the authors of the chapters. This book readily lends itself in many ways to the classroom, from carefully selected topical chapters that fit naturally with the ebb and flow of the semester, to useful aids like clinical application questions and suggested readings and resources that can be used to direct student preparation efficiently.

The experienced practicing mental health professional will find the easy-to-use structure of the chapters useful. Chapters explicitly tease out clinical implications, assessment approaches, and clinical strategies. The user-friendly aids will help the busy clinician by helping facilitate page-to-practice adoption of new ideas and techniques.

The academic researcher will benefit from the sound empirical overview of traditional psychology of religion and spirituality topics that may generate and spark ideas for further research. Typically, researchers are experts in one area, but by reading excellent summaries of other areas, they can deepen and broaden their understanding of the context for their topics of interest. Likewise, these research-oriented readers—even when reading about a field of specialized interest rather than broadening the scope of understanding—will benefit from seeing how their research might be presented to a broader audience and how their research might be more readily applied to counseling and psychotherapy.

Students will benefit from this book's concise introduction to key topics that have a rich foundation in the psychology of religion and spirituality. Furthermore, students interested in learning how to work more effectively with religious and spiritual issues in their clinical work will benefit from the plethora of assessment and clinical strategies highlighted throughout. Likewise, students interested in doing research, such as a thesis or dissertation on a psychology of religion and spirituality topic, will garner a strong theoretical and empirical background from which to develop their own ideas and studies.

With this book we are not trying to divide the psychology of religion and spirituality under applied versus experimental tents. Nor are we suggesting that one approach is better or weaker than the other, or that one is *good* and the other *bad*. Quite the contrary—our primary goal is to offer readers a book that will unite the best of what psychology of religion and spirituality researchers and clinicians who work with religious and spiritual issues have to offer—to provide a more holistic and scientifically informed approach to clinical practice. And we believe our chapter authors have accomplished just that, by making the connections and applications between research and practice more salient and explicit.

## CHAPTER OVERVIEW

In this first chapter of this volume, we provide readers with a concise historical overview of the evolution of the psychology of religion to the psychology of religion and spirituality. We also outline the goals of this book, discuss the audiences that will find this book helpful, and explain how readers might apply the lessons learned therein to their clinical practice.

In Chapter 2, Desrosiers discusses how religion and spirituality develop across the life span. Research on spiritual and religious development is highlighted that points to an inverse association between positive spiritual growth and the development of negative psychological symptoms. That is, the author brings attention to the buffering affects of faith across developmental stages, drawing from work on faith development theory, stages of religious judgment, cognitive models of spiritual development, intentional faith, women's faith development, parent and peer contextual factors in spiritual development, and attachment theory. Clinical implications are then extrapolated for readers, bringing attention to key practice-related issues. Clinical assessments to help clinicians measure spiritual and religious development are offered. Quantitative measures are discussed, including the Faith Development Scale, Ways of Faith Scale, Faith Styles Scale, and Spiritual Assessment Inventory. Guidelines and numerous examples of semistructured intake and interview questions are provided. Treatment strategies are covered to help clinicians support client spiritual development.

In Chapter 3, Wink, Adler, and Dillon bring attention to religious and spiritual identity, with a focus on developmental and narrative approaches for clinicians. William James and the spiritual me, Erikson's life span model of identity development, Marcia and ego identity status, ego identity and spirituality in adulthood, and narrative identity are discussed at length. The chapter authors draw from these perspectives to help readers develop a theoretical and empirical understanding of how religious and spiritual identity unfolds over the course of one's life. Key clinical implications follow, which help readers connect research to their practice. Several strategies for assessing client religious and spiritual identity are noted, including sample open-ended questions to more formal approaches, such as questions about religious dwelling and spiritual seeking; questions about client exploration and commitment across occupation, religion, and politics; and a four-stage model to assess level of client spiritual–religious identity. Clinical strategies are offered to help clinicians work with themes related to religious and spiritual identity, with an emphasis on working with spiritual-seeking and religious-dwelling clients.

In Chapter 4, Hill, Smith, and Sandage survey research findings about intrinsic, extrinsic, and quest religious motivational orientations. Overall, intrinsic religious motivations are largely correlated with positive mental health outcomes, whereas extrinsic religious motivations more often are correlated with poorer mental health outcomes. Quest motivations are discussed, which have been linked to more prosocial helping behaviors. The complexities of religious fundamentalism are covered. Initial open-ended questions and short screening assessments are highlighted, as well as more standardized assessments, like the Remuda Spiritual Assessment Questionnaire and Furnishing the Soul Inventory. The chapter authors offer several useful clinical strategies that emphasize motivations underlying individuals' reasons for being religious and the complex relationship such motivations have with general psychological structures. They propose that psychotherapists help clients develop a convincing life narrative that provides a cohesive sense of meaning for their lives, and to match interventions with religious motivational orientations.

In Chapter 5, Miller and Worthington offer readers a historical and theoretical context for understanding the relationship between personality with religion and spirituality. Specifically, the authors provide an overview of object relations, attachment style, Eysenck's biological theory, the five-factor model of personality, and spiritual transcendence, along with critiques of the big five model as it pertains to religious and spiritual variables. Pulling from positive psychology, the authors also bring attention to the link between character strengths, values, and virtues with religion and spirituality. Clinical implications are then covered for the big five traits and counseling, personality disorders, and religious coping styles. Guidelines for informal assessments are offered for conducting informal discussions to developing spiritual life maps. Formal assessments are also introduced, including the Neuroticism-Extroversion-Openness (NEO)-Personality Inventory Revised, Spiritual Well-Being Scale, RCOPE, Spiritual Assessment Inventory, Spiritual Transcendence Scale, Values in Action (VIA) Inventory of Strengths, and Schwartz Value Survey. Clinical strategies for incorporating personality into psychotherapy follow, such as promoting a forgiving personality, optimism and hope, and altruism.

In Chapter 6, Moriarty and Davis bring attention to client God images. The authors distinguish between God images and God concepts, and they offer an ecumenical religious and spiritual perspective on God images. Empirical research follows, focusing on God image development and dynamics and God image change through psychotherapy. The authors tease out clinical implications from the highlighted theoretical and empirical literature. Clinical assessments are then discussed. The authors provide insight into common clinical situations when it may be appropriate to assess God images. The authors advocate a rationale for a multistep assessment process, which includes clinical interview questions, projective assessments, and self-report survey-based measures. Clinical strategies for addressing and working with clients' God images are discussed utilizing an integrative-psychotherapy model. The authors highlight how God images might be addressed using a common factors, theoretical integrationist, technical eclectic, or assimilative integrationist approach.

In Chapter 7, O'Grady and Bartz present studies that provide insight into the nature of spiritually transcendent experiences and report outcomes for individuals experiencing spiritually transcendent experiences. Findings highlighted suggest that individuals who encounter these experiences report positive mental health outcomes, life transition, and spiritual growth. Assessment approaches to help clients distinguish between psychologically beneficial reports of spiritually transcendent experiences and pathological manifestations from a cultural framework are provided. The chapter authors recommend that psychotherapists support clients in making sense of transcendent experiences in a way that is psychologically beneficial, and that they help clients take advantage of the therapeutic potential inherent within such experiences. At times, it could be clinically indicated to encourage a client to consider engaging in spiritual practices from the client's spiritual and religious orientation that promote spiritual transcendence. On the whole, psychotherapists are encouraged to be aware of the role of spiritual transcendence in their own lives, including ways in which spiritual transcendence may enhance their effectiveness as clinicians.

In Chapter 8, Slattery and Park bring attention to a meaning perspective to understanding religious and spiritual beliefs in psychotherapy. The meaning-making framework highlighted offers insight into how religious and spiritual beliefs can affect clients' mental and physical health. Empirical research on meaning making and on religious and spiritual beliefs is reviewed, from situational to global beliefs. Clinical implications are then elucidated from the highlighted body of literature. How clinicians might assess meaning-specific religious and spiritual beliefs is addressed, as well as how clinicians might detect discrepancies between clients' beliefs and experiences. Both open-ended questions and several assessment tools, like the Faith and Belief, Importance, Community, Address in Care (FICA)–Spiritual History Tool, are discussed. Clinical strategies are provided to respond to clients' beliefs, to explore the utility of beliefs and draw on adaptive beliefs, and to close discrepancies between beliefs and experiences.

In Chapter 9, Murray-Swank and Murray-Swank's chapter on spiritual struggle shares research demonstrating that spiritual struggles have been related to poor mental and physical health, in particular, when people use negative religious coping styles when dealing with life struggles. The chapter authors report, however, that working through spiritual struggles, before they become chronic, may lead to positive transformation. The ability to find meaning in a spiritual struggle was associated with posttraumatic growth and spiritual growth, and less spiritual decline across time. Clinical implications are then brought to light for readers, followed by both informal and formal assessment procedures. In regard to clinical strategies, the authors bring attention to several manualized treatment protocols to help clients work through spiritual struggles. Likewise, the authors recommend that spiritual struggles should be addressed by surveying recent research and theory on the topic, developing relevant intervention strategies, and evaluating the outcomes of such interventions.

In Chapter 10, Krumrei and Rosmarin discuss the processes of religious and spiritual coping. The authors begin by first defining religious and spiritual coping, followed by a review of the empirical research. Attention is given to religious coping as a valuable and unique resource, religious coping as a double-edged sword, and religious coping when facing individual and religious differences. Clinical implications are woven in with the review of this burgeoning body of literature followed by clinical applications. Several clinical assessment strategies are offered, including informal assessment and formal assessment approaches.

Examples of formal assessment approaches discussed include the Adolescent Coping Orientation for Problem Experiences (COPE) Inventory, Ways of Religious Coping Scale, Religious Problem Solving Scales, and RCOPE. Clinical strategies are provided that facilitate religious coping, such as manualized treatments, spiritually integrated treatments, and religion-accommodative treatments. Furthermore, the authors bring attention to common therapeutic themes that may lend opportunities for further exploring and addressing religious-coping issues.

In Chapter 11, Worthington, Davis, Hook, Gartner, Jennings, Greer, Van Tongeren, and Greer cover forgiveness and reconciliation. Many world religions teach and encourage forgiveness. Both religious and nonreligious people bring concerns over their anger, hatred, and unforgiveness to psychotherapists. Thus, forgiveness is taught and encouraged by psychotherapists in many theoretical approaches. Worthington and his colleagues review research on forgiveness that will help psychotherapists use forgiveness with religious clients. They first review the research on the secular study of forgiveness and unforgiveness—their definitions, their biological and health consequences, areas of the psychological study of forgiveness (e.g., personality, development, interactions around transgressions, and culture), and interventions to promote forgiving. Much learned from the study of forgiveness in secular settings and with secular interventions also is useful with religious people. The authors then explore the relationship between religion and spirituality and forgiveness—especially in assessing and treating people who express persistent concerns with being unable or unwilling to forgive someone who hurt or offended them. Finally, they suggest practical applications for clinicians on the basis of their review. They identify two interventions that are supported by the most empirical evidence (Enright's for psychotherapy and Worthington's for psychoeducational interventions). They draw clinical implications from current research, including providing a case study.

In Chapter 12, Wiggins brings attention to religion and spirituality in couples and families. Empirical research discussed suggests that, overall, religion and spirituality may be valuable resources for helping couples and families in psychotherapy. Clinical implications are discussed, focusing on religion and spirituality and family life-cycle transitions, forgiveness as a spiritual construct to promote couple and family healing, and the role of faith in couples and families in response to grief and loss. Several clinical assessments follow, bringing attention to such approaches as the Brief Spiritual Assessment and Spiritual Genogram. Numerous clinical strategies are provided, including viewing God as a member of the family, Milan group rituals, postmodern language approaches, and narrative therapy.

In Chapter 13, Toussaint, Webb, and Keltner demonstrate the importance of religion and spirituality to positive client mental health and well-being. Drawing from findings from more than a thousand empirical studies and reviews, the authors offer a series of clinical implications. Easy-to-use tables are provided that highlight outcomes of empirical studies and existing literature reviews on religion and spirituality pertaining to mental health. Clinical assessments are discussed, including informal and formal structured discussion questions. The authors highlight several assessment instruments, such as the Religious Commitment Inventory, Index of Core Spiritual Experiences, and Purpose in Life Test. Clinical strategies are presented that focus on psychotherapeutic considerations (e.g., development of the psychotherapeutic relationship, maintenance of the psychotherapeutic relationship) and theoretical conceptualizations.

In Chapter 14, Masters and Hooker introduce readers to the empirical literature on religion and spirituality with physical health. Helpful clinical assessments for exploring client religion and spirituality and health are provided, including the Brief Multidimensional Measure of Religion and Spirituality, Multidimensional Health Locus of Control scales, Intrinsic/Extrinsic Religious Motivation scales, and Royal Free Interview for Spiritual and Religious Beliefs. The authors then explore several different religious and spiritual pathways and clinical strategies that can facilitate improved physical health. Specifically, behavioral and lifestyle pathways, social support, religious and spiritually influenced coping, and common religious and spiritual activities with unclear relations with health are discussed.

In Chapter 15, O'Grady, Worthington, and Aten reflect on the book's primary goal, to create a resource for clinicians and researchers alike that would help translate basic research findings into useful clinical practice strategies. Furthermore, the editors explore the unique contributions of the psychology of religion and spirituality to the scientist–practitioner model and to the broader field of psychology. To conclude the chapter and book, the editors discuss future directions for moving the psychology of religion and spirituality forward.

## REFERENCES

Allport, G. W. (1950). *The individual and his religion*. New York, NY: Macmillan.

Aten, J. D., & Leach, M. M. (2008). A primer on spirituality and mental health. In J. D. Aten & M. M. Leach (Eds.), *Spirituality and the therapeutic process: A comprehensive resource from intake to termination* (pp. 9–24). Washington, DC: American Psychological Association.

Bergin, A. E. (1980). Psychotherapy and religious values. *Journal of Consulting and Clinical Psychology, 48*, 95–105.

Blazer, D. (1998). Freud vs. God: How psychiatry lost its soul and Christianity lost its mind. Downer Grove, IL: InterVarsity Press.

Brown, D., & Srebalus, D. (1996). *Introduction to the counseling profession*. Needham Heights, MA: Allyn & Bacon.

Caplan, E. (1998). *Mind games: American culture and the birth of psychotherapy*. Los Angeles, CA: University of California Press.

Emmons, R. (2003). *The psychology of ultimate concerns*. New York, NY: Guilford Press.

Frankl, V. (1962). *Man's search for meaning*. New York, NY: Simon & Schuster.

James, W. (1961). *The varieties of religious experience.* New York, NY: Collier. (Original work published 1902)

Jones, S. L. (1994). A constructive relationship for religion with the science and profession of psychology: Perhaps the boldest model yet. *American Psychologist, 49*(3), 184–199. doi: 10.1037/0003-066X.49.3.184

Jung, C. G. (1938). *Psychology of religion.* New Haven, CT: Yale University Press.

Rogers, C. (1951). *Client-centered therapy: Its current practice, implications and theory.* Boston, MA: Houghton Mifflin.

Shafranske, E. (Ed.). (1996). *Religion and the clinical practice of psychology.* Washington, DC: American Psychological Association.

Standard, R. P., Sandhu, D. S., & Painter, L. C. (2000). Assessment of spirituality in counseling. *Journal of Counseling and Development, 78,* 204–210.

Vande Kemp, H. (1996). Historical perspective: Religion and clinical psychology in America. In E. P. Shafranske (Ed.), *Religion and the clinical practice of psychology* (pp. 71–112). Washington, DC: American Psychological Association.

Worthington, E. L., Jr. (1989). Religious faith across the life span: Implications for counseling and research. *The Counseling Psychologist, 17,* 555–612.

Worthington, E. L., Jr. (2010). Integration of spirituality and religion into psychotherapy. In J. C. Norcross, G. R. VandenBos, & D. K. Freedheim (Eds.), *History of psychotherapy: Continuity and change* (2nd ed., pp. 533–543). Washington, DC: American Psychological Association.

Worthington, E. L., Jr., Sandage, S. J., Davis, D. E., Hook, J. N., Miller, A. J., Lewis Hall, M. E., & Hall, T. W. (2008). Training therapists to address spiritual concerns in clinical practice and research. In J. D. Aten & M. M. Leach (Eds.), *Spirituality and the therapeutic process: A comprehensive resource from intake to termination* (pp. 267–291). Washington, DC: American Psychological Association.

# 2

# *Development of Religion and Spirituality Across the Life Span*

ALETHEA DESROSIERS

The interface of religious and spiritual development with psychological development and healthy functioning has been an increasingly researched area in recent years. Although Fowler's theory of faith development (1981) may be one of the most well-known theories of spiritual–religious development, several stage theories have been proposed describing the structure of faith development in a manner that is not content specific and therefore is applicable across particular religious traditions and cultures (Clore & Fitzgerald, 2002; Oser & Gmunder, 1991). Additionally, current research points to a variety of contextual factors, such as relationships with parents and friends, which appear to contribute to the development of spirituality through childhood and adolescence. Given that spiritual growth and development have been inversely associated with prevalent forms of psychopathology like depression (Desrosiers & Miller, 2007; Miller & Gur, 2002), substance abuse (Miller, Davies, & Greenwald, 2000; Piedmont, 2004; Sterling et al., 2007), and eating disorders (Richards, Berrett, Hardman, & Eggett, 2006), this chapter explores the clinical implications of spiritual and religious development, and also identifies methods for assessing spiritual and religious development during the therapeutic encounter. Finally, this chapter presents strategies for tailoring clinical interventions and illustrates them specifically through a case study.

## RESEARCH ON SPIRITUAL AND RELIGIOUS DEVELOPMENT

Although some researchers have claimed that their theories of religious and spiritual development are universal in nature (Fowler, 1981), this assertion has received minimal empirical support. In fact, theories of spiritual development omit information about religious or spiritual content that may characterize specific stages or styles of faith. An effort has been made to investigate the validity of these theories in the context of Eastern religious traditions (Oser, 1991; see Parker, 2006, for a review), but most participants in these samples represent a Judeo–Christian background. Additionally, the cognitive stage theories discussed in this chapter (Cartwright, 2001; Fowler, 1981; Oser & Gmunder, 1991) give primacy to a linear, vertical, and sequential concept of spiritual development that favors cognition over affect and experience. An alternative viewpoint stemming from feminist theory will be presented.

### Faith Development Theory: James Fowler

Seeking to formulate a theory of religious development that would apply across culture and religious tradition, Fowler (1981) focused on the concept of faith, which he defined as "our way of finding coherence in and giving meaning to the multiple forces and relations that make up our lives" (p. 4). Religion is one form through which faith finds expression, and a reciprocal relationship may develop in which religion and faith interact continually to renew and reform each other.

In developing his theory, Fowler (1981) distinguished between the *content* of faith, which may differ according to religious beliefs, and the *structure* of faith, or the psychological processes that render the content as personally meaningful. Drawing from the work of Piaget (1970), Kohlberg (1976), and Erikson (1968), Fowler attempted to integrate models of cognitive, moral, and socioemotional development into his broad theory. On the basis of data collected from 359 semistructured interviews conducted over 10 years, Fowler identified seven stages of faith corresponding to general developmental periods (rather than specific ages) throughout the life span (see Table 2.1). He maintained that progression from one stage to the next is hierarchical and sequential, with each new stage incorporating and expanding on the operations of the previous stage. Backward movement, however, also may occur, requiring reworking of faith issues in the previous stage.

### Stages of Religious Judgment: Fritz Oser and Paul Gmunder

Oser and Gmunder (1991) developed a stage theory of religious development focused on the structural components of judgment and reasoning, in which growth occurs through a sequential, hierarchical process. Movement from one stage to the next depends on the resolution of ambiguities or contradictions that raise questions about a person's relationship to the divine or about who is ultimately in control, such as freedom versus dependence, trust versus mistrust, and transcendence versus immanence. At lower stages, individuals tend to think in a dichotomous, either–or fashion about these contradictions, while at higher stages dualities and ambiguities are accepted as such and are integrated into the fabric of religious and spiritual experience. Several investigations have provided some support for this theory, in that progression through the stages of religious development was correlated positively with age in both a Christian sample (Oser & Gmunder, 1991) and a Hindu–Buddhist sample (Dick, 1982).

**Table 2.1** Fowler: Stages of Faith Development

| | Stage | Characteristics |
|---|---|---|
| Stage 1 | Intuitive–projective faith (ages 2–7) | Understanding of God based on intuitive, imaginative processes; images formed from religious narratives |
| Stage 2 | Mythic–literal faith (childhood and beyond) | Imaginative pictures organized into meaningful categories; principles of justice guide understanding of God |
| Stage 3 | Synthetic–conventional faith (adolescence and beyond) | Development of specific values and beliefs; overarching faith system remains unexamined and conforms to expectations of others |
| Stage 4 | Individuative–reflective faith (late adolescence and beyond) | Beliefs examined more critically; extrinsic, received faith is transformed into a personal, inner-faith commitment |
| Stage 5 | Conjunctive faith (midlife and beyond) | Integration of multiple perspectives and appreciation of paradoxes; relationship with God experienced as personal, active, and dynamic |
| Stage 6 | Universalizing faith | Attaining universalizing faith is rare; related to the ability to see beyond paradox through processes like ascetic actualization (e.g., Gandhi) |

Fowler also describes a stage of faith during infancy called *undifferentiated faith*, for a total of seven stages.

Although stage theories of spiritual–religious development may at first appear to have minimal relevance for clinical work, a general familiarity with these models may assist psychotherapists in certain types of clinical encounters. For example, religious doubts or crises in faith typical of particular stages may trigger considerable psychological distress or threaten significant relationships and support systems. Stage theories might provide a useful theoretical framework for conceptualizing psychological struggles associated with religious–spiritual concerns. Psychotherapists might consider that negotiating doubts and contradictions of a religious nature is a positive and healthy component of overall religious development. For clients at higher stages of religious development, improving tolerance of ambiguity and paradox could be particularly helpful.

### Cognitive Models of Spiritual Development

The idea that religious development mirrors the process of cognitive development, particularly as outlined in Piaget's model, was first investigated and supported by Elkind (1961, 1962, 1964), and then by several others (Goldman, 1964; Degelman, Mullen, & Mullen, 1984; Tamminen, 1976; Tamminen & Nurmi, 1995; Zachry, 1990). More recently, Cartwright (2001) proposed that previous attempts to apply Piaget's theory of cognitive development to spiritual development are incomplete in that they have not integrated current postformal theories of cognitive development. Theories of postformal thought contend that some individuals have the ability to contemplate multiple logical systems and choose the system that resonates most accurately with their sense of self, thus going beyond formal operational reasoning (Sinnott, 1998). In an extension of theories indicating that changes in the understanding of a relationship to the divine mirror changes in cognitive development (sensorimotor, preoperational, concrete operational, and formal operational), this understanding may continue to grow beyond formal operational thought to include a new sense of subjectivity. Cartwright further argued that at each stage, spiritual understanding transcends understanding in preceding stages through the assimilation of new cognitive abilities. Subjective experiences, such as life events and interpersonal relationships, ignite the process of transcendence by challenging individuals to engage in new modes of thinking. At postformal levels of cognitive development, individuals are able to see beyond culturally transmitted views and consider multiple perspectives before choosing one as most fitting for the self. Abstract principles (compassion, forgiveness) are understood as connecting threads between self, others, and a higher power rather than just guides for religious behavior.

### Intentional Faith: Clore and Fitzgerald

Also emphasizing the cognitive component of faith, Clore and Fitzgerald (2002) sought to refine Fowler's (1981) theory by proposing a formal theory influenced by Lonergan's (1957, 1972) cognitional theory, which specified the mechanism of adult faith development as the process of differentiation and integration. In contrast to Fowler, Clore and Fitzgerald suggested that faith development occurs through the process of integrating increasingly advanced faith concepts into an existing reservoir, rather than through a successive series of displacements. They found support for their theory suggesting four levels of faith based on four ostensible levels of knowledge: commonsense, thoughtful, responsible, and transcendent, each progressively more integrated and differentiated. Commonsense faith involves the basic use of symbols and common sense. Thoughtful faith involves reflective reasoning and integrating differing aspects of experience. Responsible faith, or self-authenticating faith, involves a sense of conviction and responsibility for right acts and also the capacity to reflect on one's own process of knowing. Finally, transcendent faith involves going beyond the human experience to arrive at insights and consider the larger context. Based on high correlations among scales (Clore & Fitzgerald, 2002), their findings also suggested that faith is too complex to identify individuals by one distinct stage. Higher levels of faith may contain elements of previous levels that have been reorganized and incorporated.

Theories of faith development formed on the basis of cognitive development might be relevant for psychotherapists in some cases. For example, it is possible that a client might experience negative thoughts about self or others that stem from religious beliefs and that trigger mood or anxiety issues. Psychotherapists might feel more confident in challenging these (maladaptive) belief systems or facilitating the development of alternative perspectives within a particular faith system if they are familiar with cognitive theories of religious development.

### Women's Faith Development

Although Fowler conceptualized faith as a dynamic, meaning-making process involving cognitive, affective, and behavioral aspects, feminist psychologists and theologians have suggested that women's faith development is inherently relational and occurs through the process of connectedness rather than through the process of separation and individuation (Heyward, 1982; Gilligan, 1982; Grey, 1999; Jordan, 1991). For example, Fowler's description of individuals who have achieved the highest level of faith development has pointed to those who have sacrificed relationships with important others for the greater good (e.g., Gandhi). With the exception of a few venerable ascetics like Mother Theresa, this notion of spiritual development may be less applicable for women.

Slee (2004) attempted to more fully understand the nuances and patterns of women's faith development through interviews of 30 Christian women. Her findings suggested a patterning of women's faith development characterized by alienation, awakening, and relationality. Experiences of alienation involved a lack of authentic connection to self, others, and God; feelings of emptiness; loss of meaning; and a sense of paralysis or lack of movement. The spiritual impasse created by alienation, however, if brought to consciousness, has the power to initiate an "awakening" in which a woman's orientation to her self and the world is reformulated. Through navigating the challenges posed by spiritual impasse, a reconnection to the self and a deeper awareness of connectedness to both others and the divine is experienced. Spiritual awakenings may be stimulated by mystical experiences, but more often, the women interviewed reported more ordinary and mundane accounts. Additionally, awakening was not necessarily a single occurrence, but something that was entered into again and again, requiring continual deconstruction and reconstruction of experience throughout the life course. Finally, women constructed their faith lives in terms of their relationship to God and strong empathic connections with others. Relationality was not so much a phase, but "a fundamental epistemology that underlies and undergirds the whole of a woman's spiritual journey" (Slee, 2004, p. 160).

### Parent and Peer Contextual Factors in Spiritual Development

Parents consistently have been shown to play a significant role in the development of spirituality and religiosity in their children. For example, parental religious beliefs and commitment have been associated with religious beliefs of offspring in a number of studies (Boyatzis, Dollahite, & Marks, 2006; Gunnoe & Moore, 2002; King, Elder, & Whitbeck, 1997; Miller, Warner, Wickramaratne, & Weissman, 1997; Smith, 2005). Particular qualities of the parental relationship appear to be important for transmission of religious beliefs or practices to occur.

Such factors as emotional closeness, parental warmth, and parental acceptance have been shown to be highly correlated with adolescent adoption of parental religious beliefs and practices (Okagaki & Bevis, 1999; Ozorak, 1989; Potvin & Lee, 1982) and also to moderate the transmission of religious beliefs and practices between parents and offspring (Bao, Whitbeck, Hoyt, & Conger, 1999).

Spiritual modeling has been proposed to explain the process of transmission of parental religiosity to offspring (Bandura, 2003; Oman & Thoresen, 2003). Applying principles from social modeling and observational learning, spiritual modeling suggests that spiritual growth transpires through the process of imitating or emulating other religious individuals, ranging from exalted spiritual figures (e.g., Muhammad, Jesus Christ) to devoted community or family members. Spiritual modeling has provided the theoretical foundation for a model of religious *transmission* in which religious beliefs and values are transmitted unidirectionally from parent to child. Although some empirical evidence supports this model (Dudley & Dudley, 1986; Flor & Knapp, 2001), current literature suggests that the process is more complex, involving reciprocal, mutual influencing between parents and children (Schwartz, 2006).

For example, a more interactive, dyadic process of internalization than that indicated by the transmission model is supported by studies exploring parental willingness to discuss spiritual and religious topics with their children. In a qualitative study investigating the process of spiritual development in a highly diverse sample of adolescents, Kelley, Athan, and Miller (2007) found that parental openness to conversations about spirituality was a principal factor contributing to the spiritual development of adolescents. With regard to specific qualities of these discussions with parents, qualitative research suggests that youth-centered, transactional (bidirectional) conversations are experienced more positively by both parents and adolescents than parent-centered, unidirectional conversations (Dollahite & Thatcher, 2008).

Psychotherapists working with parents interested in fostering spiritual development or augmenting protective factors in their children could offer psychoeducational information based on these research findings. They might more directly encourage parents to engage in exploratory conversations about spirituality and religion and to embrace questions and doubts expressed by their children. Furthermore, parents experiencing their own religious doubts or uncertainties about talking with their children could be encouraged to consult religious professionals or to explore these areas during psychotherapy sessions.

In addition to the influence of parents, peers also have a significant impact on spiritual development through adolescence. In some instances, communication with friends about spirituality and religion has been found to be of comparable importance to communication with parents (Desrosiers, Kelley, & Miller, 2011; King, Furrow, & Roth, 2002), whereas in other cases, conversations about faith with peers appear more important than conversations with parents for adolescent spiritual and religious development (Schwartz, 2006). On the basis of the cognitive-anchoring hypothesis of Ozorak (1989), parents may provide the base for communication about spiritual and religious concerns during childhood and early adolescence. Then, as friendships become increasingly important through adolescence, beliefs or questions about spirituality are further tested or elaborated through conversations with peers.

Research findings on the contribution of peers and parents suggest that psychotherapists could enhance therapeutic outcomes in work with adolescents and young adults by encouraging participation in peer groups or activities in which spiritual or religious beliefs are supported and challenged by peers through reciprocal dialogue. In the absence of a parent who is able to support spiritual growth, psychotherapists might introduce these topics into psychotherapy sessions through questions about meaning, faith, or creation, or they could identify alternative spiritual mentors.

### Applications From Attachment Theory

Drawing from the principles of attachment theory (Ainsworth, Blehar, Waters, & Wall, 1978; Bowlby, 1969, 1973, 1980), Kirkpatrick (1992) suggested that individuals may experience God as an additional attachment figure capable of providing a safe, secure base. He specified two hypotheses through which attachment theory might explain religious development. In the compensation hypothesis, a child who lacks a secure attachment to parents turns to God as a substitute attachment figure. Alternatively, according to the correspondence hypothesis, beliefs about attachment figures (including God) are a direct reflection of previous attachment experiences, meaning that a relationship with God should share the same characteristics as earlier parental relationships. The notion of correspondence also draws strength from findings showing a robust association between images of God (i.e., internal working models) and images of parental relationships (Kirkpatrick, 1997, 1998; Rizzuto, 1979).

Although modest support has been demonstrated for both hypotheses (Biergegard & Granqvist, 2004; Granqvist & Hagekull, 1999, 2001; Kirkpatrick, 1997, 1998; Kirkpatrick & Shaver, 1990), it seems that the picture may be more complex. For example, Granqvist (2002) found that insecure attachment appeared to be related more to general instability (increases or decreases) in religiosity, and proposed revised hypotheses: (a) For securely attached individuals, religiosity, developed through social learning, corresponds more to parental religiosity than to security of attachment; and (b) for insecurely attached individuals, affect regulation is the underlying mechanism through which emotional compensation or felt security is sought in a relationship with God.

In a similar vein, the concept of spiritual maturity has been articulated from an object relations perspective as a fundamentally relational phenomenon that mirrors the quality of relationship with God (Hall & Brokaw, 1995; Hall, Brokaw,

Edwards, & Pike, 1998). This idea stems from the work of Rizzuto (1979) on images of God in which she theorized that an individual's representation of God reflects internalized representations of parents and is transformed continuously throughout development as new experiences are internalized. Spiritual maturity is depicted as a mature dependence or interdependence on God that is developed through the same underlying psychological mechanisms through which mature, interdependent relationships with fellow humans are cultivated. Although existing research supports the association between spiritual maturity and maturity of relationships with other (Hall & Brokaw, 1995; Hall et al., 1998; TenElshof & Furrow, 2000), a more explicit discussion about the specific processes through which spiritual maturity is cultivated is lacking.

## CLINICAL IMPLICATIONS

Findings of previous studies have provided some insight into potential clinical implications of disruptions in spiritual development in both adolescents and adults. For example, on the basis of the greater magnitude of the protective effects of religiosity against substance abuse in adolescents compared with adults, Miller et al. (2000) suggested that a lack of support around spiritual development might generate augmented risk of substance abuse. The notion that deficiencies in support around the development of spiritual connection and understanding during adolescence might pose a risk for psychopathology also has been suggested with respect to depressive symptoms, particularly with adolescent girls (Desrosiers & Miller, 2007; Miller & Gur, 2002). With these findings in mind, psychotherapists might draw from feminist perspectives on spiritual development (see Slee, 2004) in work with adolescents (especially females) who are exhibiting symptoms of depression or endorsing substance abuse. Exploring specifically the quality of connection or extent of alienation from self, other, and God may be an important component of treatment in these populations. Psychotherapists can support spiritual development, which in turn may contribute to reducing depressive symptoms and substance abuse in some clients, by engaging in dialogue around salient spiritual and religious issues and encouraging clients to develop additional supports (friends, religious groups) that nurture their spiritual growth and sense of connectedness.

Current research also has demonstrated that higher levels of intrinsic and experiential spiritual dimensions, such as forgiveness (McCullough, Bono, & Root, 2005), positive religious coping (Pargament, 1997), and personal devotion (Kendler, Gardner, & Prescott, 1997; Kendler et al., 2003), are inversely associated with psychopathology. These findings underscore the potential importance of attending to spiritual development during the course of therapy. For example, psychotherapists might attempt to understand whether and in what ways a client turns to God for support in times of stress and how this has played out in the past. Depending on the client's religious identity and values, psychotherapists might discuss ways to augment positive religious coping, such as creating time for prayer or contemplation and then reflecting on these experiences during psychotherapy sessions.

From a different perspective, negative life events or struggles with psychiatric conditions like depression, substance abuse, or anxiety might be considered opportunities for spiritual growth. This idea is in line with the proposals of several stage theorists stating that conflict motivates the development of faith (Fowler, 1981; Oser & Gmunder, 1991). For example, in a longitudinal study of individuals ranging in age from their early 30s to mid-70s, Wink and Dillon (2002) found that experiencing adverse circumstances, such as external conflict with family or internal conflict that prompted the need for psychotherapy, facilitated spiritual development. Additionally, an association was found for women between religious commitment and negative life events in early adulthood and spiritual development in later adulthood. Implications of adversity for spiritual growth may be particularly pertinent as individuals approach old age, because typically they confront increasing losses and health concerns. Results of qualitative research with both adolescents and adults also have indicated that significant losses and experiences of trauma or adversity can serve as catalysts for increased self-awareness and spiritual growth, depending on how individuals cope (Batten & Oltjenbruns, 1999; Bryant-Davis, 2005; Cadell, Regehr, & Hemsworth, 2003; Hamilton & Jackson, 1998). Psychotherapists, of course, do not want to spin trials and struggles to sound as if they are not taking the client's struggles seriously. Psychotherapists, however, can stay alert for opportunities to ask clients to reflect on the ways they might believe they have grown from their struggles.

Furthermore, it is important to keep in mind that the relationship between adversity and spiritual growth is not necessarily straightforward; rather, trauma and adversity complexly interact with spiritual growth. For instance, some research on spirituality and eating disorders has shown that eating disorders may diminish spirituality because the disorder tends to occupy an individual's entire sphere of attention (Richards et al., 1997). On the other hand, evidence is mounting that mature spirituality can function as a resource for healing in the treatment of eating disorders (Hsu, Crisp, & Callender, 1992; Richards et al., 2006; Watkins, Christie, & Chally, 2006). For example, in a study of female inpatients diagnosed with anorexia nervosa, bulimia nervosa, or an eating disorder not otherwise specified, improvements in spiritual well-being during treatment were significantly related to gains in eating attitudes, reductions in body shape concerns, and improvements in social functioning (Smith, Hardman, Richards, & Fischer, 2003). Furthermore, indicators of lower stages of spiritual development, such as negative images of God, feelings of spiritual unworthiness, and fears of abandonment by God, have been observed in patients with eating disorders (Richards et al., 1997).

Considering these findings, psychotherapists may want to assess the level of spiritual development in clients with eating disorders and encourage clients to access and cultivate this powerful resource as an important component of treatment. They might consider incorporating into the therapeutic dialogue questions exploring spiritual beliefs or practices and challenge clients to contemplate ways in which their beliefs might explicitly help or hinder their treatment progress. Psychotherapists also should be prepared to guide and support clients through spiritual struggles and issues that might arise in relation to the eating disorder to facilitate spiritual growth as well as recovery. This guidance may include encouraging clients to engage in prayer or meditation, to seek support from religious communities or religious professionals, or to dedicate time for spiritual or religious readings.

In addition to the research on eating disorders, studies on individuals in treatment for alcohol and other drug abuse problems have shown that spiritual development and treatment progress are closely intertwined. For example, increases in spiritual well-being and other indicators of spiritual growth have been associated with length of recovery and level of recovery behaviors (Sterling et al., 2007; White, Wampler, & Fischer, 2001), and alcohol relapse has been linked to decreased spirituality (Sterling et al., 2007). The treatment outcome research on adults in Alcoholics Anonymous (AA) consistently shows that higher endorsements of spirituality, including spiritual growth, spiritual practice, and spiritual connectedness, are associated with better posttreatment outcomes (Piedmont, 2004; Sterling, Weinstein, Hill, Gottheil, Gordon, & Shorie, 2006) and longer periods of recovery (Carroll, 1993; Carter 1998). These results suggest that spiritual growth has a significant impact on treatment for substance use disorders, and neglecting the spiritual domain during the therapeutic encounter may limit the progress of individuals seeking help for alcohol or drug abuse.

That being said, findings should be interpreted judiciously. Just because spiritual growth and treatment progress were correlated, helping a client progress spiritually may not necessarily lead to better treatment outcomes. It is possible that reductions in substance abuse (or other symptoms) are necessary first, after which point individuals are more capable and interested in cultivating a spiritual life or increasing their engagement in spiritual practice. Furthermore, although correlations between spiritual growth and recovery offer some preliminary support for the incorporation of a spiritual focus in treating substance abuse, psychotherapists should be mindful of the absence of randomized clinical trials in evaluating the impact of level of spiritual development on treatment outcomes. Specific interventions intended to promote spiritual growth also are yet to be empirically tested.

Stepping outside the realm of psychopathology, spiritual development has been associated with positive mental health outcomes. For instance, in a sample of male clergy, spiritual maturity was associated with enhanced life satisfaction and improved experiences of social support (Froehlich, Fialkowski, Scheers, Wilcox, & Lawrence, 2006), and strong social support systems have been associated with lower reports of tension and anxiety (Knox, Virginia, & Lombardo, 2002). Again, in so far as higher reports of feelings of connectedness to a higher power in daily life may reflect higher levels of spiritual development, significant positive associations between spiritual development and indicators of positive functioning such as happiness and life satisfaction have been found in adult and adolescent samples (Argyle, 1999; Diener & Clifton, 2002; Diener, Suh, Lucas, & Smith, 1999; Kelley & Miller, 2007). Psychotherapists may want to consider the role of fostering spiritual development in promoting human flourishing and well-being as well as in treating or preventing psychopathology. Potential corollaries worth contemplating include the extent to which a psychotherapist should recommend spiritual practices, and the individuals for whom they would be most helpful. Additionally, if psychotherapists are uncomfortable broaching the subject of spiritual development during psychotherapy, are they denying clients a valuable resource for growth and recovery?

## CLINICAL ASSESSMENTS

Several instruments have been developed thus far to assess spiritual and religious development as conceptualized through the dominant theoretical models, including two semistructured interviews and four questionnaires. The semistructured interviews developed by Fowler (1980) and Osmer and Gmunder (1991) are labor-intensive and time-consuming instruments to administer and score, rendering them ill suited for clinical use. Furthermore, the questionnaires, although potentially useful in developmental research, have questionable applications for clinical settings, as psychometric properties of the assessments have not been investigated with clinical populations.

### Quantitative Assessments

The Faith Development Scale (Leak, Loucks, & Bowlin, 1999), a brief, seven-item scale derived explicitly from Fowler's theory and intended to generate an overall index of faith, has shown adequate internal reliability (alpha = .71) and strong test–retest reliability ($r = .96$, $p < .01$), but psychometrics were evaluated within a small sample of college students ($n = 89$). Similarly, the Ways of Faith Scale (Clore & Fitzgerald, 2002) was developed to assess the four ways of intentional faith: commonsense, thoughtful, responsible, and transcendent. Coefficient alpha values for subscales were moderate, ranging from .71 to .87, but again, the absence of psychometric research within clinically troubled populations suggests that it might not yet be appropriate for clinical use. Additionally, many practitioners might find the reliability values too low for use with patients, although values are fairly acceptable for research use. Another measure that has been widely used in developmental research to assess Fowler's stages of faith is the Faith Styles Scale (Barnes, Doyle, & Johnson, 1989). Although evidence for construct validity was reported, internal consistency and test–retest reliability were fairly low (alpha = .53; rho = .62), which is quite problematic if implemented in clinical settings.

Finally, the Spiritual Assessment Inventory (Hall & Edwards, 2002), which was developed to measure spiritual development through an object-relations theory perspective, has exhibited comparable psychometric properties with non-clinical samples (alpha = .73 to .95). If evaluated in a clinically troubled population, this scale has the potential to be more useful for clinicians, as it provides an assessment of the degree to which one's relational–emotional development is reflected in one's relationship with a higher power. For clinicians influenced by object relations theories, this type of questionnaire might facilitate conceptual integration of relational patterns manifested at the spiritual and interpersonal level. The present version of the questionnaire includes 48 items, which seems too lengthy for the time parameters of typical psychotherapy sessions.

### Intake–Interview Questions

In addition to the quantitative scales and semistructured interviews, spiritual development can be explored more broadly through open-ended questions during intake sessions. Pargament (2007) identifies several dimensions of spiritual assessment that might inform exploration of spiritual development. For example, psychotherapists might inquire about the (a) salience of spirituality, (b) salience of religious affiliation, (c) salience of spirituality to the presenting problem, and (d) salience of spirituality to the solution. Further exploration into spiritual development might be geared toward understanding the spiritual history of the client through the following questions: When did you first discover or learn about the sacred? How did you try to foster your relationship with the sacred when you were younger? How has your understanding or experience of the sacred changed since you were a child? How have your spiritual practices and beliefs changed since you were a child? How would you describe your current spiritual orientation? How do you see yourself changing spiritually in the future? Other questions proposed by Richards and Bergin (2005) include the following: Do my client's faith and spirituality promote a mature sense of spiritual identity and purpose or obscure divine potential? Do my client's faith and spirituality promote agency and choice or impairment and loss of self-control? Do my client's faith and spirituality promote integrity and congruence or deception? Do my client's faith and spirituality promote personal growth and change or stagnation?

Additionally, depending on the therapist's theoretical vantage point of spiritual and religious development, it might also be useful to glean questions from semistructured interviews, such as Fowler's faith development interview (1981). This alternative interview would save psychotherapists from the labor-intensive task of administering, scoring, and interpreting the entire interview and simultaneously would offer a resource for inquiry that is grounded in theory. The following questions drawn from Fowler's interview might prove useful clinically: What presently gives meaning to your life? Have you experienced losses, crises, or suffering that has changed your life in special ways? Have you had moments of joy, ecstasy, or breakthroughs that have shaped your life? When life seems discouraging and hopeless, what holds you up or renews your hope? Where do you feel that you are changing, growing, or struggling with doubt in your life at the present time? What is your image of mature faith?

Psychotherapists might find that implementing particular questions during the intake process or at relevant times throughout treatment is a more feasible alternative to administration of questionnaires or semistructured interviews. Open-ended questions can be tailored according to individual differences among clients and interwoven more seamlessly into the clinical hour. Asking questions about spiritual or religious development as part of the intake interview may strengthen the initial rapport by expanding the menu of therapeutic discourse and demonstrating that the psychotherapist is open and receptive to all facets of the client's life experience. In contrast, administering questionnaires might create a sense of distance or feel too evaluative for clients. Open-ended questions have the potential to provide more clinically useful information as well, because the psychotherapist is free to explore the unique ways that spiritual development might interface with treatment for each individual.

## TREATMENT STRATEGIES

In light of the range of empirical studies reporting associations between spiritual growth and many positive mental health outcomes, psychotherapists might consider expanding their approach to incorporate treatment strategies that support spiritual development in clients. Additionally, the developmental research outlined in this chapter can offer a theoretical foundation for conceptualizing the process of spiritual development in clients or assessing their level of spiritual development. To this point, some preliminary suggestions are offered about how psychotherapists might address spiritual struggles and facilitate spiritual development within the context of most therapeutic modalities (e.g., psychoanalytic, cognitive-behavioral, and interpersonal).

To begin with, psychotherapists might first focus on discerning the client's spiritual developmental level or pattern through inquiring about past and current spiritual and religious beliefs, practices, and experiences. Introducing open-ended questions such as those presented in the assessment section may best facilitate this process. Once the psychotherapist has gained some insight into the client's patterning or stage of spiritual development, he or she might then explore the ways in which presenting problems or concerns may be understood in relation to spiritual development. Psychotherapists can refer to current theories on spiritual development during this process to inform case conceptualizations and treatment approaches.

Considering that there is no single, universally agreed-on model of spiritual development, psychotherapists might find it most useful to become fluent with the various theoretical models and then formulate their approach on the basis of the model that is most reflected or embodied by each client. For example, a client whose presenting issues involve experiences of alienation or disconnection from self and others could be conceptualized from a feminist perspective on spiritual development, especially if the client is female. Psychotherapists could attempt to facilitate growth by cultivating awareness of the client's relationships and experiences that obstruct connectedness and contribute to spiritual impasse. The psychotherapist might initiate mutual exploration of experiences of self-silencing and provide a therapeutic space in which the client's voice is heard and validated. Depending on the inclinations of the client, encouraging time for contemplation, meditation, prayer, ritual, or community could promote spiritual growth and healing.

Alternatively, cognitive stage theories of spiritual and religious development posit that characteristics reflective of higher stages include the capacity to contemplate multiple logical systems and to experience abstract principles (e.g., compassion, gratitude) as connecting threads between self, other, and a higher power. Psychotherapists conceptualizing spiritual development from the cognitive perspective might facilitate growth by promoting consideration of a greater range of views or beliefs and encouraging clients to make choices that resonate with their sense of self. Another possible channel for spiritual growth could be fostering the types of qualities distinguishing higher stages, such as compassion or forgiveness. For instance, psychotherapists could assess the extent to which the client is struggling with forgiveness of self, others, and God and then could focus on the therapeutic discourse around these struggles. If clients are resistant or unable to forgive, psychotherapists might explore obstacles to forgiveness as well as personal costs of harboring anger and resentment. Once a client is ready, psychotherapists can identify particular pathways toward forgiveness that feel right for the client (i.e., writing a letter that may or may not be delivered; developing compassion for the imperfections of self, other, or God; or letting go of the past and committing to live in the present).

Based on research findings suggesting that life struggles can stimulate spiritual development (Bryant-Davis, 2005; Cadell et al., 2003; Wink & Dillon, 2002), psychotherapists might attempt to conceptualize the client's experiences of adversity from a spiritual perspective. Viewed alongside stage theories, suffering may be the catalyst to prompt growth into a new stage, at which individuals see a broader universalism, compassion, or commonality among humans. Psychotherapists might help clients reformulate their experiences of suffering as opportunities for spiritual growth. Suggesting relevant readings or referring clients to other spiritual or religious professionals might further support spiritual growth.

Drawing from the developmental research indicating that spiritual growth may be fostered through mutual dialogue and openness to doubts and questions between parents and children (Kelley et al., 2007; Schwartz, 2006), psychotherapists might model this type of dyadic discussion in the context of psychotherapy to promote spiritual development in clients (although empirical research with adults is clearly necessary to substantiate this proposition). This approach might involve encouraging the client's own questioning, offering amplified reflections in response to the client's verbal and nonverbal behavior, and improving the client's ability to tolerate ensuing fear, anxiety, sadness, or anger. Not surprisingly, these recommendations sound like good clinical practice in general; however, the difference here is in the focus of the lens, rather than the technique of treatment.

For interested psychotherapists, potential treatment strategies may be augmented through familiarity with spiritually oriented treatment models (Richards & Bergin, 2005; Sperry & Shafranske, 2005), which are ostensibly compatible with any theoretical orientation. For example, Richards and Bergin (2005) propose that healing and growth viewed from a spiritual orientation might emanate from a positive relationship with the sacred axioms in living, which they call the Spirit of Truth. Similar to physical laws of the universe, spiritual laws to human behavior transcend specific religious belief systems, such as sustaining family or upholding commitments. Living in harmony with these axioms creates the potential for thriving and growth, whereas transgressing them ignites conflict and suffering. Again, this paradigm of spiritual growth is supported by the research showing that struggles and adversity often fuel spiritual development and that attending to spiritual development, in some cases, may alleviate symptoms.

Finally, spiritual development is viewed here as a highly personal process that varies widely among individuals. Psychotherapists should remain mindful that the developmental process may not unfold according to a specific timeline and thus may not fit neatly into time-limited or manualized treatments. Openness and receptivity to the client's experience of spirituality and spiritual struggle are essential, as well as the capacity to be fully present and fully engaged with the client throughout the therapeutic journey. Given that the pathway shared between spiritual growth and mental health is not clearly delineated through existing research, psychotherapists should remain open to a multitude of possibilities that may emerge and be willing to follow the client's lead in co-constructing experience.

## CASE STUDY

### Presenting Picture

Jana, a 29-year-old Caucasian female, presented as a somewhat guarded and mistrustful but also intelligent, talented, and psychologically minded young woman when she began therapy. She had decided to seek psychotherapeutic services because she felt that she was "going through a lot of changes" and she thought it would be helpful to have someone to talk to. She was considering ending her relationship of 5 years with her boyfriend, Seth, a 46-year-old music buyer, which was causing her to experience stress and tension. She reported a history of anxiety, which she described as an "unbearable sensitivity" that would at times cause her to fear that she might lose her mind, as well as a history of symptoms of depression and dysphoria dating back to childhood. At the present time, her anxiety was experienced as a feeling of internal restlessness or "not being content."

Jana described Seth as a very talented musician who never really fulfilled his potential. They worked on writing an album together for several years, but Jana said that they could never seem to complete it. Jana stated that Seth was a "very affectionate, loving, and special man." She described him as very dependable, providing her with a sense of stability at a time when she needed it. Soon after beginning therapy, however, she realized that she had been compromising certain things to maintain the relationship, and she felt strongly that she no longer wanted to compromise concerning the things that are important to her. More specifically, she stated that "he doesn't really love himself, he doesn't actualize himself ... he drags me down and robs my spirit." She said, "He gets joy from me, but that is a huge responsibility for me." She also said that he would subtly invalidate what she said or doubt her, which made her feel belittled and disregarded. Despite her awareness of the abnegation of self required to sustain the relationship, she also felt guilty about leaving, worrying about the hurt she might inflict on Seth.

Jana described an extremely tumultuous, violent, and volatile family life. She reported having a close relationship with her sister, who was 2 years older than her, but her relationships with both of her parents were wrought with conflict. Beginning at the age of 5, she recalled that her mother and father were always "violently yelling and fighting." Her mother was an alcoholic, and when she was drinking, the violence would escalate considerably, often culminating in physical or emotional abuse. Jana stated, "She hit me, kicked me in the stomach, and strangled me until I blacked out," while her father made excuses for her mother's behavior. When Jana was 10 years old, her mother was hit by a car, suffering severe brain injury that required intensive rehabilitation lasting one year. After her mother returned from the rehabilitation center following the accident, Jana reported that she was completely "out of control." She would become "violent and combative for no reason." The family attempted to seek help and attended family therapy for several months, but Jana said that this was a "disaster." Her mother "would come to therapy drunk, sometimes not show up at all, or fight the whole time." When Jana was 15, the situation at home became too much for her to endure, and she left home and lived with various friends. She also had begun to abuse drugs to cope with the intolerable chaos in her internal and external worlds, which continued from age 11 to age 19. Jana's parents finally divorced when she was approximately 20 years old. She said that she "didn't really notice when they got divorced," adding that "they had been codependent for a long time."

At the start of treatment, Jana worked as a writer for a trend-forecasting company. She helped to write a bimonthly newsletter that covered trends in areas ranging from business to fashion. Growing up, she had always excelled in art and music and had attended a specialized high school for creative and performing arts. Throughout treatment, Jana discussed her desire to write songs and play music, affirming that song writing was her true passion, and she also spent time painting.

Although Jana's parents identified as Catholic, they never attended church or participated in religious activities. Although Jana did not consider herself to be religious, she reported a deeply felt, intrinsic sense of spirituality, which she described as an "energy" and a "connection." She viewed her spirituality as a large part of who she was and reported having many spiritual experiences throughout her life. She did not describe these in detail, but she stated that she was able to see auras and has also seen ghosts. She understood these spiritual experiences as a "gift" and something to honor. In the context of her relationship with Seth, she felt her spirituality was another area that was criticized, questioned, and invalidated by Seth.

### Assessment and Treatment

Jana's spiritual development was assessed through open-ended questions as recommended by Pargament (2007) during the intake process and throughout treatment. This approach was chosen in light of Slee's (2004) research suggesting that spiritual development in women may be more effectively explored through an open-ended conversation about their spirituality in which they have the opportunity to organize, articulate, and assert their own experience. Questions were intended to allow Jana to find her own voice and to provide her with the space to utilize her own symbols, language, and system of meaning rather than forcing her to identify with particular quantitative categories of spiritual or religious development (i.e., Do you consider yourself to be a spiritual person? Has your sense of spirituality changed over the years, and if so, how?).

Jana's sense of spirituality was a salient dimension of her life experience that was essentially interwoven through her difficulties with interpersonal relationships, depression, and anxiety and appeared somewhat thwarted and negated by important others, leading her to struggle with an authentic connection to her self. This understanding of Jana's struggles draws from the literature outlined, showing that disruptions in spiritual development may be associated with symptoms of depression and also that stressful life events hold potential for spiritual growth. In so far as Jana's struggles involved entangling and disentangling relationships in which she tended to give her entire self away to be absorbed by the other and negate her own needs in search of a deeply felt connection with others, Slee's (2004) conceptualization of the patterning of women's faith development seemed most applicable as a framework for understanding the interface of Jana's spiritual development and her presenting difficulties. With the glimmers of awareness that she had been abandoning her self for the needs of others and enduring emotional and verbal abuse in an effort to feel a spiritual connection with a partner, she began to struggle with the realization of her alienation.

During the course of treatment, Jana continually negotiated the space between alienation and awakening, struggling to work though the impasse with which she was confronted. Through this process, the therapist attempted to provide support for Jana by providing her with a safe space to begin to reclaim her self and thus reformulate her experience of spiritual connection with others and with the divine. To achieve this goal, the therapist supplied consistency through the therapeutic frame (appointment times, session length, fee schedule, etc.) as well as by providing Jana with an empathic relationship in which she was validated and affirmed through her journey, rather than starved and depleted.

Much of the content of sessions centered on her relationship with Seth and, after that, a subsequent relationship with a man named Logan. In both of these relationships, Jana's own needs were sacrificed in an effort to care for, nurture, or inspire her partner, and she experienced great difficulty asserting herself and trusting her intuition. With Logan, she initially expressed feeling like there was a spiritual connection between them or that they were "soul mates," identifying all of the experiences of synchronicity and connection that had contributed to this feeling. After several weeks, however, she began to feel that Logan was also invalidating, controlling, selfish, and manipulative. This confusing experience of feeling an intense spiritual connection and then feeling mistreated was challenging at a spiritual level and functioned as one of Jana's many mini-awakenings.

Therapy progressed always with attention and openness to the spiritual dimension of Jana's challenges as understood in relation to women's faith development theory. Through the support of the therapeutic relationship, Jana was able to begin to find a stronger voice and reaffirm and reignite her intuitive self; she began to recognize how the complete giving away of her self contributed to feelings of emptiness, depletion, and depression. In part, this involved the therapist supporting Jana's quest for self-fulfillment and actualization by devoting time to her creative passions, song writing, and painting without feeling burdened. Additionally, Jana was faced with the task of reenvisioning her sense of spirituality to include an increased care of self and a reclaiming of the parts of her self that had been given away. Through the process of reaffirming her self-in-relationship, she was able to deepen and expand the way she related to the divine. She also began to reformulate her assumptions about synchronicity and spiritual connection, continuing to view them as imbued with meaning but recognizing that their meaning could be varied and surprising, rather than static and determined (e.g., He is my soul mate). As Jana replenished her sense of self and reconstructed her sense of spirituality through the course of treatment, she observed that her experiences of depression were subsiding, and she articulated a renewed confidence and enthusiasm for the future.

## CONCLUSION

Drawing from research on cognitive and psychosocial development, a number of stage theories of spiritual and religious development have been proposed that attempt to describe distinct phases of an upward spiritual path. Further research is needed to examine the relevance of these theories across different religious traditions and nontheists using psychometrically sound assessment measures that correspond to the specific model of faith development under investigation. Additionally, combining qualitative and quantitative methods might be beneficial. Empirical research also supports the contribution of relationships with parents and friends to spiritual development, particularly in childhood and adolescence. Psychotherapists might seek to integrate these environmental and relational factors into particular models of spiritual and religious development to generate a more complete picture of the spiritual path of clients. Moreover, given that spiritual development has been associated with recovery from several forms of psychopathology and also that struggles with psychopathology and adversity might be opportunities for spiritual growth and transformation, attending to the spiritual dimension may very well facilitate positive treatment outcomes.

Although the developmental research points to some potentially useful considerations for clinical practice, it must be noted that psychotherapists should approach these considerations prudently. A wide gulf is yet to be bridged between research findings on spiritual development and implications for clinical practice. Specifically, suggestions for psychotherapists drawn from the developmental research need to be investigated empirically, with clinical populations, before recommendations for practice can be offered more resolutely. In the interim, interested psychotherapists might focus their attention on becoming familiar with the existing literature on spiritual development so that they might ask good clinical questions, such as those presented after the summary points, when therapeutically relevant.

## CHAPTER SUMMARY

- Several stage theories of spiritual and religious development have been proposed that draw largely from theory and research on cognitive and psychosocial development, such as Fowler's faith development theory and Clore and Fitzgerald's theory of intentional faith.

- Empirical research supporting various models of religious and spiritual development is somewhat lacking, and almost none has been conducted with clinical populations. Generalizing from the few cross-sectional studies conducted with nonclinical samples is extremely tenuous.
- Relationships with parents and peers characterized by warmth, acceptance, and openness to discussing spiritual concerns have been positively associated with spiritual and religious development in children and adolescents.
- Research based on attachment theory has provided some evidence for correspondence between security of attachment in childhood and the development of a relationship with a higher power through adulthood.
- Disruptions in the development of spiritual connection may pose risks for psychopathology, particularly depression and substance abuse.
- Negative life events and experiences of adversity can offer opportunities for spiritual growth and development.
- Spiritual maturity and increases in spirituality and religiosity have been linked with better treatment outcomes for eating disorders and substance abuse.
- Spiritual and religious development has been associated with positive aspects of functioning, such as life satisfaction.
- Several questionnaires are available to measure spiritual and religious development, but these have not been tested with clinical populations (i.e., the Faith Development Scale, Faith Styles Scale, and Spiritual Assessment Inventory).
- Open-ended interview questions such as "How would you describe your current spiritual orientation?" may be most clinically useful for assessing spiritual and religious development.

## CLINICAL APPLICATION QUESTIONS

1. What is my client's conceptualization of faith, and what role does faith play in his or her life?
2. What cognitive stage most appropriately corresponds to my client's spiritual or religious beliefs and understanding of faith?
3. How is my client's spiritual or religious development related to his or her presenting problem and concerns?
4. How might introducing a quantitative assessment measure of spiritual development help or hinder the therapeutic alliance and therapeutic progress?
5. What are the unique characteristics (i.e., personality traits, attachment style) of my client, and how might these influence my choice of intervention strategies?
6. What is my role as a psychotherapist in the developmental path of spirituality or religiosity traveled by my client?
7. What are the strengths and limitations of stage theories of spiritual or religious development?

8. Which contextual factors (e.g., family or friends) have contributed to or inhibited to the developmental phase of my client's faith, and how might these relationships play out within the therapeutic relationship?
9. How might my client's difficulties be understood as opportunities for spiritual growth?

## SUGGESTED READINGS AND RESOURCES

Fowler, J. W. (1981). *Stages of faith.* San Francisco, CA: Harper & Row.

Hood, R. W., Hill, P. C., & Spilka, B. (2009). *The psychology of religion: An empirical approach,* 4th ed. New York, NY: Guilford Press.

Miller, L. (2005). *Spiritual awareness psychotherapy* [DVD]. Series on spirituality and religion in psychotherapy with Jon Carlson. Washington, DC: American Psychological Association.

Pargament, K. I. (2007). *Spiritually integrated psychotherapy.* New York, NY: Guilford Press.

Shafranske, E. P. (2005). *Addressing issues of spirituality and religion in psychotherapy* [DVD]. Series on spirituality and psychotherapy with Jon Carlson. Washington, DC: American Psychological Association.

Sperry, L., & Shafranske, E. P. (Eds.). (2005). *Spiritually oriented psychotherapy.* Washington, DC: American Psychological Association.

Richards, P. S., & Bergin, A. E. (2005). *A spiritual strategy for counseling and psychotherapy.* Washington, DC: American Psychological Association.

## REFERENCES

Ainsworth, M. D. S., Blehar, M. C., Waters, E., & Wall, S. (1978). *Patterns of attachment: A psychological study of the strange situation.* Hillsdale, NJ: Erlbaum.

Argyle, M. (1999). Causes and correlates of happiness. In D. Kahneman, E. Diener, & N. Schwarz (Eds.), *Well-being: The foundations of hedonic psychology* (pp. 353–373). New York, NY: Russell Sage.

Bandura, A. (2003). On the psychosocial impact and mechanisms of spiritual modeling. *The International Journal for the Psychology of Religion, 13,* 167–173.

Bao, W., Whitbeck, L. B., Hoyt, D. R., & Conger, R. D. (1999). Perceived parental acceptance as a moderator of religious transmission among adolescent boys and girls. *Journal of Marriage and the Family, 61,* 362–374.

Barnes, M., Doyle, D., & Johnson, B. (1989). The formulation of a Fowler scale: An empirical assessment among Catholics. *Review of Research, 30,* 412–420.

Batten, M., & Oltjenbruns, K. A. (1999). Adolescent sibling bereavement as a catalyst for spiritual development: A model for understanding. *Death Studies, 23,* 529–546.

Biergegard, A., & Granqvist, P. (2004). The correspondence between attachment to parents and God: Three experiments using subliminal separation cues. *Personality and Social Psychology Bulletin, 30,* 1122–1135.

Bowlby, J. (1969). *Attachment and loss: Vol. 1. Attachment.* New York, NY: Basic Books.

Bowlby, J. (1973). *Attachment and loss: Vol. 2. Separation anxiety and anger.* New York, NY: Basic Books.

Bowlby, J. (1980). *Attachment and loss: Vol. 3. Loss.* New York, NY: Basic Books.

Boyatzis, C. J., Dollahite, D. C., & Marks, L. D. (2006). The family as a context for religious and spiritual development. In E. C. Roehlkepartain, P. E. King, L. Wagener, & P. L. Benson (Eds.), *The handbook of spiritual development in childhood and adolescence* (pp. 297–309). Thousand Oaks, CA: Sage.

Bryant-Davis, T. (2005). Coping strategies of African American adult survivors of childhood violence. *Professional Psychology: Research and Practice, 36,* 409–414.
Cadell, S., Regeher, C., & Hemsworth, D. (2003). Factors contributing to posttraumatic growth: A proposed structural equation model. *American Journal of Orthopsychiatry, 73,* 279–287.
Carroll, S. (1993). Spirituality and purpose in life in alcoholism recovery. *Journal of Studies on Alcohol, 54,* 297–301.
Carter, T. M. (1998). The effects of spiritual practices on recovery from substance abuse. *Journal of Psychiatry and Mental Health Nursing, 5,* 409–413.
Cartwright, K. B. (2001). Cognitive developmental theory and spiritual development. *Journal of Adult Development, 8,* 213–220.
Clore, V., & Fitzgerald, J. (2002). Intentional faith: An alternative view of faith development. *Journal of Adult Development, 9,* 97–107.
Degelman, D., Mullen, P., & Mullen, N. (1984). Development of abstract religious thinking: A comparison of Roman Catholic and Nazarene youth. *Journal of Psychology and Christianity, 3,* 44–49.
Desrosiers, A., Kelley, B., & Miller, L. M. (2011). Parent and peer facilitation of relational spirituality in adolescents and young adults. *Psychology of Religion and Spirituality, 3,* 39–54.
Desrosiers, A., & Miller, L. M. (2007). Relational spirituality and depression in adolescent girls. *Journal of Clinical Psychology, 63,* 1021–1037.
Desrosiers, A., & Miller, L. M. (2008). Substance use versus anxiety: Are some disorders more spiritual than others? *Research in the Social Scientific Study of Religion, 9,* 137–154.
Diener, E., & Clifton, D. (2002). Life satisfaction and religiosity in broad probability samples. *Psychological Inquiry, 13,* 206–209.
Diener, E., Suh, E. M., Lucas, R. E., & Smith, H. L. (1999). Subjective well-being: Three decades of progress. *Psychological Bulletin, 125,* 276–302.
Dollahite, D. C., & Thatcher, J. Y. (2008). Talking about religion: How highly religious youth and parents discuss their faith. *Journal of Adolescent Religion, 23,* 611–641.
Dudley, R. L., & Dudley, M. (1986). Transmission and transaction: Predicting adolescents' internalization of parental religious values. *Journal of Family Psychology, 15,* 627–645.
Elkind, D. (1961). The child's concept of his religious denomination: I. The Jewish child. *Journal of Genetic Psychology, 99,* 209–225.
Elkind, D. (1962). The child's concept of his religious denomination: II. The Catholic child. *Journal of Genetic Psychology, 101,* 185–193.
Elkind, D. (1964). Piaget's semi-clinical interview and the study of spontaneous religion. *Journal for the Scientific Study of Religion, 4,* 40–46.
Erikson, E. H. (1968). *Identity: Youth and crisis.* New York, NY: Norton.
Flor, D. L. & Knapp, N. F. (2001). Transmission and transaction: Prediction adolescents' internalization of parental religious values. *Journal of Family Psychology, 15,* 627–645.
Fowler, J. W. (1981). *Stages of faith.* San Francisco, CA: Harper & Row.
Froehlich, J. P., Fialkowski, G. M., Scheers, N. J., Wilcox, P. C., & Lawrence, R. T. (2006). Spiritual maturity and social support in a national study of a male religious order. *Pastoral Psychology, 54,* 465–478.
Gilligan, C. (1982). *In a different voice: Psychological theory and women's development.* Cambridge, MA: Harvard University Press.
Goldman, R. (1964). *Religious thinking from childhood to adolescence.* New York, NY: Seabury Press.
Granqvist, P. (2002). Attachment and religiosity in adolescence: Cross-sectional and longitudinal evaluations. *Personality and Social Psychology Bulletin, 28,* 260–270.

Granqvist, P., & Hagekull, B. (1999). Religiousness and perceived childhood attachment: Profiling socialized correspondence and emotional compensation. *Journal for the Scientific Study of Religion, 38,* 254–273.
Granqvist, P., & Hagekull, B. (2001). Seeking security in the new age: On attachment and emotional compensation. *Journal for the Scientific Study of Religion, 40,* 529–547.
Grey, M. (1999). Expelled again from Eden: Facing difference through connection. *Feminist Theology, 21,* 8–20.
Gunnoe, M. L., & Moore, K. A. (2002). Predictors of religiosity among youth aged 17–22: A longitudinal study of the National Survey of Children. *Journal for the Scientific Study of Religion, 41,* 613–622.
Hall, T. W., & Brokaw, B. F. (1995). The relationship of spiritual maturity to level of object relations development and God image. *Pastoral Psychology, 43,* 373–391.
Hall, T. W., Brokaw, B. F., Edwards, K. J., & Pike, P. L. (1998). An empirical exploration of psychoanalysis and religion: Spiritual maturity and object relations development. *Journal for the Scientific Study of Religion, 37,* 303–313.
Hall, T. W., & Edwards, K. J. (2002). The spiritual assessment inventory: A theistic model and measure for assessing spiritual development. *Journal for the Scientific Study of Religion, 41,* 341–357.
Hamilton, D. M., & Jackson, M. H. (1998). Spiritual development: Paths and processes. *Journal of Instructional Psychology, 25,* 262–270.
Heyward, I. C. (1982). *The redemption of God: A theology of mutual relation.* Washington, DC: University of America Press.
Hsu, L. K., Crisp, A. H., & Callender, J. S. (1992). Recovery in anorexia nervosa: The patient's perspective. *International Journal of Eating Disorders, 11,* 341–350.
Jordan, J. V. (1991). *Women's growth in connection: Writings from the Stone Center.* New York, NY: Guilford Press.
Kelley, B. S., Athan, A. M., & Miller, L. F. (2007). Openness and spiritual development in adolescents. *Research in the Social Scientific Study of Religion, 18,* 3–33.
Kelley, B. S., & Miller, L. (2007). Life satisfaction and spirituality in adolescents. *Research in the Social Scientific Study of Religion, 18,* 233–261.
Kendler, K. S., Gardner, C. O., & Prescott, C. A. (1997). Religion, psychopathology, and substance use and abuse: A multimeasure, genetic-epidemiologic study. *The American Journal of Psychiatry, 154,* 322–330.
Kendler, K. S., Liu, X., Gardner, C. O., McCullough, M. E., Larson, D., & Prescott, C. A. (2003). Dimensions of religiosity and their relationship to lifetime psychiatric and substance use disorders. *American Journal of Psychiatry, 160,* 496–503.
King, P. E., Furrow, J. L., & Roth, N. (2002). The influence of families and peers on adolescent religiousness. *Journal of Psychology and Christianity, 21,* 109–120.
King, V., Elder, G. H., & Whitbeck, L. B. (1997). Religious involvement among rural youth: An ecological and life-course perspective. *Journal of Research on Adolescence, 7,* 431–456.
Kirkpatrick, L. A. (1992). An attachment-theory approach to the psychology of religion. *The International Journal for the Psychology of Religion, 2,* 3–28.
Kirkpatrick, L. A. (1997). A longitudinal study of changes in religious belief and behavior as a function of individual differences in adult attachment style. *Journal for the Scientific Study of Religion, 36,* 207–217.
Kirkpatrick, L. A. (1998). God as a substitute attachment figure: A longitudinal study of adult attachment style and religious change in college students. *Personality and Social Psychology Bulletin, 24,* 961–973.

Kirkpatrick, L. A., & Shaver, P. R. (1990). Attachment theory and religion: Childhood attachments, religious beliefs and conversions. *Journal for the Scientific Study of Religion, 29,* 315–334.

Knox, S., Virginia, S., & Lombardo, J. P. (2002). Depression and anxiety in a Roman Catholic secular clergy. *Pastoral Psychology, 50,* 345–358.

Kohlberg, L. (1976). Moral stages and moralization: The cognitive-developmental approach. In T. Lickona (Ed.), *Moral development and behavior: Theory, research, and social issues* (pp. 31–53). New York, NY: Holt, Rinehart, and Winston.

Leak, G. K., Loucks, A. A., & Bowlin, P. (1999). Development and initial validation of an objective measure of faith development. *The International Journal for the Psychology of Religion, 9,* 105–124.

Lonergan, B. J. (1957). *Insight: A study of human understanding.* San Francisco, CA: Harper and Row.

Lonergan, B. J. (1970). *Method in theology.* New York, NY: Seabury.

McCullough, M. E., Bono, G. & Root, L. M. (2005). Religion and forgiveness. In R. F. Paloutzian & C. L. Park (Eds.), *Handbook of the psychology of religion and spirituality* (pp. 394–411). New York, NY: Guilford Press.

Miller, L., Davies, M., & Greenwald, S. (2000). Religiosity and substance use and abuse among adolescents in the National Comorbidity Survey. *Journal of the American Academy of Child and Adolescent Psychiatry, 39,* 1190–1197.

Miller, L., & Gur, M. (2002). Religiosity, depression, and physical maturation in adolescent girls. *Journal of the American Academy of Child & Adolescent Psychiatry, 41,* 206–214.

Miller, L., Warner, V., Wickramaratne, P., & Weissman, M. (1997). Religiosity and depression: Ten-year follow-up of depressed mothers and offspring. *Journal of the American Academy of Child and Adolescent Psychiatry, 36,* 1416–1425.

Okagaki, L., & Bevis, C. (1999). Transmission of religious values: Relations between parents' and daughters' beliefs. *The Journal of Genetic Psychology: Research and Theory on Human Development, 160,* 303–318.

Oman, D., & Thoresen, C. E. (2003). Spiritual modeling: A key to spiritual and religious growth? *The International Journal for the Psychology of Religion, 13,* 149–165.

Oser, F. K. (1991). The development of religious judgment. *New Directions for Child and Adolescent Development, 52,* 5–25.

Oser, F., & Gmunder, P. (1991). *Religious judgment: A developmental approach.* Birmingham, AL: Religious Education Press.

Ozorak, E. W. (1989). Social and cognitive influences on the development of religious beliefs and commitment in adolescence. *Journal for the Scientific Study of Religion, 28,* 448–463.

Pargament, K. I. (1997). *The psychology of religion and coping.* New York, NY: Guilford Press.

Pargament, K. I. (2007). *Spiritually integrated psychotherapy.* New York, NY: Guilford Press.

Parker, S. (2006). Measuring faith development. *Journal of Psychology and Theology, 34,* 337–348.

Piaget, J. (1970). Piaget's theory. In P. M. Carmichael (Ed.), *Manual of child psychology, Vol. 1* (3rd ed., pp. 703–732). New York, NY: John Wiley & Sons.

Piedmont, R. L. (2004). Spiritual transcendence as a predictor of psychosocial outcome from an outpatient substance abuse program. *Psychology of Addictive Behaviors, 18,* 213–222.

Pierce, B. J., & Cox, W. F. (1995). Development of faith and religious understanding in children. *Psychological Reports, 76,* 957–958.

Potvin, R. H., & Lee, C. F. (1982). Adolescent religion: A developmental approach. *Sociological Analysis, 43,* 131–135.

Richards, P. S., & Bergin, A. E. (2005). *A spiritual strategy for counseling and psychotherapy.* Washington, DC: American Psychological Association.

Richards, P. S., Berrett, M. E., Hardman, R. K., & Eggett, D. L. (2006). Comparative efficacy of spirituality, cognitive, and emotional support groups for treating eating disorder inpatients. *Eating Disorders: Journal of Treatment and Prevention, 14,* 401–415.

Richards, P. S., Hardman, R. K., Frost, H. A., Berrett, M. E., Clark-Sly, J. B., & Anderson, D. K. (1997). Spiritual issues and interventions in the treatment of patients with eating disorders. *Eating Disorders: The Journal of Treatment & Prevention, 5,* 261–279.

Rizzuto, A. M. (1979). *The birth of the living God: A psychoanalytical study.* Chicago, IL: Chicago University Press.

Schwartz, K. D. (2006). Transformations in parent and friends faith support predicting adolescents' religious faith. *The International Journal for the Psychology of Religion, 16,* 311–326.

Sinnott, J. D. (1998). *The development of logic in adulthood: Postformal thought and its applications.* New York, NY: Plenum.

Slee, N. (2004). *Women's faith development: Patterns and processes.* Burlington, VT: Ashgate.

Smith, C. (2005). *Soul searching: The religious and spiritual lives of American teenagers.* New York, NY: Oxford University Press.

Smith, F. T., Hardman, R. K., Richards, P. S., & Fischer, L. (2003). Intrinsic religiousness and spiritual well-being as predictors of treatment outcome among women with eating disorders. *Eating Disorders: The Journal of Treatment & Prevention, 11,* 15–26.

Snarey, J. (1991). Faith development, moral development, and non-theistic Judaism: A construct validity study. In W. Kurtines & J. Gerwitz (Eds.), *Handbook of moral development and behavior: Vol. 2. Research* (pp. 279–306). Hillsdale, NJ: Erlbaum.

Sperry, L., & Shafranske, E. P. (Eds.). (2005). *Spiritually oriented psychotherapy.* Washington, DC: American Psychological Association.

Sterling, R., Weinstein, C. S., Hill, P., Gottheil, E., Gordon, S. M., & Shorie, K. (2006). Level of spirituality and treatment outcome: A preliminary examination. *Journal of Studies on Alcohol, 67,* 600–606.

Sterling, R. C., Weinstein, S., Losardo, D., Raively, K., Hill, P., Petrone, A., & Gottheil, E. (2007). A retrospective case control study of alcohol relapse and spiritual growth. *The American Journal of Addictions, 16,* 56–61.

Tamminen, K. (1976). Research concerning the development of religious thinking in Finnish students: A report of results. *Character Potential: A Record of Research, 7,* 206–219.

Tamminen, K., & Nurmi, K. E. (1995). Developmental theories and religious experience. In R. W. Hood, Jr. (Ed.), *Handbook of religious experience* (pp.169–311). Birmingham, AL: Religious Education Press.

TenElshof, J. K., & Furrow, J. L. (2000). The role of secure attachment in predicting spiritual maturity of students at a conservative seminary. *Journal of Psychology and Theology, 28,* 99–108.

Watkins, J. A., Christie, C., & Chally, P. (2006). Relationship between spiritual well-being and binge eating in college females. *Eating and Weight Disorders, 11,* 51–56.

White, J. M., Wampler, R. S., & Fischer, J. L. (2001). Indicators of spiritual development in recovery from alcohol and other drug problems. *Alcoholism Treatment Quarterly, 19,* 19–35.

Wink, P., & Dillon, M. (2002). Spiritual development across the adult life course: Findings from a longitudinal study. *Journal of Adult Development, 9,* 79–94.

Zachry, W. H. (1990). Correlation of abstract religious thought and formal operations in high school and college students. *Review of Religious Research, 31,* 405–412.

# 3

# *Developmental and Narrative Perspectives on Religious and Spiritual Identity for Clinicians*

PAUL WINK, JONATHAN M. ADLER,
AND MICHELE DILLON

Identity gives an individual a sense of sameness and continuity (Erikson, 1968) and provides answers to questions about the nature, purpose, and meaning of life (Kiesling, Sorell, Montgomery, & Colwell, 2006). William James (1910/1968) placed spiritual identity, encompassing intellectual, moral, and emotional development, at the center of personality. Given that the search for personal meaning is a vital component of a person's identity, it is not surprising that religion and spirituality play a key role in the identity development of many Americans. Nonetheless, because identity addresses core issues regarding human nature, many competing paradigms or models can explain identity development (see Poll & Smith, 2003). We frame our discussion of identity in terms of two separate paths of religious and spiritual engagement. According to Wuthnow (1998), religious dwellers craft their identity by adhering to tradition, emphasizing an external source of authority. For example, within the Christian tradition, believers tend to embrace a personal God, attend church, and derive solace from prayer. In contrast, spiritual seekers tend to blend various religious traditions (e.g., combine attendance at a place of worship with nature-centered rituals or Indian meditation), prioritize the self and inner experiences, and believe in an impersonal life force. Within the therapeutic context, the narratives of religious dwellers center on finding meaning in traditional scripture (e.g., the Bible or the Koran), and they appear to prioritize conventional adjustment and personal happiness as end goals. In contrast, the narratives of spiritual seekers emphasize complexity of meaning-making associated with the blending of various religious traditions and, in therapy, tend to construe progress in terms of personal growth over adjustment and life satisfaction. Although somewhat overlapping, we conceive these two ways of relating to God or to a transcendent force as manifestations of divergent ways of being in the world and negotiating identity, which Jung (1971) has foreshadowed in his distinction between the extrovert and introvert.

The relevant clinical issues highlighted in this chapter include the nature of the relationship between the psychological experience of a transcendent being and the reality of God's existence; whether the term *spirituality* should be restricted to a quest for meaning with reference to a transcendent force, or more broadly, whether it should be construed to incorporate any search for meaning; differences in psychosocial functioning and spiritual growth among religious dwelling and seekers; and the role of happiness versus personal growth as determinants of successful identity development and therapy outcomes.

## WILLIAM JAMES AND THE SPIRITUAL ME

In discussing the nature of the self or identity, William James (1910/1968) argued that the *me* or the object of our experience (as opposed to the *I* or the knower or subject of experience) can be divided into three classes: the material me, the social me, and the spiritual me. The *material me* includes our body, clothes, physical desires, family, and other world possessions, and the *social me* includes our reputation, our interpersonal relations, and the recognition we get from others. In contrast to the more external or extroverted nature of the material and social aspects of the self, the spiritual me encompasses our internal states of consciousness, including moral and religious aspirations as well as more general states of consciousness.

Apart from his general contribution to the study of identity, James's concept of the spiritual me or spiritual identity has important implications for contemporary debates on the relationship between religion and identity. James clearly used the term spirituality in a broad sense not only to include traditional religious experiences but also to encompass other mental phenomena. This usage foreshadows current debates as to whether the term *spiritual* encompasses a quest for meaning irrespective of whether it relies on secular or sacred means, or whether the term should be restricted to a search for meaning that involves some reference to God or a transcendent being or force. The broader usage of the concept of spirituality typically is found among scholars in Europe (see Stifoss-Hanssen, 1999), where church attendance has declined precipitously since the 1960s. In contrast, most American academics tend to restrict spirituality to beliefs and practices that incorporate some reference to a transcendent being or force (e.g., Dillon & Wink, 2007; Zinnbauer & Pargament, 2005).

Clearly, either the broader or narrower sense of the term spirituality can be used legitimately as long as it is clearly operationalized. The broader use of the term, however, poses the danger of diluting the meaning of spirituality and impeding the understanding of the similarities and differences in a search for meaning that is formed on the basis of secular as opposed to sacred precepts. Dillon and Wink (2007) used a narrow definition of spirituality that restricted the term to a search for meaning "focused on the transcendent or sacred nature of being" (p. 225) and compared the social–psychological similarities and differences among spiritual individuals, church-going religious individuals, and those who were secular (i.e., neither spiritual nor religious). They found some clinically relevant commonalities and differences across the three groups. For example, although highly religious church-involved older individuals showed little fear of death, this was also true of individuals who were not religious or spiritual but who found personal meaning in secular beliefs and practices. On the other hand, only the highly religious individuals were buffered against depression and the loss of life satisfaction resulting from adversity (e.g., poor physical health) (Wink, Dillon, & Larsen, 2005). Thus, a narrowly circumscribed definition of spirituality that includes acknowledgment of God or a transcendent being has the advantage of making it possible to compare the implications for therapy and for everyday life of different ways of constructing meaning and crafting a life narrative.

Another important aspect of James's (1910/1968) conceptualization of the spiritual me or identity is that it decoupled the subjective or psychological experience of the "revelation of the living substance of our Soul" (p. 43), from questions concerning the actual existence of God or a transcendent being. In adopting this agnostic approach, James drew a clear demarcation between psychology (i.e., the study of mental states and consciousness) and theology (i.e., an academic discipline that along with philosophy has a long tradition of addressing the issue of God's existence). Carl Jung (1958) adopted a similarly agnostic stance. Although his notion of an archetype acknowledges the universal propensity of the human brain to produce images of God or the Divine, he nonetheless brackets the question of God's existence as falling outside the purview of psychology. More recently, a different approach has been taken by Richards and Bergin (1997) and Poll and Smith (2003), who embraced a model of spiritual identity development and counseling based on a theistic perspective of identity "that explicitly affirms the reality of the soul" (Poll & Smith, 2003, p. 130). Furthermore, Poll and Smith (2003) argued that "without faith that God exists and that humans are in fact spiritual in nature, the concept of spiritual identity has little merit, being merely a different aspect of social identity" (p. 133).

Although these scholars emphasize that therapy is not an appropriate forum for proselytizing, and that tolerance and respect should be shown for clients' beliefs and values, these injunctions stand in tension with what appear to be some inevitable consequences of adopting a theistic approach to identity. Poll and Smith (2003), for example, stated that "the entire process of spiritual identity development is one of unlearning beliefs about God based on interactions with others and refining more accurate images of the true attributes of God by interacting directly with Him" (p. 134). This view of spiritual development reflects a strongly Protestant view on the nature of the relationship with a transcendent being that may not be accessible to clients with non-Christian beliefs. On the other hand, in therapy in which the client and therapist share the same religious weltanschauung, the theistic view has the distinct advantage of fully facilitating the use of religious resources in the process of gaining mental health.

## ERIKSON LIFE SPAN MODEL OF IDENTITY DEVELOPMENT

Whereas William James (1910/1968) pioneered the study of the self or identity in American psychology, it was Erik Erikson (1950) who contributed the most to our understanding of identity and its development, particularly as it unfolds in a given sociohistorical context. Writing in the 1950s and early to mid-1960s, Erikson prophetically foresaw that the post–World War II decades would be characterized by a growing interest in, if not preoccupation with, self-identity. For Erikson, identity constituted "a subjective sense of an invigorating sameness and continuity" (1980, p. 109), or, to paraphrase William James, an answer to the question: Who is the real me?

According to Erikson (1950), the life cycle evolves through a series of invariant stages, each marked by a psychosocial crisis as the individual confronts and attempts to master age-appropriate developmental tasks. In infancy, a successful negotiation of the trust versus mistrust polarity engenders a sense of hope. Subsequent resolution of the tension between autonomy versus shame and doubt results in the development of a sense of will and, overcoming the conflict between initiative and guilt helps develop a firm sense of purpose. Once the child enters school, she or he develops competence by experiencing a sense of industry and thus avoiding the danger of succumbing to feelings of inferiority. Erikson postulated that issues of identity come to the forefront during adolescence, a time when young men and women must begin to develop a sense of self that is independent of their family of origin. The new pride in developing a strong sense of identity frequently signifies, Erikson (1968) argued, "an inner emancipation from a more dominant group identity" (p. 22). The process of identity development involves both reflection and observation, and simultaneously entails a differentiation of the self from others and a widening of the circle of significant others expanding from that of parents to, ultimately, the whole of mankind (generativity versus despair). A secure sense of identity results in feelings of fidelity that, on a personal level, imply an accuracy of self-perception and, on an interpersonal level, leads to loyalty and faithful devotion to others and to social causes. Once developed, a firm sense of identity helps the individual to develop the capacity for intimacy and love in early adulthood, generativity or care for others at midlife, and integrity or wisdom in old age.

An important aspect of Erikson's epigenetic model is its emphasis on the importance of the interplay between psychological and social forces in understanding the developmental tasks confronted by the individual and the resources available for successful negotiation of the vicissitudes of life. The psychosocial nature of Erikson's developmental model has several important implications for understanding the process of identity development and its relationship to religiousness and spirituality. According to Erikson (1968), the process of identity formation is aided by the development of a personal ideology that provides meaning to life. Not surprisingly, religion is an important source of ideological commitment as well as providing a valuable resource in negotiating the perils of an identity crisis. As reported by Erikson (1968), William James, for example, preserved his sanity during an acute personal crisis by clinging to scripture-texts, such as "come unto me all ye that labor and are heavy laden" (Erikson, 1968, p. 153). The ideological potential of a society inspires adolescents by pointing them to worthwhile ways of living. This is a dialectical process, Erikson (1968) argues, whereby the ideology of a social system helps adolescents develop a sense of identity and cope with crisis. At the same time, the same social system is rejuvenated by the power of the youth who absorb its ideological precepts into their lifeblood.

Erikson argues that the process of identity formation involves an intricate interplay between personal (psychological) experiences and sociohistorical events. This interrelatedness is well illustrated by the life of Martin Luther whose vocational and personal identity crisis coincided with a crisis in the church associated with what were perceived as corrupt practices of the Papacy and the priesthood, and that occurred at a time of rapid economic growth and increased rationalization in Western Europe. The responsiveness of identity to the broader social context leads Erikson (1968) to argue that, unlike personality, an individual's identity, their sense of sameness and continuity, is not set in plaster but rather is subject to change throughout the life cycle. Erikson's claim regarding the fluidity of identity presciently foreshadows the advent of postmodernity and the challenge it poses to the presumption of essential personality characteristics and the stability of the self across time and different social contexts (e.g., Gergen, 1991).

Erikson's acknowledgment of fluidity in an individual's sense of identity is highlighted in Poll and Smith's (2003) model, which assumes that individuals are prone to move between different stages of identity development depending on their personal circumstances. Thus, a person not ordinarily inclined to be spiritual might recognize and feel strongly the presence of God during the months surrounding the birth of a child (awakening stage), but then gradually become preoccupied with material concern again (preawareness stage), until perhaps an encounter with a charismatic pastor may result in deeper consideration of the individual's past and current spiritual experiences (recognition stage; Poll & Smith, 2003, p. 136). Clearly, the changeable nature of spiritual identity requires the therapist to conduct a careful assessment of the client's religious background and history. It also requires clinical sensitivity to the fact that the experience of a current stressful event, be it family conflict, illness, or death, or the experience of a normative life event, such as the birth of a child, marriage, or retirement, may result in regression to a prior stage of spiritual development or, alternatively, propel the individual to progress to a higher and more integrated level of relating with God or to a transcendent force.

A final consequence of Erikson's (1968) psychosocial model of identity development is the importance of understanding an individual's sense of self against the backdrop of the surrounding cultural landscape. This means that any consideration of religious and spiritual identity among current generations of Americans has to take into account changes in the spiritual marketplace since the 1960s and the resulting trend toward the decoupling of traditional religiousness from newer forms of spiritual beliefs and practices (e.g., Roof, 1999). Up until the 1960s, it made little sense to differentiate spirituality from religiousness because within mainstream American culture an individual's spiritual life typically revolved around the beliefs and worship practices of a well-established religious or denominational tradition (although movement between Protestant denominations was not uncommon). Recent years, however, have witnessed a significant increase in the proportion of Americans who describe themselves as spiritual but not religious. This is a varied group, but individuals who self-describe in this way typically reject institutionalized religion. Although they may or may not reject the notion of a personal God, they tend to acknowledge the existence of a transcendent force that can be known through a variety of practices drawn from both Western and Eastern religious traditions (Pew Forum, 2008). The increasing diversity of the American spiritual marketplace highlights the importance of a goodness of fit between client and therapist in therapy focused on change through spiritual development.

## MARCIA AND EGO IDENTITY STATUS

In his model of identity development, Erikson (1968) was primarily concerned with differentiating between individuals who attain a firm sense of personal continuity and sameness versus those who experience identity confusion and who, as a result, are not able to commit to a firm ideology, personal goals, and a sense of self. In particular, Erikson was interested in identity crises among creative individuals who, like Bernard Shaw and William James, grappled productively with personal vulnerability and the restraint of convention, as well as among delinquents who, as a result of childhood deprivation, developed a negative sense of identity by spitefully spurning roles and expectations offered them by the surrounding community. James Marcia (1966) elaborated Erikson's model of identity by interposing additional developmental stages or statuses between achieved identity and identity confusion.

Marcia's (1966, 1993) model of identity consists of two axes. The vertical axis is anchored by identity achieved versus identity diffused on the basis of whether the person has committed to a sense of identity. The horizontal axis is anchored by moratorium versus foreclosure on the basis of whether the individual has undergone a process of self-exploration. Achieved individuals are able to commit to an identity following a process of exploration, whereas diffused individuals show evidence of neither exploration nor commitment. The remaining two statuses are considered transitional, with foreclosed individuals showing commitment without exploration and individuals in moratorium engaging in exploration without commitment. Marcia's model is both developmental and hierarchical with the presumption that individuals progress from identity diffusion to achievement via the way stations of foreclosure and moratorium. Marcia (1993) acknowledged that his model deviates from Erikson's (1968) model. Erikson had little to say about foreclosure, and he discussed identity moratorium primarily in the context of social arrangements affording youth a reprieve from entering adulthood (e.g., an American college education that does not require students to declare a major until their junior year could be seen as an example of identity moratorium).

Marcia's (1966, 1993) conceptualization of ego identity and his interview-based method of scoring identity status through the assessment of an individual's commitment and exploration in the realm of ideology, vocation, and relationships have generated a wide body of research evidence, especially on adolescence. Hunsberger, Pratt, and Pancer (2001), for example, found that among high school seniors, identity achievement as opposed to identity diffusion was positively related to healthy personal adjustment. Whereas moratorium was related to religious doubting, foreclosed individuals were less doubtful of religious teachings. Achievement and foreclosure have been associated with higher rates of church attendance (Markstrom-Adams, Hofstra, & Dougher, 1994), and youth with achieved identity tend to exhibit intrinsic rather than extrinsic religious motivation (Markstrom-Adams & Smith, 1996). In addition, Markstrom (1999) found a relationship among adolescents between frequency of church attendance and ego strength characterized by fidelity. Among Christian college students, achieved identity has been found to be associated with greater understanding of Christian identity, God's purpose for life, and commitment to a Christian vocation (Feenstra & Brouwer, 2008).

## EGO IDENTITY AND SPIRITUALITY IN ADULTHOOD

In contrast to adolescence, little is known about the relationship between identity development and spirituality in adulthood. The most comprehensive findings come from Kiesling et al. (2006), who content analyzed the identity interview responses of devout men and women (ages 22 to 70) in a snowball sample. The structured interview explored salience (commitment) and flexibility (exploration) in the development of the religious or spiritual role as well as of the roles of partner, parent, wage worker, and homemaker. In support of Marcia's (1966, 1993) model of ego identity, the highly devout participants could be classified as spiritually achieved, foreclosed, or in moratorium. The absence of an identity-diffused group was expected given that the sample was selected purposively with positive identity development in mind.

The approximately 40% of men and women in Kiesling et al.'s (2006) study who were classified as foreclosed "had few questions or doubts about their identity commitments and tended to be unreflective" (p. 1272). Foreclosed individuals showed little sign of questioning their spiritual identity as they adopted most of their beliefs, values, and practices from their family and the religious tradition in which they grew up. One participant, for example, commented on his Christianity by saying, "I was born with it," and others provided the rationale for their current spiritual beliefs and practices by stating, "Because that's the way I was taught." Most foreclosed respondents described their spiritual identity as based on a relationship with a personal God and used terms such as "having a sense of being in the will of God," "jumping into a father's lap," and "having a childlike faith" (all quotes from Kiesling et al., 2006, p. 1272). Spiritual turning points for these men and women tended to coincide with normative life events, such as being baptized as adolescents or being ordained as a priest. When confronted with change, the foreclosed individuals typically saw it as an opportunity to deepen their faith using traditional religious practices such as prayer and worship in a like-minded community, to take them "further up and deeper in" (Kiesling et al., p. 1273).

Kieslieng et al. (2006) found that "whereas foreclosed persons emphasized intimacy and security in their relationship to a deity, individuals in moratorium were driven either by psychological benefit (e.g., self-expression, personality change, recovery from crisis, purpose) or by philosophical and ethical concerns and intellectual pursuits (e.g., to be true to their conscience)" (p. 1273). In describing their spiritual identity, men and women in moratorium tended to emphasize its creative potential and the possibility of self-realization and openness to new experiences and growth. In contrast to foreclosed individuals, who tended to associate spiritual identity with feelings of security, grace, and divine favor, those in moratorium tended to focus on feelings of nirvana, fascination, harmony, and letting go. Whereas foreclosure was associated with the need to avoid feelings of shame and social embarrassment, for individuals in moratorium, the main danger to the self arose from feelings of inauthenticity and intellectual or existential stagnation. Rather than relying on external authority, as did foreclosed individuals, those in moratorium "relied on themselves as sole arbiters of truth" (Kiesling et al., 2006, p. 1273). Spiritual practices associated with moratorium ranged from church attendance to individual personal rituals drawing on non-Western practices. In sum, identities characterized by foreclosure and moratorium appear to constitute two distinct approaches to spirituality, or two spiritual types that differ in their ways of relating to tradition and authority, practices, and attitudes toward the self.

In contrast to individuals classified as either foreclosed or in moratorium, those exhibiting achieved identity in Kiesling et al.'s study (2006) tended to show greater strength of spiritual commitment and religious commitment, but otherwise they appeared to share common characteristics with either foreclosed individuals or those in moratorium. For example, whereas spiritual striving among some of the achieved individuals was motivated by relationships and the need for connectedness, among others, it was driven by psychological or other intrinsic benefits. The spiritual practices associated with achieved identity included traditional prayer as well as nature worship and trance dancing.

Achieved identity, unlike foreclosure and moratorium, may not constitute an independent way of incorporating spiritual issues into the fabric of the self but, rather, primarily demarcates strength of spiritual beliefs and practice. Hence, one could argue that the achieved individuals are likely to be an amalgam of foreclosed and in-moratorium men and women who are highly realized in their distinct developmental paths. Although highly realized spiritual individuals may be characterized by some emergent qualities, such as a particularly strong equanimity or commitment to social justice, we would argue that these new characteristics are likely to be grafted onto a sense of identity that either prizes relationships and conventionality or prioritizes self-investment and nonconformity.

### Two Pathways to Spiritual Identity

Wink and Dillon (2003; Dillon & Wink, 2007) investigated spiritual identity using in-depth personal interviews and quantitative data in a longitudinal community study. They differentiated between traditional church-based religious belief and participation (religious dwelling) and non-church-centered engagement in intentional spiritual practices (spiritual seeking). Not surprisingly, religion was a vital component of the identity of the highly religious individuals, and, analogously, spiritual seeking was a central aspect of highly spiritual individuals' identity. The findings pointed to a clear differentiation among the study participants on a number of psychosocial characteristics, practices, and attitudes that map closely onto Kiesling et al.'s (2006) distinction between foreclosed and in-moratorium identity. Most notably, religious dwellers were characterized as warm, protective of others, likeable, dependable, ethically consistent, and prone to overcontrol their personal needs and impulses (Wink, Ciciolla, Dillon, & Tracy, 2007)—all characteristics that fit with a foreclosed identity. Similarly, they tended to uphold conventional beliefs regarding the status of women and gays in American society and emphasized the importance of maintaining law and order and existing societal traditions (Wink, Dillon, & Prettyman, 2007). In contrast, spiritual seekers showed characteristics indicative of a moratorium identity. They were intellectually independent, introspective, and creative, and had wide interests. Furthermore, they had relatively low scores on authoritarianism, thus indicating that they accepted nonconventional gender roles and sexual preferences and, in general, demonstrated independence from traditional social rules and sources of authority.

In older adulthood, the study participants were actively engaged in an array of everyday activities or life tasks. Spiritual seekers, however, reflecting their openness to experience, tended to engage more in creative life tasks (e.g., writing, sculpting, playing an instrument) and activities aimed at self-improvement. In contrast, religious dwellers showed a preference for activities involving family, friends, and community (Dillon & Wink, 2007; Wink & Dillon, 2003). Although both religious dwellers and spiritual seekers were more satisfied with life than other study participants (i.e., the nonreligious and the nonspiritual; Dillon & Wink, 2007), dwellers showed greater overall evidence of personal well-being than seekers. In particular, religious dwelling was related negatively to depression and only dwellers (as noted earlier) were buffered against depression associated with the stress of poor physical health. These findings are indicative of a connection between religious dwelling and hedonic well-being (an emphasis on maintaining high levels of positive affect; Ryan & Deci, 2001). In contrast, spiritual seeking appears to be associated with eudaimonic well-being that prioritizes personal growth over life satisfaction; thus older seekers, unlike dwellers, saw adversity as an opportunity for personal growth, and they tended to engage in life review designed to provide a new perspective on past experiences. Perhaps because of their openness to experience, spiritual seekers experienced a greater number of conflict-laden relationships and stressful life events in the first half of adulthood, and they were more likely than religious dwellers to seek therapy in early and middle adulthood (Dillon & Wink, 2007).

Although these findings on religious dwelling and spiritual seeking parallel and extend those reported by Kiesling et al. (2006) for individuals with foreclosed and in-moratorium identity statuses, the two approaches to spiritual identity differ in an important way. The former assumes that religious dwelling and spiritual seeking, or R-spiritual identity and S-spiritual identity (Wink, 2010), denote two separate ideal typical developmental paths, each with its own distinct goals and characteristics (although in individual lives, the two can overlap). The distinction between two separate paths of development allows clinicians to treat both as equally mature. Thus, a sense of identity formed on the basis of acceptance of existing traditions and conventional religious beliefs and practices without intense self-exploration can be as developmentally appropriate as one that involves crafting a more individual sense of identity based on an emphasis on self-growth, exploration, and reliance on personal feelings as the arbiter of truth. Kiesling et al (2006), by contrast, wedded to Marcia's (1966) model of ego development, allow for only one type of mature spiritual identity, that is, one necessitating both exploration and commitment. As a result, foreclosed individuals who accept traditional beliefs, values, and practices without extensive exploration, and those in moratorium who continue to be open to new possibilities, are considered lacking and in need of further growth to achieve a truly mature sense of identity.

Feminist scholars (e.g., Ray & McFadden, 2001) have criticized the notion that spiritual development necessitates exploration before commitment. They prefer the notion of a quilt or web that acknowledges a more intuitive and relational pattern of development over the rational and individualistic pattern epitomized by the popular image of a hero's journey. Similarly, Erikson's contention that the capacity for mutuality and intimacy is based on the development of a firm sense of identity has been challenged as doing injustice to those individuals—women and members of collectivist societies—who might use relationships as an opportunity to grow and develop a firmer sense of self.

The contention that two distinct lines of identity development are associated with dwelling and seeking gains support from a variety of sources. According to Otto Rank (1945), *adapted* individuals maintain throughout their lives an identification with the will of their parents that differentiates them from *creative* individuals who emphasize individuality over identification with parental or societal authority. Blatt and Shichman (1983) portrayed the anaclitic (object-directed) line of development as emphasizing satisfying interpersonal relations, intimacy, caring, and love. Chief concerns are those of closeness, affection, cooperation, and dependability. In contrast, the primary concerns of the introjective (self-directed) line of development, Blatt and Shichman (1983) argued, deal with issues of self-definition, self-worth, and autonomy. The emphasis is on thinking and action, work, and power and control, rather than on feelings and people. A similar distinction between self- and other-directedness was made by Heinz Kohut (1977) in his psychoanalytic study of the self and narcissism.

Empirical support for the psychoanalytically derived notion of distinct lines of development was provided by Wink (1991). He found that whereas self-directedness was associated with creativity, norm questioning, undercontrol of impulses, independence, and work orientation, other-directedness was characterized by prosocial inclinations, emphasis on interpersonal relationships, ego control, and readiness to accept life demands. More recently, Keyes, Shmotkin, and Ryff (2002) provided evidence of differences in psychological functioning between subjective well-being (SWB) versus psychological well-being (PWB). Whereas individuals high on SWB tended to emphasize life satisfaction and positive overall affect, those scoring high on PWB derived their sense of well-being from personal growth and purpose in life. Keyes et al.'s (2002) findings support research into different types of maturity that contrasts ego complexity or differentiation (eudaimonic well-being) with competence or happiness (hedonic well-being) (e.g., see Helson & Wink, 1987).

## NARRATIVE IDENTITY AND THE TWO PATHWAYS

Another contemporary framework for conceptualizing identity is that of *narrative identity* (e.g., McAdams, 2001). From this perspective, identity is understood as an internalized and evolving story of the self that connects the reconstructed past to the perceived present and to the anticipated future. The psychological job of narrative identity is fundamentally to provide the self with a sense of unity and purpose. In terms of unity, selves must be integrated across time, show thematic coherence, and draw from the *master narratives* outlining the typical and expected course of a life within the person's cultural context (e.g., Adler & McAdams, 2007; Habermas & Bluck, 2000; Hammack, 2008). Narratives that achieve such unity provide a deep sense of integration for the individual, and high levels of narrative coherence have been shown to correlate with a variety of positive psychological outcomes (e.g., Adler, Wagner, & McAdams, 2007).

In terms of providing the self with a sense of purpose, narratives also explain what a life means to the person living it. Personal narratives typically are characterized by a variety of themes that reveal the primary concerns that have been important to the person. McAdams, Hoffman, Mansfield, and Day (1996) pointed to *agency* and *communion* as the two central superordinate thematic clusterings in life narratives. The theme of agency is concerned with the individual's autonomy, achievement, mastery, and the ability to influence the course of their life. In contrast, the theme of communion is concerned with love, friendship, connection, and togetherness. Although agency and communion are regarded as central themes, they are by no means the only indications of purpose in one's life; a wide variety of narrative themes have been investigated, including redemption (McAdams, 2006), contamination (Adler, Kissel, & McAdams, 2006), growth (Bauer & McAdams, 2004), and many others. Each of these themes has distinct and important relationships with psychological well-being.

Researchers focused on narrative identity typically develop hypotheses about the distinctive contours of personal stories that distinguish them from others in meaningful ways. For example, McAdams (2006) identified a constellation of themes that characterizes the life stories of midlife American adults who are especially generative, that is, they are heavily invested in the well-being of future generations (Erikson, 1968). McAdams (2006) labeled this thematic clustering *the redemptive self*, as the theme of redemption is one of its organizing characteristics. These generative adults tend to describe their lives as beginning with a sense of their own advantage, set against an early awareness of the suffering of others. The narrators typically discuss their childhood and adolescence as having been imbued with a clear set of values, sometimes from religious or spiritual sources, and sometimes from family or community. This relative lack of ideological conflict is followed by grappling in the adult years with the dual demands of work and love. As these midlife adults bring their personal narratives into the present day, their stories are characterized by an emphasis on future growth and fulfillment. Throughout, these life stories are rich in scenes of redemption—their signature theme—stories that describe how specific episodes with unfortunate beginnings yield to positive endings. Redemption sequences can be highly significant, such as a cancer scare leading one to the realization of what is truly important to a person, or they can be more minor, such as a failed exam leading to a productive connection with a teacher. Regardless of the scope, these highly generative midlife adults narrate their lives as having been marked by a series of these redemption episodes.

Although the redemptive self refers to the narrative style of a broad group of individuals, these themes bear obvious connection to religious and spiritual identity. Stories of atonement are ubiquitous in religious discourse and the language of atonement fundamentally reveals a redemptive turn (McAdams, 2006). The shift from suffering to salvation is a key emphasis of religious life, particularly in the Christian-dominated United States, and this cultural narrative of redemption infuses the personal stories of many religious individuals (McAdams, 2006). In another example, Colby and Damon (1992) found that moral exemplars, many of whom espoused a richly developed spiritual identity, echoed the ideological commitment and certainty that McAdams (2006) noted. These American adults who exemplified moral virtue and who dedicated their lives to making a positive difference in the world shared the clarity of vision that is associated with the redemptive self.

In addition to the specific connections with the redemptive self, other approaches to narrating one's life relate to religious and spiritual identity development. For example, it seems that highly religious Christians shape their stories in distinct ways depending on their political affiliation. Religious conservative Christians' personal narratives tend to feature strong authority figures who are strict enforcers of moral rules and to tell stories of learning lessons in self-discipline (McAdams et al., 2008). In contrast, religious liberal Christians' narratives are not distinguished by characters of authority figures and described learning lessons regarding empathy and openness (McAdams et al., 2008). When asked to imagine a life without faith, religious conservative Christians describe scenes of unrestrained impulses and human selfishness upsetting the social order, whereas religious liberal Christians wove stories of an empty, barren, and dull world, indicating that faith serves somewhat different psychological roles for highly religious Christian conservatives and liberals (McAdams & Albaugh, 2008).

In another example, the stories of people who changed their religious affiliation were characterized by themes that related differentially to different psychological outcomes (Bauer & McAdams, 2004). In these stories of transition, themes of integration, when new perspectives of self and other were adopted, were associated with psychological maturity, as operationalized by the construct of ego development (e.g., Hy & Loevinger, 1996). In other words, those individuals whose religious transitions were narrated as being concerned with the integration of novel ways of looking at the world were found to be deeply nuanced and differentiated in their general approach to meaning-making. In contrast, those individuals whose narratives were rich in themes of intrinsic motivation—those that emphasize the importance of achieving happiness—were found to be high in overall subjective well-being and life satisfaction. Thus, different thematic profiles in these narratives of religious transitions were associated with distinct psychological outcomes (Bauer & McAdams, 2004).

This last example connects quite directly to our earlier discussion of the two pathways to religious and spiritual identity. Although Bauer and McAdams (2004) did not explore differences in religious versus spiritual transitions, their identification of narrative themes that relate differentially to affective–life satisfaction outcomes versus meaning-focused outcomes resonates with the findings we discussed earlier concerning religious dwelling's association with hedonic well-being and spiritual seeking's association with eudiamonic well-being. Indeed, scholars focused on narrative identity have embraced these two dimensions of psychological functioning in their work. If religious dwelling and spiritual seeking are routes to distinct psychological outcomes, a variety of narrative strategies also characterize these two pathways.

A large body of empirical literature suggests that ego development, or the complexity and nuance of meaning-making, is uncorrelated with subjective well-being and life satisfaction (i.e., Bauer & McAdams, 2004; King & Raspin, 2004; Pals, 2006). The ways in which these two dimensions of psychological functioning are associated with narrative strategies of self-making have been investigated in a variety of ways. For example, a series of studies by King and Raspin (2004) investigating people's adaptations to significant life transitions reveals that different approaches to storytelling relate differently to subjective well-being and ego development. When an individual undergoes a significant transition, they are faced with the psychological task of grappling with the self that they will no longer become, what King calls *lost possible selves*. For instance, when a person gets divorced, they must make sense of the married self they no longer are (King & Raspin, 2004). In studies focused on transitions ranging from the coming out process in gay individuals to coping with the prospect of having a child with Down's syndrome, King and Raspin have found that the salience of the lost possible self—how often participants thought about it—was negatively related to subjective well-being. In contrast, the elaboration of the lost possible self—the amount of vivid detail in people's narratives about this self—was related to ego development, both concurrently at the time of the narrative and years down the road. In sum, happiness appears to be associated with the ability to selectively suppress certain life events or to keep them at bay, but not repress (e.g., Vaillant, 1977). In contrast, personal growth requires an active exploration of trauma or stress to produce a change in the self or personal identity through the process of accommodation or modification of existing cognitive and emotive structures.

Another series of studies investigated the unique ways in which subjective well-being and ego development relate to narrative themes; this series focused on stories of psychotheraphy and thus is of special relevance to this book's objective. Regardless of the presenting problem the client brings to treatment, all therapies kick off with the client's story. Clients must represent their lives and problems to the therapist and, over the course of treatment, the way they story their lives evolves. A theoretical approach to treatment that explicitly focuses on the contours of clients' stories has evolved, representing the emerging school of *narrative therapy* (e.g., White & Epston, 1990). Yet regardless of the therapist's theoretical orientation, narrative offers a productive metaphor for understanding the therapeutic experience. Indeed, as with other types of significant life transitions like those described (e.g., Bauer & McAdams, 2004; King & Raspin, 2004), therapy represents a change experience that must get storied for the individual to make meaning out of it. Thus, when therapy is over, clients have a new story to tell—that of the therapeutic change episode. As in other studies of change narratives, different ways of narrating psychotherapy relate differentially to subjective well-being and ego development.

In a pair of studies by this chapter's second author (Adler & McAdams, 2007; Adler, Skalina, & McAdams, 2008), the theme of agency was associated with SWB among former therapy clients, whereas the overall coherence of their narratives was associated with ego development. That is, the extent to which clients' narratives portrayed the protagonist as having the ability to influence his or her circumstances, as opposed to being subject to the whims of the environment, was significantly positively associated with SWB. After treatment, those who narrated therapy in an agentic way were happier than those whose stories were less rich in agentic themes. As a counterpoint, those individuals whose therapy stories lacked a high degree of coherence (i.e., did not provide a clear structural flow or sense of why the narrative was salient) were found to be lower in ego development. These people whose meaning-making processes were more straightforward crafted less coherent stories about their experience in therapy (also see Adler et al., 2007). Returning to the thrust of this chapter, it seems that the two pathways to religious and spiritual identity resonate with a great deal of the work that has been done on narrative identity development, and particularly as it pertains to SWB and ego development. Just as the religious dwelling pathway may result in greater happiness while the spiritual seeking pathway may result in greater complexity of meaning-making, the distinguishing narrative themes of agency and coherence also relate differentially to these important psychological outcomes.

## CLINICAL IMPLICATIONS

Our review of religious and spiritual identity development has a number of important implications for clinical practice. The key points are as follows:

1. Adult psychological health is related to the construction of a narrative that provides the individual with a continuous and coherent sense of identity and offers meaning to life. Consequently, therapeutic success depends on helping the client develop a personally relevant and compelling life narrative. No one master narrative is related to psychological health. Personal well-being has been related to a wide range of life stories, including themes of redemption and atonement, and growth.
2. Individuals can develop a cohesive and congruent sense of identity using both religious and secular resources. When broadly construed, the term spirituality subsumes any type of quest for meaning, but when narrowly construed, it is restricted to meaning-making that includes a reference to a transcendent force or being. Successful therapy can draw on either secular or religious source to construct a meaningful life narrative.
3. A person's sense of identity does not remain static; it is subject to fluctuations based on personal experiences, stage in the life cycle, and broader changes in the sociocultural and historical context. It is imperative, therefore, to conduct a thorough assessment before the onset of therapy to develop the client's current identity status. At the same time, a radical reformulation of one's life narrative that may be appropriate in early adulthood may be counterproductive in the second half of life. In our research, we (Wink & Dillon, 2002) found that stressful or disequilibrating life events such as divorce or conflict with children promoted spiritual growth when occurring in early to middle adulthood but not later in life (presumably because of diminished opportunities to make significant life changes).
4. Spiritual identity development proceeds along two separate developmental lines. Religious dwellers or individuals high in foreclosure (preservers) adhere to tradition, tend to embrace a personal God, and place an emphasis on feelings of happiness. In contrast, spiritual seekers embrace nontraditional and eclectic ways of relating to the sacred, embrace an impersonal transcendent force, and emphasize personal growth over happiness.
5. Therapeutic interventions need to be matched with the client's religious and spiritual identity. That is, religious dwellers and spiritual seekers are likely to benefit from different types of therapeutic interventions that match their respective personality style, respect for tradition, and emphasis on hedonic versus eudaimonic well-being. In particular, religious dwellers are likely to find personal meaning and to grow through reliance

on conventional religious resources such as prayer and Bible reading. In contrast, seekers are likely to use more unorthodox religious resources to aid their spiritual journey and derive stronger solace from the sheer process of personal change and a new self-understanding than increase their life satisfaction through adjustment to societal norms and expectations.

## CLINICAL ASSESSMENT

We can assess religious-dwelling and spiritual-seeking orientations and identify individuals with a foreclosed or in-moratorium identity status in several ways. In the context of therapy, the simplest way to assess these distinctions is to ask clients first whether they are religious and subsequently whether they are spiritual. A vast majority of Americans identify themselves as both religious and spiritual, reflecting the traditional usage of the term spirituality as a marker of religious commitment (Wink, 2010). Most individuals in this group endorse traditional religious beliefs and practices and therefore would be classified as religious dwellers or foreclosed. Recent years have witnessed, however, a growing number of individuals who report being spiritual but not religious (e.g., Pew Forum, 2008). This latter group is likely to consist mainly of spiritual seekers who embrace personal autonomy from traditional religious beliefs and practices. In addition, religious dwelling can be differentiated from spiritual seeking in the Judeo-Christian tradition by asking respondents to endorse either the belief that "there is a personal god" or that "there is some sort of spirit or life force" (Houtman & Aupers, 2007, p. 311). Spiritual seekers are more likely than religious dwellers to believe that meaningful spirituality requires a combination of different religious ideas and practices, and the belief that all religious traditions and ideas refer to the same inner truth (Houtman & Mancini, 2002). Psychometrically valid measures of religious dwelling are abundant and include the Religious Commitment Inventory (Worthington et al., 2003) and the Religious Index for Psychiatric Research (Koenig, Parkerson, & Meador, 1997).

In our research, we probed for religious dwelling and spiritual seeking by asking participants about their everyday religious and spiritual experiences. Sample questions include the following: Could you describe the beliefs, values, and philosophies that guide your life? Do you consider yourself a religious person? Does the transcendent or spiritual have a place in how you think about yourself? How often do you ever attend religious services? What becomes of us when we die?

In describing his everyday beliefs and values, for example, a high scorer on our measure of religious dwelling stated, "I believe totally in scripture. I think we can always learn from it." Another highly religious participant stated, "When death comes, the last breath, my security is in my firm belief in what Jesus taught in the Bible, and that I am immediately with him in Paradise, Heaven" (Dillon & Wink, 2007, p. 228). These statements exemplify the adherence to tradition and belief in the existence of a personal God that characterizes both religious dwellers and individuals high on foreclosure. In contrast, a spiritual seeker in our sample indicated that "[she] has a very close connection to nature, ... and God or spirit is not something out there. It is mine, ... and I am co-creator of the spirit.... We are all one." In response to a question about belief in an afterlife, another spiritual individual commented, "I do believe that I'm part of the universe, and that I get returned somehow—my spirit or my consciousness—to something that is, hopefully, more worthwhile, at a higher level." Such responses are typical of the priority given to self, personal truth, and belief in an impersonal life force that typifies both spiritual seekers and individuals in moratorium.

A similar diagnostic strategy has been used to assess ego identity statuses. Marcia (1966), for example, probed for the extent of an individual's exploration and commitment in three domains: occupation, religion, and politics. The domain of religion typically is assessed by determining the extent to which the person is or is not religious in a conventional sense and inquiring about their personal philosophy of life including issues of ethics and social responsibility. Sample questions include the following: "What form and frequency of religious observances, including attendance at religious services, should be maintained? Should involvement with an organized religion be maintained, or does one need to develop a highly personal religious orientation? What positions should be taken on any of various doctrinal issues?" (Waterman, 1993, p. 158). In each of the domains, exploration is determined by evidence of a period of struggle or active questioning in arriving at decisions about goals, values, and beliefs. In contrast, commitment "involves making a relatively firm choice about identity elements and engaging in significant activity directed toward implementation of that choice" (Waterman, 1993, p. 164).

Poll and Smith (2003) provided an important four-stage model for gauging the level of spiritual or religious identity development in therapy. Clients at the *preawareness* stage "have limited recognition of spirituality" (p. 137). Poll and Smith argued, however, that many clients seeking therapy are "in want" (p. 138) but have minimal resources to draw from to further their strivings toward spiritual identity development. These individuals in the *awakening* stage are to be distinguished from those in the *recognition* stage, who have developed basic trust in a transcendent force or being. Clients at the *integration* stage of identity development perceive themselves as spiritual beings and strive to act in a way that reflects their deep sense of faith. When seen in therapy, however, these individuals are likely to have faith that is stronger in some areas of functioning than others. As previously discussed, a strength of Poll and Smith's model is its premise that clients can fluctuate between the various stages of identity development depending on their life circumstances. In addition, Poll and Smith (2003) reaffirmed the importance of the narrative approach to identity by stating that the "spiritual narrating process provides the very foundation of spiritual identity:

Storytelling may be a step towards wholeness and therefore a part of the healing activity of God" (p. 139).

## CLINICAL STRATEGIES AND CASE STUDIES

We would like to argue that knowing whether the client is a spiritual seeker or a religious dweller has important implications for the process, aims, and goals of therapy. In constructing or reconstructing their life narrative, spiritual seekers are much more likely to use the self and what feels right as the final arbiter of truth, draw on disparate religious traditions to define their relationship with a transcendent force, and emphasize personal growth and narrative coherence as markers of therapeutic progress. In contrast, religious dwellers are more likely to be guided in the process of growth and narrative development by absolute truths and an image of an external and personal God. For them, the ultimate goal of therapy is likely to center on developing a sense of agency and personal happiness and personal growth that is bound within the context of the prevailing convention. In other words, for the spiritual seeker, the divine spark is to be uncovered by a personal odyssey aimed at stripping away the norms of conduct inculcated by the process of socialization and maintained by existing cultural norms of behavior. This process of finding ultimate meaning and constructing a life narrative typically draws on beliefs and practices taken from various religious traditions, including Christianity, Buddhism, Hinduism, and Shamanism. In contrast, the task of religious dwellers is not to discover unique religious truth but rather to incorporate the precepts of an existing and well-established faith. Clearly, both tasks have their own challenges and rewards.

Although therapy choice is driven by a variety of factors and, therefore, is hard to predict, we would like to hypothesize that spiritual seekers are more likely to gravitate toward and benefit from psychodynamic and existentialist–humanist type therapies. It is not surprising, for example, that Jungian therapy (Rieff, 1966)—with its emphasis on individuation, self-seeking, the constraining effect of social norms and traditions, and the underlying unity and covalidity of all religious beliefs—holds particular sway among New Agers (Roof, 1999). The same is true of psychoanalytic therapy with its emphasis on challenging the ultimate veracity of all consciously felt experiences and norms of social conduct, and humanist therapy with its emphasis on self-actualization, personal growth, and blending of Western and Eastern therapeutic practices. Wink, Dillon, and Fay (2005) found that spiritual seeking in old age was particularly characteristic of individuals who, as adolescents, were characterized by openness to experience and personal autonomy and who in early to middle adulthood went into therapy. These longitudinal findings, in support of Rieff's (1966) contention, suggest that therapy may play an important role in the development of spiritual beliefs and practices and that for spiritual seekers the *therapist* has taken over the role of the *priest*. Although all forms of therapy aim at both the alleviation of symptoms and personal change or growth, the latter aim is better served by more global types of therapy that specifically link change with the understanding of symptoms within a broader context of personality and the nature of the client's being in the world. The nature of the relationship between therapy and self-seeking is well illustrated in Dillon and Wink's (2007) longitudinal study of lives by the cases of Jane and Melissa.

### Case of Jane[1]

Between the ages of 40 and 43 (1968–1971), Jane, her husband Jim, and their oldest son Jack sought therapy because of Jack's drug abuse. The threesome, but at times only Jane and Jim, attended encounter groups and family marathons with the aim of "trying to work out new systems for living rather than these old things that were causing the problems." Jane thought that family therapy was effective in getting Jack to change because having the parents involved conveyed to Jack the message that "we have a heck of a lot to learn ourselves and we can change too, and we don't expect it to just be you." The therapy had an existentialist bent, and participants used the "empty chair technique" to actively get involved with their problems and to get in touch with how they were feeling in the here and now. "No digging up of anxiety history. We don't go back to how did your mother treat you.... We talk about the here and now."

At the time while she was undergoing family therapy, Jane did not have strong religious beliefs. In response to the question (asked in 1972) whether she believed in God, Jane responded:

> I don't know. Not ... as some force behind the universe I sort of do, but it's very nebulous. And I sort of have a feeling that all this reaching out and exploring space and all is leading man to some kind of a greater understanding of this force, but I can't say that this force is directed to our moral lives or ... I don't feel responsible to a God.

Having grown up in a nonreligious family, Jane entertained a vague sense of a larger transcendent force since early adolescence. It was not until her next therapeutic experience that Jane, then in her early 50s, developed a much deeper sense of spirituality (as recounted in her 1982 interview). Having become a licensed therapist, Jane started to attend the ashram where as a result of profound experiences in meditation, her whole attitude toward life changed. "It became very positive, very upbeat, very cheerful, altruistic, excited, and with very little dismay." When one of her daughters was about to have her first baby, Jane had an extraordinary dream in which the daughter, Kate, was the diva in an opera. As part of the spectacle, Kate "resplendent with belly" was brought on stage in a divan and to the accompaniment of a chorus of heavenly, angelic voices, gave birth to a

[1] All quotes in the following three cases are taken from original interview transcripts.

baby, a baby that happened to be Jane herself. Interpreting the dream as a sign of rebirth, Jane really wanted to be present at Kate's delivery but also felt obliged to take care of a sick son. Consumed with fear and guilt, Jane ended up attending a prolonged meditation session with hundreds of other individuals at an ashram visited by a prominent guru. During the meditative state, after being singled out by the guru, Jane had a revelatory peak experience. Feeling intense heat all over her body and with perspiration running down her face, Jane felt "like a ripe fruit dropping into—being released from its bonds, and dropping into the regenerative womb." In this state Jane gave up all her guilt, pain, and suffering and felt "like some great physical blockage was just leaving and moving out."

When interviewed 20 years later (in 1998) at age 72, Jane described a very close connection to nature. She meditated on a regular basis, sometimes by simply going inside the house and being completely still and, at other times, meditating on love or compassion. She described God or spirit as "not something out there. It's in me. And that I'm a co-creator of the spirit. There's no judgments. We are, you know, as one. All one. And god is our external appearances and ways of thought." Following the death of her husband after a prolonged illness, Jane retired to spiritual community in New Mexico in the late 1990s.

### Case of Melissa

In crafting a meaningful life, Melissa, like Jane, was helped by therapy and spirituality. As an adult, Melissa had to come to terms with childhood trauma and conflict with both of her parents, who were perceived by Melissa as narrow-minded and unsympathetic to her needs and aspirations. Melissa divorced her emotionally distant husband and had to support herself and her two young children at a time (the 1970s) when career opportunities for women were limited. Grappling with depression and self-doubt, Melissa sought answers to her problems by blending Western and Eastern religious beliefs and practices, including meditation, Shamanistic rituals, and participation in a drumming circle. She relied on dreams to provide a running commentary on her life and to allow her to get in touch with the universal archetypes hidden behind Maya's veil. Like Jane, Melissa described mystical experiences. For example, when initially considering divorcing her husband, Melissa looked one day at him asleep and saw his head turn into a brilliant white light—like something, as she said, out of Castaneda's novel. She interpreted this sign to mean that the relationship had hope because her husband's persona was more than just the surface.

At age 70, Melissa described her philosophy of life as centered on finding out what is true versus illusory and the need to "consider possibilities, but believe nothing." When asked how she had changed over the years, she stated that "it is like having a screen in front of your eyes that you could hardly see through. So I have to get the screen back, and back. It is now pretty far back, but maybe you never get rid of it." Despite her emphasis on the unknown, Melissa was prepared to believe in some kind of a life force, which, however, she was hesitant to call "God." She had a vision of the world as a total ecosystem, with all its living organisms equally sacred. In her words: "A person is part of everything that is alive, part of the [sacred] total." Having adopted aspects of Hindu philosophy, Melissa was able to reconcile herself with her deceased parents by coming to the realization that it is "you who chooses your own parents or—in this philosophy—you set yourself these parameters, or the difficulties, and then see what you can do with them."

From a therapeutic perspective, the cases of Jane and Melissa vividly illustrate the spiritual seeker's need to weave a complex narrative that integrates the self with a transcendent force that permeates the world at large. As a result, neither woman sought solutions to her immediate problems; rather, striving for self-understanding and narrative coherence took precedence over the demands of external reality. For both women, dreams became an important aspect of therapy as they facilitated their encounter with the unconscious and archetypical substratum lying beneath the level of awareness. Although at age 70 both Jane and Melissa were highly functioning, as befits Jungian (1971) introverts, neither stressed happiness as a central goal in life. Rather, their adult lives can be construed as a never-ending quest to craft an increasingly individuated life story that freed them from the shackles of convention.

Unlike that of spiritual seekers, the life narrative of religious dwellers in the Judeo–Christian tradition tends to be based on the acknowledgment of the existence of an external and personal God who is the source of morality and world order. As suggested by Poll and Smith (2003), for the Christian counselor, "when one's story is told, identity and resolution found, God has been encountered in God's self-revelation" (p. 140). The fact that religious dwellers are guided by a belief in the reality of an external God and the validity of scriptural truth does not mean that they are not prone to internal struggle or personal growth. The main difference, after all, between religious dwellers and spiritual seekers revolves not around the quest for deeper self-understanding but around the parameters of growth: the allegiance to an external versus internal source of truth and authority. In addition, and perhaps a consequence of the divergent ways of relating to the external world, religious dwellers are much more likely than spiritual seekers to construe the aim of spiritual development in terms of personal life satisfaction and satisfactory relationships with others. Dillon and Wink (2007) found that religious dwelling was related in late adulthood to a sense of well-being from personal relationships, whereas spiritual seeking was related to well-being from personal growth. Given the external criteria for growth and an emphasis on happiness and satisfactory relationships with others, religious dwellers are more likely than spiritual seekers to benefit from cognitive-behavioral therapies and certain types of emotion-focused therapies that emphasize adjustment to the external world and personal well-being. As indicated by Poll and Smith (2003), from a theistic perspective (Richards & Bergin, 1997), it is important for therapists working with religious dwellers to assist their clients in recognizing or reaffirming a spiritual identity based on the acceptance of God's will.

### Case of Anne

Anne, another of Dillon and Wink's (2007) study participants, entered therapy with a psychiatrist in her late 30s. The initial reason for therapy was depression following a hysterectomy that the gynecologist felt had a psychological component and the psychiatrist attributed primarily to hormonal changes. According to Anne, the main benefit of the therapy was that she developed a better understanding of the dynamics in her family. In particular, she became more objective about her relationship with her husband and mother-in-law. Previously, Anne was hurt by the fact that her mother-in-law seemed to shun her family and more frequently visit her other children. As a result of therapy, Anne became more philosophical about the relationship and this made her life more pleasant. Realizing that the tension in the relationship with her mother-in-law had more to do with her husband than herself, Anne learned not to initiate inviting her mother-in-law to visit but rather to wait until the initiative came from her husband. Anne was glad to have been in therapy because she otherwise would have felt guilty following the death of her mother-in-law, thinking she had done something wrong and wondering why she never "made the grade." Instead, as a result of therapy, Anne realized that the problem was not with her but had something to do with the relationship between her husband and his mother that caused them to be distant and over which she had no control.

At the time of her therapy, Anne, a Catholic, attended church regularly and believed in an afterlife of "a state of everlasting happiness, whatever that might be." When reinterviewed more than 30 years later at age 69, Anne said that religion was an invaluable source of strength and comfort in her life in general and more specifically was a great support to her in her 35-year battle with cancer. Even though she was on a morphine drip and hooked up to an oxygen tank, Anne rated her life satisfaction as high and was looking forward to a big family party celebrating her 70th birthday. In response to the question "What is the purpose of life?" Anne stated, "Well we're taught in the church the purpose of life is to know, love, and serve God, and save our own souls. And I think I've served that purpose by the life I've led." She went on to describe Catholicism as not just a Sunday religion but also

> a religion that you're living and you're practicing every day of your life. I can't take pieces out of it because it's all one piece, a part of the whole.... I mean I can be out digging in the garden and saying my prayers. If there is something bothering me I don't have to run to church and kneel down in front of the altar to say my prayers. It's a living religion, and if you live your religion, really live it, I think it automatically solves a lot of problems for you. I wouldn't say automatically, but it does solve problems for you.

And although Anne strongly believed that her religious outlook was true and that Jesus Christ came to this earth as the Son of God, she was tolerant and had great respect for other religions.

In contrast to Jane and Melissa, Anne's description of her therapeutic experience as well as her attitude toward religious teachings was characterized by a deferential tone and a conviction that both the therapist and the priest imparted fundamental truths about life. Her view of the afterlife emphasized the theme of happiness. At the same time, her life narrative was devoid of the complexity characteristic of spiritual seekers. Instead, Anne used therapy and religion to enhance life satisfaction and prop up her self-esteem and sense of agency. In turn, the latter helped her to deal more effectively with the demands of the external world and negotiate the relationship between her husband and mother-in-law. Given the fact that Anne's life is guided by the belief in an external truth and a personal God, she is likely to be much more willing to seek and accept advice from a therapist than either Jane or Melissa for whom the self constitutes the final arbiter of truth.

It is important to keep in mind, of course, that the boundaries between spiritual seeking and religious dwelling are never clear-cut, and the same applies to distinctions between hedonic and eudaimonic well-being and narratives based on agency and coherence. At the same time, it needs to be acknowledged that the spiritual seeker's emphasis on a complexity of life narrative can be a double-edged sword. On the one hand, it offers the promise of developing a psychologically nuanced sense of self that does not easily succumb to external pressures to conform. On the other hand, however, an emphasis of the primacy of inner life can alienate the person from others and can result in a paralysis detracting from the ability to attain desired life goals. Conversely, a religious dweller's focus on the external world can come at a price of relative lack of differentiation and complexity of life narrative.

## CONCLUSION

A meaningful sense of identity or narrative is vital to crafting a purposeful and satisfying life. Historically, religion has played a vital role in the identity development of many individuals even though the self has undergone considerable transformation since the dawn of modernity (Taylor, 1989). Clearly, there is more than one way of incorporating religion into a life narrative just as there are many ways of being in the world. The contemporary American religious landscape has witnessed the emergence of religious dwelling and spiritual seeking as overlapping but alternative ways of incorporating the sacred into an individual's sense of identity. Whereas religious dwellers emphasize an external source of authority and tend to uphold a traditional religious and social order, spiritual seekers prioritize the self and inner experiences and a belief in an impersonal life force.

The distinction between these two types of religious orientation is important for therapy as religious dwellers tend to derive their sense of well-being from feelings of happiness and life satisfaction and, in contrast, spiritual seekers tend to emphasize personal growth. Even though most religion scholars tend to use the terms religiousness and spirituality interchangeably, a growing body of research disentangling the nature and implications of church-centered religion from individualized spirituality (e.g., Dillon & Wink, 2007; Roof 1999) suggests that researchers and therapists can well benefit from awareness of the different ways by which individuals incorporate the sacred into their self-identity.

## CHAPTER SUMMARY

- Identity gives an individual a sense of sameness and continuity and therefore is vital for well-being and healthy psychological functioning.
- Research on identity has focused largely on Marcia's ego identity statuses. In contemporary American religious landscape, identity development follows two lines of development associated with either religious dwelling or spiritual seeking. This distinction reflects Marcia's dichotomy between identity foreclosed and in moratorium.
- Religious dwellers craft their identity by adhering to tradition, emphasizing an external source of authority, for example, within the Christian tradition by embracing the notion of a personal God, attending church, and deriving solace from prayer.
- Spiritual seekers, in contrast, tend to blend various religious traditions, prioritize the self and inner experiences, believe in an impersonal life force, and be eclectic in their religious practices.
- Although only moderately overlapping, religious dwelling and spiritual seeking share important characteristics in common, including a generative concern for others and, in old age, vital involvement in everyday activities.
- In terms of assessment, religious dwellers tend to describe themselves as both religious and spiritual and tend to endorse a belief in a personal God. In contrast, spiritual seekers tend to portray themselves as spiritual but not religious, and they are likely to believe in an impersonal and transcendent spirit.
- In therapy, the narratives of religious dwellers center on finding meaning in traditional scripture (e.g., the Bible or the Koran). In contrast, narratives of spiritual seekers emphasize complexity of meaning-making associated with a blending of various religious traditions.
- In terms of therapeutic goals, religious dwellers prioritize conventional adjustment and happiness (hedonic well-being), whereas spiritual seekers tend to emphasize personal growth (eudaimonic well-being).

- In general, the theme of redemption (turning adversity into growth or fulfillment) characterizes personal narratives of highly functioning religious Americans irrespective of their specific religious orientation.

## CLINICAL APPLICATION QUESTIONS

1. Given your client base, what is your estimate of the number of religious dwellers and spiritual seekers? Do you adjust your therapeutic technique or strategies on the basis of this differentiation?
2. Do you think that happiness and personal growth go hand in hand, or are the two in tension? Can an emphasis on happiness and life satisfaction be detrimental to self-exploration?
3. What adjustments, if any, do you make in therapy based on your client's age? Do you think that a person's sense of identity or life narrative changes with age? Was Erikson correct in assuming that generative concerns and wisdom come to the forefront in the second half of the adult life cycle?
4. What kinds of life narratives have you come across among your clients? Are the themes of redemption and atonement important for understanding Americans' sense of self? Do the salience of these themes have cultural variations? Have you observed ethnic difference in life narratives?
5. What client characteristics predispose him or her to posttraumatic growth?
6. One could argue that what matters in dealing with stress and adversity is not whether one is religious/spiritual or agnostic/atheistic but rather the strength and conviction of the belief. Do you agree with this statement? What might help an agnostic individual deal with death anxiety?

## SUGGESTED READINGS AND RESOURCES

Dillon, M., & Wink, P. (2007). *In the course of a lifetime: Tracing religious belief, practice, and change*. Berkeley: University of California Press.

Erikson, E. H. E. (1968). *Identity: Youth and crisis*. London, England: Faber.

Heelas, P., & Woodhead, L. (2005). *The spiritual revolution: Why religion is giving way to spirituality*. Oxford, England: Blackwell.

McAdams, D. P. (2006). *The redemptive self: Stories Americans live by*. New York, NY: Oxford University Press.

Rieff, P. (1966). *The triumph of the therapeutic: Uses of faith after Freud*. Middlesex, England: Penguin University Books.

Roof, W. C. (1999). *Spiritual marketplace: Baby boomers and the remaking of American religion*. Princeton, NJ: Princeton University Press.

## REFERENCES

Adler, J. M., Kissel, E. C., & McAdams, D. P. (2006). Emerging from the CAVE: Attributional style and the narrative study of identity in midlife adults. *Cognitive Therapy and Research, 30*, 39–51.

Adler, J. M., & McAdams, D.P. (2007). Time, culture, and stories of the self. *Psychological Inquiry, 18*, 97–99.

Adler, J. M., Skalina, L. M., & McAdams, D. P. (2008). The narrative reconstruction of psychotherapy and psychological health. *Psychotherapy Research, 18,* 719–734.

Adler, J. M., Wagner, J. W., & McAdams, D. P. (2007). Personality and the coherence of psychotherapy narratives. *Journal of Research in Personality, 41,* 1179–1198.

Bauer, J. J., & McAdams, D. P. (2004). Personal growth in adults' stories of life transitions. *Journal of Personality, 72,* 573–602.

Blatt, S., & Shichman, S. (1983). Two primary configurations of psychopathology. *Psychoanalysis and Contemporary Thought, 6,* 187–254.

Colby, A., & Damon, W. (1992). *Some do care: Contemporary lives of moral exemplars.* New York, NY: Free Press.

Dillon, M., & Wink, P. (2007). *In the course of a lifetime: Tracing religious belief, practice, and change.* Berkeley: University of California Press.

Erikson, E. H. E. (1950). *Childhood and society.* New York, NY: Norton.

Erikson, E. H. E. (1968). *Identity: Youth and crisis.* London, England: Faber.

Erikson, E. H. E. (1980). *Identity and the life cycle.* New York, NY: Norton.

Feenstra, J. S., & Brouwer, A. M. (2008). Christian vocation: Defining relations with identity status, college adjustment, and spirituality. *Journal of Psychology and Theology, 36,* 83–93.

Gergen, K. (1991). *The saturated self.* New York, NY: Basic Books

Habermas, T., & Bluck, S. (2000). Getting a life: The emergence of the life story in adolescence. *Psychological Bulletin, 126,* 748–769.

Hammack, P. L. (2008). Narrative and the cultural psychology of identity. *Personality and Social Psychology Review, 12,* 222–247.

Helson, R., & Wink, P. (1987). Two conceptions of maturity examined in the findings of a longitudinal study. *Journal of Personality and Social Psychology, 53,* 531–541.

Houtman, D., & Aupers, S. (2007). The spiritual turn and the decline of tradition: The spread of post-Christian spirituality in 14 Western countries, 1981–2000. *Journal for the Scientific Study of Religion, 46,* 305–320.

Houtman, D., & Mancini, P. (2002). Why do churches become empty, while New Age grows? Secularization and religious change in the Netherlands. *Journal for the Scientific Study of Religion, 41,* 455–473.

Hunsberger, B., Pratt, M., & Pancer, S. M. (2001). Adolescent identity formation: Religious exploration and commitment. *Identity: An International Journal of Theory and Research, 1,* 365–386.

Hy, L. X., & Loevinger, J. (1996). *Measuring ego development* (2nd ed.). Hillsdale, NJ: Erlbaum.

James, W. (1968). The self. In C. Gordon & K. J. Gergen (Eds.), *The self in social interaction* (Vol. 1, p. 41–49). New York, NY: Wiley. (Original work published in 1910)

Jung, C. G. (1958). Psychology and religion: West and east. In H. Read, M. Fordham, and G. Adler (Eds.), *The Collected Works of C. G. Jung.* Princeton, NJ: Princeton University Press.

Jung, C. G. (1971). *Psychological types.* Princeton, NJ: Princeton University Press.

Keyes, C. L. M., Shmotkin, D., & Ryff, C. D. (2002). Optimizing well-being: The empirical encounter of two traditions. *Journal of Personality and Social Psychology, 82,* 1007–1022.

Kiesling, C., Sorell, G. T., Montgomery, M. J., & Colwell, R. K. (2006). Identity and spirituality: A psychosocial exploration of the sense of spiritual self. *Developmental Psychology, 42,* 1269–1277.

King, L. A., & Raspin, C. (2004). Lost and found possible selves, subjective well-being, and ego development in divorced women. *Journal of Personality, 72,* 603–632.

Koenig, H. G., Parkerson, G., & Meador, K. (1997). Religion index for psychiatric research. *American Journal of Psychiatry, 153,* 885–886.
Kohut, H. (1977). *The restoration of self.* New York, NY: International Universities Press.
Marcia, J. (1966). Development and validation of ego-identity status. *Journal of Personality and Social Psychology, 3,* 551–558.
Marcia, J. E. (1993). The ego identity status approach to ego identity. In J. Marcia, A. Waterman, D. Matteson, S. Archer, & J. Orlofsky (Eds.), *Ego identity: A handbook for psychosocial research* (pp. 3–21). New York, NY: Springer-Verlag.
Markstrom, C. A. (1999). Religious involvement and adolescent psychosocial development. *Journal of Adolescence, 22,* 205–221.
Markstrom-Adams, C., Hofstra, G., & Dougher, K. (1994). The ego-virtue of fidelity: A case for the study of religion and identity formation in adolescence. *Journal of Youth and Adolescence, 23,* 453–469.
Markstrom-Adams, C., & Smith, M. (1996). Identity formation and religious orientation among high school students from the United States and Canada. *Journal of Adolescence, 19,* 247–261.
McAdams, D. P. (2001). The psychology of life stories. *Review of General Psychology, 5,* 100–122.
McAdams, D. P. (2006). *The redemptive self: Stories Americans live by.* New York, NY: Oxford University Press.
McAdams, D., & Albaugh, M. (2008). What if there were no God? Politically conservative and liberal Christians imagine their lives without faith. *Journal of Research in Personality, 42,* 1668–1672.
McAdams, D. P., Albaugh, M., Farber, E., Daniels, J., Logan, R.L., & Olson, B. (2008). Family metaphors and moral intuitions: How conservatives and liberals narrate their lives. *Journal of Personality and Social Psychology, 95,* 978–990.
McAdams, D. P., Hoffman, B.J., Mansfield, E.D., & Day, R. (1996). Themes of agency and communion in significant autobiographical scenes. *Journal of Personality, 64,* 339–378.
Pals, J. L. (2006). Narrative identity processing of difficult life experiences: Pathways of personality development and positive self-transformation in adulthood. *Journal of Personality, 74,* 1079–1110.
Pew Forum. (2008). *U.S. religious landscape survey.* Washington, DC: Pew Research Center.
Poll, J. B., & Smith, T. B. (2003). The spiritual self: Toward a conceptualization of spiritual identity development. *Journal of Psychology and Theology, 31,* 129–142.
Rank, O. (1947). *Will therapy and truth and reality.* New York, NY: Knopf.
Ray, R. W., & McFadden, S. H. (2001). The web and the quilt: Alternatives to the heroic journey toward spiritual development. *Journal of Adult Development, 8,* 201–211.
Richards, P. S., & Bergin, A. E. (1997). *A spiritual strategy for counseling and psychotherapy.* Washington, DC: American Psychological Press.
Rieff, P. (1966). *The triumph of the therapeutic: Uses of faith after Freud.* Middlesex, England: Penguin University Books.
Roof, W. C. (1999). *Spiritual marketplace: Baby boomers and the remaking of American religion.* Princeton, NJ: Princeton University Press.
Ryan, R. M., & Deci, E. L. (2001). On happiness and human potentials: A review of research on hedonic and eudaimonic well-being. *Annual Review of Psychology, 52,* 141–166.
Stifoss-Hanssen, H. (1999). Religion and spirituality: What a European ear hears. *The International Journal for the Psychology of Religion, 9,* 25–33.
Taylor, C. (1989). *Sources of the self: The making of the modern identity.* Cambridge, MA: Harvard University Press.
Vaillant, G. (1977). *Adaptation to life.* Boston, MA: Little, Brown.

Waterman, A. S. (1993). Developmental perspectives on identity formation: From adolescence to adulthood. In J. Marcia, A. Waterman, D. Matteson, S. Archer, & J. Orlofsky (Eds.), *Ego identity: A handbook for psychosocial research* (pp. 42–68). New York, NY: Springer-Verlag.

White, M., & Epston, D. (1990). *Narrative means to therapeutic ends.* New York, NY: Norton.

Wink, P. (1991). Self and object-directedness in adult women. *Journal of Personality, 59,* 769–791.

Wink, P. (2010). Trouble with spirituality. *Research in the Social Scientific Study of Religion, 21,* 49–70.

Wink, P., Ciciolla, L., Dillon, M., & Tracy, A. (2007) Religiousness, spirituality, and personality; Findings from a longitudinal study. *Journal of Personality, 75,* 1051–1070.

Wink, P., & Dillon, M. (2002). Spiritual development across the adult life course: Findings from a longitudinal study. *Journal of Adult Development, 9,* 79–94.

Wink, P. & Dillon, M. (2003). Religiousness, spirituality, and psychosocial functioning in late adulthood: Findings from a longitudinal study. *Psychology and Aging, 18,* 916–924.

Wink, P., Dillon, M., & Fay, K. (2005). Spiritual seeking, narcissism, and psychotherapy: How are they related? *Journal for the Scientific Study of Religion, 44,* 143–158.

Wink, P., Dillon, M., & Larsen, B. (2005). Religion as moderator of the depression-health connection. *Research on Aging, 27,* 197–220.

Wink, P., Dillon, M., & Prettyman, A. (2007). The relation between religiousness, spiritual seeking and authoritarianism: Findings from a longitudinal study. *Journal for the Scientific Study of Religion, 46,* 321–335.

Worthington, E. L. Jr., Wade, N. G., Hight, T. L., Ripley, J. S. McCullough M. E., Berry, J. W., et al. (2003). The Religious Commitment Inventory—10: Development, refinement, and validation of a brief scale for research and counseling. *Journal of Counseling Psychology, 50,* 84–96.

Wuthnow, R. (1998). *After heaven: Spirituality in America since the 1950s.* Berkeley: University of California Press.

Zinnbauer, B. J., & Pargament, K. I. (2005). Religion and spirituality. In R. F. Paloutzian & C. L. Park (Eds.), *Handbook of the psychology of religion and spirituality* (pp. 21–42). New York, NY: Guilford Press.

# 4

# *Religious and Spiritual Motivations in Clinical Practice*

PETER C. HILL, EVONNE SMITH,
AND STEVEN J. SANDAGE

Motivation, whether or not guided by religious concerns, is a highly complex phenomenon and one that is difficult for scientific study. Broadly defined, to motivate is to set into motion; the energization of behavior and its direction toward a goal. Psychologists speak of motivation as a state or drive, and different states or drives have different goals. Although this chapter will focus specifically on the concept of religious motivation, we cannot escape other aspects of religious experience entirely because motivation will be influenced by beliefs, values, and especially emotions. Ultimately, our goal is to understand how the motivational basis of religion can function in ways that sometimes lead to a personally enriching growth and at other times result in an overwhelming burden.

## RELIGIOUS AND SPIRITUAL PERSPECTIVE

Most of the research on religious motivation has been conducted within a Judeo-Christian context (primarily Christian) in North America and the United Kingdom. The God of Judaism and Christianity has been construed as a transcendent, yet also anthropomorphic, figure who, depending on the theology of the particular tradition, often is perceived to be personally involved and vitally interested in human affairs. Islam, as the other major Western monotheistic religion, shares many of these assumptions. Such perceptions of God, including interpretations of how God chooses to be known by humans, have important implications for religious motivation. This is not to say that motivations emanating from other religious traditions or motivations of those who identify their spiritual experiences outside any religious tradition should be considered any less important or relevant to the psychological study of religion and spirituality. What will be presented in this chapter, however, represents the psychology of religious motivation literature to date, which largely reflects the Judeo–Christian tradition. This is slowly changing, and a similar chapter written 10 years from now may have a broader research base from which to draw.

## THEORETICAL MODELS AND EMPIRICAL RESEARCH

In this section, we will explore religious motivation in light of four religious orientations: intrinsic, extrinsic, quest, and religious fundamentalism. Each orientation will be described and discussed in terms of motivational components, and selected research will be presented with suggestions to benefit clinical practice.

### Intrinsic and Extrinsic Religious Motivations

The most influential theory in contemporary psychology of religion over the past half century is a theory of motivation: Allport's (1950; Allport & Ross, 1967) theory of religious orientation. Allport posited two primary religious orientations that are best conceptualized in terms of motivation: an intrinsic and an extrinsic orientation. This distinction is made on the basis of the recognition that although two individuals may engage in similar religious behavior—attend church, engage in religious rituals, take a spiritual pilgrimage, and so on—they may do so for different reasons, with some reasons reflecting more mature religious motivations than other reasons. An *intrinsic* orientation is the tendency to view religion as the reference point or framework from which other aspects of life are perceived and understood; it is a devout and strongly personal commitment to an ethic that stresses love of neighbor; the sentiment itself is of primary importance to the individual and is of ultimate concern and significance (Emmons, 1999). Religion is the supreme value, the final good, and the ultimate answer to life's most important questions. In short, it is a master motive, an internalized and sincere desire to serve the object of devotion.

In contrast, individuals with an *extrinsic orientation* approach religion as a tool that can be used for self-justification and to fulfill certain needs, such as security, a sense of belonging, and even community status. Faith and beliefs are selectively held and frequently superficial; an extrinsic religious orientation is a religion of convenience and expediency that is called on only when needed and, therefore, is not well integrated into daily life. In contrast to the end orientation of an intrinsic orientation, an extrinsically motivated faith is a means to some other end. This means that extrinsic religiosity involves limited religious motivation for coping with suffering or drawing on faith during stressful life transitions.

## QUEST RELIGIOUS MOTIVATION

Although our understanding of intrinsic and extrinsic orientations has changed little over the last 30 years, what has changed during this period is the development of a third religious orientation. *Quest* was proposed as an orientation that involves "honestly facing existential questions in all their complexity, while at the same time resisting clear-cut, pat answers" (Batson, Schoenrade, & Ventis, 1993, p. 166). The quest construct was designed to address three factors included in Allport's original conceptualization of mature religion that, according to Batson and his colleagues, were neglected in subsequent research. These factors are (1) being prepared to confront existential questions without simplifying them, (2) viewing doubts as healthy, and (3) demonstrating openness to change. Quite simply, Batson's concern was that the disregard of these important components of a mature religiousness or spirituality could result in an approach and measure of maturity that reflect only a devout endorsement of religious teachings (i.e., the intrinsic religion's "master motive" quality) at the expense of a fuller, richer conceptualization. Batson and colleagues' conceptualization, reflecting an open-ended existential and process philosophy, emphasizes complexity, doubt, and tentativeness as significant aspects of religious maturity.

Yet Batson et al.'s (1993) approach, too, has been criticized on the grounds that doubt and questioning are less reflective of a mature religion than they are indicative of a religious faith that is still in process (Hood & Morris, 1985), suggesting that, for some, an intrinsic orientation may be the end result of the questing search. A classic study by Thouless (1935) found that people tend to hold religious beliefs with considerable conviction, suggesting that religious doubt is fleeting and temporary for most people. Watson, Howard, Hood, and Morris (1988) found that a quest orientation tends to peak in late adolescence and early adulthood and then declines throughout adulthood, suggesting a temporary orientation rather than a pervasive motivation through the life span. It is also possible that intrinsic and quest forms of religiosity could increase and even be integrated over the course of faith development, as evidenced in a longitudinal study with adult Christian seminary students (Williamson & Sandage, 2009). The sustainability and development of any religious orientation over time remains an open research question.

It is likely that the role of questing or doubting as a religious motivation differs considerably between people, and the clinician needs to consider possible influences of skepticism and questioning in the life of the religious client. Given that flexibility often is viewed as a hallmark of mental health, one can rightfully assume that, in some cases, questing represents a form of openness and a tolerance of ambiguity that reflects religious maturity and, indeed, doubt has been shown to be an important part of psychological and cognitive development (Krause, Ingersoll-Dayton, Ellison, & Wulff, 1999). It often takes a high level of courage, strong sense of self and personal competence, and high ability to tolerate ambiguity to seriously entertain thoughts of religious doubt. Religious questing has been shown to increase following exposure to tragedy, as profound existential questions might press for a spiritual transformation involving a new system of meaning (Krauss & Flaherty, 2001). On the other hand, religious doubting can increase feelings of psychological distress and decreased feelings of personal well-being depending on the religious and family contexts (Krause et al., 1999), perhaps because of a number of factors or consequences such as strong social disapproval or stressful family patterns (Hunsberger, Alisat, Pancer, & Pratt, 1996). A study with Christian undergraduates found moderate levels of family triangulation were associated with the highest levels of existential questioning, suggesting that limited questing might emerge in young adults from families with very low or very high levels of enmeshment (Rootes, Jankowski, & Sandage, 2009). Quest religiosity also has been associated with lower levels of sexual guilt and masturbation discomfort, which is a contrast with the positive correlation for both intrinsic and extrinsic religiosity with both those variables and other sexual concerns (Crowden & Bradshaw, 2007). For many individuals, religion has been shown to be an effective coping mechanism (Pargament, 1997), so newfound doubting may undermine such adaptive means, particularly if those means include healthy social support. Questing may adversely affect self-esteem by inducing feelings of guilt or shame if it feels disloyal to a conservative religious tradition or results in marginalization (Krause et al., 1999). On the other hand, people typically will not quest for new meaning unless their prior methods of coping have some limitation. It would be an oversimplification to declare a quest religious orientation as necessarily healthy or unhealthy, and quest is best viewed as a motivation that potentially can be part of spiritual and religious development.

## Research Findings on Intrinsic-Extrinsic-Quest Religious Motivations

### *Early Research Findings*

The intrinsic–extrinsic distinction originated in the study of prejudice. Donahue's (1985) meta-analysis concluded that research has rather consistently supported the Allport and Ross (1967) finding that extrinsics are more prejudiced than intrinsics, although perhaps not as strongly as predicted by Allport. Across nine studies reviewed by Donahue, the mean correlation between prejudice and intrinsic orientation was –.09 and was .28 with an extrinsic orientation. Although now dated, Donahue's meta-analysis remains the most systematic analysis of religious orientation to date, and Donahue's conclusions have largely been supported by subsequent research (Hood, Hill, & Spilka, 2009).

### *Clinical Findings*

In a meta-analytic study of 147 investigations, Smith, McCullough, and Poll (2003) found that religiousness is mildly associated with fewer depressive symptoms ($r = -10$), and that religious orientation is a key moderating variable. They also found that extrinsic religious orientation was positively correlated ($r = .16$) whereas intrinsic religious orientation was negatively correlated ($r = -.18$) with depressive symptoms. Research on anxiety shows similar results (e.g., Baker & Gorsuch, 1982). One of the more interesting studies compared the extrinsic and intrinsic orientations of both Thai Buddhists and Canadian Christians (Tapanya, Nicki, & Jarusawad, 1997). The relationship between anxiety and religious orientation was approximately the same in both samples, with intrinsic religion being negatively correlated and extrinsic religion positively correlated with anxiety and worry. A number of other negative psychological constructs such as ego weakness, poor social integration, and suspiciousness show the same correlational pattern with both intrinsic and extrinsic religion (Bergin, Masters, & Richards, 1987), a pattern now replicated with Muslims (Watson et al., 2002).

The preponderance of evidence suggests that intrinsic religious orientation is positively associated with mental health. In contrast, extrinsic religion does not fare nearly as well on most mental health measures and has been positively correlated with narcissism, particularly among males (Watson, Jones, & Morris, 2004). One possible implication of this general finding is that individuals who seek God or religious involvement as an ends in itself (intrinsic religiosity) are more likely to have increased social functioning (because of lower levels of suspiciousness and greater social integration) and possibly better therapeutic prognosis (because of greater ego strength and lower levels of anxiety and worry). Intrinsic motivations, whether religious or otherwise, are more likely to be associated with developmental maturity than are extrinsic motivations. As the particular relationship between extrinsic religiosity and these possible areas of difficulty may vary between individuals, therapists are encouraged to explore each dynamic with individual clients.

### *Moral Decision Making*

Much of the research on religious orientation as motivation has focused on such topics of morality as prejudice, discrimination, and helping behavior. Hunsberger and Jackson's (2005) review of the literature indicates that as long as the object of prejudice or discrimination is based on a characteristic that does not involve a moral issue (such as race or gender), then the religiously prescribed intrinsic orientation is negatively associated and the utilitarian-guided extrinsic orientation is positively associated with intolerance. If, however, the object of intolerance involves a moral issue (such as homosexuality), then intrinsics show as much, or even more, prejudice as extrinsics. In contrast, the quest orientation is negatively associated with prejudice, regardless of the object to which the attitude or behavior is being expressed.

A similar pattern of results can be found from the research on religious orientation and helping behavior. Not surprisingly, a number of studies found a positive correlation between *self-reported* measures of both intrinsic and quest religious motivations and helping behavior (Bernt, 1989; Watson, Hood, Morris, & Hall, 1984). In two separate studies, however, Batson and his colleagues (Batson,

Eidelman, Higley, & Russell, 2001; Batson, Floyd, Meyer, & Winner, 1999) found that only a quest orientation seems to be a good predictor of *actual* (versus self-reported) helping behavior (see Hood et al., 2009, for a review of this complex literature). In general, extrinsics were the least likely to *report* (and actually engage in) helping behavior, presumably because such behavior may involve costs with little self-advantage.

The differences between intrinsics and questers in helping are especially evident if helping the person may involve a value-violating behavior. Batson et al. (2001) found that intrinsics were not only less likely to help someone engage in a behavior they viewed as morally wrong (e.g., give money to help finance a trip to a gay-pride rally if they believe homosexuality is wrong), but also likely to express antipathy toward that person. In contrast, the high-quest participants were less likely to give money to a person when doing so would promote a value-violating intolerance (e.g., giving money for the individual to attend an antigay rally because it suggests a closed-minded mentality), but they were equally likely to give money to a person who held "intolerant" or "close-minded" values (e.g., an individual who was antigay) when giving money to the individual would not promote intolerance (e.g., money given to visit the individual's grandparents). Yet Goldfried and Miner (2002) questioned Batson et al.'s (2001) conclusion that questing correlates with a universally empathic stance, based on their finding that individuals high on a measure of quest religiosity were less likely to help an individual who was a fundamentalist than an individual who was not. Goldfried and Miner's findings instead suggested that quest may correlate positively with empathy only toward others who hold similar values, in this case open-mindedness. Finally, it should be noted that Batson, Denton, and Vollmecke (2008) failed to replicate the Goldfried and Miner's findings, suggesting that this will remain a fertile topic of research.

One can draw a number of clinical implications from this line of research. First, it is important to recognize the importance of one's value system as a religious motivator, particularly with regard to moral decision making. For the intrinsic, this value system may be defined by religious teachings; for the quester, this value system may include the ideal of open-mindedness and flexibility. The therapist, of course, should respect the values contained within each motivational system and try to understand, *in the client's own terms*, why she or he takes a specific approach to moral decision making and altruistic behavior. Either intrinsic or quest religious orientations might motivate helping others, depending on the person.

Second, all people, whether religious or not, are subject to biases defined through their own value system, and these findings seem to apply to all forms of religious motivation. Thus, it is likely that even the most open-minded of religious questers are subject to the biases of their own value system and, therefore, are less tolerant of people who do not match their ideal of intellectual openness and flexibility. Clinicians are not immune to bias that might favor either intrinsic or quest motivations, which suggests that regular attention to countertransference is wise.

Third, the distinction found in various studies between what a religious person says they believe they would do (often reflecting strongly held religious values) and what the research indicates that a person actually does, may cause a certain level of dissonance and discomfort for the individual, especially the intrinsically oriented individual. Of course, this clinical implication relies on what may be a questionable assumption that the person is aware of such incongruence in his or her own life—an assumption that, if not met, may indicate an important need to be addressed. Although considerable research in social psychology suggests that people often go to great lengths to justify their behavior and thereby reduce any dissonance associated with it, it also is likely that some individuals will experience guilt and possibly even shame over the difference between their self-reported and actual behavior. This discrepancy may be especially distressing to individuals prone to guilt- or shame-based reactions (e.g., individuals with a depressive personality structure) or those with low self-esteem.

Finally, a universally compassionate religious style is unlikely, although one can surmise from the research with North American Christian samples that the extrinsic orientation may be a good candidate for an *un*compassionate religious motivation (although this conclusion may not apply to other religious contexts; see Cohen & Hill, 2007). It is premature and likely incorrect to think that questers are, by nature, more or less compassionate than intrinsics.

### *Summary*

Perhaps the most important question for consideration is not the degree to which the *categories* of intrinsic, extrinsic, or quest religious motivations reflect mature religion or spirituality, but rather how well a person functions with whatever religious orientation he or she may have. Consider the intrinsically oriented person. That person may have, as Batson et al. colleagues (1993) have argued, mindlessly adopted (for whatever reason) a religious orthodoxy that only *appears* to be a mature orientation. Or, that person may have, as suggested by Hood and Morris (1985), arrived at a religious or spiritual conviction after deep and careful consideration of life's most perplexing existential questions. Likewise, the quester may represent a religious maturity by his or her willingness to grapple with life's difficult questions without resorting to simple and easy answers (Hunsberger et al., 1996). On the other hand, the ability of the quester to differentiate but not integrate into broader theoretical structures, such as that potentially provided by religious or spiritual meaning systems, may create confusion, isolation, and even existential crisis. Although clients may seldom seek therapy directly because of these existential crises, this confusion may be reflected in clients' core beliefs or schemas underlying psychological disorders, such as depression (e.g., "Life is meaningless.") or anxiety disorders (e.g., "Am I going to be condemned?"). Even the self-serving extrinsic religious orientation at times may be useful if it helps the person cope with demands of everyday living (Pargament, 1992). Indeed, in some religious cultures that are particularly communal, an extrinsic religion may be endorsed as a more mature religious motivation than it is in Christianity (Cohen & Hill, 2007). Thus, it may be less important to argue the superiority of one orientation over another as much as to determine the degree to which any religious orientation can be used in a healthy or unhealthy manner.

### Religious Fundamentalism

We propose that religious fundamentalism could be considered yet another religious motivation with important implications for therapy. Religious fundamentalists may be at increased risk for various psychopathologies (e.g., depression, anxiety, guilt, or low self-esteem) yet, because of religious schemas, they either may be less likely to seek help or may seek help only from certain therapists (Hartz & Everett, 1989; Worthington, Kurusu, McCullough, & Sandage, 1996). For instance, highly religious Protestant and Jewish clients may be more likely to seek therapists who hold similar religious orientations, values, and commitments than other clients (Worthington et al., 1996).

The need to understand this group of clients is heightened by the impact of therapists' possible biases. Research on therapist religious bias in clinical settings is limited and the results are mixed; some studies (e.g., Reed, 1992) find no evidence for therapist bias, whereas other studies (e.g., Gartner, Harmatz, Hohmann, Larson, & Gartner, 1990) indicate that nonreligious therapists (or therapists with religious orientations that differ from their clients) may be more likely to perceive fundamentalist clients as presenting with higher levels of psychopathology and stress and lower levels of empathy and psychological maturity than other clients with the same symptoms (Worthington et al., 1996). Religious issues also may play more central roles in therapy for these individuals, regardless of the religious nature of their presenting problems. The role of religiosity in therapy thus may be more complicated when working with these clients and may require therapists to adjust their clinical approaches accordingly. Therefore, understanding the motivations underlying religious fundamentalism is important for therapists working with this client population. Some therapists may need to come to grips with their own biases, either favorable or unfavorable, regarding fundamentalist forms of religion.

#### *Fundamentalism as Cognitive Style*

Although there are other definitions of religious fundamentalism, the following definition offered by Altemeyer and Hunsberger (1992) has generated the most research attention:

> [T]he belief that there is one set of religious teachings that clearly contains the fundamental, basic, intrinsic, essential, inerrant truth about humanity and deity; that this essential truth is fundamentally opposed by forces of evil which must be vigorously fought; that this truth must be followed today according to the fundamental, unchangeable practices of the past; and that those who believe and follow these fundamental teachings have a special relationship with the deity. (p. 118)

It is within this definitional framework that the authors developed a 20-item Likert-type measure for research purposes of religious fundamentalism (and in 2004 developed a shortened 12-item version). Based on this conceptualization and measure, these researchers found that people who score high on fundamentalism also tend to score high on a measure of right-wing authoritarianism (RWA; Altemeyer, 1988), suggesting that the two tendencies seem to "feed" on each other in that both encourage conventionalism, self-righteousness, feelings of superiority, and obedience to authority.

Hunsberger and Jackson's (2005) review of 16 published articles (some with multiple samples) found that religious fundamentalism, mostly measured by the Altemeyer and Hunsberger (1992, 2004) instrument, positively correlated with different types of intolerance (racial/ethnic, gay/lesbian, women, communists, religious out-groups, and RWA) in 44 of 50 studies. In the other six studies, religious fundamentalism was uncorrelated with racial and ethnic intolerance. In no study was this measure of religious fundamentalism negatively correlated with intolerance. Jackson and Esses (1997) found that those high in religious fundamentalism tended to attribute the suffering of those whose behavior violated conservative norms (i.e., homosexuals and single mothers) to internal rather than external causes and believed that such moral violators should be left to help themselves if in need. The increased risk and prevalence of intolerance and prejudice may impair social and emotional functioning of these individuals and indicate a decreased psychological flexibility and more rigid cognitive approach that can be detrimental to psychological health.

Fundamentalists may filter their world in a manner that seeks confirmation for intolerant views, discounting discrepant information in the process. Therapeutically, these clients may be less open to information that contradicts their established schemas. Fundamentalism can be described as resistance to modernity, so those high in fundamentalism may be more suspicious of professionals and large social systems (e.g., a mental health care system) than other clients.

### *Fundamentalism as Meaning-Making*

An alternative conceptualization to the Altemeyer and Hunsberger (1992, 2004) conceptualization of religious fundamentalism has been offered by Hood, Hill, and Williamson (2005). They argue that the rigid dogmatic cognitive style captured so well by Altemeyer and Hunsberger applies to only some fundamentalists. For them, the bigger issue surrounds the question "*Why* do fundamentalists so strongly adhere to their belief system?" To answer this question, the authors propose a "hermeneutical" approach (see Sandage, Cook, Hill, Strawn, & Reimer, 2008) whereby fundamentalists are studied on their own terms.

Hood et al. (2005) proposed that fundamentalists are driven by what they call an *intratextual* model of meaning-making; that is, a single sacred text is the provider of absolute truth and therefore should be viewed as supremely authoritative. For fundamentalist Christians, of course, this text is the Bible, but virtually every religious or spiritual tradition has some text (usually written, but sometimes oral) that is accorded sacred status. Other nonfundamentalist adherents also might believe in the same sacred text; the difference, however, is that for the fundamentalist the text itself contains absolute truths that inform and regulate all beliefs, even those beliefs not directly addressed by the text itself. No other text is necessary for an understanding of absolute truth, although perhaps the text points to other sources of knowledge (e.g., experiential knowledge, knowledge gained through the senses). Any other potential source of truth, including science, must align with the claims of the sacred text to be legitimate. Thus, for the intratextualist, the sacred text is a filter through which all aspects of life, not just those directly related to religious issues, are understood. It is therefore important that therapists be sensitive to the concerns of such religiously conservative clients who nevertheless seek therapy despite serious reservations, emanating from an intratextually driven meaning system, about the wisdom of entering into a therapeutic relationship with a professional. This might feel like a compromise of core convictions or even a lack of faith for the fundamentalist. It also may be the case that therapeutic interventions likely will not be accepted unless they can be legitimated by the client's understanding of the sacred text.

In contrast, the religiously committed *non*fundamentalist utilizes the principle of *intertextuality,* whereby multiple texts can speak authoritatively and deriving truth may involve the consultation of several, possibly interrelated, sources of knowledge. Consider, for example, whether one should allow contemporary psychology to inform such issues as how the husband–wife relationship should be structured, whether divorce should be considered a legitimate option, or the degree to which sexual orientation is genetically determined. To the intertextually driven nonfundamentalist (including those strongly committed to a religious or spiritual tradition), it might seem ludicrous to consider such issues without the benefit of psychological science and clinical wisdom. To the fundamentalist, however, such allowance violates what is subjectively determined to be an even more important principle—that the sacred text be granted ultimate authority and that its authority cannot be questioned. In this sense, fundamentalism can be viewed as a relatively closed system that tends to conserve prior meanings and rigorously controls new input from outside the system, suggesting that it could be considered an opposite religious motivation to quest.

These are extreme types on which a typology is described. Hood et al. (2005) recognized that, in reality, even the intratextualist often relies on multiple sources of knowledge. The key point is that these other sources of knowledge must be consistent with the sacred text—or at least do not challenge it, either directly or by implication.

### *Clinical Issues*

The clinical implications of a fundamentalist religious motivation are numerous. First, the defensiveness displayed by fundamentalists, although sometimes reflecting a personality characteristic, is no doubt exacerbated by the fact that fundamentalists accurately perceive themselves continuously at odds with an inhospitable culture that, in itself, has an impact on social and emotional functioning. For example, a continuous defensive posture is likely to lead to decreased flexibility of thought and experience and elevated anxiety. The fundamentalist may surround himself or herself with only other intratextualists (e.g., Bible-believing Christians) and, in fact, in-group and out-group distinctions mark one of the key characteristics of fundamentalists in their desire to remain separate from the world (Ammerman, 1987). Although Hood et al. (2005) argued that such defensiveness reflects, in part, the influence of a subculture with strong historical reactionary roots to a culture that is hostile to conservative Christianity, it also appears that fundamentalists see the world in absolutistic terms and that this may reflect a closed cognitive style (Hunsberger et al., 1996; Kirkpatrick, Hood, & Hartz, 1991). Beck (2006) found that those Christians who display what he called a *defensive religion*, where religious beliefs "are motivated primarily by the goal of providing existential comfort and solace" (p. 208), were likely not only to resist confronting existential realities but also to demonstrate a strong in-group bias.

To the extent that clinical psychology may be seen to represent a culture at odds with their religious values and as an enterprise that may challenge their source of existential comfort, fundamentalist clients may come to therapy in a primed defensive mode. Early in the clinical relationship, therapists should cautiously attempt to disarm and reduce such defensiveness to increase therapeutic effectiveness. Religious defense serves similar purposes to those of other defenses (e.g., to keep painful thoughts, feelings, memories, and so on from conscious awareness) and can be addressed similarly. To avoid undermining clients' religious beliefs or unnecessarily increasing defenses in reaction to a perceived attack on their religion, therapists can first affirm healthy parts of a client's faith. For therapists who share religious frameworks with their client, are familiar with the sacred texts of their clients, and are comfortable doing so, the use of a short verse of a sacred text or biblical language in challenging, clarifying, and interpreting defensive uses of faith may be helpful in addressing these religious defenses, especially for fundamentalist clients. The clinician who does so should remain cognizant that the fundamentalist client may deeply respect the power of these sacred texts and may resist an attitude that seems too casual about the meaning of such texts.

Second, fundamentalists are more likely than their other religious counterparts to display a strong need for certainty and to avoid religious doubt (Hunsberger et al., 1996), a religious orientation that can lead to resistance to change. To the extent that a religious fundamentalist motivation is maladaptive and in need of change, the clinician should expect such change to be unusually difficult and strongly resisted. After all, for the religious fundamentalist, the issues at stake in therapy may be perceived to be of ultimate significance. Or, paradoxically, a fundamentalist belief that, for example, the end of the world is eminent might limit their motivation to address "temporal" issues, such as marital conflicts.

Therapists, therefore, should exercise caution in challenging fundamentalists' core religious beliefs (e.g., textual inerrancy, the authority of scripture and religious leaders) and corresponding religious values (e.g., views on evolution, abortion) that emanate from those core beliefs (Worthington et al., 1996). Issues of sexuality and gender might be particularly anxiety provoking. Disappointed ideals related to God or the sacred can be a powerful source of pain or narcissistic injury (Jones, 2002). Fundamentalist clients might leave a session in which they cried over a spiritual disappointment and later feel tremendous shame for implying a lack of faith to the therapist.

Third, religious fundamentalists tend to value obedience in children, are more likely to endorse the use of corporal punishment in child rearing (Mahoney, Pargament, Tarakeshwar, & Swank, 2001), and manifest other authoritarian attitudes and values (Altemeyer & Hunsberger, 1992), largely because they see such values as biblically grounded. Should such issues arise in therapy, the clinician should be sensitive to the fact that they likely are rooted deeply in a comprehensive belief system that the individual finds strongly compelling and one that often is at odds with popular culture. Defensive or "paranoid" perceptions thus may contain a rational element, and therapists need to carefully differentiate between cognitive processes that are concordant with the religious schemas of these clients and more paranoid or defensive cognitive reactions. Although many fundamentalists might strike some outside evaluators as paranoid, narcissistic, or compulsive, clinicians should consider the social context as well as within-group differences when making diagnoses. Therapists will be wise to avoid unnecessary power struggles with fundamentalists, especially early in therapy. Their authoritarian preference in leadership, however, means they likely will prefer a directive over a nondirective therapist and an initial focus on practical issues over insight.

## CLINICAL IMPLICATIONS

### Understanding Risk Factors

Understanding clients' religious motivations on both conscious and unconscious levels has important clinical implications. Although religion in general has been found to positively affect mental health (Bergin et al., 1987; Smith et al., 2003), this beneficial effect may depend on motivations underlying religious activity. Keeping in mind that correlations do not imply causal relationships, particular types of religious motivation (most notably extrinsic and fundamentalist orientations) appear to exhibit positive associations with psychopathology or constructs detrimental to mental health.

#### *Extrinsic Religious Motivation*

As already noted, Smith et al.'s (2003) meta-analysis of 147 studies found that, although religiousness overall has a weak negative relationship with depressive symptoms, extrinsic religious motivation is positively correlated with depressive symptoms. Across a range of studies and populations (e.g., Nelson, 1989), extrinsic religious motivation has been found to be positively related to symptoms of depression, higher stress levels among missionaries (Navara & James, 2005), and neurotic thinking and behavior within clinical populations (Strommen, Brekke, Underwager, & Johnson, 1972). Many researchers maintain that religion is in a unique position to provide clients with a sense of purpose or meaning in life (Hood et al., 2009; Park, 2005). Perhaps extrinsic religion, with its utilitarian and narcissistic focus, is less successful as a meaning system at times of distress or loss, which require a religious orientation that can be used to tolerate distress and to find meaning in suffering. Thus, extrinsic religiosity may fail to provide the adaptive reframing or coping resources that intrinsic motivations or questing can offer, thereby facilitating limited protection against affective disorders. Extrinsic religiosity involves using religion primarily for personal benefits, so this can correlate with a religious worldview focused on luck, obtaining spiritual privileges, or entitlement to spiritually generated health and wealth. There is little room in such worldviews for the spiritual benefits of struggles, which may produce shame and hopelessness.

Several clinical strategies might be useful for those high in extrinsic religiosity. First, some clients may be going through a faith development transition and moving from an extrinsic to a more intrinsic orientation. Such clients might be responsive to reframes or invitations to consider how their spirituality or religion might be useful to them in coping with their struggles. For example, a client might be asked, "How does your Buddhist tradition understand suffering and ways of coping with suffering?" Many high extrinsics probably have limited experience with empathic and nonjudgmental figures who probe in this way. They might be helped to move toward internalizing more mature elements of their spiritual or religious traditions to cope with the issues at hand.

Second, clients high in the social approval aspects of extrinsic religiosity might be helped through (a) the use of idealized leaders or historical figures, or (b) questioning the need for social approval. If they idealize certain clergy, leaders, or even religious figures in their tradition, the therapist might be able to utilize those persons intersubjectively with the client to move from idealization to practical benefit and internalization. For example, if the client grants a release of information, the therapist might consult with a clergy member or spiritual leader the client trusts. This could be particularly useful if the client loses motivation for therapy and the clergy member or spiritual leader can offer accountability to continue treatment. Historical figures the clients admire might even be used in therapy dialogue (e.g., "What do you think Gandhi would do if he were struggling with panic disorder?"), which can help motivate more realistic use of religious ideals in support of practical coping strategies. Clients who are only moderately narcissistic in this idealizing way and moving toward internalization might be more directly questioned about the need for social approval or validation from others in their religious community. Most spiritual and religious traditions offer narratives and teachings that promote personal integrity and differentiation rather than focusing on the need to managing social impressions.

Finally, some extrinsically religious clients might simply need other motivations for therapeutic change besides explicit use of religion or spirituality. Perhaps their ability to internalize constructive religious or spiritual motivations is too limited, at least early in therapy. Others might find greater intrinsic motivation through art, music, nature, sports, political themes, or some other source they may not consciously recognize as sacred. Some extrinsics simply may need to utilize external motivators at the outset of therapy, such as avoiding certain aversive consequences (e.g., hospitalization, job loss, incarceration, or divorce). Intrinsic motivations may develop over time through therapeutic progress.

### *Fundamentalism*

A number of studies support the conclusion that fundamentalism is detrimental for psychological health. Possibly because of a rigid cognitive style that often characterizes fundamentalism, problems such as elevated prevalence rates of depression, suicidality, anxiety, guilt, low self-esteem, sexual inhibitions, and "fears of divine punishment" are associated with fundamentalism (Hartz & Everett, 1989). Many of these relationships have been found both for individuals who come from strict religious or fundamental backgrounds and for individuals who leave fundamentalist groups (Hartz & Everett, 1989). The relationship with fundamentalism, however, is more complicated than it might initially appear, as fundamentalism also has been positively associated with hope and optimism (Sethi & Seligman, 1993).

The discrepancies in findings may be due to a number of factors. We have noted that definitions of "fundamentalism" often vary widely between studies.

Sometimes the term is used in place of religious orthodoxy or conservatism (e.g., Sethi & Seligman, 1993), and at other times, it is used to capture a rigid and dogmatic religiousness (e.g., Altemeyer & Hunsberger, 1992). Also, not all people who are classified as fundamentalists are necessarily irrational and rigidly dogmatic (Hood et al., 2005). Even so, a fundamentalist orientation represents those with a strict set of beliefs that are relatively impermeable and that often maintain implications far beyond the religious teachings. Common among virtually all models, fundamentalists tend to employ schemas that typically judge the world in dichotomous evaluative terms, such as good or bad, all or none, insider or outsider, believer or nonbeliever, and so forth (Park & Paloutzian, 2005). Given that dichotomized and polarized thinking or "splitting" is often detrimental to psychological health, this may indicate an area of clinical concern. Cognitive therapists might help such clients engage in more dialectical thinking by partially agreeing with a statement and adding some new meaning or question (e.g., "I see your point, and I also wonder about ..."). Psychodynamic therapists might explore ambivalent feelings beneath rigid positions. Even if these approaches prove beneficial, they likely require patience and multiple interventions over time rather than trying to dislodge such thinking patterns all at once. Moreover, it is important for therapists to keep in mind that the presenting problems for a fundamentalist may be due to a rigid cognitive style, the content of specific theological beliefs, a specific cultural or religious context, or any combination of the above.

*Defense Against Reality*

Religious motivations may be especially maladaptive when they are driven by underlying extrinsic motivations to meet other desires or needs. This is especially problematic in individuals who use religion or religious beliefs to deny reality or to *counter therapy* (Southard, 1956). Such an illusory defense against reality (Ostow, 1990) may explain how some forms of religious involvement satisfy unconscious desires, something particularly prevalent among individuals attracted to fundamentalist groups (Hood et al., 2009). As Hill and Hood (1999) explained, however, the claim that religious beliefs function as an illusory defense against reality rests on the assumptions that religious beliefs are false (thus acceptance of such claims cannot be accounted for by objective reality) and that unconscious affect is the basis for religious representations. The first assumption regards truth claims, the evaluation of which falls outside the purview of psychology and within the scope and purpose of other disciplines, such as philosophy and theology. We contend, however, that the second assumption, unconscious affect as a basis for religion, not only is useful, but also may provide insight into the difficult to articulate experiential realm of religious knowing. That is, religious motivations may be affected by unconscious motivations, even if the validity of religious truth claims is granted. In particular, when the use of religion for self-serving needs is not consciously admitted, a conflicting set of unconscious and conscious religious motivations may result. For instance, although the reported motivations may be intrinsic (e.g., identifying with one's higher power), the underlying religious motivations may be extrinsic and self-serving (e.g., avoidance of aversive aspects of reality).

### Understanding Detrimental Motivations

Religion may create or encourage detrimental motives and beliefs. For example, in religious frameworks emphasizing moral perfection, religious members may be highly motivated by a desire to expunge themselves of aversive sin, guilt, and shame (Clark, 1929). This motivation may lead members to ruminate and obsess about perceived inadequacies and transgressions, which result in diminished self-esteem and feelings of self-worth and increased narcissistic self-involvement, scrupulosity, and possibly even self-mutilation. Yet it is crucial that we consider the possible bidirectional relationship entailed. The need to expunge oneself of sin may come from a need to project or rid oneself of undesirable parts of the self, an extrinsically oriented motivation typical of insecure attachment or impaired development of object constancy. Thus, impaired emotional and psychological development, including the need to rid oneself of "sinful" parts of the self through religion, might be the primary motivation that could produce the elevations in mysticism, conversion, and prayer often observed in individuals motivated by the presence of sin and guilt.

To illustrate the complexity of these relationships, consider Sorotzkin's (1998) discussion of perfectionism in Orthodox Jewish adolescents that illustrates the role of early developmental experiences in religious motivation. Religious pressures and unrealistic expectations augmented a perfectionist psychological structure resulting from early childhood experiences. These adolescents then exhibited increased perfectionism in religious contexts and responded to emotional distress with intensified religiosity. Attributing emotional difficulties to religious standards also enabled adolescent perfectionists with extrinsic religious motivation to avoid exploring underlying psychological dynamics, serving as an illusory defense against reality.

### Understanding Beneficial Motivations

Similar to the need to understand the risk factors associated with religious motivations, it is also important to understand the strengths imparted by religious motivations. As discussed, intrinsic religious orientation shows a positive relationship with psychological health, including greater ego strength, optimism or happiness, and social integration, and a negative relationship with anxiety, depression, and other psychopathology (Baker & Gorsuch, 1982; Bergin et al., 1987; Nelson, 1989; Smith et al., 2003; Tapanya et al.,1997; Watson et al., 2002). Quest religious orientation may impart similar benefits and has been found to predict lower levels of stress (Navara & James, 2005). Even fundamentalism, though often associated with psychopathology, may confer some psychological benefits, such as increased optimism and hope and a sense of meaning (Hood et al., 2005; Sethi & Seligman, 1993). Most religious and spiritual traditions offer teachings or practices intended to promote maturity, relational virtue, and social justice, which can parallel many of the ideals of contemporary positive psychology and psychotherapy.

### *Self-Esteem and Gratitude*

Both self-esteem and gratitude have been identified as protective and beneficial factors for mental health (Emmons & McCullough, 2003). The general positive correlation found between these factors and religious involvement appears to be a function of intrinsic religious motivation (McCullough, Emmons, & Tsang, 2002). It is therefore important for clinicians to understand the type of religious motivation underlying religious involvement. For example, individuals reporting an intrinsic religious motivation may present with underlying extrinsic motivations, thereby lowering the association of self-esteem or gratitude with religiousness. Such individuals might desire to practice gratitude and related virtues like compassion or forgiveness but simply lack the internalized psychological and spiritual skills to do so. Perhaps they have simply prayed or performed rituals in extrinsic ways they hoped would change their character, but they have not been helped to form a sustained commitment to working on such virtues over time.

### *Empathy*

The relationship between religious orientation and empathy has important therapeutic implications. Empathy has been linked to a number of positive psychological factors, such as greater interpersonal functioning (Pierce & Zarle, 1972), frequency of prosocial behaviors or altruistic acts (Duane & Hill, 1996; Mehrabian & Epstein, 1972), and likelihood of forgiving offenses (McCullough, Worthington, & Rachal, 1997), as well as negatively correlated with aggression (Mehrabian & Epstein, 1972). Research generally has found positive associations between intrinsic religious motivation and empathy. A study by Watson et al. (1984) found that intrinsic religious orientation has a stronger positive correlation with empathy than did extrinsic or indiscriminate antireligious orientations (i.e., people who scored low on both intrinsic and extrinsic religiousness), even when controlling for social desirability. In particular, intrinsic religious motivation was associated with higher vicarious emotional responses, a greater tendency to assume personal similarity with others, and greater intellectual understanding of others than other religious motivations. The development of capacities for empathy is particularly important for couples and families, who may share strong religious values about good relationships but lack the empathy or compassion to forgive offenses and realize the ideals. Other couples or families may struggle with religious differences that prove estranging unless they develop the humble and empathic ability to accept the perspective of others even when they do not agree. Clients who experience their therapists as empathic may begin to internalize that relational dynamic and, over time, this may begin to help the clients develop compassionate forms of relational spirituality (Shults & Sandage, 2006).

## CLINICAL ASSESSMENT

As with other clinical issues, addressing religious motivations in therapy first requires an adequate clinical assessment. Given the limited time clinicians can allot to assessment, it is recommended that clinicians begin by asking clients two questions suggested by Tan (1996): (1) Do you have spiritual or religious commitments that would be helpful for me to know about? If the answer is some form of "yes," then (2) are there ways you see those commitments as relevant to what we do in therapy? These two basic questions often can yield good information about a client's style of spiritual or religious motivation and their expectations or preferences about how those issues will be addressed in therapy. When working with couples and families, these questions can reveal important motivational differences within the system if each person is given an opportunity to speak for themselves. The value of assessing spiritual or religious motivations is that the clinician can move beyond simple demographics and begin to conceptualize the role those motivations may need to play in the therapeutic process, as well as strategize about ways to avoid unnecessarily offending the client and compromising the therapeutic alliance. Therapists also have an ethical responsibility to ensure that they can accommodate clients' values and goals in treatment planning or offer a referral to an appropriate practitioner.

Beyond these initial questions, short assessments designed to screen for the presence of impairment or difficulty in clients' spiritual functioning can be useful if indicated by initial answers, particularly for assessing difficulties arising from religious motivations. If clients perceive difficulties in their spiritual lives, it is useful to find out whether they believe that spiritual or religious beliefs, practices, or issues may be affecting their presenting problem. As with other clinical issues, therapists can evaluate the conscious and unconscious level of clients' religious motivations through clinical interviewing, which may involve exploring the spiritual history of their clients and taking particular note of transitions or transformational experiences. In addition to exploring clients' early spiritual experiences, God images, religious beliefs, and religious practices, therapists are encouraged to assess various factors that could reveal clients' religious motivations. This may involve explicitly asking clients about the motivations underlying religious activities, but also could involve assessing the role religious practices and beliefs play in such issues as clients' self-image, sense of control, emotional coping, and meaning-making. This process of interested and nonjudgmental assessment can be a way to build the therapeutic relationship with clients, particularly those with intrinsic or quest religious motivations. Extrinsically religious clients might find in-depth assessment in these areas to be tangential, and fundamentalist clients might find them intrusive without sufficient rapport building.

Fitchett (2002) emphasized that religious assessments be multidimensional, assessing the various ways religiosity is manifested in beliefs, attitudes, behaviors, experiences, and activities. Although the time limitations faced by clinicians often precludes a complete assessment in all these areas, therapists are encouraged to interpret and conceptualize the impacts of religious motivation within the context of these other elements, as religious motivation is heavily influenced by the various spiritual and psychological processes discussed throughout this chapter. Thus, a holistic assessment that seeks to understand medical, psychological, psychosocial, family systems, multicultural issues, gender, and societal issues is required (Fitchett, 2002).

As an example of the importance of interpreting religious motivation within a holististic understanding of clients, consider the interaction of ethnicity with religious motivation. Jackson and Coursey (1988) unexpectedly found a positive correlation between God control and internal locus of control for Black participants (a negative correlation between these variables had been found in previous studies for Whites) and a positive correlation between both these constructs and intrinsic religious orientation. Despite the high incidence of Black churches playing greater political and cultural roles within the Black community and providing more social service to church members (e.g., health care or education programs) (Brown & Adamczyk, 2009), Black individuals may have significantly higher levels of intrinsic religious motivation than White individuals, although differences were not found for extrinsic motivation (Nelson, 1989). Gender also affects and interacts with religious motivation, as evidenced by findings of an interaction between gender and religious motivation in predicting discrimination (McFarland, 1989).

Therapists should use both substantive approaches, which focus on clients' religious behaviors or beliefs, and functional approaches, which focus on how client's religious behaviors, beliefs, or attitudes work in their lives (Fitchett, 2002). These approaches need not be extensive and may be incorporated into brief screening measures, but it is important that therapists' assessments incorporate both approaches to assess conscious and underlying religious motivations. If brief or detailed screening measures indicate difficulties stemming from or affecting religious motivation, more extensive clinical assessments are recommended for diagnosis, conceptualization, and prognosis purposes. Unfortunately, most of the measures developed for assessing religious motivations have been validated for research purposes but seldom are used within clinical samples. Two measures utilized within clinical populations, although designed only for use with conservative Christians, include the Remuda Spiritual Assessment Questionnaire

(RSAQ; Darden, 2005) and (though more limitedly used within clinical samples) the web-based Spiritual Transformation Inventory (STI; http://drtoddhall.com/index.php/spiritual-assessment/).

## CLINICAL INTERVENTIONS

In addition to completing an adequate assessment of religious motivation that can be incorporated into case conceptualizations, therapists can help clients gain greater awareness of various aspects of their religiousness. These include the development of driving motivations, how religiosity may be used or motivated by emotions, unconscious needs, desires, and strivings, and possible conflicts between various motivations on both conscious and unconscious levels (Shafranske, 2009). Such an approach respects clients' autonomy by facilitating greater awareness of their available choices and encouraging greater ownership of the desires underlying extrinsic motivations (Shafranske, 2009).

As discussed, religious motivations may be utilized to defend against certain dynamics, deny reality, or meet unconscious desires; alternatively, these motivations may benefit clients' psychological health, self-esteem, and optimism. Yet it is crucial that clients' religious and spiritual experiences be regarded as unique, important experiences and not reduced simply to psychological phenomena. To do so would be to dismiss the possibility of intrinsic religious motivation that underlies what is otherwise an apparent extrinsic orientation. Psychoanalyst Sorenson (2004) spoke to this need by urging therapists to not view clients' religiosity as merely arising from psychological structures, but rather including the possibility of clients' religious experiences as "real experiences with an otherness beyond ourselves that is accepted as 'real'" (p. 114). Sorenson further argued that a failure to do so precludes therapists from fully understanding clients' religious beliefs and experiences, thus missing their clients. Rather, therapists should work to appreciate the role religious experiences and motivations play in clients' lives, including both the possible strains or conflicts and the resources and benefits such faith might produce (Shafranske, 2009). In exploring the motivations driving religious involvement, therapists should examine their own value judgments. Therapists' reported spirituality is often lower than that of their clients, which may increase the possibility of minimizing or disregarding clients' spirituality (Hathaway, Scott, & Garver, 2004).

To the degree that conscious and unconscious motivations do not match, clients may attempt to meet unconscious religious motivations in maladaptive ways, such as the use of religion to defend against clinical interventions. Similar to the general approach to other unconscious desires, beliefs, or drives, psychoanalytic or psychodynamic approaches may be particularly helpful in addressing these unconscious motivations and helping clients gain greater self-awareness if they are open to that type of exploration.

The relationship between religious experiences and psychological distress is often complex. Intrinsic religious motivations may require some prerequisite ego capacities. For instance, a capacity for object constancy may be required for individuals to tolerate frustration with God. The ability to pursue and engage in a relationship with God for the relationship itself (intrinsic motivation) may similarly depend on secure internal working models of attachment, which likely operate and affect religious motivations outside individual awareness (Hall, Fujikawa, Halcrow, Hill, & Delaney, 2009). Especially for therapists working within a psychodynamic modality, this may involve helping clients gain greater insight into nonintrinsic motivations (Shafranske, 2009). Therapists working within a cognitive or cognitive-behavioral modality may appeal to positive religious values, identify religious issues affecting psychopathology (e.g., motivations to avoid guilt and shame especially prevalent with eating disorders), and address maladaptive underlying assumptions and schemas that were motivated by or involved with clients' religious beliefs and motivations (Bergin et al., 1987; Darden, 2005).

To the extent that the requisite psychological capacities for intrinsic motivation are impaired, addressing these capacities through traditional therapeutic approaches and interventions may benefit clients' religious lives. In addition, it is possible that encouraging such clients to engage in spiritual or religious practices for the goal of self-regulation, even if a broader spiritual or religious framework is not yet internalized, may be beneficial. When experiencing intense distress, clients may be explicitly encouraged to engage in spiritual disciplines, such as prayer, worship, or meditation, which may provide soothing, comfort, and hope (Shafranske, 2009). For instance, clients with borderline personality disorder often lack sufficient distress tolerance skills, which may be enhanced through religious coping, even when motivated by the personal benefits of self-regulation. Ironically, for some clients who previously have had an extrinsic religious orientation, responsibly using healthy spiritual practices to regulate their own emotional well-being might initially feel "selfish" to them, yet the effects often are appreciated by relational partners and family members. Possibly in recognition of a broader spiritual context to such practices, identification of clients' "higher power" is included in distress tolerance skills addressed in McKay, Wood, and Brantley's (2007) *Dialectical Behavior Therapy Skills Workbook*. Wagner and Rehfuss (2008) suggested that while religious beliefs may sometimes augment inflexible or invalidating experiences, exploration of clients' faith may decrease self-injurious behaviors.

## CASE STUDY

The following case study was developed to illustrate the role of spiritual and religious motivations in therapy and the clinical interventions discussed. It is based on a compilation of a number of clients, among whom none of the authors was the treating therapist.

### Presenting Problem

Andrea was a 27-year-old, single, Caucasian female who was a graduate student seeking therapy to address feelings of depression and anxiety, distress over feeling disconnected from God, and an increasing avoidance of intimacy in relationships. She felt she was a "burden" to others if she expressed her true feelings and, as a result, often performed care-taking roles with others starting with her triangulated role with her parents' frequent conflicts during her childhood. When she experienced care from others, she often felt overwhelming sadness and a sense of loss, which she found confusing, unaware that the emotional connection reminded her of the lack of connection during her childhood and increased her awareness of her longing for greater connection with others. This longing and loss also were felt when she engaged in spiritual disciplines, and she reported feeling desperate for a sense of God being with her as she often felt numb and described no longer experiencing the "felt presence of God."

Andrea cited her relationship with God and religious beliefs as an overriding motivation in her life. This intrinsic religious orientation provided her perceived purpose in life and life goals, and directed a number of her life decisions. Her desire for a closer relationship with God also appeared to be a longing for closeness with God as an end in itself, rather than a means to another end. However, a number of extrinsic religious motivations also were identified, such as engaging in spiritual disciplines to gain approval from her parents or the religious community.

### Background

Andrea portrayed a distant relationship with her mother, who was described as dismissive of Andrea's emotional needs throughout childhood and generally disconnected from her own emotional experience. Throughout Andrea's childhood, her mother reportedly experienced frequent depression, which resulted in increased emotional withdraw from Andrea and Andrea's younger brother. Andrea's father was described as "self-absorbed" and highly critical. To avoid criticism or her father's emotional withdrawal, Andrea believed she had to attune to her father's feelings, empathize with him, and agree with his opinions. Andrea also attempted to consistently be "nice" to others, carefully follow rules, receive high grades in school, and excel in numerous extracurricular sports and activities to be "someone [her father] could be proud of."

Spiritually, Andrea "accepted Christ" at age 10 and attended a conservative Protestant church with her family until she was in middle school. At that time, the family stopped attending church together after her father disagreed with a church decision, and her father expressed that he no longer considered himself a Christian. This launched him on something of an intermittent spiritual quest, in which he would temporarily explore a new religion or meditative practice and seemingly drop it after a few months. This was a frequent source of conflict with Andrea's mother, who then found a conservative church to accompany her developing fundamentalist religious orientation. Andrea began attending church individually in college and led a number of youth groups throughout her years in college and graduate school; however, she often wondered whether she should be attending church with her mom to support her even though her own church preferences were different.

Andrea described a high degree of anxiety around academics and often feared she was not doing her best on assignments. She believed that doing less than her best was "poor stewardship" of the abilities God gave her, and she frequently experienced resulting feelings of guilt in her relationship with God. This was augmented by her perception that her decreased experience of "the felt presence of God" was an indication that God no longer liked her. Andrea also believed God had failed to act on her prayers for her father to renew his faith in God, for which she felt responsible. She expressed that her father's disbelief was further evidence that God had forgotten her or that she was insignificant to God, which reflected the belief in spiritual contingencies that characterizes extrinsic religiosity (i.e., "If I pray correctly, God will do what I want"). Andrea responded to these feelings by increasing her time spent in various spiritual disciplines that she felt she "should" do, such as Bible study, meditation, and contemplation. Andrea was confused by her anger at God as she did not cognitively blame God for her father's apostasy, attributing it to her father's free will instead. At the same time, she also worried that her mother's form of religiosity seemed to be alienating her father even more. From a relational perspective, her feelings of burden and responsibility for her parents' spirituality and relationship reflected her triangulated role in the family system and sources of extrinsic motivation that hindered her own spiritual development and functioning. Her projection that God's presence was contingent on her own academic performance also paralleled family dynamics in which her achievements provided validation for her parents' ego needs. Andrea felt she needed to explore her spiritual conflicts and possibly even new practices for connecting with God, yet her father's example of ineffectual spiritual questing and the marital conflicts it created raised anxiety for her own questing process.

### Interventions

Andrea was seen in weekly psychotherapy within a primarily psychodynamic modality that emphasized object relations theory. Although treatment focused on many aspects surrounding her attachment style and feelings of guilt and depression, those aspects relevant to the discussion of this chapter will be explicated. During therapy, Andrea was able to identify and explore her difficulty expressing emotions and needs to others, and her avoidance of experiential spiritual disciplines (e.g., focusing on the felt presence of God, worship, and mindfulness). This involved interpreting Andrea's religious defenses and helping Andrea gain insight into her extrinsically motivated use of spiritual disciplines (e.g., to reduce guilt feelings, make God lead her father back to a Christian faith, and reduce or avoid aversive feelings), which all were based on actual relational experiences in her family of origin. Andrea's therapist helped Andrea realize that she had frequently felt alone as a child and often turned to God as a source of comfort. As a result, at the time of therapy, Andrea avoided experiencing God alone and wanted to experience God in the presence of another person to avoid recapitulating her early childhood experiences. Andrea's experience of God within the therapy session provided a contrasting experience to her prior experiences of closeness with God alone. In addition to the insights Andrea gained, the healthy relational dynamics she experienced with her therapist shifted her relational templates about herself and the sacred.

Andrea's therapist encouraged Andrea to find a healthy spiritual community outside therapy (e.g., a Bible study group) to genuinely express and experience her emotions with others and to engage in spiritual disciplines with others. As positive changes emerged, her therapist suggested that Andrea seek out spiritual direction and engage in more experiential spiritual disciplines, such as finding God in nature, focusing on bodily awareness, and mindfulness. Andrea found that these experiences increased her awareness of her emotional experiences in seeking God, which, in turn, helped her connect with God in ways that differed from her lonely and often helpless experiences as a child.

Psychotherapy helped Andrea explore how she often used spiritual disciplines in attempts to be "perfect" for God. Andrea realized that she often felt her parents "loved" her by providing for her physical needs (e.g., food, clothing), but she believed her parents "didn't like her." Andrea's therapist helped Andrea recognize that she felt that she was a burden to others and subsequently worked hard to be likable, as reflected in her academic achievement, care for others' emotional needs, and attention to physical appearance. Through exploration in therapy and therapeutic interpretations, Andrea was able to recognize a similar dynamic in her relationship with God, in which she attempted to "pay God back" for her salvation through her involvement in spiritual disciplines, various religious ministries, and efficient utilization of her "gifts," as reflected by her academic achievement. Andrea also realized she attempted to be "nice" to God and seldom expressed her anger or genuine emotions to God.

Through psychotherapy, Andrea also became aware of her attempts to reduce God's "resentment" of her by attempting to convert those around her to her Christian faith. She often felt guilty if individuals in her life did not choose to convert and feared God's subsequent rejection of her. The therapist helped Andrea reach these realizations through various psychodynamic interventions, which included interpretation, empathic exploration, and the providing of a corrective relationship, which was accepting and validating of Andrea's emotional experience. This experience then encouraged Andrea to more honestly express her feelings to God in prayer. Additionally, the therapist encouraged reflection on biblical passages expressing God's unconditional acceptance.

In working through Andrea's grief surrounding her father's disbelief in God, Andrea's anger at God was explored as well. While intellectually adhering to belief in free will, Andrea struggled with her simultaneous belief that God can "soften people's hearts" but had not done so with her father. Her therapist was able to help Andrea realize that this was related to a belief that God either failed to see Andrea's desire for her father to renew his spiritual faith or disregarded her desire as it contrasted with God's own desire not to do so. Andrea was able to recognize how this reflected her own dynamics with her mother and father, respectively, which allowed her to begin to explore the possibility that these beliefs reflected her parents rather than God. Andrea began to develop more frustration with her mother and her fundamentalist orientation, and this began to balance her appraisals of her parents. Eventually, this softened into sadness that both parents had limitations in relating to the sacred and difficulty connecting with others in their spiritual process. She also began to differentiate by letting go of her felt responsibility to manage their lives and relationship.

Through psychotherapy, Andrea was able to identify underlying extrinsic motivations (e.g., emotional coping, enhancement of self-esteem) that were seemingly intrinsic in nature. Andrea's increased awareness of these underlying extrinsic motivations and subsequent acceptance of these more "selfish" motivations enabled her to later engage in a more intrinsically motivated relationship with God. Andrea gained greater awareness of her extrinsic religious motivations, including her attempts to be a "good Christian" to counter feelings of worthlessness or shame within her relationship with her father. She further gained awareness of her extrinsic motivations in seeking God to meet emotional needs for connection, decreasing feelings of helplessness by attributing control to God who she attempted to "control" through petitionary prayer, and engaging in religious activities for the social community provided by youth groups and Bible study groups.

## CONCLUSION

Although complicated to study and identify, religious motivations play significant roles in individuals' spiritual and religious experiences. Yet it is clear that not all religious and spiritual experiences are created equal—some provide more benefits or reflect greater spiritual maturity than others. As evidenced by this suggestion, religious motivations are complicated and may be best understood through a variety of approaches, including intrinsic versus extrinsic distinctions, quest motivation, and fundamentalism distinctions. Understanding the various motivations that underlie *why* people are religious, religion and spirituality in light of these motivations, and the likely intricate relationships such motivations have with psychological structures has important clinical implications and requires thorough clinical assessments and conceptualizations. We encourage therapists and researchers alike to consider not just the relationship of religion and mental health, but also the underlying motivations at both conscious and unconscious levels to truly move our understanding of these complex dynamics forward.

## CHAPTER SUMMARY

- Motivation is often influenced by beliefs, values, and emotions.
- Most research on religious motivation has been conducted within the Judeo–Christian context. More research from other diverse faith traditions is needed.
- Religious orientation can be conceptualized in terms of motivation.
- Intrinsic orientation is the tendency to view religion as the reference point from which all of life is perceived and understood.
- Extrinsic orientation is used for self-justification and to fulfill needs like belongingness and community status.
- Quest orientation is characterized by the search for the sacred.
- It is important to recognize the importance of one's value system as a religious motivator, particularly with regard to moral decision making.
- All people, whether religious or not, are subject to biases defined through their own value system, and these findings seem to apply to all forms of religious motivation.
- The distinction found in various studies between what a religious person says they believe they would do (often reflecting strongly held religious values) and what the research indicates that a person actually does, may cause a certain level of dissonance and discomfort for the individual, especially the intrinsically oriented individual.
- Religious fundamentalism could be considered yet another religious motivation with important implications for therapy.
- Religious fundamentalists may be at increased risk for various psychopathologies, yet because of religious schemas, they may be either less likely to seek help or seek help only from certain therapists.
- Fundamentalists may filter their world in a manner that seeks confirmation for intolerant views, discounting discrepant information in the process.
- Addressing religious motivations in therapy first requires an adequate clinical assessment.
- Therapy should begin with brief open-ended probing questions or brief-screening assessments.
- Religious assessments should be multidimensional, assessing the various ways religiosity is manifested in beliefs, attitudes, behaviors, experiences, and activities.

- Examples of standardized measures include the Remuda Spiritual Assessment Questionnaire and Furnishing the Soul Inventory.
- It is crucial that clients' religious and spiritual experiences be regarded as unique, important experiences and not reduced simply to psychological phenomena.
- To the degree that conscious and unconscious motivations do not match, clients may attempt to meet unconscious religious motivations in maladaptive ways.

## CLINICAL APPLICATION QUESTIONS

1. To what extent am I, as a therapist, genuinely open to a new understanding of the unique meaning that religion or spirituality can provide to the spiritually sensitive client?
2. Is the spiritually questing client engaging in a healthy search that seems to be moving toward spiritual and psychological growth, or does the questing seem to create only more anxiety, confusion, and stress?
3. Is a client's intrinsic spirituality a genuine representation of a strongly held conviction after a deep and careful consideration of difficult questions? Or is it simply an uncritical adoption of what that person has been taught?
4. Should I assume that a potential client who self-identifies as a religious fundamentalist will present with higher levels of psychopathology? What might be some of the strengths of religious fundamentalism? What are some potential challenges?
5. To what extent is the religious client willing to confront and able to handle religious doubt if maladaptive religious beliefs or practices are challenged?
6. Am I open to helping clients explore resources within their spiritual or religious tradition for questing and handling ambiguity? For dealing with psychological stress?
7. Am I aware of key relational figures who have influenced my clients' spiritual or religious orientation?
8. What factors in my own background have influenced my personal views on spiritual and religious motivations?

## SUGGESTED READINGS AND RESOURCES


Allport, G. W. (1950). *The individual and his religion*. New York, NY: Macmillan.

Batson, C. D., Schoenrade, P., & Ventis, W. L. (1993). *Religion and the individual: A social psychological perspective*. New York, NY: Oxford University Press.

Donahue, M. J. (1985). Intrinsic and extrinsic religiousness: Review and meta-analysis. *Journal of Personality and Social Psychology, 48*, 400–419.

Emmons, R. A. (1999). *The psychology of ultimate concerns*. New York, NY: Guilford Press.

Hood, R. W., Jr., Hill, P. C., & Williamson, W. P. (2005). *The psychology of religious fundamentalism*. New York, NY: Guilford Press.

Maehr, M. L. (2005). The meaning that religion offers and the motivation that may result. In W. R. Miller & H. D. Delaney (Eds.), *Judeo-Christian perspectives on psychology* (pp. 133–144). Washington, DC: American Psychological Association.

Pargament, K. I. (2007). *Spiritually integrated psychotherapy: Understanding and assessing the sacred*. New York, NY: Guilford Press.

Pargament, K. I., Murray-Swank, N. A., Magyar, G. M., & Ano, G. G. (2005). Spiritual struggle: A phenomenon of interest to psychology and religión. In W. R. Miller &

H. D. Delaney (Eds.), *Judeo-Christian perspectives on psychology* (pp. 245–268). Washington, DC: American Psychological Association.

Richards, P. S., & Bergin, A. E. (1997). *A spiritual strategy for counseling and psychotherapy.* Washington, DC: American Psychological Association.

Sorenson, R. L. (2004). *Minding spirituality.* Hillsdale, NJ: Analytic Press.

Thurston, N. S. (2000). Psychotherapy with evangelical and fundamentalist protestants. In P. S. Richards & A. E. Bergin (Eds.), *Handbook of psychotherapy and religious diversity* (pp. 131–153). Washington, DC: American Psychological Association.

## REFERENCES


Allport, G. W. (1950). *The individual and his religion.* New York, NY: Macmillan.

Allport, G. W., & Ross, J. M. (1967). Personal religious orientation and prejudice. *Journal of Personality and Social Psychology, 5,* 432–443.

Altemeyer, B. (1988). *Enemies of freedom: Understanding right-wing authoritarianism.* San Francisco, CA: Jossey-Bass.

Altemeyer, B., & Hunsberger, B. (1992). Authoritarianism, religious fundamentalism, quest, and prejudice. *The International Journal for the Psychology of Religion, 2,* 113–133.

Altemeyer, B., & Hunsberger, B. (2004). A revised Religious Fundamentalism Scale: The short and sweet of it. *The International Journal of the Psychology of Religion, 14,* 47–54.

Ammerman, N. T. (1987). *Bible believers: Fundamentalists in the modern world.* New Brunswick, NJ: Rutgers University Press.

Baker, M., & Gorsuch, R. L. (1982). Trait anxiety and intrinsic-extrinsic religiousness. *Journal for the Scientific Study of Religion, 21,* 119–122.

Batson, C. D., Denton, D. M., & Vollmecke, J. T. (2008). Quest, religion, anti-fundamentalism, and limited versus universal compassion. *Journal for the Scientific Study of Religion, 47,* 135–145.

Batson, C. D., Eidelman, S. H., Higley, S. L., & Russell, S. A. (2001). "And who is my neighbor?": II. Quest religion as a source of universal compassion. *Journal for the Scientific Study of Religion, 40,* 39–50.

Batson, C. D., Floyd, R. B., Meyer, J. M., & Winner, A. L. (1999). "And who is my neighbor?": Intrinsic religion as a source of universal compassion. *Journal for the Scientific Study of Religion, 38,* 445–457.

Batson, C. D., Schoenrade, P., & Ventis, W. L. (1993). *Religion and the individual: A social psychological perspective.* New York, NY: Oxford University Press.

Beck, R. (2006). Defensive versus existential religion: Is religious defensiveness predictive of worldview defense? *Journal of Psychology & Theology, 34,* 142–152.

Bergin, A. E., Masters, K. S., & Richards, P. S. (1987). Religiousness and mental health: A study of an intrinsically religious sample. *Journal of Consulting Psychology, 34,* 197–204.

Bernt, F. M. (1989). Being religious and being altruistic: A study of college student volunteers. *Personality and Individual Differences, 10,* 663–669.

Brown, R. K., & Adamczyk, A. (2009). Racial/ethnic difference in the provision of health-related programs among American religious congregations. *Journal of Sociology and Social Welfare, 36,* 105–123.

Clark, E. T. (1929). *The psychology of religious awakening.* New York, NY: Macmillan.

Cohen, A. B., & Hill, P. C. (2007). Religion as culture: Religious individualism and collectivism among American Catholics, Jews, and Protestants. *Journal of Personality, 75,* 709–742.

Crowden, C.R., & Bradshaw, S.D. (2007). Religiosity and sexual concerns. *International Journal of Sexual Health, 19,* 15–24.
Darden, R. A. (2005). Spiritual assessment and treatment strategies. *The Remuda Review: The Christian Journal of Eating Disorders, 4,* 14–16.
Donahue, M. J. (1985). Intrinsic and extrinsic religiousness: Review and meta-analysis. *Journal of Personality and Social Psychology, 48,* 400–419.
Duan, C., & Hill, C. E. (1996). The current state of empathy research. *Journal of Counseling Psychology, 43,* 261–274.
Emmons, R. A. (1999). *The psychology of ultimate concerns.* New York, NY: Guilford Press.
Emmons, R. A., & McCullough, M. E. (2003). Counting blessings versus burdens: An experimental investigation of gratitude and subjective well-being in daily life. *Journal of Personality and Social Psychology, 84,* 377–389.
Fitchett, G. (2002). *Assessing spiritual needs: A guide for caregivers.* Lima, OH: Academic Renewal Press.
Gartner, J., Harmatz, M., Hohmann, A., Larson, D., & Garner, A. F. (1990). The effect of patient and clinician ideology on clinical judgments: A study of ideological countertransference. *Psychotherapy, 27,* 98–106.
Goldfried, J., & Miner, M. (2002). Quest religion and the problem of limited compassion. *Journal for the Scientific Study of Religion, 41,* 685–695.
Hall, T. W., Fujikawa, A., Halcrow, S. R., Hill, P. C., & Delaney, H. (2009). Internal working model correspondence in implicit spiritual experiences. *Journal of Psychology & Theology, 37,* 227–244.
Hartz, G. W., & Everett, H. C. (1989). Fundamentalist religion and its effect on mental health. *Journal of Religion and Health, 28,* 207–217.
Hathaway, W. L., Scott, S. Y., & Garver, S. A. (2004). Assessing religious/spiritual functioning: A neglected domain in clinical practice? *Professional Psychology: Research and Practice, 35,* 97–104.
Hill, P. C., & Hood, R. W., Jr. (1999). Affect, religion, and unconscious processes. *Journal of Personality, 67,* 1015–1046.
Hood, R. W., Jr., Hill, P. C., & Spilka, B. (2009). *The psychology of religion: An empirical approach* (4th ed.). New York, NY: Guilford Press.
Hood, R. W., Jr., Hill, P. C., & Williamson, W. P. (2005). *The psychology of religious fundamentalism.* New York, NY: Guilford Press.
Hood, R. W., Jr., & Morris, R. J. (1985). Conceptualization of quest: A critical rejoinder to Batson. *Review of Religious Research, 26,* 391–397.
Hunsberger, B., Alisat, S. Pancer, S. M., & Pratt, M. (1996). Religious fundamentalism and religious doubts: Content, connections, and complexity of thinking. *The International Journal for the Psychology of Religion, 6,* 201–220.
Hunsberger, B., & Jackson, L. (2005). Religion, meaning, and prejudice. *Journal of Social Issues, 61,* 807–826.
Jackson, L. E., & Coursey, R. D. (1988). The relationship of God control and internal locus of control to intrinsic religious motivation, coping and purpose in life. *Journal for the Scientific Study of Religion, 27,* 399–410.
Jackson, L. M., & Esses, V. M. (1997). Of scripture and ascription: The relation between religious fundamentalism and intergroup helping. *Personality and Social Psychology Bulletin, 23,* 893–906.
Jones, J. W. (2002). *Terror and transformation: The ambiguity of religion in psychoanalytic perspective.* New York, NY: Brunner-Routledge.
Kirkpatrick, L. A., Hood, R. W., Jr., & Hartz, G. W. (1991). Fundamentalist religion conceptualized in terms of Rokeach's theory of the open and closed mind: New perspectives

on some old ideas. In M. L. Lynn & D. O. Moberg (Eds.), *Research in the social scientific study of religion* (Vol. 3, pp. 157–179). Greenwich, CT: JAI Press.
Krause, N., Ingersoll-Dayton, B., Ellison, C. G., & Wulff, K. M. (1999). Aging, religious doubt, and psychological well-being. *Gerontologist, 39*, 525–533.
Krauss, S. W., & Flaherty, R. W. (2001). The effects of tragedies and contradictions on religion as Quest. *Journal for the Scientific Study of Religion, 40*, 113–122.
Mahoney, A., Pargament, K. I., Tarakeshwar, N., & Swank, A. B. (2001). Religion in the home in the 1980s and 1990s: A meta-analytic review and conceptual analysis of links between religion, marriage, and parenting. *Journal of Family Psychology, 15*, 559–596.
McCullough, M. E., Emmons, R. A., & Tsang, J. (2002). The grateful disposition: A conceptual and empirical topography. *Journal of Personality and Social Psychology, 82*, 112–127.
McCullough, M. E., Worthington, E. L., Jr., & Rachal. K. C. (1997). Interpersonal forgiving in close relationships. *Journal of Personality and Social Psychology, 73*, 321–336.
McFarland, S. G. (1989). Religious orientations and the targets of discrimination. *Journal for the Scientific Study of Religion, 28*, 324–336.
McKay, M., Wood, J. C., & Brantley, J. (2007). *Dialectical behavior therapy skills workbook: Practical DBT exercises for learning mindfulness, interpersonal effectiveness, emotion regulation, and distress tolerance.* Oakland, CA: New Harbinger.
Mehrabian, A., & Epstein, N. (1972). A measure of emotional empathy. *Journal of Personality, 40*, 525–543.
Navara, G. S., & James, S. (2005). Acculturative stress of missionaries: Does religious orientation affect religious coping and adjustment? *International Journal of Intercultural Relations, 29*, 39–58.
Nelson, P. B. (1989). Ethnic differences in intrinsic/extrinsic religious orientation and depression in the elderly. *Archives of Psychiatric Nursing, 3*, 199–204.
Ostow, M. (1990). The fundamentalist phenomenon: A psychological perspective. In N. J. Cohen (Ed.), *The fundamentalist phenomenon* (pp. 99–125). Grand Rapids, MI: Eerdmans.
Pargament, K. I. (1992). Of means and ends: Religion and the search for significance. *The International Journal for the Psychology of Religion, 2*, 201–229.
Pargament, K. I. (1997). *The psychology of religion and coping.* New York, NY: Guilford Press.
Park, C. L. (2005). Religion and meaning. In R. F. Paloutzian & C. L. Park (Eds.), *Handbook of the psychology of religion and spirituality* (pp. 295–314). New York, NY: Guilford Press.
Park, C. L., & Paloutzian, R. F. (2005). One step toward integration and an expansive future. In R. F. Paloutzian & C. L. Park (Eds.), *Handbook of the psychology of religion and spirituality* (pp. 550–564). New York, NY: Guilford Press.
Pierce, R. M., & Zarle, T. H. (1972). Differential referral to significant others as a function of interpersonal effectiveness. *Journal of Clinical Psychology, 28*, 230–232.
Reed, P. R. (1992). Psychologists' views of a patient's religiousness. *Psychological Reports, 70*, 1031–1036.
Rootes, K. M. H., Jankowski, P. J., & Sandage, S. J. (2009). Bowen family systems theory and spirituality: Exploring the relationship between triangulation and religious questing. *Contemporary Family Therapy.* Advance online publication. doi:10.1007/s10591-009-9191-y
Sandage, S. J., Cook, K. V., Hill, P. C., Strawn, B. D., & Reimer, K. S. (2008). Hermeneutics and psychology: A review and dialectical model. *Review of General Psychology, 12*, 344–364.
Sethi, S., & Seligman, M. E. P. (1993). Optimism and fundamentalism. *Psychological Science, 4*, 256–259.

Shafranske, E. P. (2009). Spiritually oriented psychodynamic psychotherapy. *Journal of Clinical Psychology*, 65, 147–157.

Shults, F. L., & Sandage, S. J. (2006). *Transforming spirituality: Integrating theology and psychology*. Grand Rapids, MI: Baker Academic.

Smith, T. B., McCullough, M. E., & Poll, J. (2003). Religiousness and depression: Evidence for a main effect and the moderating influence of stressful life events. *Psychological Bulletin, 129*, 614–636.

Sorenson, R. L. (2004). *Minding spirituality*. Hillsdale, NJ: Analytic Press.

Sorotzkin, B. (1998). Understanding and treating perfectionism in religious adolescents. *Psychotherapy: Theory, Research, Practice, and Training 35*, 87–95.

Southard, S. (1956). Religious concern in the psychoses. *Journal of Pastoral Care, 10*, 226–233.

Strommen, M. P., Brekke, M. L., Underwager, R. C., & Johnson, A. L. (1972). *A study of generations*. Minneapolis, MN: Augsburg.

Tan, S.-Y. (1996). Religion in clinical practice: Implicit and explicit integration. In E. P. Shafranske (Ed.), *Religion and the clinical practice of psychology* (pp. 365–387). Washington, DC: American Psychological Association.

Tapanya, S., Nicki, R., & Jarusawad, O. (1997). Worry and intrinsic/extrinsic religious orientation among Buddhist (Thai) and Christian (Canadian) elderly persons. *International Journal of Aging and Human Development, 44*, 73–83.

Thouless, R. H. (1935). The tendency to certainty in religious belief. *British Journal of Psychology, 26*, 16–31.

Wagner J., & Rehfuss, M. (2008). Self-injury, sexual self-concept, and a conservative Christian upbringing: An exploratory study of three young women's perspectives. *Journal of Mental Health Counseling, 30*, 173–188.

Watson, P. J., Ghorbani, N., Davison, H. K., Bing, M. N., Hood, R. W., Jr., & Ghramaleki, A. F. (2002). Negatively reinforcing personal extrinsic motivations: Religious orientation, inner awareness, and mental health in Iran and the United States. *The International Journal for the Psychology of Religion, 12*, 255–276.

Watson, P. J., Hood, R. W., Jr., Morris, R. J., & Hall, J. R. (1984). Empathy, religious orientation, and social desirability. *Journal of Psychology, 117*, 211–216.

Watson, P. J., Howard, R., Hood, R. W., Jr., & Morris, R. J. (1988). Age and religious orientation. *Review of Religious Research, 29*, 271–280.

Watson, P. J., Jones, N. D., & Morris, R. J. (2004). Religious orientation and attitudes toward money: Relationships with narcissism and the influence of gender. *Mental Health, Religion and Culture, 7*, 277–288.

Williamson, I. T., & Sandage, S. J. (2009). Longitudinal analyses of religious and spiritual development among seminary students. *Mental Health, Religion, and Culture, 12*, 787–801.

Worthington, E. L., Kurusu, T. A., McCullough, M. E., & Sandage, S. J. (1996). Empirical research on religion and psychotherapeutic processes and outcomes: A 10-year review and research prospectus. *Psychological Bulletin, 3*, 448–487.

# 5

# *Connection Between Personality and Religion and Spirituality*

ANDREA J. MILLER AND
EVERETT L. WORTHINGTON, JR.

This chapter examines the relationship between personality and religion and spirituality. *Religion* is defined as a set of beliefs and practices regarding a higher power that commonly is associated with a church, organized group, or community that embraces a shared core of beliefs, values, and practices. *Spirituality* is defined as experiences and feelings related to a search for (and living within) meaning and purpose in life (Henningsgaard & Arnau, 2008). It involves a search for the sacred and experience of the sacred; however, the sacred is not necessarily thought of as God as defined in religious traditions (Saroglou & Muñoz-García, 2008)—although it might be. The majority of people in the United States identify as both religious and spiritual (Zinnbauer et al., 1997), which suggests that they believe, value, and behave within some defined religious community, and yet they also have a sense of connection and closeness to the sacred. However, approximately 20% of individuals describe themselves as spiritual but not religious. These individuals tend to have a focus on connectedness and oneness with a higher power and searching for personal and existential meaning (Wink, Dillon, & Fay, 2005).

Religion plays an important role in many people's lives around the world. In the Gallup International Millennium Survey (Gallup International Association, 2010) of people in 60 countries, 87% of people worldwide belong to a religious domination. Sixty-three percent reported that God was very important in their lives. Thirty percent of people reported that God is a force or spirit, and that sacred object to which they feel connected leads to some experience that is more similar to spirituality than to religious spirituality in some specific religion (Gallup International Association, 2010).

People may have different orientations to religion or spirituality, which speaks to their religious motivations. For instance, Allport made a distinction between intrinsic orientation to religion and extrinsic orientation to religion (Allport & Ross, 1967). An individual with an extrinsic orientation to religion is motivated to participate in religious activities for nonreligious and often self-serving goals (e.g., social interactions or community), whereas an individual with intrinsic orientation to religion is motivated to participate in religious activities for its own sake and it is central to his or her identity (Henningsgaard & Arnau, 2008; Taylor & MacDonald, 1999). Batson (1976) theorized a third orientation named *quest*. Quest orientation involves a continuous and shared search for enlightenment, truth, or transcendent meaning. Quest orientation can also occur in times of religious upheaval and is often transient until a person resolves the upheaval, settling into some stance toward, against, or away from religion. It can also be a life position—a statement of unsettled faith or agnosticism—that does not change any more than stable positions of religious faith or spirituality do. This quest orientation is more similar to spirituality—in seeking the sacred—than to religion.

Intrinsic, extrinsic, and quest orientations are general styles and patterns toward religion, spirituality, and the sacred. General styles of responding, such as attitudes, motivations, and behaviors also may be affected by religion and spirituality. For instance, individual differences in religious constructs consistently relate to personality traits and values (Saroglou & Muñoz-García, 2008). A religious person often thinks, feels, and behaves differently than a nonreligious person when faced with stressful situations or negative emotions. Furthermore, religious people may value different things in life than nonreligious people. However, Worthington (1988) has theorized (and accumulated evidence that generally supports) that only the highly religiously committed seem to consistently use a religious perceptual lens. For instance, someone who is highly religiously committed will be more likely to use religious beliefs and values when responding to conflict, challenges, and interpersonal problems than someone who identifies as slightly or moderately religiously committed.

The goals of the current chapter are to (a) summarize the historical and theoretical context of personality, religion, and spirituality; (b) discuss empirical research on the Big Five Factor model of personality as it relates to religion and spirituality (and a major critique of the Big Five); (c) examine how positive psychology constructs relate to religious and spiritual variables; (d) discuss clinical implications based on personality, religion, and spirituality research; (e) describe clinical assessments that may be useful when dealing with religion, spirituality, and character strengths; (f) discuss clinical strategies and suggestions for working with religious and spiritual clients; and (g) present a case study illustrating how to assess and use strategies to work with religious and spiritual clients.

## RELIGIOUS AND SPIRITUAL PERSPECTIVE: HISTORICAL AND THEORETICAL CONTEXT OF PERSONALITY, RELIGION, AND SPIRITUALITY

Spiritual constructs represent cognitive and affective genetically influenced traits that have behavioral implications throughout one's lifetime (Piedmont, 2005). For instance, genetics can affect religious attitudes and practices (see D'Onofrio, Eaves, Murrelle, Maes, & Spilka, 1999). Thus, individuals may be more or less likely to have particular religious attitudes and behaviors based on genetic factors in addition to environmental influences. Several major theories of personality, religion, and spirituality will be reviewed.

### Object Relations

#### *Theory*

Object relations theory addresses how children form representations of important people (e.g., parents) internally and how that influences their perception of the environment and relationships with people throughout their lives (see Kernberg, 1966). Internal representation early in life could affect spiritual and religious constructs (see Rizzuto, 1979). Internal representations of significant individuals (e.g., caregivers) influence not only how a child interacts with specific caregivers but also how the child interacts with other similar objects (e.g., God). Thus, these internal objects can guide patterns of thinking and behavior, similar to personality traits. Internal objects can be flexible or rigid. Rigid internal objects tend to be viewed as either good or bad, whereas more flexible internal objects allow for simultaneous experience of conflicting emotions toward one object. For instance, a person can feel angry at an object but still love the object. Rigid, dichotomous thinking involves strict categorizations related to an object, such as thinking a caregiver either loves me or hates me.

#### *Personality, Religion, and Spirituality*

Internal representations may affect religious internal objects. As children develop internal representations from early interactions with caregivers, they are also developing images of God. These images of God then guide them throughout portions of their lives (or throughout their whole lives). Therefore, early internal representations of God that develop as a child can affect functioning and well-being into adult life (Piedmont, 2005). The representations of God may result in one having a positive or negative sense of religiosity. If an individual has a rigid view of God, he or she may have a different relationship with God and style of coping (e.g., God is punitive, I should fear God) than someone who has a more flexible internal representation (e.g., God guides me, sometimes I may not understand God) or more positive representations (e.g., I can trust God, God is compassionate). These patterns of rigid or flexible behavior also may parallel or influence personality traits. For instance, an individual with rigid internal representations may have more rigid, inflexible personality traits that guide behaviors and attitudes. Lawrence (1997) created a measure that attempted to assess unconscious representations of a God image—the God Image Inventory. Unconscious processes are difficult to measure, however, because they are out of conscious awareness. Yet, object relations still provide a framework for examining a client's relationship with God despite the difficulty in assessing unconscious internal representations.

## Attachment Style

### *Theory*

Religious and spiritual development has been conceptualized from the perspective of attachment style (see Piedmont, 2005). Attachment occurs early in life as a result of interactions with caregivers. The patterns and quality of the early caregiving relationships then influence how people organize thoughts, emotions, and behaviors in close relationships, which often persists (to some degree) throughout their lives. Three general personality styles have been described as they relate to attachment (see Ainsworth & Bowlby, 1991). Through interactions with caregivers, children can develop a secure (i.e., confidence in dependability of caregiver to meet the child's needs), avoidant (i.e., lack of trust in ability of caregiver to meet the child's needs), or anxious–ambivalent style (i.e., desire to be close to the caregiver, but fear of rejection).

### *Personality, Religion, and Spirituality*

Attachment interactions result in a framework for later relationships, including spiritual and religious attachment. Kirkpatrick (1998) proposed that one's relationship with God will be related to his or her attachment style from other relationships. Securely attached individuals will see God as comforting. Avoidantly attached individuals will feel insecure about their relationship with God, thus avoiding a close relationship with God (Piedmont, 2005). Anxiously attached people will fear and worry about God's stability. Unlike stable patterns of personality, attachment style to God is thought to be more flexible. It can change over time. Piedmont (2005) has summarized extensive research on attachment style and relationship to God. He concluded that although much research has been conducted, the findings have been mixed. Attachment styles may be compensatory (insecurely attached people seek out a secure attachment with God) or corresponding (insecurely attached people have an insecure attachment with God). As psychotherapists know, clients often adopt personal attachments to them during treatment. Those attachments can mirror attachments with parents, and not surprisingly one might expect that attachment to God (or the sacred) might be parallel.

## Eysenck's Biological Theory

### *Theory*

Eysenck (1967) proposed a biological theory of personality that has been extensively researched. The three factors include neuroticism (i.e., tendency to experience negative emotions), extraversion (i.e., tendency to experience positive emotions), and psychoticism (i.e., hostility and a tendency to have lack of desire for social interactions; Piedmont, 2005). The Eysenck Personality Inventory was developed to measure these personality constructs. Eysenck proposed that each of these three factors have neurological structures that result in these personality tendencies. Low arousal in the ascending reticular activation system (located near the lower brain stem that regulates arousal) accounted for extraversion. High visceral brain activation (emotion-associated brain structures, including the limbic system and hypothalamus) undergirded neuroticism. Eysenck (1990) explained psychoticism as being affected by high testosterone and low levels of enzymes (e.g., monoamine oxidase). Eysenck (1967) found some biological bases for personality (e.g., ascending reticular activation system visceral brain activation). If personality and religious and spiritual constructs are related, it is possible that religious and spiritual constructs also have some biological basis.

### *Personality, Religion, and Spirituality*

Research with Eysenck's three-factor personality theory has focused on how religious variables are related to the three personality factors. For example, Francis and Jackson (2003) examined the relationship between religion and seven components of neuroticism from the Eysenck Personality Questionnaire (Eysenck, 1990). A positive correlation existed between religiosity and guilt, a negative correlation existed between religiosity and unhappiness, and no correlations existed between religiosity and low self-esteem, anxiety, dependency, hypochondriasis, or obsessiveness. Overall, most research suggests that religious attitude scales, religious orientation measures, and frequency of religious behaviors are related to low levels of psychoticism (Maltby & Day, 2001).

Spirituality and Eysenck's factors also have been studied. Maltby and Day (2001) discovered that belief in a greater power, internal beliefs and growth, attitudes toward existential issues, humility, and application of spiritual beliefs had positive correlations with extraversion. This suggests that spirituality is most closely related to extraversion. In summary, most research with Eysenck's biologically based three-factor theory demonstrates that (a) religiosity is most related to low psychoticism, and (b) spirituality is most related to extraversion.

## Big Five Factor Model of Personality

### *Theory*

The Big Five Factor model of personality includes the constructs of Extraversion (i.e., amount and intensity of interpersonal interactions), Agreeableness (i.e., range of compassionate to antagonistic interpersonal interactions), Conscientiousness (i.e., persistence, orderliness, and goal-directed actions), Neuroticism (i.e., tendency to experience negative emotions), and Openness to Experience (i.e., seeking out and enjoyment of new experiences). Research demonstrates that these five factors are stable across the life span once one reaches adulthood (Costa & McCrae, 1992). They also have a genetic basis. That is, the five factors are heritable, not just learned behaviors (Piedmont, 1999). The five factors also have been consistently identified in many different cultures, such as American, German, Portuguese, Hebrew, Chinese, Korean, and Japanese (McCrae & Costa, 1997). The Neuroticism Extraversion Openness Personality Inventory-Revised (NEO PI-R) is the most common measure of these five traits (Costa & McCrae, 1992).

### *Personality, Religion, and Spirituality*

In the 1980s, the Big Five Factor model of personality theory began to be the most frequently used model to study personality and religion. Similar to research with Eysenck's theory of personality, research has focused primarily on how religious variables are related to these five personality traits. For instance, Saroglou (2002) used a meta-analysis of more than 15 studies to examine the relationship between the five factors and measures of intrinsic–general religiosity, spiritual and religious maturity, religious fundamentalism, and extrinsic religion. Agreeableness and Conscientiousness had the strongest relationship with religiosity. Spiritual and religious maturity and intrinsic–general religiosity were associated with Extraversion and low Neuroticism. Extrinsic religiosity was associated with high Neuroticism. Spiritual and religious maturity was related to high Openness, whereas religious fundamentalism was related to low Openness. However, many of the correlations had small effect sizes ($r$ = .04–.24). Therefore, religion and spirituality are related to the five factors, but the relationship is not strong enough to indicate that the five factors fully explain religion and spirituality.

Piedmont (2005) summarized additional correlations between spiritual and religious measures and Big Five traits. Religious problem-solving scales were related to Neuroticism and Extraversion. Religious well-being scales were related to low Openness and high Agreeableness and Conscientiousness. Spirituality scales were associated with Openness and Agreeableness, and religious behaviors were related to Agreeableness and Conscientiousness. This pattern of relationships suggests that although spirituality and religiosity have some overlap (i.e., Agreeableness), they are distinct constructs (Hill & Pargament, 2003).

Relationships between religion and personality have been studied in individuals with varying religious backgrounds. For instance, Taylor and MacDonald (1999) examined the relationship between personality and religion with participants who identified as Catholic, other Christian, other religion, or no religion. Agreeableness and Conscientiousness were positively correlated with religion in

Catholic, other Christians, and other religions, but not with individuals identifying as not religious. Additionally, Neuroticism was most strongly positively related with religion in individuals identifying as not religious. Therefore, it seems differences in personality traits may exist in people who identify as religious versus nonreligious.

Religious constructs consistently are related to high Agreeableness, high Conscientiousness, and low Neuroticism. Spiritual constructs consistently are related to high Openness, Agreeableness, and Conscientiousness, and to low Neuroticism. Furthermore, the diversity of variables examined in these studies illustrates the many ways in which religion and spirituality can be examined within the context of personality.

### Does the Big Five Factor Model Explain Religious and Spiritual Variables?

McCrae (1999) suggested religion and character strengths might simply be a shared variance of previously established personality constructs (i.e., Big Five Factors). This would indicate that character strengths and religions have limited incremental validity above and beyond what the Big Five Factor model of personality already explains. McCrae stated religious and forgiving personality constructs simply may overlap with Agreeableness or Conscientiousness. Thus, Piedmont (2005) recommended that personality measures be included whenever studying religious and spiritual constructs to demonstrate that religious and spiritual variables contribute to psychological processes above and beyond personality constructs.

Henningsgaard and Arnau (2008) did just this. They examined how much variance the Big Five could account for with measures of spiritual meaning, extrinsic religiosity, and intrinsic orientation. For spiritual meaning, the Big Five traits accounted for 9.9% of the variance, largely because of the positive correlation of Conscientiousness. The Big Five traits accounted for 7.7% of the variance in intrinsic orientation, mostly because of the positive correlations with Agreeableness and Conscientiousness. The Big Five traits accounted for 8.0% of variance in quest orientation, largely because of the positive correlations with Neuroticism and Openness, and a negative correlation with Conscientiousness. These results demonstrate that personality traits play a role in religious and spiritual variables. This role is small (i.e., less than 10% of the variance), however, indicating religion and spirituality cannot be simply accounted for completely by the Big Five.

Ciarrocchi, Dy-Liacco, and Deneke (2008) examined character strengths (i.e., relational faith, spiritual discontent, and religious practices as predictors of hope and optimism) and personality. Results demonstrated that relational faith, spiritual discontent, and religious practices had significant incremental variance in optimism, pessimism, and hope (both agency and pathways) above and beyond the variance accounted for by personality. This result suggests that personality traits only partially affect hope and optimism, and that religious and spiritual constructs can explain additional, unique variance.

A large research base of evidence supports the relationship between spiritual and religious constructs with the Big Five Factor model of personality. However, Piedmont (2005) emphasized that the numinous variables are not redundant with personality. That is, religious and spiritual variables consistently explain additional information about individuals that are not explained by traditional personality models.

### Spiritual Transcendence

Piedmont (1999) proposed that a possible sixth factor to the Big Five Factor model of personality theory might be spiritual transcendence. Spiritual transcendence is the capacity to stand outside of one's current sense of time and place to view life from a broader, more objective viewpoint. It involves the ability to be aware of one's limited view and to consider existence beyond individual consciousness (Piedmont, 1999). Spiritual transcendence differs from religion; religion is a social encounter with the divine, whereas spiritual transcendence is the individual's pursuit of a connection with a larger sacredness. Piedmont (1999) further differentiated these two constructs by emphasizing that spiritual transcendence focuses on the connectedness one has with humanity, the universality of life, and satisfaction from personal encounters with transcendence. He identified three factors related to transcendence that were independent of the other Big Five: prayer fulfillment, universality, and connectedness (see Emmons & Paloutzian, 2003). Piedmont (1999) demonstrated that spiritual transcendence was a measure independent from the Big Five Factor model and that spiritual transcendence was related to many important psychological outcomes, such as prosocial behavior, perceived social support, vulnerability to stress, and health.

Spiritual transcendence as an additional personality trait has been documented cross-culturally. Piedmont and Leach (2002) found that spiritual transcendence had predictive validity independent of personality factors even in varying religions (e.g., Hindus, Muslims, and Christians). Additionally, Rican and Janosova (2010) found that the new spirituality factor did not load higher than .40 with any of the five factors from the NEO PI-R scales in a sample of college students from the Czech Republic. This provides support for the universality of spirituality. Therefore, spirituality cannot be entirely accounted for by personality traits.

### McAdams's Critique of Personality Psychology and the Big Five in Particular

Like much of personality psychology, in this chapter, we have generally taken the Big Five as being an important characterization of personality. Despite impressive advances in recent years with respect to theory and research in personality,

McAdams and Pals (2006) suggested that personality psychology has yet to articulate clearly a comprehensive framework for understanding the whole person—the Big Five notwithstanding. The issue is not as simple as merely including a spirituality dimension to personality as Piedmont (e.g., 1999) has suggested. Instead, McAdams and Pals (2006) have suggested a new theoretical approach to personality. They review personality research and theory within the framework of five *processes of personality*—a new big five, in contrast to McRae and Costa's (1997) Big Five personality traits. McAdams and Pals suggested, in fact, that the Big Five traits are best thought of as five dimensions for assessing strangers, but that they are inadequate for describing the whole person. McAdams and Pals described promising empirical and theoretical trends in personality psychology to articulate five big *principles* that can serve as a basis for an integrative science of the whole personality. They conceptualized personality as an individual's unique variation of a hypothesized evolutionary design for human nature (first principle). They suggested that personality develops as an integrated pattern of dispositional traits (second principle), personalized adaptations (third principle), and self-defining life narratives (fourth principle) that are situated in culture and social context (fifth principle).

In a subsequent theoretical review and model, McAdams and Olson (2010) furthered this conceptualization by tracing the development of personality across the human life course. They suggested that development may be observed from three different standpoints: the person as behaving actor, striving agent, and narrating author. Traits and dispositions, they argued, are evident even in the temperaments of infancy. Large differences in the way infants and children in early childhood relate to others foreshadow the ways those traits and dispositions are likely to become adult dispositions. Personal strivings—including spiritual strivings (Emmons, 1999)—and other motivations suggest that people often act as agents. Those personal traits and dispositions reach initial importance during childhood as children develop a sense of self as an agent who has the capabilities to act meaningfully. The emergence of a sense of self results in, or develops in parallel with, relatively stable valued goals for which to strive. Values, beliefs, and practices coalesce during childhood and the emergence into adolescence. Children begin to narrate a coherent life story, and their story-telling sense of a narrative self-accelerates during adolescence and young adulthood. Some sense of meaning of life emerges, and religious conversions (and conversions away from religious upbringings) are common during adolescence. McAdams and Olson (2010) summarized the development of traits, goals, and life narratives throughout five crucial transition points in development: (1) age 2, (2) transition to adolescence, (3) emerging adulthood, (4) passage through midlife, and (5) moving through old age.

With this reconceptualization of personality psychology, we can ponder its significance for the understanding of religion and spirituality. First, characteristics likely emerge even within infant temperaments and in early childhood that aim people toward religion and spirituality. We see this in light of research on attachment to God and images of God. Second, in childhood, as children develop a sense of self and personal strivings, children are aimed—intentionally or unintentionally by parents, community, culture, or serendipitous events and processes—toward or away from virtue. During adolescence, religion may be used as a primary source of identity, guiding choices and behaviors. In emerging adulthood, as more life experiences and challenges are encountered, a young adult may convert or question religious beliefs. During midlife, individuals may look back on their lives and experience a renewed sense of purpose or spirituality. As people age, religious and spiritual beliefs can provide comfort.

## POSITIVE PSYCHOLOGY

Positive psychology is the study of adaptive behaviors and constructive dispositions that promote health (Snyder & Lopez, 2002). Positive psychology often incorporates the study of life satisfaction, strengths, flourishing, psychological well-being, and *eudaimonia* (defined as virtue for self and other). For instance, individuals who are more satisfied with life tend to be better at solving problems, perform better at work, are more resilient in the face of stress, and report better physical health (Park, Peterson, & Seligman, 2004). Thus, the topics of character strengths, values, and virtue are core areas of positive psychology. Character strengths, values, and virtues are often related to religion and spirituality.

### Character Strengths

Character strengths are positive aspects that can be identified in thoughts, feelings, and behaviors, and they are a source of individual differences, similar to traits (Park et al., 2004). Twenty-four character strengths have been identified: (1) appreciation of beauty and excellence, (2) bravery, (3) citizenship, (4) creativity, (5) curiosity, (6) fairness, (7) forgiveness and mercy, (8) gratitude, (9) hope, (10) humor, (11) integrity, (12) judgment, (13) kindness, (14) leadership, (15) love, (16) love of learning, (17) modesty and humility, (18) persistence, (19) perspective, (20) prudence, (21) self-regulation, (22) social intelligence, (23) spirituality, and (24) zest. (Note that spirituality is included as a strength important to life satisfaction.) Park et al. (2004) found that of these 24 strengths, having hope, zest, gratitude, love, or curiosity as one of the top five strengths was significantly related to self-reported life satisfaction. Having modesty, creativity, judgment, appreciation of beauty, love of learning, or prudence in one's top five strengths was related to lower self-reported life satisfaction. Character strengths often are related to religious and spiritual constructs. For instance, hope, optimism, and spirituality are important constructs in positive psychology that relate to transcendence (Peterson & Seligman, 2004). Hope and optimism also have a rich tradition in most major world religious (Ciarrocchi et al., 2008).

Character strengths have been examined in the context of personality. Park et al. (2004) hypothesized some ways personality and character strengths are likely related based on previous research of correlations with the Big Five personality traits with life satisfaction (see Ryan & Deci, 2000). They suggest (a) love and gratitude are related to Agreeableness, (b) curiosity and zest are related to Extraversion, and (c) low hope is related to Neuroticism. Park et al. (2004) demonstrated, however, that even after controlling all Big Five personality traits, curiosity, zest, hope, gratitude, and love still strongly predicted life satisfaction. Therefore, character strengths supplement personality in accounting for and predicting variance in life satisfaction.

### Values

Values are abstract goals that individuals use to guide them throughout life (Saroglou & Muñoz-García, 2008). Values are similar to but distinct from personality. Traits have been described as enduring dispositions; similarly, values are enduring goals (Emmons, 1999). Furthermore, personality traits are viewed as having high heritability, whereas values are more environmentally influenced (Saroglou & Muñoz-García, 2008). Ten basic values have been identified: self-direction, stimulation, hedonism, achievement, power, security, conformity, tradition, benevolence, and universalism (Schwartz, 2005).

To clarify the relationships between religion, spirituality, personality, and values Saroglou and Muñoz-García (2008) administered the NEO PI-R, the Schwarz Values Survey, and an eight-item scale measuring religiousness and spirituality (i.e., personal classic religiosity, emotional religion, and spirituality) to more than 200 college students. Religiosity measures were related to values of conformity, tradition, and benevolence and low valuing of self-enhancement, achievement, hedonism, and self-direction. Spirituality measures were related to the value of benevolence and low valuing of self-enhancing. Values of conservatism and tradition were not as important to spiritual people as they were to religious people. Furthermore, Saroglou and Muñoz-García (2008) examined the relationship between personality and values. Extraversion was correlated positively with hedonism and stimulation, primarily because of the facets of activity and excitement seeking. Openness was positively correlated with benevolence and universalism and negatively correlated with power and achievement. Agreeableness was positively related to benevolence and conformity and negatively related to power and achievement.

Conscientiousness was correlated positively with benevolence and conformity. Neuroticism was unrelated to values. Saroglou and Muñoz-García (2008) concluded that values predicted religious and spiritual variables, but also accounted for unique variance that does not overlap with personality dimensions.

Additionally, a meta-analysis of 21 studies from 15 countries found that religious people tend to ascribe more importance to conservative values (e.g., tradition, conformity) and ascribe little importance to values of openness to change and self-enhancement (e.g., self-direction, hedonism; Saroglou, Delpierre, & Dernelle, 2004). Thus, religion may be related to or influence individual values.

In summary, values seem to be related to religion and spirituality. Furthermore, different values may be associated with religion versus with spirituality. Because values guide thoughts and behaviors, and likely interact with religion and spirituality, it is important to clinically assess values along with religion, spirituality, and personality. We now highlight how several character strengths and values relate to personality, religion, and spirituality.

### *Forgiveness*

Forgiveness can be considered a character strength or a value related to benevolence. Multiple definitions of forgiveness can be given depending on the context and type of relationship (see Chapter 11, this volume).

Forgiveness is one coping response to unforgiveness that can aid mental and physical health (Worthington, Witvliet, Peitrini, & Miller, 2007). Forgiveness is encouraged and taught in many world religions, especially in the monotheistic traditions, such as Judaism, Christianity, and Islam (McCullough & Worthington, 1999). Forgiveness and religion have been consistently positively correlated (e.g., Mullet, Neto, & Riviere, 2005), as have forgiveness and spiritual well-being (Rye et al., 2001).

The relationship between forgiveness and personality has been explored. Mullet et al. (2005) summarized correlations between forgiveness and the Big Five traits from 27 studies. Forgiveness was most strongly positively associated with Agreeableness and negatively associated with Neuroticism. A weak positive correlation was associated with Conscientiousness and a weak negative correlation was associated with Extraversion. Personality factors only explained 15% to 40% of variance in forgiveness (Mullet et al., 2005), suggesting that although there is some overlap in forgiveness and the Big Five traits, forgiveness is a unique personality construct.

### *Altruism*

Altruism is prosocial behavior toward someone without receiving benefit or compensation in return (Saroglou, Pichon, Trompette, Verschueren, & Dernelle, 2005). A large survey of Christians in the United States revealed that individuals who engaged in more altruistic, giving behaviors reported better mental health than those receiving help (Schwartz, Meisenhelder, Ma, & Reed, 2003). Altruism is important throughout the life span. Adolescents and older adults reported better mental health when engaging in more altruistic behaviors (Musick & Waggoner, 2007; Wink & Dillon, 2007). Altruistic personality has been associated with empathy, sympathy, social responsibility, and perspective taking (Carlo, Eisenberg, Troyer, Swizter, & Speer, 1991) and with Agreeableness (Ashton, Paunonen, Helms, & Jackson, 1998).

### *Hope*

Hope is a belief that one can remain motivated and can find a way to meet desired goals (Snyder, Rand, & Sigmon, 2002). Hope is not wishing for good things to happen, but is creating ways to meet one's goals and being motivated to work to meet goals. Spirituality and religiosity have been shown to predict hope (Ciarrocchi et al., 2008). In addition, hope has been used as an intervention for coping with mental health difficulties in spiritual individuals (Revheim & Greenberg, 2007). A structured group to encourage hope and positive spiritually-based coping skills used readings from the book of Psalms, as well as reading prayers, writing prayers, and sharing stories from varying faith perspectives. The group helped people decrease negative coping, increase positive coping, and cognitively reappraise from victimization to resilience.

### *Optimism*

Optimism is a person's general tendency to view life and outcomes favorably (Salsman, Brown, Brechting, & Carlson, 2005). Optimism has been linked with positive outcomes, such as physical health (Seligman, 1991), effective coping (Scheier, Weintraub, & Carver, 1986), and lower depression (Puskar, Sereika, Lamb, Tusaie-Mumford, & McGuinness, 1999). Religiosity and spirituality often are linked with positive psychological functioning (Salsman et al., 2005). Spirituality and religiosity also predict optimism (Ciarrocchi et al., 2008). In fact, Salsman et al. (2005) proposed that the relationship between religion and mental health may be explained by optimism. They examined the relationship between religiousness, optimism, and life satisfaction. Optimism fully mediated the relationship between intrinsic religiousness and psychological distress. Optimism partially mediated the relationship between intrinsic religiousness and satisfaction with life. Optimism also partially mediated the relationship between prayer fulfillment and satisfaction with life. This suggests that individuals with higher levels of intrinsic religiousness and higher levels of prayer fulfillment likely will also have higher levels of optimism and satisfaction with life (Salsman et al., 2005).

## CLINICAL IMPLICATIONS

### Big Five Traits and Counseling

Personality traits can affect how individuals interact in psychotherapy. For instance, extraverted clients may feel comfortable with counselors more quickly than introverted clients. Additionally, clients who score high on Neuroticism may be more prone to negative emotions, negative thinking, negative coping strategies, and psychological disorders. These traits may also affect clients' expectations when entering psychotherapy, hope for getting better, and interactions with the counselor. Openness to new experiences may affect comfort with and outcomes of counseling and willingness to try new strategies and styles of coping. Spiritual and religious clients may be more likely to go along with the psychotherapist (because of high Agreeableness and Conscientiousness) than are nonreligious clients. Clinicians should be aware of this possibility and check in often with clients about how they think the psychotherapy is going.

The psychotherapist often considers clients' personality in deciding which interventions to use with patients dealing with particular issues. For instance, clients low on Agreeableness or high on Neuroticism may not easily forgive or cope with negative events. A forgiving personality may help people to request and receive forgiveness by God and other people and to forgive those who have harmed them (McCullough & Worthington, 1999). People with forgiving personalities may respond differently to offenses they have experienced in their lives. Thus, it is helpful to be aware of and understand clients' dispositions (e.g., Agreeableness, Conscientiousness, Neuroticism, Openness, Extraversion, and/or forgivingness) because that can affect counseling.

## Religion and Personality Disorders

### *Narcissistic Personality Disorder*

Narcissism is broadly defined as investment in oneself (Wink et al., 2005). It has been suggested that in the United States there is a trend of a psychotherapeutic, self-centered, narcissistic individuality replacing socially responsible individualism (Wink et al., 2005). Too much focus on oneself may impair the relationship an individual can have with God or on his or her ability to engage and experience spiritual transcendence. For example, a diagnosis of a narcissistic personality disorder entails specific features of grandiosity, lack of empathy, sense of entitlement, preoccupation with fantasies of power and success, and feelings of emptiness (American Psychiatric Association, 2000). These features may distance an individual from God or spiritual connection with others. Emotions commonly experienced with this disorder include rage, shame, and irritability. These emotions may also lead to a strong defensiveness in psychotherapy. Burijon (2001) theorized (on the basis of self-psychology and object relations) that lack of empathy stems from the inability to incorporate grace into interpersonal interactions, which perpetuates a negative, insecure view of oneself as faulty. These underlying views of being defective can lead to the engagement in compensatory grandiose views and fantasies. Therefore, Burijon has advised psychotherapists to express empathy and treat clients with grace. Through experiencing empathy and grace, the underlying insecurity and sense of oneself as faulty can be corrected so that the grandiose sense of self and fantasies will no longer be needed as defenses.

### *Borderline Personality Disorder*

Borderline personality features typically include a pattern of unstable interpersonal relationships, self-image, and affect with frantic efforts to avoid real or perceived abandonment, extremes of idealization and devaluation, recurrent suicidal or self-harm behaviors, and chronic feelings of emptiness (American Psychiatric Association, 2000). Therefore, individuals diagnosed with borderline personality disorder may have an unstable relationship with God, believe God has abandoned them, and experience alternating extremes between idealization and devaluation of God. Goodman and Manierre (2008) designed a psychoanalytically oriented spirituality group that explored representations of God with nine hospitalized female patients. The representations of God included God as punitive, judgmental, and rigid or God as depersonified, inanimate, and abstract (yet with many idealized aspects). Patients with punitive God representations were able to transform their relationship with God from punishing and harsh to a more compassionate or benevolent God. Patients with depersonified God representations could not. This suggests that spiritual or religious individuals with punitive representations of God may benefit from treatment that transforms these representations into benevolent representations. These changes in representations of God can then be repeated in other interpersonal relationships and provide a way to treat individuals diagnosed with borderline personality disorder.

## Religious Coping

Coping styles are patterns that individuals construct over time while attempting to overcome difficult situations (Bassett et al., 2008). Spiritual and religious variables likely affect coping ability and style, thus directly and indirectly affecting mental health. Also, disturbances in one's relationship with the transcendent may result in psychological distress (Piedmont, 2005). In fact, spiritual and religious variables seem to play a significant role in adaptation, coping, and growth. Therefore, clinicians often can use religious and spiritual strategies to promote positive change in clients (Piedmont, 2005).

Many people may use religious or spiritual beliefs and practices as resources during stress. Pargament (2007) summarized a variety of religious coping methods. Benevolent religious reappraisal entails redefining a stressor through religion as benign or possibly having benefits. In contrast, a punishing-God reappraisal involves redefining a stressor as a punishment from God because of one's sins. Collaborative religious coping involves problem solving with God. Seeking spiritual support involves searching for comfort in God's love and care. Religious purification entails spiritual cleansing through religious rituals or actions. Seeking support from clergy or members of the congregation, attempting to provide spiritual support to others, and utilizing religious beliefs in aiding letting go of negative emotions after being harmed also are listed as religious coping methods.

Religious coping has been shown to account for unique variance in stress-related growth, religious outcome, physical health, mental health, and emotional distress, even after controlling for demographic effects (Pargament, Koenig, & Perez, 2000). Religious coping can be positive or negative (Pargament et al., 2000). A meta-analysis of more than 40 studies on religion and coping demonstrated that religious coping had positive stress-buffering effects in 34% of the studies and had negative effects of increasing stress in 4% of studies (Pargament, 1997).

### *Positive Religious Coping*

Positive religious coping typically involves the following: (a) benevolent religious reappraisals, (b) collaborative religious coping, (c) seeking out spiritual support, (d) spiritual connection, (e) religious purification rituals, (f) seeking help from clergy or congregation members, (g) religious helping, and (h) religious forgiving (Pargament et al., 2000). In fact, collaboration with God during times of stress, seeking connection with God, and seeking support from clergy or congregation have been related to better mental health, more psychological and spiritual growth as a result of a stressor, and life satisfaction (Pargament et al., 2000). More specifically, positive religious coping can buffer negative effects, such as depression, in the face of stressful events. In general, positive religious coping predicts better psychological well-being (Bassett et al., 2008). Clients with personality traits of Extraversion and Openness may be more likely to use positive religious coping. Also, clients who score high on Agreeableness may have an easier time utilizing religious forgiving during times of stress.

### *Negative Religious Coping*

Negative religious coping typically involves the following: (a) punishing religious appraisals, (b) demonic and negative religious reappraisals, (c) expressions of spiritual and interpersonal religious discontent, and (d) self-directed as opposed to collaborative religious coping (Pargament et al., 2000). Negative religious coping predicts a tendency to experience depression, lower quality of life, and callousness toward others (Bassett et al., 2008). More specifically, reappraisals of God as punishing and negative attitudes toward God, clergy, or church have been associated with poorer physical health, lower quality of life, and depression (Pargament, 1997). Clients who score high on Neuroticism and low on Extraversion may be more likely to use negative religious coping strategies. For instance, these individuals may be more likely cope with stress and problems on their own, have more negative appraisals, and may feel more spiritual and interpersonal religious discontent.

## CLINICAL ASSESSMENTS

Religion and spirituality are complex and multifaceted. Just because people report that religion or spirituality is central to their identity and that they attend church weekly does not give the clinician specific information about religious or spiritual coping, religious or spiritual well-being, relationship with God or the transcendent, or character strengths and values. Therefore, it is important to include informal and formal assessment with religious and spiritual clients.

### Informal Assessment

#### *Informal Discussion*

Assessing important religious and spiritual aspects of a client's life can be done with informal discussion. Clinicians can ask clients how they use their religious and spiritual framework during stressful or challenging times. This can give the psychotherapist an idea of religious coping strategies. Other topics that may be helpful to explore include asking what a client's relationship with God is like, motivations or reasons for religious and spiritual beliefs, and meaning that is gained from spiritual or religious beliefs. Psychotherapists can also ask clients to identify their virtues and character strengths so the psychotherapist can see what motivations (e.g., altruism, hope, or forgiveness) drive clients' lives besides religion and spirituality.

Additionally, it behooves the psychotherapist to seek more than a cursory understanding of a client's religious or spiritual commitments. Thus, the psychotherapist might employ a series of branching screening questions, such as "Do you consider yourself to be primarily religious and identified with some religious faith perspective, organization, or denomination?" If yes, the psychotherapist might ask, "Do you believe that religion plays a part in your psychological struggles that have brought you to counseling?" If no, the psychotherapist might ask, "Do you consider yourself spiritual and not religious?" and "What sacred object or experience do you hold most sacred?" and "How does this affect your life and the psychological difficulties you are having?" Importantly, the wise clinician does not accept a client's report that he or she is "religious" or "spiritual" or "not religious" at face value without seeking a bit more nuanced understanding and a sense of whether the client desires to have religion or spiritual considerations discussed explicitly in treatment.

#### *Spiritual Life Map*

Hodge (2005) described an informal, collaborative assessment for spiritual or religious clients. A client lists major events (including religious and spiritual ones) in his or her life from birth to present (and beyond to the afterlife) on the life map. The goal is to describe spiritually significant events. The events contain struggles and resources used to cope with difficulties. The clinician is in the background supporting, assisting, and encouraging the client. Once the spiritual life map is completed, the clinician asks the client to explain it. This can help clients identify (a) spiritual strengths, (b) patterns of coping, (c) resources, and (d) areas needing spiritual or cognitive reframing (Hodge, 2005). Clinicians can explore alternative ways to view the meaning of events or to view their current problems through a spiritual lens.

## Formal Assessment

### *Personality*

Personality can be assessed formally with the NEO PI-R. It contains 240 items on a scale ranging from "strongly disagree" to "strongly agree" (Costa & McCrae, 1992). Sample items include "I am easy-going and lackadaisical" and "I keep my belongings neat and clean." The NEO PI-R is designed for use with clients without personality pathology. It provides a general description of the five factors and 30 specific personality domains (six within each of the five factors).

### *Spiritual Well-Being Scale*

The Spiritual Well-Being Scale (SWBS; Paloutzian & Ellison, 1991) is a general measure of an individuals' perceived spiritual quality of life. It includes subscales of Religious Well-Being (RWB; i.e., sense of well-being in relationship with God) and Existential Well-Being (EWB; i.e., overall purpose of life and satisfaction with life). The SWBS has 20 items, 10 for each subscale. Typical items are "I don't feel much satisfaction in private prayer with God" (RWB) and "I feel that life is a positive experience" (SWB). Responses are made on a six-point scale that ranges from "strongly agree" to "strongly disagree." The scale can be used to assess a client's spiritual health, identify religious issues related to a client's disorder or coping, and identify spiritual resources for coping. Personality traits may be helpful in interpreting and improving an individual's perceived spiritual quality of life (e.g., openness or agreeableness).

### *RCOPE*

The Religious Coping Scale (RCOPE; Pargament et al., 2000) assesses positive and negative religious coping with 104 items. Positive religious coping includes measures of religious purification or forgiveness, religious direction or conversion, religious helping, seeking spiritual support, collaborative religious coping, religious focus, active religious surrender, benevolent religious appraisal, spiritual connection, and marking religious boundaries. Sample items include "Saw my situation as part of God's plan" and "Sought God's love and care." Negative religious coping measures are spiritual discontent, punishing-God reappraisals, pleading for direct intercession, passive religious deferral, interpersonal religious discontent, demonic reappraisal, and reappraisal of God's power. Sample items include "Questioned God's love for me" and "Felt the situation was the work of the devil." Responses range from 0 = *not at all* to 3 = *a great deal*. The RCOPE can be used to identify a need for increasing positive religious coping, reinforcing current use of positive religious coping strategies, or decreasing negative religious coping. Personality assessments may be helpful when paired with the RCOPE to explain and work with negative religious coping (e.g., neuroticism) and positive religious coping (e.g., openness).

### *Spiritual Assessment Inventory*

The Spiritual Assessment Inventory (SAI) is a relational measure of spiritual development (Hall & Edwards, 2002). The scale assesses awareness and quality of relationship with God along with five factors of Awareness ("I have a sense of how God is working in my life"), Disappointment ("There are times when I feel frustrated with God"), Realistic Acceptance (Follow-up question to feeling frustrated: "When I feel this way, I still desire to put effort into our relationship"), Grandiosity ("I seem to have a unique ability to influence God through my prayers"), and Instability ("I am afraid that God will give up on me"). An impression management scale also can identify individuals who report unrealistic or idealistic relationship with God ("I always seek God's guidance for every decision I make"). Fifty-four items are rated on a five-point scale from "Not at all true" to "Very true." This scale can be used to measure positive and negative aspects of relationship with God, discuss expectations of one's relationship with God, and provide specific areas for improving one's relationship with God. Personality measures may help inform results on this inventory, such as neuroticism being related to Instability or Disappointment subscales.

### Spiritual Transcendence Scale

The Spiritual Transcendence Scale (STS) measures intrinsic motivation to find deeper meaning in life by looking past individual needs to focus on the needs of a larger group or cause (Piedmont, 1999). The STS has 24 items and three subscales. Responses range from "strongly agree" to "strongly disagree." Connectedness measures how much a person feels a sense of community and association with others (e.g., "I feel that on a higher level, all of us share a common bond"). Prayer Fulfillment measures traditional religion or spirituality ("I have experienced deep fulfillment and bliss through my prayers and meditations"). Universality measures a person's meaning and purpose in life ("I believe there is a larger plan to life"). This measure can be used to assess strengths and areas of growth for spirituality and spiritual coping, and it may identify possible existential issues. Personality traits of openness and agreeableness may be helpful in interpreting Spiritual Transcendence results.

### VIA Inventory of Strengths

The VIA Inventory of Strengths (VIA-IS; Peterson & Seligman, 2004) measures the degree to which individuals perceive specific strengths apply to them. The VIA-IS assesses 24 strengths with 240 items (10 items per strength): (1) appreciation of beauty and excellence, (2) bravery, (3) citizenship, (4) creativity, (5) curiosity, (6) fairness, (7) forgiveness and mercy, (8) gratitude, (9) hope, (10) humor, (11) integrity, (12) judgment, (13) kindness, (14) leadership, (15) love, (16) love of learning, (17) modesty and humility, (18) persistence,

(19) perspective, (20) prudence, (21) self-regulation, (22) social intelligence, (23) spirituality, and (24) zest. A sample item for the strength of hope is "I know that I will succeed with the goals I set for myself." A sample item for the strength of gratitude is "At least once a day, I stop and count my blessings." Responses range from 1 = *very much like me* to 5 = *very much unlike me*. Many character strengths are related to religious and spiritual concepts, such as forgiveness and mercy, hope, modesty and humility, and spirituality. This measure can be used to identify strengths, create coping strategies that capitalize on strengths, and identify possible areas of growth. Personality traits may inform strengths. For instance, people scoring high in openness may be more likely to value creativity and appreciation of beauty and excellence, whereas someone scoring high in conscientiousness may place more value on the strengths of citizenship and self-regulation.

### Schwartz Value Survey

The Schwartz Value Survey (SVS; Schwartz, 2005) measures 10 values: self-direction, stimulation, hedonism, achievement, power, security, conformity, tradition, benevolence, and universalism. The SVS contains 57 items made up of two lists of value items. The first list has 30 items that describe desired end states, and the second list contains 27 items with potentially desirable ways of acting. Each item reflects one of the 10 values. Each item is rated to the extent that it is "a guiding principle in *my* life." Item responses are on a nine-point scale and range from 1 = *opposed to my values* to 7 = *of supreme importance*. Sample words for universalism include *social justice* and *broad-minded*. Sample words for achievement include *ambitious* and *successful*. The SVAS has been translated into 47 different languages and has been used across the world. This measure can identify values that may be helpful to discuss and utilize in psychotherapy and to recognize areas of growth or issues related to values that may be contributing to a client's current problems. Similar to strengths, personality may help inform values. For instance, high conscientiousness may be related to achievement and extraversion may be related to hedonism.

## CLINICAL STRATEGIES

### Incorporate Personality Into Psychotherapy

Psychotherapists can facilitate discussions with clients of how their personality traits affect religious coping, character strengths, values, and perceptions of psychotherapy. This can be done through informal discussions or through discussion of collaborative formal assessment. Possible topics of discussion include how extraversion and openness—perhaps to religious or spiritual ideas—might affect pscyhotherapy. Other topics of discussion might include the following: (a) how personality factors may affect social interactions or styles of religious coping,

(b) how neuroticism might affect psychological disorders and symptoms, or (c) how to counteract personality tendencies toward neuroticism.

### Encouraging Personality-Based Character Strengths

#### *Promoting a Forgiving Personality*

If clients are experiencing unforgiveness related to others, self, or God, forgiveness can be discussed and promoted within the clinical context. Forgiveness as a topic frequently comes up in clinical problems. It is a positive psychology construct that overlaps with the Psychology of Religion and Spirituality, clinical psychology, and personality psychology. A chapter within the current volume (see Chapter 11, this volume) deals with it specifically, so we will not discuss it further at this time.

#### *Promoting Optimism and Hope*

Optimism and hope can help people cope during challenging or stressful situations. Bassett et al. (2008) found that optimism is closely related to positive reappraisal coping. Therefore optimism can be used when evaluating stressors, resources, goals, and outcomes. For instance, when clients face a negative event, in addition to exploring the negative effects of the event, the psychotherapist can facilitate discussions in several ways. Topics of looking back to other difficult times and highlighting how the client overcame previous obstacles can engender optimism or hope. Also, the psychotherapist may encourage reflection on possible positive outcomes or benefits that may arise from the stressor. Creating a sense of optimism or hope can promote positive expectations for clients, thus increasing the likelihood that they will want to participate and engage in the psychotherapy and problem-solving process. By practicing more optimistic and hopeful reappraisals, over time, a general optimistic or hopeful attitude can be created.

#### *Promoting Altruism*

Participating in altruistic acts can help people to feel more connected to community, God, or the transcendent; give people a sense of appreciation; and reduce people's tendencies to overfocus on self. Many religions and spiritual communities promote or expect altruistic behaviors. Altruism can be promoted informally or formally. Psychotherapists can encourage clients to act altruistically with family, friends, acquaintances, or strangers several times a week. They can encourage clients to volunteer within the community and talk about how it affects spiritual and religious well-being. For example, a client can volunteer his or her time to help build houses for families in need. This altruistic act and the discussion of the altruistic act can help clients feel more connectedness with others as well as develop an appreciation for what he or she has. Altruism can be practiced in group counseling by asking members to help each other during sessions.

## CASE STUDY

### Background

Jenny (a disguised composite of several clients seen by the senior author) was a 45-year-old white female who presented with symptoms of depression and anxiety. She recently had left a physically and emotionally abusive marriage of 20 years. She had a negative view of herself. She actively helped her parents and siblings in any way she could, and she described her family as "tight knit." As a teacher, she worked long hours, often taking on more than was expected. She said she wanted to have children, but she was unable to because of infertility. Cognitive-behavioral therapy (CBT) was used in conjunction with the following treatment to treat symptoms of depression, anxiety, and poor self-image.

### Assessment

First, Jenny was informally assessed regarding her religious and spiritual views in the intake session. She was asked what role, if any, religion and spirituality played in her life. She stated that religion was central to her life, and it was very important for her to be a good Christian. She was also asked whether she had spiritual or religious concerns. She reported that she attends church weekly and feels guilty when she misses. After the intake, Jenny completed the (a) RCOPE to identify religious coping patterns, (b) VIA strengths inventory to identify strengths in order to improve self-image, and (c) NEO-PI-R to better understand her approach to counseling, religion, and relationships.

The RCOPE indicated Jenny was using few positive religious coping strategies. She had low scores on religious forgiveness, seeking spiritual support, collaborative religious coping, spiritual connections, religious purification, and benevolent religious appraisal. She was relying heavily on punishing-God appraisals, however. She redefined her stressors as a punishment from God because of her sins. The VIA indicated that Jenny's top five strengths were (1) industry, diligence, and perseverance; (2) kindness and generosity; (3) spirituality, sense of purpose, and faith; (4), self-control and self-regulation; and (5) zest, enthusiasm, and energy. The NEO-PI-R indicated Jenny was high on Conscientiousness, Agreeableness, and Neuroticism; average on Openness; and low on Extraversion. High Neuroticism and low Extraversion suggested that Jenny (a) experienced negative emotions, such as anxiety and depression; (b) preferred to spend time alone; (c) lacked assertiveness; (d) had little desire for excitement seeking; and (e) had a tendency to not experience many positive emotions. Thus, Jenny was expected to be slow to warm toward her psychotherapist and might resist compliments, encouragement, and positive affirmations. High Agreeableness and Conscientiousness were consistent with individuals who report being highly religious or spiritual. Jenny's average Openness indicated that she would be able to discuss concerns and applying new techniques and strategies to her life.

### Strategies

First, the RCOPE, VIA, and NEO-PI-R results were analyzed and collaboratively discussed with Jenny. She confirmed the results identified during her assessment. Second, her personality patterns and how they might affect psychotherapy were discussed. She agreed that she has a difficult time believing people when they say nice things about her. She also agreed that she was nervous about counseling, and opening up to someone with all of her private thoughts and concerns—especially with something as important to her as religion—but she was ready to make changes in her life. Jenny had a hard time admitting her strengths based on the VIA. With encouragement from her psychotherapist, she provided examples supporting her five top strengths. For instance, she could view herself as kind and generous because she frequently volunteered for causes and also often helped people in need. She brainstormed ways she could use her strengths in coping with her depression and anxiety. She said she could use her zest for life to combat her negative thoughts and depression. She admitted that she *should* be kind and generous to herself like she is with others. She agreed to try to be less harsh on herself.

Next, her religious coping strategies were explored. The psychotherapist focused on increasing benevolent reappraisals and decreasing appraisals of God as punishing. The psychotherapist redefined a stressor through religion as benevolent or potentially having benefits. For example, Jenny reported that she viewed stress and difficulties as ways of being punished by God for sinning. Reasons for these negative appraisals were explored and alternative appraisals were encouraged (e.g., I am "given" stress and difficulties because God wants to teach me something; and God believes I am resilient, and this can bring me closer to God). Jenny was encouraged to explore why she was hesitant to seek support from clergy or members of the congregation even though she was so involved in giving to others in her congregation. She said that (a) she was an introvert, and (b) she felt that her concerns were not as important as other people's problems. The psychotherapist challenged her negative appraisal that her problems were not important. After discussion, Jenny agreed to try to make more positive appraisals. She also talked about her lack of collaborative religious coping. She tended to pray and wait for signs and guidance. She was encouraged to think of problem solving by more actively interacting with God. She said she would read scripture to gain insights and concrete guidance. Jenny was asked to brainstorm some positive religious purification rituals. She came up with the idea of waking earlier so she could add times of meditation after her morning prayer.

Jenny struggled to maintain her positive intentions throughout psychotherapy. Over time, however, her mood modulated and her anxiety symptoms lowered. She attributed it to some of the cognitive skills she had learned through the CBT, and also to a revitalized spiritual life. She particularly expressed how helpful it was to change the way she used her religious beliefs in coping (i.e., increasing positive religious coping skills). Additionally, she reported that discussing her strengths helped her to view herself in a more positive light.

## CONCLUSION

We believe that the psychology of religion and spirituality has a lot to offer psychotherapists who work with religious and spiritual clients. We briefly reviewed major theories of personality as they related to religion and spirituality and empirical research on personality and positive psychology as they relate to religion and spirituality, especially with religious and spiritual clients. We described religious coping in psychotherapy and suggested useful assessment tools that can be used with religious and spiritual clients. We also recommended specific clinical strategies. Finally, we presented a brief case study to demonstrate clinical assessments and strategies.

Personality style can affect problem solving, religious coping, approach to counseling, and tendency to experience positive or negative emotions. A focus on personality can help facilitate discussions and understandings of client's character strengths, values, and coping. Therefore, clinicians are encouraged to incorporate personality and character strengths into their work with religious and spiritual clients. We strongly encourage clinicians to utilize structured assessments not only at the beginning of, but also throughout, the counseling process.

## CHAPTER SUMMARY

- Object relations, attachment style, Eysenck's biological theory, and the Big Five Factor model of personality provide useful frameworks for examining and understanding the interactions between personality and spirituality and religion.
- According to the Big Five Factor model of personality, religious constructs consistently are related to high Agreeableness, high Conscientiousness, and low Neuroticism. Spiritual constructs consistently are related to high Openness, Agreeableness, and Conscientiousness, and to low Neuroticism.
- Character strengths and values are often associated with religious and spiritual constructs.
- Forgiveness, altruism, hope, and optimism are important constructs that are related to both personality and religious and spiritual constructs.
- A thorough understanding of a client's personality can help clinicians to use better interventions with patients dealing with particular issues.
- Religious coping can have positive stress-buffering or negative effects that may increase stress. Type of religious coping is often influenced by personality factors.

- Informal and formal assessment of personality, character strengths, values, and religious and spiritual constructs can improve quality of counseling.
- Incorporating personality into psychotherapy and encouraging personality-based character strengths can be beneficial to clients and provide an additional perspective of treatment.

## CLINICAL APPLICATION QUESTIONS

1. In assessing clients, do you consider religion? How? Do you consider spirituality, and if so, with whom? Do you have some kind of implicit "theory" for deciding who might benefit and who might not benefit from inclusion of religious and spiritual issues explicitly?
2. Do you find the Big Five Factor model traits—Openness to Experience, Conscientiousness, Extraversion-Introversion, Agreeableness, and Neuroticism—helpful in deciding how you will approach religious and spiritual topics with clients? McAdams and Pals described the Big Five traits as most useful as a way to assess a stranger. That is what you are doing at the beginning of psychotherapy. But, as you get to know the client, do you find that the client's personal narrative makes more sense? McAdams and Pals suggested that themes of redemption often are associated with successful life stories. Do you find that clients change their narratives over the course of psychotherapy from victimization to redemption?
3. Are traits like humility (and some of its opposites—narcissism, pride, and entitlement)—meaningful to how your clients deal with religious issues?
4. Are you able to keep your own personality out of the discussion when the client deals with religious or spiritual issues? Do you think that is therapeutically wise?
5. Do you have one or more peers who have different perspectives on religion and personality than you do, with whom you can consult on difficult cases?
6. The research shows that clinicians regularly do not refer to religious professionals. Do you? Do you get or give more referrals to religious professionals?

## SUGGESTED READINGS AND RESOURCES

### Books for Psychotherapists

Pargament, K. I. (2007). *Spiritually integrated psychotherapy: Understanding and assessing the sacred.* New York, NY: Guilford Press.

Richards, P. S., & Bergin, A. E. (2000). *Handbook of religious diversity.* Washington, DC: American Psychological Association.

### Books for Researchers (With Articles of Interest to Psychotherapists)

Post, S. (Ed.). (2007). *Altruism and health: Perspectives from empirical research.* New York, NY: Oxford University Press.

Snyder, C. R., & Lopez, S. J. (Eds.). (2002). *Handbook of positive psychology.* New York, NY: Oxford University Press.

### Books for Clients

Emmons, R. A. (1999). *The psychology of ultimate concerns: Motivation and spirituality in psychology.* New York, NY: Guilford Press.

### Videos

Martin Doblmeier (Director). (2007). *The power of forgiveness* [DVD]. Journey Films. Available from http://www.journeyfilms.com

### Websites

American Psychological Association. Psychology of religion. http://www.apa.org/about/division/div36.aspx

Beliefnet. http://www.beliefnet.com

BorderlineCentral. Borderline personality disorder and religion. http://www.borderline-central.com/articles/bpdandreligion.php

Northwestern University, Department of Psychology. Psychology faculty profiles: Dan P. McAdams. http://www.wcas.northwestern.edu/psych/people/faculty/faculty_individual_pages/McAdams.htm

## REFERENCES

Ainsworth, M., & Bowlby, J. (1991). An ethological approach to personality development. *American Psychologist, 46*(4), 333–341.

Allport, G., & Ross, J. (1967). Personal religious orientation and prejudice. *Journal of Personality and Social Psychology, 5*, 432–443.

American Psychiatric Association. (2000). *Diagnostic and statistical manual of mental disorders* (4th ed., text rev.). Washington, DC: Author.

Ashton, M., Paunonen, S., Helmes, E., & Jackson, D. (1998). Kin altruism, reciprocal altruism, and the Big Five personality factors. *Evolution and Human Behavior, 19*, 243–255.

Bassett, R., Garrick, I., Fogarty, M., Giacalone, S., Kapuscinski, A., Olmstead, M., et al. (2008). Walking down the sunny side of the street: Three studies developing a spiritually nuanced measure of optimism. *International Journal for the Psychology of Religion, 18*, 330–352.

Batson, C. (1976). Religion as prosocial: Agent or double agent? *Journal for the Scientific Study of Religion, 15*, 29–45.

Burijon, B. (2001). Narcissism and grace: Inherent incompatibility. *Pastoral Psychology, 49*, 181–186.

Carlo, G., Eisenberg, N., Troyer D., Swizter, G., & Speer, A. L. (1991). The altruistic personality: In what context is it apparent? *Journal of Personality and Social Psychology, 61*, 450–458.

Ciarrocchi, J. W., Dy-Liacco, G. S., & Deneke, E. (2008). Gods or rituals? Relational faith, spiritual discontent, and religious practices as predictors of hope and optimism. *Journal of Positive Psychology, 3*, 120–136.

Costa, P. T., Jr., & McCrae, R. R. (1992). *The NEO-PI-R professional manual.* Odessa, FL: Psychological Assessment Resources.

D'Onofrio, B. M., Eaves, L. J., Murrelle, L., Maes, H. H., & Spilka, B. (1999). Understanding biological and social influences on religious affiliation, attitudes and behaviors: A behavior genetic perspective. *Journal of Personality, 67*, 953–984. doi:10.1111/1467-6494.00079

Emmons, R. A. (1999). *The psychology of ultimate concerns: Motivation and spirituality in psychology*. New York, NY: Guilford Press.

Emmons, R., & Paloutzian, R. (2003). The psychology of religion. *Annual Review of Psychology, 54*, 377–402.

Eysenck, H. J. (1967). *The biological basis of personality*. Springfield, IL: Thomas.

Eysenck, H. J. (1990). Biological dimensions of personality. In L. A. Pervin (Ed.), *Handbook of personality: Theory and research* (pp. 244–276). New York, NY: Guilford.

Francis, L., & Jackson, C. (2003). Eysenck's dimensional model of personality and religion: Are religious people more neurotic? *Mental Health, Religion and Culture, 6*, 87–100.

Gallup International Association. (2010). Millennium survey: Religion. Retrieved from http://www.gallup-international.com

Goodman, G., & Manierre, A. (2008). Representations of God uncovered in a spirituality group of borderline inpatients. *International Journal of Group Psychotherapy, 58*, 1–16.

Hall, T., & Edwards, K. (2002). The Spiritual Assessment Inventory: A theistic model and measure for assessing spiritual development. *Journal for the Scientific Study of Religion, 41*, 341–357.

Henningsgaard, J., & Arnau, R. (2008). Relationships between religiosity, spirituality, and personality: A multivariate analysis. *Personality and Individual Differences, 45*, 703–708.

Hill, P., & Pargament, K. (2003). Advances in the conceptualization and measurement of religion and spirituality: Implications for physical and mental health research. *American Psychologist, 58*, 64–74.

Hodge, D. (2005). Spiritual lifemaps: A client-centered pictorial instrument for spiritual assessment, planning, and intervention. *Social Work, 50*, 77–87.

Kernberg, O. (1966). Structural derivatives of object relationships. *International Journal of Psychoanalysis, 47*, 236–253.

Kirkpatrick, L. (1998). God as a substitute attachment figure: A longitudinal study of adult attachment style and religious change in college students. *Personality and Social Psychology Bulletin, 24*, 961–973.

Lawrence, R. (1997). Measuring the image of God: The God Image Inventory and the God Image Scales. *Journal of Psychology and Theology, 25*, 214–226.

Maltby, J., & Day, L. (2001). Spiritual involvement and belief: The relationship between spirituality and Eysenck's personality dimensions. *Personality and Individual Differences, 30*, 187–192.

McAdams, D. P., & Olson, B. D. (2010). Personality development: Continuity and change over the life course. *Annual Review of Psychology, 61*, 517–542.

McAdams, D. P., & Pals, J. L. (2006). A new Big Five: Fundamental principles for an integrative science of personality. *American Psychologist, 61*, 204–217.

McCrae, R. (1999). Mainstream personality psychology and the study of religion. *Journal of Personality, 67*, 1209–1218.

McCrae, R., & Costa, P. (1997). Personality trait structure as a human universal. *American Psychologist, 52*, 509–516.

McCullough, M., & Worthington, E. L., Jr. (1999). Religion and the forgiving personality. *Journal of Personality, 67*, 1141–1164.

Musick M. A., & Waggoner M. R. (2007). Self-initiated volunteering and mental health. In S. G. Post (Ed.), *Altruism and health: Perspectives from empirical research* (pp. 82–96). New York, NY: Oxford University Press.

Mullet, E., Neto, F., & Riviere, S. (2005). Personality and its effects on resentment, revenge, forgiveness, and self-forgiveness. In E. L. Worthington, Jr. (Ed.), *Handbook of forgiveness* (pp. 159–181). New York, NY: Brunner-Routledge.

Paloutzian R., & Ellison C. (1991). *Manual for Spiritual Well-Being Scale*. Nyack, NY: Life Advance.

Pargament, K. I. (1997). *The psychology of religion and coping: Theory, practice, research*. New York, NY: Guilford Press.

Pargament, K. I. (2007). *Spiritually integrated psychotherapy: Understanding and assessing the sacred*. New York, NY: Guilford Press.

Pargament, K. I., Koenig, H. G., & Perez, L. M. (2000). The many methods of religious coping: Development and initial validation of the RCOPE. *Journal of Clinical Psychology, 56*, 519–543.

Park, N., Peterson, C., & Seligman, M. (2004). Strengths of character and well-being. *Journal of Social and Clinical Psychology, 23*, 603–619.

Peterson, C., & Seligman, M. (2004). Universal virtues? Lessons from history. *Character strengths and virtues: A handbook and classification* (pp. 33–52). New York, NY: American Psychological Association.

Piedmont, R. (1999). Does spirituality represent the sixth factor of personality? Spiritual transcendence and the five-factor model. *Journal of Personality, 67*, 985–1013.

Piedmont, R. (2005). The role of personality in understanding religious and spiritual constructs. In R. F. Paloutzian and C. L. Park (Eds.), *Handbook of the psychology of religion and spirituality* (pp. 253–273). New York, NY: Guilford Press.

Piedmont, R., & Leach, M. (2002). Cross-cultural generalizability of the Spiritual Transcendence Scale in India: Spirituality as a universal aspect of human experience. *American Behavioral Scientist, 45*, 1888–1901.

Puskar, K. R., Sereika, S., Lamb, J., Tusaie-Mumford, K., & McGuinness, T. *(1999)*. Optimism and its relationship to depression, coping, anger, and life events in rural adolescents. *Issues in Mental Health Nursing, 20,* 115–130.

Revheim, N., & Greenberg, W. M. (2007). Spirituality matters: Creating a time and place for hope. *Psychiatric Rehabilitation Journal, 30*, 307–310.

Rican, P., & Janosova, P. (2010). Spirituality as a basic aspect of personality: A cross-cultural verification of Piedmont's model. *International Journal for the Psychology of Religion, 20*, 2–13.

Rizzuto, A. M. (1979). *The birth of the living god*. Chicago, IL: University of Chicago Press.

Ryan, R. M., & Deci, E. L. (2000). On happiness and human potentials: A review of research on hedonic and eudaimonic well-being. *Annual Review of Psychology, 52,* 141–166.

Rye, M. S., Loiacono, D. M., Folck, C. D., Olszewski, B. T., Heim, T. A., & Madia, B. P. (2001). Evaluation of the psychometric properties of two forgiveness scales. *Current Psychology, 20*, 260–277.

Salsman, J., Brown, T., Brechting, E., & Carlson, C. (2005). The link between religion and spirituality and psychological adjustment: the mediating role of optimism and social support. *Personality and Social Psychology Bulletin, 31*, 522–535.

Saroglou, V. (2002). Religion and the five factors of personality: A meta-analytic review. *Personality and Individual Differences, 32*, 15–25.

Saroglou, V., Delpierre, V., & Dernelle, R. (2004). Values and religiosity: A meta-analysis of studies using Schwartz's model. *Personality and Individual Differences, 37*, 721–734.

Saroglou, V., & Muñoz-García, A. (2008). Individual differences in religion and spirituality: An issue of personality traits and/or values. *Journal for the Scientific Study of Religion, 47*, 83–101.

Saroglou, V., Pichon, I., Trompette, L., Verschueren, M., & Dernelle, R. (2005). Prosocial behavior and religion: New evidence based on projective measures and peer ratings. *Journal for the Scientific Study of Religion, 44*, 323–348.

Scheier, M. F., Weintraub, J. K., & Carver, C. S. (1986). Coping with stress: Divergent strategies of optimists and pessimists. *Journal of Personality and Social Psychology, 51*, 1257–1264.

Schwartz, C., Meisenhelder, J., Ma, Y., & Reed, G. (2003). Altruistic social interest behaviors are associated with better mental health. *Psychosomatic Medicine, 65*(5), 778–785.
Schwartz, S. H. (2005). Basic human values: Their content and structure across countries. In A. Tamayo & J. B. Porto (Eds.), *Values and behavior in organizations* (pp. 21–55). Petrópolis, Brazil: Vozes.
Seligman, M. E. P. (1991). *Learned optimism*. New York, NY: Knopf.
Snyder, C., & Lopez, S. (Eds.). (2002). *Handbook of positive psychology*. New York, NY: Oxford University Press.
Snyder, C. R., Rand, K. L., & Sigmon, D. R. (2002). Hope theory: A member of the positive psychology family. In C. R. Snyder & S. J. Lopez (Eds.), *Handbook of positive psychology* (pp. 257–267). New York, NY: Oxford University Press.
Taylor, A., & MacDonald, D. (1999). Religion and the five factor model of personality: An exploratory investigation using a Canadian university sample. *Personality and Individual Differences, 27*, 1243-1259.
Wink, P., & Dillon, M. (2007). Do generative adolescents become healthy older adults? In S. Post (Ed.), *Altruism and health: Perspectives from empirical research* (pp. 43–54). New York, NY: Oxford University Press.
Wink, P., Dillon, M., & Fay, K. (2005). Spiritual seeking, narcissism, and psychotherapy: How are they related? *Journal for the Scientific Study of Religion, 44*, 143–158.
Worthington, E. L., Jr. (1988). Understanding the values of religious clients: A model and its application to counseling. *Journal of Counseling Psychology, 35*, 166–174.
Worthington, E. L., Jr., Witvliet, C. V. O., Pietrini, P., & Miller, A. J. (2007). Forgiveness and health. *Journal of Behavioral Medicine, 30*, 291–302.
Zinnbauer, B., Pargament, K., Cole, B., Rye, M., Butter, E., Belavich, T., et al. (1997). Religion and spirituality: Unfuzzying the fuzzy. *Journal for the Scientific Study of Religion, 36*, 549–564.

# 6

# *Client God Images*

## Theory, Research, and Clinical Practice

GLENDON L. MORIARTY AND EDWARD B. DAVIS

Most mainstream psychotherapy centers on issues of relationship and attachment (Badenoch, 2008; Slade, 2008). When it comes to working with religious and spiritual clients, such a focus often includes an emphasis on the client's ongoing personal, interactive relationship with one or more divine attachment figures, such as God, Allah, Jesus, Buddha, and Krishna (Davis, 2010; Granqvist & Kirkpatrick, 2008). This chapter helps inform psychotherapy with religious and spiritual clients who report having this type of relationship. More specifically, the chapter concentrates on understanding, assessing, and treating client *God images*.

To begin, we will expound on what God images are, partly by contrasting them with the related construct of *God concepts*. Next, we will highlight the religious and spiritual bases for God images, from an ecumenical perspective. We will provide an overview of empirical work on God images, concentrating on studies that are particularly relevant to psychotherapy with religious and spiritual clients. Subsequently, we will explore the clinical implications of the research we have reviewed, followed by a discussion of various ways to clinically assess and treat God images. Last, we will share a case study that illustrates this process of assessing and treating client God images.

Before we begin, we would like to briefly address the issue of language. In this chapter, we often use the term *God* to generically refer to divine attachment figures. We certainly acknowledge that other divine attachment figures exist and serve similar psychological functions (cf. Davis, 2010; Granqvist & Kirkpatrick, 2008). We have decided to use this term merely for convenience's sake, feeling that much of the research and recommendations we discuss in this chapter are equally applicable to clinical work with clients who espouse a relationship with a divine attachment figure besides or in addition to God.

## GOD IMAGES DEFINED AND CONTRASTED WITH GOD CONCEPTS

*God images* are the mental representations that underlie individuals' personal, emotional, embodied experiences in relationship with God or another divine attachment figure. They are internal working models of God and the self as experienced in relationship with God. These relational schemas underlie a person's actual experiences in that relationship. Simply put, God images are a person's heart knowledge of God (Gibson, 2006). As Hall (2004) theorized, God images are primarily composed of *implicit relational knowledge* (i.e., gut-level procedural knowledge of how to perceive and be in relationship with a general or specific relational partner; Lyons-Ruth et al., 1998; cf. Noffke & Hall, 2007). These images guide and integrate how a person experiences God at an emotional, physiological, largely nonverbal, and usually implicit level (i.e., outside of conscious awareness; Davis, 2010; cf. Fogel, 2009; Noffke & Hall, 2007).

As Gibson (2007) noted, individuals tend to have multiple God images, and some images are utilized more frequently than others. Christian author J. B. Phillips (1952) described several potential God images, including God as Resident Policeman, Parental Hangover, Grand Old Man, Heavenly Bosom, or Managing Director. It is notable that one or more God image can become activated at a given time, reflecting the operation of what has been called a "working God schema" (Gibson, 2007, p. 232). Which God images are active at a certain time will shift dynamically, based on the presence of certain learned internal cues (e.g., active moods, schemas, needs, and goals) and external cues (e.g., features of the immediate spiritual environment, such as the people who are present; Davis, 2010; cf. Mischel & Shoda, 2008).

In explaining God images, it is helpful to contrast them with a related construct—God concepts. God concepts are abstract, conceptual, doctrinal understandings of God or another divine attachment figure. They are theological beliefs about God's traits; about how God relates with, thinks about, and feels toward humans (including the self); and about how humans (including the self) should relate with, think about, and feel toward God. These schemas underlie a person's factual knowledge about God (Davis, 2010). Simply put, God concepts are a person's head knowledge of God (Gibson, 2006).

## AN ECUMENICAL RELIGIOUS AND SPIRITUAL PERSPECTIVE ON GOD IMAGES

Scholarship on God images has its historical roots in the broad Christian faith tradition, from which most God-image theory, research, and instrumentation have emanated (e.g., Benson & Spilka, 1973; Rizzuto, 1979). The lack of empirical emphasis on other traditions is lamentable but understandable, particularly considering that a relational view of the divine is perhaps most amenable to Christian theology, when compared with the theologies of the world's other major religions.

This point is underscored by the findings of the Pew Research Center's (2008) recent *U.S. Religious Landscape Survey*. Using a nationally representative sample, the Pew Research Center found that 92% of adult Americans believe in "the existence of God or a universal spirit" (Pew Research Center, 2008, p. 5), with 60% of adult Americans believing in a *personal* God (the belief that "God is a person with whom people can have a relationship" [Pew Research Center, 2008, p. 5]) and 25% believing in an *impersonal* God (the belief that "God is an impersonal force" [Pew Research Center, 2008, p. 5]). According to the Pew Research Center's data, the religious and spiritual traditions whose adult American followers are most apt to believe in a personal God are Mormon (91% of Mormons reported having this view of God), Jehovah's Witness (82%), evangelical Protestant Christian (79%), historically black churches (71%), mainline Christian churches (62%), and Catholic Christian churches (60%). Each of these traditions emanates from the wider Christian tradition.

Conversely, the traditions whose adult American followers are most prone to believe that God is an impersonal force are Hindu (53% of Hindus reported having this view of God), Jewish (50%), and Buddhist (45%). Adult American members of these three traditions are approximately twice as likely to view God as an impersonal force (31%, 25%, and 20%, respectively) as they are to view God as a personal God. In comparison, adult Muslim Americans are roughly just as likely to believe that God is an impersonal force (42%) as they are to believe that God is a personal God (41%; Pew Research Center, 2008, p. 5).

Not only do a large portion of adult Americans believe in a personal God, but also a sizeable majority view *relationship with God* as central to what it means to be religious or spiritual. For instance, in a 1989 U.S. Gallup poll, a nationally representative sample of adult Americans were asked, "Which of the following four statements comes closest to your own view of 'faith': a set of beliefs, membership in a church or synagogue, finding meaning in life, or a relationship with God?" (Gallup & Jones, 1989, as cited in Granqvist & Kirkpatrick, 2008, p. 907). Fifty-one percent of respondents chose *relationship with God*. In contrast, 19% chose *a set of beliefs*; 4%, *membership in a church or synagogue*; and 20%, *finding meaning in life* (Gallup & Jones, 1989).

## EMPIRICAL RESEARCH

Empirical research on God images began in the 1950s and since that time, researchers have investigated many aspects of God-image development, dynamics, and change. In this section, we summarize major findings from these domains. See Davis (2010), Kirkpatrick (2005), and Moriarty and Hoffman (2007) for more comprehensive reviews.

## GOD-IMAGE DEVELOPMENT AND DYNAMICS

The vast majority of scholarship on God-image development and dynamics has emanated from the psychodynamic tradition. In particular, it has emanated from classical psychoanalytic theory (Freud, 1913/1950, 1930/1962), object relations theory (Rizzuto, 1979), and attachment theory (Davis, 2010; Granqvist & Kirkpatrick, 2008; Kirkpatrick, 2005; Noffke & Hall, 2007).

### Classical Psychoanalytic Theory

According to classical psychoanalytic theory, God images develop early in life, from "a recapitulation of the patriarchal, Oedipal father of guilt and authority" (Jones, 2007, p. 37). On the basis of his case studies of clients and historical figures, Freud (1913/1950, 1930/1962) argued that during the Oedipal–Electra period, children's ambivalent feelings of guilt and longing toward their father become displaced onto their God images. God becomes an "exalted father" figure (Freud, 1913/1950, p. 244), an object with whom the child longs to relate but whose exacting demands for moral obedience engender fear and guilt. Thus, in Freud's estimation, religion becomes an obsessional or compulsive neurosis (Freud, 1913/1950) emerging from and fueled by the superego (Davis, 2010; cf. Jones, 2007).

Early quantitative research on God images sought to determine whether adults' images of God are more similar to either their father images (as Freud, 1913/1950, had suggested) or their mother images. The findings from these early studies were decidedly mixed (see Davis, 2010, for a review). More recently, studies have shown that God images are best conceptualized as a composite of maternal and paternal images (Birky & Ball, 1988; Dickie et al., 1997), bringing Granqvist and Kirkpatrick (2008) to the conclusion that "God is neither an exalted father figure nor an exalted mother figure, but rather an exalted attachment figure" (p. 908).

### Object Relations Theory

According to object relations theory (Fairbairn, 1952; Greenberg & Mitchell, 1983), one of the primary mechanisms by which God-image development occurs is the process of *internalization* (Davis, 2010; Moriarty, 2006), which Moriarty (2007) has described as "the gradual process by which people learn to treat themselves as others treat them" (p. 89). To illustrate, if children repeatedly experience their early caregivers as critical, then object relations theory predicts that they will internalize the parents' criticalness—that is, they will imbue images of others, the self, and eventually God with characteristic criticalness toward the self (Davis, 2010; cf. Mikulincer & Shaver, 2004).

Psychoanalyst Ana-Maria Rizzuto (1979) has studied this process of internalization. In her seminal work *The Birth of the Living God*, Rizzuto presented case-study findings of 20 psychiatric inpatients. Many of Rizzuto's research-based conclusions were either extensions or revisions of theoretical insights that Freud (1913/1950, 1930/1962), Erikson (1959), Fairbairn (1952), and Winnicott (1951/1975, 1971) had previously proposed. On the basis of her case material, Rizzuto argued that God images are formed during the first years of life, through (a) the establishment of a basic sense of trust or mistrust (Erikson, 1959); (b) the internalization of various other-representations and self-representations, based on how the infant and toddler was treated by early caregivers (Fairbairn, 1952); and (c) the development of a relationship with a "living" (Rizzuto, 1979, p. 41) God representation, through creative, symbolic interaction in the *transitional space* (Winnicott, 1951/1975, 1971) between the toddler's inner and outer world. Rizzuto thought that God images ideally help children (and later, adults) establish and maintain an internal sense of balance and calm (e.g., felt security). She also recognized that on the other end of the spectrum, God images can become a source of inner conflict and turmoil (Davis, 2010).

### Attachment Theory

In the past 20 years, attachment theory (Bowlby, 1969/1982, 1973, 1980) has become a popular framework for conceptualizing and studying God-image tendencies (Davis, 2010; Granqvist & Kirkpatrick, 2008; Kirkpatrick, 2005; Noffke & Hall, 2007). According to attachment theory, *internal working models* (Bowlby, 1973) are the mental representations that underlie people's feelings, thoughts, behaviors, sensations, and motivations in any type of relationship, including relationships with divine attachment figures. Internal working models include two components—one referring to the other and one referring to the self (Bowlby, 1973). As Collins, Guichard, Ford, and Feeney (2004) have explained: "The former characterizes whether the [attachment figure] will be available, sensitive, and responsive when needed, and the latter characterizes the self as either worthy or unworthy of love and care" (p. 198). Stated differently, internal working models are a type of mental "software" that people employ to figure out and predict how others will respond to them. These expectations are initially learned through early relationships with primary caregivers, but they remain open to revision across the life course, through subsequent experiences in attachment relationships (Badenoch, 2008; Davis, 2010).

In attempts to explain God-image development and dynamics, four attachment-based hypotheses have emerged: (1) the *internal-working-model correspondence hypothesis* (Kirkpatrick, 1992; Kirkpatrick & Shaver, 1992), (2) the *emotional compensation hypothesis* (Kirkpatrick, 1992; Kirkpatrick & Shaver, 1990), (3) the *socialized correspondence hypothesis* (Granqvist, 1998, 2002; Granqvist & Hagekull, 1999), and (4) the *implicit-relational knowledge correspondence hypothesis* (Hall, 2004; Hall, Fujikawa, Halcrow, Hill, & Delaney, 2009). The internal-working-model correspondence hypothesis (Kirkpatrick, 1992;

Kirkpatrick & Shaver, 1992) posits that the attachment tendencies people develop and exhibit in human attachment relationships come to correspond to the attachment tendencies they develop and exhibit in emotional relationship with God. The emotional compensation hypothesis (Kirkpatrick, 1992; Kirkpatrick & Shaver, 1990) suggests that an insecure attachment history with caregivers leads to the development of an insecure global attachment style with humans (undergirded by negative, global internal working models of self or others) and a subsequent compensatory emotional relationship with God. The socialized correspondence hypothesis (Granqvist, 1998, 2002; Granqvist & Hagekull, 1999) argues that extensive experience with religious or spiritual caregivers who are emotionally available and responsive leads to the development of a secure global attachment style with humans (undergirded by positive, global internal working models of self and others) and a subsequent adaptive emotional relationship with God (undergirded by positive, relationship-specific internal working models of God and self-in-relationship-with-God).

Research on these first three hypotheses has revealed somewhat inconsistent findings, given that all three hypotheses have received substantial research support (see Davis, 2010; Granqvist & Kirkpatrick, 2008; Kirkpatrick, 2005; and Noffke & Hall, 2007, for reviews), and no one of them has accumulated relatively more support than the others (Davis, 2010). Recently Hall and his colleagues (Hall, 2004; Hall et al., 2009) sought to reconcile these discrepant findings via their implicit-relational-knowledge correspondence hypothesis. They suggested that God-image development chiefly occurs as individuals develop implicit relational knowledge (cf. Lyons-Ruth et al., 1998) via their experiences in human relationships (cf. Badenoch, 2008) and then develop corresponding implicit relational knowledge in their relationship with God. According to this hypothesis, implicit relational knowledge is reflected in people's implicit religious and spiritual functioning (i.e., their felt religious and spiritual experience at a relational, motivational, emotional, and physiological level; cf. Badenoch, 2008; Fogel, 2009). In contrast, it is not necessarily reflected in people's explicit religious or spiritual functioning (i.e., the elements of their religion and spirituality that do not directly tap into implicit relational knowledge, such as religious or spiritual commitment or church attendance; Davis, 2010).

Preliminary research supports the implicit-relational-knowledge correspondence hypothesis (Davis, 2010; Hall et al., 2009). Importantly, Hall et al. (2009) have argued that many of the research findings that are commonly used to support the emotional compensation model (e.g., instances of insecurely attached individuals reporting sudden religious conversion or increased religiousness following an interpersonal crisis; see Granqvist & Kirkpatrick, 2008) actually support the implicit-relational-knowledge correspondence model, because such phenomena reflect the operation of characteristic affect-regulation strategies that are associated with high-attachment avoidance or anxiety (see Davis, 2010, for a review).

In the study of God-image dynamics, one major replicated finding is that how people view themselves is significantly related to how they view God (Benson & Spilka, 1973; Buri & Mueller, 1993). In other words, levels of global self-esteem are positively related to adaptive God images (e.g., images of God as loving, nurturing, caring, or forgiving) and negatively related to maladaptive God images (e.g., images of God as rejecting, controlling, punishing, or distant). Evidence indicates that adult God-image dynamics are more explainable in terms of self-referencing effects (how a person feels toward himself or herself; Gibson, 2006; Yarborough, Gibson, & Moriarty, 2009) as opposed to parent-referencing effects (how a person feels toward his or her parents), whereas the opposite is true in the case of child God-image dynamics (Buri & Mueller, 1993; Dickie et al., 1997), presumably reflecting the process of internalization.

Ample research has shown that adults' current level of object relations maturity is positively related to the adaptiveness of their God images (Brokaw & Edwards, 1994; Tisdale et al., 1997). Research also has shown that persons with impaired object-relations functioning tend to have maladaptive God images and tend to experience elevated rates of depressive symptoms (Brokaw & Edwards, 1994; Tisdale et al., 1997; Yarborough et al., 2009; cf. Davis, 2010).

## GOD-IMAGE CHANGE THROUGH PSYCHOTHERAPY

Unfortunately, to date, there is only limited research on facilitating God-image change through psychotherapy participation. Three notable exceptions are Tisdale et al. (1997); Thomas, Moriarty, Davis, and Anderson (2011); and Cheston, Piedmont, Eanes, and Lavin (2003). First, in Tisdale et al.'s (1997) seminal study, psychiatric inpatients participated in religiously based, object-relations-oriented psychotherapy (individual and group formats) and completed assessments of object-relations functioning, religious and spiritual functioning, self-concept characteristics, and God-image characteristics. Assessments were completed at admission, discharge, and 6 and 12 months after discharge. Psychotherapy participants tended to experience significant adaptive shifts in their God images; that is, on average, they grew to experience God emotionally as more loving, close, present, and accepting. Furthermore, these adaptive God-image shifts were maintained over the course of the year following discharge. It is notable that psychotherapy participants also tended to experience adaptive shifts in their self-images (i.e., they felt more positively toward themselves), and these changes were maintained over the 12-month follow-up period as well.

More recently, Thomas et al. (2011) examined the impact of religiously based, outpatient group-psychotherapy on God images, for Christians reporting a clinically significant disparity between their cognitive understanding of God and their emotional experience of God. Thomas et al.'s community sample ($n$ = 26) completed an 8-week manualized curriculum that included mainly psychoeducational and cognitive-behavioral interventions, although it also included allegorical-bibliotherapy and art-and-music interventions. Group participants reported experiencing adaptive God-image shifts, when their pre- and posttest scores were compared. On average, they tended to experience God emotionally as *more* intimate, accepting, and supportive and as *less* distant, disapproving, and harsh, compared with how they experienced God before group participation. They also reported experiencing significantly less attachment anxiety with God and attachment avoidance with God, as measured by the Attachment to God Inventory (Beck & McDonald, 2004). Overall, participants indicated that the two interventions that were most effective in promoting God-image change were allegorical-bibliotherapy (*The Chronicles of Narnia*, Lewis, 1950–1956/2001) and cognitive-restructuring interventions. Of note, Thomas et al. had no control group, but their results were consistent with Tisdale et al.'s (1997) findings, suggesting that psychotherapy participation was the factor that chiefly explained participants' adaptive God-image change.

In a related study, Cheston et al. (2003) demonstrated the potential for adaptive God-image change via participation in general, outpatient individual-psychotherapy (that is, psychotherapy that was not necessarily religiously based). Compared with a control group, psychotherapy participants tended to experience positive shifts in their God images. Here, self- and clinician ratings indicated that, following treatment, psychotherapy participants grew to experience God emotionally as *higher* in trait agreeableness and as *lower* in trait neuroticism, compared with pretreatment ratings. This effect, however, was moderated by the degree of adaptive emotional growth that participants evidenced, as per clinician rating. Stated differently, psychotherapy participants who demonstrated high emotional change tended to experience God as "more emotionally stable, less assertive, and more compassionate and loving" (Cheston et al., 2003, p. 103) post psychotherapy, whereas participants who demonstrated low emotional change did not. Importantly, Cheston et al.'s study suggests the possibility that the common factors of psychotherapy (e.g., empathy and positive regard) may facilitate God-image change indirectly, via other forms of emotional change, such as improvements in self-image and adaptive shifts in implicit relational knowledge (Davis, 2010; cf. Mikulincer & Shaver, 2004; Norcross, 2002).

## CLINICAL IMPLICATIONS

Several clinical implications emerge from this research on God-image development, dynamics, and change. Before proceeding, however, we provide a rationale for clinically addressing God images in the first place. The main rationale is that religion and spirituality are important to the vast majority of Americans (Pew Research Center, 2008), and for many religious or spiritual persons, *relationship with God* is central to their faith (Gallup & Jones, 1989). Furthermore, for religious or spiritual clients, God-image difficulties often contribute to the development and maintenance of their presenting concerns. In fact, in Allmond's (2010) survey study of Christian psychologists ($n$ = 29), pastoral counselors ($n$ = 40), and spiritual directors ($n$ = 42), the combined sample of participants ($N$ = 111) indicated that, on average, 50% of their clients present for psychotherapy with God-image-related difficulties. Moreover, on average, Allmond's respondents affirmed that God-image assessment is an important part of the overall client assessment process.

Yet one more reason to address client God images is that the experience of a mental disorder can cause *clinically significant religious impairment*—that is, "a reduced ability to perform religious activities, achieve religious goals, or to experience religious states, due to a psychological disorder" (Hathaway, 2003, p. 114). In such cases, it often becomes necessary to address God-image difficulties, even as one would address occupational or social difficulties if those domains were functionally impaired by the client's experience of psychopathology.

Given this rationale for addressing God-image difficulties, a synthesis of the aforementioned research suggests that the psychotherapeutic treatment of God images should center on facilitating adaptive changes in clients' internal working models of self and of self-in-relationship-with-attachment-figures (human and divine; Davis, 2010). Consistent with the implicit-relational-knowledge correspondence hypothesis (Hall, 2004; Hall et al., 2009) and with various empirical findings (e.g., Cheston et al., 2003; Davis, 2010; Hall et al., 2009), it is possible that any substantive adaptive shifts in implicit relational knowledge will lead to corresponding adaptive shifts in client God images. Stated differently, to promote adaptive God-image change, clinicians should strategically facilitate security-enhancing relational experiences (Badenoch, 2008; Davis, 2010; Mikulincer & Shaver, 2004). Such a strategy would place the client–psychotherapist relationship at the crux of God-image change (cf. Norcross, 2002), at least when it comes to the individual-psychotherapy treatment of client God images. With respect to group-psychotherapy treatment, the relationships among group members likely would prove to be a vital change mechanism. Clinicians who are working to facilitate security-enhancing relational experiences via individual psychotherapy may find *Psychotherapy Relationships That Work* (Norcross, 2002) and *Being a Brain-Wise Therapist* (Badenoch, 2008) especially helpful.

Another implication of this research on God-image change is that it may not matter which psychotherapeutic format or approach is used to treat clients who have God-image difficulties. In other words, preliminary research evidence suggests that different formats (e.g., individual psychotherapy, bibliotherapy, and group psychotherapy) are each effective in facilitating adaptive God-image change (Cheston et al., 2003; Thomas et al., 2009; Tisdale et al., 1997). Furthermore, treatments that are based on different theoretical approaches (e.g., cognitive-behavioral, psychodynamic, or interpersonal) are likely equally effective as well (see Moriarty & Hoffman, 2007). Thus, it seems reasonable to conclude that the best way to treat client God images is to select the psychotherapeutic formats and approaches that are most likely to facilitate change for a given client, based on a variety of client variables (e.g., presenting concerns, functional impairment, client characteristics, and preferences; Norcross, 2002). Toward this end, Systematic Treatment Selection (InnerLife) is an excellent framework for guiding the treatment-relevant decision-making process (Harwood, Beutler, Williams, & Stegman, 2011; see http://www.innerlife.com).

## CLINICAL ASSESSMENTS

Generally speaking, in-depth religious or spiritual assessment is recommended in four clinical situations: (1) when religion or spirituality is clinically relevant to the client's presenting concerns and treatment goals (Richards & Bergin, 2005), (2) when religion or spirituality is one of the primary informers of the client's worldview (Shafranske, 2005), (3) when religion or spirituality is likely to either facilitate or hinder psychotherapeutic progress (Shafranske, 2005), and (4) when religion or spirituality is significantly impaired by the client's presenting concerns (Hathaway, 2003; cf. Richards & Bergin, 2005). Given that so many adult Americans view *relationship with God* as central to religious and spiritual functioning (Gallup & Jones, 1989; Granqvist & Kirkpatrick, 2008), clinicians conducting an in-depth religious or spiritual assessment should also assess (a) whether the client actually has a relationship with a divine attachment figure, and (b) if so, whether this relationship warrants clinical attention.

To assess the former, it may prove helpful to use Bowlby's (1969/1982) and Ainsworth's (1985) criteria for differentiating an attachment relationship from any other relationship. Bowlby and Ainsworth originally offered these criteria to help determine the presence of an infant–caregiver attachment relationship, but Granqvist and Kirkpatrick (2008) adapted the criteria to guide the detection of an attachment relationship with a divine attachment figure. Here, we summarize these latter criteria:

- The client regularly seeks and maintains felt proximity to the divine attachment figure, through proximity-seeking attachment behaviors such as prayer or worship.
- The divine attachment figure acts as a haven of safety when the client (a) experiences a frightening or alarming event; (b) suffers from injury, illness, or fatigue; or (c) feels separation from, the threat of separation from, or the loss of the divine attachment figure.
- The divine attachment figure acts as a source of felt security, a secure base from which the client can explore his or her interpersonal and religious or spiritual environments.

- Whenever the client feels separation from or the threat of separation from the divine attachment figure, he or she experiences anxiety, and whenever the client feels the loss of the divine attachment figure (e.g., a dark night of the soul; St. John of the Cross, 2008), he or she experiences grief.
- The client perceives the divine attachment figure as both stronger and wiser than himself or herself.

If all these criteria are met, then the client has an attachment relationship with the divine attachment figure, and thus in-depth religious or spiritual assessment should include some degree of God-image assessment.

God-image assessment is a multistep process that is used to identify and conceptualize a person's God images. It can be completed using a variety of tools, chiefly including (a) clinical-interview questions; (b) projective assessments; and (c) self-report, survey-based measures. Each set of tools has particular advantages and drawbacks, and therefore including each type of assessment is recommended, if it is feasible to do so (Brokaw & Edwards, 1994; Gibson, 2007). The follow sections outline these three tools, discuss their respective strengths and weaknesses, and provide examples of how psychotherapists can use them to assess client God images.

### Clinical-Interview Questions

Relevant information about client God images can be gleaned from the general clinical interview and from a follow-up, God-image-focused clinical interview. In the former interview, relationships with caregivers and significant others are most important to consider. For example, as clients share details about their life, psychotherapists can form tentative hypotheses about how clients' past relationships have influenced their God-image development and continue to influence their God-image dynamics through internalized forces (Badenoch, 2008; Davis, 2010).

Once a general clinical interview has been completed, psychotherapists can transition to a more God-image-focused interview. Various lists of clinical-interview questions are available for use (e.g., O'Grady & Richards, 2007; Pargament, 2007; Rizzuto, 1979), and recently Granqvist and Main (2003) have created an Attachment to God Interview, modeled after the popular Adult Attachment Interview (George, Kaplan, & Main, 1996). These clinical-interview tools all are helpful because they allow clients to describe their relationship with God in their own words. They share, however, the drawback of being time-consuming (Gibson, 2007).

### Projective Assessments

Projective assessment tools also are useful for assessing client God images, particularly given that God images appear largely right-brain-mediated (Davis,

2010) and projective assessments are especially helpful for assessing right-brain-mediated mental contents and dynamics. For example, clients can be asked to interpret pictorial representations of God (e.g., Bassett et al., 1990) or to fill out a projective sentence-stem completion test (e.g., the God Image Sentence Blank; Moriarty, 2006). For a theistic population, another particularly helpful projective tool is the Draw-a-God exercise (Moriarty, 2006). This instrument requires only a pencil and three pieces of paper. To administer it, use the following steps:

1. Give the client the first piece of paper and instruct him or her: "Please draw a picture of you and God." Once this first drawing is completed, move on to Step 2.
2. Give the client the second piece of paper and instruct him or her: "On this piece of paper, draw a picture of how you *feel* that you and God look when you do something wrong. Draw what you *feel*, not what you *think*."
3. When the client is done with the second drawing, ask him or her: (a) "How do you feel?" (b) "How does God feel?" (c) "How close or distant do you feel from God, on a scale of 1 to 10, with 1 being *very close* and 10 being *very distant*?" and (d) "If you feel distant from God, what usually happens or has to happen for you to feel close to God again?"
4. After you have processed the second picture with the client, present the third piece of paper and instruct him or her: "Draw a picture of how you *would like to feel* you and God look when you do something wrong. Again, draw how you would honestly *like to feel*, not necessarily how you think you *should* feel." Then process this drawing.

This projective exercise is helpful in that it allows clients and their psychotherapists to identify contrasts between clients' God concepts and God images. The first drawing typically displays scenes reflecting love, kindness, wisdom, or compassion, whereas the second drawing commonly depicts scenes reflecting abandonment, distance, anger, or withdrawal. The second drawing provides an entryway into exploring how caregivers have influenced the client's God images, particularly via internalized disciplinary mechanisms. The third drawing provides an opportunity for clients to begin to emotionally imagine God images that are healthier and more reflective of their faith tradition's orthodox beliefs about the divine attachment figure.

A major advantage of projective God-image assessments is that they are able to tap into implicit (e.g., nonconscious, nonlinear, largely right-brain-mediated) mental contents and dynamics, including implicit relational knowledge and salient intrapsychic drives. As such, another advantage of these tools is their rich grounding in decades of psychodynamically informed theory and research (Gibson, 2007). Moreover, in being able to assess implicit mental contents and dynamics, projective assessments are perhaps more likely to validly assess God images than are techniques that tend to assess explicit (e.g., conscious, linear, largely left-brain-mediated) mental content and dynamics, such as self-report questionnaires. The primary disadvantage of projective God-image assessments is that they require subjective interpretation, because their interpretation is not standardized. Therefore, they are able to provide only data that are tentatively interpretable at best (Richards & Bergin, 2005).

### Self-Report, Survey-Based Measures

Among clinicians, perhaps the most popular way to assess client God images is via quantitative assessment, particularly the use of self-report, survey-based measures. Several measures are available, including the Attachment to God Inventory (Beck & McDonald, 2004), Attachment to God Scale (Kirkpatrick & Shaver, 1992), Adjective Ratings of God Scale (Gorsuch, 1968), God Adjective Checklist (Gough & Heilbrum, 1983), Loving and Controlling God Scales (Benson & Spilka, 1973; see Francis, Robbins, & Gibson, 2006, for an updated version), and God Image Inventory (Lawrence, 1991; see Hill and Hood, 1999, for reprinted copies of many of these measures).

In clinical practice, survey-based measures of God images, God concepts, and related constructs are advantageous for several reasons. First of all, they are typically quick and easy to administer, score, and interpret. Second, they often have a literature base from which to derive clinically useful hypotheses, to assist case formulation and treatment planning. Third, they usually are obtained free of cost. Indeed, survey-based research has led to great advances of understanding in the psychology of religion and spirituality field and in clinical practice (Hill, 2005). As Gibson (2007) and others (e.g., Hill, 2005; Hill & Pargament, 2003) have noted, however, survey-based measures have several serious drawbacks that deserve mention.

As it relates to the assessment of God images, survey-based measures may tend only to assess God concepts (i.e., head knowledge of God), even if they explicitly purport to assess God images. In other words, survey-based measures might commonly fail to assess heart knowledge of God, thereby becoming invalid measures of actual God images (Gibson, 2007). Furthermore, survey-based measures usually have little explanatory power for clarifying the underlying cognitive, affective, and motivational mechanisms that are involved in a client's salient God-image and God-concept psychodynamics. In addition, the existing psychometric data on self-report, survey-based God-image assessments typically are based on research with college students or "normal" community members; thus, virtually no published psychometric data are available on how reliable and valid survey-based God-image assessments are with clinical populations.

Despite these limitations, psychotherapists can continue to use self-report God-image assessments in several ways. For instance, Gibson (2007) has suggested (a) manipulating the schemas that are active when the measure is administered, (b) focusing on measuring relationship variables and not doctrinal beliefs, and (c) incorporating adjunctive qualitative measures as well. Moreover, Zahl and Gibson (2009) have recommended that clinicians adapt instruments in ways that help respondents discriminate between their head knowledge and their heart knowledge. Using two large independent samples of university students, Zahl and Gibson have found research evidence that supports the validity and utility of this recommendation. In particular, their data support the use of adapted adjective checklists (e.g., Gorsuch, 1968; Gough & Heilbrum, 1983) whereby each adjective is presented separately, and respondents are asked to rate the adjective in terms of (a) "What is theologically true about God?" (to assess God concepts) and (b) "My personal experience of what God is like" (to assess God images). As of yet, only minimal research supports this assessment strategy with clinical populations (e.g., Yarborough et al., 2009); however, to date, Zahl and Gibson's data offer the best available research evidence for informing the quantitative assessment of client God images.

## CLINICAL STRATEGIES

A limited but growing body of theory and research suggests that God images can be directly and indirectly changed through psychotherapy participation. Psychotherapists can use a variety of approaches to facilitate adaptive God-image change (see Moriarty & Hoffman, 2007, for a review). Rather than cover each of the existing approaches, we instead will recommend that psychotherapists adopt a *psychotherapy–integrationist approach* (Norcross & Goldfried, 2005) to treating client God images.

Psychotherapy integration itself can take on one of four forms: (1) a *common factors* approach, (2) a *theoretical integrationist* approach, (3) a *technical eclectic* approach, or (4) an *assimilative integrationist* approach. The common factors approach emphasizes the psychotherapeutic factors (e.g., client–psychotherapist alliance, empathy, and positive regard) that are shared across orientations and that reliably result in clients making treatment progress. The theoretical integrationist approach takes two or more theoretical frameworks and integrates their theoretical conceptualizations and psychotherapeutic techniques to maximally understand and strategically treat the client. The technical eclectic approach treats the client's presenting concerns using whichever empirically supported techniques exist for treating those concerns, regardless of the theoretical framework from which those techniques hail. Last, the assimilative integrationist approach grounds case formulation and treatment in one particular theoretical framework, while selectively incorporating views and techniques from other frameworks (Norcross & Goldfried, 2005).

The psychotherapy-integrationist treatment of God-image difficulties likewise can follow these four lines. For instance, from a common factors perspective, with enough empirical evidence, researchers may be able to identify the common factors that most effectively facilitate adaptive God-image change. From a theoretical integrationist perspective, clinicians may find substantial benefit from approaching the case formulation and treatment of client God images from different theoretical approaches (e.g., how a client's automatic thoughts and internal working models interact to fuel problematic God-image dynamics). From a technical eclectic perspective, researchers may find empirical support that long-term dynamic-interpersonal approaches are most effective in treating complex or chronic God-image difficulties, whereas short-term cognitive-behavioral approaches are most effective in treating less complex or chronic God-image concerns. From an assimilative-integrationist perspective, clinicians working with a client who is struggling to find freedom in his or her relationship with God may find it helpful to ground psychotherapy in an existential-integrative framework, while selectively incorporating narrative-experiential techniques.

Toward the end of promoting the psychotherapy-integrationist treatment of God images, we will cover the three approaches that appear most promising for treating client God images: dynamic-interpersonal, cognitive-behavioral, and narrative-experiential. To date, dynamic-interpersonal and cognitive-behavioral approaches have received the most attention in the God-image literature (Moriarty & Hoffman, 2007); thus, we will cover them in more detail. Recent scholarship (Davis & Badenoch, 2010; Hall, 2007), however, calls for the use of narrative-experiential approaches, so this approach will be reviewed briefly as well.

### Dynamic-Interpersonal Approaches

This cursory review of psychodynamic and interpersonal schools of thought does not highlight the differences between these approaches but rather underlines their major similarities. For example, psychodynamic and interpersonal psychotherapies share a number of common assumptions (Greenberg & Mitchell, 1983), including the idea that problematic interpersonal patterns are learned in past relationships, maintained in present relationships, and enacted in and healed through the client–psychotherapist relationship (Moriarty, 2006; Strength, 1998). Another common thread between dynamic and interpersonal approaches is the idea that people crave consistency and thus tend to unconsciously recreate certain interpersonal problems, with different relationship partners and in different relational contexts. This need for maintaining consistency also affects clients' God-image functioning. Here again, the idea is that the same interpersonal problems that clients learn in the past are maintained in the present, both in the client–psychotherapist relationship and in clients' relationship with God (Moriarty, 2006; Strength, 1998).

Broadly speaking, psychodynamic and interpersonal approaches assert that God-image change occurs through the internalization process—the process whereby people gradually learn to treat themselves similarly to how attachment figures have treated them previously (Davis, 2010; Mikulincer & Shaver, 2004; Moriarty, 2006). Clients raised by harsh parents tend to treat themselves in a harsh manner and correspondingly experience God as harsh. Through the psychotherapy relationship, psychodynamic psychotherapy seeks to facilitate the same process of internalization that occurs in the caregiver–child relationship. The idea is that by having *corrective emotional experiences* (Alexander & French, 1946) in the client–psychotherapist relationship, clients will come to emotionally experience themselves, others, and God in more adaptive ways. More specifically, the aim is for clients to internalize the acceptance, empathy, and compassion that the psychotherapist displays toward them, so that they might begin to treat themselves with the same acceptance, empathy, and compassion. Ideally, these so-called *security-based self-representations* (Mikulincer & Shaver, 2004) become generalized to the client's God images and start to characterize how God is perceived and experienced at a relational, motivational, emotional, and physiological level (Davis, 2010).

In addition, the staple psychodynamic intervention of offering interpretations can be used to facilitate adaptive God-image change. For instance, Strength (1998) has suggested offering interpretations about the interrelationships among a client's past relationships, current relationships, relationship with God, and relationship with the psychotherapist. According to Strength, adaptive God-image change occurs by calling attention to these interrelationships and by providing strategic corrective emotional experiences via the client–psychotherapist relationship (Alexander & French, 1946). Here again, corrective emotional experiences in the client–psychotherapist relationship ideally become generalized to clients' relationship with God and to their relationships with other humans. Such corrective emotional experiences lead to adaptive shifts in implicit relational knowledge (Lyons-Ruth et al., 1998), whereby old, unhealthy relationship patterns are replaced by new, healthy relationship patterns (Davis, 2010).

### Cognitive-Behavioral Approaches

Cognitive-behavioral psychotherapies seek to change the way people think and behave, so that people can change the way they feel. In particular, these approaches tend to target the faulty beliefs (e.g., maladaptive schemas) from which God-image difficulties have developed and been maintained (Johnson, 2007). According to this frame, the resolution of God-image-related issues occurs by identifying and challenging maladaptive beliefs about God, oneself, and others.

When using a cognitive-behavioral approach, one challenge is to remain ever mindful of the central role of emotions in God-image change. Stated differently, while treating God-image concerns with cognitive-behavioral interventions, it is easy to focus solely on thoughts and behaviors, thereby fostering surface-level shifts in client God concepts instead of promoting deeper level changes in client

God images. Fortunately, cognitive-behavioral techniques can be used in ways that affirm and involve both cognition and emotion (cf. Cozolino, 2010), a possibility we seek to highlight in the following review.

*God Image Automatic Thought Record*

The first cognitive-behavioral intervention that we suggest using is the *God Image Automatic Thought Record* (GIATR; Moriarty, 2006; see Table 6.1). This intervention is designed to identify and change the automatic thoughts that underlie problematic emotional experiences of God (or of another divine attachment figure). To complete a GIATR, clients are instructed as follows:

1. Briefly describe an actual event that made you feel like God was probably having negative thoughts about you or negative feelings toward you.
2. List any negative feelings that you felt as a result (e.g., sadness, shame, abandonment, rejection, anxiety, fear, anger). Then rate the strength of each feeling, on a scale from 0 to 100, with 0 indicating *total absence of the emotion* and 100 indicating *overwhelming presence of the emotion.*
3. Now list any negative thoughts or feelings that you felt like God was probably having about you or toward you in that moment. Then rate the degree to which you believed God was thinking or feeling that way toward you at that time, on a scale from 0 to 100, with 0 indicating "I was *not at all confident* that God was thinking or feeling that way toward me" and 100 indicating "I was *100% confident* that God was thinking or feeling that way toward me."
4. Next, knowing what you know about the Real God (as described by your religious scriptures, teachings, or leaders), what do you think God was perhaps more realistically thinking and feeling toward you in that moment? Write out the more plausible Real God response. Then rate the degree to which you believe that the Real God response is probably how God *really* thought and felt toward you at that time, on a scale from 0 to 100, with 0 indicating "I am *not at all confident* that the Real God was thinking or feeling that way toward me" and 100 indicating "I am *100% confident* that the Real God was thinking or feeling that way toward me."
5. Now close your eyes and get a mental picture of the Real God—whatever God may look like to you, whether a person such as Papa from *The Shack*, the father in the Prodigal Son parable, or perhaps even a mythological figure such as Aslan from *The Chronicles of Narnia*. Look into the eyes of the Real God. Allow yourself to experience whatever emotions and bodily sensations arise as you gaze into each other's eyes. Then allow yourself to experience the Real God responding to you in the way you described. Let that response fully sink in—let it spread throughout

**Table 6.1** God Image Automatic Thought Record

| Situation | Feelings | Automatic Thought(s) | Real God Response | Outcome |
|---|---|---|---|---|
| Briefly describe an actual event that made you feel like God was probably having negative thoughts about you and/or negative feelings toward you. | Any negative feelings that you felt as a result—rate the strength of each feeling from 0 to 100. | Any negative thoughts and/or feelings you felt like God was probably having about you or toward you in that moment—rate the degree to which you believed God was thinking/feeling that way toward you at that time from 0 to 100. | Knowing what you know about the Real God, as described by your religious scriptures, teachings, or leaders, what do you think God was perhaps more realistically thinking and feeling toward you in that moment—rate the degree to which you believe that the Real God response is probably how God *really* thought and felt toward you at that time from 0 to 100. | Relist the negative emotions that you originally felt as a result of the situation—now rate the strength of each feeling, after imagining God thinking/feeling the Real God response, from 0 to 100. |

your mind, fill your heart, and soak into your body. Stay in this experience for a minute or two, and then slowly open your eyes.

6. Finally, relist the negative emotions that you initially felt, as a result of the original situation. Then rate the strength of each feeling, after imagining the Real God's thoughts or feelings toward you, on a scale from 0 to 100, with 0 indicating *total absence of the emotion* and 100 indicating *overwhelming presence of the emotion.*

The GIATR is a cognitive-behavioral tool that facilitates adaptive shifts in God images and self-images by helping clients learn more about the Real God and begin to intentionally interact more with that divine attachment figure, especially in the face of negative emotional experiences. The GIATR will help clients dispute their irrational God-image automatic thoughts, encouraging them to examine whether those thoughts are coming from the Real God or from a maladaptive God image. After clients complete the GIATR several times, they will start to see how negative emotions in their relationship with God are typically self-imposed, resulting from inaccurate (and ultimately unhealthy) God images. Experiencing the Real God over and over helps clients think about God and themselves in more healthy ways, thereby improving their feelings toward God and toward themselves. In this way, repetitive experiences of the Real God can promote changes in the dysfunctional automatic thoughts that previously impaired the client's emotional experience of God. After clients complete a GIATR on paper several times, they often start to complete GIATRs in their head. Ultimately, the goal is that they experience recurrent positive emotions (e.g., joy, interest, contentment, and love) in their relationship with God, thereby experiencing enhanced fulfillment, health, and resilience (Fredrickson & Cohn, 2008).

### *Imagery*

*Imagery* is another cognitive-behavioral intervention that can be used to foster God-image change (Moriarty, 2006; Propst, 1987). This tool is particularly powerful because it taps into both head and heart—the cognitive and the emotional. Another strength of imagery is that it is easily incorporated into the practice of the spiritual disciplines (Boyd, 2004). Some of the most common spiritually oriented imagery techniques involve meditating on scriptures or popular narratives from a person's faith tradition, a practice that is especially common in the Christian traditions (Propst, 1987). For instance, Christian clients often find Psalms 23 and 139 and parables such as the Prodigal Son to be quite meaningful (Johnson, 2007). Imagery assists the client in entering into the scripture or scene experientially, at an emotional and embodied level (cf. Fogel, 2009). To help clients prepare for this process, psychotherapists can instruct clients to get comfortable, close their eyes, and center their mind by taking several deep breaths and beginning to focus on the present moment (Badenoch, 2008).

Imagery is often most effective when it incorporates multiple senses and involves as many imaginational details as is possible. For example, clients can imagine what it is like to actually *be* the Prodigal Son (or daughter)—to see the father (God) running toward them, to feel his warm embrace, and to hear his compassionate and forgiving words. In so doing, theological beliefs (e.g., God is loving and forgiving) can begin to have more personal relevance and emotional import. Having clients visualize emotionally meaningful scenes thereby can facilitate the healing of maladaptive God images, helping them experience God's love and acceptance at a deep emotional and embodied level (cf. Davis, 2010; Davis & Badenoch, 2010; Fogel, 2009).

#### *Bibliotherapy*

The final cognitive-behavioral intervention that we will discuss is *bibliotherapy*, an expressive psychotherapy whereby the client's reaction to and interaction with written literature (e.g., books and poetry) are explored and highlighted, to facilitate adaptive psychotherapeutic change. For example, for clients who believe in a loving God, a perennial difficulty is coming to terms with the reality of suffering. Painful experiences can leave them feeling angry at and abandoned by God (Exline & Rose, 2005). In this case, discussing theological explanations can sometimes be helpful, but we have found that allegorical stories are often a far more effective and efficient way of providing a corrective emotional experience. With a Christian population, reading and discussing the *Chronicles of Narnia* series (Lewis, 1950–1956/2001) is commonly transformative and has some preliminary research support of effectiveness (Thomas et al., 2011). Christian clients readily identify with the characters who interact with Aslan (i.e., God). Through identification with these characters, clients learn to make sense of difficult personal situations and to experience God emotionally as more affirming and experience-near, particularly during trying times (Thomas et al., 2011). Of note, we have anecdotally found that Young's (2007) *The Shack* is also a highly effective bibliotherapy tool.

### Narrative-Experiential Approaches

Another strategy for treating God-image difficulties is to use narrative-experiential approaches. Using these techniques, the psychotherapist promotes the client's understanding, articulation, and crafting of his or her *God-image narrative identity*—that is, his or her "internalized, evolving, and integrative story of the self" (McAdams, 2008, p. 242) in relationship with a divine attachment figure (Brokaw, Davis, Carafa, & Hudson, 2009; Davis & Badenoch, 2010).

More specifically, the client and psychotherapist dissect the client's God-image narrative into its salient chapters and settings, characters, plots and subplots, themes and tones, images and metaphors, milestones, and conflicts (Davis, 2009; cf. McAdams, 1993). Experiential techniques (e.g., Gestalt empty-chair exercises, psychodrama, spiritual journaling, sandplay, and art or music psychotherapy) are used to evoke the emotions and physiological sensations that are associated with the client's implicit relational knowledge of self, God, and self-in-relationship-with-God (cf. Badenoch, 2008; Davis, 2009, 2010; Davis & Badenoch, 2010). Thoughtful verbal, artistic, or written reflection is then used to attach words, images, and metaphors to these feelings and sensations (Davis, 2009, 2010; Davis & Badenoch, 2010; Hall, 2007; cf. Bucci, 1997), promoting the construction of a coherent narrative of the client's spiritual journey with the God. Next, the client and psychotherapist work to coconstruct the storylines that most likely will lead to adaptive growth in the client's relationship with God, based on client-specified life goals. Last, psychotherapy centers on empowering the client to live out these coconstructed storylines, as the author of his or her God-image narrative identity (Davis, 2009; Davis & Badenoch, 2010; cf. Cozolino, 2010; Siegel, 1999).

In sum, we suggest that the treatment of client God images proceeds according to a nuanced, psychotherapy-integrationist approach, as opposed to a rigid, orientation-specific approach. Stated differently, we recommend that psychotherapists use a variety of theories and techniques to conceptualize and treat God-image-related difficulties, rather than using a one-size-fits-all approach. Toward this end, we have described three types of approaches: dynamic-interpersonal, cognitive-behavioral, and narrative-experiential. In the following case study, we illustrate how all three approaches can synergistically promote God-image change.

## CASE STUDY

Jane Pennington, a fictitious amalgam client, was a 48-year-old White, married, evangelical Protestant Christian who was employed as a full-time administrative assistant at her church. When I (GLM) saw her, her presenting concerns were a dependent personality style and generalized anxiety. Jane was a self-described "people pleaser," having a hard time making her own decisions and consistently looking to others for direction and affirmation. She described herself as a "worrywart" and indicated that she most frequently worried about keeping her husband and her pastor–boss happy. Additionally, Jane complained of difficulties in her relationship with God; she always felt like she was letting God down. Theologically, she believed that God loved her unconditionally, but this belief was highly disconnected from how she actually experienced God emotionally, and it had been for as long as she could remember.

Jane grew up in a traditional home and was the only child of two hardworking parents. Her parents were neither emotionally available nor responsive; on the contrary, they both were emotionally unavailable and punitive. Early in life, Jane learned that, to keep her parents from getting angry with her, she had to remain quiet, agreeable, and happy.

Jane married at age 19. Her husband was 6 years her senior, and like her parents, he was quite difficult to please. Their marriage was fairly patriarchal in that Jane's husband made most decisions unilaterally, and he managed all their finances. While at home, Jane would work tirelessly to complete her "wifely duties," but it was never enough to please her husband. Jane dependably blamed herself for their marital difficulties.

Jane started psychotherapy mainly because her anxiety about pleasing others was becoming unbearable. At work, she always worried about whether or not her pastor–boss was satisfied with her job performance, and at home, she was constantly afraid that she was not doing enough to please her husband. Jane was also struggling in her emotional relationship with God. She desperately wanted to know and experience God's grace, love, and acceptance—all of which continued to elude to her.

I saw Jane weekly for twenty-five 50-minute sessions. I used a psychotherapy-integrationist approach to treatment. Specifically, I used dynamic-interpersonal and narrative-experiential interventions to treat Jane's dependent relational patterns, and I employed cognitive-behavioral interventions to treat her generalized anxiety. As psychotherapy progressed, Jane experienced adaptive shifts in her images of herself, God, and others.

The beginning stages of treatment were characterized by building rapport and by clinical assessment. I conducted a general clinical interview and a follow-up, God-image-focused clinical interview. For homework, Jane completed a self-report, survey-based measure, assessing her God-image versus God-concept discrepancies. To this end, she also completed the Draw-a-God projective exercise. Both types of assessments helped elucidate similarities between her experiences of her parents and her experiences of God. During our next few sessions, we explored how Jane's chief interpersonal problem—a maladaptive dependent personality pattern—had developed with her parents, was maintained with her husband and her pastor–boss, and influenced her emotional experience of God.

As psychotherapy progressed through the middle stages of treatment, we began to explore how Jane's dependent personality pattern was being enacted in our psychotherapy relationship. For example, we noticed how she habitually minimized her own thoughts and feelings, while readily agreeing with mine. I used my own experience of Jane to try to help her gain a new understanding of herself, offering several interpretations along these lines:

> When you talk about your relationships with your parents growing up (past relationships) it seems like you always felt like you weren't able to meet their demands and keep them happy. Similarly, when you talk about your husband and your pastor–boss, I hear a theme of feeling like you don't measure up—like they might be frustrated with you because you aren't doing enough (present relationships). With me too, you've expressed worry that I'm upset with you for not working hard

> enough (psychotherapy relationship). Likewise, when you describe your relationship with God it sounds like you often experience God as a sort of taskmaster—like you can never meet God's demands. Across each of these relationships, there appears to be a theme in which you feel guilty and worry that you are not fulfilling what you think others expect of you. Does that fit with your experience?

Multiple curative encounters helped Jane to gradually have a new experience of herself, others (including me), and God. With me, she began to share her own thoughts and feelings, even disagreeing with me at times. With her husband, she began to behave in a more assertive manner. Finally, with her pastor–boss, she began to rest more securely in the fact that she was performing well on the job. These adaptive shifts in Jane's internal working models of self and others also affected her God images. God did not feel as harsh and distant to her anymore; instead, God began to feel more patient, loving, and gracious. In fact, Jane gradually started to feel like God actually *liked* her and even *enjoyed* interacting with her in prayer and worship.

I used cognitive-behavioral interventions to treat Jane's generalized anxiety. Psychoeducation and basic cognitive-behavioral techniques (e.g., progressive muscle relaxation and deep diaphragmatic breathing) helped her understand how thinking, feeling, and behaving were intimately related and how they influenced one another. I also used cognitive-behavioral interventions to treat Jane's God-image difficulties. In particular, we used GIATRs to help her challenge and modify her problematic God images. Imagery techniques (imagining interacting with the Real God) were used to incorporate emotional involvement into this cognitive-restructuring process.

The final weeks of treatment involved strengthening the changes that Jane had made, facilitating the articulation of her God-image narrative identity, and empowering her to move forward as the author of her spiritual and life narratives. Jane and I explored termination issues, reflected on her growth, and went through the process of saying goodbye. In the end, Jane had participated in 25 sessions of psychotherapy and had worked hard to produce real changes in herself and in her emotional experiences of God and of others.

## CONCLUSION

This chapter focused on God-image theory and research, with a view toward clinical applications. We began by contrasting God images and God concepts. *God images* are the mental representations that underlie individuals' personal, emotional, embodied experiences in relationship with a divine attachment figure, such as God, Jesus, or Allah. In contrast, *God concepts* are the abstract, conceptual, doctrinal understandings that underlie individuals' beliefs about a divine attachment figure. Next we explored the religious and spiritual bases for

God images from an ecumenical perspective. We then provided an overview of relevant empirical research on God images, focusing on studies that are applicable to psychotherapy with religious or spiritual clients. We discussed ways to address God images in psychotherapy, suggesting the use of a psychotherapy-integrationist approach and highlighting the particular promise of using dynamic-interpersonal, cognitive-behavioral, or narrative-experiential interventions. We closed with a case example illustrating how theory and research can inform the assessment, conceptualization, and treatment of client God images.

## CHAPTER SUMMARY

- *God images* are the mental representations that underlie individuals' personal, emotional, embodied experiences in relationship with a divine attachment figure, such as God, Jesus, or Allah. *God concepts* are the abstract, conceptual, doctrinal understandings that underlie individuals' beliefs about a divine attachment figure. Simply put, *God images* are a person's heart knowledge of God, whereas *God concepts* are a person's head knowledge of God (Gibson, 2006).
- Scholarship on God images has its historical roots in the broad Christian faith tradition, from which most God-image theory, research, and instrumentation has emanated.
- The vast majority of scholarship on God-image development and dynamics has emanated from the psychodynamic tradition. In particular, it has emanated from classical psychoanalytic theory (Freud, 1913/1950, 1930/1962), object relations theory (Rizzuto, 1979), and attachment theory (Davis, 2010; Granqvist & Kirkpatrick, 2008; Kirkpatrick, 2005; Noffke & Hall, 2007).
- In the study of God-image dynamics, one major replicated finding is that how people view themselves is significantly related to how they view God (Benson & Spilka, 1973; Buri & Mueller, 1993). Ample research has shown that adults' current level of object relations maturity is positively related to the adaptiveness of their God images (Brokaw & Edwards, 1994; Tisdale et al., 1997).
- The main rationale for clinically addressing God images is that religion or spirituality is important to the vast majority of Americans (Pew Research Center, 2008), and for many religious or spiritual persons, *relationship with God* is central to their faith (Gallup & Jones, 1989). Furthermore, for religious or spiritual clients, God-image difficulties often contribute to the development and maintenance of their presenting concerns.
- A synthesis of this research suggests that the psychotherapeutic treatment of God images should facilitate adaptive changes in clients' internal

working models of self and of self-in-relationship-with-attachment-figures (human and divine; Davis, 2010). To promote adaptive God-image change, clinicians should strategically facilitate security-enhancing relational experiences (Badenoch, 2008; Davis, 2010; Mikulincer & Shaver, 2004). Such a strategy would place the client–psychotherapist relationship at the crux of God-image change (cf. Norcross, 2002).

- Preliminary research evidence suggests that different formats (e.g., individual psychotherapy, bibliotherapy, and group psychotherapy) are each effective in facilitating adaptive God-image change (Cheston et al., 2003; Thomas & Moriarty, 2009; Tisdale et al., 1997). Furthermore, treatments that are based on different theoretical approaches are likely equally effective as well (see Moriarty & Hoffman, 2007). In sum, it seems reasonable to conclude that the best way to treat client God images is to select the psychotherapeutic formats and approaches that are most likely to facilitate change for a given client, based on a variety of client variables (e.g., presenting concerns, functional impairment, and client characteristics and preferences; Harwood et al., 2011; Norcross, 2002).
- We suggest that the treatment of client God images proceeds according to a nuanced, psychotherapy-integrationist approach, as opposed to a rigid, orientation-specific approach. Stated differently, we recommend that psychotherapists use a variety of theories and techniques to conceptualize and treat God-image-related difficulties, rather than using a one-size-fits-all approach. Toward this end, we have described three types of approaches that appear most promising for treating client God images: dynamic-interpersonal, cognitive-behavioral, and narrative-experiential.
- God-image assessment is a multistep process that is used to identify and conceptualize a person's God images. It can be completed using a variety of tools, chiefly including (a) clinical-interview questions; (b) projective assessments; and (c) self-report, survey-based measures. Including each type of assessment is recommended, if it is feasible to do so (Brokaw & Edwards, 1994; Gibson, 2007).

## CLINICAL APPLICATION QUESTIONS

1. What are God images and God concepts, and what are the differences between them?
2. How might discrepancies between God images and God concepts lead to clinically significant client distress? What might this distress look like clinically?
3. What influences God image development and dynamics? How do self-images relate to God images? Does research evidence indicate that psychotherapy participation can lead to adaptive God-image change?
4. What types of interview questions and assessment instruments would you use to assess client God images, and why?

5. How might dynamic-interpersonal, cognitive-behavioral, and narrative-experiential interventions lead to adaptive God-image change? What are the similarities and differences among these approaches? What types of God-image difficulties might respond best to each respective approach and why? Which of the described interventions do you feel most comfortable using and why?

## SUGGESTED READINGS AND RESOURCES

God Image Therapy Video Demonstrations. http://www.regent.edu/admin/media/fms/vod/multiVideoURL.cfm?address=2000002

Jones, J. W. (1991). *Contemporary psychoanalysis and religion*. New Haven, CT: Yale.

Moriarty, G. (2006). *Pastoral care of depression: Helping clients heal their relationship with God*. Binghamton, NY: Haworth Press.

Moriarty, G. L., & Hoffman, L. (Eds.). (2007). *God image handbook for spiritual counseling and psychotherapy: Research, theory, and practice*. Binghamton, NY: Haworth Press.

Rizzuto, A. M. (1979). *The birth of the living God*. Chicago, IL: University of Chicago Press.

## REFERENCES

Ainsworth, M. D. S. (1985). Attachments across the life span. *Bulletin of the New York, NY Academy of Medicine, 61*, 792–812.

Alexander, F., & French, T. M. (1946). *Psychoanalytic psychotherapy: Principles and applications*. New York, NY: Ronald Press.

Allmond, J. (2010). *God images in Christian psychology, spiritual direction, and pastoral counseling*. (Doctoral dissertation, Regent University). Available from ProQuest Dissertations & These (AA 3370134).

Badenoch, B. (2008). *Being a brain-wise therapist: A practical guide to interpersonal neurobiology*. New York, NY: Norton.

Bassett, R. L., Miller, S., Anstey, K., Crafts, K., Harmon, J., …, & Stevenson, D. H. (1990). Picturing God: A nonverbal measure of God concept for conservative Protestants. *Journal of Psychology and Christianity, 9*, 73–81.

Beck, R., & McDonald, A. (2004). Attachment to God: The Attachment to God Inventory, tests of working model correspondence, and an exploration of faith group differences. *Journal of Psychology and Theology, 32*, 92–103.

Benson, P., & Spilka, B. (1973). God image as a function of self-esteem and locus of control. *Journal for the Scientific Study of Religion, 12*, 297–310.

Birky, I. T., & Ball, S. (1988). Parental trait influence on God as an object representation. *The Journal of Psychology, 122*, 133–137.

Bowlby, J. (1969/1982). *Attachment and loss: Attachment* (Vol. 1). New York, NY: Basic Books.

Bowlby, J. (1973). *Attachment and loss: Separation* (Vol. 2). New York, NY: Basic Books.

Bowlby, J. (1980). *Attachment and loss: Loss, sadness and depression* (Vol. 3). New York, NY: Basic Books.

Boyd, G. A. (2004). *Seeing is believing: Experience Jesus through imaginative prayer*. Grand Rapids, MI: Baker Books.

Brokaw, B., Davis, E. B., Carafa, M., & Hudson, P. (2009, April). *Storying God images: Narratives and neurobiology*. Presentation at the annual CAPS International Conference, Orlando, FL.

Brokaw, B. F., & Edwards, K. J. (1994). The relationship of God image to level of object relations development. *Journal of Psychology and Theology, 22*, 352–371.

Bucci, W. (1997). *Psychoanalysis & cognitive science: A multiple code theory.* New York, NY: Guilford.

Buri, J. R., & Mueller, R. A. (1993). Psychoanalytic theory and loving God concepts: Parent referencing versus self-referencing. *The Journal of Psychology, 127,* 17–27.

Cheston, S. E., Piedmont, R. L., Eanes, B., & Lavin, L. P. (2003). Changes in clients' images of God over the course of outpatient psychotherapy. *Counseling and Values, 47,* 96–108.

Collins, N. L., Guichard, A. C., Ford, M. B., & Feeney, B. C. (2004). Working models of attachment: New developments and emerging themes. In W. S. Rholes & J. A. Simpson (Eds.), *Adult attachment: Theory, research, and clinical implications* (pp. 196–239). New York, NY: Guilford.

Cozolino, L. (2010). *The neuroscience of psychotherapy: Healing the social brain* (2nd ed.). New York, NY: Norton.

Davis, E. B. (2009). *God image narrative therapy: A treatment manual.* Unpublished manuscript, School of Psychology and Counseling, Regent University.

Davis, E. B. (2010). *Authenticity, inauthenticity, attachment, and God-image tendencies among adult evangelical Protestant Christians* (Doctoral dissertation, Regent University). Retrieved from http://caps.net/communities/christian-psychoanalysts/cp-continued-learning

Davis, E. B., & Badenoch, B. (2010). Storying God images: Bringing narrative integration to our experience of the divine. *Winter 2009 GAINS Quarterly* (pp. 14–24, 63–65). Global Association of Interpersonal Neurobiology Studies (GAINS).

Dickie, J. R., Eshleman, A. K., Merasco, D. M., Shepard, A., Wilt, M. V., & Johnson, M. (1997). Parent–child relationships and children's images of God. *Journal for the Scientific Study of Religion, 36,* 25–43.

Erikson, E. H. (1959). *Identity and the life cycle.* New York, NY: International University Press.

Exline, J. J., & Rose, E. (2005). Religious and spiritual struggles. In R. F. Paloutzian & C. L. Park (Eds.), *Handbook of the psychology of religion and spirituality* (pp. 315–330). New York, NY: Guilford.

Fairbairn, W. R. D. (1952). *Psycho-analytic studies of the personality.* New York, NY: Basic Books.

Fogel, A. (2009). *The psychophysiology of self-awareness: Rediscovering the lost art of body sense.* New York, NY: Norton.

Francis, L. J., Robbins, M., & Gibson, H. M. (2006). A revised semantic differential scale distinguishing between negative and positive God images. *Journal of Beliefs and Values, 27,* 237–240.

Fredrickson, B. L., & Cohn, M. A. (2008). Positive emotions. In M. Lewis, J. M. Haviland-Jones, & L. F. Barrett (Eds.), *Handbook of emotions* (3rd ed., pp. 777–796). New York, NY: Guilford.

Freud, S. (1950). *Totem and taboo* (J. Strachey, Trans.). New York, NY: Norton. (Original work published 1913)

Freud, S. (1962). *Civilization and its discontents* (J. Strachey, Trans.). New York, NY: Norton. (Original work published 1930)

Gallup, G., Jr., & Jones, S. (1989). *One hundred questions and answers: Religion in America.* Princeton, NJ: Princeton Religious Research Center.

George, C., Kaplan, N., & Main, M. (1996). *Adult Attachment Interview protocol* (3rd ed.). Unpublished manuscript, University of California at Berkeley.

Gibson, N. J. S. (2006). *The experimental investigation of religious cognition* (Doctoral dissertation, University of Cambridge, Cambridge, England). Retrieved from http://divinity.npsl.co.uk/prrg/people/staff/staff.acds?context=1609849&instanceid=1609850

Gibson, N. J. S. (2007). Measurement issues in God image research and practice. In G. L. Moriarty & L. Hoffman (Eds.), *God image handbook for spiritual counseling and psychotherapy: Research, theory, and practice* (pp. 227–246). Binghamton, NY: Haworth/Routledge.

Gorsuch, R. L. (1968). The conceptualization of God as seen in adjective ratings. *Journal for the Scientific Study of Religion, 7,* 56–64.

Gough, H. G., & Heilbrum, A. B. (1983). *The adjective check list manual.* Palo Alto, CA: Consulting Psychologists Press.

Granqvist, P. (1998). Religiousness and perceived childhood attachment: On the question of compensation or correspondence. *Journal for the Scientific Study of Religion, 37,* 350–367.

Granqvist, P. (2002). Attachment and religiosity in adolescence: Cross-sectional and longitudinal evaluations. *Personality & Social Psychology Bulletin, 28,* 260–270.

Granqvist, P., & Hagekull, B. (1999). Religiousness and perceived childhood attachment: Profiling socialized correspondence and emotional compensation. *Journal for the Scientific Study of Religion, 10,* 254–273.

Granqvist, P., & Kirkpatrick, L. A. (2008). Attachment and religious representations and behavior. In J. Cassidy & P. R. Shaver (Eds.), *Handbook of attachment: Theory, research, and clinical applications* (2nd ed., pp. 906–933). New York, NY: Guilford.

Granqvist, P., & Main, M. (2003). *The Attachment to God Interview.* Unpublished manuscript, Uppsala University, Uppsala, Sweden.

Greenberg, J. R., & Mitchell, S. A. (1983). *Object relations in psychoanalytic theory.* Cambridge, MA: Harvard University Press.

Hall, T. W. (2004). Christian spirituality and mental health: A relational spirituality framework for empirical research. *Journal of Psychology and Christianity, 23,* 66–81.

Hall, T. W. (2007). Psychoanalysis, attachment, and spirituality part II: The spiritual stories we live by. *Journal of Psychology and Theology, 35,* 29–42.

Hall, T. W., Fujikawa, A., Halcrow, S. R., Hill, P. C., & Delaney, H. (2009). Attachment to God and implicit spirituality: Clarifying correspondence and compensation models. *Journal of Psychology and Theology, 37,* 247–242.

Harwood, T. M., Beutler, L. E., Williams, O. B., & Stegmans, R. S. (2011). Identifying treatment-relevant assessment: Systematic treatment selection/InnerLife. In T. M. Harwood, L. E. Beutler, & G. Groth-Marnat (Eds.), *Integrative assessment of adult personality* (3rd ed., pp. 61–79). New York, NY: Guilford.

Hathaway, W. L. (2003). Clinically significant religious impairment. *Mental Health, Religion & Culture, 6,* 113–129.

Hill, P. C. (2005). Measurement in the psychology of religion and spirituality: Current status and evaluation. In R. F. Paloutzian & C. L. Park (Eds.), *Handbook of the psychology of religion and spirituality* (pp. 43–61). New York, NY: Guilford.

Hill, P. C., & Hood, Jr., R. W. (1999). *Measures of religiosity.* Birmingham, AL: Religious Education Press.

Hill, P. C., & Pargament, K. I. (2003). Advances in the conceptualization and measurement of religion and spirituality. *American Psychologist, 58,* 64–74.

Johnson, B. (2007). Rational emotive behavior psychotherapy and the God image. In G. L. Moriarty & L. Hoffman (Eds.), *God image handbook for spiritual counseling and psychotherapy: Research, theory, and practice* (pp. 157–181). Binghamton, NY: Haworth/Routledge.

Jones, J. (2007). Psychodynamic theories of the evolution of the God image. In G. Moriarty & L. Hoffman (Eds.), *God image handbook for spiritual counseling and psychotherapy: Research, theory, and practice* (pp. 33–55). Binghamton, NY: Haworth/Routledge.

Kirkpatrick, L. A. (1992). An attachment-theoretical approach to the psychology of religion. *International Journal for the Psychology of Religion, 2*, 3–28.
Kirkpatrick, L. A. (2005). *Attachment, evolution, and the psychology of religion*. New York, NY: Guilford.
Kirkpatrick, L. A., & Shaver, P. R. (1990). Attachment theory and religion: Childhood attachments, religious beliefs, and conversion. *Journal for the Scientific Study of Religion, 29*, 315–334.
Kirkpatrick, L. A., & Shaver, P. R. (1992). An attachment-theoretical approach to romantic love and religious belief. *Personality and Social Psychology Bulletin, 18*, 266–275.
Lawrence, R. T. (1991). *The God Image Inventory: The development, validation, and standardization of a psychometric instrument for research, pastoral and clinical use in measuring the image of God.* Unpublished doctoral dissertation, Catholic University of America, Washington, DC.
Lewis, C. S. (2001). *The chronicles of Narnia*. New York, NY: HarperCollins. (Original works published 1950–1956)
Lyons-Ruth, K., Bruschweiler-Stern, N., Harrison, A. M., Morgan, A. C., Nahum, J. P., Sander, L., … Tronick, E. Z. (1998). Implicit relational knowing: Its role in development and psychoanalytic treatment. *Infant Mental Health Journal, 19*, 282–289.
McAdams, D. (1993). *The stories we live by*. New York, NY: Guilford.
McAdams, D. (2008). Personal narratives and the life story. In O. P. John, R. W. Robins, & L. A. Pervin (Eds.), *Handbook of personality: Theory and research* (3rd ed., pp. 242–262). New York, NY: Guilford.
Mikulincer, M., & Shaver, P. R. (2004). Security-based self-representations in adulthood: Contents and processes. In W. S. Rholes & J. A. Simpson (Eds.), *Adult attachment: Theory, research, and clinical implications* (pp. 159–195). New York, NY: Guilford.
Mischel, W., & Shoda, Y. (2008). Toward a unified theory of personality: Integrating dispositions and processing dynamics within the Cognitive-Affective Personality System. In O. P. John, R. W. Robins, & L. A. Pervin (Eds.), *Handbook of personality: Theory and research* (3rd ed., pp. 208–241). New York, NY: Guilford.
Moriarty, G. L. (2006). *Pastoral care of depression: Helping clients heal their relationship with God.* Binghamton, NY: Haworth/Routledge.
Moriarty, G. L. (2007). Time-limited dynamic psychotherapy and God image. In G. L. Moriarty & L. Hoffman (Eds.), *God image handbook for spiritual counseling and psychotherapy: Research, theory, and practice* (pp. 79–104). Binghamton, NY: Haworth/Routledge.
Moriarty, G. L., & Hoffman, L. (Eds.). (2007). *God image handbook for spiritual counseling and psychotherapy: Research, theory, and practice.* Binghamton, NY: Haworth/Routledge.
Noffke, J. L., & Hall, T. W. (2007). Attachment psychotherapy and God image. In G. L. Moriarty & L. Hoffman (Eds.), *God image handbook for spiritual counseling and psychotherapy: Research, theory, and practice* (pp. 57–78). Binghamton, NY: Haworth/Routledge.
Norcross, J. (Ed.). (2002). *Psychotherapy relationships that work: Psychotherapist contributions and responsiveness to patients.* New York, NY: Oxford University Press.
Norcross, J. C. & Goldfried, M. R. (Eds.). (2005). *Handbook of psychotherapy integration.* New York, NY: Oxford University Press.
O'Grady, K., & Richards, P. S. (2007). Theistic psychotherapy and the God image. In G. L. Moriarty & L. Hoffman (Eds.), *God image handbook for spiritual counseling and psychotherapy: Research, theory, and practice* (pp. 183–209). Binghamton, NY: Haworth/Routledge.

Pargament, K. I. (2007). *Spiritually integrated psychotherapy: Understanding and addressing the sacred.* New York, NY: Guilford.

Pew Research Center (2008). *U.S. religious landscape survey, religious beliefs and practices: Diverse and politically relevant, June 2008.* Retrieved from http://religions.pewforum.org/pdf/report2-religious-landscape-study-full.pdf

Phillips, J. B. (1952). *Your God is too small* [E-text]. Retrieved from http://www.new-churches.com/mediafiles/YourGodisTooSmall-Phillips.pdf

Propst, L. R. (1987). *Psychotherapy in a religious framework: Spirituality in the emotional healing process.* New York, NY: Human Sciences Press.

Richards, P. S., & Bergin, A. E. (2005). *A spiritual strategy for counseling and psychotherapy* (2nd ed.). Washington, DC: American Psychological Association.

Rizzuto, A. (1979). *The birth of the living God.* Chicago, IL: University of Chicago Press.

Shafranske, E. P. (2005). The psychology of religion in clinical and counseling psychology. In R. F. Paloutzian & C. L. Park (Eds.), *Handbook of the psychology of religion and spirituality* (pp. 496–514). New York, NY: Guilford.

Siegel, D. J. (1999). *The developing mind: How relationships and the brain interact to shape who we are.* New York, NY: Guilford.

Slade, A. (2008). The implications of attachment theory and research for adult psychotherapy. In J. Cassidy & P. R. Shaver (Eds.), *Handbook of attachment: Theory, research, and clinical applications* (2nd ed., pp. 762–782). New York, NY: Guilford.

St. John of the Cross (2008). *Dark night of the soul* (E. A. Peers, Trans.). Radford, VA: Wilder.

Strength, J. M. (1998). Expanding Davanloo's interpretive triangles to explicate the client's introjected image of God. *Journal of Psychology and Theology, 26,* 172–187.

Thomas, M. J., Moriarty, G. L., Davis, E. B., & Anderson, E. L. (2011). The effects of a manualized group-psychotherapy intervention on client God images and attachment to God: A pilot study. *Journal of Psychology and Theology, 39,* 44–58.

Tisdale, T. T., Key, T. L., Edwards, K. J., Brokaw, B. F., Kemperman, S. R., Cloud, H., Townsend, J., & Okamato, T. (1997). Impact of treatment on God image and personal adjustment, and correlations of God image to personal adjustment and object relations development. *Journal of Psychology and Theology, 25,* 227–239.

Winnicott, D. W. (1975). Transitional objects and transitional phenomena. In D. W. Winnicott (Ed.), *Through pediatrics to psycho-analysis* (pp. 229–242). New York, NY: Basic Books. (Original work published 1951)

Winnicott, D. W. (1971). *Playing and reality.* New York, NY: Basic Books.

Yarborough, C. A., Gibson, N. & Moriarty, G. (2009, August). *Depression and the emotional experience of God.* Paper presented at the International Congress for the Psychology of Religion, Vienna, Austria.

Young, W. P. (2007). *The shack.* Los Angeles, CA: Windblown Media.

Zahl, B., & Gibson, N. (2009 , August). *Measuring God representations: Improving paper and pencil measures of God representations.* Paper presented at the International Congress for the Psychology of Religion, Vienna, Austria.

# 7

# *Addressing Spiritually Transcendent Experiences in Psychotherapy*

Kari A. O'Grady and Jeremy D. Bartz

According to some scholars, transcendent influences in psychological processes are exempt from scientific investigation because of the intangible qualities of such experiences (Delaney & DiClemente, 2005). Other scholars have suggested that transcendence is a basic human trait that cuts across most demographic variables and represents the truest essence and highest achievement of the human experience (Maslow, 1971; Kroll, Bachrach, & Carey, 2002; Plante & Sherman, 2002; O'Grady & Richards, 2007, 2009). Various labels have been attached to such experiences (e.g., *religious experiences, spiritual experiences, mystical experiences,* and *anomalous experiences*), therefore we wish to delineate the term *spiritually transcendent experience* for remainder of the text. Seidlitz et al. (2002) described spiritual transcendence as "a subjective experience of the sacred that affects one's self-perception, feelings, goals, and ability to transcend difficulties" (p. 441). We also like the secular definition of transcendent given by *Merriam-Webster Collegiate Dictionary* (1993): "extending or lying beyond the limits of ordinary experience, or transcending the universe or material existence"; and the term *experience* can be thought of as a "modification of consciousness" itself (Rankin, 2008, p. 9). Thus *spiritually transcendent experiences* can be operationlized as a spiritual modification of consciousness that extends beyond the ordinary vicissitudes of everyday life.

Spiritually transcendent experiences are unique within the study of psychological processes, as such experiences seem to defy or move beyond the typical ways in which we conceptualize psychological change or development (Koss-Chioino & Hefner, 2006; Goldstein, 2007). Such experiences can generate a sense of spiritual awakening or transformation that abruptly alters the expected trajectory of people's lives. Spiritually transcendent experiences can impute significant and enduring meaning, motivation, and movement for many individuals. For example, a Gallup survey (Gallup, CNN, & *USA Today*, 2003) found that 41% of Americans indicated that they had encountered a profound religious experience or awakening that changed the direction of their lives. The peculiar effects of spiritually transcendent experiences on psychological processes makes this aspect of spirituality particularly evocative and worthy of consideration.

Given the frequency with which they occur and the powerful influence that spiritually transcendence experiences can have on individuals' lives, it is not surprising that they can emerge as clinically relevant issues during the course of psychotherapy, especially in therapeutic environments in which the client feels safe discussing spiritual matters (West, 2000). Transcendence is a spiritual or religious goal, but many psychotherapists would not consider it to be a clinical goal per se. For many religious and spiritual people, however, achieving states of transcendence has a number of mental health implications, such as providing a sense of meaning and life purpose (Goldstein, 2007). Likewise, a great deal of evidence suggests that those who engage in spiritual activity experience a variety of mental health benefits, such as increases in the following: (a) happiness, (b) life satisfaction, (c) hope, (d) personal control, (e) marital satisfaction, and (f) positive social conduct. Other mental health benefits include decreases in the following: (a) depression, (b) anxiety, and (c) suicidal behavior and ideation (Koenig, McCullough, & Larson, 2001). Studies have demonstrated a positive relationship between transcendent experiences and subjective well-being (Gehlert & Dy-Liacco, 2010; Goldstein, 2007; Pargament, Smith, Koenig, & Perez, 1998). In addition, for spiritually oriented clients who present with insecure attachment styles, achieving transcendence can help them develop a healthy attachment to a higher power, thus providing a sense of security and consistency to sustain them through the inconsistencies of life. A healthy relationship with God can provide a template for other relationships in their lives (e.g., relationships with self, siblings, partner, children, and others; O'Grady & Richards, 2007). Achieving spiritual transcendence has also been found to reduce stress and improve relationships (Goldstein, 2007; Hardy, 1979). Therefore, when clients identify themselves as spiritual or religious, psychotherapists occasionally may find it clinically relevant to assist them in understanding or achieving spiritually transcendent experiences.

Although most spiritually transcendent experiences have positive effects on those experiencing them, they also can produce negative residual consequences that require therapeutic attention. For instance, Miller and C'de Baca (2001) reported that they had worked with a woman who felt such a dramatic personal transformation from a spiritually transcendent experience that she was no longer able to tolerate some of the dysfunction in her marital relationship. She insisted on immediate remediation in her marriage, including marriage counseling. Her husband was unwilling to consider changes or to seek help, and 3 days following her request for change, he ended their relationship. One of the results of this woman's spiritually transcendent experience was the loss of her marriage. In situations such as these, clients may need to process their experiences with their psychotherapist to make sense of the seemingly negative consequences.

Thus, psychotherapists should familiarize themselves with spiritually transcendent experiences for several reasons, including the following: to help maintain a therapeutically open environment, to differentiate between psychopathology and transcendent experiences, to help clients make sense of transcendent experiences in a way that is psychologically beneficial, and to help clients take advantage of the therapeutic potential inherent within such experiences. At times, it may be clinically indicated to assist clients in facilitating spiritually transcendent experiences, including when clients are struggling with crises of faith and would like to achieve transcendence, when clients' psychological issues are being affected by unhealthy God images, and when clients have insecure attachment styles and need a sense of secure love in their lives.

## HISTORICAL OVERVIEW OF TRANSCENDENT EXPERIENCES

Historical texts of cultures from around the world are replete with accounts of burning bushes, angelic apparitions, nirvana, shamanic journeys, stigmata, channeling, near-death experiences, exorcisms, and more. The debate as to whether these experiences are manifestations of spiritual realities or psychopathology has coexisted with these accounts for centuries. With some exceptions, premodern thought has tended to err on the side of assuming a spiritual etiology of such experiences. For example, in the Middle Ages many cases of anorexia nervosa were mistaken for miraculous manifestations of fasting saints (Bell, 1985). Until the end of the eighteenth century, individuals with dissociative identity disorder (DID) were understood to be afflicted with various forms of possession and, accordingly, were treated with exorcism (Kluft, 1996). With the advent of modernism and the scientific method, the pendulum swung to the opposite extreme, and reports of authentic transcendent experiences often are viewed as nothing more than psychopathology. For example, several 20th-century scholars have proposed that near-death experiences are nothing more than psychological defense mechanisms generated to protect individuals from the prospect of death (see Greyson, 2000).

This chapter is written based on the assumption that some accounts of transcendent experiences might in fact be grounded in spiritual realities that go beyond what empirical technology is able to observe or measure. We also believe that in some cases what individuals perceive as transcendent is rather a product of psychopathology or the power of suggestion, which can be quite misleading and disruptive to healthy functioning. Additionally, some reports of spiritually transcendent experiences may involve both elements of transcendence and psychopathology.

Transcendence has been involved in the treatment of psychological ailments dating back to the beginning of recorded history. One of the oldest examples of transcendent healing is found in shamanism, which involves the ability of a shaman to enter into an altered state of consciousness (e.g., trance) so that he or she can communicate with spirit entities and receive information regarding how to heal sick or troubled individuals. Shamanism has been practiced around the world throughout history (Ingerman, 2004) and remains a major form of healing in many cultures around the world today (Moodly & West, 2005).

Other historical examples of healing practices that rely on transcendent phenomena include exorcism, the laying on of hands, Santeria, and faith healings. Because individuals have been relying on transcendent forms of healing for millennia, it should come as no surprise that one of the main historical traditions of healing in which modern psychotherapies are rooted is the religiomagical tradition (Frank & Frank, 1991). Recently, several modern psychotherapy orientations have begun to more explicitly integrate transcendence into their healing practices (Richards & Bergin, 2003). When such integration is done carefully, we believe that it potentially can enhance traditional psychotherapy.

## REVIEW OF EMPIRICAL LITERATURE

Spiritual transcendence is an encompassing term that has been empirically demonstrated to contribute to multiple facets of psychological functioning. Acknowledging that it is not reasonable to offer a comprehensive coverage of all possible transcendent experiences that clients might report in therapy, we will focus on two types of spiritually transcendence—mystical experiences and experiences of spiritual guidance. We also address spiritual transcendence and the psychotherapist. In this section, we provide an overview of the empirical literature related to these types of experiences along with suggestions for clinical application. It is important to note that most research on spiritually transcendent experiences is qualitative in nature, and therefore the findings will be reported mainly in terms of themes with reference to the nature of mystical experiences and their impacts on those who report these experiences. After reviewing these areas of focus, we present clinical considerations for working effectively with spiritually transcendent experience in psychotherapy, followed by a case study. We assume that many of the concepts that we describe will apply to other transcendent experiences not discussed in this chapter, including near-death experiences, miraculous healings, and apparitions.

### Mystical Experiences

To guide clinicians toward effectively assessing and considering the clinical implications of spiritually transcendent experiences, we will discuss common features of mystical experiences as they tend to represent the most widely explored area of spiritual transcendence. One of the challenges of understanding clinical implications of mystical experiences is the ineffable nature of such experiences. William James, one of the original discussants about mystical experiences, provided a comprehensive review of the nature of mystical experiences in his seminal work *Varieties of Religious Experiences* (1902/1997). James's explorations of the subject provided a framework for understanding mystical experiences in a way that allowed researchers and clinicians to consider the psychological impacts and correlates of these experiences. For instance, Hood, Spilka, Hunsberger, and Gorsuch (1996) utilized William James's (1902/1997) categories of mystical experiences (see Hood, 1974) and found strong correlations between James's descriptions of mystical experiences and healthy psychological functioning.

After an extensive analysis of mystical experiences, James identified several characteristics of mystical experiences, including the following: (1) ineffability, (2) noetic quality, (3) transiency, and (4) passivity. James observed that individuals who encounter mystical experiences express that their experience was *ineffable*, or beyond description. These individuals have difficulty finding sufficient language to articulate their experiences. James explains that these incidents are only fully understood by those who experience them. According to James, mystical experiences have a *noetic essence*, being more than just an emotional state, but rather a state of knowing. They are illumative and carry a sense of authority for the individual. Furthermore, James described these experiences as transient in that they are discrete rather than developmental. Despite their brevity, mystical experiences tend to have an enduring effect. Finally, James noted that whether or not the experiencers engaged in preparatory work before the mystical experience, once they encountered the experience, a state of passivity took place in which they felt as they were not in control of the experience, but rather were recipients of an unmediated happening. Mystical experiences typically are thought of as unbidden; however, in some cases, specific precursors have been identified, such as meditation, prayer, religious rituals, sacred places, chanting, religious ceremony, blessings, contemplation, fasting, pilgrimages, despair, "hitting rock bottom," accident, illness, nature, and the prospect of death (Brown & Miller, 2005; Rankin, 2008).

Miller and C'de Baca (2001) contributed additional insights into mystical experiences through their qualitative analysis of "quantum change." They conducted in-depth interviews with 59 participants who were attracted to the study by an article posted in a mainstream journal. After extensive interviewing and careful analysis of the transcripts, they found some common themes among those who reported quantum change experiences, including (a) vividness, (b) emotion, (c) surprise, (d) benevolence, and (e) permanence. The majority of mystical experiences that were reported by participants indicated psychosocial health benefits in addition to spiritual transformations. Unlike many traditional psychotherapy interventions in which outcomes can be temporary and inconsistent, participants overwhelmingly reported that the changes brought about by their mystical experiences were permanent. They described themselves as being dramatically and enduringly changed in some meaningful way by the experience, as if having gone through a one-way door. For instance, one participant reported:

> When I heard the voice say, "You don't have to do that anymore; I will be with you always," I knew I could quit drinking. How can I tell anyone that I was able to stop that day and never have the desire to drink again? Who would believe me? ... I wonder why this happened to me? (Miller and C'de Baca, 2001, pp. 16–17)

In addition to reports of overcoming addictions, respondents reported that their experiences prompted value shifts, reduction in anxiety about specific concerns as well as a decrease in generalized anxiety symptoms, decrease in depressive symptoms, increase in social activism, improved emotional regulation, and increase in life satisfaction. Thus, when clinicians provide a safe and open environment for clients to share their mystical experiences and process the meaning of these experiences in session, they may be activating an important resource for overcoming symptoms of depression and anxiety, and encouraging health-promoting behaviors.

After empirically and systematically categorizing responses of 3,000 reports of mystical experiences. Hardy (1896–1985), concluded that spirituality was a natural and universal part of the human experience (Hardy, 1979). Hardy identified themes of antecedents to these experiences, including prayer, meditation, religious worship, sacred places, natural beauty, silence and solitude, music, and life crisis. He also identified consequences of these experiences for those reporting them. In order of occurrence, these consequences are as follows: (a) sense of purpose or new meaning to life, (b) changes in religious beliefs, and (c) changes in attitudes toward others. Such consequences have obvious mental health implications. For example, gaining a sense of life's purpose can greatly improve mood and lessen symptoms of anxiety (Yalom, 1980). When deleterious religious beliefs are replaced by healthy religious beliefs (e.g., replacing harsh God images with compassionate ones), individuals are better able to part with destructive tendencies, such as perfectionism and obsessive compulsive behaviors. And when individuals experience positive changes in their attitudes toward others, it can lead to improvements in interpersonal relationships.

Additionally, spiritually transcendence can help people cope with many life challenges including health concerns. Ironson, Kremer, and Ironson (2006) conducted in-depth interviews of 96 people diagnosed with HIV to learn more about the spiritual and psychological transformations of people with HIV. One third of participants reported a spiritually transcendent experience that resulted in life changes. These changes included positive transformations in cognition, attitudes, beliefs, behaviors, God image, self-view, worldview, levels of religiosity, and spirituality. Additionally, they reported that the most common alteration in participants was dramatic changes in lifestyle. Many participants shifted from a life of drugs, criminal activity, and living on the streets to a life of self-care and engagement in positive relationships with others. Participants reported that they exchanged negative emotions for more positive emotions, such as love, acceptance, and inner peace; and experienced a reduction in feelings of fear, anxiety, anger, tension, and depression following their spiritual transformations. Perhaps the most important implication of the spiritually transcendent experiences was that these experiences increased participants' abilities to cope with the psychological and physical health challenges associated with their diagnosis of HIV. For spiritually oriented clients, encouraging activities that foster spiritual transcendence may activate healthy coping mechanisms and provide a framework of meaning that supports positive lifestyle choices and transitions.

### Spiritual Direction

Prayer is integral to spirituality for many individuals, and for spiritually oriented clients perceived guidance from God can trump all other directives in their lives. Psychotherapists should use caution when responding to reports of spiritual guidance and avoid slipping into the role of clergy. Psychotherapists do not necessarily need to determine whether or not the report is valid, but rather, assess whether or not the experience is conducive to health or illness. For instance, psychotherapists can help clients determine whether the spiritual direction empowers or restricts them from healing and growth. If the spiritual direction restricts them from progress, it may be therapeutically advantageous to further explore the nature of the guidance with the client. Likewise clinicians may be able to extrapolate other underlying issues from client reports of spiritual guidance (e.g., if God's voice is consistently punitive, this may suggest that the client views himself or others critically). It is necessary to attend to clients' claims to determine whether the "voice of God" is a symptom of psychopathology.

After extensive review of people's reported experiences of "hearing" God's voice, Rankin (2008) noted that most individuals described God's voice as being *felt* or *perceived* rather than actually heard through the auditory system. We do not suggest that clients who report actually hearing God's voice out loud should be assumed to be hallucinating, but rather that the norm for most populations is that the voice is perceived internally. When a report falls outside of the norm, other factors should be considered in discerning the meaning of the client report. Suggestions for evaluations of this nature will be addressed more thoroughly in the assessment section of our chapter.

One guideline for determining pathology of a spiritual claim is by establishing whether the report is normative within the individual's faith tradition and cultural background. (Richards & Bergin, 2000). For instance, Dein and Littlewood (2007) conducted 25 in-depth interviews with members of the Pentecostal faith tradition. All 25 individuals reported experiencing an answering voice from God, with 15 reporting hearing God's voice externally. Respondents mentioned a number of criteria that helped them distinguish God's voice from their own voice, pathology, or evil influences. One indicator was the tone of communication. They reported that God's voice was gentle, encouraging, authoritative, clear, edifying, soft, distinct, and unique.

Respondents also indicated that God's voice was accompanied by positive affective and physical changes such as peace, certainty, sense of well-being, warmth, and lightheadedness. The element of "choice" may be a useful criterion for clinicians in differentiating between spiritual experiences and mental illness: The following example from the previous study illustrates this defining principle.

David learned to distinguish between psychotic voices and God's voice because he had experienced both. After experiencing a difficult childhood, including bullying at school, David had become an angry man who abused drugs and was often in trouble with the law. Following a marital breakdown that resulted in a period of depression, he started to hear voices. They were persistent and worsened when he felt particularly low. He described these voices as "quite nasty and aggressive thoughts and voices in my head, which I didn't know how to handle. These were very forceful and pushy, like a nagging woman, so to speak" (Dein & Littlewood, 2007, p. 224). In contrast, when he was not struggling with psychosis, he had several transcendent experiences that he interpreted as communication from God. Notice the difference in the way he describes these experiences. "God says something and doesn't force you, so you do what you like with it. It is much easier to respond than with a negative voice" (Dein & Littlewood, 2007, p. 224). David's experience elucidates the need for psychotherapists to be cautious in their diagnosis and treatment planning when dealing with clients who previously have experienced psychotic hallucinations or dissociations. When working with clients who do have a history of mental illness, it is important to avoid unilateral dismissal of all reports of spiritual communication as pathological. Instead, psychotherapists can assess whether they or the client can differentiate between the current report and past reports of hearing voices.

## Spiritual Transcendence and the Psychotherapist

In addition to considering spiritual direction in the lives of clients, we believe it is important that psychotherapists examine the role that spiritual transcendence plays in their own lives and in the psychotherapy that they provide. Psychotherapists' sensitivity to client reports of spiritually transcendent experiences likely relates to the psychotherapist's state of awareness concerning issues of spirituality in their own lives, and their openness to spiritual enlightenment during the psychotherapy process (O'Grady & Richards; 2010; Wiggins, 2009). Wiggins (2009) has suggested that

> [t]herapists can explore a variety of means for cultivating a sense of transcendence and wonder in their own lives. That is not to say therapists should become religious. Instead, it is to suggest a way of being in the world that invites the luminous and mysterious to sit next to the cognitive and the scientific in one's construction of reality. (p. 54)

Research indicates that some psychotherapists and other helping professionals do invite and experience divine influences in their work with clients, by praying for their clients in and out of session, meditating, attuning themselves to God's voice in the psychotherapy process, and experiencing deep spiritual connection with their clients (O'Grady & Richards, 2010; Richards & Potts, 1995; Shafranske, 2000).

It can be valuable for psychotherapists to evaluate their personal and professional stance about spiritual experiences occurring in therapy and their role in facilitating them. Hickson, Housley, and Wages (2000) investigated the attitudes of 147 licensed professional counselors (LPCs) in two southeastern states concerning *spirituality* in the therapeutic process. Spirituality was defined as the acknowledgment of a transcendent dimension of life that includes a sense of connectedness and the sacred. Of these respondents, 90% indicated that they had an awareness of the counselor's spiritual self as a powerful psychological change agent within the counseling process. Hickson et al. (2000) also reported that 86% of the participants indicated that they strongly agreed that all humans had a universal yearning to tap into their spiritual selves. The majority of *counselors* ($n$ = 105) indicated that using a spiritual component in a therapeutic relationship is either vitally important or important (73%).

A number of clinicians interested in augmenting their work with clients by tapping into their own sense of spiritual transcendence have offered suggestions for others who wish to do so in their sessions. O'Grady and Richards (2010) recently conducted a qualitative study examining the ways that helping professionals including psychotherapists experience divine inspiration or guidance in their therapeutic work. This study also explored their beliefs about how helping professionals can seek inspiration in their work. Open-ended survey questions from 333 respondents from a variety of religious and professional backgrounds were qualitatively analyzed. On the two closed-ended questions, 284 (86.6%) of the respondents indicated they believe that God may inspire helping professionals as they work with their clients, 16 (4.9%) indicated they were uncertain about this, and 19 (5.8%) indicated they do not believe God inspires helping professionals. Two hundred and forty-five (74.7%) of the respondents indicated they have personally felt God's inspiration in their professional practice, 31 (9.5%) indicated they were uncertain about this, and 39 (11.9%) said they have not experienced God's inspiration in their professional practice. A number of themes emerged regarding the ways that helping professionals experienced God's inspiration in their work with clients and patients. Some of the themes included (1) way of being, (2) state of sacredness, (3) inspired insights, and (4) heightening of attributes or abilities. A few participants described feeling a sacred presence during a counseling session or through the encounter, as related by a licensed certified social worker:

> I feel there is a mystical quality to the therapeutic process. In that I am referring to a third force. There's the client, the therapist, and something else present. It's almost palpable when, what appears to be all of sudden, the client "gets it"—the "aha" experience. It is important to pay attention to all the subtleties present. (O'Grady & Richards, 2010, p. 61)

Participants made a number of suggestions about how psychotherapists and other helping professionals can be open to God's transcendent influence in their work with clients and patients. For instance, one psychologist stated, "I believe the inspiration is always available. What we need to do is tune in by being in a place of compassion and love, listen for it, and then step aside" (O'Grady & Richards, 2010, p. 62). Other suggestions included (a) developing a relationship with God or a higher power, (b) engaging in spiritual practices, (c) actively seeking inspiration, (d) living a virtuous life, (e) being open minded about the role of inspiration in clinical work, and (e) being present in their relationship with clients.

These studies suggest that spiritually oriented psychotherapists may find value in developing openness to spiritual influences in their own lives and in their work with clients. Likewise, some scholars suggest that psychotherapists and other helping professionals who are able to experience spiritual direction and transcendence are more fulfilled in their careers, more creative in their treatment planning, more likely to create strong therapeutic alliances, and more resilient to secondary stress than if they neglect this aspect of their lives (McBride, 1998; Wicks, 2008; Young, Dowdle, & Flowers, 2009; O'Grady, 2011).

## CLINICAL ASSESSMENT

Not all claims of spiritual transcendence promote psychological benefits, and some reports actually may be indicative of mental illness regardless of the psychotherapist's openness to such experiences. Therefore, it is important for clinicians to be able to distinguish between psychologically beneficial transcendent experiences and psychopathology. Mistaking transcendent experience for psychopathology can lead to misdiagnoses, overmedication, stigmatization, and invalidation. Conversely, mistaking psychopathology for transcendent experience can lead to undertreating and possibly reinforcing pathological beliefs and behaviors. Because of the occasional overlap between psychopathology and transcendent experiences, differentiating between the two can be a challenging task (Berenbaum, Kerns & Raghavan, 2000). This task is highly contextual in the sense that what is considered transcendent in one culture often would be considered psychopathological in another and vice versa. Because this book is targeted for a primarily Western Hemisphere audience, we explore how such differentiation could take place within the contextual parameters of the Western contemporary culture.

In Western society, mental disorders are associated with at least one of the following: present distress; impairment in functioning; increased risk of death, pain, or disability; or an important loss of freedom (American Psychiatric Association [APA], 2000, p. xxxi). Therefore, the absence of all of these factors is an indication that the experience in question may not be a manifestation of mental illness. The presence of any one of these factors does not necessarily implicate psychopathology. As stated by the *Diagnostic and Statistical Manual of Mental Disorders* (DSM-IV-TR), "Each is a useful indicator for a mental disorder, but none is equivalent to the concept.... In addition, [the] syndrome or pattern must not be merely an expectable and culturally sanctioned response to a particular event" (APA, 2000, p. xxxi). Given the complexity and ambiguity involved in discerning between the two types of experiences, we provide some tools to guide practitioners in this task.

Given the current status of the field, we recommend using open-ended questions that illicit spiritual narratives, as opposed to strictly relying on formal measures that do not yet meet industry standards and were designed for researchers rather than clinicians (Richards, Bartz, & O'Grady, 2009). Additionally, we recommend less traditional, creative assessments that could induce evaluative information, such as encouraging client's to create a spiritual life map in which the client illustrates how specific life experiences contributed to pivotal transcendent experiences (Hodge, 2005). These types of activities can serve as an assessment and as an intervention, allowing individuals alternative forms of expression outside of paper-and-pencil formats or traditional talk therapy.

### Informal Assessment

When presented with a spiritually transcendent experience in the course of a psychotherapy, a psychotherapist may use the following questions to guide their differentiation efforts. It is important to note that decisions should not be made on the basis of an answer to any single item, but rather, clinicians should look for overall patterns in the data. In addition, clinicians should be careful not to fall into a dichotomous mind-set, viewing experiences as either transcendent *or* pathological. Berenbaum et al. (2000) have suggested that an overlap often occurs between psychopathology and anomalous experiences such as transcendence. This overlap may be the result of the dissociative quality of positive transcendent experiences. Transcendence requires dissociation from the ego to achieve a sense of unity. Pathological dissociative experiences often are accompanied by neuroticism and psychosomatic symptoms and have been found to trigger defensive reactions (Garfield, Gracz, & Moore, 2010). We recommend carefully investigating each question, one by one, and then stepping back to see whether a picture that emerges is more pathological than transcendent or more uplifting than disabling.

The questions are followed by some information concerning the rationale for their importance in distinguishing between transcendence and pathology. In Table 7.1, each of the questions are presented in a list form for easier application to clinical situations:

1. Is the experience clinically distressing to the client?
2. Does the experience impair their social or vocational functioning?
3. Does the experience increase the client's risk for death, pain, disability, or an important loss of freedom?
4. Is the experience a culturally accepted phenomenon given the client's circumstances (e.g., seeing spirits of deceased loved ones shortly after their passing in the Latino culture)?

These first four questions are derived from the DSM-IV-TR (APA, 2000) definitional criteria of mental illness. They provide a well-accepted starting point for differentiation.

The next four questions further clarify the clinical picture.

*Question (5)*

Have family, friends, or coworkers expressed concern about the client's experience? This question is particularly important when performing this type of differential task because individuals that are experiencing psychopathology in the guise of transcendence often do not experience it to be distressing, and they may lack the insight to see how such experiences are interfering with their social or vocational functioning. For example, patients suffering with psychosis may pride themselves on their special ability to see spirits and may mistake the

**Table 7.1** Assessment Questions for Differentiating Transcendence From Psychopathology

1. Is the experience clinically distressing to the client?
2. Does the experience impair their social or vocational functioning?
3. Does the experience increase the client's risk for death, pain, disability, or an important loss of freedom?
4. Is the experience a culturally accepted phenomenon given the client's circumstances?
5. Have family, friends, or coworkers expressed concern about the client's experience?
6. Does the content of the client's account emphasize illness and deviance themes?
7. Has this type of experience been reported by other individuals who do not suffer from mental illness?
8. If the experience can be classified by a DSM diagnosis, are the client's demographics consistent with the typical demographics for the condition in question?

social ridicule that they receive as adulation. For this reason, consulting with the client's loved ones can shed valuable light on the situation. Of course, when consulting with the client's family, one must be careful to adhere to ethical standards of confidentiality.

*Question (6)*

Does the content of the client's account emphasize illness and deviance themes? A content analysis of the subjective experience of various altered states of consciousness, such as schizophrenic, hallucinogenic, and mystical experiences, demonstrated that the accounts of individuals with schizophrenia emphasized illness and deviance themes, whereas the accounts of mystical experiences focused on religious and spiritual issues (Oxman, Rosenberg, Schnurr, Tucker, & Gala, 1988). This suggests that experiences that are laden with illness and deviance themes may be more likely to be pathological than transcendent in nature.

*Question (7)*

Has this type of experience been reported by other individuals who do not suffer from mental illness? Near-death experiences are a good example of one type of transcendence that has been reported by "psychologically healthy individuals who do not differ from non-experient comparison groups on measures of mental health" (Greyson, 2000, p. 321).

*Question (8)*

If the experience can be classified by a DSM-IV-TR (APA, 2000) diagnosis, are the client's demographics consistent with the typical demographics for the condition in question? For example, if a client is reporting experiences consistent with psychosis before adolescence, it calls into question the appropriateness of such a diagnosis because psychosis rarely occurs in children.

### Formal Assessment

For an assessment instrument to be clinically useful, it needs to meet criteria of reliability and validity, have sufficient normative data, and provide clear administrative and scoring instructions (Richards, Bartz, & O'Grady, 2009). It is also important that spiritual and religious measures of transcendence are nondenominational and culturally sensitive. Much work still is needed to elevate current measures of spirituality and religion to these standards. With that caveat in mind, a few measures could provide useful information for psychotherapists in their assessment of spiritually transcendent experiences in psychotherapy. These assessment instruments should be used as an addendum to informal assessment, and responses to questions on these instruments should be considered additional information to that which is obtained from the clinical interview. When employing measures designed primarily for research purposes, we recommend that psychotherapists consider analyzing individual question responses of the instruments, rather than overall scores because the insufficiencies mentioned previously.

One measure that could provide some clinically relevant information is the Index of Core Spiritual Experiences (INSPIRIT; Kass, Friendman, Leserman, Zuttermeister, & Benson, 1991). It is a seven-item reliable and valid measure of one's personal conviction of God's existence and the perception of a deep connection to God's presence within. It is designed specifically to measure individuals' religious experiences, sense of closeness to God, and view of themselves as religious or spiritual. INSPIRIT was created with the intention of investigating spiritual experiences and mental health correlates. INSPIRIT is suitable for use with secular, religious, and spiritual clients. It has reported high (.90) internal consistency reliabilities.

Another pertinent and promising clinical instrument for assessing spiritual transcendence is the Assessment of Spirituality and Religious Sentiments (ASPIRES; Piedmont, 2004, 2005). ASPIRES is a nondenominational instrument measuring two dimensions: Religious Sentiments and Spiritual Transcendence. This instrument was developed by a team of theological experts from both Eastern and Western faith traditions and has proven predictive value. ASPIRES is a useful assessment instrument for clients in health care settings as well as being a psychometrically robust outcome measure across cultures. It is one of the few spiritual or religious assessment instruments that provides a technical manual with administrative and interpretive guides. This scale is relevant to both Western and Eastern faith traditions. The Spiritual Transcendence subscales include Universality, Prayer, Fulfillment, and Connectedness. The ASPIRES manual also comes with a short (13-item) form.

Hood's (1974) research measure, the Religious Experience Episodes Measure (REEM) is based on a number of open-ended studies of spiritually transcendent experiences (including the 1979 Hardy study). Hood (1975) also constructed the Mysticism Scale (M Scale): The Influence of Stace. Both of these measures demonstrate reasonably sound psychometric properties, but they are limited in their usefulness to clinicians as they are research measures (Hood et al., 1996). Likewise, Underwoods's Daily Spiritual Experiences Scale (DSES) was designed to measure everyday spiritual experiences not restricted by a particular religious tradition (Underwood & Teresi, 2002). The shorter six-item version of this measure has high internal consistency (.90), includes questions that are pertinent to the assessment of spiritual transcendence, and is brief enough to administer to clients in session. The REEM, M Scale, and DSES tools have not been validated for clinical use; however, psychotherapists and other clinicians could consider utilizing these measures either formally or informally to supplement the informal interview as long as they are conservative in the clinical conclusions they draw from such instruments.

Psychotherapists might also consider administering a Minnesota Multiphasic Personality Inventory (MMPI-2) or other measures of pathology in addition to measures of spirituality. Results from a measure of this nature could augment information obtained informally through the questions listed in Table 7.1, assisting psychotherapists as they seek to determine the mental health implications of reported spiritually transcendent experiences. For instance, an MMPI-2 profile that indicates problems with reality testing and psychotic traits may raise doubts about the client's perceptions of their reported transcendent experiences. On the other hand, if the profile is indicative of good reality testing and lacks indications of distorted perceptions, the client's reported transcendent experience may have more therapeutic utility.

## CLINICAL STRATEGIES

In our review of the research, we noted that some studies of spiritually transcendent experiences assert that the "unbidden" nature of these experiences make it difficult to prepare to receive such experiences. Other researchers found that people could engage in preparatory practices to cultivate spiritual transcendence in their lives. Likewise, the review of the literature provides reason to believe that psychotherapists can thoughtfully and creatively foster a therapeutic atmosphere that invites transcendent dimensions into psychotherapy and that respects the mystical domain of some religiously and spiritually oriented clients (Goldstein, 2007). Additionally, psychotherapists can provide a climate in which clients feel safe to explore the meaning and implications of spiritually transcendent experiences when they do occur.

In this spirit, we present a few suggestions for clinical strategies that have been reported to lead to a "way of being" that is most conducive to achieving spiritually transcendent states. The following strategies also provide interventions that may help clients develop a state of awareness about the transcendent aspects of their lives and to reflect on spiritually transcendent experience that they have had. As is appropriate for all interventions, the client's well-being must supersede the psychotherapist's personal interests in an intervention, and psychotherapists need to work within the client's value structure and goals (Richards & Bergin, 2005). The following interventions are intended for use only with spiritually oriented clients who are interested in experiencing and reflecting on spiritual transcendence within their religious and spiritual framework. We caution psychotherapists and other helping professionals to be clear about their own clinical competence and to be sensitive to the multicultural aspects of their client before assuming a particular approach for treatment (Richards & O'Grady, 2004). Psychotherapists may wish to collaborate with spiritual leaders or guides to help facilitate and respond to spiritual transcendence, whereas the psychotherapist focuses on the psychological aspects of the reported experiences.

### Spiritual Space

Many helping professionals believe that psychotherapists can cultivate spiritual experiences in psychotherapy by creating room for spiritual transcendence in the clinical office. This is most likely to occur when the psychotherapist is open to mystical influences, develops sensitivity to intuitive impressions, and allows for silence and reflection in psychotherapy (O'Grady & Richards, 2010; Richards & O'Grady, 2007). This suggestion is consistent with West's (2000) recommendation that psychotherapists create a *spiritual space* for psychotherapy. West (2000) suggested several things that can help psychotherapists do this, including (1) acknowledging that treatment can be a spiritual space, (2) tolerating silence so that the spiritual space can unfold, (3) "listening" in a deep and holistic manner to spiritual impressions, (4) speaking authentically by appropriately sharing feelings of the heart, and (5) accepting the spiritual experiences that occur. Communicating empathy, respect, and connectedness with the client also encourages spiritual space in psychotherapy. When appropriate, psychotherapists could follow a period of silence with the question "What did you experience in the silence?" Questions of this nature can foster sensitivity to internal and spiritual processing.

The nature of the therapy office environment can contribute to or detract from feelings of safety for the client. Décor should reflect warmth and denominational neutrality. Overall, the office space environment should welcome all forms of spiritual and religious expression (O'Grady & Richards, 2009; Richards & O'Grady, 2004).

### Spiritual Self-Reflection Exercises

Spiritual transcendence typically is experienced inwardly, and therefore interventions that help clients tune into their internal world could enhance their sensitivity to such experiences. Several practices and interventions encourage such inward awareness, including mindfulness practices. Mindfulness allows clients to move to a state of awareness of their inner thoughts and feelings without judging them or trying to change them (Segal & Williams, 2002). Psychotherapists might begin by using traditional mindfulness exercises such as breathing and relaxation exercises to help clients slow down and move inward during sessions (Humphrey, 2009). As clients become practiced at calming down and tuning into their internal functioning, they often are able to connect more easily to their spirituality in the moment (Walsh, 1999). Yumus Emre, an Islamic sage, is quoted as saying, "When you seek God, seek Him in your heart" (Walsh, 1999, p. 1). As such, psychotherapists could encourage clients, when they are in a quiet state of awareness, to place their hand on their heart and ask themselves what their heart feels, or what their heart is communicating to them (Richards, Hardman, & Berrett, 2007; Richards & O'Grady, 2007). Psychotherapists and other helping professionals might consider guided imagery in which the psychotherapist moves the client into a state of relaxation and then guides them to a place of safety and peace. The psychotherapist then asks the client to become aware of any spiritual symbols or insights that emerge in their safe place. It is essential that guided imagery themes are suitable to the culture, context, spirituality, religious orientation, background, and interests of the client.

The first author used a similar intervention with a client who was struggling with issues of childhood abandonment. The client frequently engaged in regrettable behaviors in an effort to escape her fear of being alone. This particular client had recently read *The Chronicles of Narnia* series (Lewis, 1950–1956/2001) and had expressed her enthusiasm about the books. The psychotherapist integrated the client's interest, clinical themes, and spirituality into a guided imagery intervention. After her client reached a state of relaxation, she guided the client to walk through a door that opened up into a snowy world void of additional stimuli. The psychotherapist asked her to imagine a warm, fur coat wrapping itself around her. The psychotherapist encouraged her to sit in the silence of the moment. Next, she asked her to become aware of anything that emerged in her surroundings. Finally, she told her client that it was time to walk back through the door and that she could bring anything back from her visit that she would like. The client shared with the psychotherapist that she initially felt deep loneliness, followed by warmth and peace, and then she saw a box sitting in the snow. She opened the box and inside was a drawing of a heart that generated feelings of safety. The client said that she brought the heart back with her and expressed her belief that the heart symbolized her need to reach out in love to others.

### Spiritual Solo Time

Another intervention that may help clients to achieve spiritually transcendent experiences that promote mental health is a technique known as spiritual solo time. This involves encouraging clients to set aside some time each day for contemplation, prayer, and journaling about their feelings and spiritual impressions. Hardman, Berrett, and Richards (2003) illustrated how this intervention helped a patient named Jan overcome anorexia nervosa and major depression. Jan's eating disorder and depression were fueled by feelings of irrational guilt and a sense of never being good enough. Additionally, "Jan superficially or 'theoretically' believed that God loved her and was concerned about her problems, but in her heart she felt that God viewed her in a disapproving, condemning manner" (Hardman et al., 2003, p. 67). Her therapists encouraged her to engage in daily spiritual solo time, which played a powerful role in her healing. They explained, "On several occasions as she contemplated and prayed, Jan received personal witnesses that God loved her and that it was okay for her to speak the truth about the sexual abuse that she had experienced" (Hardman et al., 2003, pp. 67–68). In this case, spiritual solo time literally helped Jan to have a relational corrective experience with God. The authors explained that once Jan felt supported by God, she gained the courage to take significant risks that were needed for her healing. Although simple, spiritual solo time can be a powerful way to help patients work through their issues with deity and to invite spiritual transcendence. Furthermore, research evidence supports the idea that contemplative prayer relates strongly with mystical awareness (Hood et al., 1996).

### Sacred Moment Time

Goldstein (2007) conducted a study in which he used an intervention that he referred to as a "sacred moments" exercise. Clients are encouraged to choose a personal object that represents something special or sacred to them. They are instructed to sanctify the object to reimbue the object with what the client considers to be special, holy, or cherished. The object can be tangible or intangible (e.g., a special memory or a mantra). Then, for 3 weeks or more, clients are encouraged to spend 5 minutes daily focusing on the object in a relaxed state. Finally, clients are encouraged to journal about their experience, recording whether they would deem their experience a sacred experience, and their description of aspects of the experience that were significant to them.

In his study, Goldstein (2007) randomly assigned 73 participants to one of two groups: (1) a 3-week intervention group in which participants were instructed in cultivating sacred moments as described above, or (2) a 3-week control group in which participants were instructed in writing about daily activities. Of those assigned to the sacred moments intervention group, 89% reported feeling that the spiritual intervention was conducive to experiencing sacred moments. These experiences are described as feelings of connection with and support from the transcendent (e.g., God, Higher Power, and all of life), and connection with others. Participants described these experiences as engendering purpose, gratefulness, awe, compassion, mercy, and a deep sense of inner peace. They also characterized these experiences as precious, dear, blessed, cherished, and holy.

The emotional and spiritual achievements expressed by participants in this exercise have subsequent mental health and existential benefits (Plante & Sherman, 2001). For instance, people who feel gratitude and a sense of awe tend to have greater life satisfaction, an increased likelihood for emotional well-being, and improved social relations (McCullough & Emmons, 2003; McCullough, Kimeldorf, & Cohen, 2008; Wood, Maltby, Stewart, Linley, & Joseph, 2008). Sacred moments have also been positively linked to well-being constructs and negatively to stress (Underwood & Teresi, 2002). Goldstein (2007) suggested that an important impetus for the success of this exercise may be that it allows for an inclusive definition of spirituality. He also noted that focusing on experiencing spiritual transcendence may not only increase the occurrence of such experiences but also increase the individual's awareness of transcendent experiences that occur regularly.

### Spiritual Practice Interventions

A number of practices in both Western and Eastern religious traditions help foster spiritually transcendent experiences in ways that produce mental health benefits (Keller, 2000). For instance, many religious traditions encourage adherents to ponder or meditate regularly. Meditation practices vary widely between religious and spiritual traditions, but most involve some form of separation from external stimuli, relaxation, freeing of the mind, letting go, and surrender (Richards & Bergin, 2005). Spiritual transcendence achieved through meditative practices can reduce negative stress reactions and encourage states of well-being (Yang, Su, & Huang, 2009).

Finally, many people consider prayer to be the predominant way to receive spiritual guidance and to develop spirituality in their lives (O'Grady & Richards, 2010). Although we hesitate to suggest praying in session with clients, we have found it useful to discuss client's prayer life when it seems pertinent and if the client is interested in doing so (Miller & Thoresen, 2003). Clients can be circumvented from experiencing meaningful prayer and spiritual guidance for a variety of reasons, including distorted God images, poor habits, mental illness and other mental health stressors, and unrealistic or unhealthy expectations about prayer. Exploring clients' experiences with seeking and receiving spiritual guidance can provide valuable insight into a variety of areas of functioning for the client. After clients have identified that they do pray, psychotherapists might consider asking their clients such questions as "Would you like to tell me about your prayer life?" or "In what way is praying similar/different than your experiences with other types of communication?" It is important that psychotherapists refrain from pressuring clients to participate in prayer not only because it is unethical to do so but also because it may exacerbate dysfunctional beliefs that already exist about prayer (e.g., "I am a failure because I can't experience God during prayer," or "I cannot move forward with my life until God gives me clear direction about what I should do").

### Collaboration With Clergy

Many psychotherapists or other mental health professionals do not feel adequately trained to address spiritual and religious issues in psychotherapy, especially spiritually transcendent experiences (Richards & Bergin, 2005). Even those who have obtained adequate training may determine that some client concerns will be best addressed through collaborative efforts with the client's faith community. Collaboration can mean referring clients to their religious leaders to address specific aspects of their spirituality, but it also may include working in tandem with clients' religious leaders. For instance, after consulting with the client, the psychotherapist can obtain written consent from the client to consult with the client's religious leader either over the phone or in person. The consultation would include sharing concerns and ideas specific to the client and her or his religious or spiritual concern. Collaboration also could include inviting clergy to attend a psychotherapy session with the client and psychotherapist. In the session, client, clergy, and psychotherapist work together to better understand the client's transcendent experience and possible mental and spiritual health implications. It is imperative that psychotherapists treat clergy respectfully to promote a positive working relationship with the religious leader and the religious community, and also to show support for this important member of the client's life (Edwards, McMinn, & Dominguez, 1999; Richards & Bergin2005).

### Psychotherapist Spiritual Care

Spiritual transcendence can provide and maintain a sense of meaning for people. People who describe their lives, including their careers, as meaningful are much less likely to suffer from professional and personal burnout (Hansen, 2001; O'Grady, 2011). Psychotherapists have found a variety of ways to experience the renewal that comes from spiritual transcendence, such as taking part in retreats or pilgrimages, praying, reading sacred texts, meditating, spending time in nature, attending worship services, and being receptive to the luminous (O'Grady & Richards, 2010; McBride, 1998; Wiggins, 2009). We encourage psychotherapist to explore ways in which their own sense of spirituality, whatever that may be, can help them transcend the ordinary and open up windows of insight into their work with clients. Psychotherapists often encourage their clients to create space for quiet and reflection: we believe psychotherapists and other helping professionals likewise should engage in such practices.

## CASE STUDY

### Client History and Background

Jack, a 28-year-old male from a religiously devout Christian background, sought out psychotherapy to find relief from a variety of intrusive and disturbing thoughts that were making it difficult for him to concentrate and work toward his life goals. These thoughts often were religious in nature and provoked intense feelings of guilt and fear of condemnation. Upon taking a thorough history, Jack's therapist came to the conclusion that he was struggling with obsessive-compulsive disorder. She encouraged him to seek psychiatric care and proceeded to provide him with psychotherapy.

In psychotherapy, Jack explained that sometimes when sexual thoughts would come into his mind, he would start to obsessively worry that he was morally flawed and that in the future he might commit some type of sexual sin. In these moments, Jack would experience a compulsive impulse to prove his righteousness and discipline by engaging in rituals that were very time-consuming and physically exhausting. The therapist dedicated time to reassuring Jack that it was normal to have sexual thoughts and feelings and that he was not morally flawed, thus reducing the power of the "forbiddenness" of such thoughts and feelings. She also encouraged him to resist the urges to prove his righteousness by engaging in rituals, as she viewed them as unnecessary.

### Relevant Treatment Processes

Several months into his treatment, Jack watched a movie about schizophrenia, which reminded him of an anomalous experience that he had when he was a child. For many years he had interpreted the experience to be spiritual in nature; however, this movie caused him to worry that the experience might be an indication that he either was schizophrenic or at risk for developing psychosis. Because his psychotherapist had a reputation for being open to discussing spiritual issues and Jack knew that she was accepting, he felt that it would be safe to discuss the details of his experience with her. In his next session, he decided to share the experience to get her professional opinion. He explained that when he was about 10 years old, he was struggling with several philosophical questions, and among them the question of whether or not God existed. During this era of his life, he was attending church regularly with his parents. He related that one day after attending a Sunday service with his family, he walked outside before the rest of the congregation was dismissed. Not thinking about anything in particular and finding himself all alone in the church parking lot, he suddenly heard a serene male voice above him in the air say, "It is true." He turned around in the direction of the voice to see who was talking to him but saw no one. Once again the voice repeated, "It is true." At this point, he started to wonder whether he was hearing the voice of God because it was coming, as it seemed, out of thin air and because it had an ultracrisp tonal quality that he had never before experienced or imagined. He was struck by how young the voice sounded, however, as he had always imagined that God was an old man with a white beard. After thinking this, he heard the voice one more time say, "It is true." Upon realizing that he may actually have heard the voice of God, he suddenly burst into tears. He was surprised by his tears. When his family met up with him, he tried to hide the fact that he had been crying. He explained that he felt a strong reluctance to share this experience with anyone, because he did not feel like he deserved to hear the voice of God and feared that others would be critical of him for thinking that he had.

### Assessment and Intervention

In evaluating Jack's experience, the therapist compared the data that Jack had provided with relevant diagnostic information contained in the DSM-IV-TR (APA, 2000). She took into consideration that the experience occurred at age 10. She was aware that the onset of schizophrenia usually occurs between late teens and the mid-30s (APA, 2000, p. 307). She also was aware that the onset of childhood schizophrenia usually has a severe and disabling impact on the individual's development. Jack had experienced a relatively normal development and, 18 years after the event, was successfully finishing a graduate program with no evidence of disorganized thinking. She believed that if this incident had been the onset of psychotic symptoms, it would have been likely that he would have experienced other abnormal developmental patterns and that he likely would not have been able to excel in his chosen field of study.

Jack's psychotherapist also took into consideration his cultural background. She knew that Jack's experience was consistent with his religious teachings. She also understood that the DSM-IV-TR stipulates, "In some cultures, visual or auditory hallucinations with a religious content may be a normal part of religious experience (e.g., seeing the Virgin Mary or hearing God's voice)" (APA, 2000, p. 306). In addition, the client lacked several of the classic symptoms of schizophrenia. For example, he never reported any ideas of reference, thought projection, thought insertion, bizarre delusions, disorganized speech, or disorganized behavior. Likewise, he never experienced symptoms of mania, such as loose associations, flight of ideas, distractibility, poor judgment, excessive involvement in pleasurable but dangerous activities, or severe depression, which could contribute to hallucinations. She also recognized that schizophrenia usually has a prodromal period of deterioration, and this patient was doing very well with exception to his struggle with obsessive-compulsive disorder (OCD).

On the basis of this data, Jack's psychotherapist determined that this client's experience was not psychotic but rather transcendent in nature. Therefore, she endeavored to help the client understand this experience in the context of his own life, culture, values, experiences, and beliefs. Using the client's own belief system, she asked whether he thought it could be possible that God gave him this experience because God understood that the client had a tendency to obsessively question things and wanted him to have a very strong manifestation of God's existence and love to compensate for his neurological tendency to doubt. Although he had never considered this possibility, it made sense to him and helped him to understand the experience in a way that promoted his emotional well-being and improved his relationship with God.

### Outcomes

Because of his psychotherapist's reassurance, Jack ceased to worry that he was going to develop schizophrenia. In addition, he started to develop a more merciful and caring perception of God, which helped to ameliorate his feelings of guilt and fears of condemnation. Developing a more compassionate view of God played an instrumental role in reducing the frequency and intensity of Jack's obsessive concerns. Several years following this disclosure, the patient continued free of schizophrenic symptoms and his obsessive-compulsive tendencies had greatly reduced.

### Commentary

Having a belief in the possibility of transcendent experiences enabled Jack's psychotherapist to respond to his disclosure in a way that both normalized the experience and helped the client to take advantage of the therapeutic potential inherent within it. Had the therapist been alarmed or even surprised by Jack's experience, she may not have been able to respond as effectively. Pathologizing his experience may have exacerbated his presenting symptoms, and thus, his spirituality would have proven a hindrance rather than a contributor to his emotional well-being and growth. This example demonstrates the importance of possessing an appreciation of the clients' cultural background, familiarity with the DSM-IV-TR (APA, 2000), and openness to the possibility of spiritually transcendent experiences when working with such issues in psychotherapy.

## CONCLUSION

Spiritual transcendence indeed may represent the truest essence and highest achievement of the human experience and very well could be a basic human trait. These claims are lofty and difficult, if not impossible, to verify. However, we can confidently assert that spiritual transcendence provides meaning and can produce life-changing outcomes for many individuals. As such, this area of the psychology of religion is likely to manifest in therapy and can be tapped into as a resource to promote mental health and spiritual fulfillment. Responding appropriately to spiritual transcendent themes that emerge in therapy is an essential attribute of therapeutic competence. We agree with Hood, Spilka, Hunsberger, and Gorsuch (1996): "Religious traditions cannot be adequately understood without the assumption that transcendent objects of experience are believed to be real by those who experience them. It is also possible that not only are they believed to be real, but also that they are in fact real" (p. 227).

The mere fact that some individuals occasionally may have beneficial spiritually transcendent experiences makes it critical that clinicians acquire an understanding of transcendence so that they effectively can navigate this important and oftentimes ambiguous territory of their clients' lives. For example, a client who reports hearing voices from God may be experiencing psychotic symptoms or relating a sacred, transformative experience with a higher power. If clinicians assume only one or the other of these possibilities, treatment may be inappropriate and avenues for growth ignored. We assert that as psychotherapists become more open to the role of spiritually transcendent experiences in both their lives and the lives of their clients, their capacity to help will be greatly improved. Furthermore, when clients experience their psychotherapist's genuine interest in their reports of transcendence, the therapeutic relationship is likely to be enhanced (O'Grady & Richards, 2009; Wiggins, 2009).

## CHAPTER SUMMARY

- Spiritually transcendent experiences have been characterized as (a) ineffable, (b) noetic, (c) transient, (d) unmediated, (e) unexpected, (f) vivid, (g), benevolent, (h) peaceful, (i) edifying, and (j) permanent in their impact.
- Research findings suggest that individuals who encounter spiritually transcendent experiences report positive mental health outcomes, life transition, and spiritual growth.
- Spiritually transcendent experiences can be a powerful source of meaning, guidance, and support to individuals.
- To fully understand individuals, it may be important to understand the role that spiritually transcendent experiences play in their lives.
- Assessment approaches for helping clients distinguish between psychologically beneficial reports of spiritually transcendent experiences and pathological manifestations should be conducted from a cultural framework.
- Psychotherapists should support clients in making sense of transcendent experiences in a way that is psychologically beneficial, and help clients to take advantage of the therapeutic potential inherent within such experiences.
- At times, it could be clinically indicated to encourage a client to consider engaging in spiritual practices from the client's spiritual and religious orientation that promote spiritual transcendence.
- In some cases, it may be useful to consult with clergy or to encourage clients to discuss their spiritually transcendent experiences with clergy.
- Psychotherapists are encouraged to be aware of the role of spiritual transcendence in their own lives, including ways in which spiritual transcendence may enhance their effectiveness as clinicians.

## CLINICAL APPLICATION QUESTIONS

1. How open am I to the possibility that clients may experience authentic transcendent experiences?
2. How open am I to personally experiencing transcendent experiences?
3. How comfortable do I feel helping clients to achieve transcendent experiences?
4. What questions should I ask myself if a client reports that he or she occasionally receives visits from spirits?
5. What are some differential criteria for schizophrenic experience as opposed to spiritual transcendent experience?
6. How can I open myself up to receiving spiritual guidance to improve the quality of psychotherapy?
7. What is at the root of any resistance I may experience in discussing clients' spiritually transcendent experiences?

## SUGGESTED READINGS AND RESOURCES

### Books

Cardeña, E., Lynn S. J. & Krippner S. (Eds.). (2000). *Varieties of anomalous experience: Examining the scientific evidence.* Washington, DC: American Psychological Association.

Frank, J. D., & Frank, J. B. (1991). *Persuasion and healing: A comparative study of psychotherapy* (3rd ed.). Baltimore, MD: Johns Hopkins University Press.

Moodly, R. & West, W. (2005). *Integrating traditional healing practices into counseling and psychotherapy.* Thousand Oaks, CA: Sage.

Tart, C. T. (2009). *The end of materialism: How evidence of the paranormal is bringing science and spirit together.* Oakland, CA: New Harbinger.

### Websites

Allister Hardy Trust. http://www.tsd.ac.uk/en/lrc/librariesandcentres/alisterhardyreligious experienceresearchcentre/alisterhardytrust/

## REFERENCES

American Psychiatric Association. (2000). *Diagnostic and statistical manual of mental disorders* (4th ed., text rev.). Washington, DC: Author.

Bell, R. (1985). *Holy anorexia.* Chicago, IL: University of Chicago Press.

Berenbaum, H., Kerns, J. & Raghavan, C. (2000). Anomalous experiences, peculiarity and psychopathology. In E. Cardeña, S. J. Lynn, & S. Krippner (Eds.), *Varieties of anomalous experience: Examining the scientific evidence* (pp. 25–46). Washington, D.C.: American Psychological Association.

Brown, S., & Miller, W. R. (2005). Transformational change. In W. R. Miller and H. D. Delaney (Eds.) *Judeo-Christian perspectives on psychology: Human nature, motivation, and change* (pp.167–183). Washington, DC: American Psychological Association.

Dein, S., & Littlewood, R. (2007). The voice of God. *Anthropology and Medicine, 14,* 213–228.

Delaney, H. B., & DeClemente, C. C. (2005). Implication of Judeo-Christian vies of human nature, motivation, and change for the sciences and practices of psychology. In W. R. Miller & H. D. Delaney (Eds.), *Judeo-Christian perspectives on psychology* (pp. 31–54). Washington, DC: American Psychological Association.

Edwards, L, Lim, B. R. K. B., McMinn, M. R., & Dominguez, A. W. (1999). Examples of collaboration between psychologists and clergy. *Professional Psychology: Research and Practice, 30,* 547–551.

Frank, J. D., & Frank, J. B. (1991). *Persuasion and healing: A comparative study of psychotherapy* (3rd ed.). Baltimore, MD: Johns Hopkins University Press.

Gallup, CNN, & *USA Today.* (2003, January 14). [Poll]. New York, NY: Gallup Organization.

Garfield, A. M., Gracz, M. D., & Moore, C. F. (2010, March 26). *Mysticism, mental health, and religiosity.* Poster presented for APA Division 36 Mid-Winter Conference in Columbia, Maryland.

Gehlert, N. C., & Dy-Liacco, G. S. (2010, April 26). *Validity of spiritual transcendence as a personality factor and its implications on subjective well-being.* Paper presented at "Emerging Scholars: A Celebration of Graduate Research," a conference presented by Loyola University Maryland, Baltimore.

Goldstein, E. D. (2007). Sacred moments: Implications on well-being and stress. *Journal of Clinical Psychology, 63(10),* 1001–1019.

Greyson, B. (2000). Near-death experiences. In E. Cardeña, S. J. Lynn, & S. Krippner (Eds.), *Varieties of anomalous experience: Examining the scientific evidence* (pp. 315–352). Washington, DC: American Psychological Association.
Hansen, L. S. (2001). *Integrative life planning: Critical tasks for career development and changing life patterns.* New York, NY: Jossey-Bass.
Hardman, R. K., Berrett, M. E., & Richards, P. S. (2003). A theistic inpatient treatment approach for eating disorder patients: A case report. In P. S. Richards and A. E. Bergin (Eds.), *Casebook for a spiritual strategy in counseling and psychotherapy* (pp. 55–73). Washington, DC: American Psychological Association.
Hardy, A. (1979). *The spiritual nature of man.* New York, NY: Oxford Press.
Hickson, J., Housley, W., & Wages, D. (2000). Counselors' perceptions of spirituality in the therapeutic process. *Counseling and Values, 45*(1), 58–59.
Hodge, D. R. (2005). Spiritual life maps: A client-centered pictorial instrument for spiritual assessment, planning, and intervention. *Social Work, 50,* 77–87.
Hood, R. W., Jr. (1974). Psychological strength and the report of intense religious experience. *Journal for the Scientific Study of Religion, 13,* 192–196.
Hood, R. W., Jr. (1975). The construction and preliminary validation of a measure of reported mystical experience. *Journal for the Scientific Study of Religion, 12,* 29–41.
Hood, R. W., Spilka, B., Hunsberger, B., & Gorsuch, R. (1996). *The psychology of religion: An empirical approach* (2nd ed.). New York, NY: Guilford Press.
Humphrey, K. M. (2009). *Counseling strategies for loss and grief.* Alexandria, VA: American Counseling Association.
Ingerman, S. (2004). *Shamanic journeying: A beginner's guide.* Boulder, CO: Sounds True.
Ironson, G., Kremer, H., & Ironson, D. S. (2006). Spirituality, spiritual experiences, and spiritual transformations in the face of HIV. In J. D. Koss-Chioino. & P. Hefner (Eds.), *Spiritual transformation and healing: Anthropological, theological, neuroscientific, and clinical perspectives* (pp. 241–260). Lanham, MD: AltaMira Press.
James, W. (1902/1997). *Varieties of religious experience.* New York, NY: Simon & Schuster.
Kass, J. D., Friedman, R., Leserman, J., Zuttermeister, P. C., & Benson H. (1991). Health outcomes and a new index of spiritual experience. *Journal of the Scientific Study of Religion, 30,* 203–211.
Keller, R. R. (2000). Religious diversity in North America. In P. S. Richards & A. E. Bergin (Eds.), *Handbook of psychotherapy and religious diversity* (pp. 27–56). Washington, DC: American Psychological Association.
Kluft, R. P. (1996). Dissociative identity disorder. In L. K. Michelson & W. J. Ray (Eds.), *Handbook of dissociation: Theoretical, empirical, and clinical perspectives* (pp. 337–366). New York, NY: Plenum Press.
Koss-Chioino, J. D. & Hefner, P. (Eds.). (2006). *Spiritual transformation and healing: Anthropological, theological, neuroscientific, and clinical perspectives.* Lanham, MD: AltaMira Press.
Koenig, H. G., McCullough, M. E., & Larson, D. B. (2001). *Handbook of religion and health.* New York, NY: Oxford University Press.
Kroll, J., Bachrach, B., & Carey, K. (2002). A reappraisal of medieval mysticism and hysteria. *Mental Health, Religion and Culture, 5,* 83–98.
Lewis, C. S. (2001). *The chronicles of Narnia.* New York, NY: HarperCollins. (Original works published 1950–1956)
Maslow, A. H. (1971). *The farther reaches of human nature.* New York, NY: Viking.
McBride, J. L. (1998). *Spiritual crisis: Surviving trauma to the soul.* New York, NY: Haworth Pastoral Press.

McCullough, M. E., & Emmons, R. A. (2003). Counting blessing versus burdens: An experimental investigation of gratitude and subjective well-being in daily life. *Journal of Personality and Social Psychology, 84*(2), 377–389.

McCullough, M. E., Kimeldorf, M. B., & Cohen, A. D. (2008). An adaptation for altruism? The social causes, social effects, and social evolution of gratitude. *Association for Psychological Science, 17*(4), 281–285.

*Merriam-Webster's collegiate dictionary* (10th ed.). (1993). Springfield-MA: Merriam-Webster. Retrieved from http://www.merriam-webster.com/dictionary/transcendent

Miller, W. R., & C'de Baca, J. (2001). *Quantum change: When epiphanies and sudden insights transform ordinary lives.* New York, NY: Guilford Press.

Miller, W. R., & Thoresen, C. E. (2003). Spirituality, religion, and health: an emerging research field. *American Psychologist, 58,* 24–35.

Moodly, R., & West, W. (2005). *Integrating traditional healing practices into counseling and psychotherapy.* Thousand Oaks, CA: Sage.

O'Grady, K. A. (2011). The role of inspiration in organizational life. *Journal of Management, Spirituality & Religion, 8*(3), 257–272.

O'Grady, K. A., & Richards, P. S. (2007). God image and theistic psychotherapy. *Journal of Spirituality and Mental Health, 9,* 183–209.

O'Grady, K. A., & Richards, P. S. (2009). Case study showing inclusion of spirituality in the therapeutic process. In J. D. Aten & M. M. Leach (Eds.), *Spirituality and the therapeutic process: A comprehensive resource from intake to termination* (pp. 241–265). Washington, DC: American Psychological Association.

O'Grady, K.A., & Richards, P. S. (2010). The role of inspiration in the helping professions. *Psychology of Religion and Spirituality, 2,* 57–66.

Oxman, T. E., Rosenberg, S. D., Schnurr, P. P., Tucker, G. J., & Gala, G. (1988). The language of altered states. *Journal of Nervous Mental Disease, 176*(7), 401–408.

Pargament, K. I., Smith, B. W, Koenig, H. G., & Perez, L. (1998). Patterns of positive and negative religious coping with major life stressors. *Journal for the Scientific Study of Religion, 37*(4), 710–724.

Piedmont, R. L. (2004). *Assessment of spirituality and religious sentiments, technical manual.* Baltimore, MD: Author.

Piedmont, R. L. (2005). The role of personality in understanding religious and spiritual constructs. In R. F. Paloutzian & C. L. Park (Eds.), *The handbook of the psychology of religion* (pp. 253–273). New York, NY: Guilford Press.

Plante, T. B., & Sherman, A. C. (Eds.). (2001). *Faith and health: Psychological perspectives.* New York, NY: Guilford Press.

Rankin, M. (2008). *An introduction to religious and spiritual experience.* New York, NY: Continuum.

Richards, P. S., Bartz, J. D., & O'Grady, K. A. (2009). Assessing religion and spirituality in counseling: Some reflections and recommendations. *Counseling and* Values, *54,* 65–79.

Richards, P. S., & Bergin, A. E. (Eds.). (2000). *Handbook of psychotherapy and religious diversity.* Washington, DC: American Psychological Association.

Richards, P. S., & Bergin, A. E. (Eds.). (2003). *Casebook for a spiritual strategy in counseling and psychotherapy.* Washington, DC: American Psychological Association.

Richards, P. S., & Bergin, A. E. (2005). *A spiritual strategy for counseling and psychotherapy* (2nd ed.). Washington DC: American Psychological Association.

Richards, P. S., Hardman, R. K., & Berrett, M. E. (2007). *Spiritual approaches in the treatment of women with eating disorders.* Washington DC: American Psychological Association.

Richards, P. S., & O'Grady K. A. (2004). Treating the religiously committed client. In G.P. Koocher, J. C. Norcross, & S. S. Hill (Eds.), *Psychologist's desk reference* (2nd ed., pp. 338–341). New York, NY: Oxford Press.

Richards, P. S., & O'Grady, K. A. (2007). Theistic counselling and psychotherapy: Conceptual framework and application to counselling practice. *Counselling and Spirituality, 26*(2), 79–102.

Richards, P. S., & Potts, R. W. (1995). Using spiritual interventions in psychotherapy: Practices, successes, failures, and ethical concerns of Mormon psychotherapists. *Professional Psychology: Research and Practice, 26*, 163–170.

Segal, Z. V., & Williams, M.G. (2002). *Mindfulness-based cognitive therapy for depression: A new approach to preventing relapse*. New York, NY: Guilford Press.

Seidlitz, L., Abernethy, A. D., Duberstein, P. R., Eveinger, J. S., Chang, & Lewis, B. L. (2002). Development of the spiritual transcendence index. *Journal for the Scientific Study of Religion, 41*, 439–453.

Shafranske, E. P. (2000). Religious involvement and professional practices of psychiatrists and other mental health professionals. *Psychiatric Annals, 30*, 525–532.

Underwood, L., & Teresi, J. (2002). The daily experience scale: Development, theoretical description, reliability, exploratory factor analysis, preliminary construct validity using health related data. *Annals of Behavioral Medicine, 24*, 22–33.

Walsh, F. (Ed.) (1999). *Spiritual resources in family therapy*. New York, NY: Guilford Press.

West, W. (2000). *Psychotherapy and spirituality: Crossing the line between therapy and religion*. Thousand Oaks, CA: Sage.

Wicks, R. J. (2008). *The resilient clinician*. New York, NY: Oxford University Press.

Wiggins, M. I. (2009). Therapist self-awareness of spirituality. . In J. D. Aten & M. M. Leach (Eds.), *Spirituality and the therapeutic process: A comprehensive resource from intake to termination* (pp. 53–74). Washington, DC: American Psychological Association.

Wood, A. M., Maltby, J., Stewart, N., Linley, P. A., & Joseph, S. (2008). A social-cognitive model of trait and state levels of gratitude. *Emotion, 8*, 281–290.

Yalom, I. (1980). *Existential psychotherapy*. Basic Books: New York.

Yang, K., Su, W., & Huang, C. (2009). The effect of meditation on physical and mental health in junior college students: A quasi experimental study. *Journal of Nursing Research, 17*, 261–269.

Young, J. S., Dowdle, S., & Flowers, L. (2009). How spirituality can affect the therapeutic alliance. In J. D. Aten & M. M. Leach (Eds.), *Spirituality and the therapeutic process: A comprehensive resource from intake to termination* (pp. 167–191). Washington, DC: American Psychological Association.

# 8

# *Religious and Spiritual Beliefs in Psychotherapy*

## A Meaning Perspective

JEANNE M. SLATTERY AND CRYSTAL L. PARK

This chapter uses a meaning framework to describe how various types of religious and spiritual beliefs can affect one's general state of mental health and one's responses to stressful experiences, such as change, loss, or trauma. In a variety of ways, religious and spiritual beliefs are implicated in creating, exacerbating, or easing human difficulties. These beliefs may be the focus of psychotherapeutic work and the key to improved functioning and well-being. We begin with a review of the empirical literature on the relations between well-being and religious and spiritual beliefs, ranging from broad global beliefs to specific situational beliefs, particularly noting how discrepancy among beliefs or between beliefs and experience can lead to distress and attempts to make meaning to reduce these discrepancies. We elaborate on the clinical implications of this research, describe specific strategies for the assessment of religious and spiritual beliefs and discrepancies among them, and then highlight strategies for using religious and spiritual beliefs, closing discrepancies, and making meaning in psychotherapy. We illustrate this clinical approach with a case presentation and conclude with recommendations for further research and clinical applications.

### RELIGIOUS AND SPIRITUAL PERSPECTIVE

Religious meaning, as reflected in beliefs about the nature of God and the universe, as well as the many other beliefs (e.g., life is fair, people can be trusted) that follow from these fundamental beliefs, have been the focus of theologians and philosophers for millennia. Beliefs are a central component of every religious system (Hood, Hill, & Spilka, 2009), and evidence from a variety of disciplines, such as neuroscience, anthropology, evolutionary biology, and cognitive science, is converging on the notion that religious beliefs are a universal aspect of human beings (e.g., Barrett & Lanman, 2008; Sanderson, 2008). Only recently, however, have psychologists of religion taken up this area of study, and research is just beginning on the roles that religious beliefs of clients and psychotherapists play in psychotherapy.

## EMPIRICAL RESEARCH

Although a tremendous amount of research has been conducted on the associations between religion and well-being in recent decades (e.g., for reviews, see Lee & Newberg, 2005, 2010; Moreira-Almeida, Lotufo Neto, & Koenig, 2006), little of this research has focused explicitly on religious *beliefs*. This lack of attention is puzzling, because beliefs are considered to be a major component of religion (e.g., Hackney & Sanders, 2003; Stark & Glock, 1968). Religious beliefs often form, in large part, the foundation of the individuals' fundamental meaning systems. That is, religious beliefs often serve as the basis for individuals' understanding of the world and their framework for interpreting reality (McIntosh, 1995), and religious beliefs thereby influence other basic beliefs such as one's locus of control or belief in a just world (Moreira-Almeida et al., 2006). By influencing individuals' perceptions of themselves and the world, religious beliefs also influence other aspects of their meaning systems, such as their values (i.e., things on which people place subjective importance) and behaviors (i.e., whether and why they act in particular ways). Thus, understanding the role of religious beliefs on well-being and functioning is critically important to understanding people and is essential for sound clinical work.

Religious beliefs exist on a continuum, ranging from broad general or global beliefs (e.g., in the existence and nature of God) to more situation-specific appraisals based, in part, on these global beliefs (e.g., attributions for a specific occurrence; Park, 2005). Global religious beliefs are part of one's global meaning system (McIntosh, 1995) and, along with the particular situational context, influence situational beliefs. Situational religious beliefs involve the meanings that people assign to the specific events or experiences in their lives and are the level of beliefs with which most clients consciously struggle (e.g., *not* why does God allow suffering, a global existential problem, but why did God allow *this specific traumatic experience* to happen to *me*?). From a meaning perspective, both global and situational beliefs are important determinants of subsequent feelings and behaviors (Park, 2010; Park & Folkman, 1997). The following section reviews the empirical literature on the relations of religious beliefs and well-being and highlights some important points that are relevant for psychotherapy.

### Research on Global Religious Beliefs and Well-Being

#### *Belief in God*

Perhaps the most fundamental belief in an individual's meaning system concerns the existence of God (or deity, or transcendent being), given that other specific religious beliefs typically follow from this belief. As can be seen in Table 8.1, recent polls indicate that, in the United States, the vast majority of adults report having a belief in God (Harris Interactive, 2008; Pew Forum, 2009). Such polls tend to show that the prevalence of these beliefs differ by sociodemographic characteristics. For example, more women than men endorse believing in God, and people with some graduate education are less likely to report beliefs in God than are those with a high school education. Republicans are more likely to report believing in God than are either Democrats or Independents (Harris Interactive, 2008).

In spite of the prevalence of a belief in God, surprisingly few studies have specifically focused on the influence of beliefs in God. Those studies generally have found that beliefs in God are positively linked to well-being. For example, a recent study found that beliefs in a benevolent God were related to lower levels of depression among Protestant and Jewish college students (Rosmarin, Pirutinsky, Pargament, & Krumrei, 2009). A study of women who recently had experienced the death of their infant, however, did not find a belief in God comforting; belief was unrelated to grief (Cowchock, Lasker, Toedter, Skumanich, & Koenig, 2009). Grief reactions might be better predicted by beliefs about the nature of God and afterlife (e.g., Exline, 2003; Flannelly, Ellison, Galek, & Koenig, 2008; Flannelly, Koenig, Ellison, Galek, & Krause, 2006; Smith, Range, & Ulmer, 1991–1992).

**Table 8.1** Beliefs Reported in Recent U.S. Nationally Representative Polls

| | Believe In (%) | Don't Believe In (%) | Not Sure/Don't Know (%) |
|---|---|---|---|
| God | 80–93 | 6–10 | 1–10 |
| Heaven | 70–81 | 11–15 | 8–15 |
| Miracles | 73–75 | 14–16 | 11–12 |
| Survival of the soul after death | 68–70 | 12–15 | 17–18 |
| Angels | 68–75 | 14–17 | 11–15 |
| The devil | 61–70 | 21–26 | 8–13 |
| Hell | 59–69 | 22–25 | 8–16 |
| The Bible is the actual word of God and is to be taken literally | 30 | 67 | 3 |
| The Bible is the inspired word of God, but not everything in it should be taken literally | 46 | 51 | 3 |
| Reincarnation – that you were once another person | 21–24 | 53–54 | 23–25 |

Ranges reflect estimates from different polls. Data are drawn from Gallup (2009), Harris Interactive (2005, 2008), and Pew Forum (2009).

### *Belief in Life After Death*

As seen in Table 8.1, the vast majority of U.S. adults in a national poll indicated believing in heaven, hell, and the survival of the soul after death. A substantial minority of this sample also reported beliefs in reincarnation. In another large nationally representative survey in the United States, an inverse relationship between belief in life after death and a variety of psychopathology symptoms (i.e., anxiety, depression, obsession-compulsion, paranoia, phobia, and somatization) was observed, even after controlling for demographic and other variables known to influence mental health (Flannelly et al., 2006). A follow-up article reported on the relationships among a number of specific positive and negative views of the afterlife and found that, as expected, beliefs in a pleasant afterlife were associated with better mental health, whereas beliefs in an unpleasant afterlife were associated with poorer mental health (Flannelly et al., 2008). Higher beliefs in the afterlife, however, were linked with higher posttraumatic stress disorder (PTSD) avoidance symptoms in a sample of elderly German survivors of the Dresden bombing (Maercker & Herrle, 2003).

Afterlife beliefs have been found to relate to better psychological well-being in the context of bereavement (e.g., Smith et al., 1991–1992) and may influence physical health as well. For example, in a study of bereaved Japanese elders, holding beliefs in a good afterlife predicted lower risk of developing hypertension assessed 2 years later (Krause et al., 2002).

### *Karma*

The notion that one's deeds in a previous life might influence one's current experiences has been associated with poorer well-being in several studies. In a community survey of Americans, those who believed in karma had worse self-rated physical and mental health than did those who did not believe in karma (Connor, Davidson, & Lee, 2003; Lee, Connor, & Davidson, 2008). Further analysis of those data showed that among those who had a personal history of exposure to violent trauma, beliefs in karma also were related to higher levels of PTSD symptoms (Davidson, Connor, & Lee, 2005). In a study of Indonesian survivors of the 2004 tsunami, belief in karma was associated with poorer health, but not with a diagnosis of PTSD (Levy, Slade, & Ranasignhe, 2009).

### *Beliefs About Forgiveness*

Forgiveness can be thought of as a means of coping or as a behavior, but in keeping with our focus on beliefs in this chapter, we focus on people's *beliefs* about forgiveness, such as whether they should offer forgiveness and whether they can be forgiven for transgressions. Although these issues are complex and this discussion necessarily simplifies those issues, most religions encourage and expect forgiveness. As Rye and his colleagues describe (Rye et al., 2000), forgiveness may be demanded (Judaism) or inspired by God (Christianity). It can be perceived as a source for ending suffering for both oneself and others (Buddhism, Hinduism), but also as a way of creating happiness and approaching the divine (Buddhism, Christianity, Hinduism, Islam, Judaism). Some religions promote the view that forgiveness does not need to be earned (Buddhism, Christianity), others promote the view that forgiveness should not be freely given and must be earned (Judaism), and still others promote the view that it be freely given but that one should also act to bring others into righteousness (Islam).

In summarizing the literature, McCullough and Worthington (1999) observed that people identifying as religious were more likely to value forgiveness, hold sophisticated views of forgiveness and its consequences, and report forgiving others and acting in positive ways in response to a transgression. Many religious clients perceive forgiveness as something that *should* be granted, regardless of their personal reactions or feelings (Wade, Johnson, & Meyer, 2008). Nonetheless, some people do not grant forgiveness, even though they believe they should forgive and predict they will (Barnes & Brown, 2010; McCullough & Worthington, 1999). In fact, McCullough and Worthington concluded that there is "little unqualified evidence that religious people are more forgiving for specific transgressions" (p. 1150). As a result, clients may perceive their lack of forgiveness as a moral shortcoming and may experience distress stemming from this perception (Wade et al., 2008).

Forgiveness and beliefs about its importance are related to various positive outcomes (further discussed in Chapter 11, this volume), so its relevance should be considered in the course of psychotherapy. For example, Lawler-Row (2010) reported that measures of trait and state forgiveness fully or partially mediated the positive effects of religion and prayer on health, well-being, and successful aging. Degree of forgiveness is related to decreased depression and anxiety, increased hope, higher self-esteem, better relationship adjustment, stronger life satisfaction, and measures of physical health (summarized in McCullough & Worthington, 1999). Similarly, degree of self-forgiveness was also related to lower levels of self-blame and depression when considering an unwanted end to a relationship (Wohl, DeShea, & Wahkinney, 2008).

### *Other Religious Beliefs*

Many other global religious beliefs have been documented as having fairly high levels of adherents in the United States, including the existence of angels, the devil, miracles, and ghosts (see Table 8.1). In addition, researchers have examined a number of other religious beliefs that people hold, such as the following: (1) Suffering can bring one closer to God, (2) the devil causes temptation and suffering, (3) one's own behavior in this life determines one's afterlife, (4) people deserve what happens to them (e.g., AIDS as God's punishment), (5) scripture is literal truth, and (6) there is one true religion or way to God (e.g., Exline, 2008). Minimal literature exists regarding the extent to which these beliefs affect coping with stressors, such as loss and trauma, or how they relate to well-being.

Unfortunately, many studies that have assessed religious beliefs and related them to well-being combined the scores regarding the different beliefs reviewed above, producing a general measure of beliefs, before reporting results of their analyses. Such studies, although interesting, cannot be informative regarding the influence of any *particular* beliefs. For example, in a study of cardiac surgery patients, an omnibus measure of religious beliefs (e.g., in God, an afterlife, a responsibility to respond to suffering) was related to fewer complications and shorter hospital stays (Contrada et al., 2004), although a more recent study of the same population showed this belief measure to be related to higher levels of depression and anxiety (Contrada et al., 2008). Similarly, in a large national survey, a summary measure of "Western spiritual beliefs" that included beliefs in God, the afterlife, and life after death was unrelated to physical health, but fairly strongly correlated with *poorer* mental health (Lee et al., 2008). Clearly, given the variety of different religious beliefs that people hold, a more fine-grained analysis is needed to understand their role in well-being.

This research on global beliefs offers several points for psychotherapists to consider. First, assessing global beliefs about the nature of God can be helpful in predicting client outcomes. Second, for some particular problems, such as people who are grieving, it might be necessary to inquire about a client's beliefs in an afterlife and its expected nature. Third, in some contexts, it may be useful to inquire about beliefs about forgiveness and self-forgiveness and to consider to the degree to which one's current behavior matches these beliefs. Finally, for problems that can be construed to challenge perceptions of fairness and justice—such as perceived unfairness of God, perceived unfairness of natural and human events (e.g., earthquakes, war, and so on), and interpersonal transgressions—it might be helpful to inquire about clients' views on karma, the role of the devil, and beliefs in a just world.

### Research on Situational Religious Beliefs and Well-Being

Global religious beliefs may influence individuals' understandings of the specific stressful experiences that they encounter (Moreira-Almeida et al., 2006; Pargament & Hahn, 1986; Park, 2005) affecting their well-being. For example, religious beliefs may allow individuals to make benign interpretations of potentially stressful events and thereby protect them against the daily wear and tear of stressors (Pargament, 1997). Certain religious beliefs, however, may lead to situational interpretations that are associated with greater stress, guilt, and self-blame (e.g., if one holds beliefs in karma and perceives trauma as resulting from mistakes in this or past lives). Although research linking global and situational levels of religious belief is scarce (Park, 2005), evidence is accumulating that the nature of people's situational religious beliefs can predict how well they adjust to stressful situations.

Religious attributions, or explanations for why an event occurred, are probably the most widely examined aspect of situational religious beliefs. Such beliefs are common following many different types of stressful experiences (e.g., Gall, 2004; Mickley, Pargament, Brant, & Hipp, 1998; Pargament et al., 1990; Pargament, Koenig, Tarakeshwar, & Hahn, 2004). Depending on their specific nature, religious attributions can alleviate distress or increase it. For example, in a study of caregivers of terminally ill patients, those who appraised their situation as part of God's plan or as a means of gaining strength or understanding from God reported positive outcomes, whereas those who viewed their situation as unjust, as unfair punishment from God, or as desertion from God scored lower on measures of mental and spiritual health (Mickley et al., 1998). Religious appraisals made a significant and unique contribution to the prediction of well-being in this sample, above and beyond the effects of nonreligious appraisals. In a community sample, attributions of a recent major stressor to God's will were unrelated to mental health, whereas attributions to a punishing God were related to poorer mental health (Pargament et al., 1990). Similarly, in a sample of prostate cancer survivors, attributing the cancer to God (e.g., God's love, or a spiritual force) was related negatively to physical and psychological well-being, with the exception that attributions of the cancer to God's will were unrelated to well-being (Gall, 2004). The strongest relationships were found with attributions of the cancer to an angry God. Curiously, however, a recent study of perinatal bereavement found that attributions of the baby's death to God's will (the only type of religious attribution assessed) were unrelated to grief shortly after the loss and at 1 and 2 years after the loss (Cowchock et al., 2009). A study of bereaved college students found that attributing the death of a loved one to a purposeful God was related to less distress, whereas attributions to a loving God were related to more personal growth from the loss (Park & Cohen, 1993). Although most research suggests attributions to a benign God are most helpful, one study of older adults found that attributing illness to the devil (rather than God) was positively related to well-being (Pargament et al., 2004).

There are many other types of situational religious beliefs in addition to attributions. For example, one may interpret a particular behavior as sinful or God-like, and various events can be interpreted as indicating one's likely eventual fate or as a message from God to change one's ways. Little research has been conducted, however, on these situational religious meanings or their impact on well-being.

Overall, the influence of situational religious beliefs on physical and psychological well-being is unclear. In fact, they may have both positive and negative effects. Self-regulation provided by religious interpretations may be useful for keeping people out of trouble, making good decisions, and resisting temptation (McCullough & Willoughby, 2009). Conversely, some types of situational religious beliefs, such as religious fatalism or beliefs that God is responsible for one's health, have been related to lower levels of cancer-screening behaviors (e.g., Mitchell, Lannin, Mathews, & Swanson, 2002) and poorer adherence to treatment regimens (Kremer, Ironson, & Porr, 2009; Parsons, Cruise, Davenport, & Jones, 2006). Attributing illness and trauma to God (e.g., Gall, 2004; Pargament et al., 1990) may interfere with other beliefs, including that the world is safe, predictable, and controllable through goodness, prayer, and good works. Paradoxically, attributing trauma, loss, or illness to the devil (e.g., Pargament et al., 2004) might allow people to continue believing that the world is fair and to retain their sense of control.

All of the research in this area is correlational, and much of it is cross-sectional; it is impossible to determine whether poorer adjustment leads to more negative global and situational religious beliefs or vice versa. The few longitudinal studies that have been conducted have demonstrated the ability of religious meanings to predict subsequent well-being. The mechanisms that may account for this impact are plausible, but the causal links remain speculative.

Psychotherapists may want to pay careful attention to the possible influences of situational religious beliefs on clients' physical and psychological well-being. For example, depending on their specific nature, religious attributions can alleviate distress or increase it. Attributions about God's nature and actions may lead clients to feel safe and confident that life is predictable and controllable or that life is unpredictable, unsafe, and uncontrollable.

### Changes in Religious Beliefs

Global beliefs such as those regarding the existence of a loving God or of an afterlife are considered to be fairly resistant to change, whereas situational beliefs regarding the meaning of a particular occurrence may be easier to modify (e.g., Janoff-Bulman, 1992). Both situational and global beliefs tend to change only when they are forced to. Such changes are brought about by encountering discrepancies, that is, beliefs that are in conflict with one another (Slattery & Park, in press). Such conflicts can occur in a number of different ways. For example, two global beliefs may conflict (e.g., the beliefs that God is all loving and all powerful, and that vast suffering exists in the world; Hall & Johnson, 2001). Or a global belief may conflict with one's perception of or belief about a specific situation (e.g., the belief that God is all loving and all powerful, yet let a terrible harm happen to me).

Regardless of how they come about, discrepancies can create enormous distress and be overwhelming, anxiety provoking, or depressing (Dalgleish & Power, 2004; Higgins, 1987; Higgins, Bond, Klein, & Strauman, 1986; Janoff-Bulman & Frantz, 1997). This distress can negatively affect behavior and overall functioning. In turn, this distress tends to motivate individuals to try to alleviate or close the underlying discrepancies. People can attempt to close these discrepancies in positive and adaptive ways (e.g., by problem solving or bringing opposing beliefs into alignment) or less adaptive ones (e.g., by avoiding, devaluing, or ignoring a problem).

Little research to date has explicitly examined discrepancies among religious beliefs or between religious beliefs and experiences. Some inferences can be drawn, however, from research on changes in global religious beliefs as a result of trauma. In particular, religious conversions, when they do occur, have been reported to be triggered by highly stressful or traumatic circumstances that presumably challenge one's meaning system beyond its ability to accommodate (for a review, see Paloutzian, 2005).

Religious discrepancies may be an important part of clinical work. For example, trauma and other events may lead clients to perceive discrepancies between their current experience and their previous global religious beliefs. Furthermore, the levels of distress that clients experience may be a result of the perceived discrepancy. When indicated, psychotherapists may want to consider normalizing the distress as an appropriate and temporary reaction to a stressor. Psychotherapists can monitor when clients are choosing maladaptive ways of closing discrepancies and help them to discover more positive ways of closing discrepancies.

## CLINICAL IMPLICATIONS

As described in the last section, global and specific religious beliefs are implicated in creating, exacerbating, or easing human difficulties; addressing religious issues in the course of treatment can increase treatment effectiveness (Propst, 1996). Because global beliefs are believed to be more difficult to change than situational beliefs (Janoff-Bulman, 1992), situational religious beliefs may be the more appropriate focus of psychotherapeutic work and the key to improved functioning and well-being (Pargament, 1997; Pargament et al., 1990; Park, Cohen & Herb, 1990).

Understanding global and situational religious beliefs helps psychotherapists to recognize the importance that religion plays in their clients' lives and how their clients are perceiving life events. This understanding also provides psychotherapists with guidance in terms of how they can effectively intervene with clients to help them meet their goals (Nielsen, Ridley, & Johnson, 2000). Furthermore, some situational religious beliefs may be discrepant from global religious beliefs (Slattery & Park, in press), causing distress and leading to problematic cycles in perception, cognition, and behavior (Park, Edmondson, & Mills, 2010). Clients can reduce this distress by closing these discrepancies, which may be achieved by meaning-making (i.e., changing situational or global beliefs or behaviors to reduce discrepancies; Slattery & Park, in press). From a religious meaning perspective, psychotherapists need to pay attention to six related issues:

1. Clients may enter treatment with global or situational religious beliefs that cause them distress and impair their well-being. Psychotherapists should be especially concerned about religious beliefs that seem extreme,

rigid, demanding, and pessimistic in tone, just as they would be about other extreme beliefs with a negative valence.

2. Previous trauma and other events also affect global and situational religious beliefs (Park et al., 2010); these effects are then carried into other settings, influencing the interpretation of other events (Slattery & Park, 2011a). Assessing the broader context (e.g., previous trauma, loss, or oppression) can help psychotherapists recognize their clients' global and situational beliefs and identify places to intervene (Park & Slattery, 2009; Slattery & Park, 2011a).
3. Psychotherapists should identify maladaptive beliefs; help clients interrupt negative cycles in perception, cognition, and behavior; and work with clients to shift these maladaptive beliefs and negative cycles in more adaptive directions.
4. From their own spiritual, religious, or secular framework, psychotherapists might see a client's global and situational religious beliefs as maladaptive, although these beliefs might not cause clients to experience either a discrepancy or distress (e.g., clients might attribute suffering to God's role as a responsive parent or to Satan's actions, in either case allowing them to maintain coherent and comfortable worldviews). Therefore, psychotherapists should focus on (a) situational religious beliefs that are discrepant from the client's global religious beliefs and (b) global and situational religious beliefs related to more negative outcomes. As noted, beliefs linked with negative outcomes tend to be those that are more extreme, rigid, demanding, and negatively valenced.
5. Psychotherapy needs to help clients resolve discrepancies in adaptive ways. Change can be introduced in a number of ways, such as helping clients develop new attributions about the event or their behavior, reframing the event, changing their behavior, or gathering new evidence that changes the meanings they draw (Beck, 1976).
6. The meaning-making process can be difficult for many people and sometimes is related to decreased psychological adjustment, at least in the short term (Exline, 2002; Pargament, Murray-Swank, Magyar, & Ano, 2005). Psychotherapists can help clients perceive this distress as normal and even adaptive when it is in the service of achieving a deeper and more satisfying resolution of problems.

## CLINICAL ASSESSMENTS

Gonsiorek, Richards, Pargament, and McMinn (2009) observed that "predicting attitudes, beliefs, and behavior from denominational affiliation is imprecise … and impossible in individual cases" (p. 387). Instead, psychotherapists should pay attention to global and situational beliefs that are related to more positive aspects of adjustment (e.g., growth, resiliency, adjustment, well-being, and ultimate sense of purpose), and to others that typically are related to more negative aspects of adjustment (e.g., rumination, anxiety, and withdrawal). In this section, we highlight open-ended questions and assessment tools that are useful in exploring client religious and spiritual constructs during the assessment process and throughout treatment.

Psychotherapists should listen carefully to their clients' perceptions of God, an afterlife, and the possibility of forgiveness, especially as these beliefs affect the issues for which they asked for treatment. How do their beliefs decrease or increase their pain? How do they bring them closer to God and to the people in their lives or create a sense of alienation and feelings of hopelessness? Psychotherapists should also consider the following (Propst, 1996): Do clients' religious beliefs lead them to distort reality or avoid responsibility? In what ways do their religious beliefs reflect false expectations of God? How do clients' religious beliefs lead to self-destructive behavior? As is true with various types of secular beliefs, religious beliefs that interfere with healthy functioning can be problematic and should be a focus of psychotherapy.

The FICA Spiritual History Tool (FICA) can be used to begin a discussion of spiritual issues (Borneman, Ferrell, Otis-Green, Baird, & Puchalski, 2010; George Washington Institute for Spirituality and Health [GWISH], n.d.). The FICA can be used to gather faith and spiritual beliefs (F), their importance (I), the presence of a spiritual community and the support the community offers (C), and whether and how the person wants these beliefs addressed in treatment (A). Faith and beliefs can be assessed with questions such as the following: "Do you consider yourself spiritual or religious?" "Do you have spiritual beliefs that help you cope with stress?" and "What gives your life meaning?" (GWISH, n.d., para. 3). These questions can be asked early in treatment as well as at other points in treatment as indicated and to assess change.

This early assessment has three implications. First, as described by Krumei and Rosmarin (Chapter 10, this volume), clients reporting noninvolvement with the religious and spiritual practices that are important to them also are not able to use the religious and spiritual coping strategies that previously may have been helpful to them. This assessment process opens a conversation about whether clients want to consider their use of religious and spiritual coping strategies. Second, some clients identify an important discrepancy during this assessment (e.g., "My spiritual beliefs are important to me, but I do not act on them because …"). This discrepancy can be further explored and closed during the course of psychotherapy, perhaps by helping clients act on their beliefs, recognizing that they already are acting, or deciding that they do not want to act, on their beliefs. Third, it can be important to pay attention to clients' situational religious beliefs and observe how these may differ from their global religious beliefs. For example, a woman might believe that God is good and forgiving, yet find it difficult to believe that God could forgive *her* (e.g., Chapter 11, this volume).

Although this intake and assessment process opens the door to explore religious and spiritual beliefs that may contribute to current problems, it frequently only touches the tip of the iceberg. Often, clients are attempting to make meaning about the trauma, loss, or event that brought them to treatment (Park, 2010). During this period, they may struggle to find an answer to the question "Why?" Answers to this question can take various forms, some of which cause little distress (e.g., "He went to a better place"), whereas others cause considerable distress (e.g., "This was a punishment from God because of my sinful nature"). Clients can be encouraged to become more self-reflective and monitor their thoughts, a process that is consistent with many religious traditions (Propst, 1996). As with other psychotherapies, clients can be actively involved in the assessment process and guided to observe the relationships among their thoughts and beliefs, antecedent situations, and consequent emotions and behaviors.

While assessing clients' answers to the question "Why?" psychotherapists should attend to two different issues. First, psychotherapists must identify global and situational religious beliefs that unduly increase distress and that are unlikely to have positive consequences such as becoming aware of moral conflicts. For example, as mentioned, one study found that attributing one's illness to the devil was associated with more positive outcomes than attributing illness to God (Pargament et al., 2004). See Table 8.2 for examples of religious beliefs, attributions that may follow from these beliefs, and adjustment associated with these attributions. Presumably, attributing bad things to the devil does not violate beliefs about God and one's relationship with God, while attributing bad things to God may sometimes lead people to feel unsafe and unprotected or abandoned by God. Ellis (2000), in a reversal of his previous writings about religion, argued that religion per se was not problematic in terms of mental health outcomes, but that the extremeness, demandingness, rigidity, and negativity of some religious beliefs put people at risk. This is consistent with our review elsewhere in this chapter.

Second, although psychotherapists may pay special attention to beliefs that unduly increase distress without probable positive consequences, this raises the issue of value conflicts and how to handle them. Psychotherapists may see a client's situational attribution as having negative consequences, whereas a client might see it as consistent with his or her global beliefs. For example, a psychotherapist may be disturbed when a client perceives an illness as an act of God, although this may not cause the client distress as she perceives God to be a responsive parent who justly metes out punishments with His flock's best interests in mind. When clients see themselves as being punished for no reason (e.g., they believe that they had lived good and godly lives), however, this perception likely would be discrepant with their global meaning, creating distress. They may attempt to

**Table 8.2** Some Religious and Spiritual Beliefs and Associated Client Outcomes

| Religious Beliefs | Moderating Attributions | Possible Outcomes |
|---|---|---|
| My problems are part of God's plan. I can gain strength and understanding from God's plan. | | Good things will come from this. I can trust in God. |
| God is unjustly punishing me. I do not deserve this. | | I am bad, but God is fair. The world is punitive. |
| The devil is punishing me. | | The devil is evil, but God is not. I can trust in God. |
| God couldn't or wouldn't stop this punishment. | | God is not in my corner. The world is not safe. |
| I trust in God, who will take care of me. | | What happens to me in this life is God's plan. I do not need to do things to influence that plan. |
| I believe in karma and will get what I deserve. | Things are good in this life. | I am good; my karma reflects this. |
| | Things are bad in this life. | I must have been bad and am undeserving. I cannot do anything to change my karma. |
| I believe in heaven and hell. | I believe that I (or my loved one) will go to heaven. | I can be calm about this approaching death. |
| | I expect I will go to hell. | I feel anxious and afraid. I will try to do what I can to get into heaven. |
| | My loved one will not go to heaven. | I must do everything I can to help my loved one get into heaven. |

close the discrepancy by concluding either that they are bad or that God is unfair, thus leaving them with more negative global beliefs. As another example, J. Aten (personal communication, December 30, 2009) observed that a colleague who is a Buddhist holds spiritual beliefs about the role of suffering that interfere with his willingness to attend to his physical well-being. He argues that his spiritual growth, which may derive from his physical suffering, is of more importance than alleviating his pain. These examples highlight the tension that can sometimes develop when psychotherapists and clients hold different values and goals, as well as the value conflicts that sometimes occur between religion and psychotherapy (for further discussion, see American Psychological Association, 2008; Gonsiorek et al., 2009; McMinn, Aikins, & Lish, 2003). Furthermore, they raise the difficult question of whether and under what conditions psychological goals should "trump" spiritual goals and vice versa.

## CLINICAL STRATEGIES

After assessing maladaptive global or situational religious beliefs and identifying discrepancies, treatment should focus on shifting beliefs in more adaptive directions and resolving discrepancies well. Many spiritual interventions used in clinical settings (e.g., reframing, prayer, yoga, meditation, and involvement in religious communities) can be thought of as influencing how clients see themselves, others, and God (Slattery & Park, 2011b).

### Responding to Clients' Beliefs

As Carone and Barone (2001) observed, religious beliefs are relatively stable and difficult to change. Clients, religious and otherwise, tend to look for evidence supporting their beliefs and avoid evidence disconfirming them. Furthermore, Carone and Barone observed that religious clients tend to believe that they are to blame for their problems and that they should either fix them (which Brickman et al., 1982, called the moral model) or that they are unable to fix them without intervention from a higher power (the enlightenment model). Psychotherapists, however, are more likely to believe that clients are not responsible for their problems, although they should be held responsible for solving them (the compensatory model). Because of these differences in orientation, religious clients may enter treatment focused on their guilt and worthlessness, whereas many psychotherapists may believe in their clients' personal worth and focus on helping their clients change (Carone & Barone, 2001). These differences in viewpoints may interfere with psychotherapists' abilities to intervene effectively with their religious clients.

People in spiritual or psychological pain may choose one of several paths in attempting to reduce their pain—they may attempt to work through it on their own, or they may turn to their spiritual guide, a psychotherapist who identifies as taking a spiritual approach, or a secular healer. In choosing to go to a secular helper rather than to their spiritual guide, some clients may be indicating their willingness to consider secular intervention, although their choices may also be guided or constrained by such factors as perceived availability of resources or insurance coverage. Nonetheless, as with other multicultural issues, psychotherapists who challenge their clients' (religious) worldview or are perceived as being disrespectful of it are judged more negatively by outside observers and presumably are less successful (Morrow, Worthington, & McCullough, 1993). Instead, psychotherapists can listen to clients and nonjudgmentally help *them* gather evidence either supporting or challenging their global or specific religious beliefs. For example, a psychotherapist working with a client struggling with the question of why God would have allowed a bad thing to befall her might ask, "What is the evidence that God only allows bad things to happen to bad people?" Most clients are able to identify good people who have had bad things happen to them, as well as "bad people" who have had extraordinarily easy lives. From a Judeo-Christian viewpoint, this question might be explored by looking at the lives of religious figures, including Jesus, Job, Moses and the Israelites, and many saints. Books like Kushner's (1981) *When Bad Things Happen to Good People* and Sittser's (2004) *A Grace Disguised: How the Soul Grows Through Loss* can be used to help clients explore these questions from within their own religious framework.

Psychotherapists can reframe events to help clients develop a more helpful understanding of religious doctrine. For example, some religious clients passively accept fate, believing that this is what God would want (i.e., the enlightenment model; Brickman et al., 1982). Some might be reminded of this story:

> One day Prophet Muhammad (peace be upon him) noticed a Bedouin leaving his camel without tying it and he asked the Bedouin, "Why don't you tie down your camel?" The Bedouin answered, "I put my trust in Allah." The Prophet then said, "Tie your camel first, then put your trust in Allah." (At-Tirmidhi)

With people whose values and belief systems might not make them receptive to this or similar stories, psychotherapists could talk with clients about developing wisdom, the internal process of discerning God's will, or following God's grace (depending on the client's belief system). Regardless, psychotherapists should be aware of their clients' belief systems and use their beliefs to inform clinical interventions.

The goal, as with other psychotherapies, is not to tell clients what to believe, which might, justifiably, increase their negative reactions (Morrow et al., 1993), but rather to explore with them whether other ways of looking at problems might be less extreme and also more complete and helpful. This can be done using stories from the client's religious tradition. Stories in all religious traditions address issues of sin, forgiveness, relationships with others, helping, ways of being moral, and submitting to God's will, for example. Although it is helpful for psychotherapists to know and understand the religious beliefs and traditions of other religions, sometimes it can be useful to ask clients what stories in their religious tradition address their presenting issue. If it appears that they perceive that story overly narrowly or even inaccurately, it usually is useful to refer clients to their religious or spiritual guides rather than becoming embroiled in theological interpretations. This works best when clients are receptive to this referral, their guide is sensitive to mental health issues and shares similar goals to the client–psychotherapist team, and both psychotherapist and guide trust each other and respect each other's contributions (McMinn et al., 2003). Such a trusted religious or spiritual leader may be able to help clients develop a more sophisticated and helpful understanding of religious doctrines and texts.

Sometimes it can be helpful to ask clients to take a different perspective on the presenting issue. For example, if a client is having difficulty with self-forgiveness, psychotherapists can ask clients what they would think about a friend or family member in the same situation; under what circumstances could that person be forgiven? Such questions can be asked about saints or religious figures when a parallel situation is available from the client's religious background (Propst, 1996). Religious memoirs, such as Kidd's (1990) *When the Heart Waits: Spiritual Direction for Life's Sacred Questions*, can be helpful, as many writers have sensitively and insightfully described how they experienced and responded to adversity and periods of spiritual struggle.

### Explore the Utility of Beliefs and Facilitate Drawing on Adaptive Beliefs

A client's system of religious beliefs can influence how people cope with stress, suffering, and life problems. Religious beliefs can provide support by enhancing acceptance and helping clients develop a positive self-image, endurance, and resilience. They can help to generate peace, self-confidence, purpose, and forgiveness for others or for oneself for perceived transgressions or the individual's own failures. Importantly, religious beliefs can provide a sense of order and coherence in an otherwise chaotic and confusing world (Carone & Barone, 2001). Conversely, religious beliefs can lead clients to feel rejected by God and their religious community; experience anxiety, guilt, and shame; and believe that they will be unable to change or are not worth changing. People of all sorts of religious and spiritual backgrounds tend to approach complex situations using heuristics to help them make rapid judgments; they may look for religious passages and doctrines that support their beliefs, while rejecting those that seem to contradict their beliefs. As a result, religious beliefs can be difficult to change (Carone & Barone, 2001). Nonetheless, in choosing to go to a psychotherapist rather than their spiritual guides, clients may be indicating their willingness to consider another way of thinking about the presenting problem.

Many people believe in a God who is personally involved in their lives (cf. Table 8.1; Slattery & Park, 2011b). Helping clients draw on this resource for self-acceptance and peace can be a major focus of psychotherapy, whether clients are struggling with a particular trauma or more generally dealing with issues of self-esteem or depression. Clients' specific views of God, however, should be assessed carefully and considered in treatment, particularly regarding whether they perceive God as a merciful and all-loving presence, a responsive parent, or a punishing one (see Table 8.2). Especially when perceptions of God are more punitive in nature (see Chapter 6, this volume), clients may need to consider whether and how they can gain forgiveness from God to gain or regain a more positive relationship with God (Rye et al., 2000).

Religions differ in their requirements to forgive others, and, in addition, people within a single religion differ in their perceptions of the importance of forgiveness (Exline, 2008). Psychotherapists might assess their client's perceptions of how transgressions should be handled—with vengeance or by "turning the other cheek." In a study of beliefs involving a sample of Baptists, for example, Exline (2008) reported that few expressed a belief that God endorsed vengeance. Beliefs about forgiveness can serve as guides when clients struggle with how to respond to family members and friends who have wronged them in some way. Assessing and activating religious beliefs about the value of forgiveness can help clients develop empathy for others—and themselves. Doing so can preserve and strengthen relationships and decrease the distress associated with holding a grudge (Carone & Barone, 2001).

Similarly, when clients or their loved ones face death, their beliefs in an afterlife (e.g., heaven and hell) can determine their reactions to impending death. People who believe in heaven may be comforted by their belief, yet those who also believe in hell may experience greater distress. If they experience religious struggle, they might not be happy about any afterlife (Chapter 9, this volume). Exline (2003) suggested that psychotherapists should specifically assess afterlife beliefs for client's facing death (as well as their own). Depending on the situation, clinicians might assess clients' beliefs about conditions under which they can go to heaven (e.g., repenting, living a good life, and accepting Jesus Christ as one's personal savior). They might assess whether clients believe punishment in the afterlife is permanent or temporary and whether a particular client felt a responsibility for evangelizing and saving the dying person or in saying indulgences to release the dead friend or family member from Purgatory. Nonetheless, some of these questions can be socially awkward. For example, in asking whether God can offer forgiveness so a person can go to heaven, one also suggests that not everyone will go to heaven and that without this forgiveness the person will go to hell (Exline, 2003).

### Closing Discrepancies

Psychotherapists working with clients' religious meaning systems can help clients develop new skills, normalize current behavior, reframe their understanding of the problem, draw new attributions, provide information that changes the perceived meaning of symptoms, or provide new evidence about the problem (Beck, 1976). These various techniques may be used for the ultimate aim of closing discrepancies that are causing distress (Slattery & Park, in press).

Some clients' situational religious beliefs may be discrepant from global religious beliefs, other global and situational beliefs, values, goals, sense of purpose, and behavior (Slattery & Park, in press), causing distress and leading to problematic cycles in perception, cognition, and behavior (Park et al., 2010). This distress can be reduced by closing the discrepancies—through attempts at making meaning—which may allow clients to change their perceptions, beliefs, or behavior (Slattery & Park, in press). For example, a man diagnosed with cancer may experience distress, partially because of his perceptions that God has abandoned him and is punishing him unfairly. He can close this discrepancy in several ways, including drawing new attributions about the cancer (e.g., that the cancer is a test of his godliness or that the cancer is outside God's purview) and increasing his involvement in actions that demonstrate his faith and godliness to both himself and God.

As sometimes noted in the literature, people who attempt to make meaning after a loss or trauma often experience *greater* levels of distress than either people who already have made meaning (e.g., Tolstikova, Fleming, & Chartier, 2005) or people who did not attempt to make meaning (Davis, Wortman, Lehman, & Silver, 2000). Psychotherapists should discuss this process with their clients, helping them distinguish between maladaptive rumination and adaptive cognitive processing that occurs in the course of exploring and closing discrepancies to make meaning, normalizing some kinds of distress following a loss or trauma.

## CASE STUDY

The following case study illustrates these ideas about the ways that religious meanings can influence clients' understanding of themselves and the world, and how this meaning can be an important focus of effective psychotherapy.

Teeney,[1] a 24-year-old European American woman, entered treatment significantly overweight, reporting that she was currently engaging in both bingeing and purging. She perceived her weight and problematic eating as the most significant issues, only later reporting that she also frequently dissociated, engaged in self-injurious behaviors several times a day (mostly cutting, and also some wrist-banging), rarely left her home, and spent little time with anyone other than her roommate. In addition, she was seriously depressed and often suicidal, although did not believe that she had the "guts" to kill herself.

Teeney had a significant history of incest by both her brother and uncle over most of her childhood and teenage years. When entering treatment, she had next to no involvement with any of her family members, who she believed blamed her for breaking up their family when she attempted to report the incest to her mother. Teeney was living with another woman in what she sometimes described as being a lesbian relationship. Despite this relationship, she primarily identified as a heterosexual and believed that homosexuality was sinful. She reported that, although they cuddled, by her definition they did not have sex. Teeney self-identified as an evangelical Christian, which she said meant that she believed in a literal interpretation of the Bible and that she should attend services two to three times a week. However, she reported that she had not been to church in the last 6 years.

Consistent with most recommendations about working with survivors of sexual abuse (e.g., Gray, Maguen, & Litz, 2007; Linehan, 1993), treatment focused on

[1] Teeney is a pseudonym. This case study is actually a composite of several clients' stories. Permission to use case material was given by clients.

decreasing Teeney's avoidance of trauma stimuli, normalizing her experience, identifying distortions, developing more effective coping mechanisms, and strengthening her support system. During this process, we explored ways that her religious beliefs informed her perceptions of the incest and negative attitudes about herself. She believed that she was dirty and, like many abuse victims, felt guilty, as she attributed responsibility for the incest to herself. In addition to feeling guilty and ashamed, indications that she had violated perceived "ought" messages (Higgins, 1987), she also believed she was unforgiveable and deserved to be punished.

Although the incest had begun when she was 5 years old, Teeney blamed herself for her actions. She related these appraisals of the incest to her interpretation of the Bible. She believed that she should be held responsible for everything that she did and thought. She believed that she should be punished harshly; nonetheless, she was readily able to see her roommate as blame-free in her own history of sexual abuse by an older boy from her neighborhood. In recognizing this, we began to distinguish between her feelings about herself, which we validated and accepted, and her attributions about the abuse, which we gently explored.

Teeney's beliefs about God and God's ability to forgive her were more consistent with the meaning she derived from several Old Testament passages than with messages found in many New Testament references. She had selectively focused on biblical passages that reinforced her feelings of guilt and was genuinely surprised when we discussed biblical stories that emphasized forgiveness and unconditional acceptance to a much greater degree (e.g., the prodigal son). As she and I came from different religious traditions, we explored these issues in her own reading of the Bible.

Teeney and I considered her understanding of suffering—"God won't give me anything that I can't handle"—and also helped her draw positive meanings from her suffering (e.g., "Although clearly incest is not something that you would ever wish on anyone, I wonder if there were any positive outcomes for you"). In response to this and similar questions, Teeney observed that she was more aware of her strength, had become more protective of and compassionate toward others, and was clearer about how she wanted to parent her own children. In describing these changes, her self-perceptions became less extreme and more complex, acknowledging both her weaknesses and her strengths. As she developed a more sophisticated perception of herself and the incest, she experienced fewer vacillations between rumination and avoidance, as well as fewer intrusive symptoms. Other trauma symptoms also decreased during this period, and she reported using more effective coping strategies.

I encouraged Teeney to discuss her concerns with her minister, who also suggested more benign attributions of the incest, God's role in the incest, and God's judgments of her than she previously had drawn. Talking to her minister, of course, also had the advantage of decreasing several other discrepancies in her life (e.g., I *should* go to church, but am not; I want to be part of a religious community, but am not), and helped her slowly regain the social and spiritual support that she wanted and sorely needed.

Although not a primary focus of treatment, Teeney was ambivalent about her sexuality. She managed this ambivalence by focusing on the fact that her relationship with her roommate was not sexual and most of the time she identified her roommate as such rather than as her partner or lover. She believed that if she were to identify as a homosexual, admit sexual feelings for her roommate, or act on these feelings, she would be rejected by God. Using an approach of respectful curiosity, we explored her beliefs and considered how to act on them (e.g., "How might Jesus have responded to you? How do you know?" "How did Jesus believe that his followers should behave toward others? Why?" and "How do you feel about your roommate's history of abuse? Do you blame her for it?"). She believed that Jesus responded to others with unconditional acceptance and began to give this message greater priority than other, less forgiving or accepting biblical interpretations. Doing so helped her develop an attitude of unconditional and compassionate self-acceptance. Despite becoming less judgmental about her sexuality and her sexual behavior, she began to explore the ways that this particular relationship was unhealthy for her—in particular, she believed it supported her social withdrawal and avoidance. She ultimately decided against staying in this relationship.

### Analysis

Teeney had been judgmental toward herself, especially in response to her history of incest and her possibly homosexual relationship with her roommate. She perceived herself in a dichotomous and extreme manner, saw few things changing, and felt little hope for the future.

Teeney's judgmental attitudes seemed to be related to her (mis)understanding of several biblical passages; this misunderstanding seemed to reflect her own attitudes and feelings about the abuse that she was projecting onto God, her religion, and others. Hearing more benign interpretations of the incest from her minister, interpretations that were similar to my own, removed significant barriers to change (e.g., beliefs that she was bad and dirty, and that God was unforgiving). In addition, we sometimes considered how her religious beliefs supported or failed to support her. At other points, we externalized the discussion and considered whether she applied the same beliefs and conclusions to others that she did to herself (she did not). Her sense of meaning and purpose had been damaged, and we worked to develop a sense of meaning that informed her life and allowed her to reengage with others and with life.

The effectiveness of our work together probably stemmed, in part, from the fact that our work was collaborative in nature, respectful, and nonjudgmental about her and her beliefs. Treatment goals were her own and our exploration of her goals were from within her own worldview and belief system (e.g., see Wade et al., 2008). Rather than ridiculing her beliefs and invalidating her feelings, we explored them and considered other ways that she could perceive herself and her life. Similarly, we accepted her symptoms as making sense given where she was at that point in time, while also considering the possibility that other ways of responding might be possible.

## CONCLUSION

In sum, like other multicultural work, skillful translation of the ideas and techniques of secular psychotherapy into the client's own faith language can help psychotherapists understand and engage clients in treatment, make treatment more powerful and effective, and reduce religiously based fears that may be barriers to change. To do so, psychotherapists should recognize and acknowledge differences between their own worldview and beliefs and those of their clients, respect clients' beliefs (unless they are damaging), and take their clients' beliefs into account when designing treatment goals and interventions (Johnson, Ridley, & Nielsen, 2000). In particular, psychotherapists should address the negative effects of clients' religious beliefs, especially those beliefs that are demanding, extreme, rigid, and negative. To do so, psychotherapists may need to help clients differentiate between true religious beliefs and their distorted perceptions of religious beliefs.

Psychotherapists should not, however, trivialize or uncritically dispute clients' religious beliefs—just as they would not trivialize, discount, or reject other cultural beliefs (Johnson et al., 2000; Slattery & Park, 2011a). Furthermore, religious stories and texts should not be used cleverly to trick clients into changing. Instead, they should explore beliefs with clients in a collaborative fashion; stories and texts may be used to help clients examine the demandingness and judging qualities of their religious beliefs.

The ideas presented in this chapter remain speculative, because a paucity of data are available that examine specific religious and spiritual beliefs and their relationship to psychological and physical outcomes. Furthermore, people have multiple religious and spiritual beliefs that may interact to affect outcomes from illness, loss, or trauma. So far, evidence about these types of interactions is very limited, although they should be studied further. Nonetheless, it is clear that religious beliefs are an important part of the inner life of many clients and that both religious and nonreligious psychotherapists must be open to working with this material to sensitively and holistically treat their clients effectively.

## CHAPTER SUMMARY

- Religious beliefs often are the basis for clients' understanding of the world and their framework for interpreting reality; thus, religious beliefs may influence other basic beliefs, including locus of control or belief in a just world.

- Along with the situational context, global religious beliefs influence situational beliefs. From a meaning perspective, both global and situational beliefs are important determinants of subsequent feelings and behaviors.
- Some religious beliefs predispose individuals to make benign interpretations of potentially stressful events and protect them against the daily wear and tear of stressors, while other religious beliefs lead to situational interpretations associated with greater stress, guilt, and self-blame. In either case, situational religious beliefs can predict how well people will adjust to stressful situations.
- Situational beliefs regarding the meaning of a particular occurrence are easier to modify than global beliefs, which are fairly resistant to change and generally change only when one is forced to change them (e.g., when one belief conflicts with another and causes a discrepancy).
- Discrepancies between beliefs can create enormous distress and negatively affect behavior and overall functioning. This distress tends to motivate individuals to close the underlying discrepancies.
- Global beliefs are thought to be more difficult to change than situational beliefs, but global and situational religious beliefs may both be the appropriate focus of psychotherapeutic work and key to improved functioning and well-being.
- Psychotherapists might see a client's global and situational religious beliefs as maladaptive, although these beliefs might not cause clients to experience either a discrepancy or distress; instead, psychotherapists should focus on (a) situational religious beliefs that are discrepant from the client's global religious beliefs and (b) global and situational religious beliefs related to more negative outcomes.
- Using clients' own faith language can help psychotherapists understand and engage clients in treatment, make treatment more powerful and effective, and reduce religiously based fears that may be barriers to change.

## CLINICAL APPLICATION QUESTIONS

1. How might you approach assessing the degree to which a client's religious and spiritual beliefs are related to the client's current symptoms and goals?
2. How might you respond to a client whose religious and spiritual beliefs appear to be related to psychological symptoms and distress? Why? How would you respond to a client whose lack of religious and spiritual beliefs appear related to symptoms and distress? Why?

3. How would you approach working with a client whose religious and spiritual background is very different from yours? What if that client's religious and spiritual beliefs were related to symptoms and level of distress? What if the client's beliefs were unrelated to symptoms and levels of distress?

## SUGGESTED READINGS AND RESOURCES

Carone, D. A., & Barone, D. F. (2001). A social cognitive perspective on religious beliefs: Their functions and impact on coping and psychotherapy. *Clinical Psychology Review, 21,* 989–1003. doi:10.1016/S0272-7358(00)00078-7

George Washington Institute for Spirituality and Health. (n.d.). FICA Spiritual History Tool. Retrieved from http://www.gwumc.edu/gwish/clinical/fica.cfm

Lee, B. Y., & Newberg, A. B. (2010). The interaction of religion and health. In D. A. Monti & B. D. Beitman (Eds.), *Integrative psychiatry* (pp. 408–444). New York, NY: Oxford University Press.

## REFERENCES

American Psychological Association. (2008). Resolution on religious, religion-based and/or religion-derived prejudice. *American Psychologist, 63,* 431–434.

Barnes, C. D., & Brown, R. P. (2010). A value-congruent bias in the forgiveness forecasts of religious people. *Psychology of Religion and Spirituality, 2,* 17–29.

Barrett, J. L., & Lanman, J. A. (2008). The science of religious beliefs. *Religion, 38,* 109–124.

Beck, A. T. (1976). *Cognitive therapy and the emotional disorders.* New York, NY: International Universities Press.

Borneman, T., Ferrell, B., Otis-Green, S., Baird, P., & Puchalski, C. (2010). Evaluation of the FICA Spiritual Assessment Tool (501). *Journal of Pain & Symptom Management, 39,* 406–407.

Brickman, P., Rabinowitz, V. C., Karuza, J., Coates, D., Cohn, E., & Kidder, L. (1982). Models of helping and coping. *American Psychologist, 37,* 368–384.

Carone, D. A., & Barone, D. F. (2001). A social cognitive perspective on religious beliefs: Their functions and impact on coping and psychotherapy. *Clinical Psychology Review, 21,* 989–1003.

Connor, K. M., Davidson, J. R. T., & Lee, L. C. (2003). Spirituality, resilience, and anger in survivors of violent trauma: A community survey. *Journal of Traumatic Stress, 16,* 487–494.

Contrada, R. J., Boulifard, D. A., Hekler, E. B., Spruill, T. M., Krause, T. J., Labouvie, E. W., & Idler, E. L. (2008). Psychosocial factors in heart surgery: Presurgical vulnerability and postsurgical recovery. *Health Psychology, 27,* 309–319.

Contrada, R. J., Goyal, T. M., Cather, C., Idler, E. L., Krause, T. J., & Rafalson, L. (2004). Psychosocial factors in outcomes of heart surgery: The impact of religious involvement and depressive symptoms. *Health Psychology, 23,* 227–238.

Cowchock, F. S., Lasker, J. N., Toedter, L. J., Skumanich, S. A., & Koenig, H. G. (2009, August 19). Religious beliefs affect grieving after pregnancy loss. *Journal of Religion and Health.* Retrieved from http://www.springerlink.com/content/0022-4197

Dalgleish, T., & Power, M. J. (2004). Emotion-specific and emotion-non-specific components of posttraumatic stress disorder (PTSD): Implications for a taxonomy of related psychopathology. *Behaviour Research and Therapy, 42,* 1069–1088.

Davidson, J. R. T., Connor, K. M., & Lee, L. C. (2005). Beliefs in karma and reincarnation among survivors of violent trauma: A community survey. *Social Psychiatry and Psychiatric Epidemiology, 40,* 120–125.

Davis, C., Wortman, C. B., Lehman, D. R., & Silver, R. (2000). Searching for meaning in loss: Are clinical assumptions correct? *Death Studies, 24,* 497–540.

Ellis, A. (2000). Can rational emotive behavior therapy (REBT) be effectively used with people who have devout beliefs in God and religion? *Professional Psychology: Research and Practice, 31,* 29–33.

Exline, J. J. (2002). Stumbling blocks on the religious road: Fractured relationships, nagging vices, and the inner struggle to believe. *Psychological Inquiry, 13,* 182–189.

Exline, J. J. (2003). Belief in heaven and hell among Christians in the United States: Denominational differences and clinical implications. *Omega: Journal of Death and Dying, 47,* 155–168.

Exline, J. J. (2008). Beliefs about God and forgiveness in a Baptist Church sample. *Journal of Psychology and Christianity, 27,* 131–139.

Flannelly, K. J., Ellison, C. G., Galek, K., & Koenig, H. G. (2008). Beliefs about life-after-death, psychiatric symptomology and cognitive theories of psychopathology. *Journal of Psychology and Theology, 36,* 94–103.

Flannelly, K. J., Koenig, H. G., Ellison, C. G., Galek, K., & Krause, N. (2006). Belief in life after death and mental health: Findings from a national survey. *Journal of Nervous and Mental Disease, 194,* 524–529.

Gall, T. L. (2004). Relationship with God and the quality of life of prostate cancer survivors. *Quality of Life Research: An International Journal of Quality of Life Aspects of Treatment, Care & Rehabilitation, 13,* 1357–1368.

Gallup. (2009). *Religion.* Retrieved from http://www.gallup.com/poll/1690/Religion.aspx

George Washington Institute for Spirituality and Health. (n.d.). *FICA Spiritual History Tool.* Retrieved from http://www.gwumc.edu/gwish/clinical/fica.cfm

Gonsiorek, J. C., Richards, P. S., Pargament, K. I., & McMinn, M. R. (2009). Ethical challenges and opportunities at the edge: Incorporating spirituality and religion into psychotherapy. *Professional Psychology: Research and Practice, 40,* 385–395.

Gray, M. J., Maguen, S., & Litz, B. T. (2007). Schema constructs and cognitive models of Posttraumatic Stress Disorder. In L. P. Riso, P. L. du Toit, D. J. Stein, & J. E. Young, (Eds.), *Cognitive schemas and core beliefs in psychological problems: A scientist-practitioner guide* (pp. 59–92). Washington, DC: American Psychological Association.

Hackney, C. H., & Sanders, G. S. (2003). Religiosity and mental health: A meta-analysis of recent studies. *Journal of the Scientific Study of Religion, 42,* 43–55.

Hall, M. E. L., & Johnson, E. L. (2001). Theodicy and therapy: Philosophical/theological contributions to the problem of suffering. *Journal of Psychology and Christianity, 20,* 5–17.

Harris Interactive. (2005, December 14). *The religious and other beliefs of Americans 2005.* Retrieved from http://www.harrisinteractive.com/harris_poll/index.asp?PID=618

Harris Interactive. (2008, December 10). *More Americans believe in the devil, hell and angels than in Darwin's theory of evolution.* Retrieved from http://www.harrisinteractive.com/harris_poll/index.asp?PID=982

Higgins, E. T. (1987). Self-discrepancy: A theory relating self and affect. *Psychological Review, 94,* 319–340.

Higgins, E. T., Bond, R. N., Klein, R., & Strauman, T. (1986). Self-discrepancies and emotional vulnerability: How magnitude, accessibility, and type of discrepancy influence affect. *Journal of Personality and Social Psychology, 51,* 5–15.

Hood, R. W., Hill, P. C., & Spilka, B. (2009). *The psychology of religion: An empirical approach* (4th ed.). New York, NY: Guilford.

Janoff-Bulman, R. (1992). *Shattered assumptions: Towards a new psychology of trauma.* New York, NY: Free Press.

Janoff-Bulman, R., & Frantz, C. M. (1997). The impact of trauma on meaning: From meaningless world to meaningful life. In M. J. Power & C. R. Brewin (Eds.), *The transformation of meaning in psychological therapies: Integrating theory and practice* (pp. 91–106). Hoboken, NJ: Wiley.

Johnson, W. B., Ridley, C. R., & Nielsen, S. L. (2000). Religiously sensitive rational emotive behavior therapy: Elegant solutions and ethical risks. *Professional Psychology: Research and Practice, 31,* 14–20.

Kidd, S. M. (1990). *When the heart waits: Spiritual direction for life's sacred questions.* New York, NY: HarperCollins.

Krause, N., Liang, J., Shaw, B. A., Sugisawa, H., Kim, H. K., & Sugihara, Y. (2002). Religion, death of a loved one, and hypertension among older adults in Japan. *Journals of Gerontology Series B: Psychological Sciences and Social Sciences, 57,* 96–107.

Kremer, H., Ironson, G., & Porr, M. (2009). Spiritual and mind–body beliefs as barriers and motivators to HIV-treatment decision-making and medication adherence? A qualitative study. *AIDS Patient Care and STDs, 23,* 127–134.

Kushner, H. S. (1981). *When bad things happen to good people.* New York, NY: Avon Books.

Lawler-Row, K. A. (2010). Forgiveness as a mediator of the religiosity–health relationship. *Psychology of Religion and Spirituality, 2,* 1–16.

Lee, B. Y., & Newberg, A. B. (2005). Religion and health: A review and critical analysis. *Zygon, 40,* 443–468.

Lee, B. Y., & Newberg, A. B. (2010). The interaction of religion and health. In D. A. Monti & B. D. Beitman (Eds.), *Integrative psychiatry* (pp. 408–444). New York, NY: Oxford University Press.

Lee, L. C., Connor, K. M., & Davidson, J. R. T. (2008). Eastern and Western spiritual beliefs and violent trauma: A U.S. national community survey. *Traumatology, 14,* 68–76.

Levy, B. R., Slade, M. D., & Ranasignhe, P. (2009). Causal thinking after a tsunami wave: Karma beliefs, pessimistic explanatory style and health among Sri Lankan survivors. *Journal of Religion and Health, 48,* 38–45.

Linehan, M. M. (1993). *Cognitive-behavioral treatment of borderline personality disorder.* New York, NY: Guilford.

Maercker, A., & Herrle, J. (2003). Long-term effects of the Dresden bombing: Relationships to control beliefs, religious belief, and personal growth. *Journal of Traumatic Stress, 16,* 579–587.

McCullough, M. E., & Willoughby, B. L. B. (2009). Religion, self-regulation, and self-control: Associations, explanations, and implications. *Psychological Bulletin, 135,* 69–93.

McCullough, M. E., & Worthington, E. L. (1999). Religion and the forgiving personality. *Journal of Personality, 67,* 1141–1164.

McIntosh, D. N. (1995). Religion-as-schema, with implications for the relation between religion and coping. *The International Journal for the Psychology of Religion, 5,* 1–16.

McMinn, M. R., Aikins, D. C., & Lish, R. A. (2003). Basic and advanced competence in collaborating with clergy. *Professional Psychology: Research and Practice, 34,* 197–202.

Mickley, J. R., Pargament, K. I., Brant, C. R., & Hipp, K. M. (1998). God and the search for meaning among hospice caregivers. *Hospice Journal, 13,* 1–17.

Mitchell, J., Lannin, D. R., Mathews, H. F., & Swanson, M. S. (2002). Religious beliefs and breast cancer screening. *Journal of Women's Health, 11,* 907–915.

Moreira-Almeida, A., Lotufo Neto, F., & Koenig, H. G. (2006). Religiousness and mental health: a review. *Revista Brasileira de Psiquiatria, 28,* 242–250.

Morrow, D., Worthington, E. L., & McCullough, M. E. (1993). Observers' perceptions of a counselor's treatment of a religious issue. *Journal of Counseling and Development, 71,* 452–456.

Nielsen, S. L., Ridley, C. R., & Johnson, W. B. (2000). Religiously sensitive rational emotive behavior therapy: Theory, techniques, and brief excerpts from a case. *Professional Psychology: Research and Practice, 31,* 21–28.

Paloutzian, R. (2005). Religious conversion and spiritual transformation: A meaning-system analysis. In R. F. Paloutzian and C. L. Park (Eds.), *Handbook of the psychology of religion and spirituality* (pp. 331–347). New York, NY: Guilford.

Pargament, K. I. (1997). *The psychology of religion and coping.* New York, NY: Guilford.

Pargament, K. I., Ensing, D. S., Falgout, K., Olsen, H., Reilly, B., Van Haitsma, K., & Warren, R. (1990). God help me: I. Religious coping efforts as predictors of the outcomes to significant negative life events. *American Journal of Community Psychology, 18,* 793–824.

Pargament, K. I., & Hahn, J. (1986). God and the just world: Causal and coping attributions to god in health situations. *Journal for the Scientific Study of Religion*, 25, 193–207.

Pargament, K. I., Koenig, H. G., Tarakeshwar, N., & Hahn, J. (2004). Religious coping methods as predictors of psychological, physical and spiritual outcomes among medically ill elderly patients: A two-year longitudinal study. *Journal of Health Psychology. 9,* 713–730.

Pargament, K. I., Murray-Swank, N. A., Magyar, G. M., & Ano, G. G. (2005). Spiritual struggle: A phenomenon of interest to psychology and religion. In W. R. Miller & H. D. Delaney (Eds.), *Judeo-Christian perspectives on psychology: Human nature, motivation, and change* (pp. 245–268). Washington, DC: American Psychological Association.

Park, C. L. (2005). Religion and meaning. In R. F. Paloutzian & C. L. Park (Eds.), *Handbook of the psychology of religion and spirituality* (pp. 295–314). New York, NY: Guilford Press.

Park, C. L. (2010). Making sense of the meaning literature: An integrative review of meaning making and its effects on adjustment to stressful life events. *Psychological Bulletin, 136,* 257–301.

Park, C. L., & Cohen, L. H. (1993). Religious and non-religious coping with the death of a friend. *Cognitive Therapy and Research, 17,* 561–577.

Park, C., Cohen, L. H., & Herb, L. (1990). Intrinsic religiousness and religious coping as life stress moderators for Catholics versus Protestants. *Journal of Personality and Social Psychology, 59,* 562–574.

Park, C. L., Edmondson, D., & Mills, M. A. (2010). Religious worldviews and stressful encounters: Reciprocal influence from a meaning-making perspective. In T. W. Miller (Ed.), *Handbook of stressful transitions across the lifespan* (pp. 485–501). New York, NY: Springer.

Park, C. L., & Folkman, S. (1997). Meaning in the context of stress and coping. *Review of General Psychology, 1,* 115–144.

Park, C. L., & Slattery, J. M. (2009). Including spirituality in case conceptualizations: A meaning system approach. In J. Aten & M. Leach (Eds.), *Spirituality and the therapeutic practice: A comprehensive resource from intake to termination* (pp. 121–142). Washington, DC: American Psychological Association.

Parsons, S. K., Cruise, P. L., Davenport, W. M., & Jones, V. (2006). Religious beliefs, practices and treatment adherence among individuals with HIV in the southern United States. *AIDS Patient Care and STDs, 20,* 97–111.

Pew Forum on Religious and Public Life. (2009, October 3). *U.S. religious landscape survey.* Retrieved from http://religions.pewforum.org/reports#

Propst, L. R. (1996). Cognitive-behavioral therapy and the religious person. In E. P. Shafranske (Ed.), *Religion and the clinical practice of psychology* (pp. 391–407). Washington, DC: American Psychological Association.

Rosmarin, D. H., Pirutinsky, S., Pargament, K. I., & Krumrei, E. J. (2009). Are religious beliefs relevant to mental health among Jews? *Psychology of Religion and Spirituality, 1*, 180–190.

Rye, M. S., Pargament, K. I., Ali, M. A., Beck, G. L., Dorff, E. N., Hallisey, C., … & Williams, J. G. (2000). Religious perspectives on forgiveness. *Forgiveness: Theory, research, and practice* (pp. 17–40). New York, NY: Guilford.

Sanderson, S. K. (2008). Adaptation, evolution, and religion. *Religion, 38,* 114–156.

Sittser, J. (2004). *A grace disguised: How the soul grows through loss* (expanded ed.). Grand Rapids, MI: Zondervan.

Slattery, J. M., & Park, C. L. (in press). Clinical approaches to discrepancies in meaning: Conceptualization, assessment, and treatment. In P. T. P. Wong (Ed.), *Human quest for meaning* (2nd ed.). New York, NY: Routledge.

Slattery, J. M., & Park, C. L. (2011a). Meaning making and spiritually oriented interventions. In J. Aten, M. R. McMinn, & E. V. Worthington (Eds.), *Spiritually oriented interventions for counseling and psychotherapy.* (pp. 15–40) Washington, DC: American Psychological Association.

Slattery, J. M., & Park, C. L. (2011b). *Empathic counseling: Meaning, context, ethics, and skill.* Pacific Grove, CA: Brooks/Cole.

Smith, P. C., Range, L. M., & Ulmer, A. (1991–1992). Belief in afterlife as a buffer in suicidal and other bereavement. *Omega: Journal of Death and Dying, 24*, 217–225.

Stark, R., & Glock, C. Y. (1968). *American piety.* Berkeley, CA: University of California Press.

Tolstikova, K., Fleming, S., & Chartier, B. (2005). Grief, complicated grief, and trauma: The role of the search for meaning, impaired self-reference, and death anxiety. *Illness, Crisis and Loss, 13*, 293–313.

Wade, N. G., Johnson, C. V., & Meyer, J. E. (2008). Understanding concerns about interventions to promote forgiveness: A review of the literature. *Psychotherapy: Theory, Research, Practice, Training, 45,* 88–102.

Wohl, M. J. A., DeShea, L., & Wahkinney, R. L. (2008). Looking within: Measuring state self-forgiveness and its relationship to psychological well-being. *Canadian Journal of Behavioural Science/Revue canadienne des sciences du comportement, 40,* 1–10.

# 9

# *Navigating the Storm*

## Helping Clients in the Midst of Spiritual Struggles

NICHOLE A. MURRAY-SWANK AND
AARON B. MURRAY-SWANK

According to Yalom (2000), "It is best not to *pursue* purpose explicitly but to allow it to *ensue* from meaningful and authentic engagement, from plunging into an enlarging, fulfilling, self-transcending endeavor" (para. 43). Spirituality provides people with a worldview, a blueprint, for how to live life fully, while also encountering the inevitability of loss, illness, suffering, and death. In this process, spiritual beliefs and practices often provide comfort, hope, meaning, support, and connection. One's spiritual worldview, however, also can result in struggle, strain, isolation, and doubt. A recent client described such a struggle when he started the session: "I am searching for some way to address my anger at God and the alienation I feel. I feel completely empty inside, like I have no purpose." Clients' question why difficult life events happen, grapple with how to cope in times of change, and wrestle with concerns about divine intervention and support.

The purpose of this chapter is to explore how to help clients in the midst of spiritual struggles. As such, we make no claims to comprehensively address the theological questions of suffering, evil, or the afterlife. We will draw from the theoretical literature in psychology, diverse spiritual perspectives, the empirical literature in the psychology of religion, and our clinical experience of working with people with spiritual struggles. More specifically, we draw extensively from prior work on religious coping and Yalom's (1980) model of existential psychotherapy. We hope to provide a framework that integrates these perspectives, while suggesting ways to think about and intervene in the lives of clients with spiritual struggles.

First, we discuss the framework underlying our approach to working with spiritual struggles. Next, we review recent empirical research on spiritual struggles, negative religious coping, anger toward God, and attachment to God. In addition, we highlight some promising interventions that address spiritual struggles and religious strain. We also discuss assessment strategies and clinical interventions for working with spiritual and religious strain. Finally, we present case studies of working with spiritual struggles, including a discussion about how to work with value conflicts in psychotherapy.

## RELIGIOUS COPING AND EXISTENTIAL PSYCHOTHERAPY: AN INTEGRATIVE FRAMEWORK

Pargament, Koenig, and Perez (2000) suggested five ways that religion and spirituality serve the coping process: They help people (1) make meaning, (2) gain control, (3) seek comfort, (4) gain intimacy, and (5) achieve life transformation. Similarly, Yalom's (1980, 2000) psychotherapy model elucidates four existential questions that every human encounters: (1) meaning in life versus meaninglessness, (2) isolation, (3) freedom versus responsibility, and (4) death (see Table 9.1). While Yalom (2000) discusses religion as an immature way to "quell existence anxiety" (para. 34), we emphasize the relevance and importance of spirituality in coping with life's existential themes. In fact, we propose four types of spiritual struggles based on an integration of the religious coping framework and existential psychotherapy: (1) spiritual meaning, (2) spiritual control and responsibility, (3) spiritual isolation and disconnection, (4) death and impermanence (see Table 9.1).

### Death and Impermanence

Let us begin with the end in mind: Everyone physically dies. According to Yalom's (1980) existential model, the inevitability of this reality creates the ultimate form of anxiety. Similarly, within Buddhism, the notion of impermanence is paramount. Goldstein (2002) wrote, "A first aspect to consider is that *the end of birth is death*" (p. 33). Recognizing the fact that all things change, including life itself, allows a person to let go of clinging and suffering and to experience awakening

**Table 9.1** Religious Coping, Existential Themes, and Categorization of Spiritual Struggles

| Pargament's Religious Functions | Yalom's Existential Themes | Four Types of Spiritual Struggles |
|---|---|---|
| Make meaning | Meaning in life versus meaninglessness | Spiritual meaning |
| Gain control | Freedom versus responsibility | Spiritual control and responsibility |
| Gain intimacy | Isolation | Spiritual isolation and disconnection |
| Seek comfort | Religion serves to assuage anxiety | Related to spiritual connection |
| Life transformation | Death | Death and impermanence |

and ultimate freedom. Thus, according to Buddhist thought, life involves suffering because of one's attachment to solidness, desires, and even life itself. Overall, we consider the final physical frontier of death as a common time of spiritual struggle for people across diverse faith traditions.

In addition to death is the dying process itself. From an empirical perspective, numerous studies have explored the role of spirituality at the end of life. For example, in a national survey of seriously ill patients, recently bereaved family members, and physicians and other care providers, 89% of the seriously ill patients responded that being at peace with God was very important at the end of life (Steinhauser et al., 2000). In fact, for both patients and recently bereaved family members, being "at peace with God" was ranked as the second most important consideration in the dying process, second only to freedom from pain (Steinhauser et al., 2000). Additionally, 85% of seriously ill patients indicated that the ability to pray was very important in the dying process. Finally, talking about the meaning of death was very important, especially for those who considered spirituality as important in their lives.

### Spiritual Meaning

The meaning of death, whether sooner or later, will become significant for most people. Likewise, finding meaning while living represents a central human goal. People seek to live meaningful lives and find ways to maintain a sense of purpose and value. From a spiritual perspective, people draw from religious and spiritual perspectives to create and sustain meaning in life. As exemplified in the quote used to begin this chapter, "I feel completely empty inside, like I have no purpose." For many, spirituality is inextricably tied to meaning in life.

Numerous theorists and researchers have emphasized the value of spiritual meaning in the coping process. For example, in a review of religion and meaning, Park (2005) described how religion plays a central role in finding global meaning in life as well as in meaning-making in the midst of crises or difficult times. Clinically, Park and Slattery (2009) reviewed the relevance of spirituality and religion in a meaning-systems approach to case conceptualization. From an Eastern perspective, Phillips, Cheng, et al. (2009) highlighted the importance of spiritual meaning (e.g., right understanding) in how Buddhists cope with stress.

Exline, Park, Smyth, and Carey (2011) demonstrated that difficulty finding meaning in negative life events predicted increased anger toward God. In addition, anger toward God predicted poor mental and physical health across diverse samples (Exline et al., 2011). On the other end of the continuum, finding spiritual meaning in events may lead to improved outcomes. For example, in an empirical study on people experiencing spiritual struggles, increased meaning in the struggle was related to post-traumatic growth, life satisfaction, spiritual growth, and struggle resolution, as well as less spiritual decline (Desai, 2006). Thus, the ability to create spiritual meaning reflects a primary motivation for many people, and assists people in coping with life's challenges. Subsequently, difficulties in the spiritual meaning-making process represent one important type of spiritual struggle to assess and work through with clients.

### Spiritual Control and Responsibility

The third type of spiritual struggle involves a certain aspect of the spiritual meaning-making process: spiritual responsibility and control. Countless clients have entered our offices with the explicit or underlying question "Who is in charge?" More specifically, religious clients frequently ask, "Is God to blame?" "Is this the result of actions in past lives?" or "Am I to blame?" From an existential perspective, a psychotherapist would help a client discover that he or she is ultimately responsible in one's life and thus experience freedom. However, spiritual worldviews are more complex. In Western spiritual traditions, people frequently believe in a loving, all-powerful God. They may also attribute responsibility to the devil. From an Eastern perspective (e.g., Hindu, Buddhist), an individual might believe in the role of karma or might struggle with the role of ego.

Exline et al. (2011) examined the problematic role of certain types of attributions about spiritual control and responsibility. For example, holding God responsible for difficult life events (e.g., loss of a loved one) and cruelty attributions (e.g., "God wanted to hurt me, did not care about me, was not responding to me, had abandoned me, and/or turned away from me") were associated with poor outcomes. As we will review, other types of beliefs about spiritual responsibility and control (e.g., punishment by God) can lead to decreased well-being. In general, working with a client's questions and concerns about spiritual responsibility and control is paramount in psychotherapy.

### Spiritual Disconnection and Isolation

Finally, we suggest that feelings of spiritual isolation and disconnection abound as clients face difficulties in life. Some people come in to psychotherapy with the question "Did God abandon me?" Recently, one of our therapy clients who was a survivor of sexual abuse asked God, "Where were you in the midst of my suffering? Where are you now?" The spiritual isolation and disconnection from God and others can be profound and long-lasting. From an existential perspective, Yalom (1980) has contended that humans are fundamentally alone. However, from a spiritual perspective, people frequently believe in a higher power or divine source that is available for connection. Kirkpatrick (2005) described one's attachment to God as a real attachment relationship, and as one that is adaptive for human functioning. The perceived loss of this attachment relationship results in grief, suffering, and anxiety. Within certain Eastern perspectives, spiritual seekers may encounter disconnection from one's True Nature, Inner Self, Buddha-nature, or from fellow Sangha or members of a spiritual community. Working with a client's sense of spiritual isolation and disconnection can facilitate the psychotherapy process.

To summarize, we describe four types of spiritual struggles that are important to assess and work with in psychotherapy: difficulties in spiritual meaning, questions about spiritual control and responsibility, the experience of spiritual isolation and disconnection, and struggles with death and impermanence. These struggles are not mutually exclusive; they often are experienced simultaneously and they frequently are interrelated (as seen in the following case studies). We use these categories to help psychotherapists identify, think about, and work with spiritual struggles. As mentioned, this categorization results from the integration of prior work on religious coping (e.g., Pargament et al., 2000) and existential psychotherapy (Frankl, 1984; Yalom, 1980). We turn next to an empirical review, considering what psychotherapists can learn from recent research findings.

## EMPIRICAL REVIEW OF NEGATIVE RELIGIOUS COPING, RELIGIOUS STRAIN, AND ATTACHMENT TO GOD

There is a vast body of empirical literature on the psychological and physical implications of spirituality in the coping process. Although not exhaustive, we provide an illustrative review of research on spiritual struggles, with particular attention to the impact on mental health. More specifically, we focus on the literature regarding negative religious coping, spiritual and religious strain, anger toward God, and attachment to God.

### Negative Religious Coping

As people attempt to cope with spiritual struggles by making meaning out of difficult life events, gaining control and freedom, seeking intimacy and connection, or facing death, certain forms of coping appear to be problematic. Overall, Pargament et al. (2000) described seven types of negative religious coping: spiritual discontent, demonic reappraisal, passive religious deferral, interpersonal religious discontent, reappraisal of God's power, punishing God reappraisal, and pleading for direct intercession. Krumrei and Rosmarin (Chapter 10, this volume) offer a fuller treatment on the literature on negative religious coping. Generally, the empirical research repeatedly demonstrates a link between these types of negative religious coping styles and poor mental and physical health. In a meta-analysis on 49 studies of religious coping, negative religious coping (22 studies) significantly predicted negative adjustment, such as depression, anxiety, and mortality (Ano & Vasconcelles, 2005).

To highlight, negative forms of religious coping (e.g., feeling abandoned by, angry with, or punished by God) have been associated with posttraumatic stress disorder (PTSD) and psychological distress among trauma survivors (e.g., Fallot & Heckman, 2005; Gall, 2006; Murray-Swank, Kohn, & Doehring, 2007).

In longitudinal studies across diverse samples, negative religious coping predicted psychological distress, poor physical health, and even mortality across time (e.g., Pargament, Koenig, Tarakeshwar, & Hahn, 2001; Sherman, Plante, Simonton, Latif, & Anaissie, 2009). Finally, negative religious coping has been related to poor emotional health, such as increased depression, anxiety, and anger and less life satisfaction, purpose, and well-being among Jewish, Buddhist, Hindu, and Islamic participants (e.g., Abu Raiya, Pargament, Mahoney, & Stein, 2008; Khan & Watson, 2006; Phillips , Hietbrink, et al., 2009; Rosmarin, Pargament, Krumrei, & Flannelly, 2009; Tarakeshwar, Pargament, & Mahoney, 2003). Taken together, the research indicates that negative forms of religious coping are related to negative physical and mental health across diverse spiritual traditions and cultures.

One important component when considering the psychological and spiritual impact of negative religious coping may be *time*. For example, in a study of medically ill elderly patients, only the participants who reported "chronic" negative religious coping (i.e., reporting negative religious coping at baseline and 2 years later) demonstrated a deterioration in mental and physical health (Pargament, Koenig, Tarakeshwar, & Hahn, 2004). In a similar vein, Exline et al. (2011) found that chronic anger toward God (across 1 year) predicted worse outcomes for cancer survivors.

Additionally, facilitating the spiritual meaning-making process appears to be one promising way to help clients work through chronic spiritual struggles. Empirically, difficulty finding meaning was associated with increased spiritual struggles among college students and cancer survivors (Exline et al., 2010). In another study, the ability to find meaning in a spiritual struggle was associated with posttraumatic and spiritual growth, and less spiritual decline across time, in a sample of college students (Desai, 2006). Thus, it appears that helping people *work through* spiritual struggles before they become chronic is a key consideration in psychotherapy. Slattery and Park (Chapter 8, this volume) offer a more extensive review of meaning-making research.

### Religious Strain, Anger Toward God, and Attachment to God

In a related line of empirical work, researchers have examined religious strain and anger toward God as important predictors of poor mental and physical health. In one study, Exline, Yali, and Sanderson (2000) identified three factors of religious strain: alienation from God (e.g., "Feeling that God is far away"), fear of guilt (e.g., "Belief that you have committed a sin too big to be forgiven"), and religious rifts (e.g., "Disagreement with a family member or friend about religious issues"). In this study, religious strain was associated with depression and suicidality in college student and clinical outpatient samples (e.g., Exline et al., 2000). In another study, difficulty forgiving God (e.g., "I sometimes find it difficult to forgive God for things that happen") predicted depression and anxiety, after controlling for difficulties with forgiving self and others (Exline, Yali, & Lobel, 1999).

Feelings of alienation from God partially mediated the link between difficulty forgiving God and depressed mood (Exline et al., 1999).

In a recent report on five studies on anger and negative feelings toward God, anger toward God was a frequent response to difficult life events (Exline et al., 2011). Additionally, holding God responsible and attributions of cruel intent (spiritual control and responsibility), and difficulty finding meaning (spiritual meaning), were associated with increased anger toward God. Next, increased anger toward God was related to poor mental health (e.g., depression and negative emotions) and general well-being (e.g., decreased life satisfaction) across diverse samples. Finally, chronic anger was associated with the worst outcomes for cancer survivors.

Anger, abandonment, and alienation reflect emotions within relationships. Kirkpatrick (2005) has focused on relational attachment with God as a useful way to think about an individual's spirituality, especially for individuals who espouse a theistic worldview (i.e., belief in a personal God available for connection). From this perspective, people can develop secure or insecure attachments to God or other deities (see Moriarty & Davis, Chapter 6, this volume). More specifically, an avoidant attachment reflects a relationship in which God is seen as impersonal, distant, and uncaring. An anxious attachment reflects an inconsistent God; sometimes God seems warm and responsive, and other times God seems uncaring and unresponsive (Kirkpatrick, 2005). A secure relationship involves the belief that God is stable, consistent, and responsive. As with any attachment figure, individuals seek proximity and comfort when facing threatening or challenging situations, and experience anxiety and grief at the threat of losing their relationship or separation from God. Researchers have examined attachment to God as an important variable related to emotional functioning and how individuals cope with challenges. For example, Rowatt and Kirkpatrick (2002) found that an anxious attachment style, viewing God as inconsistent, was related to higher levels of negative affect and neuroticism, even when controlling for social desirability and a range of religious variables.

In general, spiritual struggles have been related to poor mental and physical health, and even death. However, working through spiritual struggles, before they become chronic, may lead to growth and transformation.

## MANUALIZED INTERVENTIONS FOR NEGATIVE RELIGIOUS COPING, SPIRITUAL STRUGGLES, AND RELIGIOUS STRAIN

Recent manualized, spiritually integrated interventions in psychology have been developed to specifically help clients work through spiritual struggles, such as negative religious coping, religious strain, and disconnection from God. In addition, researchers have begun to examine the effectiveness of this work. For example, *Solace for the Soul: A Journey Toward Wholeness* (Murray-Swank, 2003) addresses diverse spiritual struggles surrounding sexual abuse. In this 8-week manualized, theistic intervention, clients explore such themes as spiritual disconnection, abandonment and anger at God, and feelings of spiritual shame. For example, in a session entitled "God where are you?" psychotherapists normalize spiritual struggles (e.g., "It is normal to feel angry at God") and clients read a poem about a spiritual struggle written by a survivor of sexual abuse ("I know that you can hear my silent screams.... Meet me in the wasteland of my tears, wrap me up in your mighty arms, and rock me to sleep"; Flaherty, 1992, p. 51). They are asked to reflect upon, write about, and discuss times they too have ever felt abandoned by God or angry with God, or experienced times of spiritual disconnection. Psychotherapists guide clients through a two-way journaling-to-God exercise, as a way to express struggles, work through them, and gain new insights. The next session focuses on ways of enhancing spiritual connection (with God, self, and others). For example, clients are asked to reflect upon times they have felt God's presence in life. Psychotherapists guide clients in a visualization of divine light exercise, and practice a loving kindness meditation (see Murray-Swank, 2003). Overall, this theistic intervention explicitly addresses spiritual struggles and negative religious coping. It also focuses on three of the spiritual struggles we have outlined: spiritual meaning, spiritual responsibility and control, and spiritual isolation and disconnection.

In an outcome study on the Solace for the Soul program, female survivors of sexual abuse experienced decreases in psychological distress (e.g., depression and anxiety) and trauma symptoms across the course of intervention and at 1- to 2-month follow-up intervals (Murray-Swank & Pargament, 2008). In a study focused on the spiritual impact of the Solace for the Soul program, clients with spiritual struggles demonstrated increases in positive religious coping, spiritual well-being, and positive images of God (Murray-Swank & Pargament, 2005). From a qualitative perspective, clients reconstructed narratives about spiritual meaning, as well as their histories of sexual trauma. For example, one client commented at the end of the intervention, "Although I haven't let go of the anger completely, I am working towards God ... I notice the anger coming down. I know now that God is not the person to be angry at. I am angry at the person whose fault it is ... my dad" (Murray-Swank & Pargament, 2005, p. 197). This client began to reconstruct her narrative about spiritual control and responsibility, shifting blame from herself and God to the perpetrator of the abuse (her stepfather).

In another example, Harris et al. (2007) developed an eight-session, spiritually integrated group intervention for veteran military trauma survivors. Building spiritual strength was developed to address religious strain, reduce spiritual distress, and enhance religious meaning-making. For example, clients explore feelings of anger at God, abandonment at God, and punishment by God, and explore their feelings of guilt and beliefs about evil. They also explore ways to reduce spiritual disconnection, and discuss how to increase forgiveness. For example, during the fifth session, psychotherapists teach clients different spiritual strategies for coping with trauma (e.g., seeking calm and focus, seeking assistance, and seeking acceptance). In a pilot study on this intervention, participants in the Building Spiritual Strength group demonstrated decreases in PTSD symptoms as compared with a wait-list control group (Harris et al., 2011).

Cole's psychotherapy program Re-Creating Your Life: During and After Cancer explicitly integrates existential themes (i.e., control, identity, relationships, and meaning) with spirituality (Cole, 2005; Cole & Pargament, 1999). For example, in one session, clients are guided through a visualization process about the spiritual significance of an experience and are asked to visualize a symbol of the spiritual meaning of their cancer. Cole and Pargament (1999) described how one client described an image of a pretzel: "She shared that she had learned about herself through her cancer experience, that she was wound too tightly and wrapped up in herself.... Cancer was teaching her to let go and more fully enjoy significant others in life" (Cole & Pargament, 1999, p. 404). In a study on the efficacy of this intervention, depression and pain severity remained stable across time for the spiritually focused psychotherapy group, and they increased in a no-treatment control group (Cole, 2005).

From an Eastern perspective, Avants and Margolin (2004) developed an intervention based on the Four Noble Truths and the Eightfold Path of Buddhism. Spiritual Self-Schema (3-S) therapy was developed for people with addictions and HIV risk behaviors. Psychotherapists utilize aspects of cognitive psychotherapy and Buddhist principles to help clients move from an "addict self-schema" to a "spiritual self-schema" (Avants & Margolin, 2003, p. 1). For example, in the first session, psychotherapists teach clients the difference between the addict self, a habit pattern of mind that is causing suffering, and the real self, the spiritual self that is always available. Clients are taught to identify the addict self, interrupt the addict autopilot, and activate the spiritual self (Avants & Margolin, 2003, p. 6). One example of activating the spiritual self is the use of a "spiritual stretch exercise" (Avants & Margolin, 2003, p. 13) that combines movement with affirmations of a client's spiritual nature, as well as mindfulness practices.

This spiritually integrative intervention primarily focuses on craving as the root cause of suffering. More specifically, the intervention includes an in-depth training in mastery of the mind, morality, and wisdom (see Avants & Margolin, 2003). Also, the intervention aims to increase the 10 qualities of generosity, morality, renunciation, wisdom, effort, tolerance, truth, strong determination, loving kindness, and equanimity. Although this approach was developed from Buddhist principles, the authors discuss how the treatment remains compatible with the world's major religions, and the spiritual schema is tailored to an individual's belief system.

In a preliminary study of 3-S therapy, drug-dependent clients demonstrated decreased use of cocaine and heroin at the end of the intervention (Avants,

Beitel, & Margolin, 2005). In addition, participants demonstrated increases in daily spiritual experiences, private religious practices, use of spiritual coping, and expressions of spiritual qualities in daily life (Avants et al., 2005). In another study of HIV-positive drug users, the treatment group (3-S group) demonstrated decreases in impulsivity and intoxicant use when compared with a standard care control (Margolin et al., 2007). Additionally, participants in the 3-S group demonstrated greater increases in spiritual experiences, values, and private spiritual practice such as meditation and prayer (Margolin et al., 2007).

These studies highlight some promising interventions for working through spiritual struggles and facilitating the growth process, including many of the themes we have discussed (e.g., spiritual meaning, isolation, control and responsibility, and death and impermanence). We turn next to the clinical implications of this research, and general strategies for working with spiritual struggles and religious strain in psychotherapy.

### Clinical Implications of Research Findings

To summarize briefly, certain ways of making meaning and ascribing spiritual responsibility and control have been found to be problematic, such as viewing events as a punishment from God or attributing events to the Devil. In addition, feeling spiritually isolated and disconnected, abandoned by God, and angry with God and having an insecure relationship with God can lead to worse outcomes (e.g., depression, anxiety, and poor health), particularly if chronic. Finally, recent research on addressing spiritual struggles through manualized interventions has shown promise in helping clients improve spiritual and psychological health.

These research findings have important implications for psychotherapists working with individuals facing difficult life challenges. First, the repeated associations between spiritual struggles and mental health, physical health, and mortality highlight the importance of assessing and addressing spiritual and religious strain in the psychotherapy process. Next, we believe that it is useful to have a guiding framework for assessing and intervening in the lives of clients with spiritual struggles. We contend that this process is threefold: (1) surveying recent research and theory on the topic, (2) developing relevant intervention strategies, and (3) evaluating the outcomes of such interventions. We turn next to our framework for intervening in the lives of clients with spiritual struggles.

## CLINICAL INTERVENTION STRATEGIES

We emphasize five key components when helping others work through spiritual struggles: Assess, normalize, express, create meaning, and seek connection. As clients create meaning, we listen for spiritual narratives and embedded theologies about spiritual control and responsibility. In addition, our intervention strategies are consistent with an emotion-focused, humanistic-existential perspective.

First, as in any psychotherapeutic endeavor, the assessment of spiritual struggles is important, which we will discuss more thoroughly in the section to follow. Second, although spiritual traditions often emphasize emotions such as reverence, joy, gratitude, and peace, humans also experience sadness, anger, disappointment, and loneliness. We stress that all emotions are OK to have, experience, and accept. In addition, most intimate relationships include times of conflict. Therefore, one's relationship with the divine or one's spiritual path most likely will include times of conflict and strain. Normalizing spiritual struggle is primary.

Third, we believe that the emotional expression of spiritual struggles and the creation of meaning are helpful to clients. Here, our assumptions are consonant with an emotion-focused, existential framework (e.g., Greenberg, 2004). Within this perspective, psychotherapists help clients become aware of and accept the diverse emotions they feel. Psychotherapists help clients make meaning of their emotional experiences (Greenberg, 2004). Key components involve arriving and leaving: "Arriving" includes awareness of and acceptance, whereas "leaving" involves determining whether the emotion is healthy for the person, and helping transform and find alternative responses and a "new inner voice" (Greenberg, 2004, p. 7). In a similar vein, researchers have demonstrated that expression alone or catharsis is insufficient. For example, Kelly and colleagues (Kelly, 1999; Kelly, Klusas, von Weiss, & Kenny, 2001) have demonstrated that disclosure or expression by the client is important when an individual can gain a new perspective or insight. Thus, at those times when the psychotherapist judges that the client is on the verge of an insight, he or she can encourage full expression by the client. In general, emotional expression coupled with cognitive insight lead to the most improvement in clients.

Therefore, from a spiritual perspective, once a client can accept a negative emotion such as abandonment by God, the next step involves finding a way to express it. For example, this can include words, pictures, music, or art. A client who had experienced a gang rape as an adolescent expressed how she was "left hung to dry" by God. For her, a T-shirt on a laundry line with words and pictures of innermost expressions of anger and despair helped her "see" and feel her spiritual emotions. After actually painting her T-shirt, she included this as part of a rape awareness week at a local college. This facilitated her sense of connection, especially as she saw hundreds of other T-shirts hanging throughout the school.

In many of the interventions described above, the use of writing facilitated the expression and meaning-making process. In one of the following case studies, we describe a spiritually based empty chair technique to encourage emotional expression. Once the client has expressed an emotion, psychotherapists can listen for and assist clients in creating spiritual meaning within their struggles. *Spiritual meaning* is a broad notion, and we support the use of a client-centered, existential approach. This includes an awareness of and respect for diverse spiritual beliefs, practices, and theological underpinnings. In addition, this approach includes the clinical determination of whether a worldview remains healthy and beneficial for a client.

Finally, we believe that seeking spiritual connection is important. Clients can connect with the self (e.g., one's spiritual center, heart, and inner wisdom) and others (e.g., friends, family, spiritual communities, and Sangha). In addition, they can connect with the sacred, in whatever form a client believes in (e.g., God, Allah, Jesus, the Inner Self, Ganesh, Shiva, and/or Nature). Psychotherapists can support this process by helping clients create and sustain spiritual connection. For example, N. A. Murray-Swank has used spiritual imagery exercises with clients. For one childhood incest survivor, the image of a waterfall (see Murray-Swank, 2003), representing the spirit of love cascading over her, allowed her to feel the presence of the sacred in her life. Another client from a Hindu religion pictured herself sitting in the lap of her guru. Numerous options are available depending on the forms and images with which clients connect.

Overall, working with diverse spiritual beliefs and practices can be complex and challenging, and can involve numerous ethical threats because of the power differential inherent in psychotherapy. We attempt to respect the diverse manifestations of the spiritual dimension in a client's life. More specifically, we maintain a pluralist and client-centered approach. In this assumptive worldview, psychotherapists "recognize the existence of a religious or spiritual absolute reality but allow for multiple interpretations and paths towards it" (Zinnbauer & Pargament, 2000, p. 167). Generally, this type of approach values cultural competence when working with spiritual issues in psychotherapy. For example, Sue and Sue (2008) recommended the following competencies when working within a cultural framework: (a) awareness of one's own assumptions, values, and biases; (b) understanding the worldview of culturally diverse clients; and (c) developing culturally appropriate intervention strategies and techniques. From a spiritual perspective, this type of cultural competence involves continued self-awareness, openness, training, and experience in working with spiritually diverse clients. We turn next to a more thorough discussion of the assessment process, and conclude with case studies highlighting work with spiritual struggles in psychotherapy.

## ASSESSMENT AND CASE CONCEPTUALIZATION

Assessment of any problem begins with understanding the difficulty through the client's eyes. Although general assessment processes might vary depending on the setting (e.g., medical, psychiatric, or pastoral care, or private practice), the key point is that a solid understanding of the individual, his or her background, and his or her concerns is primary. The assessment should provide an overall picture of the client's spiritual background as well as current involvement in a spiritual community or spiritual practices. In their texts on spiritually integrated psychotherapy, Pargament (2007), Aten and Leach (2009), and Plante (2009) provided helpful frameworks to guide this initial assessment of spirituality. The psychotherapist can listen for the salience of the client's religion and spirituality and for his or her unique spiritual strengths and resources. The psychotherapist can assess whether spirituality is related to the presenting problems and begin to listen for any areas of spiritual struggle.

For individuals who appear to be experiencing spiritual struggle and strain, a more detailed assessment is needed, which we will explore in the following case studies. This area may be assessed over several sessions. In addition, psychotherapists may wish to include quantitative assessment measures that assess domains of spiritual struggle. For example, Pargament's Religious Coping Scale (RCOPE; Pargament et al., 2000) includes 35 negative religious coping items that assess the degree to which an individual is using a range of negative religious coping strategies in dealing with a difficult event. Example subscales include punishing God reappraisal, demonic reappraisal, and spiritual discontent. One advantage of this scale is that it has been adapted and used with diverse religious populations, with specific versions for Jewish (Rosmarin et al., 2009), Muslim (Khan & Watson, 2006), Buddhist (Phillips, Vonnegut, et al., 2009), and Hindu (Tarakeshwar et al., 2003) populations. A brief version of the RCOPE (14 items; Pargament, Smith, Koenig, & Perez, 1998) is clinically relevant. Another example of a promising assessment measure is the Attitudes Towards God Scale (ATGS-9; Wood et al., 2010), a nine-item instrument that assesses both positive attitudes toward God (five items) and disappointment and anger at God (four items). This measure may be particularly useful for clinicians as a marker of spiritual struggle and strain in relation to God. For those interested a more extensive review of quantitative assessment measures, Pargament (2007) and Aten and Leach (2009) have provided a comprehensive review of measures for psychotherapists in clinical practice.

## CASE STUDIES

### Assessment Illustration: Dying of Breast Cancer

To describe and illustrate our assessment model, we will consider the case of RS, a 60-year-old White female who sought psychotherapy following a diagnosis of end-stage metastatic breast cancer.[1] By describing the assessment process with RS, we hope to illustrate how our model can be used to organize the assessment of spiritual struggles. Table 9.2 provides an example of a case conceptualization form that can be used to guide the assessment process and treatment planning.

[1] For the cases presented in this chapter, a pseudonym is used, and identifying details have been altered for confidentiality.

**Table 9.2** Spiritual Struggles: Assessment and Intervention

Presenting problem (from the client's perspective): "I have breast cancer and I'm struggling emotionally."

Spiritual background and history (include current beliefs and/or affiliation, significant history, current involvement in spiritual community, or other religious and/or spiritual practices): Lifelong connection with Presbyterian Church; attends weekly services; religious practices include reading scripture and religious books, prayer, and healing rituals for cancer.

Spiritual resources and strengths: Strong sense of spiritual connection with church, minister, and spiritual community; felt sense of connection with God and Jesus.

**Prominent Areas of Spiritual Struggle and Potential Intervention Strategies**

| Type of Spiritual Struggle | Key Assessment Areas and Questions | Prominent Themes and Struggles | Possible Intervention Strategies |
|---|---|---|---|
| Spiritual meaning | How does individual make sense of the event(s) spiritually?<br>How does circumstance challenge existing spiritual beliefs? | Client has belief that God will heal her and is struggling with worsening cancer.<br>There is conflict between these beliefs. | Reflect and normalize struggle.<br>Help client create meaning and spiritual narrative that includes a sense of connection and reality of death. |
| Spiritual control and responsibility | Who is in charge?<br>Who is to blame?<br>Did God cause events?<br>Is event perceived as part of God's plan?<br>Are there beliefs about Karma? | Client holds strong belief that God is in control and can heal her.<br>God is responsible for intervening with cancer. | Exploration of spiritual beliefs regarding control.<br>Identification and expression of underlying emotions.<br>Work with theology of spiritual. |
| Spiritual isolation and disconnection | Abandonment by God?<br>Anger at God?<br>Disconnection from others or spiritual community? | Client feels abandoned by God at times.<br>Client feeling more separated and distant from others. | Two-way journaling to express emotion.<br>Utilize spiritual strengths to enhance connection with God and others. |
| Death and impermanence | What are beliefs about death and the afterlife (e.g., heaven, reincarnation, etc.)?<br>Spiritual beliefs about dying process? | Client facing worsening prognosis and likely death from cancer.<br>Client struggling to let go of belief that she will be healed. | Explore client's beliefs about death and dying.<br>Facilitate emotional expression.<br>Normalize areas of struggle.<br>Help client find spiritual support and connection in the dying process.<br>Visualization and imagery exercises. |

When I (AMS) asked RS what prompted her to seek psychotherapy, she tearfully described feelings of sadness and anxiety about her cancer diagnosis and what the future would hold: "I wake up every day with a knot in my stomach, and break down sobbing at the smallest things.... I think, how can this be happening to me?" After gaining some further background and history, it was clear that the presenting problem was RS's daily struggle with feeling emotionally overwhelmed related to her cancer diagnosis and the paralyzing effects this was having on her life and relationships. Although she alluded to involvement in her church and religious practices (and her presentation suggested issues with spiritual meaning were prominent), RS did not spontaneously identify spiritual struggle as a reason for seeking psychotherapy.

RS's presentation provided a natural transition into assessing her religious background and history, as she made a number of references to her church as she described her presenting problem. To make the transition into assessing her religious and spiritual life, I remarked, "It sounds like your involvement in church is important to you. I would like to learn more about your religious and spiritual life, if that would be OK." She then proceeded to describe herself as a "very religious person," noting that she had been member of the Presbyterian Church since early adulthood. I asked her to describe what types of activities she participated in at church, and also about her religious practices at home. As she described her extensive involvement in church and her daily practices of reading scripture and prayer, I began to note a number of spiritual resources and strengths—clearly, her connection with her church and God was a source of support for her.

When moving into the specific assessment of spiritual struggle, it is helpful for the psychotherapist to consider the types of spiritual struggles that may be present. Table 9.2 provides examples of questions (e.g., How does individual make sense of the event(s) spiritually?) to consider in each of the domains of spiritual struggle. It is important for the psychotherapist to tailor specific assessment questions to the individual client, a task that requires careful attunement to the client's spiritual experiences and an empathic, nonjudgmental presence.

With RS, I began by assessing how her religious beliefs were involved in understanding and coping with her cancer diagnosis:

*AMS:* I am wondering how your religious beliefs have been involved in dealing with your cancer?

*RS:* I try to turn to God and Jesus and put all my belief in Him. If I have enough faith, I believe that He will heal me.

*AMS:* Jesus will heal you if you have enough faith ...

*RS (tearfully):* I mean, I believe so. But I mean, I have lived a good life, I have been faithful. I had just retired from my job and was looking forward to the future. I don't know why God would allow this to happen to me right now.

RS's responses to these questions provided important information about spiritual meaning and control and responsibility, and suggested that RS may have important struggles in these areas. As noted in Table 9.2, RS is struggling to make meaning, as she believes that God can (and will) heal her, but her cancer is getting worse. In a related vein, the assessment suggests that RS holds an underlying belief that God is in control and can heal her. An important indicator of struggle in these areas is RS's strong emotions around these topics. In assessing spiritual struggle, the psychotherapist can stay attuned to the client's emotional experience, as strong affect is often an indicator that something important is going on. When strong emotions arise, it can be helpful for the psychotherapist to reflect this and use this to inform the assessment process. For example, in a subsequent session with RS, I reflected the struggle she described and asked her to describe her emotional experience:

*AMS:* You are struggling to make sense of how God could allow this to happen. I see how painful this is for you. Can you say what you are feeling right now, in this moment?

*RS (quietly):* I feel lonely, like I'm all alone in this. It is a horrible feeling, like I am in a dark, empty hole. Sometimes, I feel like even God has left me …

At this point, RS began to express underlying struggles with feeling abandoned by God. I continued to explore this area by asking RS about her image of God, and how her relationship with God had been affected by her experience of cancer. She described relating to God through Jesus, "like a purely loving presence," and noted how she now felt "further from that presence" in the midst of her illness, which was painful and distressing for her. I also asked about her relationship with her minister and other members of her religious community, and she described also feeling more distance from others as her illness had worsened.

As the assessment of RS continued, she received more discouraging news about the extent and rapid spreading of her cancer, and her doctors estimated that she would have 3 to 6 months to live. Assessing clients' spiritual struggles around end-of-life issues is a sensitive and complex task. For those interested in a more in-depth discussion of this topic, we refer the reader to recent discussions of assessment of spiritual needs in end-of-life care (e.g., Sulmasy, 2006) as well as a recent review of interventions to address existential issues in the care of persons with terminal and life-threatening illness (e.g., LeMay & Wilson, 2008). To identify spiritual struggles around dying, it is helpful to learn about clients' religious and spiritual beliefs and practices regarding death, their feelings related to dying, and spiritual beliefs and concerns about the dying process. These questions can help the psychotherapist identify areas of spiritual struggle related to death and understand what is important to the client facing the prospect of dying. In working with RS, I initially asked her whether she had particular religious beliefs around death. She talked about a belief in "heaven," describing this as "a place to be reunited with God and with loved ones." When I asked about her feelings regarding her doctor's prognosis, she was silent, and then remarked, "I'm not ready to talk about that yet."

Overall, the goal of assessment is to provide direction to inform clinical intervention. The information collected during this assessment points to a number of specific avenues for the psychotherapy process. For illustrative purposes, we have provided examples of clinical interventions and techniques in Table 9.2 that could be used to address the identified areas of spiritual struggle. In the following case examples, we will focus more specifically on working with spiritual struggles in the process of psychotherapy.

### Clinical Case Study: Spiritual Struggles and Sexual Abuse

CT entered psychotherapy at the age of 24 feeling like she was "dying inside." As a result of her history of childhood sexual abuse by her stepfather between the ages of 6 and 10, CT described feeling "pointless pain." She declared, "I don't like to feel," as feelings to her represented a "deep pit of despair." She said, "If I fall in, I will never get out." From a spiritual perspective, CT was active in her faith community. She served at homeless shelters, volunteered at Bible camps, and regularly attended worship services. She relied on her religious beliefs, and felt this represented the one thing that "kept her going."

Despite the strength of CT's religious convictions, she came in one day saying,

*CT:* If I am honest with God, then everything sucks.
*NMS:* Everything sucks if you are honest with God.
*CT:* Yes, EVERYTHING.
*NMS:* What does being honest with God mean to you?
*CT:* Telling him how I really feel.
*NMS:* How you really feel. The real truth.
*CT:* Yes, the truth.
*NMS:* That can be really hard, to do that.
*CT:* Yeah, I'm afraid. I want to trust, but I can't.
*NMS:* What would it feel like to trust?
*CT:* To believe that God really is there for me.
*NMS:* That would mean a lot, to really know deep down that you are loved and that God is there for you.
*CT:* I want to believe that.
*NMS:* I am wondering if we can try something together, to tell God how you really feel.
*CT:* Like what?
*NMS:* Like what we did with your stepfather, but with God. We can ask God to be present, maybe even in this chair here. And I will be here too. And you can talk to God, telling God how you feel.

CT agreed and began talking to God, in a spiritual empty chair technique. After a couple of minutes, she began to express her anger and her pain. She asked,

"Have I done something wrong to deserve this? Why didn't you protect me? I was a little girl. I hate you, yet I love you. You can heal me, why don't you? Where is the justice? All I feel is alone and in despair. There is no end to the pain."

Before discussing how we proceeded, we would like to highlight the themes of spiritual control and responsibility, spiritual meaning, and spiritual isolation that CT expressed. CT voiced her confusion and anger about spiritual control: Why didn't God protect her? Why didn't God heal her? She expressed anger and isolation: "All I feel is alone and in despair." For CT, this represented her worst fear, to feel alone in a pit of despair. Therefore, I viewed it as essential to normalize and support her, as well as end the session with a sense of connection. Many clients fear that expressions of such intense anger and loss will result in punishment from God or even more abandonment. However, the avoidance of the pain and spiritual concerns actually worsen their outcomes, often leaving them in a deep state of isolation, shame, and disconnection. Therefore, I supported CT in her expression:

*NMS:* That took a lot of courage what you just did. A lot of courage. How do you feel right now?
*CT:* I feel tired, but good. I feel like God was really listening to me.

I wanted to take the opportunity to encourage the spiritual support CT began to experience.

*NMS:* God was listening to you?
*CT:* Yeah, I could feel it.
*NMS:* Where?
*CT:* I just felt a warmth, almost like a quietness inside.
*NMS:* I wonder if we can just focus on that feeling for a moment, on God being present with us. That warmth and quietness.

I asked her to focus on that feeling, and to really experience it. Then we breathed in silence for several minutes with that presence and support.

This brief session example was not the end for CT. It was more like a new beginning.

After CT was able to fully express her anger, she began to reenvision the spiritual meaning around her sexual abuse and her spiritual path in general. God became someone she really related to, someone who could tolerate both her pain and her love. In this way, she actually deepened her connection with God.

CT also wrestled with her thoughts about freedom and free will, particularly God's role in stopping sexual abuse. As I have seen in other trauma survivors, she began to shift responsibility and control away from herself and God. Originally, she asked, "Did *I* do something wrong to deserve this?" She thought that perhaps really, deep down, she was to blame. However, as we worked with this in psychotherapy, I asked her to observe children at her Church who were her age at the time of the abuse. She came in stating, "They are so small, so innocent. And they seem so happy." Of course, this resulted in a deep grieving process for the loss of both her innocence and her happiness. It also resulted in a sense that children are not to blame; therefore, *she* wasn't to blame.

In addition, CT wondered about and questioned God's ability to intervene in the world. She stated during one session, "I felt so special in the beginning, like he [her stepfather] *really* loved me. Until things got worse and worse. How could he do that to me?" I used this question to explore her beliefs about spiritual control and responsibility more fully. I too wondered out loud about how someone whom she felt loved her could choose to harm her in that way. Working with beliefs about divine intervention can be challenging, and an awareness of a psychotherapist's own beliefs remains crucial. In this case, CT arrived at a personal understanding that God did not protect her because God gave humans free will. Therefore, humans can choose to harm others, even innocent children whom they "love." As her psychotherapist, I supported this belief for her as it seemed to allow her to feel God's connection and shifted blame for the abuse off herself.

I normalized CT's experiences and feelings (e.g., anger, hate, love, pain, loss, and loneliness). She expressed these in numerous ways throughout our sessions together. In addition, she created a new spiritual understanding of her sexual abuse in which she was not to blame and God was not to blame. Instead, her stepfather made a choice to abuse her, and God remained available for connection, relationship, and support in the midst of pain and suffering. Overall, this resulted in a deeper connection with herself, others, and with God.

### Clinical Case Study: Spiritual Struggles and Traumatic Brain Injury

BF was a 56-year-old married male with three adult children. He practiced as an internal medicine physician for 20 years before enduring a traumatic brain injury (TBI) in a car accident. As a result of the traumatic brain injury, BF experienced word-finding difficulties, short-term memory loss, and personality changes, including emotional swings and hostility. He began to abuse alcohol, and his marriage to his wife and relationships with his children deteriorated. BF sought therapy 2 years after his TBI, as he began to fully experience the long-term effects and losses.

In the third session, BF raised a spiritual struggle as one of his main concerns in his life:

*BF:* I used to feel so connected to God. Everything is so different now. I had such a strong faith. I even started new churches! Now all I feel is angry and alienated.

*NMS:* You were really connected to God before. But now with everything that has happened to you, you feel angry and alone. That must feel really hard and difficult.

*BF:* I feel completely empty inside. Like my life lacks any purpose to it.

*NMS:* What an enormous amount of losses you have endured. *(Normalize.)*

*BF:* I just don't understand why this happened? I don't know how I am supposed to live like this? What can I do?

BF describes spiritual struggles in most of the categories we have discussed: spiritual meaning, spiritual isolation and disconnection, and, to a lesser extent, spiritual control and responsibility. In this case, the lack of meaning and spiritual isolation represent the main sources of difficulties for BF.

From an intervention perspective, I continued to normalize and convey empathy for the feelings of loss, emptiness, anger, and hopelessness that BF experienced. I also continually assessed BF for suicidal thoughts and desires. Overall, I encouraged the expression of these struggles and listened for any sources of connection and meaning.

In the last quote from BF, he asks, "Why?" and "How?" For us, these questions lead easily into emotional expression and action about coping.

*NMS:* It can be really helpful to continue to give voice to your struggles, just like you are doing now.

*BF:* I don't know what you mean, give voice.

*NMS:* I just mean finding a way to say out loud or write about what you are going through. It is not to keep you in it, but I heard you ask, "What can I do?" Through all of this, even though it is hard, we can find the *what to do* that may help you.

*BF:* I still don't really know what you mean.

*NMS:* I'm sorry to be unclear. I know you mentioned last week that you keep a journal. I am wondering if it might be helpful to use a two-way journaling-to-God exercise this next week. This is where you write a letter to God, about the things that we are talking about right now, or any other concerns you have, and then you listen for God's response. In whatever way that comes: words, pictures. The important part is that you write your concerns and then write down anything you hear.

At this point, I decided to use a two-way journal to God practice because BF was seeking connection and meaning. Similar to the Gestalt exercise, two-way journaling to God can help clients express spiritual emotions, create new meaning, and facilitate spiritual connection.

The next session, BF returned:

*BF:* I tried the journaling, and all I heard was silence.

*NMS:* Silence. God was silent?

*BF:* I don't think he was silent; he was ignoring me.

*NMS:* What happened next?

*BF:* I got mad.

*NMS:* You were mad at God.

*BF:* Yes I was. No good God would ever do something like this. I used to have a life.

*NMS:* You used to have a life, and now all you have is loss and more loss. Loss of a career you loved, loss of a marriage, loss of the way you think, your memory, and a new person in your body that you are learning who he is.

To note, working with clients with TBIs can be challenging because of the cognitive and emotional changes that can result from the injury itself. For this client,

I requested a copy of the neurocognitive report to ensure that our work aligned with his capabilities and goals. Consultation with a neuropsychologist, or other appropriate professionals, is encouraged to facilitate this process.

Psychotherapy with BF continued with exploring the traumatic grief that he experienced on many levels, including career aspirations, relationships, and spirituality. The spiritual struggle was clearly intertwined with his depression, emptiness, and loss of meaning. BF was a very motivated client; he *wanted* to work through his struggle and feel meaning and connection again. From our perspective, this had to first include an acknowledgment of the losses, and an expression of grief and anger, and it also had to build on strengths and connections. I encouraged him to seek support with a TBI support group, which helped with his feeling of isolation. In this group, they focused on acknowledging losses, giving time to grieve, and finding ways to move forward, including learning to appreciate his *new self*. From a spiritual perspective, we, too, focused on creating a new spiritual narrative that included his TBI and all the subsequent changes that resulted.

We cannot describe the entire process of spiritual change in detail, but we would like to highlight one aspect that seemed to help BF create new spiritual meaning and connection. During the course of discussing the medical process with his TBI, and given his prior background as a physician, I wondered out loud in one session,

*NMS:* You know, I have heard you talk about how important you think it is for the medical professions to take spiritual issues seriously, and how you felt that this was neglected in your own treatment. I am wondering if there might be a way to do something about this?

*BF:* What can be done? People seem to just think the spiritual stuff is a brain problem.

*NMS:* I'm not sure what can be done. It just seems like something that would be really important to get out there. Maybe tell medical people about how it is important to take spiritual matters seriously?

At this point in therapy, I wanted to help BF find a way to create some meaning and build on the idea of finding a new self after a TBI, an idea that was emphasized in his group. Even with the word-finding difficulties and difficulties with short-term memory, BF was articulate and reflective. As mentioned, he was also motivated. I provided support in sessions when he first went to his TBI organization to discuss adding resources about spiritual problems on the website. He used his prior medical connections and gave a seminar to internal medicine physicians about his own experiences and the importance of taking spiritual matters seriously in patients. Although this seminar did not take the grief away, it did help him build a sense of spiritual meaning and connection. It follows the process we described: Normalize, express, create meaning, and seek connection.

## WORKING WITH VALUE CONFLICTS IN SPIRITUALLY INTEGRATED PSYCHOTHERAPY

When working with the spiritual dimension of living, particularly spiritual struggles, value conflicts are inevitable. The next case provides an example of a value conflict that developed in a case during which N. A. Murray-Swank supervised a master's-level counseling student.

A couple in their early 40s started psychotherapy with concerns about their son and parenting. They had been married for 14 years and had an 8-year-old son with behavioral problems (e.g., difficulties at school and aggression). Both parents were practicing Hindus who attended an area temple. They were deeply involved in their spiritual practices and devoted to the importance of spirituality in family life.

As psychotherapy continued, the mother described a spiritual struggle related to her experience with a chronic illness. She wondered about living fully in the midst of pain and illness, and while parenting a young, active child. She turned to her spiritual practice for support, and also harbored the belief that if she just meditated enough, her illness would go away.

After the fourth session, the following dialogue ensued between the psychotherapist and the mother:

*Client (C):* I really started to feel something integrate for me this week.
*Psychotherapist (P):* Oh, what was that?
*C:* I was sitting during Satsang at our temple. My teacher spoke about how we can work with emotional blockages and physical problems, but there is always a spiritual energy beyond that. It is this spiritual energy I wish to connect with.
*P (pauses):* Now, know that I am not trying to change what you believe, but can I mess with your world for a little bit?
*C:* OK.

The psychotherapist proceeded to try to encourage the client to expand her thinking to see that there really were no differences between mind, body, and spirit. He emphasized how all energy, whether spiritual, emotional, or physical, were really the same. Therefore, trying to connect with a spiritual energy beyond the physical and emotional remained useless. The mother left this session visibly upset.

At the beginning of the next session, the client stated right away:

*C:* I think our spiritual difference keeps coming back into the room. Last time, I felt that I *finally* came to some sort of peace about where I was at. I said I was happy about things starting to integrate for me, and you challenged that.

The psychotherapist heard her dismay and remarked in a nondefensive manner:

*P:* Did you feel disrespected?
*C:* I did.
*P:* I apologize. I didn't mean to disrespect your beliefs. I view it as my role to challenge and help you grow.
*C:* That didn't seem like the place, as I was happy about finally integrating some things.
*P:* I hear you saying that you were finally starting to integrate things, and I disrespected that. I am sorry.

Interestingly, in this case, the psychotherapist and client's spiritual beliefs were actually not that different from each other. As the client began to create her own sense of spiritual meaning and connection (i.e., uniting with a spiritual energy beyond her physical illness), the psychotherapist challenged this. He stated, "Know that I am not trying to change what you believe ... *but can I mess with your world for a little bit*?" In actuality, he attempted to modify what she believed.

Working with value conflicts can be complex and challenging. As psychotherapists, we always bring our values into the room, whether values about emotions, behaviors, or spirituality. For example, we may value emotional expression in clients, healthy thought patterns, or honest communication among couples. In addition, we often try to expand a client's way of thinking or challenge people for the purpose of growth. Determining when to challenge and when to encourage and support a client can remain a delicate venture.

This case study highlights useful aspects of working with value conflicts. First, the client was able to articulate her discomfort: "I think our *spiritual difference* keeps coming back into the room." Sometimes clients are unable to do this and may leave psychotherapy feeling dismayed or may stay in psychotherapy feeling overpowered. In this case, voicing her concern opened the door for the psychotherapist to respond: "Did you feel disrespected?" Ultimately, the psychotherapist *heard* her concern, did not become defensive, and *apologized.*

Earlier we discussed some ethical and cultural considerations in working with spirituality in psychotherapy. We maintain a pluralistic, client-centered approach when addressing value conflicts regarding spirituality. In this case study, some of the ethical guidelines can be highlighted. For example, one of the Competencies from the Association for Spiritual, Ethical, and Religious Values in counseling (2009), a division of the American Counseling Association, states, "The professional counselor continuously evaluates the influence of his or her own spiritual and/or religious beliefs and values on the client and the counseling process" (Competency 4). Similarly, both the cultural competencies of Sue and Sue (2008), as well as the guidelines from APA's Division 36 (e.g., Hathaway & Ripley, 2009), discuss the importance of self-awareness of religious and spiritual values, and how these might influence clients. For example, the preliminary APA practice guidelines for working with religious and spiritual issues state, "Psychologists do not seek to proselytize or otherwise impose their worldview on the client"

(Guideline M-3; Hathaway & Ripley, 2009, p. 48). In this case study, the psychotherapist would never have imagined that he might impose a worldview on a client. However, these types of value differences and conflicts can be subtle and complex. Therefore, a psychotherapist's own self-awareness, humility, and openness can facilitate the process. In addition, seeking continuous education, training, and consultation can be helpful.

At times, clients and psychotherapists will disagree about how to create spiritual meaning and connection, how to answer questions about spiritual control and responsibility, and how to confront death and impermanence. Personally, I (N. A. Murray-Swank) struggle when my client survivors of traumatic events believe "This is God's will for me" or "This is the result of karma, something I did in another lifetime." However, I have seen numerous clients find peace and purpose, and draw strength, from these meaning systems. Ultimately, we advocate for ongoing therapist self-awareness and cultural competence, respecting spiritual and religious diversity, and utilizing a client-centered perspective for working with value conflicts.

## CONCLUSION

In this chapter, we have provided a framework, based on an integration of theory and research, for assisting clients in the midst of spiritual struggles. In the quote that begins this chapter, Yalom (2000) noted that purpose *ensues* "from meaningful and authentic engagement, from plunging into an enlarging, fulfilling, self-transcending endeavor" (para. 43). This quote exemplifies our goal as psychotherapists and as human beings. As psychotherapists, the ability to assist people in the midst of spiritual struggles represents a meaningful and self-transcending endeavor that requires a true "plunging" into authentic engagement, both with the realities of life and death and with fellow human beings. As human beings, we acknowledge that life involves pain, change, suffering, and death. We also recognize the human ability to transcend the self and seek ultimate meaning, fulfillment, connection, and freedom.

## CHAPTER SUMMARY

- Spiritual struggles may be present when clients encounter issues with (a) spiritual meaning, (b) spiritual responsibility and control, (c) spiritual disconnection and isolation, and (d) death and impermanence. These themes provide a framework for assessment and intervention when working with clients with spiritual struggles.
- Research on negative religious coping and religious strain suggests that spiritual struggles can lead to diminished mental and physical health.

- Manualized, spiritually integrated interventions have been developed to help clients work through spiritual struggles, such as negative religious coping, religious strain, and disconnection from God. These interventions illustrate promising strategies for addressing spiritual struggles in psychotherapy.
- Our intervention model emphasizes five key components when helping clients work through spiritual struggles in psychotherapy: Assess, normalize, express, create meaning, and seek connection.
- Psychotherapists who work with spiritual struggles in therapy must attend to ethical issues and cultural competence. This requires a respect for diverse beliefs, ongoing therapist self-awareness, and a client-centered approach in working with value differences in addressing spiritual struggles in the therapy process.

## CLINICAL APPLICATION QUESTIONS

1. How do I feel about addressing spiritual struggles with my clients in psychotherapy?
2. How have my own spiritual or existential struggles influenced me? How might this affect my work as a therapist?
3. As a therapist, are there certain types of spiritual struggles that I find harder to address?
4. What are some therapeutic strategies in working with clients who feel angry with or abandoned by God?
5. How might I work with the spiritual struggles of clients who hold religious and spiritual values that are very different than my own? What would be important to consider in navigating these value differences?

## SUGGESTED READINGS AND RESOURCES

### Books

Aten, J. D., & Leach, M. M. (Eds.). (2009). *Spirituality and the therapeutic process: A comprehensive resource from intake to termination.* Washington, DC: American Psychological Association.

Pargament, K. I. (2007). *Spiritually integrated psychotherapy: Understanding and addressing the sacred.* New York, NY: Guilford Press.

Plante, T. G. (2009). *Spiritual practices in psychotherapy: Thirteen tools for enhancing psychological health.* Washington, DC: American Psychological Association.

Richards, P. S., & Bergin A.E. (2005). *A spiritual strategy for counseling and psychotherapy* (2nd ed.). Washington, DC: American Psychological Association.

### DVD Resources

The following DVDs are all part of the American Psychological Association's Spiritual Video Series and provide clinical examples and guidance for working with spirituality in psychotherapy and are available at http://www.apa.org/pubs/videos:

- *Addressing Issues of Spirituality and Religion in Psychotherapy* (by Edward Shafranske)

- *Theistic Integrative Psychology* (by P. Scott Richards)
- *Christian Counseling* (by Mark McMinn)
- *Spiritual Awareness Psychotherapy* (by Lisa Miller)
- *Mindful Therapy* (by Lorne Ladner)

## REFERENCES


Abu Raiya, H., Pargament, K. I., Mahoney, A., & Stein, C. (2008). A psychological measure of Islamic religiousness: Development and evidence for reliability and validity. *The International Journal for the Psychology of Religion, 18,* 291–315.

Ano, G. G., & Vasconcelles, E. B. (2005). Religious coping and psychological adjustment to stress: A meta-analysis. *Journal of Clinical Psychology, 61,* 461–480.

Association for Spiritual, Ethical and Religious Values in Counseling. (2009). *Competencies for addressing spiritual and religious issues in counseling.* Retrieved from http://www.aservic.org/resources/spiritual-competencies/

Aten, J. D., & Leach, M. M. (Eds.). (2009). *Spirituality and the therapeutic process: A comprehensive resource from intake to termination.* Washington, DC: American Psychological Association.

Avants, S. K., Beitel, M., & Margolin, A. (2005). Making the shift from the "addict self" to "spiritual self": Results from a Stage 1 study of Spiritual Self-Schema (3-S) therapy for the treatment of addiction and HIV risk behavior. *Mental Health, Religion & Culture, 8,* 167–177.

Avants, S. K., & Margolin, A. (2003). Spiritual Self Schema Therapy: Individual therapy treatment manual. Retrieved from http://info.med.yale.edu/psych/3s/3-S_ind_manual.html

Avants, S. K., & Margolin, A. (2004). Development of Spiritual Self-Schema (3-S) therapy for the treatment of addictive and HIV risk behavior: A convergence of cognitive and Buddhist psychology. *Journal of Psychotherapy Integration, 14,* 253–289.

Cole, B. (2005). Spiritually-focused psychotherapy for people diagnosed with cancer: A pilot outcome study. *Mental Health, Religion & Culture, 8,* 217–226.

Cole, B., & Pargament, K. I. (1999). Re-creating your life: A spiritual/psychotherapeutic intervention for people diagnosed with cancer. *Psycho-Oncology, 8,* 395–407.

Desai, K. M. (2006). *Predictors of growth and decline following spiritual struggles.* Master's thesis, Bowling Green State University. Retrieved from http://www.ohiolink.edu/etd/send-pdf.cgi?bgsu1133545979

Exline, J. J., Park, C. L., Smyth, J. M., & Carey, M. P. (2011). Anger toward God: Social-cognitive predictors, prevalence, and links with adjustment to bereavement and cancer. *Journal of Personality and Social Psychology, 100*(1), 129–148.

Exline, J. J., Yali, A. M., & Lobel, M. (1999). When God disappoints: Difficulty forgiving God and its role in negative emotions. *Journal of Health Psychology, 4,* 364–379.

Exline, J. J., Yali, A. M., & Sanderson, W. C. (2000). Guilt, discord, and alienation: The role of religious strain in depression and suicidality. *Journal of Clinical Psychology, 56,* 1481–1496.

Fallot, R. D., & Heckman, J. P (2005). Religious/spiritual coping among trauma survivors with mental health and substance abuse disorders. *Journal of Behavioral Health Services & Research, 31,* 215–226.

Flaherty, A. M. (1992). *Woman why do you weep? Spirituality for survivors of childhood sexual abuse.* Mahwah, NJ: Paulist Press.

Frankl, V. E. (1984). *Man's search for meaning.* New York, NY: Washington Square Press.

Gall, T. L. (2006). Spirituality and coping with life stress among adult survivors of childhood sexual abuse. *Child Abuse & Neglect, 30,* 829–844.

Goldstein, J. (2002). *One dharma: The emerging western Buddhism.* New York, NY: HarperCollins.

Greenberg, L. S. (2004). Emotion-focused therapy. *Clinical Psychology and Psychotherapy, 11,* 3–16.

Harris, J. I., Erbes, C. R., Engdahl, B. E., Thuras, P., Murray-Swank, N., Grace, D., ... & Le, T. V. (2011). The effectiveness of trauma focused spiritually integrated intervention for veterans. *Journal of Clinical Psychology, 67,* 1–14.

Harris, J. I., Murray-Swank, N., Engdahl, B. E., Erbes, C. R., Olson, R. H. A., & Bacon, R. (2007). *Building spiritual strength for military veteran trauma survivors.* Treatment manual. Department of Veterans Affairs, VA Medical Center, Minneapolis, MN.

Hathaway, W. L., & Ripley, J. S. (2009). Ethical concerns around spirituality and religion in clinical practice. In J. D. Aten & M. M. Leach (Eds.), *Spirituality and the therapeutic process: A comprehensive resource from intake to termination* (pp. 25–52). Washington, DC: American Psychological Association.

Kelly, A. E. (1999). Revealing personal secrets. *Current Directions in Psychological Science, 8,* 105–109.

Kelly, A. E., Klusas, J. A., von Weiss, R. T., & Kenny, C. (2001). What is it about revealing secrets that is beneficial? *Personality and Social Psychology Bulletin, 27,* 651–665.

Khan, Z. H., & Watson, P. J. (2006). Construction of the Pakistani religious coping practices scale: Correlations with religious coping, religious orientation, and reactions to stress among Muslim university students. *The International Journal for the Psychology of Religion, 16,* 101–112.

Kirkpatrick, L. A. (2005). *Attachment, evolution, and the psychology of religion.* New York, NY: Guilford Press.

LeMay, K., & Wilson, K. G. (2008). Treatment of existential distress in life threatening illness: A review of manualized interventions. *Clinical Psychology Review, 28*(3), 472–493.

Margolin, A., Schuman-Olivier, Z., Beitel, M., Arnold, R. M., Fulwiler, C. E., & Avants, S. K. (2007). A preliminary study of Spiritual Self-Schema (3-S +) therapy for reducing impulsivity in HIV-positive drug users. *Journal of Clinical Psychology, 63,* 979–999.

Murray-Swank, N. A. (2003). *Solace for the soul: A journey towards wholeness.* Treatment manual for female survivors of sexual abuse. Baltimore, MD: Loyola College.

Murray-Swank, N. A., Kohn, M., & Doehring, C. (2007, November). *Spirituality, religious coping, and psychological functioning in clergy sexual abuse.* Poster presented at the annual meeting of the International Society for Traumatic Stress Studies, Baltimore, MD.

Murray-Swank, N. A., & Pargament, K. I. (2005). God, where are you? Evaluating a spiritually-integrated intervention for sexual abuse. *Mental Health, Religion & Culture, 8,* 191–203.

Murray-Swank, N. A., & Pargament, K. I. (2008). Solace for the soul: Evaluating a spiritually-integrated counselling intervention for sexual abuse. *Counselling and Spirituality, 27*(2), 157–174.

Pargament, K. I. (2007). *Spiritually integrated psychotherapy: Understanding and addressing the sacred.* New York, NY: Guilford Press.

Pargament, K. I., Koenig, H. G., & Perez, L. (2000). The many methods of religious coping: Development and initial validation of the RCOPE. *Journal of Clinical Psychology, 56,* 519–543.

Pargament, K. I., Koenig, H. G., Tarakeshwar, N., & Hahn, J. (2001). Religious struggle as a predictor of mortality among medically ill elderly patients: A two-year longitudinal study. *Archives of Internal Medicine, 161,* 1881–1885.

Pargament, K. I., Smith, B. W., Koenig, H. G., & Perez, L. (1998). Patterns of positive and negative religious coping with major life stressors. *Journal for the Scientific Study of Religion, 37*, 710–724.

Park, C. L. (2005). Religion and meaning. In R. F. Paloutzian & C. L. Park (Eds.), *Handbook of the psychology of religion and spirituality* (pp. 295–314). New York, NY: Guilford Press.

Park, C., & Slattery, J. M. (2009). Including spirituality in case conceptualizations: A meaning-systems approach. In J. D. Aten & M. M. Leach (Eds.), *Spirituality and the therapeutic process: A comprehensive resource from intake to termination* (pp. 121–142). Washington, DC: American Psychological Association.

Phillips, R. E., Cheng, C. M., Pargament, K. I, Oemig, C., Colvin, S. D., Abarr, A. N., … & Reed, A. S. (2009). Spiritual coping in American Buddhists: An exploratory study. *The International Journal for the Psychology of Religion, 19*, 231–243.

Phillips, R. E., Hietbrink, L., Ussher, R., Turner, H., Cheng, C., & Oemig, C. (2009, May). *Predictive and incremental validity of a Buddhist coping measure.* Poster presented at the meeting of the Midwestern Psychological Association, Chicago, IL.

Phillips, R. E., Vonnegut, E., Hietbrink, L., Ferris, D., Hickman, W., McQuinn, N., Oemig, C. (2009, May). *Initial validation of a measure of Buddhist coping.* Poster presented at the meeting of the Midwestern Psychological Association, Chicago, IL.

Plante, T. G. (2009). *Spiritual practices in psychotherapy: Thirteen tools for enhancing psychological health.* Washington, DC: American Psychological Association.

Rosmarin, D. H., Pargament, K. I., Krumrei, E. J., & Flannelly, K. J. (2009). Religious coping among Jews: Development and initial validation of the JCOPE. *Journal of Clinical Psychology, 65*, 670–683.

Rowatt, W. C., & Kirkpatrick, L. A. (2002). Two dimensions of attachment to God and their relation to affect, religiosity, and personality constructs. *Journal for the Social Scientific Study of Religion, 41*, 637–651.

Sherman, A. C., Plante, T. G., Simonton, S., Latif, U., & Anaissie, E. J. (2009). Prospective study of religious coping among patients undergoing autologous stem cell transplantation. *Journal of Behavioral Medicine, 32*, 118–128.

Steinhauser, K. E., Christakis, N. A., Clipp, E. C., McNeilly, M., McIntyre, L., & Tulsky, J. A. (2000). Factors considered important at the end of life by patients, family, physicians, and other care providers. *Journal of the American Medical Association, 284*, 2476–2482.

Sue, D. W., & Sue, D. (2008). *Counseling the culturally diverse: Theory and practice* (5th ed.). Hoboken, NJ: John Wiley.

Sulmasy, D. P. (2006). Spiritual issues in the care of dying patients: "It's OK between me and God …". *Journal of the American Medical Association, 296*(11), 1385–1392.

Tarakeshwar, N., Pargament, K. I., & Mahoney, A. (2003). Initial development of a measure of religious coping among Hindus. *Journal of Community Psychology, 31*, 607–628.

Wood, B. T., Worthington, E. L., Exline, J .J., Yali, A. M., Aten, J. D. & McMinn, M. R. (2010). Development, refinement, and psychometric properties of the Attitudes toward God Scale (ATGS-9). *Psychology of Religion and Spirituality, 2*, 148–167.

Yalom, I. D. (1980). *Existential psychotherapy.* New York, NY: Basic Books.

Yalom, I. D. (2000, May). *Religion and psychiatry.* Award speech presented at the meeting of the American Psychiatric Association, New Orleans, LA. Retrieved from http://www.yalom.com/lec/pfister

Zinnbauer, B. J., & Pargament, K. I. (2000). Working with the sacred: Four approaches to religious and spiritual issues in counseling. *Journal of Counseling and Development, 78*, 162–171.

# 10

# *Processes of Religious and Spiritual Coping*

ELIZABETH J. KRUMREI AND DAVID H. ROSMARIN

Historically, psychologists have viewed religious issues as marginal to the practice of psychotherapy (Pargament, 2007) and have largely excluded religion and spirituality from research on sources of strength and support (Sheridian, Bullis, Adcock, Berlin, & Miller, 1992). The past decade, however, has shown a growing awareness of the importance of religion in Americans' lives (see Gallup Poll, 2008), resulting in a greater recognition in the field of psychology for the importance of transcendent meaning and the sacred (Smith, Bartz, & Richards, 2007). This has been accompanied by a rapid development of theory and research on religious coping. In this chapter, we look at empirical research and clinical implications related to people incorporating religion into their responses to stressful life events. We include a discussion of therapeutic assessment and intervention strategies relevant to religious coping.

## DEFINITIONS OF RELIGIOUS AND SPIRITUAL COPING

Coping has long been a central theme in the field of psychology. Coping has not been described as a homogeneous concept but rather as an umbrella term that includes a range of strategies, responses, cognitions, and behaviors (Schwarzer & Schwarzer, 1996). In the classic transactional model of stress, coping is defined as "constantly changing cognitive and behavioral efforts to manage specific external and/or internal demands that are appraised as taxing or exceeding the resources of the person" (Lazarus & Folkman, 1984, p. 141).

Pargament (1997) defined religious coping as a proactive process of searching for significance in times of stress. He differentiated religious coping from other forms of coping in that it occurs in ways related to the sacred. The sacred is based on concepts such as God, the divine, and transcendence, and spans into other aspects of life (e.g., people, activities, objects, symbols) that are perceived to be sacred through their association with divinity (Pargament & Mahoney,

2005). Thus, unlike other personal and social forms of coping, religious coping involves beliefs, experiences, rituals, and institutions that are associated with supernatural forces. Psychotherapists are likely to encounter a variety of different types of attempts by clients to cope with stress. Pargament, Smith, Koenig, and Perez (1998) described 21 distinct religious coping strategies that represent ways in which individuals attempt to achieve a sense of meaning, control, spiritual comfort, connection with others, or spiritual transformation in times of stress. For example, individuals can find meaning by redefining a stressor in spiritual terms, such as seeing it as part of God's plan. Individuals might seek control by turning the situation over to God or praying for a miracle. People might seek comfort by seeking a spiritual connection with other people or a larger spiritual force. Finally, individuals may seek a spiritual reawakening or religious life transformation. Although various conceptualizations have been proposed for the distinction between religion and spirituality (e.g., Hill et al., 2000; Zinnbauer et al., 1997), we use the terms in tandem in this chapter as we explore the role of religion and spirituality in people's efforts to respond to stress.

## EMPIRICAL LITERATURE

Hundreds of empirical studies have been published on religious coping with a wide variety of stressors, including loss of loved ones, serious medical conditions, imprisonment, abuse, adjustment concerns, car accidents, war, natural disasters, racism, and other major life events (Pargament, 1997). Because a majority of these studies have been conducted among groups of individuals in the general population, the findings are probabilistic and cannot form the basis for direct inferences about individual clients in treatment. Nevertheless, the information generated by this line of research is clinically useful for increasing insight into the potential outcomes of various forms of religious coping. To this end, we highlight some of the themes that have emerged in the empirical literature on religious coping.

### Religious Coping as a Valuable and Unique Resource

Prati and Pietrantoni (2009) synthesized information from 103 studies about the psychosocial factors related to posttraumatic growth. In this analysis, religious coping emerged as the strongest predictor of positive psychological changes in the aftermath of extremely stressful events (effect size = 0.38; based on 31 studies with 6,188 participants). Importantly, it surpassed other forms of coping, such as interpersonal (e.g., social support) and intrapersonal (e.g., optimism) coping. Psychotherapists may gather from this that religious coping is a potentially valuable resource in times of stress.

Research has highlighted that religious coping is not only valuable, but also unique when it comes to predicting mental health outcomes. For example, use of private prayer as a coping mechanism by 151 patients experiencing their first coronary bypass surgery was predictive of lower levels of general distress one year later (Ai, Dunke, Peterson, & Bolling, 1998). This finding remained significant after controlling the effects of noncardiac health conditions, levels of depression during the first postoperative month, and social support. Similarly, among 150 individuals who were waiting in hospitals while a relative underwent artery bypass surgery, religious coping methods used to achieve a sense of control, such as seeing oneself as working collaboratively with God to achieve a goal, accounted for significant, unique amounts of variance in participants' levels of anxiety and depression, beyond the effects of secular control-oriented coping methods (Pargament et al., 1999). In addition, Tix and Frazier (1998) found that religious coping measured 3 months after kidney transplant surgery was predictive of greater life satisfaction a year after surgery for patients ($n = 239$) and their significant others ($n = 179$). This link was not attributable to the effects of secular forms of coping, such as cognitive restructuring, social support, and perceived control.

Thus, a pattern among the research is that religious coping accounts for significant portions of variance in well-being, beyond the variance attributable to other important nonreligious coping methods. This suggests that religious coping is important to people's adjustment to stressors and that the religious nature of coping is essential to this relationship. Because many studies have shown that religious coping methods are not redundant with secular methods of coping, but account for unique variance, it seems that religious coping is not merely a proxy for coping in general. Rather, it seems that religion adds a distinctive dimension to the coping process.

### *Implications for Clinical Application*

Psychotherapists may be inclined to ask whether religious coping truly influences people's adjustment to crises, or whether empirical studies are merely detecting correlations. A respectable amount of research on this topic has been longitudinal, providing insight into temporal precedence and directionality of religious coping predicting change in outcome measures over time. Although drawing causal inferences remains a core challenge, Prati and Pietrantoni (2009) further supported that religious coping functions as a true predictor of posttraumatic growth by highlighting that significant differences did not exist between estimates derived from longitudinal versus cross-sectional studies in their meta-analyses. This strengthens confidence in religious coping being an active agent in posttraumatic growth, as stronger links would be expected in cross-sectional studies compared with longitudinal studies if religious coping were a correlate rather than a determinant.

As religious coping seems to add a distinctive dimension to coping in the general population, religion also may offer psychotherapy clients an array of coping strategies that are not redundant with secular forms of coping. However, we acknowledge that using or promoting religious coping as a therapeutic intervention might not produce the same effects as individuals employing identical coping strategies spontaneously. In addition, individuals in psychotherapy may possess distinctive characteristics from those who do not seek psychotherapy that can have a bearing on religious coping, such as the severity of their stressors or the intensity of their reactions to them.

### Religious Coping as a Double-Edged Sword

Psychotherapists should keep in mind that religious coping is an umbrella term that encompasses a wide array of religious responses to stress. Many religious coping methods have been empirically linked to greater physical, psychological, emotional, and spiritual well-being (e.g., Pargament, Koenig, & Perez, 2000; Pargament et al., 1998). These methods therefore have been termed *positive religious coping* (e.g., interpreting a stressor as being used by God for good, seeking support from one's Church, or searching for a new direction in life through religion). Other methods have been empirically linked to poorer mental and physical health outcomes, even including greater risk of mortality (Pargament, Koenig, Tarakeshwar, & Hahn, 2001). These forms of religious coping have been termed *negative religious coping* (e.g., interpreting a stressor as the work of the devil or a punishment from God, passively waiting for God to solve a problem, or becoming dissatisfied with one's church). Because negative religious coping methods sometimes are also associated with personal and spiritual growth (Pargament et al., 1999; Pargament et al., 2000) they have been conceptualized as spiritual struggles that have complex implications for people's lives (Exline & Rose, 2005; Pargament, Murray-Swank, Magyar, & Ano, 2005).

Ano and Vasconcelles (2005) provided structure to the body of research on religious coping by statistically combining the results of 49 studies (105 effect sizes) examining the relationship between religious coping and psychological adjustment for a total of 13,512 participants dealing with stressful life situations. Their meta-analysis indicated that positive religious coping was associated with positive psychological adjustment (effect size = 0.33; fail-safe number = 10,040), and inversely related to negative psychological adjustment (effect size = −0.12; fail-safe number = 1,059) to stressful events. That is, those who used positive religious coping experienced somewhat greater stress-related growth, spiritual growth, positive affect, and self-esteem, as well as modestly less depression, anxiety, and distress. Negative religious coping, however, was associated with negative psychological adjustment to stress (effect size = 0.22; fail-safe number = 2,190). Those who used negative religious coping experienced somewhat more depression, anxiety, and distress.

In the previous section, we highlighted empirical studies showing that religious coping can be a unique predictor of beneficial outcomes. Psychotherapists should be aware that religious coping also can be unique in harmful ways. For example, Burker, Evon, Sedway, and Egan (2005) found that negative religious coping contributed unique variance beyond negative secular coping in predicting depression and anxiety among 81 patients with end-stage lung disease who were being evaluated for lung transplants. Similar results have surfaced for individuals with mental health disorders. For example, among 48 young adults diagnosed with schizophrenia or bipolar disorder, interpreting one's mental illness as a punishment from God or as an indication that God lacked power was associated with higher levels of psychological distress and personal loss (Phillips & Stein, 2007).

Therefore, understanding the effects of religious coping in a person's life is in part contingent on considering the specific form of religious coping that he or she employs. Many studies have revealed the duality of religious coping. For example, Mickley, Pargament, Brant, and Hipp (1998) gathered information from 92 caregivers of terminally ill patients. They found that the use of positive religious appraisals, such as seeing the situation as part of God's plan or as a means of gaining strength from God, were associated with experiencing greater meaning in life and spiritual well-being, whereas negative religious appraisals, such as viewing the situation as a punishment from God, were associated with greater anxiety and depression. This finding held even after controlling the effects of parallel, nonreligious appraisals, such as interpreting the situation as an opportunity for growth or blaming the doctor or a loved one.

Gall (2006) examined coping with life stressors among 101 adult survivors of childhood sexual abuse. She found that negative forms of religious coping (e.g., spiritual discontent) were related to greater distress, whereas positive forms of religious coping (e.g., spiritual support and religious forgiveness) were related to less distress. Religious coping predicted levels of anxiety, anger, and depression beyond the contribution of similar secular coping methods (e.g., cognitive appraisals) even when controlling factors such as the severity of abuse. Along similar lines, Krumrei, Mahoney, and Pargament (2009) found among 100 recently divorced adults that negative religious coping was associated with higher levels of depression and positive religious coping was associated with higher levels of posttraumatic growth, above and beyond the effects of parallel, nonreligious coping methods.

### *Implications for Clinical Application*

This research provides a hopeful picture about the potential for positive religious coping to promote mental health. Yet, the research literature also indicates the effects of negative religious coping are equally powerful in an alarming direction. Because these studies have not been conducted among samples of psychotherapy clients, it is unclear how well we can generalize the findings to those who seek treatment for psychological disorders. Nevertheless, this information can be used to broaden psychotherapists' basis for hypotheses formation, allowing them to ask clients relevant questions. For example, of clinical utility is the item analysis of a study that found that negative religious coping was predictive of increased risk of mortality (Pargament et al., 2001). Three items in particular raised elderly patients' risk of dying within a 2-year period by up to 28%: "Wondered whether God had abandoned me," "Questioned God's love for me," and "Decided the devil made this happen." These items verbalize specific spiritual struggles that psychotherapists can inquire about with clients who are facing major life stressors.

The empirical research shows that particular forms of religious coping are tied to either favorable or unfavorable outcomes, and in some instances both. Psychotherapists likely will be in a position to observe clients engaging in attempts to cope that incorporate religion in both positive and negative ways. The varied research findings suggest that psychotherapists should not jump to conclusions about specific religious coping methods, but rather should form a clinical interpretation on the basis of each client's unique situation. Perhaps the most important theme to psychotherapists in the empirical literature is that religious coping has diverse implications for people's mental health, depending on the "fit" between the stressor and the religious coping method employed (Pargament, 1997; Pargament et al., 1998). Next we consider how people's individual and religious differences are related to religious coping.

### Individual and Religious Differences

A small empirical basis suggests that religious coping has widespread relevance among many world religions and perhaps even secular societies (Pargament, 2011). Of course, religious coping behaviors are closely tied to a person's religious dispositions (Belavich & Pargament, 2002). Those who are more religious have greater access to religious coping methods (Park & Cohen, 1992).

The vast majority of religious coping research has been conducted among samples of predominantly Christians. In recent years, research has begun to highlight that individuals in each of the major world religions use religious resources to cope with life's challenges. Although commonalities exist among the world religions, different philosophical and theological tenets can influence the nature and implications of religious coping. For example, Hindu's may emphasize karma, yoga, and detachment (Tarakeshwar, Pargament, & Mahoney, 2003), Muslim may emphasize religious behaviors such as giving *Sadaqah* (alms) in the name of Allah (Khan & Watson, 2006), and Jews may rely heavily on community involvement (Rosmarin, Pirutinsky, Pargament, & Krumrei, 2009). Psychotherapists need to understand religious coping among individuals of many different faiths.

Recent research has revealed many commonalities and also some distinctive forms of religious coping among Hindus (Tarakeshwar et al., 2003), Muslims (Abu Raiya, Pargament, Mahoney, & Stein, 2008), and Jews (Rosmarin, Pargament, Krumrei, & Flannelly, 2009). The functions of religious coping have been shown to be largely similar across religions (i.e., the functions of gaining meaning, control, comfort, closeness with God, intimacy with others, and life transformation). In addition, the overarching structure of religious coping has many parallels. Studies of Muslims (Khan & Watson, 2006) and Jews (Rosmarin, Pargament, et al., 2009) confirmed the use of positive and negative religious coping in these populations. Factor analyses of religious coping strategies used by Hindus revealed the use of negative religious coping along with two distinct forms of positive religious coping (God focused and spirituality focused) that presumably reflected forms of Hindu worship (ritual-based idol worship and reverence of the formless Universal Spirit, Brahman; Tarakeshwar et al., 2003). Similar to Christian samples, more use of positive religious coping strategies was tied to better outcomes, while more use of negative religious coping strategies was tied to poorer outcomes among each religious group. For example, greater Islamic religiousness such as Islamic positive religious coping and identification was associated with less anger, while greater Islamic religious struggle and interpreting stressors as a punishment from Allah were associated with greater anger.

The differences in religious coping among each of these major religions were found primarily in the specific nature of the techniques employed. Some forms of religious coping observed in Christian samples were not reported among the other religions (e.g., Hindus did not endorse religious forgiving, dissatisfaction with members in the religious community, and attributing stressful events to the Devil). Furthermore, the essence of similar types of religious coping was unique to the group under examination. For example, the religious coping strategy of looking for a stronger connection with a higher power may represent building a personal relationship with Christ for one individual and represent searching for the formless Brahman for another (Tarakeshwar et al., 2003).

In addition to differences across religions, studies have shown religious affiliations within the same religion moderate the impact of religious coping on distress (e.g., Rosmarin, Pirutinsky, et al., 2009). A few studies have observed differences in the use and effects of religious coping between Protestants and Catholics. For example, receiving emotional support from church members when faced with breast cancer longitudinally predicted less distress for Evangelicals and more distress for Catholics (Alferi, Culver, Carvery, Arena, & Antoni, 1999). Furthermore, religious coping is shaped by nonreligious individual and contextual factors. For example, the persistence with which individuals engage in religious coping over time is related to outcomes (Krumrei, Mahoney, & Pargament, 2008; Pargament, Koenig, Tarakeshwar, & Hahn, 2004).

### *Implications for Clinical Application*

These studies highlight that there are group similarities and differences in religious coping across religions. In psychotherapy, it is essential to use an approach that is sensitive to the theological principles of a client's religious tradition. This is particularly true when working with religious minorities in one's locale. To this end, we must not forget that seemingly similar religious coping methods may hold different meaning for individuals of different faiths. For example, the religious coping tactic of focusing on one's purpose in living may involve a wide range of foci that are unique to the religious goals of the individual client: loving God and neighbor, mindfulness, enlightenment, interior illumination, and so on. Continued development of conceptual frameworks is needed to understand the uniqueness of non-Christian forms of religious coping. In addition, the individual and contextual differences related to religious coping highlight that merely understanding an individual's religious background is not sufficient for understanding the role of religious coping in his or her life. Thus, religious coping should be assessed on an individual basis in psychotherapy.

## CLINICAL APPLICATION

The body of empirical literature on religious coping provides a tentative basis for a three-pronged clinical approach: exploration of religious coping, bolstering positive religious coping, and working through negative religious coping.

Exploration involves considering the ways in which clients incorporate aspects of their religion and spirituality into their thoughts, feelings, and behaviors surrounding a stressful life event. I (EJK) recently asked a client how she was managing to cope with the loss of her job and her home. Her response was a simple: "It's God." Rather than brushing off this comment, I reflected that her faith seemed to be very important to her. This opened the door for her to share about the strength and security she gained from a steadfast God in the midst of upheaval in her life. She described the peace and calmness she received from being able to speak to God at any time, without constraints. Religious coping often involves the way clients think about their stressors. One client described her experience of grappling with her husband's affair as follows:

> I credit Him [God] for the strength to endure. Knowing that there is a bigger picture that I cannot see is what keeps me going—knowing that god knows the plans He has for me and my kids, and that those are plans to prosper me and not to harm us.

This is an example of a client forming a benevolent religious reappraisal in which she trusts that God will bring good out of her crisis.

Second, psychotherapists can also explore with clients whether there are helpful religious coping resources that they are overlooking. For example, a client with dysthymia once shared, "I feel drained and don't really make plans outside of work anymore. I've even stopped going to [church] choir practice on Wednesday nights. That used to be the one thing that I had for me—the one thing I truly enjoyed." I (EJK) asked the client how the choir might fit into her goal of engaging in activities that improved her mood. She agreed to make it a priority to go that week. When I asked her about it in our next session, a genuine smile came across her face. She described how she had felt alive for the first time in a while when she had joined others to sing worship songs.

Finally, it may be crucial in psychotherapy to explore the negative religious coping methods that clients employ. For some individuals, religion and spirituality can raise stumbling blocks in the midst of life's stressors. For example, when getting divorced, one client indicated that he felt "rejected by my spouse and God." It is not uncommon for clients to experience a sense of abandonment from God, or to wrestle with deep anger at God. Frequently, clients also feel abandoned or judged by their religious communities. Some clients may grapple with questions of how God could let something terrible happen to them. Others may experience a deep sense of shame that keeps them from turning to God in their time of need. Bringing these negative religious coping experiences into the conversation can shed new light on a client's presenting concerns and can provide rich therapeutic conversations.

As we further consider clinical assessment and intervention related to positive and negative religious coping in the following sections, let us highlight this point: It is not uncommon for positive and negative religious coping to co-occur. Some studies have reported high base rates for both phenomena within community samples, suggesting that individuals are employing positive and negative religious coping techniques simultaneously. The implication is that an either–or schema for positive and negative religious coping methods is too simplistic and may cause psychotherapists to overlook important experiences among their clients. For example, a client with posttraumatic stress disorder (PTSD) may engage in the negative religious coping method of reappraising God's powers as insufficient to control the traumatic event. Simultaneously, he may attempt to engage in problem solving in partnership with God, known as the positive method of collaborative religious coping. Or, a client may experience dissatisfaction with her religious community (negative religious coping), while receiving comfort from God (positive religious coping) or visa versa. The message for psychotherapists is that it is essential to assess both of these forms of religious coping and to consider greater use of positive religious coping and the resolution of spiritual struggles as concurrent points of intervention.

## CLINICAL ASSESSMENT

The research literature has highlighted that religious coping is relevant to a wide variety of stressors and typically is endorsed highly in community samples. From this endorsement, we can tentatively infer that religious coping might be relevant to many clients in psychotherapy. At minimum, psychotherapists have the incentive to listen for and inquire about the ways in which clients incorporate their religion into the coping process. Religious coping has been shown to predict outcomes beyond the effects of conventional religiousness (e.g., self-rated religiousness and spirituality, church attendance, and so on). Thus, merely inquiring about general religious beliefs and practices in isolation from concrete life situations may obscure the powerful ways in which religious coping is at work in a client's life. For this reason, we will highlight informal and formal methods in which psychotherapists can gather information on the substantively religious and spiritual cognitions and behaviors that clients experience in response to stressful life events.

### Informal Assessment

Inquiry into positive and negative methods of religious coping can provide valuable clinical information. Exploring the topic informally in the therapeutic relationship is perhaps the most valuable avenue for therapeutic intervention. Psychotherapists can make use of a host of informal, open-ended questions (see Table 10.1). Psychotherapists should use clinical judgment to select questions that are appropriate to the individual client, particularly attending to whether a client identifies with explicitly religious and spiritual experiences.

Many clients will make use of explicitly religious and spiritual language to describe their experiences. For such clients, it is effective to match their use of terms and directly inquire into the religious and spiritual cognitions and behaviors they employ in response to life's stressors (e.g., "In what ways has your spirituality helped you deal with your problems?"). Other clients, however, may draw on coping methods that are infused with spirituality in a more subtle or covert manner. These individuals may connect more with implicit religious coping questions (e.g., "For what are you deeply grateful?" or "What are your deepest regrets?" see Pargament & Krumrei, 2008). Here, too, it is beneficial to mirror the client's language, perhaps using terms such as "force" or "energy" rather than "God." For clients who are overtly or covertly religious, psychotherapists can use informal assessment strategies to demonstrate genuine interest in clients' spiritual lives. This is invaluable for determining how spirituality may impact distress, well-being, and functioning.

Some psychotherapists are reticent to address issues of spirituality. We have found that, when asked, many clients readily report that spirituality is important in their lives and that they use religious coping strategies. Some clients have voiced the notion that simply discussing their spirituality in psychotherapy has decreased stress. We also have found that clients who are not particularly religious or spiritual are not offended when asked about religious coping. For this reason, we believe that informal assessment of client religious coping poses the potential for great benefit with little risk. Thus, it is incumbent on psychotherapists to approach this topic as any other aspect of a client's life.

### Formal Assessment

Psychotherapists may desire to augment informal assessment with the use of quantitative measures. Most quantitative coping instruments do not include

**Table 10.1** Unstructured Assessment of Religious Coping[a]

| | |
|---|---|
| **Positive Religious Coping** | |
| Explicit questions | • What spiritual beliefs do you find especially meaningful?[b]<br>• What spiritual rituals or practices are important to you?<br>• Why are you involved in spirituality?<br>• How has your spirituality changed your life for the better?<br>• To what degree has your spirituality given you pleasure? Meaning? A sense of connectedness to others? Hope for the future? Confidence? A feeling of being loved? Compassion for others?<br>• Has your spirituality or religion been involved in the way you have responded to your problem? If so, in what way?<br>• In what ways has your spirituality helped you understand or deal with your problems?<br>• Has your problem affected you spiritually or religiously? In what way?<br>• How has your understanding of the sacred changed? |
| Implicit questions | • What sustains you in the midst of your troubles?<br>• From what sources do you draw the strength or courage to go on?[c]<br>• When you are afraid or in pain, how do you find comfort or solace?[c]<br>• Who truly understands your situation?[c]<br>• For what are you deeply grateful?[c] |
| **Negative Religious Coping** | |
| Explicit questions | • Has your problem affected you spiritually or religiously? In what way?<br>• How has your understanding of the sacred changed?<br>• Do you ever have mixed thoughts and feelings about the sacred? What are they like?<br>• How has your spirituality changed your life for the worse?<br>• To what degree has your spirituality been a source of pain? Guilt? Anger? Confusion? Doubt? Anxiety? Fear? Feelings of insignificance? Feelings of alienation from others?<br>• In what ways has your spirituality been harmful in understanding or dealing with your problems? |
| Implicit questions | • What are the deepest questions your situation has raised for you?<br>• What causes you the greatest despair or suffering?<br>• How has this experience changed you at your core?<br>• What have you discovered about yourself that you find disturbing?<br>• What has this experience taught you that you wish you had never known?<br>• What are your deepest regrets?<br>• What would you like to be able to let go of in your life? |

[a] Adapted from Pargament and Krumrei (2008)
[b] Drawn or adapted from Hodge (2001).
[c] Drawn or adapted from Griffith and Griffith (2002).

specific religious coping items or embed these items within other scales. Among the 13 leading coping measures reviewed by Schwarzer and Schwarzer (1996), only three contain subscales that are religious in nature. These are (1) the three-item "seeking spiritual support" subscale of the Adolescent Coping Orientation for Problem Experiences Inventory (Patterson & McCubbin, 1987) that assesses going to church, praying, and talking to a minister; (2) the six-item "religion" category of the Measure of Daily Coping (Stone & Neale, 1984) that assesses such actions as seeking spiritual comfort and support; and (3) the four-item "religious coping scale" of the COPE Inventory (Carver, Scheier, & Weintraub, 1989) that assesses seeking God's help, putting trust in God, seeking comfort in religion, and praying. The first two measures are not geared toward use in psychotherapy because they are concerned with coping with general life stress and daily problems and were validated with nonclinical samples of adolescents and adult community members respectively. The COPE Inventory was normed among a nonclinical sample of college students. It has been employed in research among some groups of clinically troubled individuals (although not among psychotherapy clients specifically) and the religious coping scale has demonstrated internal consistency that meets minimum requirements for clinical use ($\alpha = .92$). An advantage of administering a broad coping measure is that it provides the psychotherapist with information about many different forms of coping in which a client is engaged (e.g., social support, planning, denial, or disengagement) and offers insight into how religious coping fits into this larger picture.

In addition to general coping scales, several self-report inventories are specifically religious in nature. The Ways of Religious Coping Scale (WORCS; Boudreaux, Catz, Ryan, Ameral-Melendez, & Brantley, 1995) uses 40 items ($\alpha = .95$) to assess religious coping strategies. The measure provides information on two domains: internal and private religious coping ($\alpha = .97$), which involves such activities as prayer and basing decisions on one's religious beliefs; and external and social religious coping ($\alpha = .93$), which involves receiving and giving support within a religious community. Because the measure is written at a fourth-grade reading level, the applicability of this measure is broad. It was developed, however, for research purposes and was validated among college students. Further research is needed to establish its utility among psychotherapy clients.

An early measure of religious coping is the Religious Problem Solving Scales (RPSS; Pargament et al., 1988). It was developed to understand various ways in which individuals incorporate their relationship with God into the problem-solving process to deal with difficult events in their lives. The RPSS provides information on three styles of coping: collaborative, self-directing, and deferring. Collaborative problem solving ($\alpha = .94$) involves an active, personal exchange with God. This style of religious coping is associated with a committed, internalized religion and greater levels of competence in responding to life's problems. The self-directing style ($\alpha = .94$) emphasizes active coping within the freedom

God gives individuals to direct their own lives. This style of coping is associated with lower levels of traditional religious involvement and is considered a generally effective style of functioning. Deferring problem solving ($\alpha = .94$) involves waiting for solutions from God, which has been associated with externally oriented religion and lower levels of competence. The RPSS was validated among a community sample of Christian church members. It has been used to understand coping among individuals adjusting to serious circumstances, such as cancer (Nairn & Merluzzi, 2003).

The Religious Coping Scale (RCOPE; Pargament et al., 2000) includes the religious problem-solving concepts of the RPSS in addition to many other forms of religious coping. It provides comprehensive assessments of religious approaches to coping with 99 items across 17 subscales. This multidimensional inventory can provide an objective starting point for assessing and quantifying client use of religious coping. Its condensed version, the Brief RCOPE (Pargament et al., 1998), contains 18 items with the two subscales of positive and negative religious coping (e.g., seeking support from or struggling with religious communities, and appraising God's involvement as benevolent or malevolent). These measures frequently have been used in research settings among clinically troubled individuals.

A limiting factor of these scales is that they were designed for use with Christian populations and draw heavily on Christian doctrine and terminology. For example, the WORCS uses, "I think about Jesus as my friend," and the RCOPE notes, "Looked for spiritual support from clergy." In recent years, alternative versions have been developed that are theologically and culturally relevant to Hindus (Tarakeshwar, et al., 2003), Muslims (Abu Raiya et al., 2008), and Jews (Rosmarin, Pargament, et al., 2009).

Although measures of religious coping have by enlarge been developed for research purposes, several show clinical promise (Pargament, 2007). For each of the tools discussed, more research is needed on their use in psychotherapy. Nonetheless, when used with caution, they can provide objective data about how religion relates to appraisals of stressors and attempts to cope. In addition to providing such clinically relevant information, religious coping measures can provide structure for discussing spirituality in psychotherapy. Administering a brief questionnaire to clients about religious coping sends a message that religion and spirituality are not taboo and that they are open for discussion in psychotherapy. Reviewing clients' responses to a measure in session can provide further ground for exploring how religion can be part of a client's problems and solutions.

## CLINICAL STRATEGIES

The field of clinical psychology has recognized that religious populations generally underutilize conventional treatments, as many religious individuals prefer spiritually based treatment (Puchalski, Larson, & Lu, 2001). Consequently, research efforts have been made in recent years to examine psychological treatments that attempt to facilitate religious coping. We will mention some spiritually integrated interventions with initial empirical support and then discuss more broadly how religious coping can be an additive layer to general therapeutic efforts.

### Treatments That Facilitate Religious Coping

Religious coping interventions have been designed specifically to address spiritual struggles and facilitate the use of religious resources in a number of populations, including adults with HIV (Tarakeshwar, Pearce, & Sikkema, 2005), survivors of sexual abuse (Murray-Swank & Pargament, 2005), cancer patients (Cole, 2005), individuals with social anxiety (McCorkle, Bohn, Hughes & Kim, 2005), adults with addictions (Beitel, et al., 2007), and college students experiencing spiritual struggles (Gear et al., 2008). These manualized interventions draw on such techniques as spiritual autobiographies, spiritual genograms, visualization exercises, meditation, and surrender rituals to help clients explore spiritual struggles and their use of religious coping. Initial outcome studies of such interventions have shown promising results (Pargament, 2007).

Smith et al. (2007) examined 31 outcome studies of structured and nonstructured spiritual therapies (71% group psychotherapy, 26% individual psychotherapy) for a range of clinical issues, including depression, trauma, stress, anxiety, and eating disorders. Many of the interventions made active use of religious coping methods, such as prayer (42%) and religious imagery or meditation (32%). The meta-analysis revealed that spiritual approaches to psychotherapy were moderately effective in the treatment of psychological problems (effect size = 0.56). Furthermore, among the smaller number of studies that used well-being as an outcome measure, the effect size of spiritually integrated treatments was large (0.96). In particular, clients seemed to benefit from interventions that explicitly taught spiritual concepts and related them to their situation or well-being.

Another meta-analysis of studies comparing religion–accommodative treatments with standard cognitive-behavioral therapy (CBT) for depression indicated that both methods were equally effective in reducing depression (McCullough, 1999). On this basis, spiritually integrated psychotherapy can be offered to clients without compromising treatment efficacy. In fact, recently analyzed data of a randomized treatment outcome study among Jewish individuals with elevated levels of stress and worry indicated that psychotherapy incorporating religious coping produced large treatment effects in a short period (2 weeks) and may have greater utility than conventional treatments among religious clients (Rosmarin et al., 2011).

### Incorporating Religious Coping Into Psychotherapy

In addition to drawing from manualized treatments, psychotherapists may consider infusing religious coping into psychotherapy sessions in a less structured fashion. This involves listening for opportunities to reinforce positive religious coping methods and to resolve issues related to negative religious coping. Specific efforts can be woven into a variety of common therapeutic themes, including meaning, pain, control, and change.

### *Meaning*

The cognitive model of psychotherapy emphasizes that the way in which individuals interpret the meaning of life phenomena will influence their affect. Often, negative schema and automatic thoughts underlie painful emotional states (Beck, 1972). Thus, the psychological impact of any event will depend on how a person appraises the meaning of the given event (Lazarus & Folkman, 1984). Some clients will possess schema and automatic thoughts of a religious nature. They may interpret the meaning of stressful events through a spiritual lens, which can have implications for the way they view themselves and the world. For example, clients may interpret stressors as a punishment from God, or view traumatic events as evidence that God is not fully in control.

In Beck's cognitive approach, the therapist becomes involved with the client's specific cognitive patterns that lead to or sustain a disorder such as depression. This same approach can be taken with clients who attempt to cope through negative religious meaning-making. Cognitions of a religious nature are amenable to the same cognitive techniques that have been used in many empirically supported treatments, such as identifying and questioning illogical thinking (Beck & Alford, 2009). Juxtaposing clients' negative religious appraisals with their larger God image or faith system may help clients to discover faulty meanings that they are ascribing to their experiences. For example, a client who deeply believes that God is compassionate may simultaneously be burdened by anger or shame stemming from the appraisal that God created a crisis to punish him or her. Beck (1972) suggested that discovering the faulty meanings a client ascribes to his or her experiences can lead to "new meaning" (p. 142) in life that helps the client to be satisfied and meet goals. Clients' negative religious appraisals may be influencing them without their conscious awareness. When clients gain insight into their unspoken interpretations, they gain the opportunity to critically evaluate their cognitions, employ strategies such as thought stopping, and replace negative religious appraisals with more helpful beliefs. Richards, Hardman, and Berrett (2007) have provided examples of incorporating spiritual discussions and education into treatment of women with eating disorders to help them become aware of, examine, and modify distorted and dysfunctional religious beliefs that are contributing to their emotional distress. They discuss a variety of spiritual concepts with their clients such as God's love and grace, forgiveness, prayer, service, honesty, human suffering, and imperfections to examine whether the clients' beliefs may be inconsistent with their personal theology and having an unhealthy impact on their lives.

By the same token, religious cognition can consist of positive rather than negative coping methods. For example, religious reappraisals provide an opportunity for the client to supply an event with positive spiritual meaning. Clients may benefit from using a spiritual lens to reinterpret a stressor in a potentially beneficial light. For example, a client may be able to see how God is strengthening him or her through a difficult experience. Religious meaning-making can be one way in which clients gain insight and closure about difficult situations in the therapeutic process (e.g., Exline, Smyth, Gregory, Hockemeyer, & Tulloch, 2005).

### *Pain*

Clients often present to psychotherapy in emotional turmoil. Religious coping can provide a deep reservoir of comfort. In the midst of distress, clients may find a new capacity to make spiritual connections with God and others. One study showed that incorporating spirituality into meditation practices was effective in helping clients cope with painful life experiences (Wachholtz & Pargament, 2008). Psychotherapists might ask the client to call to mind a spiritually supportive image or experience. Psychotherapists also can draw on guided imagery exercises in which the client visualizes God's love.

Kaori and Jeeseon (2009) have described ways in which psychotherapists can draw on Buddhist approaches in grief counseling. They highlight that the Western emphasis on intrapersonal experiences in grief models can mislead grieving individuals to engage in self-pity or self-criticism. They make use of the Buddhist conceptualization of compassion as "[a] non-dualistic view of the self and others [that] helps one recognize that all individuals are the same in their struggle with suffering and their pursuit for happiness" (pp. 671–672). Moving toward such a conceptualization can help bereaved clients shift from self-pity and self-criticism to the rebuilding of connections with others.

For many sources of pain, psychotherapists can help clients find ways to gain support from religious sources, including their relationship to a higher power and organized religious groups. For example, psychotherapists can consider encouraging clients to seek spiritual support, comfort, and reassurance within a religious community.

### *Control*

Difficult circumstances can challenge a client's equilibrium in life. The concerns that bring people to psychotherapy often are accompanied by a sense of powerlessness that is one of the most painful emotions to experience (Baugh, 1988). It is essential to differentiate situations in which clients should be empowered to take action from situations in which clients will benefit from acceptance and giving up control. This distinction relates to the nature of the stressor in comparison with the client's abilities and resources. Some situations can be changed by the client, while others cannot. Some struggles are effective (e.g., those related to the choices, behaviors, and attitudes of the client), whereas some battles are impossible to win (e.g., those related to the choices, behaviors, and attitudes of others; life circumstances and events; and occurrences in the past).

Religious coping methods can be powerful tools to help clients reestablish a sense of control. Psychotherapists may observe some individuals shifting responsibility for change to God. Putting their situation in God's hands can function as a way to shirk responsibility, shift blame, or be avoidant. Clients may feel overwhelmed to the point that they throw up their hands and wait for God to control the situation.

On the other extreme, psychotherapists may recognize that their clients are going through life with clenched fists, anxiously clamping onto the experiences and events that are affecting them. They may be living in regrets from the past or be consumed by anger or bitterness about wrongs that have been done to them. Pursuit of personal control to the exclusion of other goals and values can become dysfunctional (Cole & Pargament, 1999). In such instances, psychotherapists can work with clients to relinquish negative emotions and events by actively surrendering control to God. Baugh (1988) emphasized that clients can gain a sense of control by giving up a desired control that is beyond their power or ability. Cole and Pargament (1999) described spiritual surrender as the paradoxical way to achieve control and cite empirical support of this coping method.

Psychotherapists can help clients move beyond passive religious deferral or attempts to control the uncontrollable by considering ways the client can engage in a collaborative partnership with God to resolve their problems. Baugh (1988) described a mental image that may help clients in these efforts. The client pictures two desks: one belonging to themselves and one belonging to God. All of the client's present concerns are pictured as stacks of paper requiring attention. The client identifies the stacks that are within his or her control and places them on his or her personal desk. The rest of the stacks of work are placed on God's desk. The client must then decide to focus on his or her own tasks and to let God decide when and how to work on the others.

For clients who are less inclined to mental imagery, this same activity can be done by asking them to list their concerns under either a *controllable* or *uncontrollable* column on a sheet of paper. This is followed by discussing what surrender of the uncontrollables would look like in behavioral terms. Cole and Pargament (1999) pointed out that surrender involves an experience of self-transcendence in which the individual stops "playing God" and starts "seeking God" (p. 185). This is both a cognitive and experiential shift that involves changes in motivation, affect, values, perception, thought, and behavior.

Research has offered preliminary suggestion that spiritual surrender is associated with more positive adjustment than other approaches for achieving control (Cole & Pargament, 1999). Psychotherapists can help clients demarcate their decision to relinquish control by incorporating a surrender exercises into a session (see Richards et al., 2007, for further examples). When clients give up the desire to control matters that are beyond their power, they often experience a greater sense of stability, tranquility, and perhaps ironically: control. Nevertheless, psychotherapist should be cautious about the way spiritual surrender is addressed in psychotherapy. Cole and Pargament (1999) offered the clinical wisdom that surrendering control for the explicit purpose of gaining control will not be successful. Thus, rather than taking a utilitarian approach to surrender, this concept can be processed as a therapeutic aspect of the healing process when a client experiences an illness, death, or other event that forces him or her to face the limits of his or her control in life.

### *Change*

Points of crisis can also mark points of decision. Clients may be grappling for new direction in life after losing a job, marriage, or loved one. Clients may reevaluate their lives after being diagnosed with a mental or physical illness. The first response of a psychotherapist to a client in crisis is to focus on safety concerns and stabilization (Oakley, 2009). Research indicates that in the time that follows, many people respond to difficult life events by experiencing posttraumatic growth (see Linley & Joseph, 2004, for review). Individuals commonly attribute psychosocial and spiritual growth following a crisis to spiritual resources, such as having a loving relationship with God or obtaining support from fellow-believers (Pargament, 2007).

Clients may view a psychological problem or difficult life event not only as personally devastating but also as the loss or violation of something they hold sacred. For example, a person who views his or her divorce as the violation of a holy covenant or the loss of a sacred family unit can experience the event as a "spiritual trauma" (Mahoney, Krumrei, & Pargament, 2008, p. 105).

Both personal and spiritual traumas can mire people down in painful spiritual struggles. The deep discomfort created by the difficult situation, however, can push people to turn to God or seek out new spiritual resources. In this way, religious coping may facilitate long-range psychological and spiritual growth in the healing process (Mahoney et al., 2008).

When psychotherapy addresses existential questions, clients are more likely to experience traumatic events as an impetus for greater awareness of existence in and through relation (Oakley, 2009). Drawing on the client's religious framework can be particularly helpful in exploring the bigger questions of life and existence. Some religious coping tactics are particularly suited to people's attempts to achieve change. For example, clients can draw on religious guidance to seek new direction in life. This may involve attending to an inner spiritual compass or listening to God through prayer. Psychotherapists may choose to incorporate religious metaphors that offer insight and strength to the client during uncertain times.

The therapeutic approaches discussed here will be meaningful only if they fit within a client's individual understanding and experience of the sacred. Of course, similar to other forms of therapeutic intervention, addressing religious thoughts and behaviors will take time. For further reading, Pargament (2007) has provided an extensive discussion of spiritually integrated psychotherapy.

## CASE STUDY: FAYE[1]

Faye was a nontraditional aged college student who self-identified as a Christian. She was referred to counseling by a professor when she "broke down" during a talk after class. She laughed frequently to cover her nerves and spoke in a French accent, having come from the Congo. Faye identified that she was "stressed out" and didn't know how to make herself a priority. Her adult brother had recently moved into her one-bedroom apartment with her (a plan devised by her family). Not much later she lost her job. Both situations caused financial strain. Her brother did not contribute financially, and even expected Faye to give him spending money. Faye sighed as she explained that it was impossible for her to say "no" to anyone in her life. Simultaneously, she reported being extremely hesitant to form new relationships and stated point blank that she did not trust anyone. We spent the first couple of sessions discussing her relationships and working on skills related to boundaries, assertiveness, and self-care. Our work took on new depth when Faye decided to open up about her past.

### Faye's Story

Faye had been the black sheep in her large family. Or in this case, "white sheep" may be more descriptive. Although her complexion would be considered dark by American standards, she had been the light-skinned child in her African tribe. She had other physical characteristics that set her apart, and she had the tendency to keep to herself. For these reasons, tribe leaders told her mother that she was a witch. For years her family accepted this and Faye described in detail how she "went through at least 20 different ministers trying to cast out the witchcraft in me" involving church rituals centered on beatings, pouring hot wax on her, and sacrificing animals over her.

#### *Meaning*

As Faye shared one ritual story after another, it quickly became clear that religion was integrally interwoven into her sociocultural context and life experience. Exploring the spiritual meaning Faye attached to her experiences was key to our treatment theme related to Faye's sense of identity. In her tribe, Faye had been viewed as a witch. As a western psychologist, my explicit assumption was that

[1] Several weeks following termination, I contacted the client to inquire about describing her case in a publication. She willingly agreed and signed her permission. Her name and other identifying details have been changed to maintain confidentiality.

Faye was not a witch and that she had experienced emotional, physical, psychological, and spiritual trauma as the result of a false interpretation. However, I listened carefully to Faye's personal interpretations of herself and her experience:

> They would ask me a series of questions, like, "do you have this kinds of dreams at night?" And I would say, "nope, nope" and I really didn't! But the more I said no, the more they beat me up, so after a while I just started saying yes. They told my mom that I was a very quiet kid because in the witchcraft world I was thirty-something. And I was a really arrogant kid because I was so confidant in my powers. And at that moment, for a second I actually did believe them. I'm like, maybe I'm a witch after all, because all these people are saying I am.

When Faye moved to the United States as a teenager, she was surprised to find that she blended in within the range of skin tones and was embraced as a "normal" person. On an intellectual level, Faye did not believe she had been a witch. She forced a laugh at the stupidity of the accusation. Nevertheless, I pointed out that there seemed to remain a part of her that lived down to the spiritual view that had been placed on her. When she let others walk over her or treat her badly, she was acting as if she were not a complete human being. Exploring Faye's spiritual identity took our work on boundaries to a new level. When I asked her to describe how she viewed herself at her core, she explained that she and a small group of women at her church had decided to focus on positive affirmations from scripture. Pulling out a list, she described that she was choosing to see herself as a fearfully and wonderfully made creation of God.

We explored in session what it meant to be fearfully and wonderfully made. This new grounding for her identity helped to heal the sense of shame resulting from the ostracism she had experienced. I encouraged her to draw on her new spiritual view of herself when she was having difficulty setting or maintaining healthy boundaries. We role played stressful situations in which family members placed unreasonable expectations on her, or friends asked for unreasonable favors. This allowed her to practice repeating helpful phrases to herself about her God-given worth and to formulate responses that were fitting with this new spiritual view of herself.

### *Pain*

Faye was stoic during her initial disclosures about the abuse. As a child, she had cried but no one had attended to her confusion and pain. Over time, she stopped expressing emotions. Early in treatment, Faye reported that she had never been angry at those who had hurt her because they had done what they believed was best for her by trying to "purify me from evil spirits." In our sessions, we explored how it had been adaptive for her to shut down the emotional pain as a child, but that it had come at a cost. Faye had never learned how anger or hurt could help her to judge situations and make decisions about how to respond. As a child, she could not make choices for herself, but as an adult she had the right, and even the responsibility, to respond to the world around her. Her emotions, even the difficult ones (perhaps particularly the difficult ones), could be a gift to help guide her in forming healthy relationships.

Our work involved exploring Faye's emotional response to key figures in her life. When Faye shared stories of mistreatment, I would ask her to reflect on the feelings she experienced. She started by acknowledging that she had experienced some anger toward her mother. When I probed further, she described:

> I think what I was mad about with [my mom] was the fact that she would lie to me to get me to all these places. I remember there was this one [time], she told me I was going to visit friends on Christmas break. … So I was so happy. I was like, "I haven't seen them in such a long time!" Not knowing that she was taking me to a church [pause]. Then something just didn't feel right. We went to this church service for Christmas and my mom just left me there. She just went home. And when [the service] was done my traveling bag was already in the pastor's office upstairs and my mom was gone. So, then I knew why I was there. I knew I wasn't there because of vacation or nothing. … They beat me up with a broom. So, it was like, literally, picking out toothpicks out of someone's skin [pause] like on my back, my skin, like, three days later. And my mom was crying as she was taking it out afterwards. She was crying. She was like, "I can't believe I did this. I cannot believe I did this."

Out of all of the stories of physical, emotional, and sexual abuse, the mental image of Faye in the moment that she realized her mother had lied to her about going on vacation to get her to a witchcraft ceremony and had abandoned her there was particularly heartbreaking for me. In the absence of Faye displaying emotion as she described the experience, I intentionally paused to reflect on what this story stirred in me. I disclosed to Faye that I was feeling deeply hurt about what she had gone through. I connected my statements to the themes we had been working on related to her views of herself. Her experience was worthy of taking pause and feeling emotion. In this way, I hoped to model emotional expression to Faye and to emphasize her worth.

I reflected the irony that the betrayals Faye had experienced came from those who should have protected her. I asked Faye at whom else she felt mad besides her mother. Faye disclosed that she experienced confusion and anger directed toward God about the way she had been treated. In the religious coping literature, this is referred to as spiritual discontent. Faye described that sometimes she felt abandoned by God and questioned God's love for her. When she had been powerless to change her situation, she had questioned God's power. She wondered whether God was in control, and if so, why He was not intervening in her situation. I encouraged Faye to allow herself to reconnect with the emotion behind her big questions about God. We worked on feeling identification, and I witnessed Faye develop a new awareness of her emotional experience. During this process, we built on Faye's self-care resources to help her manage her emotions and keep from being swept under by them. She identified prayer, exercise, and music as her most helpful resources. For the first time, Faye could be in control of when and how to experience the pain and anger that had been so far beneath the surface.

### *Change*

Given her background, it may seem amazing that Faye identified as a Christian when she presented for psychotherapy. She reported that it had taken her a long time to rededicate her life to God because of what she had been through. Despite her past, she described drawing great strength from her faith in her adult life. She identified her church as her main source of support. Nevertheless, she grappled with the role of clergy in her life. She maintained a strong conviction that no person could speak for God. She prioritized her personal, direct connection to God. During the course of treatment, Faye commonly sought comfort and reassurance from God's love to cope with her memories from the past and her present life stressors. I encouraged Faye to focus on strengthening this connection. Feeling valued by God helped to facilitate a healing experience. Feeling accepted by God, regardless of what she had gone through in the past, placed Faye in a greater position to accept herself. We explored how Faye could continue to draw strength, peace, and reassurance from her positive connection with God. One session, Faye described how positive religious coping had transformed her to the extent that it had a greater influence on her than the abuse of her past. She reported, "my belief system is reshaping my functioning and my way of viewing things. … That's how I switched from who I was to who I am now."

### *Control*

As Faye became more in touch with her emotional experience, we were able to draw on her faith to process and let go of anger and bitterness. One method was to draw on the concept of surrender. We made use of an activity in which Faye identified the "burdens" that she had been carrying with her as a result of her past experience. She identified that she was angry at the faulty logic of her accusers and was resentful that she had lost a happy childhood.

Facing her burdens meant having to face her own powerlessness—the fact that she could not do anything to right the wrong. We explored how Faye had been powerless to stop the abuse as a child, and that as an adult she remained powerless to correct the events from the past. We processed the bitterness, anger, and resentment that Faye had been keeping at bay. Rather than rejecting these aspects of her experience, I encouraged Faye to accept the feelings as a natural and healthy response to the wrong she had experienced. The goal, however, was not to remain stuck in those feelings, but to move toward letting them go.

We explored the notion of active religious surrender. I asked Faye to monitor her thoughts and feelings during the days between sessions. When she found that she was ruminating about the wrong that had been done to her and feeling "stuck" in the associated anger and bitterness, she was to intentionally relinquish these factors to God. Faye reported that turning her "uncontrollables" over to God relieved her distress in the moment, but that she found it difficult to maintain a state of acceptance. We decided to use a surrender ritual to emphasize Faye's desire to let go of the things she could not change. I gave Faye two circles of paper. On one she wrote the issues that she could control: "how I respond to my emotions, what I do when I feel anxious, who I let into my life, how I expect others to treat me, how I spend my time." On the other, she wrote the struggles that she could not control: "that I was treated as a witch, that I had to endure rituals, that I was hurt, that my mother did not protect me, that I feel angry, that people ask things of me." Faye decided that she wanted to relinquish her uncontrollables to a greater power. I placed a bowl of water between us, and when she was ready, she put her circle of uncontrollables in the bowl, allowing the ink to run in the water. This symbolized her giving these items to God to take care of. She was left with only *her* circle of control in her hands.

Watching her uncontrollables wash away in the water allowed Faye to grieve for the losses she had experienced: the loss of innocence, the loss of a childhood, the loss of confidence. In addition, giving up the control that was beyond her, cleared room for Faye to exert control where she did have it—in her daily decisions, mood management, and current relationships.

### Discussion

Faye provides an example of how religion and spirituality can be at the heart of pain, abuse, rejection, and ostracism. Simultaneously, Faye provides an example of how religion and spirituality can contribute hope, connectedness, healing, and powerful transformation. This case also illustrates how positive and negative religious coping methods can flow naturally out of attempts to cope and can be intertwined in a person's life at a given time.

Religion and spirituality were important undertones in our therapeutic work related to trauma, trust, boundaries, and self-care. Because Faye's spiritual narrative unfolded as a natural component of her life story, I did not engage in a comprehensive spiritual assessment but rather used open-ended questions to explore Faye's spiritual interpretations of herself and her experiences, and her use of religious coping methods. Much of the intervention related to religious coping consisted of reinforcing Faye's positive religious coping methods and exploring, and at times challenging, her negative religious coping methods.

## CONCLUSION

In this chapter, we have considered the clinical implications of empirical research on religious and spiritual coping in response to stressful life events. Because the majority of studies on this topic have been conducted among groups within the general population, strong inferences cannot be made about individual clients in treatment. We have tentatively offered ways that psychotherapists can infuse religious coping into psychotherapy related to a variety of common therapeutic themes. Research has provided preliminary support for some of the methods we have explored. In addition, initial outcome studies of religious coping interventions for clinical populations have shown promising results. With a strong body of research on religious coping in the general population, directions for future research involve gathering empirical evidence regarding the role of religious and spiritual coping during the course of psychotherapy.

## CHAPTER SUMMARY

- Religious coping occurs when people incorporate their religion or spirituality into efforts to respond to stressors. This process is influenced by contextual and individual factors.
- Empirical studies have been conducted on many different religious coping strategies in response to a wide variety of stressors. This research has shown that religious coping methods relate to both positive and negative outcome measures, depending on the nature of the religious coping strategy and the fit between the strategy and the situation.
- Not much research is available on the use of religious coping specifically by psychotherapy clients. Based on research in the general population, religious coping is likely relevant to many individuals seeking psychotherapy.
- More research is needed on the use of therapeutic techniques involving religious coping. Initial empirical support has been offered for a number of treatments that incorporate a focus on religious coping, and some manualized treatments on this topic are available.
- Psychotherapists may wish to attend to the substantively religious and spiritual cognitions, behaviors, and emotions that clients experience in response to stressful life events. Explicit and implicit open-ended questions are helpful for assessment. Some quantitative measures of religious coping are also available for use in psychotherapy.
- Psychotherapists may choose to incorporate religious coping techniques or exercises into therapeutic work on themes such as meaning, pain, control, and change. It may be beneficial to reinforce and explore helpful religious coping methods and working through religious or spiritual struggles that compound client distress.
- Incorporating religious coping into psychotherapy will be meaningful only if the approach fits within a client's individualized understanding and experience of the sacred.

## CLINICAL APPLICATION QUESTIONS

1. Research has suggested that religious coping methods are not redundant with secular methods of coping, but add a distinctive dimension to the coping process. Is this sufficient evidence to support incorporating religious coping into psychotherapy?
2. What does it mean to focus on clients' substantively religious and spiritual cognitions and behaviors that occur during times of stress? What is the clinical utility of doing so? How does this differ from assessing global indicators of religiosity (e.g., religious affiliation, frequency of prayer)?
3. What are the advantages and disadvantages of using formal versus informal means to assess religious coping (e.g., quantitative measures versus unstructured, open-ended questions)?
4. How does the topic of religious coping relate to multicultural competence?
5. What are some ways that religious coping can be infused as an additive layer to the therapeutic process?
6. What are some specific ways in which to tailor a therapeutic emphasis on religious coping to a client's individualized understanding and experience of the sacred?

## SUGGESTED READINGS AND RESOURCES

Aten, J. D., & Leach, M. M. (Eds.). (2008). *Spirituality and the therapeutic process: A comprehensive resource from intake to termination.* Washington, DC: American Psychological Association.

Miller, W. R. (Ed.). (1999). *Integrating spirituality into treatment: Resources for practitioners.* Washington, DC: American Psychological Association.

Miller, W. R., & Martin, J. E. (Eds.). (1988). *Behavior therapy and religion: Integrating spiritual and behavioral approaches to change.* Thousand Oaks, CA: Sage.

Pargament, K. I. (1997). *The psychology of religion and coping: Theory, research, practice.* New York, NY: Guilford Press.

Pargament, K. I. (2007). *Spiritually integrated psychotherapy: Understanding and addressing the sacred.* New York, NY: Guilford Press.

## REFERENCES

Abu Raiya, H., Pargament, K. I., Mahoney, A., & Stein, C. (2008). A psychological measure of Islamic religiousness (PMIR): Development and evidence for reliability and validity. *International Journal for the Psychology of Religion, 18*, 291–315.

Ai, A. L., Dunkle, R. E., Peterson, C., & Bolling, S. F. (1998). The role of private prayer in psychological recovery among midlife and aged patients following cardiac surgery. *Gerontologist, 38*, 591–601.

Alferi, S. M., Culver, J. L., Carvery, C. S., Arena, P. L., & Antoni, M. H. (1999). Religiosity, religious coping, and distress; A prospective study of Catholic and evangelical Hispanic women in treatment for early-stage breast cancer. *Journal of Health Psychology, 4*, 343–356.

Ano, G. G., & Vasconcelles, E.B. (2005). Religious coping and psychological adjustment to stress: A meta-analysis. *Journal of Clinical Psychology, 61*, 461–480.

Baugh, J. R. (1988). Gaining control by giving up control: Strategies for coping with powerlessness. In W. R. Miller & J. E. Martin (Eds.). *Behavior therapy and religion: Integrating spiritual and behavioral approaches to change* (pp. 125–138). Thousand Oaks, CA: Sage.

Beck, A. T. (1972). *Depression: Causes and treatment*. Baltimore, MD: University of Pennsylvania Press.

Beck, A. T., & Alford, B. A. (2009). *Depression: Causes and treatment* (2nd ed.). Baltimore, MD: University of Pennsylvania Press.

Beitel, M., Genova, M., Schuman-Olivier, Z., Arnold, R., Avants, S. K., & Margolin, A. (2007). Reflections by inner-city drug users on a Buddhist-based spirituality-focused therapy: A qualitative study. *American Journal of Orthopsychiatry, 77*, 1–9.

Belavich, T. G., & Pargament, K. I. (2002). The role of attachment in predicting spiritual coping with a loved one in surgery. *Journal of Adult Development, 9*, 13–29.

Boudreaux, E. L., Catz, S., Ryan, L., Ameral-Melendez, M., & Brantley, P. J. (1995). The ways of religious coping scale: reliability, validity, and scale development. *Assessment, 2*, 233–244.

Burker, E. J., Evon, D. M., Sedway, J. A., & Egan, T. (2005). Religious and nonreligious coping in lung transplant candidates: Does adding God to the picture tell us more? *Journal of Behavioral Medicine, 28*, 513–526.

Carver, C. S., Scheier, M. F., & Weintraub, J. K. (1989). Assessing coping strategies: A theoretically based approach. *Journal of Personality and Social Psychology, 56*, 267–283.

Cole, B. S. (2005). Spiritually-focused psychotherapy for people diagnosed with cancer: A pilot outcome study. *Mental Health, Religion and Culture, 8*, 217–226.

Cole, B. S., & Pargament, K. I. (1999). Spiritual surrender: A paradoxical path to control. In W. R. Miller (Ed.), *Integrating spirituality into treatment: Resources for practitioners* (pp. 179–198). Washington, DC: American Psychological Association.

Exline, J. J., & Rose, E. (2005). Religious and spiritual struggles. In R. F. Paloutzian, & C. L. Park (Eds.), *Handbook of the psychology of religion and spirituality* (pp. 315–330). New York, NY: Guilford Press.

Exline, J. J., Smyth, J. M., Gregory, J., Hockemeyer, J., & Tulloch, H. (2005). Religious framing by individuals with PTSD when writing about traumatic experiences. *International Journal for the Psychology of Religion, 15*, 17–33.

Gall, T. L. (2006). Spirituality and coping with life stress among adult survivors of childhood sexual abuse. *Child Abuse and Neglect, 30*, 829–844.

Gallup Poll. (2008). *Religion*. Retrieved from http://www.gallup.com/poll/1690/Religion.aspx

Gear, M. R., Faigin, C. A., Gibbel, M. R., Krumrei, E., Oemig, C., McCarthy, S. K., & Pargament, K. I. (2008). The Winding Road: A promising approach to addressing the spiritual struggles of college students. *Spirituality in Higher Education Newsletter, 4*, 1–8.

Griffith, J. L., & Griffith, M. E. (2002). *Encountering the sacred in psychotherapy: How to talk with people about their spiritual lives*. New York, NY: Guilford Press.

Hill, P. C., Pargament, K. I., Hood, R. W., Jr., McCullough, M. E., Swyers, J. P., Larson, D. B., & Zinnbauer, B. J. (2000). Conceptualizing religion and spirituality: Points of commonality, points of departure. *Journal for the Theory of Social Behaviour, 30*, 51–77.

Hodge, D. R. (2001). Spiritual assessment: A review of major qualitative methods and a new framework for assessing spirituality. *Social Work, 46*, 203–214.

Kaori, W., & Jeeseon, P. (2009). Integrating Buddhist psychology into grief counseling. *Death Studies, 33*, 657–683.

Khan, Z. H., & Watson, P. J. (2006). Construction of the Pakistani Religious Coping Practices Scale: Correlations with religious coping, religious orientation, and reactions to stress among Muslim university students. *International Journal for the Psychology of Religion, 16*, 101–112.

Krumrei, E. J., Mahoney, A., & Pargament, K. I. (2008). Turning to God to forgive: More than meets the eye. *Journal of Psychology and Christianity, 27*, 302–311.

Krumrei, E. J., Mahoney, A., & Pargament, K. I. (2009). Divorce and the divine: The role of spirituality in adjustment to divorce. *Journal of Marriage and Family, 71*, 373–383.

Lazarus, R. S., & Folkman, S. (1984). *Stress, appraisals, and coping.* New York, NY: Springer.

Linley, P. A., & Joseph, S. (2004). Positive change following trauma and adversity: A review. *Journal of traumatic stress, 17*, 11–21. doi: 0894-9867/04/0200-0011/1

Mahoney, A., Krumrei, E. J., & Pargament, K. I. (2008). Broken vows: Divorce as a spiritual trauma and its implications for growth and decline. In S. Joseph & P. A. Linley (Eds.), *Trauma, recovery, and growth: Positive psychological perspectives on posttraumatic stress* (pp. 105–124). Hoboken, NJ: Wiley.

McCorkle, B. H., Bohn, C., Hughes, T., & Kim, D. (2005). "Sacred Moments": Social anxiety in a larger perspective. *Mental Health, Religion and Culture, 8*, 227–238.

McCullough, M. E. (1999). Research on religion-accommodative counseling: Review and meta-analysis. *Journal of Counseling Psychology, 46*, 92–98. doi:10.1037/0022-0167.46.1.92

Mickley, J. R., Pargament, K. I., Brant, C. R., & Hipp, K. M. (1998). God and the search for meaning among hospice caregivers. *Hospice Journal, 13*, 1–17.

Murray-Swank, N. A., & Pargament, K. I. (2005). God, where are you? Evaluating a spiritually-integrated intervention for sexual abuse. *Mental Health, Religion, and Culture, 8*, 191–204.

Nairn, R.C., & Merluzzi, T. V. (2003). The role of religious coping in adjustment to cancer. *Psycho-Oncology, 12*, 428–441.

Oakley, S. (2009). Creating safety for the client: The London 7/7 bombings. In L. Barnett (Ed.), *When death enters the therapeutic space: Existential perspectives in psychotherapy and counselling* (pp. 89–101). New York, NY: Routledge.

Pargament, K. I. (1997). *The psychology of religion and coping: Theory, research, practice.* New York, NY: Guilford Press.

Pargament, K. I. (2007). *Spiritually integrated psychotherapy: Understanding and addressing the sacred.* New York, NY: Guilford Press.

Pargament, K. I. (2011). Religion and coping: The current state of knowledge. In S. Folkman (Ed.), *The Oxford handbook of stress, health, and coping* (pp. 269–288). New York, NY: Oxford University Press.

Pargament, K. I., Cole, B., VandeCreek, L., Belavich, T., Brant, C., & Perez, L. (1999). The vigil: Religion and the search for control in the hospital waiting room. *Journal of Health Psychology, 4*, 327–341.

Pargament, K. I., Kennell, J., Hathaway, W., Grevengoed, N., Newman, J., & Jones, W. (1988). Religion and the problem-solving process: Three styles of coping. *Journal for the Scientific Study of Religion, 27*, 90–104.

Pargament, K. I., Koenig, H.G., & Perez, L.M. (2000). The many methods of religious coping: Development and initial validation of the RCOPE. *Journal of Clinical Psychology, 56*, 519–543.

Pargament, K. I., Koenig, H. G., Tarakeshwar, N., & Hahn, J. (2001). Religious struggle as a predictor of mortality among medically ill elderly patients: A two-year longitudinal study. *Archives of Internal Medicine, 161*, 1881–1885.

Pargament, K .I., Koenig, H. G., Tarakeshwar, N., & Hahn. J. (2004). Religious coping methods as predictors of psychological, physical, and social outcomes among medically ill elderly patients: A two-year longitudinal study. *Journal of Health Psychology, 9*, 713–730.

Pargament, K. I., & Krumrei, E. J. (2008). Clinical assessment of clients' spirituality. In J. D. Aten & M. M. Leach (Eds.), *Spirituality and the therapeutic process: A comprehensive resource from intake to termination* (pp. 93–120). Washington, DC: American Psychological Association.

Pargament, K. I., & Mahoney, A. (2005). Sacred matters: Sanctification as a vital topic for the psychology of religion. *International Journal for the Psychology of Religion, 15,* 179–198.

Pargament, K. I., Murray-Swank, N. A., Magyar, G. M., & Ano, G. G. (2005). Spiritual struggle: A phenomenon of interest to psychology and religion. In W. R. Miller & H. D. Delaney (Eds.), *Judeo-Christian perspectives on psychology: Human nature, motivation, and change* (pp. 245–268). Washington, DC: American Psychological Association.

Pargament, K. I., Smith, B. W., Koenig, H. G., & Perez, L. (1998). Patterns of positive and negative religious coping with major life stressors. *Journal for the Scientific Study of Religion, 37,* 710–724.

Park, C., & Cohen, L. H. (1992). Religious beliefs and practices and the coping process. In B. N. Carpenter (Ed.), *Personal coping: Theory, research, and application* (pp. 185–198). New York, NY: Praeger.

Patterson, J. M., & McCubbin, H. F. (1987). *Adolescent coping* style and behaviors: Conceptualization and measurement. *Journal of Adolescence, 10,* 163–186.

Phillips, R. E., & Stein, C. H., (2007). God's will, God's punishment, or God's limitations? Religious coping strategies reported by young adults living with serious mental illness. *Journal of Clinical Psychology, 63,* 528–540.

Prati, G., & Pietrantoni, L. (2009). Optimism, social support, and coping strategies as factors contributing to posttraumatic growth: A meta-analysis. *Journal of Loss and Trauma, 14,* 364–388.

Puchalski, C. M., Larson, D. B., & Lu, F. G. (2001). Spirituality in psychiatry residency training programs. *International Review of Psychiatry, 13,* 131–138.

Richards, P. S., Hardman, R. K., & Berrett, M. E. (2007). *Spiritual approaches in the treatment of women with eating disorders.* Washington, DC: American Psychological Association.

Rosmarin, D. H., Pargament, K. I, Krumrei, E. J., & Flannelly, K. J. (2009). Religious coping among Jews: Development and initial validation of the JCOPE. *Journal of Clinical Psychology,* 65, 1–14.

Rosmarin, D. H., Pirutinsky, S., Auerbach, R. P., Björgvinsson, T., Bigda-Peyton, J., Andersson, G., ... Krumrei, E. J. (2011). Incorporating spiritual beliefs into a cognitive model of worry. *Journal of Clinical Psychology, 67,* 691–700. doi: 10.1002/jclp.20798

Rosmarin, D. H., Pirutinsky, S., Pargament, K. I., & Krumrei, E. J. (2009). Are religious beliefs relevant to mental health among Jews? *Psychology of Religion and Spirituality, 1,* 180–190.

Schwarzer, R., & Schwarzer, C. (1996). A critical survey of coping instruments. In M. Zeidner & N. S. Endler (Eds.), *Handbook of coping: Theory, research and applications* (pp. 107–132). New York, NY: Wiley.

Sheridian, M. J., Bullis, R. K., Adcock, C. R., Berlin, S. D., & Miller, P. C. (1992). Practitioner's personal and professional attitudes and behaviors toward religion and spirituality: Issues for education and practice. *Journal of Social Work Education, 28,* 190–203.

Smith, T. B., Bartz, J. D., & Richards, P. S. (2007). Outcomes of religious and spiritual adaptations to psychotherapy: A meta-analytic review. *Psychotherapy Research, 17,* 645–655.

Stone, A. A., & Neale, J. M. (1984). New measure of daily coping: Development and preliminary results. *Journal of Personality and Social Psychology, 46,* 892–906.

Tarakeshwar, N., Pargament, K. I., & Mahoney, A. (2003). Initial development of a measure of religious coping among Hindus. *Journal of Community Psychology, 31*, 607–628.

Tarakeshwar, N., Pearce, M. J., & Sikkema, K. J. (2005). Development and implementation of a spiritual coping group intervention for adults living with HIV/AIDS: A pilot study. *Mental Health, Religion, and Culture, 8*, 179–190.

Tix, A. P., & Frazier, P A. (1998). The use of religious coping during stressful life events: Main effects, moderation, and mediation. *Journal of Consulting & Clinical Psychology, 66*, 411–422.

Wachholtz, A. B., & Pargament, K .I. (2008). Migraines and meditation: Does spirituality matter? *Journal of Behavioral Medicine, 31*, 351–366.

Zinnbauer, B. J., Pargament, K. I., Cole, B., Rye, M. S., Butter, E. M., Belavich, T. G., … Kadar, J. L. (1997). Religion and spirituality: Unfuzzying the fuzzy. *Journal for the Scientific Study of Religion, 36*, 549–564.

# 11

# *Forgiveness and Reconciliation Within the Psychology of Religion and Spirituality*

Everett L. Worthington, Jr., Don E. Davis, Joshua N. Hook, Aubrey L. Gartner, David J. Jennings, II, Chelsea L. Greer, Daryl R. Van Tongeren, and Todd W. Greer

Many world religions teach and encourage forgiveness. Both religious and nonreligious people bring concerns over their anger, hatred, and unforgiveness to psychotherapists. Thus, forgiveness is also taught and encouraged by psychotherapists in many theoretical approaches. In this chapter, we provide a review of forgiveness research that will aid psychotherapists and other clinical practitioners to use forgiveness with religious clients. First, we briefly review the research on the secular study of forgiveness because most of these findings also are applicable to forgiveness within a religious and spiritual context. Second, we explore the relationship between religion and spirituality and forgiveness. Finally, we suggest practical applications for clinicians based on our review. We draw clinical implications from current research, including spiritually oriented forgiveness models.

## REVIEW OF SECULAR FORGIVENESS RESEARCH

Historically, forgiveness has been understood within a religious context (McCullough & Worthington, 1999; Rye et al., 2000). Theologian, Lewis Smedes (1984), wrote a popular trade book, *Forgive and Forget: Healing the Hurts We Don't Deserve*. He argued that forgiveness should be undertaken, not (merely) for religious motives, but because forgiveness had benefits for oneself. That book initiated the scientific study of forgiveness. The idea that forgiveness could be therapeutic captivated the interest of both clinicians and researchers who began to investigate forgiveness within the context of secular research and psychotherapy.

Although a few researchers in the field of the psychology of religion and spirituality contributed, most early research was secular and was oriented primarily at self-focused motives to forgive offenders.

### Definitional Disputes

In the early phase of the scientific investigation of any concept, definitions are hotly contested. The study of forgiveness was no exception. Before Smedes (1984), forgiveness was largely identified with religion. One of the first battles was to disengage definitions of forgiveness with religion. This was necessary for two reasons. First, each of the major religions has different definitions of forgiveness (e.g., Rye et al., 2000). Second, as long as forgiveness was tied to a religion, only scientists interested in religion were likely to study it, and only religiously focused psychotherapists were likely to use it as an intervention. Of course, defining forgiveness in secular terms generated tension between researchers and religious adherents.

Another early controversy involved how to define *complete forgiveness.* Does complete forgiveness involve merely getting rid of negative thoughts, feelings, motives, and attitudes? Or should complete forgiveness also involve the replacement of these with positive emotions toward the transgressor? Worthington (2005) surveyed how 29 research teams defined forgiveness. Those who studied isolated transgressions (e.g., crimes or transgressions by strangers or acquaintances), series of transgressions by someone with whom one does not want to continue to interact (e.g., ex-spouse, cut-off family member, hated former boss), or transgressions by someone not available for reconciliation (e.g., one who has died or moved away) tended to define complete forgiveness as the elimination of negative feelings, thoughts, or motives. Alternatively, researchers who studied forgiveness within valued and continuing relationships (e.g., marriage, family, church, or workplace relationships) argued that complete forgiveness involved both the reduction of negative and the renewal of positive experiences.

A related controversy concerned whether forgiveness involved a restoration of the relationship with the offender (i.e., reconciliation). For the most part, psychologists have agreed on a definition of forgiveness that separates forgiveness (viewed as an *intra*personal process) from restoring a relationship (viewed as an *inter*personal process). Theologians have been more reluctant to make that distinction. The resolution of this definitional controversy might lie in understanding the central forgiving figure (i.e., humans, the divine). Psychologists primarily address forgiveness processes of individuals, and almost all (i.e., 85% or higher; McMinn et al., 2008) differentiate forgiveness from reconciliation. Typically, the ones who do not make such clear distinctions between forgiveness and reconciliation are researchers who study close relationships (e.g., Rusbult, Bissonnette, Arriaga, & Cox, 2005). Because they study relationships, they often see the interpersonal context more starkly. Most of those researchers tend to see forgiveness as individually experienced and not requiring reconciliation; occasionally, however, some tend to include reconciliation within forgiveness. Most theologians, write about relationships with the divine. In divine forgiveness, they tend to see divine forgiveness and relational repair with the divine as entwined. When theologians consider forgiveness of one human by another, about half think that relational repair completes forgiveness (McMinn et al., 2008).

Importantly, although most secular researchers tend to distinguish forgiveness and reconciliation, clients may not do so as often. Indeed, many laypeople conflate forgiveness and reconciliation (Kearns & Fincham, 2004). When this occurs, the client might experience problems in mental health. For example, if a client believes that to completely forgive a transgression, the client must reconcile with the transgressor, then this can place a client in a dangerous position. The client might feel trapped between reentering a physically abusive relationship or experiencing tension with a God who demands interpersonal forgiveness. When the client is unwilling to reconcile with the transgressor, he or she may be unable to attain personal peace because of the failure to offer "complete forgiveness." Psychotherapists can help by clarifying distinctions between decisional and emotional forgiveness and between both types of forgiveness (i.e., an intrapersonal experience) and reconciliation (i.e., a product of a relationship requiring mutually trustworthy behavior).

A final definitional issue pertains to how forgiveness unfolds over time. McCullough, Fincham, and Tsang (2003) have championed the position that forgiveness must be defined as a *change* in a person's negative motivations toward a transgressor *over time*, possibly ending in the complete elimination of negative motivations and the presence of benevolent and conciliatory motivations. McCullough et al. (2003) argued that one cannot really understand how much unforgiveness a person harbors through a single measurement. For example, two people might score equally on a forgiveness rating of their respective spouses. One score may represent a decline in forgiveness, as the spouse believes the partner is not putting forth effort to maintain a healthy marriage. The other score may represent greater forgiveness, as the spouse feels optimistic that an abysmal marriage is improving. The clinician must be aware of how the relationship is changing, rather than just focusing on how much unforgiveness currently is experienced. The momentum of change—whether the score on an inventory measuring forgiveness is getting worse, getting better, or stuck—will affect the psychotherapeutic progress. (These issues regarding measuring forgiveness are addressed in the next section.) Another clinically important consideration is the daily mood variation of clients. Sometimes people are in a fouler mood than at other times. If the client has had a recent failure, bad interaction with his or her spouse, or bad news from the doctor that one must eat low cholesterol diet for the next 3 months (cholesterol is colloquially defined as the stuff in food that makes it taste good), then the client is likely to speak more unkindly toward or about a transgressor and report more unforgiveness, vengeance, or grudge feelings than on days where things are working perfectly.

### Measurement of Forgiveness

Researchers who study forgiveness within the psychology of religion and spirituality conduct either basic research or clinical research. Measurement within a clinical setting has different standards than measurement within a research setting. A basic researcher often wants a forgiveness measure that is both reasonably reliable, so that it captures the fundamental process of forgiveness, and brief, so that participants are not burdened with a large number of items. In clinical situations, the demands are different. One main purpose of clinical assessment is to aid diagnosis (and possibly prognosis). A clinician typically wants to assess a single client (not a large group) as carefully as possible to provide a rich and accurate diagnostic understanding. Thus, clinicians desire accurate instruments. Clinicians also may use assessments for other reasons that require less accuracy. Sometimes single items can be used effectively and quickly to screen whether forgiveness is a psychotherapeutic issue. Single items also can be used during psychotherapy to focus the client's attention on psychotherapeutic goals and to provide a rough indication of progress. The appendix includes two single items that are appropriate for screening and for use during psychotherapy. These items allow clinicians to differentiate between two types of forgiveness: decisional forgiveness and emotional forgiveness (Worthington, 2006).

Several measuring instruments—assessing the forgiveness of a single offense—have been used in clinical research in the psychology of forgiveness. The longest and most reliable is the Enright Forgiveness Inventory (Enright, Rique, & Coyle, 2000). Another excellent instrument for forgiveness research, and perhaps for diagnosis, is the Transgression Related Interpersonal Motivations Inventory (TRIM; McCullough et al., 1998). The Rye Forgiveness Scale (Rye et al., 2001) is also frequently used. Each of these instruments measures how much a person has forgiven a single transgression.

Clients sometimes have different goals than forgiving a single transgression. They may wish to forgive the partner in an ongoing relationship for multiple transgressions. Gordon, Baucom, and Snyder (2004) have developed a scale for couple forgiveness, which they have used to assess forgiveness in couples dealing with extramarital affairs. Clients may wish to become more forgiving people in general. The use of a trait measure of *forgivingness* would be appropriate in this circumstance. For survey research, three trait measures often are used. The Heartland Forgiveness Scale (HFS; Thompson et al., 2005) measures a forgiving personality, as well as forgivingness of self and of situations (e.g., a natural disaster). The Trait Forgivingness Scale (TFS) is a brief, 10-item measure that assesses how forgiving a person tends to be across situations and time (Berry, Worthington, O'Connor, Parrott, & Wade, 2005). For basic research, but not clinical applications, the Transgression Narrative Test of Forgiveness (TNTF; Berry, Worthington, Parrott, O'Connor, & Wade, 2001) is a good instrument, developed using item response theory. The TNTF assesses people's responses to five increasingly difficult-to-forgive scenarios to determine their likelihood of forgiving as a disposition.

### Biology of Forgiveness

Most research on the biology of forgiveness has noted that unforgiveness is stressful, and forgiveness is a coping mechanism that can reduce stress reactions (for a review of psychological research, see Worthington & Sotoohi, 2010). Worthington (2006) described a stress-and-coping model of forgiveness, summarized the research evidence pertaining to the model, and suggested interventions to promote forgiveness, including psychotherapeutic, couple and family, psychoeducational, and group therapy interventions. Evidence that unforgiveness is stressful (see Worthington, 2006) is substantial. Forgiveness is conceptualized as one of several coping responses to unforgiveness that can positively affect both physical and mental health (Worthington, Witvliet, Peitrini, & Miller, 2007).

### Motivations for Forgiving

Individuals have many personal motivations for forgiving, which usually are centered on wanting to feel better. A person might feel tortured by grudge-holding, feel guilt for not living up to one's values, or feel condemned by others (or God) for being a bitter and unforgiving person. Researchers have examined numerous benefits that accrue to people who forgive, and to the extent that people believe they will benefit from forgiveness, they can attempt to forgive to receive those benefits. These benefits, which accumulate over time, typically fall into one of four categories: (1) physical health, (2) mental health, (3) relationship enhancing, and (4) spiritual benefits.

#### *Physical Health Benefits*

The physical health benefits of forgiveness are well-established, perhaps more strongly than any of the other salutary effects (Toussaint, Williams, Musick, & Everson, 2001; Worthington & Sotoohi, 2010; Worthington et al., 2007). Clinicians can confidently use this research to motivate clients to forgive or to persist when the clients' work on forgiveness falters. Toussaint et al. (2001) showed that health benefits accrue in people high in forgivingness after middle age relative to those who chronically hold grudges. Most researchers agree that the physical health benefits of forgiving come about largely as a result of reducing negative emotions and reducing one's sense of stress from unforgiveness (Worthington, 2006). Additionally, some benefits are hypothesized to occur as a result of experiencing positive emotions after forgiveness is granted.

Three stress-related mechanisms have been shown to affect health when one forgives. First, forgiveness reduces cardiovascular risk as a result of attenuated stressfulness when unforgiveness is replaced by a forgiving response (Williams, 1989). Second, immune system functioning is also improved (Worthington et al., 2007). Third, forgiveness may prevent the damage that occurs when stress products such as cortisol accumulate, and cortisol has pernicious negative effects on most body systems when it is chronically elevated (for a review, see Sapolsky, 1994). Psychotherapists can help clients with stress-related physical disorders by helping promote forgiveness.

### *Mental Health Benefits*

A variety of mental health benefits are associated with forgiving, including decreased symptoms of anxiety, depression, and anger. Enright and Fitzgibbons (2000) have argued strongly that anger is a major source of mental health problems and that anger is implicated in many mental health disorders. Forgiveness can reduce anger and therefore help people reduce associated psychological symptoms. A reduction in rumination—uncontrolled repetition of negative, emotion-arousing thoughts—is the mechanism that is most responsible for the mental health benefits of forgiveness. Rumination has been associated with many mental health disorders, such as depression, anxiety, anger, obsessive-compulsive disorder, posttraumatic stress disorder (PTSD), and psychosomatic disorders. Rumination tends to dominate one's mental health disorder. Depressive rumination leads to depression; anxious rumination leads to anxiety; and angry rumination leads to vengeance and anger-related disorders. When people forgive, they usually decrease depressive, anxious, vengeful, and angry rumination and no longer obsess as much about the past transgression (Berry, Worthington, O'Connor, et al., 2005).

### *Relationship Benefits*

Relationship benefits can follow forgiving. Much of the research on forgiveness in relationships has been focused within marriage. Fincham and his colleagues have conducted more than 15 studies that demonstrate that relationships improve when the partners are more forgiving of each other (for a review, see Fincham, Hall, & Beach, 2005). Gordon et al. (2004) examined forgiveness within marriage relationships in which extramarital affairs have occurred. They have developed a clinical protocol to help people forgive when a partner has been in an affair. Additionally, Rusbult et al. (2005) have studied how relationships between unmarried partners are affected by forgiveness or unwillingness to forgive. They employ a social exchange model that presumes at least unconscious processing of costs and benefits making up the calculus of acting. They examine how forgiveness shapes partners' desires to stay and talk about transgressions, to passively ignore the partner, or to leave and cut off the partner.

### *Spiritual Benefits*

Spirituality involves closeness or intimacy with an object that one considers sacred. What one considers sacred can vary considerably. Some view the sacred to be God (*religious spirituality*), humans (*humanistic spirituality*), nature (*nature spirituality*), or the cosmos (*cosmic spirituality*) (Worthington & Aten, 2009). People who are unforgiving often feel separated and disconnected from God, other people, nature, or wider existence; therefore, forgiveness can help them feel less negative and perhaps more positive toward someone or something that has alienated them. Thus, they might develop greater connection, closeness, and intimacy with the object of their spirituality. Spiritual benefits might accumulate to a person who forgives (Rye et al., 2000). For example, forgiveness has been found to be positively related to spiritual well-being (Rye et al., 2001). This is especially true when the person's religion or spirituality prescribes forgiving and has implied divine or interpersonal consequences for not forgiving.

## The Forgiving Personality

Personality researchers have found that among the Big Five Factor Model of Personality traits, the most consistently related to forgiveness are agreeableness and neuroticism (Mullet, Neto, & Riviera, 2005). Neuroticism, which is negatively related to forgiveness, is emotional instability or emotional labiality. People who are high in agreeableness, which is positively related to forgiveness, generally are hard to offend and forgive easily. Those who are low in agreeableness are often irascible and argumentative.

Secure adult attachment has been consistently linked to forgiveness (Burnette, Davis, Green, Worthington, & Bradfield, 2009). People who have insecure attachment, whether anxious-avoidant or ambivalent-unstable attachment, tend to be low in forgiveness. People who seek psychotherapy often have personality patterns (e.g., insecure attachment) and relationship difficulties that are associated with higher measures of unforgivingness (Enright & Fitzgibbons, 2000). Additional personality traits that are related to unforgiveness—such as (a) trait rumination (Berry et al., 2005), (b) vengefulness (McCullough, 2008), (c) grudge-nurturing (Mullet et al., 2005), (d) narcissism (Exline, Bauermeister, Bushman, Campbell, & Finkel, 2005), (e) low empathy (McCullough, Worthington, & Rachal, 1997), (f) high trait anger (Welton, Hill, & Seybold, 2008), and (g) high trait anxiety (Mullet et al., 2005)—are often exhibited by clients (Enright & Fitzgibbons, 2000).

## Developmental Psychology and Forgiveness

Few developmental psychologists study forgiveness. Enright and colleagues have been a noted exception. They programmatically studied the reasoning about forgiveness as it developed during childhood (for a review, see Enright & Fitzgibbons, 2000). Their results paralleled previous findings on childhood reasoning about justice. Specifically, children move through different stages as they develop their capabilities of reasoning about forgiveness. They first adopt preconventional perspectives. Then they begin viewing justice and forgiveness as social conventions, and finally they consider justice and forgiveness as universal motives.

The way that children reason about forgiveness does not, of course, necessarily predict whether they actually forgive. Some very vengeful, vindictive adults have the capacity to reason at the highest level about forgiveness but simply choose not to forgive. Therefore, the development of moral reasoning capabilities must be supplemented with consideration of the social and the emotional development of forgiveness (Denham, Neal, Wilson, Pickering, & Boyatzis, 2005). Worthington (2009) suggested that certain characteristics and processes predispose children to forgive, such as the following: (a) having an easygoing temperament, (b) developing early empathy, (c) acquiring effective emotion-regulation strategies, (d) building a varied coping repertoire (especially using emotion-focused coping), and (e) self-soothing. Child psychotherapists can teach such strategies to children or coach parents in how to do so. Practical guidance to parents on teaching children such strategies that lead directly to forgiveness is not available. Generally, though, excellent parenting books abound. Parents need to supplement the advice in those books by teaching children how to interact in ways that eventually will promote forgiving.

Parents are one of the primary sources from which children learn how to forgive (Denham et al., 2005). It is unlikely that children experience actual adult-like forgiveness before they have developed the appropriate cognitive and the emotional capacities to understand the construct. This understanding probably does not occur until around age 11 or 12; however, parents can create social scaffolds that encourage children to forgive as they are developing. Children can learn the forms of forgiveness (i.e., the external structures that encourage and support forgiveness) at an early age, and as their internal cognition and emotional control develops, they can supplement those forms with the experience of forgiving (Worthington, 2009). Psychotherapists and family therapists can help parents with child-related disorders learn to teach such social scaffolds to their child. For example, parents can coach wrongdoing children to apologize and teach them how to make a good apology and how to offer restitution. They can coach children who have been offended or harmed how to accept responsibility for their own part of misunderstandings, make good reproaches (i.e., requests for causal explanations about transgressions), and grant forgiveness (or ask for more time if they need it).

### Social Interactions Surrounding Forgiveness

The actual social interactions around the transgressions are just recently being investigated. In the past, people have studied accounts (i.e., apologies, confessions, and excuses), denials of responsibility, and justifications of one's behavior (Schönbach, 1990). The interactions around transgressions are much richer, however, than merely making reproaches and giving accounts. There are different types of reproaches, such as demands or more gentle requests for an account (see Worthington, 2006, for clinical examples). When forgiveness is offered, people might not be able to accept it. Gartner (2009) has developed an instrument to assess acceptance of forgiveness. They may feel too guilty, remorseful, or self-condemning to accept forgiveness. Feeling forgiven by God might predict one's ability to forgive oneself or to accept forgiveness from another (Krause & Ellison, 2003). Furthermore, when an offender requests forgiveness with a sincere confession, the victim still may not grant unconditional forgiveness at that moment, or even in the future. Research is just beginning to examine how offenders respond when they request forgiveness and the victim either rejects the apology, delays an answer, or grants partial forgiveness. Jennings (2009) has found, as might seem obvious, that it is hurtful when requests for forgiveness are refused directly. What is not so obvious, however, is that offenders were hurt when victims hesitated or gave anything less that full forgiveness immediately after being asked. Offenders logically can understand that making a decision to forgive or experiencing emotional forgiveness takes time. Yet if the person they hurt or offended says anything less than he or she fully forgives—for example, if he or she says, "I can forgive you, but it's going to takes more time," or "It is a bit too soon for me to tell you truthfully that I fully forgive you at this point, maybe later," or "I have forgiven you but I'm still hurt and it might take a while to get over"—then the perpetrator still feels hurt. It is as if the offender feels entitled to full forgiveness if he or she apologizes and asks for forgiveness. Nothing less than full forgiveness is good enough. Offenders who feel any rejection, can turn that around and blame the victim self-righteously.

### Business, Workplace, Organizational Psychology, and Forgiveness

Much work has been done in the last decade on workplace and organizational forgiveness (Exline, Worthington, Hill, & McCullough, 2003; Hill, Exline, & Cohen, 2005; Worthington, Greer, et al., 2010). This is important to the clinician who works in an organization because the psychologist often will serve an Employee Assistance Program or counsel members of the business. Even clinicians in practice see many clients who have experienced wounds within organizational settings.

At the beginning of the decade, organizational and workplace researchers focused on justice and injustice in organizations (Aquino, Tripp, & Bies, 2006). Organizational attention to justice is usually most important in dealing with the public (Worthington, 2006, 2009). The public expects just relations with an organization, and injustices harm public relations. Within an organization, too, justice is central, but people do not tend to leave jobs because they experience inequities in pay or perks. Mostly, they leave organizations because of conflict with and unforgiveness toward their coworkers (Zapf & Gross, 2001). They may not want to go to work where they must work alongside someone who hurt them deeply. Thus, they change jobs, which incurs huge costs to organizations as they have to replace, retrain, and recover the lost expertise. Psychotherapists and counseling psychologists who do career counseling can see people who are struggling to find and hold onto jobs when their past is dotted with frequent on-the-job conflicts and beliefs that they have experienced maltreatment from a coworker or employer. Career, emotional, and stress-related psychological problems can be, and often are, direct fallout from an unforgiving personality or relationships that tend to get repeated with parent–child-like conflicts.

### Culture and Forgiveness

The world is increasingly connected because of advances in electronic technology (e.g., Internet, e-mail, fiber-optics) and easy travel (Friedman, 2005). Thus, it is important to understand how different cultures understand and practice forgiveness. Hook, Worthington, and Utsey (2009) reviewed the existing research from different cultures and summarized the findings in a two-part model. First, they found that people in generally collectivistic cultures tended to make decisions to forbear or decide to forgive rather than being concerned with emotional forgiveness (which is characteristic of individualistic cultures). Second, they found that people from collectivistic cultures tended more often to think that forgiveness should lead to reconciliation, whereas people from individualistic cultures tended to think that forgiveness could occur more often without necessitating reconciliation. They found support for collectivistic forgiveness regardless of the country. That is, even in the United States, some people were more collectivistic (i.e., African Americans relative to Caucasians, religious people relative to nonreligious people) and others more individualistic in their orientation, and generally they adhered to the model of collectivistic forgiveness (Hook et al., 2010).

Each of the major religions understands forgiveness differently (Rye et al., 2000). Whereas most people worldwide are religious, some are not (Berger et al., 1999). Regardless of cultures being religious or not, they usually gravitate toward worldviews of individualism or collectivism. Hook, Worthington, and Utsey (2009) have proposed that collectivistic cultures are concerned with maintaining social harmony, and this may motivate their decision to forgive more strongly than the associated change in feelings that occur from experiencing emotional forgiveness (for a discussion of the two types of forgiveness, see Worthington, 2006). Although they have *decided* to forgive, certain individuals may be *emotionally* unforgiving; therefore, individuals in these cultures may nonetheless decide to maintain harmony, for the good of the collective, and to forbear vengeful and grudge-motivated acts. Cultures differ according to whether they tend to deal with transgressions through forbearance, decisional forgiveness, emotional forgiveness, or pursuit of vengeance and justice. Some cultures are cultures of honor (Nisbett & Cohen, 1996). Honor-cultures often derive from historic roots in locations that have highly mobile resources (i.e., raise cattle or sheep, have wealth concentrated in portable and thus easily stolen goods). If transgressions against self or property occur, the person must respond rapidly, harshly, and aggressively. The person must get the idea across to all observers that no transgressions will be tolerated. They will be punished vigorously. Cultures of justice, to the contrary, usually did not originate from locations with mobile resources. Agrarian cultures or those with economies based in textiles provided a strong need for fairness and justice, but they did not provide the need to defend one's reputation through violent retaliation for wrongdoing.

Men and women tend to differ starkly with respect to vengeance. Men are several times more likely to respond vengefully. Women, on the other hand, are more likely than men to hold grudges. One characteristic of cultures that can vary widely is roles of men and women. It is reasonable for a psychotherapist to expect, then, that a client from a culture with strong role stereotypes might follow more gender-role stereotype behaviors.

Relative to previous decades, psychotherapists increasingly counsel people with different cultural and religious backgrounds. Even though negative stigma about psychotherapy still exists for many cultures, more cultural minorities are entering into psychotherapy in the United States. This places more demands on psychotherapists to understand different religious and cultural viewpoints about religion and forgiveness to be able to help clients most effectively.

## RESEARCH ON FORGIVENESS IN RELIGIOUS AND SPIRITUAL CONTEXTS

### Psychology of Religion

The explicit study of forgiveness within the psychology of religion has been limited. Most early research was aimed at showing that religious people were more forgiving than were nonreligious people. In general, this was supported, although a curious problem emerged from the literature. When reporting on their disposition or tendency to forgive over time and across situations, religious people rated themselves to be more forgiving than did religious people (McCullough & Worthington, 1999). In fact, the correlation between religiousness and trait forgivingness was about .4. When reporting about the forgiveness of individual transgressions, however, the correlation between religiousness and forgiveness was only 0.2.

Several explanations of the phenomenon were hypothesized (McCullough & Worthington, 1999; Tsang, McCullough & Hoyt, 2005). First, relationships between variables are lower when measured at different levels of specificity (i.e., dispositional variables compared with variables that assess thoughts or feelings about a specific event). Tsang et al. (2005) examined this hypothesis by asking people to recall several transgressions and report how much each was forgiven. By summing across the different transgressions, they found correlations between religiousness and summed forgiveness that were as high as correlations between religiousness and forgiving dispositions. Second, religious people might not actually be more forgiving than nonreligious people. Perhaps, for many religious people, saying one is forgiving is a socially acceptable response that may not necessarily transfer to actually forgiving specific events. Third, religious people might, in fact, be more forgiving, but a measurement problem may attenuate the correlations. In most studies that have examined the relationship between religion and forgiveness, participants provide a description of a transgression that is bothering them and then rate how much they have forgiven that transgression. By directing people to recall a transgression that is, in fact, unforgiven, the resulting salient discrepancy may account for the relatively small difference between religious and nonreligious people. A fourth possibility might be that religiousness is a weak predictor, among many other factors, for predicting forgiveness of a specific offense. Finally, most religions promote both forgiveness and justice; therefore people may rationalize unforgiveness as exacting (religion-consistent) justice (which is called the *rationalization hypothesis*).

In recent years, attention has shifted away from comparing religious and nonreligious people. Davis, Hook, and Worthington (2008) have suggested a model of forgiveness and relational spirituality. They show that a person's experience of relationship with the sacred (Davis et al., 2008), the degree to which a transgression is perceived as the destruction of something sacred (Mahoney, Rye & Pargament, 2005), or the degree to which the victim sees the offender as similar or dissimilar, affect the likelihood of forgiveness (Davis et al., 2009).

Importantly, psychotherapists cannot easily predict how religion and spirituality may affect forgiveness for a specific client. Highly religious clients may (a) forgive; (b) rationalize vengeance or justice; or (c) be affected by personality, religious, or spiritual community norms, or by a power struggle with a specific person. Beyond this, religion and spirituality may be directly involved with decisions and experiences of forgiving because of the client's relationship with the sacred, type of transgression, and perceptions of the transgressor's spirituality. Careful assessment is necessary. For psychotherapists, this is the bottom line: do not assume, assess (see the appendix for a brief screening assessment tool).

## CLINICAL IMPLICATIONS

Several clinical implications for working on forgiveness issues with religious and spiritual clients arise from our review of forgiveness research. The key take-home messages for clinicians are as follows:

1. Clinicians need to understand two different types of forgiveness (i.e., decisional and emotional forgiveness) and related constructs (such as forbearance, reconciliation, justice, and honor). In addition, decisional and emotional forgiveness are internal experiences and need to be seen as distinct from talking about forgiveness.

2. Complex social and societal processes surround forgiveness—such as making reproaches for someone's wrongdoing, giving accounts for one's own wrongdoing, offering apologies and restitution and asking for forgiveness, communicating partial or full forgiveness, accepting the degree of forgiveness offered, and doing other things to promote reconciliation (such as seeking to build more trust into the relationship).
3. Forgiveness probably comes up in counseling more often with religious people simply because religious people tend to value forgiveness more than nonreligious people (Rye et al., 2000), but when forgiveness comes up in counseling, the psychotherapist should not assume that the person is necessarily religious or spiritual and likewise should not assume that the person wants forgiveness treated like a spiritual topic. The psychotherapist must find out from the client how he or she would like the issue dealt with, or if at all.
4. A rich body of literature regarding forgiveness has been studied by all subdisciplines of psychology. As we have observed explicitly in each section, understanding the basic research literature can enrich the psychotherapist's understanding of the phenomena surrounding transgressions and can give specific suggestions about how one might treat the client better.

Thus far, we have not approached the clinical literature directly. Numerous interventions to promote forgiveness with specific clientele have been studied. In the subsequent sections, we address the clinical application through evidence-based interventions and through clinical recommendations. We advise the psychotherapist–reader to keep his or her theoretical and empirical understanding of forgiveness in mind—based on the foregoing review and commentary—as he or she reads the sections dealing with direct clinical applications and established and tested intervention packages.

### Clinical Assessments

In most clinical situations, forgiveness is not the presenting problem. Rather, unforgiveness is more likely to emerge as a problem over the course of psychotherapy. Unforgiveness results from unhealed interpersonal wounds in a person's past or present life. For example, in couple therapy and family therapy, forgiveness issues can be on the surface. The partners or family members may have hurt each other multiple times and might present with a poor relationship that is characterized by conflict, communication problems, intimacy problems, and forgiveness problems.

We suggest three levels of clinical assessment. *Level-one clinical assessment* is a screening (Richards & Bergin, 2005). A screening can be as simple as asking people whether they believe that lack of forgiveness plays a central role in their problems. Often this will give the psychotherapist an initial clue about whether to address forgiveness during psychotherapy. We suggest, however, that screening for forgiveness might not be routinely applied. Typically, this would be asked only in the event that a clinician finds that the client has symptoms that include interpersonal anger or hostility, relationships problems, or interpersonal stress-related problems. It can be as simple as a quick follow-up question to a statement like "I've had problems with my father for years. He's been so judgmental and condemning."

Clients who are Christian (differentiated from other religious clients) might have guilt and self-condemnation because of their inability to forgive. Many feel such guilt because Jesus, in teaching his disciples, said, "For if you forgive men their sins, your Father in heaven will forgive your sins, but if you do not forgive men their sins, your Father will not forgive your sins." For Christians, some might (mis)understand this to mean that holding unforgiveness might result in loss of an eternal relationship with God. Most, however, will interpret this in much more limited sense that, at the final judgment of believers, their judgment of another person will be visited on them. Either way, though, persistent failure to forgive, if the person believes it is a religious obligation to do so, is guilt producing.

If the verbal probe suggests that the person struggles to forgive an event, the clinician can use the two single-item instruments in the appendix to quantify degree of decisional and emotional forgiveness. That can provide a baseline used throughout psychotherapy to track the client's forgiveness.

If forgiveness does become a major focus of psychotherapy, the clinician might want to conduct a *level-two assessment* (Richards & Bergin, 2005) of forgiveness, which occurs before addressing forgiveness issues and assesses one's desire to forgive a particular transgression or increase one's dispositional tendency to forgive. Initial assessment of one's forgiveness, or unforgiveness, surrounding a particular transgression can be obtained using questionnaires, such as the Enright Forgiveness Inventory (Enright et al., 2000) or the TRIM (McCullough et al., 1998). If the person is attempting to become a more forgiving person, rather than forgive a particular relationship or transgression, the TFS or HFS might be administered as a baseline. If forgiveness of self is a concern, the HFS might prove useful.

It is important to consider a type of assessment that Richards and Bergin (2005) did not identify. *Level-three assessment* occurs during counseling and is intended to direct the client's attention to a topic that is psychotherapeutically relevant. The psychotherapist might administer brief forgiveness instruments during the session (e.g., TFS or HFS to assess trait forgiveness; TRIM, DFS, or EFS for specific transgressions), or a single-item measure assessing unforgiving or forgiving emotions or the likelihood of making a decision to forgive. In the appendix, we have given two single-item forgiveness instruments: one to assess decisional forgiveness, the other to assess emotional forgiveness. These have been used in research and have been found to be correlated with many personality and outcome measures of mental health. Level-two assessment can serve as the baseline to which future measures of forgiveness, which occur in level three, can be compared to demonstrate change and increased forgiveness.

## CLINICAL STRATEGIES

### Should a Psychotherapist Integrate Religion and Spirituality Into Treatment?

When working with religious and spiritual clients, the psychotherapist must consider whether to integrate religion and spirituality into psychotherapy. Tan (1996) has suggested that most psychotherapists who integrate religion and spirituality into the psychotherapeutic process do so across a continuum between implicit and explicit approaches. Hall and Hall (1997) have distinguished three interconnected categories that they believe reflect the full "spectrum of clinical integration" (p. 88) for incorporating religion and spirituality into counseling and psychotherapy.

At one end of the spectrum, the psychotherapist operating from *implicit integration* understands the client's religious and spiritual beliefs and is aware of how the client's belief system may affect psychotherapy. The psychotherapist is also aware of her or his own religious beliefs and values and the effect these may have on treatment. Religion and spirituality are not routinely integrated into psychotherapy. The psychotherapist might deal with forgiveness in psychotherapy, but it likely will be discussed in secular terms rather than in a religious context unless the client explicitly discusses a religious or spiritual conceptualization. In the middle of the spectrum, a psychotherapist can *explicitly discuss, assess, and work with spiritual issues.* Typically, such a psychotherapist appeals broadly to the client to consider the client's use of forgiveness because of the humanistic or broadly spiritual motives. He or she might also discuss spiritual benefits of forgiving. The psychotherapist, however, will avoid specific doctrinal or explicitly religious framing of forgiveness. At the most explicit end of the continuum, the psychotherapist intentionally *uses spiritually oriented goals and techniques in psychotherapy.* For example, a psychotherapist using an explicit approach to integration might contextualize forgiveness within scriptural passages and pray for and with the client on matters of forgiveness.

### Which Established Treatments Are Most Efficacious?

#### *Individual Psychotherapy to Promote Forgiveness*

Enright and Fitzgibbons (2000) created a process model of forgiving that has been found to be efficacious across a variety of clinical contexts and clinical disorders, including incest, medical problems, and alcohol addiction (for reviews and a meta-analysis, see Baskin & Enright, 2004). Enright's process model is organized around four phases and 20 steps scattered across the phases. In general, most forgiveness interventions follow a similar flow, and with apologies to all of the investigators, we will (over)generalize about that flow. Psychotherapists typically talk at the beginning about the transgression. For most, psychotherapeutic work deals with the details of a single incident. Even if the client does not believe he or she can identify a single transgression, he or she usually will be asked to provide one to work with and learn the method. The assumption—often explicitly addressed and encouraged by the end of psychotherapy—is that once one learns the therapeutic method, the client must apply it repeatedly to forgive a person or become a generally more forgiving person. The client usually is asked how he or she is doing at dealing with the grudge or vengeful motives, and a report of "not so well" is followed by a discussion about whether the person would like to work on forgiving. Within this period, a clear working definition must be arrived at with the client, and forgiveness is differentiated from concepts with which it often is confused. The psychotherapist and client then work systematically through the model of 20 steps spread out over four phases. For Enright, the phases of the process model involve (1) uncovering, (2) decision, (3) work, and (4) deepening.

Greenberg, Warwar, and Malcolm (2008) have developed psychotherapeutic interventions with individuals. Much of their work is based on the Gestalt therapy method of the empty chair conversation. The clients who work with an empty chair conversation seem to end in one of two places. Either they decide that the perpetrator is not trustworthy and perhaps never will be, so the clients must autonomously rely on themselves, or they develop empathy for the perpetrators and come to forgive them.

### *Couple Therapy for Forgiveness*

Several investigators have studied forgiveness in couple therapy (DiBlasio & Benda, 2008; Greenberg et al., 2008; Gordon et al., 2004; Ripley, 2009). DiBlasio has developed a decision-based intervention to promote forgiveness, and it has been shown to be particularly efficacious in Christian couples, but also efficacious in secular couples. Greenberg et al. (2008), similarly to their work with individual clients using the empty chair, demonstrated that emotionally focused couple therapy tended to promote a sense of client autonomy and prompt partners to let go of their anger more than they forgave the transgressions. However, forgiveness-focused couple therapy promoted explicit communications of forgiveness and experiences of forgiveness. Gordon et al. (2004) have found that infidelity could be treated in couple therapy by combining explicit attention to forgiveness and psychoanalytically informed insight into the dynamics of the relationship that led to the affair. Despite the use of forgiveness in treating couple problems, no one has used forgiveness measures in controlled clinical trials in family therapy.

*Psychoeducational Group Intervention to Promote Forgiving*

Worthington and colleagues developed a psychoeducational model of forgiveness and tested it in a number of contexts (for a review and meta-analysis, see Wade, Worthington, & Meyer, 2005). Clinically, this model can be used as an adjunct to psychotherapy. For example, instead of taking time in psychotherapy, the psychotherapist can ask the client to attend a weekly forgiveness group designed to teach and promote forgiveness. Other psychoeducational models have been effective. Enright used his process model psychoeducationally (for reviews, see Baskin & Enright, 2004; Enright & Fitzgibbons, 2000). Others have used forgiveness psychoeducational interventions with divorced individuals (Rye et al., 2005), for stress reduction and cardiovascular health (Luskin, Ginzburg, & Thoresen, 2005), for stress and anger reduction (Wade & Goldman, 2006), for marriage enrichment (Ripley & Worthington, 2002; Worthington, Mazzeo, and Cantor 2005), or for parenting enrichment (Kiefer et al., 2010).

*Evaluation of Degree of Evidence Supporting Clinical Interventions*

Wade et al. (2005) reviewed 42 studies of psychoeducational groups that promote forgiveness. They found most were efficacious, and no clear distinction was made in the efficacy of the various psychoeducational treatments. The choices about which treatment to recommend involved (a) fit with the psychotherapist's approach, and (b) research support.

Typically, when treatments are evaluated as empirically supported, several conditions must be met: (1) Independent investigators must evaluate the treatments, which must be manualized (i.e., organized into a manual); (2) treatments must have been shown to be more effective than a proven alternative group or a control group; (3) at least two clinical trials to which people had been randomly assigned had to show efficacy; and (4) two independent labs must provide evidence. At this point, among psychotherapeutic approaches, only Enright's process model meets the qualifications for an empirically supported psychotherapy treatment for forgiveness. Only Worthington's and Enright's programs meet the criteria for empirically supported psychoeducational treatments. In the following sections, we provide some descriptions of specific interventions to promote forgiveness.

## CASE STUDIES

In a variety of publications, many case studies have been presented using Worthington's five steps to REACH forgiveness. We summarize a few of the cases that are available in extended versions elsewhere. This will illustrate several modalities of doing forgiveness therapy.[1]

[1] As a practitioner, you might not have the resources or patience to track down the lengthier case studies referenced in this section, so we will provide enough detail in each for you to benefit from the reading. If you are more interested in reading the extended cases, you can e-mail the senior author for a downloadable version of the cases.

### Couple Therapy

Worthington and DiBlasio (1990) described the case of a couple who had not made progress in couple therapy. The couple seemed continually stuck in their unforgiveness. They had been taught communication skills and conflict resolution skills, and were trained in producing deeper intimacy with each other using Worthington's Hope-Focused Couple Approach (see Jakubowski, Milne, Brunner, & Miller, 2004). Yet the partners kept coming back to many of their old wounds. The couple therapist, DiBlasio, suggested to the couple that because of the power of past hurts in the marriage, the couple needed to work on forgiveness. Both partners immediately agreed. DiBlasio then suggested that each one spend the week thinking of all the ways he or she had wronged the other partner. The partners expressed surprise, having expected to discuss their victimization. But having agreed to work on forgiveness, they agreed to the homework. The next week when they met, DiBlasio had the couple take turns confessing their wrongs as they held hands and faced each other. At one point, the couple became emotional as they deeply confessed their wrongdoing. DiBlasio offered to step outside and give them a private moment to deal with each other. When he returned, the floor was literally wet with tears they had shed. This exercise in confession, and the spontaneous forgiveness that arose from it, was healing medicine for this couple's problems. We observe in passing that this was the first clinical case study supporting Worthington's approach to forgiveness, and as the first, it is necessarily not as well developed as the later case studies.

### Enrichment With Early Married Couples

Worthington et al. (2005) described a case in which an early married couple worked through a psychoeducational 9-hour treatment manual with a "marriage consultant" to promote forgiveness. (The treatment manual—Forgiveness and Reconciliation through Experiencing Empathy [FREE], for couples—is available for free download at http://www.people.vcu.edu/~eworth.) The couple was part of a research study. They were assessed with a large battery of questionnaires pre- and postintervention and also at about 1-year follow-up, and their data were presented within the case. Their posttreatment gains were maintained at the follow-up. Through their interactions with the psychotherapist, the intervention focused on teaching people the five steps to REACH forgiveness, and the four planks in a bridge to reconciliation (see Worthington & Drinkard, 2000). The intent of teaching the bridge to reconciliation was to help people communicate about transgressions without inflicting additional harm on each other.

The couple, John and Jenny, had been married 2 months at the outset of treatment. Both reported being under very high job stresses, which were bleeding over into their relationship. On the Global Severity Index of a brief symptom assessment, both scored in the clinical range, reporting some depression and anxiety. Their couple satisfaction was in the troublesome range, with John reporting higher levels of marital satisfaction than did Jenny, but also reporting more verbal aggression. Jenny was a financial manager and John, though 10 years older, made substantially lower salary. In addition, John had purchased items without telling Jenny and had exceeded their budget at times. Jenny was struggling to forgive the financial betrayals. The couple went through an enrichment forgiveness and reconciliation protocol, and at the end of 9 hours of meeting with a counselor, the partners forgave, especially Jenny forgiving John the big betrayal over money. By the end of treatment, John's level of marital satisfaction had increased by 5 percent and Jenny's by 10 percent (bringing her from the clinical range to subclinical).

Worthington's model is as follows. After defining forgiveness, people talk about the hurt and then decide to forgive as much of it as possible. Then they seek to increase their emotional forgiveness. The five steps to REACH emotional forgiveness are as follows: R = recall the hurt without blaming or self-pity, E = empathize with the person who hurt you (includes sympathy, compassion, and love), A = altruistic gift of forgiveness is granted, C = commit to the emotional forgiveness you have experienced, and H = hold onto forgiveness when you doubt you have forgiven. This method is taught in psychoeducational groups and the free leader and participant manuals are available for 20 hours of group intervention for secular and Christian settings. A "best 6-hour" psychoeducational group manual for leaders and participants is available for Christian-oriented psychoeducational groups. All manuals are free and can be adapted to your own practice. Merely give citation credit. The psychoeducational groups have been shown to be efficacious in numerous studies.

The planks in the "bridge to reconciliation" include (a) decide (whether, when, and how) to reconcile, (b) discuss the transgression, (c) detoxify the relationship from emotional negativity, and (d) devote yourself to building a closer relationship. Those steps can be taught to individuals, but they work best if they are taught to couples or families. The five steps to REACH emotional forgiveness are taught within the second plank in the bridge to reconciliation.

### Individual Psychotherapy

Worthington, Hunter, et al. (2010) described an application of teaching the five steps to REACH emotional forgiveness and individual psychotherapy. The client brought up forgiveness as a major issue, and the psychotherapist taught the client the five steps, applied them to an offense the client had already forgiven, and then had the client apply the five steps to the issue that was troubling to the client.

Using a different case of forgiveness in individual psychotherapy, including verbatim transcripts involving 63 client–psychotherapist interchanges, we can get a flavor of how the conversations between psychotherapist and client might unfold in the early stages of the discussion (see Worthington, 2006). Clara (a pseudonym) began talking in psychotherapy about her inability to forgive her father for his alcoholism and all the heartache it had caused her and her family. This became the focus of psychotherapy for at least two full sessions. In the first excerpt, the psychotherapist (abbreviated T in these excerpts) begins to intervene cognitively with Clara (Cl).

*T-11:* So once your "moods" get started, how to they end?

*Cl-12:* Sometimes, like just a few minutes ago, I just get so upset that I wind down, angry, depressed, and wounded. I hate that. ... Sometimes, I just kind of grumble around and then my mind moves to something else. Not very often, I recognize that I'm about to flame out, and I stop myself.

*T-13:* How do you do that?

*Cl-14:* I think something like, "Don't go there." Or, "You know where this'll lead."

*T14:* And that helps?

*Cl-15:* Sometimes. Mostly, though, I don't recognize until I'm too far into raging.

The psychotherapist asks how often (out of 10) Clara can stop her anger from becoming rage. She says, about 1 of 20 times. Then, he tries a solution-focused therapy technique.

*T-16:* I wonder. You seem pretty resourceful. Is there anything that you might do to increase this to 2 out of 20?

*Cl-17:* Sure. I think just paying attention to it could probably up it to 5 out of 20.

After the therapist tries to get her to think of doing something different to change it merely to 2 of 20 (not the overly optimistic 5), they later come back to a different topic.

*Cl-24:* So, I want to forgive him. But I've wanted to forgive for years, and I can't make myself. Every time I try to forgive, I get angry all over again within a day or two.

*T-24:* What would it mean if you forgave him? What would be different about your life?

After discussing the benefits she presumes she would experience, they worked toward a working definition of forgiving.

*T-26:* You said that you had tried to forgive him many times. How did you try to forgive?

*Cl-27:* You know, I just said I forgave him.

*T-27:* Hummm?

*Cl-28:* What do you mean, "Hummm?"

*T-28:* Just putting together what you were saying—you'd just say you forgave him and then suddenly feel completely free of hate and anger.

*Cl-29 (laughs):* Yeah, I guess it doesn't make sense now that I think of it. It sounds a little unrealistic that I ought to feel so free of the hate jus because I said I forgave him.

*T-29:* I think it is important to decide you want to forgive. So you are on the right track. I also think it is important that you get rid of your hatred and anger toward your dad. That is a part of forgiving. But maybe those two parts of forgiving are not joined at the hip. (Worthington, 2006, pp. 161–163)

This eclectic psychotherapist uses assorted techniques and methods to help the client self-discover motivations to therapy on forgiveness, to mobilize her efforts to try to forgive, to change her thinking, and to develop a different understanding of forgiveness—as involving decisional and emotional forgiveness (without necessarily using those terms with the client).

## CONCLUSION

In this present chapter, we defined two types of forgiveness and showed that forgiveness can be linked intimately with religion in people's lives. Some people forgive and are motivated to forgive because they value forgiveness as it is often valued in secular culture. For other people, forgiveness can be a sacred duty that is taught by their religion and practiced within a religious community. That religious stamp of imprimatur on the act of forgiving can deeply motivate the client and empower the act of self-sacrificial forgiving.

The research on forgiveness is voluminous, and much of it can be applied to people who wish to attend psychotherapy or other treatments that are religiously or spiritually accommodated. The findings are useful in terms of designing assessments at levels 1 and 3, as well as for the few people for whom forgiveness becomes the major issue of psychotherapy (and for which level-two assessment is appropriate). Numerous interventions already have been developed to promote forgiveness, either in psychotherapy, including couple and family therapy, or in psychoeducation. Although a careful review and evaluation of these interventions was not conducted in this chapter, we did note that the evidence that has accumulated and has been summarized in several meta-analytic summaries (Baskin & Enright, 2004; Wade et al., 2005) has shown several treatments meet criteria that could be labeled empirically supported treatments. Treatments are available for a number of specific disorders, as well as for general application for interpersonal harms that are more generic.

We have one recommendation of paramount importance for clinicians: If your client wants to experience more forgiveness, he or she must spend more time thinking about forgiving. A reliable dose–response relationship exists between the amount of time people spend trying to forgive and the amount of forgiveness that they experience (Wade et al., 2005). The forgiveness rate in virtually any kind of treatment, whether psychotherapeutic or psychoeducational, regardless of who originated the forgiveness intervention, is about one tenth of a standard deviation improvement per hour of concentrated intervention.

We know how efficacious forgiveness interventions are, but we do not know how to create the most forgiveness in the least amount of time. Typically in psychotherapy, forgiveness is not the major focus. A psychotherapist might spend 2 or 3 hours, over the course of psychotherapy, specifically focusing on forgiveness. A crucial question is to determine which specific interventions are necessary, which are both necessary and sufficient, and which are the most powerful at inducing change the fastest. An important consideration in helping answer this question is one's religious or spiritual beliefs. A complete understanding of forgiveness must include accounting for the powerful effects of religion—one of people's most cherished beliefs.

## CHAPTER SUMMARY

- Most psychotherapy is characterized by problems stemming, sometimes directly and other times not, by interpersonal offenses or hurts.
- Most psychotherapy does not deal directly with those hurts by necessarily trying to promote forgiveness, and when it does, usually the focus in for just a session or two.
- Research findings drawn primarily from the secular literature seem relevant for the religion and spirituality context. Findings suggest that the field has come to a general consensus about what forgiveness is and several good measures exist to assess aspects of forgiveness. One good way to conceptualize forgiveness is through a stress-and-coping model, which makes research understandable on the (a) biology of forgiveness; (b) physical, mental, relational, and spiritual benefits (and costs) of forgiving; (c) motivations and emotions associated with offenses and forgiving them; (d) development of forgiveness; (e) personality dispositions predicting forgiveness (or not); and (f) social, societal, political, and cultural contexts that influence forgiveness.
- Research specifically in a religious context suggests that religious traditions value forgiveness, so personal religious faith plays a big part in many people's desire to forgive and their success in forgiving.
- We recommend that clinicians conduct a level-1 assessment of whether clients believe that (a) unforgiving responses might be playing a part in their problems, (b) such issues are related to their religion or spirituality, and (c) forgiveness should be covered in psychotherapy.
- Several treatments were summarized. Two treatments were identified as being the most firmly empirically supported—Enright's process model for many psychotherapies and Worthington's REACH forgiveness model for psychoeducational group adjuncts to treatment.
- Case studies including transcripts illustrated the REACH forgiveness method.

## CLINICAL APPLICATION QUESTIONS

1. When you work with a client on forgiveness, typically how long do you spend in psychotherapy?
2. Do you use psychoeducational groups for people in your practice who can be profitably referred to group counseling? Do you have groups about forgiving people?
3. We suggest that the best predictor of how well a client forgives is the amount of time spent working on forgiveness. If you spend little time with most clients in dealing with forgiveness, are there other ways you can get the clients to concentrate on forgiving outside of psychotherapy (i.e., books, groups, videos, etc.)?

## APPENDIX: SINGLE ITEMS TO MEASURE DECISIONAL AND EMOTIONAL FORGIVENESS

*Note:* We want you to rate two types of forgiveness. For example, a person might perhaps ***decide to grant*** complete forgiveness but still ***feel*** very unforgiving toward a person.

***Granting forgiveness*** is defined as **deciding (even if you don't say aloud) that you will not seek revenge against and not avoid the person but will try to put the relationship (if any) back on the pre-offense footing. This describes how you intend to act toward the person.** Using the scale below (from 0 = no forgiveness granted to 4 = complete forgiveness granted) estimate the current level to which you have granted forgiveness.

| 0 | 1 | 2 | 3 | 4 |
|---|---|---|---|---|
| No Forgiveness | | | | Complete Forgiveness |

***Experiencing emotional forgiveness*** is defined as **the degree to which you actually feel that your emotions have become less negative and (perhaps) more positive toward the person who offended or harmed you.** If 0 = no forgiveness experienced and 4 = complete forgiveness experienced (that is, if you have experienced complete emotional forgiveness, you have no negative feelings and perhaps even some positive feelings toward the person who offended or harmed you), then use the scale below to indicate to what degree you have experienced emotional forgiveness.

| 0 | 1 | 2 | 3 | 4 |
|---|---|---|---|---|
| No Forgiveness | | | | Complete Forgiveness |

## SUGGESTED READINGS AND RESOURCES

### Books for Psychotherapists

Enright, R. D., & Fitzgibbons, R. P. (2000). *Helping clients forgive: An empirical guide for resolving anger and restoring hope.* Washington, DC: American Psychological Association.

Worthington, E. L., Jr. (2005). *Hope-focused marriage counseling: A guide to brief therapy, with a new introduction* (Rev. ed.). Downers Grove, IL: InterVarsity Press.

Worthington, E. L., Jr. (2006). *Forgiveness and reconciliation: Theory and application.* New York, NY: Brunner-Routledge.

### Books for Researchers (With Articles of Interest to Psychotherapists)

Worthington, E. L., Jr. (Ed.). (2005). *Handbook of forgiveness.* New York, NY: Brunner-Routledge.

### Books for Clients

Enright, R. D. (2001). *Forgiveness is a choice: A step-by-step process for resolving anger and restoring hope.* Washington, DC: American Psychological Association.

Luskin, F. M. (2001). *Forgive for good: A proven prescription for health and happiness.* San Francisco, CA: Harper.

Worthington, E. L., Jr. (2001). *Five steps to forgiveness: The art and science of forgiving.* New York, NY: Crown.

Worthington, E. L., Jr. (2003). *Forgiving and reconciling: Bridges to wholeness and hope.* Downers Grove, IL: InterVarsity Press.

Worthington, E. L., Jr. (2009). *A just forgiveness: Responsible healing without excusing injustice.* Downers Grove, IL: InterVarsity Press.

### Videos/CDs

Dipersio, V. (Director). Desiderio, F. (Executive Producer). (2007). *The big question: A movie about forgiveness* [DVD]. Paulist Productions. Available from http://www.bigquestionthemovie.com

Doblmeier, M. (Director and Producer). (2007). *The power of forgiveness* [DVD]. Journey Films. Available from http://www.journeyfilms.com

### Websites

The Forgiveness Project. http://www.theforgivenessproject.com

Campaign for Forgiveness Research. http://www.forgiving.org

Fetzer Institute. http://www.fetzer.org/loveandforgive

International Forgiveness Institute. http://www.forgiveness-institute.org

Virginia Commonwealth University, Department of Psychology. http://www.people.vcu.edu/~eworth (free downloads of participant and leader manuals for forgiveness groups and couple counseling)

## REFERENCES

Aquino, K., Tripp, T. M., & Bies, R. J. (2006). Getting even or moving on? Power, procedural justice, and types of offense as predictors of revenge, forgiveness, reconciliation, and avoidance in organizations. *Journal of Applied Psychology, 91*(3), 653–668.

Baskin, T. W., & Enright, R. D. (2004). Intervention studies in forgiveness: A meta-analysis. *Journal of Counseling and Development, 82,* 79–90.

Berger, P. L., Sacks, J., Martin, D., Weiming, T., Weigel, G., Davie, G., & An-Naim, A. A. (Eds.). (1999). *The desecularization of the world: Resurgent religion and world politics.* Washington, DC, and Grand Rapids, MI: Ethics and Public Policy Center and William B. Eerdmans.

Berry, J. W., Worthington, E. L., Jr., O'Connor, L., Parrott, L. III, & Wade, N. G. (2005). Forgiveness, vengeful rumination, and affective traits. *Journal of Personality, 73,* 1–43.

Berry, J.W., Worthington, E.L., Jr., Parrott, L. III, O'Connor, L., & Wade, N.G. (2001). Dispositional forgivingness: Development and construct validity of the Transgression Narrative Test of Forgivingness (TNTF). *Personality and Social Psychology Bulletin, 27,* 1277–1290.

Burnette, J. L., Davis, D. E., Green, J. D., Worthington, E. L., Jr., & Bradfield, E. (2009). Insecure attachment and depressive symptoms: The mediating role of rumination, empathy and forgiveness. *Personality and Individual Differences, 46,* 276–280.

Davis, D. E., Hook, J. N., & Worthington, E. L., Jr. (2008). Relational spirituality and forgiveness: The roles of attachment to God, religious coping, and viewing the transgression as a desecration. *Journal of Psychology and Christianity, 27,* 293–301.

Davis, D. E., Worthington, E. L. Jr., Hook, J. N., Van Tongeren, D. R., Green, J. D., & Jennings, D. J., II. (2009). Relational spirituality and the development of the similarity of the offender's spirituality scale. *Psychology of Religion and Spirituality, 1*(4), 249–262.

Denham, S. A., Neal, K., Wilson, B. J., Pickering, S., & Boyatzis, C. J. (2005). Emotional development in children: Emerging evidence. In E. L. Worthington, Jr. (Ed.), *Handbook of forgiveness* (pp. 127–142). New York, NY: Brunner-Routledge.

DiBlasio, F. A., & Benda B. B. (2008). Forgiveness intervention with married couples: Two empirical analyses. *Journal of Psychology and Christianity, 27,* 150–158.

Enright, R. D. (2001). *Forgiveness is a choice: A step-by-step process for resolving anger and restoring hope.* Washington, DC: American Psychological Association.

Enright, R. D., & Fitzgibbons, R. P. (2000). *Helping clients forgive: An empirical guide for resolving anger and restoring hope.* Washington, DC: American Psychological Association.

Enright, R. D., Rique, J., & Coyle, C. T. (2000). *The Enright Forgiveness Inventory user's manual.* Madison, WI: International Forgiveness Institute.

Exline, J. J., Baumeister, R. F., Bushman, B. J., Campbell, W. K., & Finkel, E. J., (2004). Too proud to let go: Narcissistic entitlement as a barrier to forgiveness. *Journal of Personality and Social Psychology, 87,* 894–912.

Exline, J. J., Worthington, E. L., Jr., Hill, P. C., & McCullough, M. E. (2003). Forgiveness and justice: A research agenda for social and personality psychology. *Personality and Social Psychology Review 7,* 337–348.

Fincham, F. D., Hall, J. H., & Beach, S. R. H. (2005). "'Til lack of forgiveness doth us part": Forgiveness and marriage. In Everett L. Worthington, Jr. (Ed.), *Handbook of forgiveness* (pp. 207–225). New York, NY: Brunner-Routledge.

Friedman, T. L. (2005). *The world is flat: A brief history of the twenty-first century.* New York, NY: Farrar, Strauss and Giroux.

Gartner, A. L. (2009). *The acceptance of a communicated offer of forgiveness in romantic relationships.* Unpublished master's thesis, Virginia Commonwealth University, Richmond.

Gordon, K. C., Baucom, D. H., & Snyder, D. K. (2004). An integrative intervention for promoting recovery from extramarital affairs. *Journal of Marital and Family Therapy, 30,* 213–231.

Greenberg, L. J., Warwar, S. H., & Malcolm, W. M. (2008). Differential effects of emotion-focused therapy and psychoeducation in facilitating forgiveness and letting go of emotional injuries. *Journal of Counseling Psychology, 55,* 185–196.

Hall, M. E. L., & Hall, T. W. (1997). Integration in the therapy room: A review of the literature. *Journal of Psychology and Theology, 25*(1), 86–101.

Harris, A. H. S., & Thoresen, C. E. (2005). Forgiveness, unforgiveness, health, and disease. In E. L. Worthington, Jr. (Ed.), *Handbook of forgiveness* (pp. 321–333). New York, NY: Brunner-Routledge.

Hebl, J., & Enright, R.D. (1993). Forgiveness as a psychotherapeutic goal with elderly females. *Psychotherapy, 30,* 658–667.

Hill, P. C., Exline, J. J., & Cohen, A. B. (2005). The social psychology of justice and forgiveness in civil and organizational settings. In E. L. Worthington, Jr. (Ed.), *Handbook of forgiveness* (pp. 477–490). New York, NY: Brunner-Routledge.

Hook, J. N., Worthington, E. L., Jr., & Utsey, S. O. (2009). Collectivism, forgiveness, and social harmony. *Counseling Psychologist, 37*(6), 786–820.

Hook, J. N., Worthington, E. L., Jr., Utsey, S. O., Davis, D. E., et al. (2010). *Collectivistic forgiveness: Test of a model.* Unpublished manuscript under editorial review, Virginia Commonwealth University, Richmond.

Jakubowski, S. F., Milne, E. P., Brunner, H., & Miller, R. B. (2004). A review of empirically supported marital enrichment programs. *Family Relations, 53*, 528–536.

Jennings, D. J., II. (2010). *The transgressor's response to a rejected request for forgiveness.* Unpublished master's thesis, Virginia Commonwealth University, Richmond.

Kearns, J. N., & Fincham, F. D. (2004). A prototype analysis of forgiveness. *Personality and Social Psychology Bulletin, 30,* 838–855.

Kiefer, R. P., Worthington, E. L., Jr., Myers, B., Kliewer, W. L., Berry, J. W., … & Kilgour, J., Jr. (2010). Training parents in forgiveness and reconciliation. *American Journal of Family Therapy, 38*, 32–49.

Krause, N., & Ellison, C. G. (2003). Forgiveness by God, forgiveness of others, and psychological well-being in late life. *Journal for the Scientific Study of Religion, 42,* 77–93.

Luskin, F. M., Ginzburg, K & Thoresen, C. E. (2005) The efficacy of forgiveness intervention in college age adults: Randomized controlled study. *Humboldt Journal of Social Relations, 29,* 163–184.

Mahoney, A., Rye, M. S., & Pargament, K. I. (2005). When the sacred is violated: Desecration as a unique challenge to forgiveness. In E. L. Worthington, Jr. (Ed.), *Handbook of forgiveness* (pp. 57–72). New York, NY: Brunner-Routledge.

Malcolm, W. M., Warwar, S., & Greenberg, L. (2005). Facilitating forgiveness in individual therapy as an approach to resolving interpersonal injuries. In Everett L. Worthington, Jr. (Ed.), *Handbook of forgiveness* (pp. 379–391). New York, NY: Brunner-Routledge.

McCullough, M. E. (2008). *Beyond revenge: The evolution of the forgiveness instinct.* San Francisco, CA: Jossey-Bass.

McCullough, M. E., Fincham, F. D. & Tsang, J.-A. (2003). Forgiveness, forbearance, and time: The temporal unfolding of transgression-related interpersonal motivations. *Journal of Personality and Social Psychology, 84*(3), 540–557.

McCullough, M. E., Rachal, K. C., Sandage, S. J., Worthington, E. L., Jr., Brown, S. W., & Hight, T. L. (1998). Interpersonal forgiveness in close relationships II: Theoretical elaboration and measurement. *Journal of Personality and Social Psychology, 75,* 1586–1603.

McCullough, M. E., & Worthington, E. L. Jr. (1999). Religion and the forgiving personality. *Journal of Personality, 67,* 1141–1164.

McCullough, M. E., Worthington, E. L. Jr., & Rachal, K. C. (1997). Interpersonal forgiving in close relationships. *Journal of Personality and Social Psychology, 73,* 321–336.

McMinn, M. R., Fervida, H., Louwerse, K. A. Pop, J. L., Thompson, R. D., Trihub, B. L., & McLeod-Harrison, S. (2008). Forgiveness and prayer. *Journal of Psychology and Christianity, 27*, 101–109.

Mullet, E., Neto, F., & Riviere, S. (2005). Personality and its effects on resentment, revenge, forgiveness, and self-forgiveness. In E. L. Worthington, Jr. (Ed.), *Handbook of forgiveness* (pp. 159–181). New York, NY: Brunner-Routledge.

Nisbett, R. E., & Cohen, D. (1996). *Culture of honor: The psychology of violence in the South.* Boulder, CO: Westview.

Richards, P. S., & Bergin, A. E. (2005). *A spiritual strategy for counseling and psychotherapy* (2nd ed.). Washington, DC: American Psychological Association.

Ripley, J. S. (2009, November 7). *Hope for marriage: Randomized clinical trial comparing the Hope-focused Approach accommodated to Christianity and secular.* Keynote address presented at the meeting of the Christian Association for Psychological Studies-East region, Chambersburg, Pennsylvania.

Ripley, J. S., & Worthington, E. L., Jr. (2002). Comparison of hope-focused communication and empathy-based forgiveness group interventions to promote marital enrichment. *Journal of Counseling and Development, 80,* 452–463.

Rusbult, C. E., Bissonnette, V. L., Arriaga, X. B., & Cox, C. L. (2005). Accommodation processes during the early years of marriage. In T. N. Bradbury (Ed.), *The developmental course of marital dysfunction* (pp. 74–113). New York, NY: Cambridge.

Rye, M. S., Loiacono, D. M., Folck, C. D., Olszewski, B. T., Heim, T. A., & Madia, B. P. (2001). Evaluation of the psychometric properties of two forgiveness scales. *Current Psychology, 20,* 260–277.

Rye, M. S., Pargament, K. I., Ali, M. A., Beck, G. L., Dorff, E. N., Hallisey, C., … & Williams, J. G. (2000). Religious perspectives on forgiveness. In M. E. McCullough, K. I. Pargament, & C. E. Thoresen (Eds.), *Forgiveness: Theory, research, and practice* (pp.17–40). New York, NY: Guilford Press.

Rye, M. S., Pargament, K. I., Pan, W., Yingling, D. W., Shogren, K. A., & Ito, M. (2005). Can group interventions facilitate forgiveness of an ex-spouse? A randomized clinical trial. *Journal of Consulting and Clinical Psychology, 73,* 880–892.

Sapolsky, R. M. (1994). *Why zebras don't get ulcers: A guide to stress, stress-related diseases, and coping.* New York, NY: Freeman.

Schönbach, P. (1990). *Account episodes: The management or escalation of conflict.* New York, NY: Cambridge University Press.

Smedes, L. B. (1984). *Forgive and forget: Healing the hurts we don't deserve.* New York, NY: Harper & Row.

Tan, S.-Y. (1996). Religion in clinical practice: Implicit and explicit integration. In E. P. Shafranske (Ed.), *Religion and the clinical practice of psychology* (pp. 365–390). Washington, DC: American Psychological Association.

Thompson, L. Y., Snyder, C. R., Hoffman, L., Michael, S. T., Rasmussen, H. N., … & Roberts, D. E. (2005). Dispositional forgiveness of self, others, and situations. *Journal of Personality, 73,* 319–359.

Toussaint, L. L., Williams, D. R., Musick, M. A., & Everson, S.A. (2001). Forgiveness and health: Age differences in a U.S. probability sample. *Journal of Adult Development, 8,* 249–257.

Tsang, J., McCullough, M. E., & Hoyt, W. T. (2005). Psychometric and rationalization accounts for the religion-forgiveness discrepancy. *Journal of Social Issues, 61,* 785–805.

Wade, N. G., & Goldman, D. (2006). Sex, group composition, and the efficacy of interventions to promote forgiveness. *Group Dynamics: Theory, Research, and Practice, 10,* 297–308.

Wade, N. G., Worthington, E. L., Jr., & Meyer, J. (2005). But do they really work? Meta-analysis of group interventions to promote forgiveness. In Everett L. Worthington, Jr. (Ed.), *Handbook of forgiveness* (pp. 423–440). New York, NY: Brunner-Routledge.

Welton, G. L., Hill, P. C., & Seybold, K. S. (2008). Forgiveness in the trenches: Empathy, perspective taking, and anger. *Journal of Psychology and Christianity, 27,* 168–177.

Williams, R. (1989). *The trusting heart.* New York, NY: Random House.

Worthington, E. L., Jr. (2001). *Five steps to forgiveness: The art and science of forgiving.* New York, NY: Crown Publishers.

Worthington, E. L., Jr. (2003). *Forgiving and reconciling: Bridges to wholeness and hope.* Downers Grove, IL: InterVarsity Press.

Worthington, E. L., Jr. (Ed.). (2005). *Handbook of forgiveness*. New York, NY: Brunner-Routledge.

Worthington, E. L., Jr. (2006). *Forgiveness and reconciliation: Theory and application*. New York, NY: Brunner-Routledge.

Worthington, E. L., Jr. (2009). *A just forgiveness: Responsible healing without excusing injustice*. Downers Grove, IL: InterVarsity Press.

Worthington, E. L., Jr., & Aten, J. (2009). Psychotherapy with religious and spiritual clients: An introduction. *Journal of Clinical Psychology: In Session, 65*, 123–139.

Worthington, E. L., Jr., & DiBlasio, F. A. (1990). Promoting mutual forgiveness within the fractured relationship. *Psychotherapy, 27*, 219–223.

Worthington, E. L., Jr., & Drinkard, D.T. (2000). Promoting reconciliation through psychoeducational and therapeutic interventions. *Journal of Marital and Family Therapy, 26*, 93–101.

Worthington, E. L., Jr., Greer, C. L., Hook, J. N., Davis, D. E., Gartner, A. L., ... & Toussaint, L. (2010). Forgiveness and spirituality in organizational life: Theory, status of research, and new ideas for discovery. *Journal of Management, Spirituality and Religion, 7*(2), 119–134.

Worthington, E. L., Jr., Hunter, J. L., Sharp, C. B., Hook, J. N., Van Tongeren, D. R., ... & Monforte-Milton, M. M. (2010). A psychoeducational intervention to promote forgiveness in Christians in the Philippines. *Journal of Mental Health Counseling, 32*(1), 82–103.

Worthington, E. L., Jr., Mazzeo, S. E., & Canter, D. E. (2005). Forgiveness-promoting approach: Helping clients REACH forgiveness through using a longer model that teaches reconciliation. In Len Sperry & Edward P. Shafranske (Eds.), *Spiritually-oriented psychotherapy* (pp. 235–257). Washington, DC: American Psychological Association.

Worthington, E. L., Jr., & Sotoohi, G. (2010). Physiological assessment of forgiveness, grudges, and revenge: Theories, research methods, and implications. *International Journal of Psychology Research, 5*(3/4), 291–316.

Worthington, E. L., Jr., Witvliet, C. V. O., Pietrini, P., & Miller, A. J. (2007). Forgiveness and health. *Journal of Behavioral Medicine, 30*, 291–302.

Zapf, D., & Gross, C. (2001). Conflict escalation and coping with workplace bullying: A replication and extension. *European Journal of Work and Organizational Psychology, 10*(4), 497–522.

# 12

# *Religion and Spirituality in Couples and Families*

Marsha I. Wiggins

The last two decades have been characterized by a resurgence in interest in the role of religion and spirituality in family life. Hodge (2005) noted the topic of religion and spirituality has become prominent among couple and family psychotherapists. Indeed, Weaver et al. (2002) reviewed family counseling journals between 1995 and 1999 and found a larger percentage of articles related to religion and spirituality appeared in family counseling and psychotherapy journals rather than in journals of psychology, gerontology, or mental health nursing. These results are not surprising given that the family is the center of religious and spiritual practices, and that a relationship exists between religion and spirituality and the family. That is, religious faith and spiritual practice circumscribe and influence family values and daily life, and families are crucial for the maintenance and health of religion (Gold, 2010).

In this chapter, I focus on the role of religion and spirituality in couple and family life. First, I review the empirical research on the growth-promoting function of religion and spiritual life among couples and families. Second, I describe the challenges and benefits of managing diverse beliefs and practices that result from coupling and the joining of extended family systems, noting the impact those systems have on couples and families. Third, I discuss clinical implications of research. I highlight the role of religion and spirituality during major family life cycle transitions and the ways psychotherapists may work with clinically related issues that involve religion and spirituality. Fourth, I describe two spiritual assessment approaches that assist psychotherapists in working with couples and families to understand the relationship of religious and spiritual themes to family life. Fifth, I present clinical strategies for working with couples and families' religious and spiritual differences, and I introduce interventions that use religious and spiritual beliefs and practices to enrich couple and family relationships. These concepts are illustrated through the use of a case study that suggests how psychotherapists may apply empirical research and clinical strategies in their work with clients for whom religion or spirituality are significant.

## RELIGIOUS AND SPIRITUAL PERSPECTIVES ON COUPLE AND FAMILY LIFE

A Gallup poll, referenced by Hoogestraat and Trammel (2003) revealed that 80% of Americans claimed that religion was important in their families of origin. Seventy-five percent of respondents in that poll reported that their family relationships had been enhanced by religion. Overall, religion and spirituality may contribute to families' sense of meaning and purpose, and they may form central constructs that shape family dynamics. Thus, religion and spirituality influence a family's worldview (Frame, 2000) and inform the ways in which it will or will not engage in systemic change (Gold, 2010). Psychotherapists who take seriously families' religious and spiritual values will discover a myriad of ways a religious or spiritual perspective functions as a powerful resource for negotiating life cycle transitions and for coping with family conflict and distress.

## EMPIRICAL RESEARCH

Although most research regarding the psychology of religion and spirituality is individually focused (Mahoney & Tarakeshwar, 2005), a body of empirical research is emerging on the impact of religion and spirituality on couple and family units. One of the major ways religion and spirituality contribute to higher family functioning is by helping families make meaning of their lives together and the life events that happen to them (Griffith & Rotter, 1999; Hoogestraat & Trammel, 2003; Sperry, 2001). Religion and spirituality provide frameworks for understanding life's purpose and interpreting trauma, suffering, and loss. Park and Fenster (2004) found that stress-related growth is an outcome of meaning-making coping (see Slattery & Park, Chapter 8, this volume). Religion and spirituality also function as coping mechanisms for family members in the face of general anxiety (Griffith & Rotter, 1999; Rajagopal, Mackenzie, Bailey, & Lavizzo-Mourey, 2002). In addition to meaning-making coping, religion and spirituality often offer families a positive outlet for social support. Some researchers have found links between religion and spiritual involvement and larger or more enduring social networks (Strawbridge, Shema, Cohen & Kaplan, 2001). For example, Strawbridge et al. (2001) conducted a longitudinal study of religion and spirituality and their relationship to social support. They found those who attended worship frequently were less likely over 28 years to become socially isolated. In a survey of 200 married adults from 20 major religious denominations in the United States, Abbott, Berry, and Meredith (1990) found respondents reported that religion was helpful in family life primarily by enhancing the family's social network and activities. Moreover, Sperry (2001) suggested involvement in organized religion provides a haven for families experiencing emotional pain, including grief and loss. Sperry also noted that religious involvement among families provides increased family intimacy through ritual and tradition. Engaging in rituals and celebrations within a congregation creates the sense of "family" within the church, synagogue, or mosque. These regular observances foster stability and cohesion in family life (Griffith & Rotter, 1999).

In general, researchers have found a positive connection between religiosity and marital satisfaction (Mahoney, Pargament, Tarakeshwar, & Swank, 2001). Also, higher levels of spousal communication, lower divorce rates (Call & Heaton, 1997; Mahoney et al., 2001), greater implementation of effective communication skills (Mahoney et al., 2001), and higher levels of marital commitment (Mahoney et al., 2001; Stanley & Markham, 1992) are associated with religiosity.

Researchers have found that parenting is also affected by religion and spirituality. The birth of a child may cause parents (especially mothers) to view God and religion as more important in their lives (Becker & Hofmeister, 2001). Fathers, too, may experience more religious introspection and involvement as a result of becoming a parent (Palkovitz, 2002). Mothers who were church attenders were more likely to be married when their babies were born, were more committed to the institution of marriage, and were less likely to experience conflict with their child's father than those who were not regular church attenders (Wilcox & Wolfinger, 2007). In general, research results on the quality of parenting have revealed religion is related to parental warmth, effective parenting strategies, and family cohesiveness (Brody, Stoneman, Flor, & McCrary, 1994; Wilcox, 2002). In sum, empirical research results suggest religion and spirituality are positive factors in family life and can be considered among strengths and resources as families present for psychotherapy.

## CLINICAL IMPLICATIONS

### Religion and Spirituality and Family Life-Cycle Transitions

In addition to functioning as resources that moderate stress in family life, religion and spirituality issues arise frequently in life-cycle transitions. When couples marry or form other committed unions, one of the first questions raised is related to whether they will have a religious or civil ceremony (Walsh, 1999). How couples grapple with this question is related to their personal and family history with religious organizations, and it can trigger couples' beliefs about their relationship, commitment, and the meaning of marriage or a sacred union. Psychotherapists may find themselves triangulated with partners in the couple or between families of origin about whether or not to include a spiritual dimension in a marriage or commitment ceremony and if so, what kind. The couple may be relying on the psychotherapist to act as a "tie-breaker" when couples or families have encountered gridlock regarding these issues. Gay and lesbian couples may experience the pain of rejection if their religious authorities forbid celebrations of union, or if their family members do not approve of same-sex partnerships (Laird & Green, 1996). Again, psychotherapists may find themselves caught in a double bind between gay affirming and homophobic family members with each party expecting the psychotherapist to align with their particular value system. Concerns regarding intermarriage may arise when partners have different religious or spiritual backgrounds. If one or both families object to the marriage on the basis of religious differences, increased stress may occur and partners may feel torn between their commitment to each other and to their families of origin. Furthermore, locating clergy who are willing to perform marriage or uniting rituals outside of their particular faith traditions often is challenging.

Psychotherapists working with these power struggles are usually successful in managing couple or family conflict by maintaining a neutral stance, clarifying the issues and coaching the couple toward a workable solution. When the polarization between partners is pronounced, however, the psychotherapist may want to initiate a paradoxical intervention, such as suggesting that perhaps the couple should not get married or have a commitment ceremony. Although this intervention should be a last resort to move the couple out of entrenchment, it often has one of the following effects: either the couple colludes together against psychotherapist and solves the problem, or the couple decides they are not meant for each other and take steps to end the relationship.

A common occasion for religious issues to arise in the family is with the birth of a child. Rituals associated with new birth include baptism, christening, or dedication (Christian); circumcision (Jewish); or *jatakarma* (Hindu), which involves ritual washing followed by a naming ceremony, the *samskara namakarana* (Crompton, 1998). In fact, deciding about whether or not to participate in these religious rituals may be the impetus for couples to seek psychotherapy. Or, if in the initial stages of their relationship couples determine religion and spirituality to be peripheral or insignificant, they may discover that the birth of a child propels them to seek religious or spiritual connections (Becker & Hofmeister, 2001). In fact, 90% of adults claim they want some kind of religious or spiritual faith to be part of their children's upbringing (Mahoney et al., 2001). Psychotherapists may offer both resources and support for couples who wish to explore religious or spiritual opportunities in their communities. To be effective, they must be knowledgeable about the churches, synagogues, mosques, and spiritually oriented groups in the areas where they work. They also should be aware of ethnically diverse and gay-friendly religious and spiritual congregations and be able to make such referrals for clients.

Families with adolescents also may experience religious or spiritual concerns. Even if religion has played an insignificant role in family life during the latency period, many parents feel compelled to involve their young adolescents in religious training out of a sense of duty or loyalty to a tradition (Frame, 2003). Indeed, religious involvement has been shown to be a protective factor against health risk behaviors in adolescents. Research results reveal that religiosity is positively related to health and mental health and negatively associated with alcohol and drug use, risk-taking behaviors, and engagement in early sexual behavior (Hodge, Cardenas, & Montoya, 2001; Lammers, Ireland, Resnick, & Blum, 2000).

With more permeable boundaries around teens and their parents (McGoldrick & Carter, 2003), new opportunities emerge for adolescents to explore a variety of values and lifestyles as their peer network expands. Nevertheless, according to Gallup and Bezilla (1992), 95% of North American adolescents reported they believed in God, 75% said they tried to practice the tenets of their religions, and more than a third said they were involved in church youth groups. Youth in the 6th to 12th grades indicated "being religious or spiritual" was important to them (Benson, Roehlkepartain, & Rude, 2003, p. 208).

Adolescents are attaining a level of cognitive development that makes it possible for them to reflect on their family's religious or spiritual beliefs, and to affirm or reject these beliefs. Indeed, Fowler's (1981) model of faith development, suggests adolescence is a time when youth examine critically their system of beliefs, values, and commitments. Also, they must gradually begin to take responsibility for a worldview that they have chosen.

Parents with adolescents may experience power struggles with their teens over religion. Sometimes the struggle centers on whether the parents should require their youth to attend religious services and activities with the family. Other times, the struggle may be about whether adolescents are free to choose their own religion, especially if such a choice is significantly different from the family religion. In the case of a power struggle over religious involvement with the family, couple psychotherapists may assist parents in making the transition from parenting children to parenting adolescents. They may provide psychoeducation regarding the developmental tasks of adolescence, and they may aid parents in relaxing their level of control and giving their adolescents more latitude in their decision making. The family psychotherapist may wish to facilitate parents' and adolescents' negotiation of religious requirements, and support them as they brainstorm together about alternative solutions. In the case of adolescents choosing a religion other than the one in which they were raised, the couple psychotherapist may seek to soften parental control by asking parents what goals they have for their adolescents who are on their way to becoming adults. Many parents will indicate they hope their adolescents will become independent, responsible adults who make good decisions. Psychotherapists may leverage this parental goal by suggesting to parents that giving adolescents freedom to explore and practice decision making may help these teens develop a repertoire of effective decision-making skills that lead to responsible behavior.

Psychotherapists working with parents with more rigid goals will face more difficult challenges. These parents often want their adolescents to "stay in the fold" and appropriate their parents' values, religion, and choices. Psychotherapists may first reframe parental control as the parents' way of showing love and care for their adolescents. They may help these parents face the possibility that their excessive attempts at control may backfire, resulting in their adolescents' increasing rebellion and a potential cutoff from the family, especially their parents. Psychotherapists may wish to support these parents as they consider their "bottom-line" expectations for their youth, thus not abdicating total parental control, but loosening it enough to stay in a relationship with their adolescents. Psychotherapists may employ paradoxical interventions in families where adolescents who adopt other religions as a means of rebelling against their families. Although it can be difficult to engage parents in this exercise, and doing so requires significant parental trust in the psychotherapist, the psychotherapist can ask parents if they are willing to consider "reverse psychology" with their teens. If they agree, the psychotherapist can then coach parents to behave in ways that support their adolescents' exploration and religious expression rather than criticizing or forbidding it. In this way, parental support undercuts the need for adolescent resistance and the issue may lose some of its intensity and eventually may disappear.

Families with parents at midlife are often the same ones launching older adolescents into young adulthood. They may experience a shift in roles in relation to their children and their own parents. Couples at midlife face the challenge of redefining their relationships and creating visions for the future (McGoldrick & Carter, 2003). During this time, some partners engage in affairs as a result of a midlife crisis or a reevaluation of their life circumstances, including their intimate relationships. In addition to the pain such a relationship fracture creates, the betrayed partner may feel confused about how to respond to an affair—especially if she or he is being told by a pastor or other church authority that she or he must "forgive and forget" and move immediately toward reconciliation. Under these circumstances, psychotherapists may find themselves in a double bind: They want to share with couples all they know about the delicate and often lengthy process of forgiveness (see Worthington et al., Chapter 11, this volume), while simultaneously managing the ecclesiastically driven pressure the couple experiences to do otherwise. When working with couples caught in this dilemma, psychotherapists will want to maintain a neutral stance and refrain from doing battle with a religious authority (Frame, 2003), thus imposing one's values on clients. Instead, psychotherapists may wish to help couples understand and reflect on the process of forgiveness through bibliotherapy, invite them to engage their clergy in a conversation regarding their understanding of forgiveness and reconciliation, and create a space for each partner to explore his or her personal beliefs and current feelings about what is required of each if forgiveness and reconciliation were to occur. The psychotherapist will want to ask the couple to consider what would happen if one or both of them decided reconciliation was not what they wanted. The psychotherapist's role is not to advocate for a particular outcome, but rather to help the couple untangle conflicting messages about how to respond to an affair, to open up multiple perspectives on the situation, and to assist clients in getting in touch with their intuition and listening to the wisdom of their inner voices so they can make the best decisions.

In their later years, aging adults are challenged by adjustments to retirement, managing financial concerns, and adapting to changes in health status (McGoldrick & Carter, 2003). During this period, elders evaluate life's meaning and grapple with the prospect of death—that of their loved ones and their own. Psychotherapists working with aging couples and families may be confronted with helping them address the spiritual dimensions of end-of-life issues, including how to manage a partner's or family member's dementia or Alzheimer's disease, what to include in living wills, and most profoundly, what they believe about death and how to deal with it. At the heart of all of these issues is the reality of loss and the grief associated with death. A more detailed treatment of this topic is found in the next section. Suffice it to say that psychotherapists' knowledge about these moments when spirituality is salient, and their openness to helping clients explore these issues, may enhance their work with families.

## RELIGION AND SPIRITUALITY'S ROLE WITH CLINICAL ISSUES

Religion and spirituality may be significant forces in clients' lives when they face challenging clinical issues, such as recovering from addictions, dealing with affairs or other betrayals, and experiencing grief and loss. Clients' spiritual resources may be of help to psychotherapists who may build on them in the healing process.

### Forgiveness as a Spiritual Construct to Promote Couple and Family Healing

In Chapter 11, this volume, Worthington et al. deal with the concept of forgiveness in great detail, addressing various models and citing research regarding the clinical significance of forgiveness and its positive outcomes in interpersonal and intrapersonal relationships. The authors' discussion of forgiveness can be applied to healing among couples and in families.

In the couple relationship, forgiveness may be said to be an essential ingredient to a successful, long-term partnership (Worthington, 1994). Indeed, the concept of forgiveness has deep roots in most western religions, including Christianity, Judaism, and Islam (Frame, 2003). In eastern religions, too, forgiveness is present and often considered to be more related to ignorance than to evil. In compassionate Buddhism, forgiveness emerges from compassion (Sanderson & Linehan, 1999). Because many clients believe in the sanctity of marriage and believe God is present in their relationship, forgiveness may become an especially significant construct.

Psychotherapists may ask couples to explore their individual understandings of forgiveness, especially those understandings shaped by religious beliefs. Psychotherapists may consider brief bibliotherapy interventions by having couples read Spring's (2004) book, *How Can I Forgive You? The Courage to Forgive and the Freedom Not To.* In addition, psychotherapists may engage in psychoeducational interventions by presenting couples with the major ideas developed by Worthington et al. (Chapter 11, this volume). After couples have explored their personal beliefs about forgiveness and have been exposed to the literature on the topic, psychotherapists may engage them in a conversation about how their individual beliefs are congruent with or divergent from the ideas they encountered in the bibliotherapy and psychoeducational interventions. Psychotherapists may ask questions such as "How have your beliefs about forgiveness changed because of reading this book or hearing about how psychologists understand forgiveness?" "What steps would each of you need to take to make forgiveness a reality in your relationship?" or "How do you think God would want you to live out forgiveness in your relationship?" The challenge for psychotherapists, then, is to utilize clients' religious or spiritual leanings regarding forgiveness and to pair these beliefs or perceptions with accepted standards of mental health practice.

Some research results about forgiveness in couple relationships suggest that attributions, commitment, and empathy are associated with positive forgiveness outcomes (Fincham, Hall, & Beach, 2006). Attributions, or explanations regarding the offending behavior, are associated with greater levels of forgiveness (Boon & Sulsky, 1997), especially among women (Fincham, Paleari, & Regalia, 2002). In addition, partners with greater commitment and satisfaction in their relationships reported higher level of forgiveness (McCullough et al., 1998). Conversely, when partners are ambivalent about their relationships and less committed to remaining in the relationship's long term, forgiveness may be more challenging to employ in psychotherapy (Fincham et al., 2006). Empathy, too, is a powerful tool in the forgiveness process, especially for men (Fincham et al., 2002), presumably because "empathic behavior tends to be less common for men in relationships and therefore more influential" (Fincham et al., 2006, p. 419).

In light of these research results, psychotherapists could apply these findings to their work with couples by asking the offending male in an intimate partnership to explain to his partner how he understands what happened to cause him to do something that hurt her. In addition, psychotherapists could teach their clients to apply the skills of basic empathy, that is, how to stand inside another's experience and imagine what she or he is feeling. For example, the psychotherapist could ask the offending wife to articulate how she believes her husband feels if she has wronged him. This wife could be coached to say something like "You are feeling betrayed because I spent so much money shopping without consulting you and now we have a deficit in our checking account."

Among couples, one partner engaging in an affair is a common and painful experience that often calls for forgiveness if the couples' relationship is to survive. Spring (2004), whose writing is informed by a traditional Jewish theological approach (see Rye et al., 2000), maintained that genuine forgiveness between partners is a transaction that involves "an exchange between two people bound together by an interpersonal violation" (p. 123). It is also conditional, meaning that it must be earned. Spring claimed that if one person has been hurt by another, the offender must work very hard to earn forgiveness through repentance and restitution. The injured person must also work to let go of resentment and the desire for retribution. Spring (2004) wrote,

> While the offender is never *entitled* to be forgiven, he is more likely to earn this currency if he attempts to repair the harm he caused. While the hurt party is never *obligated* to forgive ... she is more likely to do so, and resuscitate the relationship if she gives him a chance to make good. (p. 124)

One family therapy intervention, the use of reflexive questioning, developed by Karl Tomm (1987) could be especially helpful for couples in healing when there has been an incident in the relationship that requires forgiveness. Essentially, the psychotherapist asks strategic questions aimed at having partners or family members make cognitive and behavior shifts because of a change in their levels of meaning associated with the issue at hand. For example, the psychotherapist could ask the husband, "If your wife continued to feel wounded and betrayed by you, what do you think would happen to your relationship?" Or, the psychotherapist could ask the wife, "If your husband continued to apologize and accept your need to continually check up on him as a result of his affair, how do you think that would affect your willingness to forgive him?"

With regard to issues involving family forgiveness, Madanes (1990) developed a 16-step model of interventions aimed at assisting survivors of incest to work through the trauma with family members and the offender. This process involves repentance from the offender for the abuse, an apology from the family members for failure to protect the victim, symbolic reparation on the part of the offender, and assistance for the offender in moving toward self-forgiveness. Madanes (1990) claimed this intervention was the first step toward family reunification. It is predicated on significant individual psychotherapy for the victim and the offender before implementing the approach with the entire family. Psychotherapists who employ this family psychotherapy technique can integrate the literature on forgiveness into this powerful strategy. Forgiveness is an important construct in psychotherapy with couples and in families. Psychotherapists will want to explore clients' beliefs in depth, offer psychoeducation regarding some misconceptions about forgiveness, and remind clients that forgiveness is a process that takes time.

## Grief and Loss

Loss is a fundamental underlying factor for many families who present for psychotherapy. Although death is considered to be a major, if not the most dramatic loss people encounter, many other losses have a profound impact in families: (a) loss of a birth family for those adopted and those placing children for adoption; (b) loss through divorce; (c) loss of faculties as a result of aging; (d) loss related to disabilities; (e) loss of jobs; (f) loss of community through geographic relocation; (g) loss of heterosexual privilege for those coming out as lesbian, gay, bisexual, transgendered (LGBT), or questioning, and the loss of hopes their parents had for them; and (h) loss of the dream of biological children through infertility or miscarriage, and many more.

Families must confront a variety of issues when they lose a member through death. Some of these concerns have to do with the cause of death (e.g., illness, suicide, AIDS, tragedy), timing (on or off time), the state of family communication and relationships predeath, the role of the deceased in the family, secondary losses (e.g., financial, roles, home, connection to extended family), or lawsuits or estate battles. Psychotherapists will want to inquire about all of these factors as they assess the impact of death on a family.

In addition, clients' spiritual and religious beliefs may be deeply connected to the process of coping with grief and loss. Specific belief systems and ways of making meaning of loss are inexorably linked to clients' ability to move into new ways of being in the world after experiencing significant losses. For example, clients who believe their losses are part of God's will may come to different conclusions and undergo different processes of mourning than those who believe their losses are indications of their personal deficits or that their losses are mysterious or unexplainable or part of the circle of life (Thompson, 2007). Psychotherapists may make use of meaning reconstruction theory (Neimeyer, 2001), which posits that when people undergo major losses, they lose not only the person or thing that was dear to them, but also the meaning that person or thing held for them. Psychotherapists may explore with clients their beliefs about specific losses with the goal of assisting them to construct new stories—stories that integrate old and new meanings and that may be a source of healing (Thompson, 2007).

## Clinical Assessments

One of the most underdeveloped areas of practice with regard to religion and spirituality in psychotherapy is in clinical assessment of these constructs (Bullis, 1996; Sherwood, 1998). Quantitative measures, such as paper and pencil questionnaires, are the most widely used spiritual assessment tools (Lukoff, Turner, & Lu, 1993). Most of these instruments, however, are focused on individuals and not on couples and families. Moreover, quantitative measures often are viewed as inappropriate approaches to assessing religion and spirituality because the constructs are subjective and a comprehensive understanding of clients' reality is lost. Thus, religion and spirituality are difficult to quantify (Reed, 1992). Instead, qualitative methods seem to be more appropriate and useful for families because they are process oriented, open ended, and holistic (Franklin & Jordan, 1995). They also allow clients to connect their own religious and spiritual understandings and experiences to those of their significant others and their families of origin. By so doing, they are able to provide psychotherapists with information regarding how religion and spirituality are lived out in their family relationships and what role these constructs play in exacerbating or mitigating family distress.

Two qualitative approaches for assessing religion and spirituality in families are described in the next sections: the brief spiritual assessment and the spiritual genogram. Psychotherapists may use these tools to determine the degree to which religion and spirituality are related to couple or family presenting problems and how to design interventions that address these issues.

### The Brief Spiritual Assessment

This brief spiritual assessment is an initial approach used to elicit information from clients about how spirituality functions in their lives. Psychotherapists use this abbreviated set of questions to determine the ways spirituality may be a source of strength and how clients' beliefs and practices influence their lives (Hodge, 2005). Questions included in such an assessment are as follows:

1. I was wondering if you consider spirituality or religion to be a personal strength?
2. In what ways does your spirituality help you cope with the difficulties you encounter?
3. Are there certain spiritual beliefs and practices you find particularly helpful in dealing with problems?
4. I was also wondering if you attend a church or some other type of spiritual community?
5. Do resources exist in your faith community that might be helpful to you? (Hodge, 2005, p. 343)

These questions allow the psychotherapist to gauge whether and to what degree religion or spirituality might be involved in the presenting problems or might be a resource for the family to deal with the problems. Among couples and families, responses can help inform the psychotherapist if conflict surrounds religion and, if so, the degree of the conflict present.

In addition to this brief screening assessment, psychotherapists may wish to expand the interview to include other questions. Gorsuch and Miller (1999) suggested exploring clients' purpose or meaning in life (see Slattery & Park, Chapter 8, this volume). One advantage to discussing religious and spiritual persuasions and experiences with clients is that psychotherapists can ask follow-up questions and can assist clients in making connections between their spiritual worldviews and their current life challenges. For example, a couple psychotherapist may discover that the couple has a spiritual belief that life's purpose is to be known intimately by a partner, and to have that person be a witness to his or her life. By invoking that belief as a goal for relationship enhancement or healing, the psychotherapist may use the couple's belief system as leverage for having them address the problems that threaten their relationship. Or, if a family reveals they have a deep commitment to God, the psychotherapist may employ the notion of God as a member of the family (Griffith, 1986). Then the psychotherapist may inquire as to how family members believe God would want them to behave and what changes they may need to make to live in obedience to their understanding of God's expectations.

### The Spiritual Genogram

For psychotherapists to obtain a broad picture of a family's religious and spiritual background, the spiritual genogram is an appropriate assessment approach (Frame, 2000). A *genogram* is a multigenerational map of family structure and composition that employs symbols to depict who is in the family and biological and legal relationships to one another (McGoldrick, Gerson, & Shellenberger, 1996). The psychotherapist gathers data from the couple or family regarding births, marriages, divorces, deaths, and family members' perceptions of family relationships. For example, disengagement, enmeshment, conflict, and alliances may be designated to give a richer depth to the family diagram (Friedman, Rohrbaugh & Krakauer, 1988). The psychotherapist may create the framework of the spiritual genogram in the session and then ask clients to add color coding and symbolic representations as a homework assignment. In the subsequent session, the psychotherapist asks a series of reflection questions, enabling clients to discover family of origin patterns. Then the psychotherapist uses the information to design appropriate couple or family interventions. If psychotherapists believe constructing the spiritual genogram to be too time intensive, they may adapt the reflection questions without the use of the genogram.

In the spiritual genogram, clients indicate religious or spiritual traditions through color coding (Lewis, 1989). For example, "Roman Catholics may be drawn in red, Protestants in orange, Jews in blue, Muslims in black, Mormons in gray, Buddhists in yellow, Unitarians in purple, agnostic or atheist in pink, personal spirituality in green, and no religious/spiritual affiliation in brown. If religious/spiritual heritage is unknown, no color is added" (Frame, 2003, p. 105).

Significant religious or spiritual family life should be noted on the genogram. To indicate that particular family members left a religious or spiritual organization or movement, brackets [ ] are placed around these persons on the genogram. If family members converted to other religions or joined other types of churches, synagogues, or mosques, clients add another layer of color around the family member's symbol, indicating the nature of the change. Dates for leaving and joining religious organizations should be indicated. This aspect of the genograms reveals the stability or fluidity of religious or spiritual affiliation.

The symbol ⇆ represents religious or spiritual closeness between family members (Frame, 2003). Such closeness does not have to be a reflection of a shared religious or spiritual tradition. It may also reflect the bond that grows in a family that eschews religion. The symbol ∿∿∿ represents antagonism or conflict, and clients note the specifics on their genograms. Psychotherapists attempt to uncover how religious or spiritual beliefs, experiences, rituals, and practices are connected to clients' therapeutic concerns by asking the following questions:

1. What role, if any, did religion/spirituality play in your family of origin? What role does it play now?
2. What specific religious/spiritual beliefs are most important for you now? How are they a source of connection or conflict between you and other family members?
3. How is gender viewed in your religious/spiritual tradition? Ethnicity? Sexual orientation? How have these beliefs affected you and your extended family?
4. What patterns emerge for you as you think about religion and spirituality in your family or origin and extend family? How are you currently maintaining or diverting from those patterns?
5. How does your religious/spiritual history connect with your current distress, or with the problem you presented for therapy? What new insights or solutions may occur to you based on the discoveries made through the genogram? (Frame, 2003)

One result of investigating these issues with clients is that they often develop more objectivity and a greater appreciation for the ways in which they have been shaped (consciously or unconsciously) by family religion and spirituality. Often they may suspend blaming each other to seek solutions for family problems (Frame, 2003).

## CLINICAL STRATEGIES

### God as a Member of the Family

A variety of clinical strategies may be employed by psychotherapists to address and integrate religion and spirituality into the therapeutic domain. Butler and Harper (1994) utilized the concepts of *triangles* and *triangulation* in their work with religious couples. Such couples have a real and personal relationship with God and believe that God is "stabilizing interpersonal relationships and engaging in daily family transactions" (Griffith, 1986, p. 609). Essentially, to manage the anxiety or tension in the couple relationship, one or both partners (at some time or other) brings in a third party, in this case God, to diffuse conflict and to balance the relationship. When each party in the triangle is fairly differentiated, then each of the partners can use their belief system and their relationship with God to provide support for problem-solving efforts. In this ideal state, couples take responsibility for addressing their issues and enlist God's assistance for reconciliation and problem resolution (Butler & Harper, 1994).

When individual partners are not well differentiated, God may become triangulated in the couple relationship, so that God's presence interferes with the couples' relationship development. For example, in coalition triangles each partner "competes intensely for the allegiance of God, but neither is assured that they have it" (Butler & Harper, 1994, p. 282). In this case, partners attempt to convince each other that God is on their side, sometimes citing sacred writings or revelatory experiences as evidence of their position. Rather than seeking God's help in solving their problems, they co-opt God into participating in their blaming of the other partner. In couples who present with a triangulated God, psychotherapists must assist clients in acknowledging the way God has been triangulated in their relationship and help them to free God from this untenable position. By so doing, God (or other higher power) may be available to the couple for joint problem-solving efforts.

### Strategic Family Therapy

Psychotherapists working from a strategic perspective may discover that God is an active player in family interactions. Circular questioning is a method of determining how God functions in a family system (Griffith, 1986). For example, psychotherapists using appropriate respect and neutrality might ask each family member, "When Dad stops focusing on his work and attends to his relationship with Mom, what happens to John's relationship to God?" "Does John move closer to God or farther away?" and "If John moves away from God, who else makes a similar move? Who would be the most upset if the family did not remain close to God?" (Griffith, 1986). Other examples of circular questions (Fleurides, Nelson, & Rosenthal, 1986) include the following:

> About which relationship in the family do you think God would express the most satisfaction? About which relationship do you think God would express the least satisfaction? If you worked out your sexual relationship with your husband so that you both found it to be satisfying, would you feel closer or further away from God? With whom in the family can you talk about God? With whom would it feel awkward? (Griffith & Griffith, 1992, p. 73)

In these ways, psychotherapists are able to uncover information about God as a member of the family and how the God-construct functions in the context of the family's presenting problem.

### The Milan Group: Rituals

The Milan Group, led by Selvini-Palazzoli, Coscolo, Cecchin, and Prata (1978), prescribed rituals as interventions in strategic family therapy. Rituals are symbolic acts that express values, meaning, or cultural norms (Bewley, 1995). Rituals are used in family therapy for various purposes. They involve relating (shaping, expressing, and maintaining relationships), changing (marking transitions for ourselves and others), healing (recovering from relationship betrayal, trauma, or loss), believing (voicing beliefs and making meaning), and celebrating (affirming deep joy and honoring life with festivity) (Imber-Black & Roberts, 1992). Rituals are dramatic statements that assist with self integration as one considers change, integration of self and culture through the use of popular symbols, or (for our purposes) religious symbols, and the integration of self and others through the development of community (Neu, 1995).

Because rituals are central to both religion and spirituality, they lend themselves well to being media for incorporating the sacred into secular psychotherapy. When designing spiritually informed rituals, Bewley (1995) suggested psychotherapists and clients cocreate them with attention to couple or family notions of spirituality. Together, psychotherapists and clients identify an experience embraced by the clients, find significant symbols that represent the experience, and formulate corresponding symbolic acts. Both psychotherapists and clients designate the ritual as a sacred process and set apart a space where spirit (in whatever form clients describe) can be remembered (Bewley, 1995). Rituals may be used for healing from incest, for gay and lesbian persons coming out (Neu, 1995), or for dealing with grief and loss (Bewley, 1995). A ritual may be created to address almost any therapeutic issue; however, ritual work may be contraindicated for clients with poor ego strength and those who have experienced ritual abuse (Bewley, 1995).

### Postmodern Approaches: Languaging

One of the major contributions of social constructionist thinking and psychotherapy has been the use of language systems. In the religious and spiritual realm, these ideas are particularly well suited because language, metaphor, and narrative are some of the important vehicles by which spirituality is experienced and explored. Griffith and Griffith (1992), building on the work of Tomm (1987) and White (1986), designed some reflexive questions that "invite fresh dialogue and new linguistic distinctions in the conversations between self and God-construct" (p. 73):

a. Had you possessed the relationship you now have with God when you first married, how do you suppose your different behavior might have altered the way the relationship evolved?
b. If God were to restructure this interaction, how do you think it would go?

c. If God were to see worth in this relationship which the two of you might not be able to see, what might that be?
d. If you were to discover that God had in fact been present and active in this situation all along, where might that have been? (Griffith & Griffith, 1992, p. 73)

Other questions include Outcome and Unique Account Questions (White, 1988):

a. Has there ever been even a brief moment when, contrary to your expectations, you did sense approval coming from God?
b. Can you recall a time when your husband might have criticized your relationships with God but didn't?
c. In view of all the betrayals you experienced in your life growing up, are you surprised to discover that you have learned to trust God? (Griffith & Griffith, 1992, pp. 73–74)

Unique Redescription and Unique Possibilities Questions (White, 1986, 1988) delve into clients' religious or spiritual perspectives. These types of questions require clients to think differently about the way they are framing the problem and to imagine how they might respond under circumstances they had not previously considered. Some examples of these types of questions are as follows:

a. What difference will your having learned how to trust God make in your learning how to trust your wife?
b. If you see yourself as the person God sees, what new possibilities might you imagine for this relationship?
c. If you were to agree with the outcome you believe God wants for this relationship, what might be the next step in getting there? (Griffith & Griffith, 1992, p. 74)

### Postmodern Approaches: Narrative Therapy

Another popular postmodern method of family psychotherapy is narrative therapy. Well-known writers such as White and Epston (1990) argued that working with life narratives invites clients to examine life stories that do not fit with the facts clients currently are experiencing. In fact, a major reason why people enter psychotherapy is because their life stories have become tangled up. Either their lives have lost purpose or the purpose has become derailed as a result of psychological difficulties (Vitz, 1992).

Lax (1996) argued that narrative models have much in common with Buddhist practice. In Buddhism, the notion of "a permanent self is an illusion that we cling to, a narrative developed in relation to others over time that we come to identify as who we are" (Lax, 1996, p. 200). Narrative therapy is similar in that people's lives are viewed as changing narratives to be freed from one objective, idealized version and opened to a host of possibilities. In both Buddhism and narrative therapy, "multiple voices, stories, and views are valued, with the individual's own experience given centrality" (Lax, 1996, p. 201). In addition, both Buddhism and narrative therapy share an emphasis on *reflexivity*, the "process of making oneself an object of one's own observation" (Lax, 1996, p. 206). Thus, we are shaped by and shape our own narratives. As psychotherapists, we inform and are informed by clients' narratives *and* by the changes in their narratives. Buddhist couples and families who are in the habit of insight meditation and mindfulness (Nhat Hanh, 1976) may respond well to narrative work that asks them to deconstruct their current stories and to disengage from them enough to become observers of their own narratives (Frame, 2003).

## CASE STUDY

Patrick and Sarah are a White couple in their mid-40s. They have two sons: Andrew, 20, and Stephen, 18. Both Andrew and Stephen are attending colleges in the northeastern United States. Patrick and Sarah are seeking couples' psychotherapy because Sarah discovered Patrick was having a sexual relationship with Tim, a coworker at the bank. Patrick said that Sarah had told their sons that Patrick was having an affair, but had not told them that the affair was with a man. Patrick indicated that he had "had this attraction to males ever since I could remember." However, he stated, "I couldn't begin to come out and say I was gay or anything. I still love Sarah. Besides, part of me is afraid I am going to burn in hell for this."

On the intake form, Patrick indicated he had been raised in a fundamentalist, Bible-believing nondenominational Christian church. He had been in Sunday School and the youth group, and he had even considered going into the ministry. Patrick revealed that he "was kicked out" of the church at 16 because he had been caught "messing around" with another boy on a youth retreat. Patrick confided he had never shared this incident with anyone. He had simply refused to attend church or any religious activities since his painful church dismissal. Patrick said he was seeking psychotherapy so he could "figure out who I am," "try to find some spiritual peace," and "figure out what Sarah and I are going to do now." Patrick said he was sure the Bible said homosexuality was a sin, but he could not quote the chapter and verse. He reported that whenever he would have sex with other men he would feel ashamed of his same-sex attraction and guilty for "cheating on Sarah."

Sarah reported she had been raised in a nominally religious home and attended a Presbyterian church at Christmas and Easter and a few other times with friends or with her grandparents. She told the psychotherapist she had a "deep, personal spirituality" and "believed God loved her and wanted her to be happy." Sarah offered that she and Patrick had not attended church during their married life because "Patrick was adamantly opposed to it" and that they had not raised their sons with any religion. Sarah indicated she had been "devastated" by Patrick's affair, and felt confused about what it meant for their marriage. On the one hand, she said she "wanted to banish him from their home and her life." On the other hand, she confessed she still loved Patrick and "wanted to have her husband back."

Patrick and Sarah's psychotherapist, Julia, was challenged by helping them come to terms with Patrick's sexual orientation, helping them address the religious dimensions of their fractured relationship, and make decisions about whether to stay together or to get a divorce. Julia began by asking Patrick and Sarah to construct a spiritual genogram (Frame, 2000). Each partner mapped three generations of their family of origin at the top of the large piece of paper.

Patrick's genogram reflected a line of Christian fundamentalists, traced back to his paternal great-grandparents who left the Roman Catholic Church when they emigrated from Ireland and joined a fundamentalist Christian church to "fit in" to their new community. Sarah's family tree consisted of a variety of Protestant Christians who "attended church as a family obligation and a social opportunity." She acknowledged she had a "positive connection to the church and believed God loved and accepted all people." She indicated on the genogram a close relationship with all four of her grandparents who engaged in significant service to the poor as a sign of their Christian commitment. Patrick noted his "love-hate relationship with God and the church" and "Satan who had tempted him to be unfaithful to Sarah" as spiritual dimensions of the presenting problem. Sarah indicated she was active in several social justice–focused community organizations and defined her spirituality as "service to others." She also revealed her grandparents, all of whom were deceased, continued to live on through her acts of service.

After joining with the couple and committing herself to helping them achieve their goals, Julia began working with Patrick on his sexual orientation and the religious messages about homosexuality he had received during his youth. At first, Julia asked Patrick what he thought about homosexuality. Patrick said "down deep I believe God created me this way" and revealed he "couldn't change his attractions no matter how hard he tried." Patrick told Julia he had "given up on God" because he felt his rejection from the youth group meant "God had given up on him." When Julia realized Patrick had closed himself off from God and religion, she asked him, "What do you suppose might happen if you were to discover you could be both gay and Christian at the same time?" Patrick responded, "I would be incredibly relieved about the religion part and really sad about my marriage." Julia then asked Patrick to engage in a homework assignment in which he would research the biblical passages he thought were prohibiting homosexuality. In addition, she lent him the video, *For the Bible Tells Me So* (Karslake, 2007) and asked Patrick to keep a record of his understandings, insights, and questions. Through this homework assignment, Patrick realized that in the Bible Jesus had nothing to say about homosexuality And, he learned there were alternate interpretations of scripture proscribing homosexual activity. In subsequent sessions,

Julia asked Patrick to share his discoveries with Sarah and to talk about what he thought his discoveries may mean for himself personally and for their marriage.

Julia also asked Sarah to reflect on her understanding of sexuality and what it meant for her to be married to someone who thought he might be gay. Julia helped Sarah explore her religious views about homosexuality as well. Although Patrick initially presented as extremely conflicted about his sexuality, Sarah reported she felt "solidly heterosexual" and believed that God's love for everyone was "bigger than sexual issues." She did not hold any particularly negative views about homosexuality per se, but she was both angry and grief-stricken to discover Patrick's affair with a gay coworker.

In a subsequent conjoint session, Julia asked Patrick and Sarah, "If God were to weigh in on this dilemma the two of you are facing, what do you think God would say to you?" Patrick responded, "I think God would say, 'I want each of you to be happy and to continue to be good parents for your sons.'" Sarah stated, "I believe God would say, 'Stop hurting each other and figure out how you can have a loving relationship, even if it isn't a marriage.'" Julia then asked the couple, "If you place any kind of authority on your understanding of God's will, what clues do you have about how to proceed?" Patrick stated, "I'm going to have to come to terms with being gay and deal with the heartbreak I have caused Sarah." Sarah acknowledged, "I am going to have to accept the fact that our marriage is over and find a way to heal my broken heart."

After Patrick was willing to confront his homosexuality, Julia referred him to individual psychotherapy during which he began to address both his religious beliefs and personal views that led him to believe he had to choose a single identity, either gay or Christian (Heermann, Wiggins, & Rutter, 2007). To assist Patrick in embracing his sexual orientation, his individual psychotherapist introduced him to a variety of bibliotherapy resources about being gay (Lynch, 1996), connected him to an LGBT support center in his community, and gave him a list of gay-affirming churches that would offer him a more decidedly positive religious message about his sexual orientation than the one with which he was raised.

At the beginning of couples psychotherapy, two salient themes emerged: Sarah's deep feelings of anger and betrayal and Patrick's overwhelming sense of guilt about his affair. Julia worked with Patrick and Sarah to address the feelings they each held about Patrick's infidelity. Because they genuinely loved and respected each other, after several months, Sarah was able to understand that Patrick was caught in a terrible double bind—that of either being unfaithful to the person he knew himself to be or of being unfaithful to Sarah. Patrick was able to acknowledge his fear of losing his marriage and family if he were to have been honest with Sarah about his sexuality.

Julia asked Patrick to write a letter to Sarah expressing his sincere sorrow over betraying her and her trust. She asked Patrick to include a section in the letter in which he would attempt to articulate what Sarah must be feeling as a result of both his betrayal and his acknowledgment of his sexual orientation. Then Julia asked Patrick to read the letter to Sarah in the psychotherapy session After hearing Patrick's letter, Sarah wept and said, "I didn't think you could possibly understand how much I have suffered since I found about you and Tim. But after hearing your letter, I realize you understand more than I thought you did. I am starting to see how devastated and guilty you are feeling." Sarah's response to Patrick's letter was a turning point that helped Julia's work with Sarah and Patrick around the theme of forgiveness of self and other. She helped them to separate the forgiveness journey from their difficult decision about what to do about their marriage.

The other major theme in Sarah and Patrick's psychotherapy was that of grief and loss. Each partner experienced profound sadness as they acknowledged they would never have the same kind of intimate relationship as they had enjoyed for more than 20 years, and they both were devastated as they decided to divorce so that each could seek a life and a relationship that would bring them fulfillment. During the grief work, Julia asked Patrick and Sarah each to keep a journal about their feelings and experiences and to share selections of it with each other in the psychotherapy room to foster empathy for each other's pain. The process of writing their stories helped them come to terms with the reality of their loss (Shallcross, 2009). Julia also talked with Patrick and Sarah about the reconstruction of meaning (Neimeyer, 2001) about their marriage and its ending. They were asked to use their spiritual or religious beliefs as part of their meaning-making exercise. As Sarah and Patrick crafted a story of their life together and a vision of their lives apart, they used this activity to prepare themselves to share their story with their sons, Andrew and Stephen, who had become extremely angry at their father because of the affair. It took many months of family psychotherapy for Andrew and Stephen to address their significant anger and grief over the loss of their family unit and to begin to come to terms with their father's sexuality.

Finally, Julia coached Patrick and Sarah to create a ritual for the ending of their marriage. They had come to reframe their divorce as a gift of freedom to each other. They wanted to craft a family ritual in which they would relinquish their marriage vows and their wedding rings. But they also wanted to affirm their never-ending role as parents to their sons whom they were launching into adulthood. Julia helped Patrick and Sarah write a script for a ceremony in which they would celebrate the years of their marriage as well marking its end. The ritual would conclude with Sarah and Patrick offering each other a blessing for their futures.

During her work with Patrick and Sarah, Julia began with an open and accepting posture toward each partner. She was adept at suspending her personal beliefs to empathize with her clients. Julia utilized a spiritual genogram to establish a multigenerational picture of Patrick and Sarah's families of origin. She helped

Patrick and Sarah understand how their religious or spiritual beliefs, despite being somewhat hidden from them, contributed to their challenging circumstances. Julia was able to accurately describe both Patrick and Sarah's pain and to integrate their religious and spiritual backgrounds into her overall assumptions about the couple's problems. Julia hypothesized that Patrick had been so wounded by his church and felt so ashamed of his same-sex attractions that he abandoned God and the church without ever examining his beliefs or trying to reconcile his experiences and his faith. Julia believed having Patrick confront both his spirituality and his sexuality would enable him to connect authentically with Sarah and address the fracture in their relationship. Julia was also able to leverage Sarah's openness to homosexuality and her spiritual commitment to social justice to enable her to release Patrick from their marriage so that each could live more honest and fulfilling lives. Moreover, she was able to use their spiritual beliefs to craft some of her interventions. In fact, Julia brought God into the conversation using a form of circular questioning that freed both Patrick and Sarah to express some of their truest fears and feelings. She suggested Patrick do research about his assumptions regarding the Bible, and offered him a contemporary resource that was both Christian and gay affirming. Then, Julia drew on the empirical research and clinical interventions associated with forgiveness to assist Patrick and Sarah to address the betrayal and hurt in their relationship. Julia created a space for the couple to grieve the loss of their relationship and to construct a new meaning for their story together and apart. She then enabled Patrick and Sarah to draw on the power of symbol and metaphor as they engaged in a ritual to end their marriage and move them forward on separate journeys.

## CONCLUSION

Religion and spirituality are major forces that have significant impact on couples and families across the life cycle. These constructs are potential resources for coping with life's tragedies and traumas, and they can be barriers to individual, couple, and family growth. Empirical research reveals that religion and spirituality are central constructs in many families and often are associated with well-being in general and couple satisfaction specifically. Clinical assessments that make use of multigenerational maps and showcase the role of religion and spirituality in the family can be useful tools for couples and families navigating the intersection of difficult issues and particular spiritual perspectives. Therapeutic interventions drawn from a variety of theoretical lenses can be adapted to include a spiritual or religious focus. These approaches can be use to take seriously clinical issues within a religious or spiritual context. In all of these ways, couple and family psychotherapists are able to take seriously and honor the spiritual dimensions of couple and family relationships and to harness their power for therapeutic ends.

## CHAPTER SUMMARY

### Empirical Research

- Religion and spirituality are important factors in family life that help family members create value systems and develop meaning-based coping in the face of life's traumas and tragedies.
- Religion and spirituality often offer families a positive outlet for social support.
- Religious communities provide a haven for families experiencing grief and loss.
- Religious involvement among families provides increased family intimacy through ritual and tradition.
- Researchers have found a positive connection between religiosity and marital satisfaction. Also, higher levels of spousal communication, lower divorce rates, greater implementation of effective communication skills, and higher levels of marital commitment are associated with religiosity.
- Research results on the quality of parenting have revealed that religion is related to parental warmth, effective parenting strategies, and family cohesiveness.

### Clinical Implications

- Religion and spirituality are connected to clinical issues that arise across the life span.
- One issue is the potential for the psychotherapist to become triangulated with a couple or with family members regarding religious marriage or commitment ceremonies.
- A second issue is the need for the psychotherapist to help diffuse power struggles between couples and their families of origin and between parents and adolescents when a member or members makes a religious decision that challenges family tradition.
- A third issue is the opportunity for psychotherapists to assist couples in addressing the religious beliefs that circumscribe extramarital affairs, including the couples' beliefs about forgiveness and possible conflict involving the perspectives of religious authorities.
- A fourth clinical challenge is for psychotherapists to enable families to deal with their religious belief systems in the face of end-of-life issues, including death.

### Clinical Assessment

- The brief spiritual assessment consists of exploratory questions psychotherapists may use at the beginning of psychotherapy to determine how important religion or spirituality is to a couple or family and how they (psychotherapists) may integrate these constructs into their clinical work.

- The spiritual genogram is a multigenerational map of family relationships, focusing on religion and spirituality across time. The color-coded diagram enables psychotherapists and family members to understand the religious and spiritual patterns in their extended families and how these patterns may influence them in their current relationships.

### Clinical Strategies

- Considering God as a member of the family may enable psychotherapists to help clients uncover the ways their religious and spiritual perspectives impinge on their behaviors. Psychotherapists may be able to use this strategy to address ways in which God may be triangulated in the couple or family system.
- Strategic family therapy interventions involve using circular questioning as a method of determining how God functions in a family system. Psychotherapists ask clients to imagine what would happen if they made changes in their family system by asking such questions as "About which relationship in the family do you think God would express the most satisfaction?" "About which relationship do you think God would express the least satisfaction?" and "If you worked out your sexual relationship with your husband so that you both found it to be satisfying, would you feel closer or further away from God?"
- Employing rituals that capture major client change can utilize religious and spiritual power for therapeutic intervention. Rituals involve relating (shaping, expressing, and maintaining relationships), changing (marking transitions for ourselves and others), healing (recovering from relationship betrayal, trauma, or loss), believing (voicing beliefs and making meaning), and celebrating.
- Postmodern approaches also involve languaging and narrative. Psychotherapists ask questions that require clients to think differently about the way they are framing the problem and to imagine how they might respond under circumstances they had not previously considered. For example, "If you decided to end your affair, what do you think that would do to your relationship with God?" Narrative approaches involve having clients rewrite their stories by assigning new and hopeful meanings to them.

## CLINICAL APPLICATION QUESTIONS

1. What kinds of religious or spiritual issues that emerge in couple and family therapy might be the most challenging for you personally?

2. How might you apply classic couple and family interventions when religious or spiritual issues are involved in the clients' presenting problem?
3. What might you need to do to suspend your own religious or spiritual values or beliefs to work clients with religiously different from yourself?
4. What additional circular questions besides those mentioned in this chapter might be helpful in working with families in which God is an important member?

## SUGGESTED READINGS AND RESOURCES

Hodge, D. R. (2005). Spiritual assessment in marriage and family therapy: A methodological framework for selecting from among six qualitative assessment tools. *Journal of Marital and Family Therapy, 31,* 341–356.

Karslake, D. (Director). (2007). *For the Bible tells me so* [DVD]. New York, NY: First Run Features.

Kidd, S. M. (1996). *The dance of the dissident daughter: A woman's journey from Christian tradition to the sacred feminine.* New York, NY: HarperCollins.

Spring, J. A. (2004). *How can I forgive you? The courage to forgive and the freedom not to.* New York, NY: HarperCollins.

Walsh, F. (Ed.). (1999). *Spiritual resources in family therapy.* New York, NY: Guilford.

## REFERENCES

Abbott, D. A., Berry, M., & Meredith W. H. (1990). Religious belief and practice: A potential asset in helping families. *Family Relations, 39,* 443–448.

Becker, P. E., & Hofmeister, H. (2001). Work, family, and religious involvement formen and women. *Journal for the Scientific Study of Religion, 40,* 707–722.

Benson, P. L., Roehlkepartain, E. C., & Rude, S. P. (2003). Spiritual development in childhood and adolescence: Toward a field of inquiry. *Applied Developmental Science, 8,* 205–213.

Bewley, A. R. (1995). Re-membering spirituality: Use of sacred ritual in psychotherapy. In J. Ochshorn & E. Cole (Eds.), *Women's spirituality, women's lives* (pp. 201–214). New York, NY: Haworth.

Boon, S. D., & Sulsky, L. M. (1997). Attributions of blame and forgiveness in romantic relationships: A policy-capturing study. *Journal of Social Behavior and Personality, 12,* 19–44.

Brody, G. H., Stoneman, Z., Flor, D., & McCrary, C. (1994). Religion's role in organizing family relationships: Family process in rural, two-parent African-American families. *Developmental Psychology, 32,* 696–706.

Bullis, R. K. (1996). *Spirituality in social work practice.* Washington, DC: Taylor & Francis.

Butler, M. H., & Harper, J. M. (1994). The divine triangle: God in the marital system of religious couples. *Family Process, 33,* 277–286.

Call, V. R. A., & Heaton, T. B. (1997). Religious influence on marital stability. *Journal for the Scientific Study of Religion, 36,* 382–392.

Crompton, M. (1998). *Children, spirituality, religion, and social work.* Aldershot, UK: Ashgate.

Fincham, F. D., Hall, J., & Beach, S. R. H. (2006). Forgiveness in Marriage: Current status and future directions. *Family Relations, 55,* 415–427.

Fincham, F. D., Paleari, F., & Regalia, C. (2002). Forgiveness in marriage: The role of relationship quality, attributions, and empathy. *Personal Relationships, 9,* 27–37.

Fleuridas, C., Nelson, T. S., & Rosenthal, D. M. (1986). The evolution of circular questions: Training family therapists. *Journal of Marital and Family Therapy, 12,* 113–127.

Fowler, J. W. (1981). *Stages of faith: The psychology of human development and the quest for meaning.* San Francisco, CA: Harper & Row.
Frame, M. W. (2000). The spiritual genogram in family therapy. *Journal of Marriage and Family Therapy, 26,* 211–216.
Frame, M. W. (2003). *Integrating Religion and Spirituality into Counseling: A comprehensive approach.* Pacific Grove, CA: Brooks/Cole.
Franklin, C., & Jordan, C. (1995). Qualitative assessment: A methodological review. *Families in Society, 76,* 281–295.
Friedman, H., Rohrbaugh, M., & Krakauer, S. (1988). The timeline genogram: Highlighting temporal aspects of family relationships. *Family Process, 27,* 293–304.
Gallup, G., & Bezilla, R. (1992). *The religious life of young Americans: A compendium of surveys on the spiritual beliefs and practices of teenagers and young adults.* Princeton, NJ: G. H. Gallup International Institute.
Gold, J. M. (2010). *Counseling and spirituality: Integrating spiritual and clinical orientations.* Upper Saddle River, NJ: Merrill.
Gorsuch, R. L., & Miller, W. R. (1999). Assessing spirituality. In W. R. Miller (Ed.), *Integrating spirituality into treatment* (pp. 47–64). Washington, DC: American Psychological Association.
Griffith, J. L. (1986). Employing the god-family relationship in therapy with religious families. *Family Process, 25,* 609–618.
Griffith, J. L., & Griffith, M. E. (1992). Therapeutic change in religious families: Working with the God-construct. In L. A. Burton (Ed.), *Religion and the family: When God helps* (pp. 63–86). New York, NY: Haworth Press.
Griffith, B. A., & Rotter, J. C. (1999). Families and spirituality: Therapists as facilitators. *The Family Journal, 7,* 161–164.
Heermann, M., Wiggins, M. I., & Rutter, P. A. (2007). Creating a space for spiritual practice: Pastoral possibilities with sexual minorities. *Pastoral Psychology, 55,* 711–721.
Hodge, D. R. (2005). Spiritual assessment in marriage and family therapy: A methodological framework for selecting from among six qualitative assessment tools. *Journal of Marital and Family Therapy, 31,* 341–356.
Hoogestraat, T., & Trammel, J. (2003). Spiritual and religious discussions in family therapy: Activities to promote dialogue. *The American Journal of Family Therapy, 31,*413–426.
Imber-Black, E., & Roberts, J. (1992). *Rituals for our times.* New York, NY: Harper Collins.
Karslake, D. (Director). (2007). *For the Bible tells me so* [DVD]. New York, NY: First Run Features.
Laird, J., & Green, R. H. (Eds.). (1996). *Lesbians and gays in families and family therapy.* San Francisco, CA: Jossey-Bass.
Lammers, C., Ireland, M., Resnick, M., & Blum, R. (2000). Infuences on adolescents' decision to postpone onset of sexual intercourse: A survival analysis of virginity among youths aged 13–18 years. *Journal of Adolescent Health, 26,* 42–48.
Lax, W. D. (1996). Narrative, social constructionism, and Buddhism In H. Rosen & K. T. Kuehlwein (Eds.), *Constructing realities: Meaning-making perspectives for psychotherapists* (pp. 195–220). San Francisco, CA: Jossey-Bass.
Lewis, K. G. (1989). The use of color-coded genograms in family therapy. *Journal of Marital and Family Therapy, 15,* 169–176.
Lukoff, D. Turner, R., & Lu, F. (1993). Transpersonal psychology research review: Psychospiritual dimensions of healing. *Journal of Transpersonal Psychology, 25,* 11–28.
Lynch, B. (1996). Religious and spirituality conflicts. In D. Davies & C. Neal (Eds.), *Pink therapy: A guide for counselors and therapists working with lesbian, gay and bisexual clients* (pp. 199–207). Buckingham, England: Open University Press.

Madanes, C. (1990). *Sex, love, and violence: Strategies for transformation.* New York, NY: Norton.

Mahoney, A., Pargament, K. I, Tarakeshwar, N., & Swank, A. B. (2001). Religion in the home in the 1980s and 1990s. A meta-analytic review and conceptual analysis of links between religion, marriage and parenting. *Journal of Family Psychology, 15,* 559–596.

Mahoney, A., & Tarakeshwar, N. (2005). Religion's role in marriage and parenting in daily life and during family crises. In R. F. Paloutzian & C. L. Park (Eds.), *Handbook of the psychology of religion and spirituality.* New York, NY: Guilford Press.

McCullough, M., Rachal, K., Sandage, S., Worthington, E. L., Brown, S., & Hight, T. (1998). Interpersonal forgiving in close relationships: II. Theoretical elaboration and measurement. *Journal of Personality and Social Psychology, 75,* 1586–1603.

McGoldrick, M. & Carter, B. (2003). The family life cycle. In F. Walsh (Ed.), *Normal family processes* (3rd ed., pp. 375–398). New York, NY: Guilford Press.

McGoldrick, M., Gerson, R., & Shellenberger, S. (1996). *Genograms in family assessment* (2nd ed.). New York, NY: Norton.

Neimeyer, R. A. (2001). Meaning reconstruction and the experience of loss. In R. A. Neimeyer (Ed.), *The language of loss: Grief therapy as a process of meaning reconstruction* (pp. 261–292). Washington, DC: American Psychological Association.

Neu, D. L. (1995). Women's empowerment through feminist rituals. In J. Ochshorn & E. Cole (Eds.), *Women's spirituality, women's lives* (pp. 185–200). New York, NY: Haworth.

Nhat Hanh, T. (1976). *The miracle of mindfulness!* Boston, MA: Beacon Press.

Palkovitz, R. (2002). *Involved fathering and men's adult development: Provisional balances.* Hillsdale, NJ: Erlbaum.

Park, C. L., & Fenster, J. A. (2004). Stress-related growth: Predictors and processes. *Journal of Social and Clinical Psychology, 23,* 195–215.

Rajagopal, D., MacKenzie, E., Bailey, C., & Lavizzo-Mourey, R. (2002). The effectiveness of a spiritually-based intervention to alleviate subsyndromal anxiety and minor depression among older adults. *Journal of Religion and health, 41,* 153–166.

Reed, P. G. (1992). An emerging paradigm for the investigation of spirituality in nursing. *Research in Nursing and Health, 15,* 349–357.

Rye, M. S., Pargament, K. I., Ali, M. A., Beck, G. L., Dorff, E. N., … & Williams, J. G. (2000). Religious perspectives on forgiveness. In M. E. McCullough, K. I. Pargament, & C. E. Thoresen (Eds.), *Forgiveness: Theory, research, and practice* (pp.17–40). New York, NY: Guilford Press.

Sanderson, C., & Linehan, M. M. (1999). Acceptance and forgiveness. In W. R. Miller (Ed.), *Integrating spirituality into treatment* (pp. 199–216). Washington, DC: American Psychological Association.

Selvini-Palazzoli, M., Coscolo, L., Cecchin, G., & Prata, G. (1978). A ritualized prescription in family therapy: Odd days and even days. *Journal of Family Counseling, 4,* 3–9.

Shallcross, L. (2009, September). Rewriting the 'rules' of grief. *Counseling Today,* 28–33.

Sherwood, D. A. (1998). Spiritual assessment as a normal part of social work practice: Power to help and power to harm. *Social Work and Christianity, 25,* 80–100.

Sperry, L. (2001). *Spirituality in clinical practice: Incorporating the spiritual dimension in psychotherapy and counseling.* Philadelphia, PA: Temple University Press.

Spring, J. A. (2004). *How can I forgive you? The courage to forgive and the freedom not to.* New York, NY: HarperCollins.

Stanley, S. M., & Markham, H. J. (1992). Assessing commitment in personal relationships. *Journal of Marriage and the Family, 54,* 595–608.

Strawbridge, W. J., Shema, S. J., Cohen, R. D., & Kaplan, G. A. (2001). Religious attendance increases survival by improving and maintaining good health practices, mental health, and stable marriages. *Annals of Behavioral Medicine, 23,* 68–74.

Thompson, N. (2007). Loss and grief: Spiritual aspects. In M. E. Coyle, P. Gilbert, & V. Nicholls (Eds.), *Spirituality,values and mental health: Jewels for the journey.* London, UK: Kingsley.

Tomm, K. (1987). Interventive interviewing: Part II. Reflexive questioning as a means to enable self-healing. *Family Process, 26,* 167–183.

Vitz, P. C. (1992). Narratives and counseling, Part 1: From analysis of the past to stories about it. *Journal of Psychology and Theology, 20,* 11–19.

Walsh, F. (1999). Religion and spirituality: Wellsprings for healing and resilience. In F. Walsh (Ed.), *Spiritual resources in family therapy* (pp. 3–27). New York, NY: Guilford Press.

Weaver, A. J. Samford, J. A., Morgan, v. J., Larson, D. B., Koenig, H. G., & Flannelly, K. J. (2002). A systematic review of research on religion in six primary marriage and family journals: 1995–1999. *American Journal of Family Therapy, 30,* 293–309.

White, M. (1986). Negative explanation, restraint, and double description: A template for family therapy. *Family Process, 25,* 169–184.

White, M. (1988, Winter). The process of questioning: A therapy of literary merit? *Dulwich Centre Newsletter*, 8–14.

White, M., & Epston, D. (1990). *Narrative means to therapeutic ends.* New York, NY: Norton.

Wilcox, W. B. (2002). Religion, convention, and parental involvement. *Journal of Marriage and Family, 64,* 780–792.

Wilcox, W. B., & Wolfinger, N. H. (2007). Then comes marriage? Religion, race and marriage in urban America. *Social Science Research, 36,* 569–589.

Worthington, E. L. (1994). Marriage counseling: A Christian approach. *Journal of Psychology and Christianity, 13,* 166–173.

# 13

# *Religion, Spirituality, and Mental Health*

LOREN TOUSSAINT, JON R. WEBB,
AND WHITNEY KELTNER

This chapter addresses two core questions: (1) do religious and spiritual factors influence mental health, and (2) how can this best be understood in psychotherapy? First, we provide an overview of the convincing evidence showing that religious and spiritual factors are important to mental health. Second, we summarize assessments and clinical strategies for understanding and addressing religious and spiritual issues in psychotherapy. We believe that religious and spiritual issues deserve greater attention in psychotherapy, and we argue that this is consistent with American Psychological Association (APA) guidelines (APA, 2002; 2008). With greater awareness of the evidence and clinical tools available to psychotherapists, religious and spiritual issues can be more effectively addressed in psychotherapy thereby contributing to improved mental health and well-being.

## RELIGIOUS AND SPIRITUAL PERSPECTIVE

Beginning with Freud (1989), modern psychology has consistently dismissed religion, sometimes virulently so. Meaningful segments of the field continue to question the utility of religion and spirituality; conceptually, empirically, and clinically. APA policy (APA, 2008) and ethical standards (APA, 2002) recognize and respect religion and religiousness, but it is unclear how this translates to the field as a whole. Twenty-two years ago, Bergin and Jensen (1990) showed lower levels of belief and religiousness in psychologists as compared to the general public. Eight years later, McMinn, Chaddock, Edwards, Lim, and Campbell (1998) found little mutual collaboration between clergy and psychologists. Just a few years ago, Delaney, Miller, and Bisonó (2007) found that psychologists continue to be substantially less religious than the general public. Indeed, Frazier and Hansen (2009) found a lack of belief in the importance of religious or spiritual issues among psychologists and a reluctance to discuss such issues with clients and during professional consultation. Similarly, O'Connor and Vandenberg (2005) found that psychologists were likely to view less mainstream religious beliefs as pathological.

More than a relative lack of belief, a fundamental disconnect is apparent between psychology and religion for many psychologists. The findings of McMinn, Hathaway, Woods, and Snow (2009) suggested that while the leadership of APA views religion and spirituality as important for diversity sake, the capacity for the application of scientific rigor to religion and spirituality is questionable. Furthermore, negative assumptions regarding the origin, function, and implication of religion and spirituality continue to be promulgated by a subset of psychological scholars (e.g., Carone & Barone, 2001; Henrich, 2009; Lynn, Harvey, & Nyborg, 2009; see also Cummings, O'Donohue, & Cummings, 2009).

Ironically, analogous to religion and spirituality, psychology likewise attempts to address the human condition, to the degree that it is sometimes referred to as the *secular priesthood* (Reisner & Lawson, 1992). As such, we intend to show that scientific rigor has been applied to religion and spirituality and that the findings consistently show that, through evidence-based clinical psychology and psychotherapy, it can be a constructive force in mental health.

## REVIEW OF THEORETICAL AND EMPIRICAL RESEARCH

Through the turn of the millennium, there were 1,200 studies and 400 research reviews in the area of religion, spiritually, and health (Koenig, McCullough, & Larson, 2001). Notably, 724 studies examined religiousness, spirituality, and major *mental health* outcomes, such as depression, anxiety, substance use, suicide, and psychosis. To determine the research activity since Koenig et al.'s review, we searched PsycINFO and PubMed for literature reviews and individual empirical studies. First, we examined PsycINFO using PsycINFO Thesaurus search terms, including "Religion," or "Religiosity," or "Religious Affiliation," AND "Mental Health," or "Mental Disorders," or "Emotional Adjustment." Second, we searched PubMed using the Medical Subject Headings "Religion" or "Spirituality" AND "Mental Disorders/Psychology." In both databases, we searched using hierarchically nested search terms and identified only those studies for which our concepts were a major focus of the work. We located 196 additional studies (27% growth) that have been published. We summarized empirical studies in a format similar to that used by Koenig et al. (2001), classifying by mental health outcome (detailed summary tables available upon request from the first author).

### Empirical Studies Conducted Through 2000

In the top half of Table 13.1, we summarize Koenig et al.'s (2001) review of the quantitative literature published through 2000. Each empirical study reviewed by

Koenig et al. was coded as "NA" representing no association; or "P" for at least one positive association with a better health outcome ($p < .05$); or "(P)" for borderline trend positive association, indirect effect, or qualitative results; or "NG" for at least one negative association with a better health outcome ($p < .05$); or "(NG)" for borderline trend negative association, indirect effect, or qualitative results; or "M" for mixed positive and negative associations with better health outcome ($p < .05$); or "C" for complex results. Similar to Koenig (2009), we examined studies from five different mental health outcomes, including the following: depression, suicide, anxiety, psychotic disorders, and substance use. We tabulated the frequency of "NA," "P," "NG," "M," and "C." We included "(P)" and "(NG)" in the "NA" category because these were relatively infrequent and borderline trends can be difficult to interpret.

In Table 10.1, we find that the majority (74%) of studies conducted through 2000 examining religiousness, spirituality, and mental health show at least one statistically significant positive association. The percentage of studies showing positive associations is 67%, 82%, and 89% for depression, suicide, and substance use, respectively. For anxiety (51%) and psychosis (43%), studies showing positive associations are much less prevalent. In fact, the percentage of studies reporting positive associations and the type of mental health outcome under consideration were related, $\chi^2$ (4, $N$ = 441) = 48.89, $p < .001$; *Cramer's* $\phi$ = .33. This suggests that religiousness and spirituality have a differential impact on different mental health outcomes. Studies vary widely, however, in definition and measurement of religiousness and spirituality and mental health. Hence, some caution is warranted in interpreting this analysis. Despite these limits, a preponderance of empirical studies show that religiousness and spirituality are beneficially connected to mental health.

### Empirical Studies Conducted Between 2001 and 2009

In the lower half of Table 13.1, we summarize 150 empirical studies (34% increase in published literature) on religiousness, spirituality, and mental health. As with studies done through 2000, the majority (59%) of studies published from 2001 to 2009 show at least one positive association between religiousness and spirituality and improved mental health. The percentage of studies with positive associations is 56%, 89%, and 78% for depression, suicide, and substance use, respectively. A lower percentage of studies examining anxiety (49%) and psychosis (39%) as outcomes showed positive associations. Again, the percentage of studies reporting positive associations and the type of mental health outcome under consideration were related, $\chi^2$ (4, $N$ = 150) = 11.24, $p < .05$; *Cramer's* $\phi$ = .27. Much like the body of work through 2000, studies conducted between 2001 and 2009 show the most convincing support of salutatory associations between religiousness, spirituality, and mental health when considering depression, suicide,

**Table 13.1** Outcomes of Empirical Studies: Earliest–2000 and 2001–2009

| | NA (%) | P (%) | NG (%) | M (%) | C (%) | Total (%) |
|---|---|---|---|---|---|---|
| | **Empirical studies earlier than 2000 (*n* = 441 studies)** | | | | | |
| Depression | 18 (16) | 78 (67) | 7 (6) | 12 (10) | 1 (1) | 116 (100) |
| Suicide | 12 (14) | 69 (82) | 1 (1) | 1 (1) | 1 (1) | 84 (100) |
| Anxiety | 20 (26) | 40 (51) | 10 (13) | 5 (6) | 3 (4) | 78 (100) |
| Psychotic disorders | 4 (29) | 6 (43) | 1 (7) | 2 (14) | 1 (7) | 14 (100) |
| Substance use | 10 (7) | 132 (89) | 3 (2) | 3 (2) | 1 (1) | 149 (100) |
| | **Empirical studies between 2001 and 2009 (*n* = 150 studies)** | | | | | |
| Depression | 8 (12) | 37 (56) | 10 (15) | 9 (14) | 2 (3) | 66 (100) |
| Suicide | 1 (11) | 8 (89) | 0 (0) | 0 (0) | 0 (0) | 9 (100) |
| Anxiety | 7 (20) | 17 (49) | 7 (20) | 3 (9) | 1 (2) | 35 (100) |
| Psychotic disorders | 2 (15) | 5 (39) | 4 (30) | 1 (8) | 1 (8) | 13 (100) |
| Substance use | 2 (7) | 21 (78) | 1 (4) | 2 (7) | 1 (4) | 27 (100) |

NA, no association; P, at least one positive association with a better health outcome ($p < .05$); NG, at least one negative association with a better health outcome ($p < .05$); M, mixed positive and negative associations with better health outcome ($p < .05$); C, complex results.

and substance use as the main outcomes. To date, of 591 studies, 413 (70%) have identified at least one statistically significant effect showing a positive benefit of religiousness and spirituality for mental health. Interestingly, in Figure 13.1, we show that the percentage of studies that have positive associations between religiousness and spirituality with depression, anxiety, and

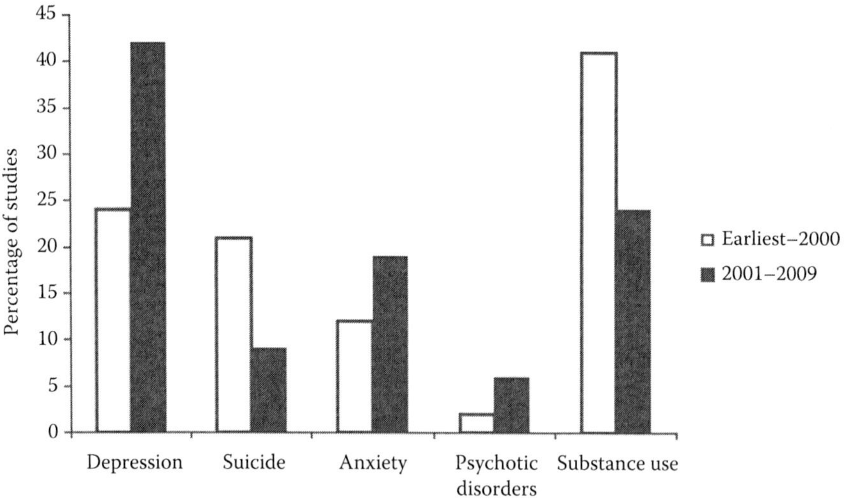


**Figure 13.1** Percentage of studies showing at least one statistically significant effect.

psychotic disorders has grown since 2000, whereas studies identifying positive relationships in suicide and substance use have lagged somewhat. This trend in the recent literature departs in a statistically significant way from the results of Koenig et al.'s (2001) prior review, $\chi^2$ (4, $N$ = 413) = 25.34, $p <$ .001; *Cramer's* $\phi$ = .25.

### Literature Reviews Conducted Between 2001 and 2009

Koenig et al. (2001) have completed exhaustive reviews of the literature encompassing over a century's worth of science. Hence, the *Handbook of Religion and Mental Health* (Koenig, 1998) and the *Handbook of Religion and Health* (Koenig et al., 2001) are required reading for many. These volumes are massive in size and broad in scope, yet it has been several years since their publication. As a brief update, we review the last 9 years of work (2001–2009) as of the time of writing.

#### *Description of Reviews*

Forty-six reviews have been published between 2001 and 2009 reflecting the ongoing interest in distilling robust conclusions in an area in which individual studies sometimes appear more conflictual than consistent. Some psychotherapists (e.g., in private practice) may not have ready access to searchable databases, and consequently, review articles may be an excellent resource. Reviews are briefly summarized in Table 13.2.

Reviews cut across multiple religious and spiritual constructs and mental health conditions. The majority ($n$ = 35) examined broad Christian religiousness and spirituality. Five examined meditation and mindfulness; two focused on Buddhism; two examined religious culture; one included forgiveness, purpose, and religiousness; and one examined indigenous healing (see Table 13.2). Most ($n$ = 28) examined global mental health, including depression, anxiety, and quality of life, or other such issues. Nine focused centrally on substance abuse, three on obsessive-compulsive disorder, and two on trauma and resilience. One review each focused on depression, anxiety, anorexia, and psychotic disorders (see Table 13.2).

#### *Conceptual Models and Mechanisms*

An especially valuable aspect of many of these reviews is the conceptual and theoretical modeling systems proposed to understand the relationship of religiousness and spirituality with mental health. Work by Koenig and Larson (2001), Baetz and Toews (2009), James and Wells (2003), and Levin and Chatters (1998) is especially useful in this regard.

Koenig and Larson (2001) have suggested that the beneficial effects of religiousness and spirituality on mental health may be the result of three things. First, religiousness and spirituality foster positive psychological characteristics, such as optimism, hope, meaning, purpose, and motivation. Together these

**Table 13.2** Summary of Existing Literature Reviews by Year and Mental Health Outcome

| Study Authors (Year) | Main Religious/Spiritual Variables | Main Mental Health Outcome |
|---|---|---|
| Ai & Park (2005) | Religiousness and spirituality | Trauma and resilience |
| Ano & Vasconcelles (2005) | Religious coping | Global mental health |
| Baer (2003) | Mindfulness | Global mental health |
| Baetz & Toews (2009) | Religiousness and spirituality | Global mental health |
| Baumann (2007) | Religiousness | Obsessive-compulsive disorders |
| Bhavsar & Bhugra (2008) | Culture's influence on religiousness | Psychotic disorders |
| Bishop, Monat, Lazarus, & Reevy (2007) | Mindfulness | Health-related stress |
| Calhoun (2007) | Spirituality | Substance use |
| Constantine, Myers, Kindaichi, & Moore (2004) | Indigenous healing practices | Global mental health |
| Cook (2004) | Spirituality | Substance use |
| Dakwar & Levin (2009) | Meditation | Substance use |
| de Bilbao & Giannakopoulos (2005) | Culture's influence on religiousness | Obsessive-compulsive disorders |
| Dew et al. (2008) | Religiousness and spirituality | Global mental health |
| D'Souza & George (2006) | Spirituality | Global mental health |
| Galanter (2006) | Spirituality | Substance use |
| Geppert, Bogenschutz, & Miller (2007) | Religiousness and spirituality | Substance use |
| Griffin & Berry (2003) | Religious and moralistic motifs | Anorexia |
| Grossman, Niemann, Schmidt, & Walach (2004) | Mindfulness | Global mental and physical health |
| Hackney & Sanders (2003) | Religiousness | Global mental health |
| Heath (2006) | Spirituality | Global mental health |
| James & Wells (2003) | Religiousness | Global mental health |
| Kaplar, Wachholtz, & O'Brien (2004) | Religiousness and spirituality | Global mental and physical health |
| Kelly (2008) | Buddhist beliefs | Global mental and physical health |
| Klein & Albani (2007) | Religiousness | Global mental health |
| Koenig (2001) | Religiousness and spirituality | Global mental health |
| Koenig (2009) | Religiousness and spirituality | Global mental health |
| Koenig & Larson (2001) | Religiousness and spirituality | Global mental health |
| Koenig, Larson, & Larson (2001) | Religiousness and spirituality | Health-related stress |
| Kuniwaki (2001) | Spirituality | Substance use |
| Larson & Larson (2003) | Religiousness and spirituality | Health-related stress |
| Longshore, Anglin, & Conner (2009) | Religiousness and spirituality | Substance use |

**Table 13.2** Summary of Existing Literature Reviews by Year and Mental Health Outcome (Continued)

| Study Authors (Year) | Main Religious/Spiritual Variables | Main Mental Health Outcome |
|---|---|---|
| Mabe & Josephson (2004) | Religiousness and spirituality | Global mental health |
| McGee (2008) | Meditation | Global mental health |
| Miller & Bogenschutz (2007) | Spirituality | Substance use |
| Miller & Kelley (2005) | Religiousness and spirituality | Global mental health |
| Moreira-Almeida, Neto, & Koenig (2006) | Religiousness | Global mental health |
| Olson (2003) | Buddhist beliefs | Obsessive-compulsive disorders |
| Sawatzky, Ratner, & Chiu (2005) | Spirituality | Quality of life |
| Schaefer, Blazer, & Koenig (2008) | Religiousness and spirituality | Trauma and resilience |
| Shreve-Neiger & Edelstein (2004) | Religiousness | Anxiety |
| Siegel, Anderman, & Schrimshaw (2001) | Religiousness and spirituality | Health-related stress |
| Smith, Bartz, & Richards (2007) | Spiritually oriented psychotherapies | Global mental health |
| Smith, McCullough, & Poll (2003) | Religiousness | Depression |
| Tonigan (2007) | Spirituality | Substance use |
| Van Dyke & Elias (2007) | Forgiveness, purpose, and religiousness | Global mental health |
| Wong, Rew, & Slaikeu (2006) | Religiousness and spirituality | Global mental health |

characteristics promote a worldview that reduces stress and enhances well-being. Second, religiousness and spirituality promote prosocial virtues (e.g., forgiveness, mercy, compassion) and other-oriented behaviors (e.g., volunteering) that may act as distractions from internal ruminations, enhance interpersonal relationships, and improve well-being by recognizing contributions to others' happiness. Third, religious beliefs and practices facilitate social support, strengthen marital and familial relationships, and broaden support networks.

Baetz and Toews (2009) recently offered explanatory models, including psychological, social, and biological factors. Psychological factors include *religious orientation* (i.e., intrinsic versus extrinsic religious perspective), which acts as a motivational mechanism, and religious coping, which is involved in the development of religious virtues, such as forgiveness, gratitude, optimism, and compassion. Social mechanisms include social control of health behavior. That is, religiousness and spirituality discourage health-compromising behaviors (e.g., substance use) and encourage health-promoting behaviors (e.g., healthy diet). Evidence of biological and genetic factors is scarce, but Baetz and Toews reviewed evidence suggesting that genetics may predispose individuals to higher religiousness and spirituality *and* improved mental health. Biological mechanisms also include *neuroendocrine dysregulation* and *hypothalamic-pituitary adrenal axis* and *sympathetic nervous system* activation (i.e., physiological stress-reaction systems) associated with religiousness and spirituality as well as mental illnesses.

James and Wells (2003) argued that religion plays a role in the development of cognitive schemata and self-regulatory mechanisms. Cognitive schemata are mental frameworks used in the appraisal of stressful life events, and hence, religious individuals reap mental health benefits from the tendencies to interpret stressful life events with more meaning, predictability, and perceived control. Religious behaviors offer a means of cognitive self-regulation through prayer, mediation, and religious rituals that provide distractions and effective coping responses in dealing with rumination, worry, and anxiety.

Levin and Chatters (1998) provided perhaps the most complete set of theoretical causal models. The *suppressor model* posits that poor physical health or general life stress activates increased religiousness and spirituality, which in turn has a direct and indirect suppressing effect on mental illness. Indirect suppressing effects are thought to be largely mediated through social, psychological, and behavioral coping responses. The *distress-deterrent model* suggests that religiousness and spirituality and poor health and life stress have independent effects on mental illness. These independent effects are opposite of one another, and hence this model is also referred to as the *counterbalancing model*. The *prevention model* suggests that religiousness and spirituality have their protective effect on mental illness through all the same indirect mechanisms in the suppressor model and also through a positive influence on physical health. The *moderator model* argues that harmful effects of poor health and life stress on mental health are mitigated by high religiousness and spirituality. The *health effects model* argues that poor health and life stress do not stimulate religiousness and spirituality, but rather interferes with it and any positive direct or indirect effects on mental health.

## CLINICAL IMPLICATIONS

Research on religiousness and spirituality and mental health continues to grow vigorously. Hence, our understanding of the efficacy of religious and spiritual therapeutic techniques will continue to improve. Two conclusions of clinical relevance can be drawn from this literature. First, several dozen reviews and hundreds of empirical studies converge on the same conclusion: Religiousness and spirituality generally help more than they harm. Helpful effects appear most pronounced for depression, suicide, and substance use. Harmful effects, though much less prevalent overall, are more common in anxiety and psychotic disorders. Second, well-developed theoretical and conceptual models explain how religiousness and spirituality can influence mental health. This is crucial because models not only provide explanations for findings but also guide research and treatment.

When using models to guide intervention with clients, psychotherapists can help their religious or spiritual clients find healing through focused, explicit, and purposeful utilization of their belief system. In particular, psychotherapists can help their clients recognize and apply the aspects of their belief systems that promote healthy motivation, socialization, interpretation, and coping. It may be useful to explicitly connect belief systems and models in cases in which assumptions are shared regarding the nature of the relationship between religion, spirituality, and health. One relevant example is from working with people from a variety of relatively *Theist*-based faith communities. Theists believe in a transcendent deity that is actively involved in human affairs. In working with Theists, explicit behavioral guidance can be given and compliance can be expected, because both are more likely to be viewed as coming directly from deity by members of such groups. Hence, it might be more efficient to focus interventions in the context of Baetz and Toews's (2009) work regarding social mechanisms or Levin and Chatters's (1998) work regarding suppression and prevention effects. As such, motivation to comply with clinical recommendations may be facilitated if the recommendations are viewed as consistent with divine guidance. Conversely, it may be more efficient to focus interventions in more naturalistic terms, such as the work of James and Wells's (2003) regarding cognitive schemata and self-regulatory mechanisms or of Baetz and Toews's (2009) regarding biological and genetic factors, when working with people from relatively *Deist*-based faith communities—that is, individuals who believe in a transcendent deity that is uninvolved in human affairs.

The practicing psychotherapist should know that theoretical and empirical evidence supports the generally positive influence of religiousness and spirituality on mental health. Obviously, these conclusions are statistical summaries. Psychotherapists deal with individuals, and thus they must assess individuals carefully to see whether religion plays a role in the life of the client and, if so, whether it is having positive or negative effects (or mixed). At a minimum, however, this evidence suggests that the psychotherapist can approach religious and spiritual assessment with an open mind, looking for possible positive involvement of religion and spirituality in the person's mental health.

## CLINICAL ASSESSMENTS

A number of methods can be used to gain information about the religious and spiritual domains of clients' lives. Some clients may initiate discussion of religious or spiritual topics spontaneously, whereas informal prompts can be helpful for others. Formal, systematic techniques and assessments also can be used.

### Informal Discussion

Informal approaches may utilize a variety of simple icebreakers or straightforward questions. For instance:

1. "Can you tell me a bit about your religious and spiritual beliefs?"
2. "How important is religion and spirituality to you?"
3. "Are there ways in which you could see your religious or spiritual beliefs helping or hurting you in the tough times you are presently facing?"
4. "Do you find comfort in your religion or spirituality?"
5. "Have your views regarding religion and spirituality always been the same?"

Questions of this nature may help clients feel more comfortable offering their views on religion and spirituality and can help the psychotherapist ethically incorporate these issues into psychotherapy. The responses to the first two questions will inform the psychotherapist of the appropriateness of probing further. For instance, for a client who has few religious or spiritual beliefs or who indicates that religion or spirituality is not important for him or her, questions 3–5 may be largely inappropriate and even may be viewed as disrespectful.

### Formal Structured Discussion

Formal approaches to understanding religiousness and spirituality may require examination of several keys areas during intake and treatment. Koenig and Larson (2001) reviewed some important issues to address:

1. What, if any, is the client's religious affiliation? Given differences in beliefs across religious traditions, this context might be crucial to successfully incorporating religious and spiritual issues into psychotherapy.
2. Does the client believe in God(s), and what is the client's God image(s) (see Moriarty & Davis, Chapter 6, this volume)? For example, is God a benevolent, loving being or an angry and punitive judge-like figure? Understanding God image(s) helps in understanding how a client approaches religious and spiritual coping (see Krumrei & Rosmarin, Chapter 10, this volume).
3. What was the client's childhood or adolescent religious experience like (see Desrosiers, Chapter 2, this volume)? Did parents strictly prescribe religion or spirituality as a part of family life? Or, were perspectives and feelings of children taken into consideration in an environment of supportive religious and spiritual encouragement? Does the client view his or her religious upbringing favorably or regretfully (see Wiggins, Chapter 12, this volume)?
4. What role do religion and spirituality play in the client's present-day life? Are they important? Do they provide meaning and purpose, or

are they merely social functions (see Slattery & Park, Chapter 8, this volume)? Are they part of the client's identity?

5. Are religion and spirituality used to cope, and how do they serve this function (see Krumrei & Rosmarin, Chapter 10, this volume)?
6. Does the client belong to a religious community? If so, how is the community viewed? Is it supportive and engaging or condemning and judgmental? What activities is the client involved in?
7. What is the client's relationship with clergy like? Does the client know the clergy and feel accepted, cared for, and supported? This may suggest types of support available and provide insight into other beliefs such as God image(s) and perceptions of the religious community.
8. Do specific religious or spiritual struggles potentially influence mental health, and how open is the client to addressing these issues (see Murray-Swank & Murray-Swank, Chapter 9, this volume)?
9. Is the client concerned that psychotherapy will not be consistent with his or her beliefs (see Slattery & Park, Chapter 8, this volume)? Or does the client believe that simply going to psychotherapy reflects self-centeredness, a weakness in faith, or lack of belief in God's power to heal?
10. Do the client's religious and spiritual beliefs affect their acceptance and adherence to psychotherapeutic or medical regimens?

The 10 issues are some of the key issues involved in a structured discussion of religiousness and spirituality in psychotherapy. Nonetheless, other structured approaches also exist. For instance, Richards and Bergin (2005) provided a two-tiered ecumenical approach. In this method, the psychotherapist initially gets basic descriptive information from the client about religious and spiritual issues and then, on the basis of this information, chooses more complete assessment and treatment options. Structured approaches offer an efficient and effective means to collect more detailed information that allows one to plan and implement religiousness and spirituality into psychotherapy.

### Assessment Instruments

A comprehensive compendium of existing religiousness and spirituality measures is Hill and Hood's (1999) *Measures of Religiosity,* which includes descriptions, reviews, and complete items for 100 different measures. Although an authoritative reference collection, it was not specifically designed to offer measures that are useful in the clinical setting. Clinically useful measures must meet four criteria. First, measures must be brief. Second, measures must possess exceptional *reliability* (i.e., minimal measurement error). Third, they must be *valid* (i.e., accurate) in clinical samples. Fourth, measures must have psychotherapeutic utility. We review three measures that meet these criteria below.

The Religious Commitment Inventory (RCI–10; Worthington et al., 2003) is a brief, ecumenical screening instrument used to determine levels of commitment to one's chosen religion. Worthington et al. have evaluated its performance in secular and Christian college students; community adults; single and married individuals; Christians, Buddhists, Muslims, Hindus, and nonreligious individuals; and psychotherapists and clients at secular and Christian counseling centers. Norms are provided based on almost 2,000 individuals. Notably, the RCI–10 has been used with more than 400 clients and more than 100 counselors (Wade, Worthington, & Vogel, 2007; Worthington et al., 2003). With high reliability (coefficient alphas > .90), a length of only 10 items, and easy administration and scoring, the RCI–10 is an ideal measure for use in psychotherapy. As religious commitment is unlikely to change much over the course of psychotherapy, we recommend the RCI–10 as a strong *screening* measure but do not recommend assessing commitment as an outcome variable.

The Index of Core Spiritual Experiences (INSPIRIT; Kass, Friendman, Leserman, Zuttermeister, & Benson, 1991) is a seven-item measure of one's personal conviction of God's existence and the perception of a deep connection to God's presence within. It is specifically designed to measure spiritual healing in psychotherapy and is suitable for use with secular, religious, or spiritual clients. Originally, the INSPIRIT was validated in 83 outpatients of a hospital-based behavioral medicine program. In this sample, the INSPIRIT showed high reliability (coefficient alpha = .90) and strong *concurrent validity* (i.e., associations with similar variables measured at the same time) with purpose in life, life satisfaction, health-promoting attitudes, and medical symptoms. Further validity has been demonstrated in higher scores on the INSPIRIT by meditating clients compared with nonmediating client controls. More recently, the INSPIRIT has been used with clients seeking treatment for opiate and cocaine abuse enrolled in a 12-week outpatient treatment program (Heinz, Epstein, & Preston, 2007). Evidence in support of the INSPIRIT's validity was offered in a number of associations with key substance abuse treatment outcomes.

The Purpose in Life Test (PIL; Crumbaugh & Henrion, 1988; McIntosh, 1999) is a 20-item measure designed to assess meaning and purpose in one's life. The PIL is conceptually grounded in Frankl's (1955) work on logotherapy, and as a result, the measure reflects the belief that finding meaning in one's life is a significant spiritual motive. The measure consists of three parts, but the first part is the most efficient and useful. Parts 2 and 3 involve sentence completion and essay writing, which potentially could be useful but is difficult to score and interpret. The 20-item scale provides a reliable (split-half reliability = .90) and valid assessment of one's search for meaning and purpose in life. Validity has been demonstrated in predicting membership to clinical versus nonclinical and inmate versus non-inmate groups. Validation and norming has been done in multiple samples, including undergraduates, a variety of outpatient psychiatric patients, and hospitalized alcoholics.

Dozens of measures of religiousness and spirituality have been developed. In our review of more than 100 measures, only these three (RCI–10, INSPIRIT, and PIL) met all four of our criteria for clinical utility. Although many measures of religiousness and spirituality are brief and possess strong reliability and potentially could be useful in psychotherapy, few have been designed specifically for psychotherapeutic use and validated in clinical samples. Assessments for use in psychotherapy can simply be hard to find and psychotherapists should exercise caution in choosing appropriate measures. Nonetheless, these three measures provide accurate and clinically relevant information with exceptional efficiency.

## CLINICAL STRATEGIES

Many authoritative books, chapters, and scientific papers have been published in the past decade regarding the interface of religious and spiritual issues with mental health and psychotherapy. Such efforts have involved the development of specific stand-alone theory and technique, integration with traditional or contemporary theory and technique, or application of traditional or contemporary theory and technique to religious or spiritual issues and clients (e.g., Aten & Leach, 2008; Miller, 1999; Nielsen, Johnson, & Ellis, 2001; Pargament, 2007; Richards & Bergin, 2000, 2005; Shafranske, 1996; Sperry & Shafranske, 2005). The bottom line in working with religious and spiritual issues and clients is to approach the client with genuine sensitivity, respect, and flexibility and to recognize that numerous resources exist to educate and assist psychotherapists in this important component of their work.

The following discussion of clinical strategies will address two broad topics. First, we will briefly discuss several issues specifically related to religious or spiritual clients, which will likely have bearing on the development and maintenance of the psychotherapeutic relationship. Second, we will briefly introduce the issue of theoretical conceptualization, particularly as it pertains to the case study that follows.

### Psychotherapeutic Considerations

#### *Development of the Psychotherapeutic Relationship*

Given the reality of religion as culture (Cohen, 2009) and the influence of religious culture on psychotherapist and client worldviews (see Richards & Bergin, 2005), it is imperative for psychotherapists to understand accurately and reasonably at least three perspectives (in order of relative importance) regarding the client's belief system. First, psychotherapists need to understand the point of view of the client regarding the nature of their espoused belief system, including the client's personal interpretation and application of these beliefs. Second, psychotherapists need to consider the normatively accepted expression(s) of the espoused belief system as expressed by the belief system itself, if it is formal and structured. Third, the psychotherapist should be aware of responsible and objective third-party alternative descriptions and interpretations of the client's belief system. Unfortunately, competing belief systems may not always characterize one another in a responsible manner, and psychotherapists should be cautious and cognizant of this. To the extent that the psychotherapist can gain insight into each of these areas, it is possible to prioritize the relevance and importance of religious and spiritual issues to the client's overall mental health and well-being.

Psychotherapists are cautioned never to impose religious or spiritual interventions or personal beliefs on clients (see APA, 2002, 2008; Richards & Bergin, 2005). The degree to which a psychotherapist identifies with his or her own religious or spiritual belief system or lack thereof in his or her professional role is important and worth contemplation. A psychotherapist's belief status need not match the client's; however, matching belief status might be helpful to and preferred by the client. Hence, many mental health care professionals are asked whether they are Christian psychotherapists, yet a difference exists between describing oneself as a Christian psychotherapist and a psychotherapist who is Christian. Moreover, this question and distinction are applicable and adaptable to all belief systems, including atheist, agnostic, religious, spiritual, monotheism, polytheism, existentialism, and others. The manner in which this question is answered, may reflect the level to which psychotherapists are able to service ethically and efficaciously the needs of their diverse clientele.

Similarly, psychotherapists are encouraged to explicitly distinguish between psychotherapy and religious or spiritual counseling (see Pargament, 2007). Although both fields seek to address the human condition and can have considerable overlap, each field has its own specific purview and expertise. We recommend that psychotherapists deliberately discuss and establish an appropriate boundary with their clients so it is abundantly clear that the psychotherapist is not acting in a dual role and not functioning as or taking the place of the client's clergy. As such, the psychotherapist's role is not to absolve sin or adjudicate doctrine, but to provide a safe, professional, and empirical psychotherapeutic environment to facilitate mental health and emotional healing, while also ethically, competently, and appropriately incorporating the religiousness and spirituality of the client.

### *Maintenance of the Psychotherapeutic Relationship*

Preserving an appropriate psychotherapist–clergy boundary with religious or spiritual clients likely will be a continuous process during psychotherapy. Some clients may seek to engage the psychotherapist in a variety of clinically inappropriate theological debates, including doctrinal topics. The content of such debates may range in nature from unorthodox to otherwise benign and mainstream to radically and inflexibly fundamentalist. Regardless of content, the psychotherapist, always maintaining appropriate professional boundaries, must seek to facilitate reasonable, constructive, adaptive, and functional client-based exploration of religious and spiritual issues in the service of the mental health of the client and the safety of society. Take, for example, a religious or spiritual client engaging in excessive alcohol use or sexually permissive behavior. Rather than the psychotherapist stating that these actions are against the client's religion, it would be more appropriate to (a) explore how these behaviors fit within the client's belief system, and (b) commence with standard psychotherapeutic interventions for compulsive or addictive behaviors.

Additionally, the psychotherapist must always be aware of potential issues and processes related to countertransference, utilize professional consultation, and refer when necessary (see APA, 2002, 2008; Nielsen et al., 2001). As another example, consider a religious or spiritual client struggling with sexual identity or sexual orientation issues who is considering homosexual marriage. If the psychotherapist is unable to objectively explore, facilitate, and support client-based decisions and solutions, a referral to another psychotherapist is imperative. If a psychotherapist is aware of this personal bias and difficulty beforehand, he or she should not accept the individual as a client but refer from the outset. Furthermore, the broad necessity for awareness, consultation, and referral exists regardless of the interaction between the biases of the psychotherapist and the biases of the client. In this example, just as the psychotherapist who is unable to ethically treat a religious or spiritual client whose decision is to pursue an alternative lifestyle must refer, so too must the psychotherapist refer if he or she feels unable to ethically treat a client who chooses to continue a traditional lifestyle. The job, as a psychotherapist, is to facilitate the mental health and well-being of autonomous individuals.

Last, when theological topics seem unavoidable, rather than discuss theology per se, it likely will be helpful to focus on the client's broader conceptualization of the issue(s) at hand. As one example, a religious or spiritual client may be struggling with the nature of sin, including defining what it is and is not. Rather than debate the theology of sin and the doctrinal definition and identification of sin(s) (the purview of clergy), the psychotherapist likely will be helpful by focusing on the client's thought processes relative to sin in the context of the client's belief system. For instance, for a Christian, it may be helpful to discuss (a) the difference between mistakes and sins, including the issue of whether Jesus made any mistakes (e.g., Did He ever stub His toe?), (b) whether God functionally expects humans to be perfect (sinless or mistake-free), and (c) whether there are functional, practical, consequential, and other differences in sin (e.g., Is there a difference between swearing and adultery?). Although such issues may approach adjudication of doctrine or absolution of sin, they fundamentally differ. That is, they allow the client the freedom to clarify personal understanding and application of debatable issues within their belief system. This can be especially useful because thought processes themselves, rather than the theological content, may be leading to emotional difficulty.

### Theoretical Conceptualization

The psychotherapeutic needs of religious or spiritual clients can be met through many, if not all, mainstream theoretical models of psychotherapy, particularly when psychotherapists follow the ethical guidelines and policies of the APA (2002; 2008) regarding respect and valuation of culture and diversity, including seeking consultation and competency training when appropriate. We primarily utilize cognitive-behavioral (CB) theory and therapy in the following clinical conceptualization and discussion. Nevertheless, we recommend that psychotherapists apply theories to a client, rather than clients to a theory. In other words, rather than pushing a particular theoretical approach on a client, psychotherapists are encouraged to allow their client(s), or the needs of the client, to pull for specific theoretical techniques from the psychotherapist. As such, psychotherapists must have basic competence in a variety of theories and techniques to avoid this, so-called *Procrustean bed approach* (i.e., rigid adherence to an arbitrary standard; see Hoffman & Rosman, 2003). Our focus on CB theory and therapy is necessitated by space constraints. Nevertheless, it is important to realize that many different theories and techniques, in actuality, may be quite similar in underlying concept and principle, with differences arising from nuance in language and application (Shedler, 2010; Webb & Trautman, 2010).

Theoretical and empirical connections exist between religiousness, spirituality, and mental health, particularly in the realm of cognitions, emotions, and behavior. It follows that CB concepts and techniques, although not the only appropriate approach, are warranted to facilitate successful and efficient treatment. In particular, the symptoms of depression and anxiety often arise and continue as a function of dysfunctional thought processes. Beck (Beck, Rush, Shaw, & Emery, 1979) has described the *cognitive triad* as the tendency for humans to become focused on negative perceptions of themselves, their experiences, and their future. Ellis (Ellis & Dryden, 1997) has described the *irrational* (i.e., self-defeating) nature of *demands and expectations* (i.e., in absolutistic terms) that humans tend to place on themselves, others, and the world. The bottom line in CB therapy is the basic, inescapable, intertwined connection between thoughts, emotions, and behaviors and the commonly accepted evidence-based view that modification of thoughts has great power in the subsequent modification of emotion and behavior. When employing such concepts and techniques with religious and spiritual clients (see the case study), psychotherapists must be careful to explain that the object of therapeutic intervention is not to change thoughts, per se, but to change thought processes. That is, the goal is not to change thoughts, beliefs, or values, but to modify thought processes or *how* clients think about what they think about—*metacognitions*.

For many religious and spiritual clients struggling with emotional difficulties, once the psychotherapist has a clear multiperspective understanding of the clients' belief system, it becomes apparent that many struggle with conceptions of deity and self. Many such clients express discrepancies between their personal perceptions of deity and self as compared with actual doctrinal conceptions of deity and what it means to be human. Often times, many cognitive distortions become apparent to the client through the recognition of the simple, yet profound, theme that the positive, optimistic, *reasonable, and rational* interpretation and application of the client's belief system applies only to others. That is, according to the client, it applies to others, but *not the client*. In addition to the individual cognitive distortions related to deity and self, each type of distortion often can lead to the other. That is, distorted views of self often arise *from* or *lead to* distorted views of others, including God. These assumptions likely are not in the client's explicit awareness, but they are automatic thoughts until identified through careful and reasoned exploration with the psychotherapist. Once identified, logic and consistent disputation can reverse their deleterious effects on mental health.

## CASE STUDY

A myriad of topics and issues may arise in the context of incorporating and addressing religiousness and spirituality in psychotherapy. The following case study briefly illustrates and addresses the two broad, yet primary, concerns regarding conceptions of deity and self.

Leeza, a 43-year-old married Caucasian woman (demographic and case-oriented details have been modified to protect the identity of this individual), presented for psychotherapy complaining of anxiety and depression. She described growing up as the youngest child in an emotionally abusive household, including parental alcoholism. Although raised with basic Christian values, she reported that during her teens and early 20s she rebelled and became sexually promiscuous and dependent on drugs and alcohol. While reporting a lifelong and consistent interest in spirituality, she reported that in her late-20s she became interested in religion and felt directed by God to convert to a conservative Christian denomination. Through her new found faith commitment, she reported that she was able to change her lifestyle, including obtaining and maintaining sexual- and substance-related sobriety. Shortly after her conversion and subsequent lifestyle modifications, Leeza married a member of her congregation following a relatively brief courtship. It was agreed that Leeza would be a stay-at-home mother, and the couple quickly had four children. Leeza's husband had great difficulty maintaining gainful employment, and the couple consistently struggled to make financial ends meet.

When she presented for therapy, Leeza complained of intense periods of uncontrollable anxiety related to confusion and anger about her familial relationships. She expressed intense frustration and disillusionment about the nature of her relationships with each member of her family of origin. She felt that each emotionally abused her and, in turn, should have protected her from the other(s). She reported that, more often than not, these types of relationships continued to this day and that she was not treated with respect or basic decency by anyone in her family. Leeza also expressed growing concern about the nature of her relationship with her husband. That is, she reported being frustrated that she must sacrifice her interests for him to be happy and reasonable in their relationship. As a result, she expressed feeling that she had lost her identity.

Once a clear multiperspective understanding of Leeza's belief system was developed, it was apparent that she, like many religious and spiritual clients, struggled with difficulties related to her conceptions of deity and self. This understanding was developed through genuine and respectful informal questions about her personal understanding, interpretation, and application of her belief system. This was coupled with the psychotherapist's research and understanding of the belief system. Given her conversion experience as an adult, further understanding was developed from formal questions about differences between early and current: (a) religious or spiritual experiences with parents and clergy, and (b) manifestations of religiousness or spirituality in the context of importance, meaning, purpose, and coping.

The discrepancies between Leeza's personal perceptions of deity and self as compared with the actual doctrinal conceptions became apparent through a simple exercise. The psychotherapist had Leeza openly and deliberately contemplate the religious and spiritual suggestions she would offer a friend or loved one hypothetically going through the same experiences. Through this exercise, Leeza was able to clearly see that she held a double standard when it came to the application of her belief system to others versus to herself. For example, God is understanding, loving, forgiving, and merciful to everyone, except to her. Similarly, everyone is loveable and worthwhile, even though they make mistakes, except her.

Although the exercise was simple, the process and outcome was not easily accomplished. Leeza resisted admitting that she felt differently regarding her view of herself and her relationship with God. Nevertheless, it became apparent that while she intellectually realized that God loved and accepted her, she did not emotionally experience or allow it. Being careful to avoid or prevent iatrogenic client recognition of this process, the psychotherapist appropriately focused Leeza's attention on recurring instances when she expressed differences in her perceptions and conceptions of deity and self as applied to herself versus others. The psychotherapist also worked to normalize discrepancies based on Western Hemisphere cultural norms and expectations, especially that individuals must be resourceful, self-sufficient, and independent to the point of holding oneself to a higher standard. Similarly, it was discussed that this higher standard leads to harsher self-judgment not only relative to how one judges others, but also in expectations of how God judges oneself.

Ironically, much of the progress was made by seeking to separate Leeza's sense of worth from her behavior. In short, growth resulted from developing an objective sense of self-worth. Although she was able to recognize and describe objective, nonbehaviorally based worth in others, initially she was unable to do so for herself. After repeated experiences with this contradiction, appropriately and constructively identified by the psychotherapist, Leeza was able to personally recognize and resonate with this fundamental difficulty and discrepancy in her conceptions of deity and self.

Through a more accurate application of her belief system to herself, including an accurate conception of deity, Leeza was able to develop a more accurate conception of self. Growth also occurred in her sense of self-worth, which in turn lead to increased self-confidence. Ultimately, she was able to restore her sense of identity, thereby meaningfully reducing her symptoms of anxiety and depression through the development and maintenance of healthy boundaries with her husband and family of origin. By viewing and accepting herself intellectually, emotionally, and spiritually as the offspring of a deity who loves, respects, and values her unconditionally, equally, and without preference, Leeza was able to view herself as inherently and objectively valuable and worthwhile. Armed with views that were more consistent with the actualities of her belief system, she was empowered to recognize and pursue her desires, preferences, and standards regarding healthy and constructive intra- and interpersonal relationships and quality of life. No longer was she at the mercy of others' unreasonable attitudes and behaviors. With her rediscovered (perhaps newfound) belief system, congruent sense of self, and relationship with deity, recognizing and pursuing her healthy and constructive desires, preferences, and standards was no longer a risk-laden fast-track to rejection and despair. Instead, she found a well-lit path of opportunity for unbridled growth and satisfaction. This shift allowed Leeza to move away from reacting to the limitations imposed by imperfect others and toward the possibilities bestowed by deity. In sum, it can be quite useful to focus on distorted conceptions of deity and self, particularly as it relates to inconsistencies between clients' personal perceptions and the ideals of many belief systems.

## CONCLUSION

This chapter provides an overview of the research conducted to date on connections between religiousness, spirituality, and mental health. Several dozen literature reviews and hundreds of individual empirical studies converge on the same conclusion. Religiousness and spirituality typically have salutary associations with mental health. Some of the best empirical studies even suggest that religiousness and spirituality play a causal role in creating improved mental health. This is especially convincing evidence and suggests that religious and spiritual factors may be addressed in psychotherapy with good effect. To help in this regard, we reviewed key assessment methods and clinical strategies that are available and effective in incorporating clients' religious and spiritual issues into psychotherapy. Undoubtedly, psychotherapists reading this chapter could enumerate many cases in which religious and spiritual issues were at the center of client struggles. We highlight one such case in the context of cognitive distortions relative to conceptions of deity and self and conclude that effectively dealing with these types of issues can result in clinically significant improvements in mental health. With continued attention to religious and spiritual issues and their connection to mental health, scientists and psychotherapists alike will grow in their understanding of how and when to best address these factors with clients and how religiousness and spirituality can best promote mental health.

## CHAPTER SUMMARY

### Literature Review

- Out of 591 studies conducted through 2009, 413 (70%) have identified at least one statistically significant effect showing a positive benefit of religiousness and spirituality for mental health.
- Evidence of the positive benefits of religiousness and spirituality for mental health are more consistently found when examining depression, suicide, and substance use as outcomes.
- A great percentage of recent studies (2001–2009) show positive benefits for depression, anxiety, and psychotic disorders, whereas older work (earliest–2000) shows a greater percentage of studies showing favorable outcomes in suicide and substance use.

### Clinical Implications

- Evidence supports the importance of addressing religious and spiritual issues in therapy.
- Theoretical and conceptual work provides excellent explanations for how the effects of religious and spiritual factors are conveyed to mental health.

### Clinical Assessments

- Formal structured discussion topics include the following: affiliation, God-image, childhood experience, current religious importance, religious coping, views of religious community, relationship with clergy, religious struggle, religious or spiritual therapy preferences, and religious beliefs and medical care.
- Self-report instruments include the following: Religious Commitment Inventory–10 (RCI–10); Index of Core Spiritual Experiences (INSPIRIT); and Purpose in Life Test (PIL).

Clinical Strategies

- Genuine cultural sensitivity, respect, and flexibility.
- Multiperspective understanding of clients' belief system: (a) client, (b) belief system, and (c) third-party.
- Metacognitions regarding self, others, and the world, including conceptions of deity and self.

## CLINICAL APPLICATION QUESTIONS

1. Are you a religious or spiritual psychotherapist or a psychotherapist who is religious or spiritual or neither?
2. What is the best way to assess religiousness and spirituality for *this* client?
   Informal initial discussion may always be most appropriate. If the client is religious or spiritual and continued discussion is warranted, is the client comfortable discussing personal religiousness or spirituality or is the client psychologically minded about the topic? If *yes*, continued informal discussion may be most appropriate. If *no*, formal discussion may be most appropriate. If so, it may be helpful to preface the discussion with words to the effect of, "I/we ask the following sorts of questions of every client as a means of gaining the most well-rounded understanding of your background and history as possible." Does the client seem to be struggling with issues of basic belief and connection, commitment, or spiritual purpose and meaning (use INSPIRT assessment tool). Is the psychotherapist having difficulty pinpointing this (use RCI 10)? Or is the psychotherapist interested in tracking this (use the PIL Test)?
3. Is the client's manifestation of religiousness and spirituality having a positive or negative impact? If positive, how can you help maintain and generalize such effects? If negative, how can you reframe it into more constructive activities (e.g., coping, negative to positive)?
4. Is the client engaging in cognitive distortions relative to their belief system?

## SUGGESTED READINGS AND RESOURCES

American Psychological Association. (Producer). (2005). *Psychotherapy video series: Spirituality* [DVD]. Available from http://www.apa.org/pubs/videos/index.aspx

Aten, J. D., & Leach, M. M. (Eds.). (2008). *Spirituality and the therapeutic process: A comprehensive resource from intake to termination.* Washington, DC: American Psychological Association.

Hill, P. C., & Hood, R. W. Jr. (1999). *Measures of religiosity.* Birmingham, AL: Religious Education Press.

Koenig, H. G. (Ed.). (1998). *Handbook of religion and mental health.* San Diego: CA: Academic Press.

Koenig, H. G. (2002). *Spirituality in patient care: Why, how, when, and what.* Philadelphia, PA: Templeton Foundation Press.

Koenig, H. G., McCullough, M. E., & Larson, D. B. (2001). *Handbook of religion and health.* New York, NY: Oxford University Press.

Miller, W. R. (Ed.). (1999). *Integrating spirituality into treatment: Resources for practitioners.* Washington, DC: American Psychological Association.

Nielsen, S. L., Johnson, W. B., & Ellis, A. (2001). *Counseling and psychotherapy with religious persons: A rational emotive behavior therapy approach.* Mahwah, NJ: Erlbaum.

Pargament, K. I. (2007). *Spiritually integrated psychotherapy: Understanding and addressing the sacred.* New York, NY: Guilford Press.
Richards, P. S., & Bergin, A. E. (Eds.). (2000). *Handbook of psychotherapy and religious diversity.* Washington, DC: American Psychological Association.
Richards, P. S., & Bergin, A. E. (2005). *A spiritual strategy for counseling and psychotherapy* (2nd ed.). Washington, DC: American Psychological Association.
Shafranske, E. P. (Ed.). (1996). *Religion and the clinical practice of psychology.* Washington, DC: American Psychological Association.
Sperry, L., & Shafranske, E. P. (Eds.). (2005). *Spiritually oriented psychotherapy.* Washington, DC: American Psychological Association.

## REFERENCES

Ai, A. L., & Park, C. L. (2005). Possibilities of the positive following violence and trauma: Informing the coming decade of research. *Journal of Interpersonal Violence, 20*(2), 242–250.
American Psychological Association. (2002). Ethical principles of psychologists and code of conduct. *American Psychologist, 57*(12), 1060–1073.
American Psychological Association. (2008). Resolution on religious, religion-based, and/or religion-derived prejudice. *American Psychologist, 63*(5), 431–434.
Ano, G. G., & Vasconcelles, E. B. (2005). Religious coping and psychological adjustment to stress: A meta-analysis. *Journal of Clinical Psychology, 61*(4), 461–480.
Aten, J. D., & Leach, M. M. (Eds.). (2008). *Spirituality and the therapeutic process: A comprehensive resource from intake to termination.* Washington, DC: American Psychological Association.
Baer, R. A. (2003). Mindfulness training as a clinical intervention: A conceptual and empirical review. *Clinical Psychology: Science and Practice, 10*(2), 125–143.
Baetz, M., & Toews, J. (2009). Clinical implications of research on religion, spirituality, and mental health. *Canadian Journal of Psychiatry, 54*(5), 292–301.
Baumann, K. (2007). Obsessive-compulsive disorders and religion in contemporary perspective. *Fortschritte der Neurologie, Psychiatrie, 75*(10), 587–592.
Beck, A. T., Rush, A. J., Shaw, B. F., & Emery, G. (1979). *Cognitive therapy of depression.* New York, NY: Guilford Press.
Bergin, A. E., & Jensen, J. P. (1990). Religiosity of psychotherapists: A national survey. *Psychotherapy, 27,* 3–7.
Bhavsar, V., & Bhugra, D. (2008). Religious delusions: Finding meanings in psychosis. *Psychopathology, 41*(3), 165–172.
Bishop, S. R., Monat, A., Lazarus, R. S., & Reevy, G. (2007). *What we really know about mindfulness-based stress reduction.* Westport, CT: Praeger/Greenwood.
Calhoun, F. J. (2007). Developmental research on alcohol and spirituality: What we know and what we don't know. *Southern Medical Journal, 100*(4), 427–429.
Carone, D. A., Jr., & Barone, D. F. (2001). A social cognitive perspective on religious beliefs: Their functions and impact on coping and psychotherapy. *Clinical Psychology Review, 21,* 989–1003.
Cohen, A. B. (2009). Many forms of culture. *American Psychologist, 64*(3), 194–204.
Constantine, M. G., Myers, L. J., Kindaichi, M., & Moore, J. L., III. (2004). Exploring indigenous mental health practices: The roles of healers and helpers in promoting well-being in people of color. *Counseling and Values, 48*(2), 110–125.
Cook, C. C. (2004). Addiction and spirituality. *Addiction, 99*(5), 539–551.

Crumbaugh, J., & Henrion, R. (1988). The PIL Test: Administration, interpretation, uses theory and critique. *The International Forum for Logotherapy: Journal of Search for Meaning 11*, 76–88.

Cummings, N., O'Donohue, W., & Cummings, J. (Eds.). (2009). *Psychology's war on religion.* Phoenix, AZ: Zeig, Tucker, & Theisen.

Dakwar, E., & Levin, F. R. (2009). The emerging role of meditation in addressing psychiatric illness, with a focus on substance use disorders. *Harvard Review of Psychiatry, 17*(4), 254–267.

de Bilbao, F., & Giannakopoulos, P. (2005). Effect of religious culture on obsessive compulsive disorder symptomatology. A transcultural study in monotheistic religions. *Revue Méd Suisse, 1*(43), 2818–2821.

Delaney, H. D., Miller, W. R., & Bisonó, A. M. (2007). Religiosity and spirituality among psychologists: A survey of clinician members of the American Psychological Association. *Professional Psychology: Research and Practice, 38*(5), 538–546.

Dew, R. E., Daniel, S. S., Armstrong, T. D., Goldston, D. B., Triplett, M. F., & Koenig, H. G. (2008). Religion/spirituality and adolescent psychiatric symptoms: A review. *Child Psychiatry and Human Development, 39*(4), 381–398.

D'Souza, R., & George, K. (2006). Spirituality, religion and psychiatry: Its application to clinical practice. *Australasian Psychiatry, 14*(4), 408–412.

Ellis, A., & Dryden, W. (1997). *The practice of rational emotive behavior therapy* (2nd ed.). New York, NY: Springer.

Frankl, V. E. (1955). *The doctor and the soul: From psychotherapy to logotherapy.* New York, NY: Knopf.

Frazier, R. E., & Hansen, N. D. (2009). Religious/Spiritual psychotherapy behaviors: Do we do what we believe to be important? *Professional Psychology: Research and Practice, 40*(1), 81–87.

Freud, S. (1989). The future of an illusion. In P. Gay (Ed.), *The Freud reader* (pp. 685–722). New York, NY: Norton.

Galanter, M. (2006). Spirituality and addiction: A research and clinical perspective. *American Journal of Addictions, 15*(4), 286–292.

Geppert, C., Bogenschutz, M. P., & Miller, W. R. (2007). Development of a bibliography on religion, spirituality and addictions. *Drug and Alcohol Review, 26*(4), 389–395.

Griffin, J., & Berry, E. M. (2003). A modern day holy anorexia? Religious language in advertising and anorexia nervosa in the West. *European Journal of Clinical Nutrition, 57*(1), 43–51.

Grossman, P., Niemann, L., Schmidt, S., & Walach, H. (2004). Mindfulness-based stress reduction and health benefits: A meta-analysis. *Journal of Psychosomatic Research, 57*(1), 35–43.

Hackney, C. H., & Sanders, G. S. (2003). Religiosity and mental health: A meta-analysis of recent studies. *Journal for the Scientific Study of Religion, 42*(1), 43–55.

Heath, C. D. (2006). A womanist approach to understanding and assessing the relationship between spirituality and mental health. *Mental Health, Religion & Culture, 9*(2), 155–170.

Heinz, A., Epstein, D., & Preston, K. (2007). Spiritual/religious experiences and in-treatment outcome in an inner-city program for heroin and cocaine dependence. *Journal of Psychoactive Drugs, 39*, 41–49.

Henrich, J. (2009). The evolution of costly displays, cooperation and religion: Credibility enhancing displays and their implications for cultural evolution. *Evolution and Human Behavior, 30*, 244–260.

Hill, P. C., & Hood, R. W. Jr. (1999). *Measures of religiosity.* Birmingham, AL: Religious Education Press.

Hoffman, S., & Rosman, L. (2003). "Procrustean psychotherapy" or differential therapeutics: Teaching treatment selection to trainees. *Journal of Contemporary Psychotherapy, 33*(4), 341–347.

James, A., & Wells, A. (2003). Religion and mental health: Towards a cognitive-behavioural framework. *British Journal of Health Psychology, 8*(3), 359–376.

Kaplar, M. E., Wachholtz, A. B., & O'Brien, W. H. (2004). The effect of religious and spiritual interventions on the biological, psychological, and spiritual outcomes of oncology patients: A meta-analytic review. *Journal of Psychosocial Oncology, 22*(1), 39–49.

Kass, J. D., Friedman, R., Leserman, J., Zuttermeister, P. C., & Benson, H. (1991). Health outcomes and a new index of spiritual experience. *Journal for the Scientific Study of Religion, 30,* 203–211.

Kelly, B. D. (2008). Buddhist psychology, psychotherapy and the brain: A critical introduction. *Transcultural Psychiatry, 45*(1), 5–30.

Klein, C., & Albani, C. (2007). Religiousness and mental health. An overview about findings, conclusions, and consequences for clinical practice. *Psychiatr Prax, 34*(2), 58–65.

Koenig, H. G. (Ed.). (1998). *Handbook of religion and mental health.* San Diego: CA: Academic Press.

Koenig, H. G. (2001). Religion and medicine II: Religion, mental health, and related behaviors. *International Journal of Psychiatry in Medicine, 31,* 97–109.

Koenig, H. G. (2009). Research on religion, spirituality, and mental health: A review. *The Canadian Journal of Psychiatry, 54,* 283–291.

Koenig, H. G., & Larson, D. B. (2001). Religion and mental health: Evidence for an association. *International Review of Psychiatry, 13*(2), 67–78.

Koenig, H. G., Larson, D. B., & Larson, S. S. (2001). Religion and coping with serious medical illness. *Annals of Pharmacotherapy, 35*(3), 352–359.

Koenig, H. G., McCullough, M. E., & Larson, D. B. (2001). *Handbook of religion and health.* New York, NY: Oxford University Press.

Kuniwaki, H. (2001). [Therapy for patients with substance abuse from point of view of brain science and spirituality]. *Seishin Shinkeigaku Zasshi, 103*(12), 1055–1060.

Larson, D. B., & Larson, S. S. (2003). Spirituality's potential relevance to physical and emotional health: A brief review of quantitative research. *Journal of Psychology & Theology, 31*(1), 37–51.

Levin, J., & Chatters, L. (1998). Research on religion and mental health: An overview of empirical findings and theoretical issues. In H. Koenig (Ed.), *Handbook of religion and mental health* (pp. 33–50). San Diego, CA: Academic Press.

Longshore, D., Anglin, M. D., & Conner, B. T. (2009). Are religiosity and spirituality useful constructs in drug treatment research? *Journal of Behavioral and Health Services Research, 36*(2), 177–188.

Lynn, R., Harvey, J., & Nyborg, H. (2009). Average intelligence predicts atheism rates across 137 nations. *Intelligence, 37,* 11–15.

Mabe, P. A., & Josephson, A. M. (2004). Child and adolescent psychopathology: Spiritual and religious perspectives. *Child and Adolescent Psychiatric Clinics of North America, 13*(1), 111–125, vii–viii.

McGee, M. (2008). Meditation and psychiatry. *Psychiatry, 5*(1), 28–40.

McIntosh, D. N. (1999). Purpose in Life Test. In P. C. Hill & R. W. Hood (Eds.), *Measures of Religiosity.* Birmingham, AL: Religious Education Press.

McMinn, M. R., Chaddock, T. P., Edwards, L. C., Lim, B. R. K. B., & Campbell, C. D. (1998). Psychologists collaborating with clergy. *Professional Psychology: Research and Practice, 29*(6), 564–570.

McMinn, M. R., Hathaway, W. L., Woods, S. W., & Snow, K. N. (2009). What American Psychological Association leaders have to say about *Psychology of Religion and Spirituality*. *Psychology of Religion and Spirituality, 1*(1), 3–13.
Miller, W. R. (Ed.). (1999). *Integrating spirituality into treatment: Resources for practitioners*. Washington, DC: American Psychological Association.
Miller, W. R., & Bogenschutz, M. P. (2007). Spirituality and addiction. *Southern Medical Journal, 100*(4), 433–436.
Miller, L., & Kelley, B. S. (2005). Relationships of religiosity and spirituality with mental health and psychopathology. In R. F. Paloutzian & C. L. Park (Eds.), *Handbook of psychology of religion and spirituality* (pp. 460–478). New York, NY: Guilford.
Moreira-Almeida, A., Neto, F. L., & Koenig, H. G. (2006). Religiousness and mental health: A review. *Revista Brasileira de Psiquiatria, 28*(3), 242–250.
Nielsen, S. L., Johnson, W. B., & Ellis, A. (2001). *Counseling and psychotherapy with religious persons: A rational emotive behavior therapy approach*. Mahwah, NJ: Erlbaum.
O'Connor, S., & Vandenberg, B. (2005). Psychosis of faith? Clinicians' assessment of religious beliefs. *Journal of Consulting and Clinical Psychology, 73*(4), 610–616.
Olson, T. (2003). Buddhism, behavior change, and OCD. *Journal of Holistic Nursing, 21*(2), 149–162.
Pargament, K. I. (2007). *Spiritually integrated psychotherapy: Understanding and addressing the sacred*. New York, NY: Guilford Press.
Reisner, A. D., & Lawson, P. (1992). Psychotherapy, sin, and mental health. *Pastoral Psychology, 40*, 303–311.
Richards, P. S., & Bergin, A. E. (Eds.). (2000). *Handbook of psychotherapy and religious diversity*. Washington, DC: American Psychological Association.
Richards, P. S., & Bergin, A. E. (2005). *A spiritual strategy for counseling and psychotherapy* (2nd ed.). Washington, DC: American Psychological Association.
Sawatzky, R., Ratner, P. A., & Chiu, L. (2005). A meta-analysis of the relationship between spirituality and quality of life. *Social Indicators Research, 72*(2), 153–188.
Schaefer, F. C., Blazer, D. G., & Koenig, H. G. (2008). Religious and spiritual factors and the consequences of trauma: A review and model of the interrelationship. *International Journal of Psychiatry in Medicine, 38*(4), 507–524.
Shafranske, E. P. (Ed.). (1996). *Religion and the clinical practice of psychology*. Washington, DC: American Psychological Association.
Shedler, J. (2010). The efficacy of psychodynamic psychotherapy. *American Psychologist, 65*(2), 98–109.
Shreve-Neiger, A. K., & Edelstein, B. A. (2004). Religion and anxiety: A critical review of the literature. *Clinical Psychology Review, 24*(4), 379–397.
Siegel, K., Anderman, S. J., & Schrimshaw, E. W. (2001). Religion and coping with health-related stress. *Psychology & Health, 16*(6), 631–653.
Smith, T. B., Bartz, J., & Richards, P. S. (2007). Outcomes of religious and spiritual adaptations to psychotherapy: A meta-analytic review. *Psychotherapy Research, 17*(6), 643–655.
Smith, T. B., McCullough, M. E., & Poll, J. (2003). Religiousness and depression: Evidence for a main effect and the moderating influence of stressful life events. *Psychological Bulletin, 129*(4), 614–636.
Sperry, L., & Shafranske, E. P. (Eds.). (2005). *Spiritually oriented psychotherapy*. Washington, DC: American Psychological Association.
Tonigan, J. S. (2007). Spirituality and alcoholics anonymous. *Southern Medical Journal, 100*(4), 437–440.

Van Dyke, C. J., & Elias, M. J. (2007). How forgiveness, purpose, and religiosity are related to the mental health and well-being of youth: A review of the literature. *Mental Health, Religion & Culture, 10*(4), 395–415.

Wade, N., Worthington, E., & Vogel, D. (2007). Effectiveness of religiously tailored interventions in Christian therapy. *Psychotherapy Research, 17*(1), 91–105.

Webb, J. R. & Trautman, R. P. (2010). Forgiveness and alcohol use: Applying a specific spiritual principle to substance abuse problems. *Addictive Disorders & Their Treatment, 9*(1), 8–17.

Wong, Y. J., Rew, L., & Slaikeu, K. D. (2006). A systematic review of recent research on adolescent religiosity/spirituality and mental health. *Issues in Mental Health Nursing, 27*(2), 161–183.

Worthington, E., Wade, N., Hight, T., Ripley, J., McCullough, M., Berry, J., et al. (2003). The Religious Commitment Inventory–10: Development, refinement, and validation of a brief scale for research and counseling. *Journal of Counseling Psychology, 50*, 84–96.

# 14

# *Impact of Religion and Spirituality on Physical Health*

Kevin S. Masters and Stephanie A. Hooker

Psychologists, epidemiologists, public health investigators, and research physicians recently have shown increased interest in issues of religion and spirituality (R/S) and their relationship with physical health. Masters (2007) demonstrated a notable increase in published scientific research addressing R/S and health. In the 5 years between 1975 and 1979, fewer than 100 published articles were located, less then 20 per year; whereas for the 7 years between 2000 and 2006, more than 650 were identified, approximately 93 per year. So what factors led to the increased interest in R/S and health?

It is clear that Americans are a religious people. The Pew Research Center (2008) survey of a representative sample of 35,000 American adults revealed that 78.4% consider themselves affiliated with some branch of Christianity, 4.7% affiliate with another religious tradition, and 16.1% are unaffiliated. Notably, just under half of the unaffiliated (5.8% of the total population) indicate that religion is either somewhat important or very important in their lives. Barnes, Powell-Griner, McFann, and Nahin (2004) studied alternative medical treatments in the United States. These treatments generally lie outside the mainstream practice of the medical profession but often are engaged in by individuals based on their own beliefs and understandings of health and illness. They found that prayer for self (43%) and prayer for others (24.4%) are the two most commonly named and being in a prayer group (9.6%) ranks fifth. Evidence from several countries outside the United States indicates that prayer is the most commonly used health intervention by the general public there as well (e.g., Edman & Koon, 2000; Samana et al., 2004). Not only are Americans, and other citizens of the world, religious but they also perceive a connection between their faith and their health.

It seems unlikely, however, that people are any more religious or spiritual now than they have been historically. What is new is the publication of large epidemiological studies and meta-analyses, some with appropriate statistical controls, demonstrating beneficial relationships between R/S (typically defined as religious service attendance) and various indexes of morbidity and mortality. Table 14.1 lists recent reviews and meta-analyses of the primary empirical literature. R/S, something that a large segment of the population deems important and participates in, and that also demonstrates relations with health outcomes, should draw the attention of researchers, practitioners, and even funding sources.

Another factor related to the increased interest in R/S and health is the growing acknowledgment of the importance of culture in psychological and physical functioning. The increased interest in cultural factors, and the inclusion of R/S as a form of culture, is reflected in definitions of evidence-based practice by both the American Psychological Association (APA Presidential Task Force on Evidence-Based Practice, 2006) and the Council for Training in Evidence-Based Behavioral Practice (2009). Both definitions include specific reference to patient values and culture. Furthermore, the accreditation guidelines (APA Commission on Accreditation, 2009) and ethical principles (American Psychological Association, 2002) of the APA both explicitly recognize the importance of professional respect and competence regarding religious issues in therapy. Even so,

**Table 14.1** Representative Reviews and Meta-Analyses of Religion and Mortality

| Study Authors | Type of Study and Focus of Article |
|---|---|
| Chida, Steptoe, & Powell (2009) | Meta-analysis; all-cause mortality in both healthy and diseased populations; cardiovascular specific mortality |
| Hall (2006) | Meta-analysis; all-cause mortality; cost per life year |
| Hummer, Rogers, Nam, & Ellison (2004) | Narrative review with focus on different aspects of religious involvement; all-cause mortality |
| Jarvis & Northcott (1987) | Narrative review with focus on religious groups/ denominations; all-cause mortality and morbidity |
| Larson, Larson, & Koenig (2002) | Narrative review including a review of meta-analyses; all-cause mortality in community and patient populations |
| Levin, Chatters, & Taylor (2005) | Narrative review focused on African Americans; all-cause mortality and morbidity |
| Levin & Vanderpool (1987) | Narrative review; health, including mortality |
| Luskin (2000) | Narrative review; focused on mortality and morbidity associated with cardiovascular and pulmonary disease |
| Masters (in press) | Narrative review; cardiovascular mortality and morbidity |
| McCullough (2001) | Narrative review but focuses on McCullough et al. (2000) meta-analysis; all-cause mortality |
| McCullough, Hoyt, Larson, Koenig, & Thoresen (2000) | Meta-analysis; all-cause mortality |
| Powell, Shahabi, & Thoresen (2003) | Narrative review; investigates several hypotheses, including attendance and all-cause mortality, cardiovascular disease, cancer mortality, and others |

Cohen (2009) has argued that R/S has not received adequate attention as a form of culture from the scientific community. Although behavioral scientists who study R/S seriously are no longer routinely derided as ancient holdovers from a prescientific era, the number of behavioral scientists involved in research on R/S and health remains relatively small, and funding opportunities for this research are still inadequate.

## R/S AND HEALTH RESEARCH LITERATURE

### Mortality Studies

This selective review of studies addresses the association between R/S and mortality. Those studies included in this text were selected on the basis of their historical importance, methodological rigor, or breadth of findings that they bring to the discussion. These findings are important for practitioners who strive to work within a scientist–practitioner model because they provide an empirical basis for considerations on the relationship between R/S and mortality. They are thus applicable to behavioral practitioners working in any number of settings, including traditional psychotherapeutic practice as well as newer behavioral practice settings, such as integrated primary health care. Patients engage with psychologically and behaviorally trained practitioners for many reasons. These reasons include stress-related disorders, psychosomatic disorders, psychopathology that manifests with accompanying physical involvement, and psychological factors that interfere with adherence to medically necessary behavioral regimens. Thus, for many, their psychological disorder is associated with health-compromising behaviors that can shorten their life and increase their risk of dying. By reviewing the research on mortality and R/S, we provide psychotherapists and other professionals who use psychological research in patient care with the ammunition needed to intervene with patients for whom R/S is important. We hope to arm practitioners with information that can be used to motivate clients and patients toward better mental and physical health.

Recent investigations into the R/S–mortality relationship used sophisticated methods and diverse samples. For example, Hummer, Rogers, Nam, and Ellison (1999) studied a representative U.S. sample of 21,204 individuals over an 8-year interval. Religious attendance was broken into four categories and 37% of the sample attended religious services at least once a week. People who never attended were at 1.87 times the risk of death compared with those who attended once a week. Based on life expectancy estimates at age 20, overall life expectancy differences between those who attended more than once per week and those who never attended were greater than 7 years. Strikingly, among African Americans there was a 14-year advantage for those who attended more than once a week. A graded relationship also existed between attendance and mortality with the largest step difference between those who never attended and those who attended less than once a week (4.4 years). When appropriate controls were included, the precise estimates changed, and generally the effect of attendance was reduced, but all models continued to show significant benefits for religious attendance.

This is a very strong study. Relationships with mortality of this magnitude are rare; if a pharmaceutical company could synthesize, bottle, and sell a pill with these results, their profits would soar. But what does it mean to a behavioral practitioner? First, it clearly suggests that R/S is "in play" in the therapeutic encounter, even to the point that, particularly for African American patients, ignoring R/S could be considered poor practice. At a minimum, assessment of social involvements should include questions regarding religious service attendance. Nevertheless, out of context, it is ethically problematic for psychotherapists to advocate that clients attend religious services. But for those clients who already are committed to a particular faith, although not regularly accessing that faith community, these research findings are relevant. Perhaps the most important implication of this study and those to follow, however, is that psychotherapists need to develop knowledge of the research literature, awareness, sensitivity, and comfort in discussing such issues as religious service attendance and be willing to consider the possibility that this knowledge may provide a useful adjunctive treatment for certain individuals.

Evidence-based practice cannot be confidently built around any one study no matter how persuasive it may be. Table 14.1 highlights additional reviews and meta-analyses in this area. Of particular note is a recent meta-analysis by Chida, Steptoe, and Powell (2009). They included 37 studies in their quantitative analysis and concluded that R/S, and in particular religious service attendance, was associated with reduced risk for mortality in initially physically healthy (i.e., not having a chronic life-threatening or life-limiting disease) populations. This effect was not found in diseased populations, although a trend was evident in the direction of a beneficial relationship and the number of studies examined was considerably smaller. It is interesting that the overall protective effect for R/S could not be accounted for by behavioral factors (smoking, drinking, exercising, and socioeconomic status), negative affect, or social support, suggesting R/S may have a direct effect on mortality. This study also established a protective effect for R/S specifically for cardiovascular mortality, the first review to do so.

Studies investigating R/S and mortality have been conducted around the world with groups from many different and varied cultures. Beneficial effects for R/S variables have been found for highly orthodox Jewish groups in Israel (Gouldbourt, Yaari, & Medalie, 1993), members of religious versus secular kibbutzim in Israel (Kark, Shemi, Friedlander, & Martin, 1996), and Finnish Lutheran males compared with Finnish Eastern Orthodox men (Räsänen, Kauhanen, Lakka, Kaplan, & Salonen, 1996). Beneficial findings for religious affiliation in Northern Ireland (O'Reilly & Rosato, 2008) and religious attendance in older adults in Denmark over 20 years (la Cour, Avlund, & Schultz-Larsen,

2006) demonstrated effects in secular societies. Research in China that included numerous controls showed the somewhat surprising finding that religious participation predicted lower risk of mortality for the oldest women and for individuals in poor health (Zhang, 2008). Finally, also in Asia, Yeager et al. (2006) studied a nationally representative sample of older Taiwanese and found that religious attendance showed the most consistent association with health outcomes and remained significantly associated with lower mortality after controlling for prior health status. This array of findings from different cultures and from groups with widely varying religious beliefs suggests that the effects of R/S on mortality are not limited to one particular group but are widespread. The findings also suggest that, for clinicians to be most effective, they would do well to properly understand important cultural and associated R/S beliefs when engaging patients.

A final group of studies in the United States investigated differences in mortality based on denomination. Mormons have been the focus of many of the studies at least in part because of the strict behavioral code that they are encouraged by their religious teachings to follow (i.e., abstinence from alcohol, tobacco, and hot caffeinated beverages; moderation in meat consumption; weekly or more often church attendance; and sexual abstinence outside of marriage). These studies found beneficial relationships between Mormon identification and mortality (Enstrom, 1989; Enstrom & Breslow, 2008; Lyon, Wetzler, Gardner, Klauber, & Williams, 1978). In an interesting analysis, Enstrom (1989) compared "Mormon-like" non-Mormons from the Alameda County Study (i.e., individuals who were white, attended church regularly, did not smoke, and resided in Alameda County, California) with U.S. population data. These comparisons indicated that the Mormon-like sample had standardized mortality ratios that were also lower than both the U.S. general population and the U.S. nonsmoking population and were the same as the Mormon sample. Consequently, this study demonstrated that (a) mortality effects found in Mormon samples generalized to a similar population that regularly attended church and did not smoke, and (b) reductions in rates of mortality were not completely explained by never having smoked but appear also to be affected by regular religious attendance.

Taken as a whole, these studies suggest a protective effect for R/S as related to mortality and that this effect is found around the world in different cultures and is sustained, although somewhat diminished in magnitude, when rigorous controls are implemented. Some of the effect is due to religious people's tendency to engage in health-promoting behaviors and their avoidance of health risk behaviors, but this does not totally explain the relationship. The strongest evidence is found when religious attendance is the measure of religion. Frequent attendees are likely to be members of a relatively stable social network and therefore receive significant social support (see "Social Support" below). Again, however, social support also does not completely account for the relationship.

### Morbidity Studies

Perhaps even more applicable to the daily lives of practitioners are research findings that relate R/S with morbidity. A wide variety of studies exist that not only offer preliminary support for the R/S–health hypothesis but also suggest mechanisms through which this effect may be achieved. It is important to note, however, that not all R/S practices have been found to be beneficial. Again, we will selectively review the literature. This section will initially look at R/S as it relates to preventive health behaviors. Then it considers R/S in regards to secondary prevention and coping among patients.

#### *Primary Prevention Among Healthy Individuals*

Behaviors that preserve health or prevent illness can be broken into two types: (1) those wherein individuals do something positive to increase the likelihood of being healthy (e.g., regular physical activity); or (2) those characterized by *not* engaging in something that puts health at risk (e.g., not smoking). The idea of a healthy lifestyle is important because many different behaviors link to health outcomes, but individuals often engage in one healthy behavior (e.g., not smoking) only to essentially "cancel out" the benefits by engaging in unhealthy behaviors in another area (e.g., overeating). Several studies are highlighted in the following paragraphs that investigate these behaviors in relation to R/S variables.

Strawbridge, Shema, Cohen, and Kaplan (2001) reported on 2,676 participants of the Alameda County Study. They investigated the likelihood of maintaining or improving good health behaviors as well as the likelihood of initiating poor health behaviors by comparing weekly religious service attendees in 1965 versus all others over the subsequent 30 years. Weekly attendance was associated with significant improvement in quitting smoking and becoming physically active and also was associated with the increase in number of personal relationships and getting married, but it was not associated with initiating annual medical checkups. Regular attendees were *less* likely to *stop* having regular checkups. This study is important because it suggests that those who attend services weekly are more likely to change their behavior in ways predictive of better health than those who do not attend.

Hill, Ellison, Burdette, and Musick (2007) specifically addressed the question of the relation between religious involvement and healthy lifestyle in a sample of 1,369 Texas adults. They included 12 different health relevant behaviors, both positive and negative, and found that religious involvement was significantly associated with a healthy lifestyle. Furthermore, the effect was larger than the effects of age, sex, marital status, education, financial strain, and self-rated health and was of about the same magnitude for both sexes and all racial and ethnic groups. This further supports the possibility that religious involvement is associated with extensive involvement in health behaviors.

Other studies (Gillum, 2005, 2006a, 2006b; Gillum & Ingram, 2006) included U.S. nationwide representative samples of between 11,820 and 18,774 respondents. They found that infrequent religious service attendees were more likely to be smokers and that, among women, those who attended services less than weekly were less likely to engage in leisure time physical activity. Benjamins and Brown (2004) reported that among a U.S. nationally representative sample of older adults assessed on six different types of preventive health care, those who reported high levels of religiosity were more likely to use these preventive services and, specifically, those affiliated with a denomination (Catholic, Protestant, Jewish) had greater utilization than those not affiliated.

Finally, Koenig and Vaillant (2009) reported a longitudinal study of 456 inner-city U.S. men beginning at age 14 with subsequent assessments at 32 and 47 years of age and outcomes measured at age 70. Religious service attendance at age 47 predicted both objective and subjective physical health and well-being but, somewhat surprisingly, did not predict mortality. The relationships between attendance and physical health variables were statistically determined to be at least partially due to smoking, alcohol abuse, depressed mood (attendees were lower on all three), and past health status. Attendance directly predicted well-being.

This series of studies strongly suggests that individuals regularly attending religious services are more likely to engage in a variety of health-enhancing activities and avoid those behaviors known to jeopardize health. In short, a healthy lifestyle appears to be associated with religious involvement. Health psychologists have long been frustrated by observing that improvements in one healthy behavior often are unrelated to changes in others and tend to be short lived. But the findings of these studies suggest that religious communities may provide a key point of integration for healthy living. This can be a vital resource for practitioners. Recent applied studies demonstrated the effectiveness of church-based preventive interventions for African Americans (Davis-Smith, 2007; Samuel-Hodge et al., 2009; Turner, Sutherland, Harris, & Barber, 1995). Practitioners should consider developing health-based enrichment or psychoeducation interventions that can be delivered and managed in religious settings (churches, synagogues, etc.) and that take specific advantage of the particular religious or cultural teachings of the group to deliver tailored and culturally sensitive interventions (i.e., ones likely to be accepted and reap particularly effective benefits). By working with clergy and developing preventive interventions, clinicians will be able to tap into a largely unexplored resource for healthy behavior change and maintenance.

### *Secondary Prevention and Coping Among Patients*

Several lines of research and associated practice can be considered regarding the effects of R/S among patient populations. What follows is a brief survey. An often hypothesized but relatively unexplored behavioral pathway concerns R/S and treatment adherence. Park, Moehl, Fenster, Suresh, and Bliss (2008) examined religious support, commitment, and positive and negative religious coping as predictors of treatment adherence in a sample of 202 patients afflicted with congestive heart failure (CHF). The most prominent finding was that religious commitment predicted greater adherence to CHF-specific behaviors over 6 months even when controlling for initial levels of adherence. Similarly, Park, Edmondson, Hale-Smith, and Blank (2009) examined relations between health behaviors and religious attendance, daily spiritual experiences, and religious struggle in a sample of 167 younger adult cancer survivors. They found that attendance had little impact on behaviors, but daily spiritual experiences positively predicted engagement in health behaviors, apparently because of the association of self-assurance with daily spiritual experiences. Religious struggle negatively predicted health behaviors, an effect mediated by guilt or shame.

Others also investigated R/S in the context of cancer. Yanez et al. (2009) found that spirituality in the form of finding meaning and peace predicted favorable adjustment during cancer survivorship and faith was related to perceived cancer-related growth. Krupski et al. (2006) studied men with early-stage prostate cancer and found that low spirituality predicted worse psychosocial adjustment as well as low health-related and disease-specific quality of life. Holt, Lukwago, and Kreuter (2003) studied cancer beliefs and mammography utilization among urban African American women and found that spiritual beliefs predicted breast cancer beliefs and mammography utilization. Fitchett et al. (2004) studied R/S struggle among cancer, diabetic, and CHF patients. Struggle includes questioning God, becoming angry at God, or being unable to reconcile one's current condition with previously held R/S beliefs. Although half of the total sample reported no R/S struggle, among those who did, it was clear that struggle was related to greater emotional distress and higher levels of depressive symptoms.

A notable study of HIV-positive patients was conducted by Ironson, Stuetzle, and Fletcher (2006). They followed 100 patients over 4 years and found that 45% increased their R/S following positive diagnosis of HIV, whereas 42% remained the same and 13% decreased. Those reporting an increase in R/S also demonstrated less disease progression on the basis of biological markers that could not be explained by likely causes.

Probably the greatest amount of research on R/S and secondary prevention or coping has been conducted with patients with cardiovascular disease (CVD). Blumenthal et al. (2007) prospectively investigated a subset of 503 patients from the Enhancing Recovery in Coronary Heart Disease trial to determine whether R/S predicted death or recurrent nonfatal myocardial infarction (MI) in this rather select group of patients. Over 18 months, R/S measures failed to predict statistically significant relationships. The simple analysis for service attendance was marginally significant, demonstrating that those who never attended church tended to have a higher event rate than weekly attendees but a *lower* event rate than those who attended several times per month. Simple analyses for spiritual experiences approached significance; however, those who had *more* spiritual experiences tended to have a *higher* event probability.

Earlier studies also examined the link between MI and R/S. Friedlander, Kark, and Stein (1986) investigated the hypothesis that religious orthodoxy among Jewish residents of Jerusalem was a negative predictor of recurrent MI. Among cases, 51% of males and 50% of females defined themselves as secular compared with 21% and 16%, respectively, among the controls. Secular males were 4.17 times more likely to have a recurrent MI than were orthodox males and secular females were 7.31 times more likely than orthodox females.

Agrawal and Dalal (1993) studied 70 male Hindu MI patients in India who had been hospitalized following their first MI. The investigators assessed the extent that patients believed in God, karma, and a just world, and they measured attributions pertaining to the causes of their MI and recovery. The findings regarding belief in God support the hypothesis that religious variables may have both beneficial and harmful effects. In this case, those who attributed the cause of their *illness* to God had worse recoveries but those who attributed their *recovery* to God fared better. A perhaps surprising finding to Western readers is that blaming oneself for the illness predicted better recovery. The authors hypothesize that in the Indian cultural context, self-blame may have induced a greater sense of perceived control over the recovery but did not induce greater moral guilt over the illness.

Several studies investigated the effects of R/S on outcomes among patients undergoing various cardiac surgeries. Oxman, Freeman, and Manheimer (1995) prospectively studied 232 older adults who had undergone elective open heart surgery. Those who received some degree of strength and comfort from their religion were at reduced risk of death during 6-month follow-up. Ai and colleagues (Ai, Dunkle, Peterson, & Bolling, 1998; Ai, Park, Huang, Rodgers, & Tice, 2007; Ai, Peterson, Bolling, & Rodgers, 2006; Ai, Peterson, Tice, Huang, et al., 2007; Ai, Peterson, Tice, Rodgers, et al., 2006) published a series of studies investigating religious variables and outcomes following cardiac surgery. In the first (Ai et al., 1998), the researchers found that prayer was commonly used by patients and that it predicted decreases in depression and general distress. They subsequently published a number of studies on the same sample of patients undergoing a variety of types of cardiac surgeries, and they investigated several aspects of faith-based coping as predictors of postsurgery outcomes. In general, they found that positive religious coping predicted better psychological and functional outcomes, whereas negative religious coping predicted worse results. This research, however, provides two additional findings of note. First, they determined that the effects of positive religious coping were mediated by hope, optimism, and social support. Second, they demonstrated the importance of longitudinal assessment. In particular, cross-sectional analyses indicated a relationship between prayer and *poorer* overall functioning; in longitudinal analysis, however, prayer predicted subsequent *better* functioning.

Finally, two recent publications by Contrada and colleagues (Contrada et al., 2004, 2008) investigated patients undergoing elective coronary bypass or cardiac valve surgery. In the first study, the researchers found that stronger presurgical religious beliefs predicted fewer postsurgery complications and shorter length of hospital stay, with complications mediating the effect on length of stay. A somewhat surprising finding, however, was that religious attendance was associated with longer hospital stay. Frequency of prayer did not predict outcomes. The authors discussed attendance in light of the possible influence of negative religious coping strategies. The study also found that relationships were stronger among women than men, and prayer and attendance tended to be less related to psychosocial variables (optimism, hostility, depression, social support) than were religious beliefs. Contrada et al. (2004) also found longer hospital stays for individuals whose frequency of religious attendance exceeded what would be predicted by the strength of their beliefs as compared with those whose attendance was less frequent than would be expected based on their beliefs. These findings are fascinating because they suggest a type of behaviorally based self-report measure of extrinsic and intrinsic religiousness, with extrinsic being exemplified by those who attended more than their beliefs would predict.

In the second study (Contrada et al., 2008), 550 elective cardiac surgery patients were interviewed before surgery. Findings indicated a number of variables had effects on hospital length of stay that were mediated by either depressive symptoms or social support. For our purposes, the effect of religious involvement on length of stay was mediated by perceived social support and the effect of sense of purpose was mediated by reduced depressive symptoms.

What do the many findings in this section mean for practitioners? Upon first encounter, they seem to provide a general, but inconsistent, case for a beneficial relationship between R/S and health outcomes, with the presence of negative findings duly noted. For example, spiritual experiences were associated with more healthy behaviors in a cancer population, but they predicted a higher probability of a subsequent cardiac event in a cardiac population. Attendance generally was associated with better health outcomes (even after adjusting for health status variables) but not always. The elective cardiac surgery study (Contrada et al., 2004) provided an insightful analysis that when attendance exceeds strength of belief, it is associated with longer hospital stays. In some cases, prayer was related to better outcomes when assessed longitudinally; but it was not related to better outcomes in other cases, particularly when assessed cross-sectionally. It seems likely that for many ill individuals, engagement in R/S-related practices is indicative of an attempt to gain control over their health and symptoms in a way that may not be entirely consistent with the content or strength of their R/S beliefs. In light of these findings, for example, we offer the following hypotheses regarding ill individuals: (a) Spiritual experiences are beneficial when they are aspects of a spiritually integrated living perspective, but they are associated with negative outcomes when they are indicative of an attempt at managing illness absent an established spiritual context; (b) religious attendance that exceeds belief may be motivated by fear and desperate hope for beneficial health intervention rather than the comfort that is found when one acts (i.e., attends services) in ways that are consistent with one's beliefs; and (c) prayer that continues over time is indicative of a practice based on long-standing belief in prayer, whereas prayer could be used short term as a distressed plea for healing.

When patients engage in negative religious coping, they experience negative outcomes and, although perhaps not as certain, when patients' R/S is associated with meaning, peace, sense of purpose, positive attributions, or comfort, it also is associated with beneficial physical and functional outcomes. This result suggests that practitioners cannot make blanket assumptions regarding the role of R/S in the patients' coping and health processes. Rather, practitioners working with individuals who are ill and have R/S beliefs need to carefully consider the entire functioning of the individual and the place of spirituality within this holistic framework. Spiritual experiences can be a source of strength and self-awareness for those with a spiritual belief system that is integrated into their world view and daily functioning. But for others they may be an indicator of desperation and poor coping. Practitioners should carefully assess the phenomenological aspects and causes for spiritual engagement in those who are ill to determine their functionality and health impact. Once this is done, clinicians can work intensely with patients to better integrate spiritual beliefs with their current physical reality in a manner that supports coping.

## Clinical Assessments

The following sections detail selected measures of R/S that may be useful for practitioners to consider. The list is far from complete but includes measures of several important constructs from the research literature that may be useful for practitioners when considering the relationship between health and R/S.

### *Brief Multidimensional Measure of Religiousness/Spirituality*

A national working group convened by the Fetzer Institute and the National Institute on Aging (NIA) developed a multidimensional measure of R/S (Idler et al., 2003) designed to become the standard in health research related to R/S: the Multidimensional Measure of Religiousness/Spirituality (MMRS; Fetzer Institute, 1999). To facilitate use, a brief 38-item version of the original measure was created (the Brief Multidimensional Measure of Religiousness and Spirituality [BMMRS]). The original individual dimensions included daily spiritual experiences, meaning, values, beliefs, forgiveness, private religious practices, religious or spiritual coping, religious support, religious spiritual history, commitment, organizational religiousness, and a statement of religious affiliation. Subsequent study (Masters et al. 2009; Neff, 2006; Piedmont, Mapa, & Williams, 2007; Stewart & Kocske, 2006) determined that the dimensions were highly intercorrelated. Masters et al. (2009) confirmed seven factors: experiential comforting faith, negative religious interaction, personal spirituality, punishing God, religious community support, private religious practices, and forgiveness.

Although practitioners, on occasion, may administer the entire scale or individual dimensions and subscales, perhaps the greatest value of this measure in the clinical setting is to provide a reasonably complete listing of important R/S dimensions. These dimensions could become the focus of assessment and could provide practitioners with sample items to incorporate into their interview or interactions with patients. This is likely to be particularly helpful for practitioners who are developing their personal comfort around inquiring about R/S concerns.

*Multidimensional Health Locus of Control (LOC)*

The Multidimensional Health LOC Scales (MHLC; Wallston, Wallston, & DeVellis, 1978) originally measured control beliefs about one's current state of health along three subscales: Internal Health LOC (IHLC), Powerful Others Health LOC (PHLC), and Chance Health LOC (CHLC). Following the development of these scales, it became apparent that religious individuals often attribute control to a fourth dimension: God. Welton, Adkins, Ingle, and Dixon (1996) developed the God Control subscale and Wallston et al. (1999) further refined the God Health LOC (GHLC) subscale to fit the MHLC (form C, scale for specific diseases). Interestingly, Wallston et al. (1999) found that the GHLC was associated with poorer psychological adjustment (greater negative affect and lower positive affect), which was somewhat different from Welton et al.'s (1996) finding that the GHLC was associated with greater levels of healthy habits. However, their samples were fundamentally different. Wallston et al. (1999) sampled disease populations, whereas Welton et al. (1996) sampled a healthy population. Wallston et al. (1999) suggested that individuals with chronic illness who have put their faith in God may be disappointed because they have not seen improvement, an observation with clear clinical relevance.

Pargament, Kennell, Hathaway, and Grevengoed (1988) offered three types of religious coping that could describe the ways someone might view the GHLC. The first type, self-directing, is when individuals perceive themselves to be actively in control of their lives and receiving support from God, who is more passive. The second type is deferring. In this style, the individual defers problem solving to God, who is an active deity, and the individual takes on a more passive role. The final type, collaborative, occurs when individuals work with God as partners; both are active. Consistent with Pargament's analysis of coping and control, participants with high internal LOC and high GHLC employed more active styles of coping (Welton et al., 1996). Thus, Welton et al. concluded that God control is actually a more active than passive form of control. Masters and Wallston (2005) found that higher scores on the GHLC were related to greater use of religious coping, whereas greater scores on the IHLC were related to more active problem-solving coping styles. Higher scores on the two external scales (CHLC and PHLC) were related to more passive coping styles and to emotional venting.

McIntosh and Spilka (1990) found that a collaborative relationship with God was negatively associated with overall sickness and 10 disease indicators. They believed this relationship was at least partially mediated by the positive affect that the collaborative individuals exuded. Conversely, they found that the deferring style of coping was positively associated with two diseases indicators.

Though practitioners may want to actually administer the scale at certain times, the more likely use is to incorporate the ideas and items into the flow of the clinician–patient interaction. Considerations need to be made about the effectiveness of the particular coping style for the particular patient in that patient's particular circumstance. Treatments for certain chronic disease processes (e.g., type II diabetes, coronary heart disease) often call for patients to engage in numerous behaviors, including dietary restriction, regular exercise, and various other daily regimens. In these cases, collaborative coping seems well suited to the task. By being active, patients are more likely to adhere to their treatment regimens, and their belief in God as a partner is likely to fuel motivation to continue the engagement. But some disease conditions progress to the point at which active types of coping are limited. In these situations having confidence that God is ultimately in control may prove comforting in the absence of any active patient coping. Again, practitioners need to carefully listen and assess how patients are incorporating their sense of God control to determine if it is being viewed in a healthy manner and not being interpreted as punishment or evidence of divine abandonment. These latter interpretations likely could have negative emotional and perhaps health consequences.

### *Intrinsic/Extrinsic Religious Motivation*

Intrinsic/extrinsic (I/E) religious orientation was originally conceptualized by Allport and Ross (1967), who developed the Religious Orientation Scale to measure the reasons why individuals engage in religious practices. Those who were intrinsically oriented were thought to view their religion as an end in itself, a master motive; those who were extrinsically oriented used their religion primarily to attain some other goal, perhaps personal comfort or social connection (Allport & Ross, 1967; Burris, 1999). Gorsuch and McPherson (1989) revised the scale after a factor analysis done by Kirkpatrick (1989) revealed extrinsically oriented items could be broken down into those that were personally oriented (Ep) or socially oriented (Es). This revision (I/E-R) created a 14-item scale that has been considered the best current measure of I/E religious motivation (Hill, 2005) and is recommended for use among individuals who express some religious sentiment.

Many studies have investigated I/E religious motivation. Some of the most significant findings have been in the area of mental health. Smith, McCullough, and Poll (2003) found an overall negative relationship between religiousness and depression symptoms in their meta-analysis; however, this effect was parceled out by I/E religiosity. Extrinsic religious motivation was positively associated with depression symptoms, whereas intrinsic motivation was negatively associated with depression symptoms, although not reaching statistical significance (Smith et al., 2003). Similar findings were reported with anxiety and obsessive-compulsive symptoms, wherein extrinsically oriented participants report more symptoms and intrinsically oriented participants report fewer symptoms (cf. Masters & Bergin, 1992).

In general, a pattern of research over many years supports the notion of beneficial relationships for psychological functioning and perhaps health for intrinsic religiousness and a deleterious relationship for extrinsic religiousness with these same variables. This again suggests that R/S is valuable to the extent that it is integrated into one's core values and worldview but when engaged in primarily for the benefits it may provide, R/S fails the test. The important implication for clinical practice is that unless intrinsic motivation, at some point, accompanies faith-based behaviors, psychological gains seem unlikely. To the extent that this activity continues with an extrinsic motivation, harm is possible. Consequently, clinicians should keep alert to the development of intrinsic or extrinsic R/S motivations in their patients. If they perceive that patients' R/S practices lack accompanying intrinsic belief, clinicians should be particularly aware, for this may be a path to disappointment and depression.

*Royal Free Interview for Spiritual and Religious Beliefs*

King, Speck, and Thomas (1995) developed the Royal Free Interview for Spiritual and Religious Beliefs (RFI) to measure strength of religious or spiritual beliefs in patients admitted to the hospital with acute physical illnesses. The interview is divided into three sections: (1) demographic characteristics, (2) clinician's assessment of patient's condition at time of admission, and (3) religious, spiritual, and philosophical beliefs. Because of the branched design of the third section, the interview can take on different forms depending on patient response.

King et al. (2001) subsequently developed a self-report version. One criticism of the interview was that it placed too much focus on intellectual assent to a faith but did not include enough emphasis on cognitive or emotional experiences of that faith (King et al., 2001). Thus, King et al. (2001) included spiritual experiences, beliefs about the afterlife, and near-death experiences in the self-report version. The authors demonstrated satisfactory internal consistency in a sample of participants who expressed R/S beliefs ($\alpha = .89$) and for a group of fundamentalist Christians ($\alpha = .74$). King et al. (2001) also demonstrated satisfactory test–retest reliability and demonstrated evidence for the criterion validity of the measure by showing that individuals who endorsed a R/S life view on the RFI reported greater intrinsic religious motivation than those who did not.

The original intention of the developers was to create a measure of religious, spiritual, or philosophical beliefs and test whether a relationship existed between those beliefs and physical illness (Seybold, 1999). Before development of the RFI, King, Speck, and Thomas (1994) found that strength of spiritual beliefs was associated with poor medical outcome, but this study had many limitations. Consequently, they addressed these limitations in a study (King, Speck, & Thomas, 1999) in which cardiology and gynecology patients were given the RFI and assessed on general psychiatric health, quality of life during illness, and social function. Patients who had stronger spiritual beliefs (but not religious or philosophical beliefs) at their first assessment were 2.2 times more likely to have a poorer health outcome at 9-month follow-up. Although they posited explanations for this finding (e.g., seriously ill patients may be more attuned to their spiritual beliefs than patients who are less severe, individuals with stronger beliefs may be less likely to struggle to recover because they believe in an afterlife, etc.), they did not measure any of the relevant variables for these possible explanations. Interestingly, the researchers found a significant decrease in strength of spiritual beliefs over the 9 months, and those who had poor outcomes had a greater decrease in strength of spiritual beliefs, something that may be clinically relevant. This decrease could reflect a spiritual struggle in those whose health is declining, which could identify a place for clinical intervention.

Few studies have used the RFI in relationship to health. McCoubrie and Davies (2006) did not find a relationship between strength of beliefs and depression and anxiety in advanced cancer patients. Giaquinto, Spiridigliozzi, and Caracciolo (2007) found a 4% and 5% decrease in anxiety and depression, respectively, for each unit increase in spiritual and religious beliefs in stroke patients, even after controlling for covariates. However, this linear relationship is not always found. For example, hemodialysis patients with no or strong spiritual beliefs reported better social functioning and greater levels of physical functioning in their daily activities than patients with weak spiritual beliefs (Kao et al., 2009). This suggests a curvilinear relationship between strength of spiritual beliefs and health-related quality of life.

## PATHWAYS AND CLINICAL STRATEGIES

These studies demonstrate that R/S variables are related to health and mental health outcomes among both healthy populations and patients, and we have highlighted the clinical implications of these findings throughout this chapter. It is clear that R/S is not a simple unidimensional construct whose influence can be easily summarized. Rather, recognition of different facets of R/S and how these interact with particular patients' and their conditions are important.

### Behavioral and Lifestyle Pathways

From a clinical perspective, it is important to understand the strong connection between R/S and healthy lifestyles and to use this to therapeutic advantage whenever possible. Impressive evidence suggests that R/S strengthens behavioral pathways that relate to better health and functioning. Notably, R/S predicts engagement in a variety of health-enhancing behaviors and avoidance of many health risk behaviors. Taken together, evidence suggests that an R/S healthy lifestyle may be most strongly characterized by abstinence from cigarette smoking and moderation or abstinence in alcohol use, but this lifestyle also includes other relevant health characteristics. To gain the greatest therapeutic leverage, it is important for clinicians to understand the theological and social factors that influence engagement in health-relevant behaviors among individuals who are members of particular faith communities *and how individual patients interpret these factors*. Are they a potential source of strength and support or are they likely to increase resistance to a behavior change plan? Through the use of sensitive and empathic query within a motivational interviewing framework, we believe therapists can be able to navigate effectively in this area. It is useful to inquire about local church-based health resources that patients can access, such as exercise groups or times of meditation. In recent years, many churches have become more actively involved in faith-based addictions treatments. These treatments may provide important support for health behavior change and maintenance. Therapists need to deliberately inquire about these possibilities with their religiously involved patients, because it is quite possible for patients to overlook or be unaware of available resources even within their own faith communities.

Psychological constructs underlying these behavioral patterns include increased conscientiousness, self-regulation skill, and agreeableness. A recent line of work investigates relations between R/S and personality constructs. Conscientiousness (Kern & Friedman, 2008) and neuroticism (Lahey, 2009) have reasonably well-established relations with health and longevity. Evidence indicates that religiousness, or certain forms of it, such as intrinsic religiousness, is associated positively with conscientiousness and agreeableness and negatively with neuroticism (Bergin, Masters, & Richards, 1987; McCullough, Tsang, & Brion, 2003; Saroglou & Fiasse, 2003; Saroglou & Munoz-Garcia, 2008; Saucier & Skrzypinska, 2006). McCullough and Willoughby (2009) noted that agreeableness and conscientiousness form the personality substrates of self-control. Their recent review suggests that self-control and self-regulation are likely pathways through which R/S influences health outcomes. It is our impression that for many years a folk-psychology conceptualization existed among therapists that too much R/S tended to make people rigid, guilt ridden, and perfectionistic-anxious. The preponderance of the research suggests instead that the more common pattern is for R/S to predict better self-control, behavioral regulation, and competence. Clinicians must carefully attend to this issue and scrutinize their own schemata for possible preexisting views or biases. Without question, religious mandates or precepts *can* be used in the service of unhealthy behavioral and cognitive patterns, but this review suggests that it is not the norm.

### Social Support

Therapists need to consider the social milieu of their patients. For the religious individual, this includes the possibility of social support sustained from their religious affiliations. Individuals involved in a religious group are likely to receive support. Given what is now known about social support and health, this is one of the more obvious mechanisms connecting R/S and health. Indeed, many studies examined the relationships between social support, R/S, and health. Some evidence suggests that individuals who regularly attend religious services have larger social networks. Ellison and George (1994) found that frequent religious service attendees had more nonfamily ties and were more likely to stay in contact with other people. Additionally, religious individuals may be more likely to have quality relationships. Ellison and George (1994) also found that frequent attendees reported feeling more valued and more integrated into their social group. Buck, Williams, Musick, and Sternthal (2009) found that congregational support, as might be expected, predicted lower levels of systolic and diastolic blood pressure. Oddly, congregational criticism also was related to *lower* diastolic blood pressure and to *lower* likelihood of hypertension.

Although social support is a clear mechanism for mediating the relationship between R/S and health, it only explains a relatively small amount of that relationship (George, Ellison, & Larson, 2002). Moreover, religious attendance is often used as a proxy for social support (Oman & Thoresen, 2002), but individuals may attend religious services for many reasons (e.g., intrinsic versus extrinsic religious motivations). Thus, the levels and types of support individuals receive through attending services likely vary, and clinicians should investigate this support. It would be a mistake to believe that anyone who attends religious services receives significant social support. Inquiries about level and degree of involvement with the faith community are more likely to yield information regarding the nature and scope of received support. It is also true that some patients have a difficult time receiving support when it is offered, perhaps out of embarrassment or fear of looking weak or even unspiritual because of their needs. These cognitions interfere with receipt of support and should be appropriately challenged in therapy. In any social context, however, giving and receiving must be done in balance, and research demonstrates that those who volunteer or provide for others also experience psychological and health benefits (Harris & Thoresen, 2005; Krause, 2009; Oman, Thoresen, & McMahon, 1999). Thus, we believe it is also good for patients to find ways wherein they can *provide* support to others in their faith communities.

### R/S-Influenced Coping

Clinicians are often concerned with how their patients cope with social, emotional, and physical stress. Coping practices, and how R/S influences them and is integrated with them, have shown relations with outcomes. Positive coping (e.g., finding strength from God, seeing self as part of a spiritual reality) predicts better outcomes and appears to be one way that R/S is beneficial to psychological and physical health. Although positive coping often has been highlighted, it is clear that, among certain individuals, R/S coping strategies are not beneficial. These efforts may be characterized by spiritual struggle and are typified by individuals who cannot reconcile their R/S beliefs with their current health condition. Consequently they become angry at God, may believe they are being punished, and can be filled with doubt, question, and despair. For these individuals, changes in R/S beliefs and coping styles are important for improved functioning. This situation may be particularly challenging for clinicians. One option is to consider the involvement of clergy. Patients often misinterpret the tenets of their faith thus involvement of sensitive and psychologically astute clergy can be a valuable resource. Cognitive therapeutic challenge strategies similar to those used in other situations in which patients are excessively harsh or judgmental of themselves may be useful. When patients feel punished by God, it is quite likely that they are judging themselves harshly and therefore believe that God has no choice but to do likewise. So challenges can be most appropriate. For example, "When your best friend was ill last year did you see that as a punishment from God?" and similar lines of questioning may help patients move from a rigid condemnation to a more fluid understanding that it is, indeed, impossible to know the mind of God. Those comfortable doing so may discuss examples of how bad things happened to great people of scripture, and many times it is explicitly clear that no punishment was involved.

### Common R/S Activities With Unclear Relations With Health

Clinicians may find themselves assessing or considering a final group of activities when treating patients. For this group of R/S activities, relations with health outcomes are less clear. These include prayer, sudden turning to God for comfort, or even increasing religious service attendance. Health-relevant outcomes from these activities are somewhat unpredictable. Many individuals turn to God or R/S in times of health crisis. What is difficult to know is the extent that this behavior actually helps with coping. Findings that increased prayer, for example, relates to increased symptom profiles are not informative. It is well understood that people pray when things are going poorly, but this does not answer the question of the effects of that prayer on these individuals. Masters and Spielmans (2007) reviewed the existing research in this particular area, but it is clear that much more needs to be done to untangle these complex relationships. The effectiveness of prayer and why some people turn to prayer when their health declines, and others do not, remain important questions. Are certain ways of praying more beneficial than others? Does the individual's prayer and faith history matter? Though it may be a relatively common human tendency to turn to God when health fails, does one's premorbid relationship with God influence outcomes? In other words, does it matter whether one has been close to God during times of good health in terms of how effective prayer will be as a coping strategy during poor health? The answers are not yet known, but clinicians would be wise to investigate all aspects of these questions when working with patients. It seems that prayer, for some, can be a calming and effective coping strategy and, for others, it may be a clear indication of their desperation and emotional pain. The same could be said for the other behaviors discussed in this chapter.

Working with awareness of these research findings and the possible mechanisms that influence them, therapists can ethically and sensitively assess and work with patients for whom R/S is relevant for their health condition. In this way, therapists may join clients in the common pursuit of better health.

## CASE STUDY

This case is of a 30-year-old White male who was overweight, lived alone, and worked at a light manual labor job. At work he injured his wrist and subsequently experienced pain in the wrist and decreased functionality, and eventually was forced on to workers' compensation. After several months, he had surgery on the wrist and though initially he experienced relief, pain returned greater than before. He was explicitly angry at his boss for "making me work so hard and being such a jerk" and his surgeon for "botching the operation." It seemed likely that he was angry at God as well, although this was not stated. He was also a long-time member of a faith community and attended services weekly, but in his particular religion, weekly attendance at services was not a sign of involvement but rather met only minimal expectations. Thus, based on his faith's practices, his involvement was peripheral, even though his church connections and faith clearly were important to him. During one particularly poignant session, he described how members of the church came to visit him, but he hid himself in the bedroom and refused to see them even though it was obvious to all that he was home. He explained that they probably did not really want to visit him and were only doing their "church duty." If they really cared, they would call him later, which they did not. Furthermore, although he wore prominent braces on his wrist, he failed to follow through with physical therapy, and consultation with his surgeon revealed that the braces were counterproductive to his healing. They were, however, a visible communication that he was injured.

### Church Involvement and Therapist Understanding

This young man had many difficulties that he was dealing with of both psychological and physical natures. It also was clear that his church was an important aspect of his life, but it was unclear how helpful or perhaps harmful his church and religious experiences were in relation to his physical healing, functioning, and psychological health. For example, his only important social contacts were through church, and yet he found these unfulfilling. To engage this issue therapeutically, it was essential to understand the church-cultural milieu in which this patient lived. At first reading, his somewhat bizarre behavior when the church members came to visit and subsequent explanation that they were only doing their duty may seem pathological. But in his faith, church members are assigned to visit those who are ill and, indeed, the church members who came to visit were doing so on that basis. They did not have a meaningful personal relationship with the patient. Knowledge of this dynamic helped the therapist acknowledge a degree of legitimacy to the patient's interpretation of the event, and this, in turn, helped establish the therapist as a helper who was not prone to reflexively side with the church members. Yet, the patient's behavior also had to be addressed. Behaving in this manner was not going to build strong social contacts and likely would have the opposite effect. Working within a cognitive–behavioral framework, his thoughts and actions surrounding church members and their reasons for visiting were challenged. Ultimately, he was able to grasp the counterproductive nature of his behavior and recognize that even though these individuals were performing a church "duty," it still was possible that they cared for him and that he could develop a closer relationship with them, but not from behind a closed door.

### Patient Anger and Therapy Process

Resolution of his anger was another important therapeutic goal. The expressed anger surrounding his current situation was the continuation of a long-term pattern of distrust and anger in interpersonal relationships. This was not a simple problem to solve and, indeed, complete success was not achieved. To address it, the therapist had to form a strong therapeutic bond with the patient and then, within that context, focus on the therapeutic process and the role that anger played within that relationship. This relationship developed by empathically listening and understanding the recitation of the many conflicts in the patient's life, but this alone was not likely to produce change. Many times, these discussions led to issues of lack of intimacy, loneliness, and essential separation from God and others. This gave power to the relationship, and the therapist was able to model a caring other while simultaneously helping the patient understand, in a healthy manner, the limitations inherent in human relations. Eventually, conversation turned to God and His (for this patient God assumed male gender) involvement in the patient's life. By virtue of the therapeutic relationship, the patient was able to begin to conceive that God, indeed, may care for the patient in a way beyond human ability, but this did not mean that God would necessarily eliminate pain or suffering from the patient's life and the presence of such was not necessarily an indicator of punishment or failure on the part of the patient. In this light, great figures from the Bible were discussed as well as more modern people of faith and the suffering they experienced (e.g., both Billy Graham and Pope John Paul experiencing Parkinson's disease). The patient agreed that it was unlikely that God was punishing these other believers and was helped to believe that, at least to some degree, the same might be true of him.

### Therapeutic Reflections

Many other concerns had to be addressed with this patient, but space prohibits a further discussion. This case demonstrates a couple important points regarding R/S and therapy in the context of pain and illness. First, although the therapist was *not* a member of the patient's religious community, he had a thorough understanding of it from both theological and social perspectives. Both are important. Members of religious groups are influenced by both and although related, they are not isomorphic. It is important to be able to perceive the similarities and differences and understand how the patient interprets and moves between these constructs. A major part of this patient's difficulty was in the interpersonal sphere, including God. To simply tell the patient that God loved and cared for him was not likely to be effective; he had heard this many times, and it seemed only to lead to doubt about both the message and the messengers (i.e., fellow congregants). Instead, the therapist modeled a different kind of relationship in session with the patient. This relationship had limits and these were openly and frankly discussed, but it also had warmth and caring. This allowed the patient to then be more receptive when the conversation of others and God became the focus and gave the therapist leverage to challenge long-held but dysfunctional expectations and beliefs about both. Finally, knowledge of the lives of important religious people both from scripture and current culture broadened the conversation and allowed for cognitive intervention around the topic of whether pain and suffering were indicative of God's punishment. Eventually, the patient realized that although he emotionally "wanted" to maintain this familiar understanding of the world, the facts simply were too persuasive to the contrary.

## CONCLUSION

This chapter discussed issues of R/S and their relevance for patients experiencing physical health concerns. Times of illness or injury are particularly stressful and patients often turn to their religious faith to cope with and make sense of their situation. This presents a unique and poignant opportunity for the trained and sensitive therapist to work within the religious–cultural framework of the patient to achieve important and lasting psychological and physical benefits.

## CHAPTER SUMMARY

- Increased interest in R/S and health are due to a greater appreciation of cultural influences and higher quality epidemiological and meta analytic studies.

- Studies conducted with many different religious groups around the world demonstrate a beneficial effect of R/S on rates of mortality. This effect may be pronounced for particular groups (e.g., African Americans).
- Evidence suggests a beneficial relationship between R/S and morbidity that is, at least in part, accounted for by greater engagement in a healthy lifestyle among individuals higher in R/S.
- Some evidence suggests that church attendance temporally predicts increased engagement in healthy behaviors.
- Relations between R/S and secondary prevention are complex and indicate that some aspects of R/S may be beneficial (e.g., daily spiritual experiences), whereas others may be harmful (e.g., negative religious coping).
- Practitioners working with medically ill patients need to perform a functional analysis of the patients' R/S practices and their relation with health and behavior outcomes.
- Several assessment instruments are available for measuring R/S and various dimensions of it. Although most were developed for research use, they are applicable in certain clinical cases.
- Pathways through which R/S may influence health include engagement and prohibition of certain behaviors, social support, and psychological coping based on R/S beliefs.
- Certain R/S practices such as prayer, turning to God for comfort, or increased religious service attendance have unclear relations with health and, in some cases, may be indicative of ineffective coping or even desperation.

## CLINICAL APPLICATION QUESTIONS

1. Do you consider R/S beliefs and practices when working with your clients? How comfortable are your interactions with the clients around these issues?
2. If you thought your client's R/S beliefs or R/S-based behaviors were related to your client's illness, would you address the issue and if so, how?
3. Clients may have R/S beliefs that are very different from your own. How would you approach R/S beliefs with these clients?
4. Perhaps you will someday have a client who has a life-limiting illness (e.g., congestive heart failure, cancer) who you think might benefit from a spiritual intervention. What factors would you consider as you deliberate about the possibility of incorporating a spiritual intervention into the treatment? How would you bring this topic into the therapy session with your client? Would you suggest to your client that this might be a beneficial therapeutic avenue?
5. Are spiritual interventions equally applicable across disease categories? Are there any particular illnesses or diseases that you would *not* want to address via R/S topics?
6. What are the potential therapeutic problems or ethical concerns with bringing up R/S topics with patients? How would you handle negative reactions from your clients?

## SUGGESTED READINGS AND RESOURCES

### Books for Psychotherapists

Koenig, H. G. (2007). *Spirituality in patient care: Why, how, when, and what.* West Conshohocken, PA: Templeton Foundation Press.

Koenig, H. G. (2008). *Medicine, religion, and health: Where science and spirituality meet.* West Conshohocken, PA: Templeton Foundation Press.

Levin, J. (2001). *God, faith, and health: Exploring the spirituality-healing connection.* New York, NY: Wiley.

### Books for Researchers (With Articles of Interest to Psychotherapists)

Koening, H. G., McCullough, M. E., & Larson, D. B. (2001). *Handbook of religion and health.* New York, NY: Oxford University Press.

### Videos

McCauley, J., & Gibbons, M.C. (Directors). (2001). *Give me strength: Spirituality in the medical encounter* [VHS]. Baltimore, MD: John Hopkins University. Retrieved from http://www.researchchannel.org/prog/displayevent.aspx?rID=3110&fID=1636

Puchalski, C. (Director). *Spiritual assessment in clinical practice* [DVD]. Washington, DC: George Washington University Medical Center. Retrieved from http://www.gwumc.edu/gwish/ficacourse/out/main.html

### Websites

Center for Spirituality and Healing, University of Minnesota. http://www.csh.umn.edu

Center for Spirituality, Theology and Health, Duke University. http://www.spiritualityandhealth.duke.edu

George Washington Institute for Spirituality and Health. http://www.gwish.org

## REFERENCES

Agrawal, M., & Dalal, A. K. (1993). Beliefs about the world and recovery from myocardial infarction. *The Journal of Social Psychology, 133*, 385–394.

Ai, A. L., Dunkle, R. E., Peterson, C., & Bolling, S .F. (1998). The role of private prayer in psychological recovery among midlife and aged patients following cardiac surgery. *The Gerontologist, 38*, 591–601.

Ai, A. L., Park, C. L., Huang, B., Rodgers, W., & Tice, T. N. (2007). Psychosocial mediation of religious coping styles: A study of short-term psychological distress following cardiac surgery. *Personality and Social Psychology Bulletin, 33*, 867–882.

Ai, A. L., Peterson, C., Bolling, S. F., & Rodgers, W. (2006). Depression, faith-based coping, and short-term postoperative global functioning in adult and older patients undergoing cardiac surgery. *Journal of Psychosomatic Research, 60*, 21–28.

Ai, A. L., Peterson, C., Tice, T. N., Huang, B., Rodgers, W., & Bolling, S. F. (2007). The influence of prayer coping on mental health among cardiac surgery patients: The role of optimism and acute distress. *Journal of Health Psychology, 12*, 580–596.

Ai, A. L., Peterson, C., Tice, T. N., Rodgers, W., Seymour, E. M., & Bolling, S. F. (2006). Differential effects of faith-based coping on physical and mental fatigue in middle-aged and older cardiac patients. *International Journal of Psychiatry in Medicine, 36*, 351–365.

Allport, G. W., & Ross, J. M. (1967). Personal religious orientation and prejudice. *Journal of Personality and Social Psychology, 5*, 432–443.
American Psychological Association. (2002). Ethical principles of psychologists and code of conduct. *American Psychologist, 57*, 1060–1073.
American Psychological Association, Commission on Accreditation. (2009). *Guidelines and principles for accreditation of programs in professional psychology*. Washington, DC: American Psychological Association.
American Psychological Association, Presidential Task Force on Evidence-Based Practice. (2006). Evidence-based practice in psychology. *American Psychologist, 61*, 271–285.
Barnes, P. M., Powell-Griner, E., McFann, K., & Nahin, R. L. (2004). Complimentary and alternative medicine use among adults: United States, 2002. *Seminars in Integrative Medicine, 2*, 54–71.
Benjamins, M. R., & Brown, C. (2004). Religion and preventative health care utilization among the elderly. *Social Science & Medicine, 58*, 109–118.
Bergin, A. E., Masters, K. S., & Richards, P. S. (1987). Religiousness and mental health reconsidered: A study of an intrinsically religious sample. *Journal of Counseling Psychology, 34*, 197–204.
Blumenthal, J. A., Babyak, M. A., Ironson, G., Thoresen, C., Powell, L., Czajkowski, S., et al. (2007). Spirituality, religion, and clinical outcomes in patients recovering from an acute myocardial infarction. *Psychosomatic Medicine, 69*, 501–508.
Buck, A. C., Williams, D. R., Musick, M. A., & Sternthal, M. J. (2009). An examination of the relationship between multiple dimensions of religiosity, blood pressure, and hypertension. *Social Science & Medicine, 68*, 314–322.
Burris, C. T. (1999). Religious orientation scale [Review]. In P. C. Hill & J. Hood (Eds.), *Measures of religiosity* (pp. 144–154). Birmingham, AL: Religious Education Press.
Chida, Y., Steptoe, A., & Powell, L. H. (2009). Religiosity/spirituality and mortality. *Psychotherapy and Psychosomatics, 78*, 81–90.
Cohen, A. B. (2009). Many forms of culture. *American Psychologist, 64*, 194–204.
Contrada, R. J., Boulifard, D. A., Hekler, E. B., Idler, E. L., Spruill, T. M., Labouvie, E. W., et al. (2008). Psychosocial factors in heart surgery: Presurgical vulnerability and post-surgical recovery. *Health Psychology, 27*, 309–319.
Contrada, R. J., Goyal, T. M., Cather, C., Rafalson, L., Idler, E. L., & Krause, T. J. (2004). Psychosocial factors in outcomes of heart surgery: The impact of religious involvement and depressive symptoms. *Health Psychology, 23*, 227–238.
Council for Training in Evidence-Based Behavioral Practice. (2009). *Evidence-based behavioral practice*. Retrieved from http://www.ebbp.org/ebbp.html
Davis-Smith, M. (2007). Implementing a diabetes prevention program in a rural African-American church. *Journal of the National Medical Association, 99*, 440–446.
Edman, J. L., & Koon, T. Y. (2000). Mental illness beliefs in Malaysia: Ethnic and intergenerational comparisons. *International Journal of Social Psychiatry, 46*, 101–109.
Ellison, C. G., & George, L. K. (1994). Religious involvement, social ties, and social support in a southeastern community. *Journal for the Scientific Study of Religion, 33*, 46–61.
Enstrom, J. E. (1989). Health practices and cancer mortality among active California Mormons. *Journal of the National Cancer Institute, 81*, 1807–1814.
Enstrom, J. E., & Breslow, L. (2008). Lifestyle and reduced mortality among active California Mormons, 1980–2004. *Preventive Medicine: An International Journal Devoted to Practice and Theory, 46*, 133–136.
Fetzer Institute. (1999). *Multidimensional measurement of Religiousness/Spirituality for use in health research: A report of the Fetzer Institute/National Institute on Aging working group*. Kalamazoo, MI: Author.

Fitchett, G., Murphy, P. E., Kim, J., Gibbons, J. L., Cameron, J. R., & Davis, J. A. (2004). Religious struggle: Prevalence, correlates and mental health risks in diabetic, congestive heart failure, and oncology patients. *International Journal of Psychiatry in Medicine, 34,* 179–196.

Friedlander, Y., Kark, J. D., & Stein, Y. (1986). Religious orthodoxy and myocardial infarction in Jerusalem: A case-control study. *International Journal of Cardiology, 10,* 33–41.

George, L. K., Ellison, C. G., & Larson, D. B. (2002). Explaining the relationships between religious involvement and health. *Psychological Inquiry, 13,* 190–200.

Giaquinto, S., Spiridigliozzi, C., & Caracciolo, B. (2007). Can faith protect from emotional distress after stroke? *Stroke, 38,* 993–997.

Gillum, R. F. (2005). Frequency of attendance at religious services and cigarette smoking in American women and men: The third national health and nutrition examination survey. *Preventive Medicine, 41,* 607–613.

Gillum, R. F. (2006a). Frequency of attendance at religious services and leisure-time physical activity in American women and men: The third national health and nutrition examination survey. *Annals of Behavioral Medicine, 31,* 30–35.

Gillum, R. F. (2006b). Frequency of attendance at religious services, overweight, and obesity in American women and men: The third national health and nutrition examination survey. *Annals of Epidemiology, 16,* 655–660.

Gillum, R. F., & Ingram, D. D. (2006). Frequency of attendance at religious services, hypertension, and blood pressure: The third national health and nutrition examination survey. *Psychosomatic Medicine, 68,* 382–385.

Goldbourt, U., Yaari, S., & Medalie, J. H. (1993). Factors predictive of long-term coronary heart disease mortality among 10,059 male Israeli civil servants and municipal employees. *Cardiology, 82,* 100–121.

Gorsuch, R. L., & McPherson, S. E. (1989). Intrinsic/extrinsic measurement: I/E-revised and single-item scales. *Journal for the Scientific Study of Religion, 28,* 348–354.

Hall, D. E. (2006). Religious attendance: More cost-effective than Lipitor? *The Journal of the American Board of Family Medicine, 19,* 103–109.

Harris, A. H. S., & Thoresen, C. E. (2005). Volunteering is associated with delayed mortality in older people: Analysis of the longitudinal study of aging. *Journal of Health Psychology, 10,* 739–752.

Hill, P. C. (2005). Measurement in the psychology of religion and spirituality: Current status and evaluation. In R. F. Paloutzian & C. L. Park (Eds.), *The handbook of the psychology of religion & spirituality* (pp. 43–61). New York, NY: Guilford Press.

Hill, T. D., Ellison, C. G., Burdette, A. M., & Musick, M. A. (2007). Religious involvement and healthy lifestyles: Evidence from a survey of Texas adults. *Annals of Behavioral Medicine, 34,* 217–222.

Holt, C. L., Lukwago, S. N., & Kreuter, M. W. (2003). Spirituality, breast cancer beliefs and mammography utilization among urban African American women. *Journal of Health Psychology, 8,* 383–396.

Hummer, R. A., Rogers, R. G., Nam, C. B., & Ellison, C. G. (1999). Religious involvement and U.S. adult mortality. *Demography, 36,* 273–285.

Idler, E. L., Musick, M. A., Ellison, C. G., George, L. K., Krause, N., Ory, M. G., et al. (2003). Measuring multiple dimensions of religion and spirituality for health research. *Research on Aging, 25,* 327–365.

Ironson, G., Stuetzle, R., & Fletcher, M. A. (2006). An increase in religiousness/spirituality occurs after HIV diagnosis and predicts slower disease progression over 4 years in people with HIV. *Journal of General Internal Medicine, 21,* S62–SS68.

Jarvis, G. K., & Northcott, H. C. (1987). Religion and differences in morbidity and mortality. *Social Science & Medicine, 25*, 813–824.

Kao, T., Chen, P., Hsieh, C., Chiang, H., Tsang, L., … & Chen, W. (2009). Correlations between spiritual beliefs and health-related quality of life of chronic hemodialysis patients in Taiwan. *Artificial Organs, 33*, 576–579.

Kark, J. D., Shemi, G., Friedlander, Y., & Martin, O. (1996). Does religious observance promote health? Mortality in secular vs religious kibbutzim in Israel. *American Journal of Public Health, 86*, 341–346.

Kern, M. L., & Friedman, H. S. (2008). Do conscientious individuals live longer? A quantitative review. *Health Psychology, 27*, 505–512.

King, M., Speck, P., & Thomas, A. (1994). Spiritual and religious beliefs in acute illness: Is this a feasible area for study? *Social Science & Medicine, 38*, 631–636.

King, M., Speck, P., & Thomas, A. (1995). The royal free interview for religious and spiritual beliefs: Development and standardization. *Psychological Medicine, 25*, 1125–1134.

King, M., Speck, P., & Thomas, A. (1999). The effect of spiritual beliefs on outcome from illness. *Social Science & Medicine, 48*, 1291–1299.

King, M., Speck, P., & Thomas, A. (2001). The royal free interview for spiritual and religious beliefs: Development and validation of a self-report version. *Psychological Medicine, 31*, 1015–1023.

Kirkpatrick, L. A. (1989). A psychometric analysis of the Allport-Ross and Feagin measures of intrinsic-extrinsic religious orientation. In D. O. Moberg & M. L. Lynn (Eds.), *Research in the social scientific study of religion* (pp. 1–31). Greenwich, CT: JAI Press.

Koenig, L. B., & Vaillant, G. E. (2009). A prospective study of church attendance and health over the lifespan. *Health Psychology, 28*, 117–124.

Krause, N. (2009). Church-based volunteering, providing informal support at church, and self-rated health in late life. *Journal of Aging and Health, 21*, 63–84.

Krupski, T. L., Kwan, L., Fink, A., Sonn, G. A., Maliski, S., & Litwin, M. S. (2006). Spirituality influences health related quality of life in men with prostate cancer. *Psycho-Oncology, 15*, 121–131.

la Cour, P., Avlund, K., & Schultz-Larsen, K. (2006). Religion and survival in a secular region. A twenty year follow-up of 734 Danish adults born in 1914. *Social Science & Medicine, 62*, 157–164.

Lahey, B. B. (2009). Public health significance of neuroticism. *American Psychologist, 64*, 241–256.

Larson, D. B., Larson, S. S., & Koenig, H. G. (2002). Mortality and religion/spirituality: A brief review of the research. *The Annals of Pharmacotherapy, 36*, 1090–1098.

Levin, J., Chatters, L. M., & Taylor, R. J. (2005). Religion, health and medicine in African Americans: Implications for physicians. *Journal of the National Medical Association, 97*, 237–249.

Levin, J. S., & Vanderpool, H. Y. (1987). Is frequent religious attendance really conducive to better health? Toward an epidemiology of religion. *Social Science & Medicine, 24*, 589–600.

Luskin, F. (2000). Review of the effect of spiritual and religious factors on mortality and morbidity with a focus on cardiovascular and pulmonary disease. *Journal of Cardiopulmonary Rehabilitation, 20*, 8–15.

Lyon, J. L., Wetzler, H. P., Gardner, J. W., Klauber, M. R., & Williams, R. R. (1978). Cardiovascular mortality in Mormons and non-Mormons in Utah, 1969–1971. *American Journal of Epidemiology, 108*, 357–366.

Masters, K. S. (2007). Religiosity/spirituality and behavioral medicine: Investigations concerning the integration of spirit with body. *Journal of Behavioral Medicine, 30*, 287–289.

Masters, K. S. (in press). Religion, spirituality, and cardiovascular disease. In W. Kop, L. Katzel, & S. Waldstein (Eds.), *Handbook of cardiovascular behavioral medicine*. New York, NY: Springer.

Masters, K. S., & Bergin, A. E. (1992). Religious orientation and mental health. In J. F. Schumaker (Ed.), *Religion and mental health* (pp. 221–232). New York, NY: Oxford University Press.

Masters, K. S., Carey, K. B., Maisto, S. A., Caldwell, P. E., France, C. R., & Himawan, L. (2009). Psychometric evaluation of the brief multidimensional measure of religiousness/spirituality among college students. *The International Journal for the Psychology of Religion, 19*, 106–120.

Masters, K. S., & Spielmans, G. I. (2007). Prayer and health: Review, meta-analysis, and research agenda. *Journal of Behavioral Medicine, 30*, 329–338.

Masters, K. S., & Wallston, K. A. (2005). Canonical correlation reveals important relations between health locus of control, coping, affect, and values. *Journal of Health Psychology, 10*, 719–731.

McCoubrie, R., & Davies, A. (2006). Is there a correlation between spirituality and anxiety and depression in patients with advanced cancer? *Supportive Care in Cancer, 14*, 379–385.

McCullough, M. (2001). Religious involvement and mortality: Answers and more questions. *Faith and health: Psychological perspectives.* (pp. 53–74). New York, NY: Guilford Press.

McCullough, M. E., Hoyt, W. T., Larson, D. B., Koenig, H. G., & Thoresen, C. (2000). Religious involvement and mortality: A meta-analytic review. *Health Psychology, 19*, 211–222.

McCullough, M. E., Tsang, J., & Brion, S. (2003). Personality traits in adolescence as predictors of religiousness in early adulthood: Findings from the Terman longitudinal study. *Personality and Social Psychology Bulletin, 29*, 980–991.

McCullough, M. E., & Willoughby, B. L. B. (2009). Religion, self-regulation, and self-control: Associations, explanations, and implications. *Psychological Bulletin, 135*, 69–73.

McIntosh, D., & Spilka, B. (1990). Religion and physical health: The role of personal faith and control beliefs. *Research in the Social Scientific Study of Religion, 2*, 167–194.

Neff, J. A. (2006). Exploring the dimensionality of "religiosity" and "spirituality" in the Fetzer multidimensional measure. *Journal for the Scientific Study of Religion, 32*, 69–89.

Oman, D., & Thoresen, C. E. (2002). Does religion cause health? Differing interpretations and diverse meanings. *Journal of Health Psychology, 7*, 365–380.

Oman, D., Thoresen, C. E., & McMahon, K. (1999). Volunteerism and mortality among the community-dwelling elderly. *Journal of Health Psychology, 4*, 301–316.

O'Reilly, D., & Rosato, M. (2008). Religious affiliation and mortality in northern Ireland: Beyond catholic and protestant. *Social Science & Medicine, 66*, 1637–1645.

Oxman, T. E., Freeman, D. H., & Manheimer, E. D. (1995). Lack of social participation or religious strength and comfort as risk factors for death after cardiac surgery in the elderly. *Psychosomatic Medicine, 57*, 5–15.

Pargament, K. I., Kennell, J., Hathaway, W., & Grevengoed, N. (1988). Religion and the problem-solving process. Three styles of coping. *Journal for the Scientific Study of Religion, 27*, 90–104.

Park, C. L., Edmondson, D., Hale-Smith, A., & Blank, T. O. (2009). Religiousness/spirituality and health behaviors in younger adult cancer survivors: Does faith promote a healthier lifestyle? *Journal of Behavioral Medicine, 32*, 582–591.

Park, C. L., Moehl, B., Fenster, J. R., Suresh, D. P., & Bliss, D. (2008). Religiousness and treatment adherence in congestive heart failure patients. *Journal of Religion, Spirituality & Aging, 20*, 249–266.

Pew Research Center. (2008). *U.S. religious landscape survey*. Washington, DC: Author.

Piedmont, R. L., Mapa, A. T., & Williams, J. E. G. (2007). A factor analysis of the Fetzer/NIA brief multidimensional measure of religiousness/spirituality (MMRS). *Research in the Social Scientific Study of Religion, 17*, 177–196.

Powell, L. H., Shahabi, L., & Thoresen, C. E. (2003). Religion and spirituality: Linkages to physical health. *American Psychologist, 58*, 36–52.

Rasanen, J., Kauhanan, J., Lakka, T. A., Kaplan, G. A., & Salonen, J. T. (1996). Religious affiliation and all-cause mortality: A prospective population study in middle-aged men in eastern Finland. *International Journal of Epidemiology, 25*, 1244–1249.

Samana, E. S. T., Goldenstein, P. T., Ribeiro, L. D. M., Lewin, F., Filha, E. S. V., Soares, H. P., et al. (2004). Praying correlates with higher quality of life: Results from a survey on complementary/alternative medicine use among a group of Brazilian cancer patients. *Sao Paulo Medical Journal, 122*, 60–63.

Samuel-Hodge, C., Keyserling, T. C., Park, S., Johnston, L. F., Gizlice, Z., & Bangdiwala, S. I. (2009). A randomized trial of a church-based diabetes self-management program for African Americans with Type 2 diabetes. *The Diabetes Educator, 35*, 439–454.

Saroglou, V., & Fiasse, L. (2003). Birth order, personality, and religion: A study among young adults from a three-sibling family. *Personality and Individual Differences, 35*, 19–29.

Saroglou, V., & Munoz-García, A. (2008). Individual differences in religion and spirituality: An issue of personality traits and/or values. *Journal for the Scientific Study of Religion, 47*, 83–101.

Saucier, G., & Skrzypińska, K. (2006). Spiritual but not religious? evidence for two independent dispositions. *Journal of Personality, 74*, 1257–1292.

Seybold, K. S. (1999). The royal free interview for religious and spiritual beliefs [review]. In P. C. Hill & J. Hood (Eds.), *Measures of Religiosity* (pp. 351–357). Birmingham, AL: Religious Education Press.

Smith, T. B., McCullough, M. E., & Poll, J. (2003). Religiousness and depression: Evidence for a main effect and the moderating influence of stressful life events. *Psychological Bulletin, 129*, 614–636.

Stewart, C., & Koeske, G. F. (2006). A preliminary construct validation of the multidimensional measurement of Religiousness/Spirituality instrument: A study of southern USA samples. *The International Journal for the Psychology of Religion, 16*, 181–196.

Strawbridge, W. J., Shema, S. J., Cohen, R. D., & Kaplan, G. A. (2001). Religious attendance increases survival by improving and maintaining good health behaviors, mental health, and social relationships. *Annals of Behavioral Medicine, 23*, 68–74.

Turner, L. W., Sutherland, M., Harris, G. J., & Barber, M. (1995). Cardiovascular health promotion in north Florida African-American churches. *Health Values: The Journal of Health Behavior, Education & Promotion, 19*, 3–9.

Wallston, K. A., Malcarne, V. L., Flores, L., Hansdottir, I., Smith, C. A., Stein, M. J., et al. (1999). Does God determine your health? The God Locus of Health Control Scale. *Cognitive Therapy and Research, 23*, 131–142.

Wallston, K. A., Wallston, B. S., & DeVellis, R. (1978). Development of the multidimensional health locus of control (MHLC) scales. *Health Education Monographs, 6*, 160–170.

Welton, G. L., Adkins, A. G., Ingle, S. L., & Dixon, W. A. (1996). God control: The fourth dimension. *Journal of Psychology and Theology, 24*, 13–25.

Yanez, B., Edmondson, D., Stanton, A. L., Park, C. L., Kwan, L., Ganz, P. A., et al. (2009). Facets of spirituality as predictors of adjustment to cancer: Relative contributions of having faith and finding meaning. *Journal of Consulting and Clinical Psychology, 77*, 730–741.

Yeager, D. M., Glei, D. A., Au, M., Lin, H., Sloan, R. P., & Weinstein, M. (2006). Religious involvement and health outcomes among older persons in Taiwan. *Social Science & Medicine, 63*, 2228–2241.

Zhang, W. (2008). Religious participation and mortality risk among the oldest old in china. *The Journals of Gerontology: Series B: Psychological Sciences and Social Sciences, 63*, S293–SS297.

# 15

# *Bridging the Gap Between Research and Practice in the Psychology of Religion and Spirituality*

Kari A. O'Grady, Everett L. Worthington, Jr., and Jamie D. Aten

The fields are ripe, already to harvest.

(John 4:35)

Many outstanding books have been written addressing research in the psychology of religion and spirituality (see Hood, Hill, & Spilka, 2009; Paloutzian & Park, 2005) making significant contributions to the field. We designed this book not only to complement this ever-growing body of research, but also and *especially* to integrate the research of the psychology of religion and spirituality into clinical practice. We think it is essential that psychotherapeutic assessment and intervention be supported by sound research findings within all areas of psychology and that the current boom of research in the psychology of religion and spirituality provides fertile ground for the expansion of evidence-based clinical interventions. The integration of research and practice within the psychology of religion and spirituality is not only a therapeutically responsible movement, but it also promotes respect and acceptance for the psychology of religion and spirituality within the general body of psychology.

Psychologists interested in the study of religious and spiritual experience in individuals and communities have had to exert tremendous effort to overcome derogatory perceptions among their peers and to earn respect as viable members of the field. For example, a poll conducted with members of the American Psychological Association (APA) in the 1980s revealed that members of APA ranked Division 36 (then known as Psychologists Interested in Religious Issues) last among the then 41 divisions (Harari & Peters, 1987). A general antireligious bias permeated the field, with the majority of psychologists opposed to the inclusion of spiritual and religious issues in psychology (Slife & Reber, 2009).

Psychology has not always regarded the study of spirituality and religious concerns as inferior to other psychological constructs. In fact, most of the founding fathers of psychology explored issues of spirituality and religiosity, considering these issues to be important and obvious aspects of the human experience (Wuff, 1997). However, during the early and mid-20th century, psychologists adopted the assumptions of modern-day science to be considered a valid branch of scientific investigation. At this time, the rise of behaviorism and the distancing from religious dogma, along with other movements in the field, dislocated religion and spirituality from its position within the field (O'Grady & Richards, 2010; Richards & Bergin, 2005). This position was evidenced by the dearth of psychological training programs and the sharp decline in literature attending to spiritual and religious issues (Belzen & Hood, 2006).

As mentioned in the introductory chapter of this volume, much effort in the later part of the 20th century and the early 21st century, resurrected spirituality and religion in psychological research. We are now in an exciting new era, marked by cutting-edge research and state-of-the art clinical advancements. This book would not have been possible if it were not for the early pioneers in the field of the psychology of religion and spirituality, as well as for those who followed, who through their personal determination brought religion and spirituality from the fringe to the front of many professional conversations.

## USING RESEARCH IN YOUR PRACTICE

We now transition into a practical evaluation of the contributions of this text. As you have read through the present volume, you have seen our effort to translate basic research findings in this important multicultural field of the psychology of religion and spirituality into firm recommendations useful in your practice of clinical or counseling psychology. Our first hope is that you have found these chapters useful. But only you can evaluate this. Consider the following questions:

- Do you have a good sense of how religious and spiritually oriented people develop (Desrosiers, Chapter 2, this volume) and how they are shaped by spiritual and mystical experiences (O'Grady & Bartz, Chapter 7, this volume)?
- Do you now understand people's basic religious and spiritual makeup—their personality (Miller & Worthington, Chapter 5, this volume), their identity as a religious or spiritual person (Wink, Adler, & Dillon, Chapter 3, this volume), their sense of meaning (Slattery & Park, Chapter 8, this volume), their image of God or the sacred (Moriarty & Davis, Chapter 6,

this volume), and the family influences on their development and current behavior (Wiggins, Chapter 12, this volume)?

- When the religious or spiritual client does things that are in line with their religion or spirituality but off the beaten path of secular culture, do you better understand their religious or spiritual motivations (Hill, Smith, & Sandage, Chapter 4, this volume)?
- When people bring up spiritual struggles, do you have a better sense of where those struggles come from and how to deal with them sensitively (Murray-Swank & Murray-Swank, Chapter 9, this volume) and can you see how it leads either to psychopathology (Toussaint, Webb, & Keltner, Chapter 13, this volume) or mental health (Masters & Hooker, Chapter 14, this volume)?
- Can you see how religious and spiritual factors affect people's physical health as well as their mental health (Masters & Hooker, Chapter 14, this volume)?
- People who grace the door of the clinical office typically have tried to cope and might have received aid or might have exacerbated their problems through their religious and spiritual coping efforts (Krumrei & Rosmarin, Chapter 10, this volume). Do you now better understand those mechanisms?
- As people cope with the stresses of life and of their intrapersonal and interpersonal conflicts, can you see how forgiveness might be of benefit both intrapersonally and interpersonally (Worthington et al., Chapter 11, this volume)?

If you can answer yes to some, most, or all of those questions, we believe that we have succeeded in our first goal of the book. We have two other goals as well for this book, however. These two other goals are more academic and intellectual. First, we want to show how the psychology of religion has contributed to and strengthens the scientist–practitioner model by providing an addition of understanding religious diversity and experience to the training and practice of clinical psychology. Second, we want you to see that, even as our authors have attempted to translate the existing findings of the psychology of religion into usable clinical recommendations and understanding of the root of intervention, our authors have added conceptual insight to the field of the psychology of religion and spirituality through thoughtful reviews. It is to these two additional goals that we turn our attention now.

## CONTRIBUTIONS OF THE PSYCHOLOGY OF RELIGION AND SPIRITUALITY TO PSYCHOLOGY

Some psychologists suggest that the increase of quality books, journal articles, special additions, and course offerings on the topic of religion and spirituality in mainstream publications and settings has generated a deeper level of respect for the necessity and contributions of the psychology of religion and spirituality (Emmons & Paloutzian, 2003; Paloutzian & Park, 2005). A little over a decade ago, Hill (1999) challenged psychologists of religion and spirituality to consider ways in which the broader field informs understanding about religious and spiritual experiences and how the study of spirituality and religion adds to an understanding of basic psychological and social processes. He asserted that the psychology of religion and spirituality must demonstrate its value by empirically advancing knowledge of cognitive and affective processes, generalizing new insights into personality findings, and providing a moral frame of reference for investigating social and psychological dynamics. We add that it will demonstrate its contribution when it evidences clinical usefulness in terms of therapeutic processes and outcomes.

Authors in this volume have attempted to respond to Hill's (1999) challenge for psychologists of religion and spirituality to mark their contribution within the field of psychology. Across the chapters emerges the theme that the psychology of religion and spirituality uniquely contributes to psychological and psychotherapeutic advancement because (a) the study of religious and spiritual experience contributes to the understanding of general psychological and social processes, and (b) the study of the psychology of religion and spirituality contributes to the understanding of distinct psychological and social processes that are not addressed in other areas of psychology, namely, the psychological and social processes of religious and spiritual experience.

For instance, motivation is a psychological process dealing with various states and drives. Psychologists of religion and spirituality contribute to the general knowledge about motivation through understanding religious and spiritual factors that contribute to various states and drives. In this way, the field of the psychology of religion and spirituality contributes understanding to a general psychological and social process. Additionally, the psychology of religion and spirituality contributes understanding about why people are motivated to be religious or spiritual, with the experience of religiosity or spirituality being a distinct psychological and social process (see Hill, Smith, & Sandage, Chapter 4, this volume). Another example of these themes is illustrated in Chapter 5, which addressed connections between personality, religion, and spirituality. Miller and Worthington share research that demonstrates a relationship between spirituality and religion and personality traits (e.g., religious maturity related to high openness) and that shows unique variance of spiritual and religious variables on psychological constructs above and beyond the effects of personality factors alone across cultures. The authors also present research that suggests that there may be characteristics within infant temperament that incline people towards spirituality and religion (see Miller & Worthington, Chapter 5, this volume).

Chapters in this volume also demonstrate that the psychology of religion and spirituality provides insight about possible deleterious effects of some approaches to spirituality and religion that contribute to the general psychological understanding of pathology and that lends specific insight into psychological contributors to spiritual and religious dysfunctions (see Toussaint, Webb, & Keltner, Chapter 13, this volume, and Murray-Swank & Murray-Swank, Chapter 9, this volume). For example, for those experiencing trauma, negative forms of religious coping were related to greater distress and slower recovery in psychological functioning, and negative religious appraisals were associated with a decrease in spiritual health (see Krumrei & Rosmarin, Chapter 10, this volume). Another example in this volume provides evidence that disruptions in the development of spiritual connection may pose risks for psychopathology, particularly depression and substance abuse (understanding about general psychological constructs and processes), and that negative life events and experiences of adversity can offer opportunities for spiritual and religious development or arrest, depending on the nature of the religious and spiritual approach utilized (understanding about religious and spiritual constructs and processes; see Desrossiers, Chapter 2, this volume).

Not all topics within the psychology of religion are as apparent in their contributions in the ways described in Chapter 2 and Chapter 10. Some areas of study appear unique to religious and spiritual experience (e.g., spiritually transcendent experiences and religious conversion), contributing to our understanding about religious and spiritual experience. These types of topics can stir critics to contend that psychologists should not be dealing with theological concerns or to declare the oft-used adage that "psychology is not in the business of proving God." Even such topics as spiritually transcendent experiences contribute to the broader knowledge of psychological and social processes that lead to mental health or psychopathology. Thus, in most cases, studies dealing with what appear to be primarily religious and spiritual phenomena are not trying to prove the existence of the divine, but rather are using psychological science in an attempt to better understand the way in which our clients experience and understand the sacred. For instance, authors in this text have reported that people who encounter spiritually transcendent experiences tend to undergo positive mental health changes such as value shifts, reduction in anxiety symptoms, decrease in depressive symptoms, increase in social activism, improved emotional regulation, and increase in life satisfaction, in addition to improvements in their relationships with the sacred (see O'Grady & Bartz, Chapter 7, this volume).

## FUTURE DIRECTIONS FOR THE PSYCHOLOGY OF RELIGION AND SPIRITUALITY

We believe that progress in the field is best achieved when clinical approaches are developed upon the basis of sound research, and when clinical work informs such research. This perspective hearkens to the scientist–practitioner model commonly employed in psychological training programs.

### Scientist–Practitioner Model

The scientist–practitioner model has a longstanding history that includes controversy about its utility and appropriateness for clinical training programs. Much of the controversy revolves around the feasibility of psychologist and other mental professionals being able to split themselves into two even components: half scientist, half clinician. Research indicates that few psychologists are able to maintain this dualism. Time constraints as well as personal interest and aptitude limit active engagement in both roles. Although the majority of graduate students enter graduate programs with clinical interests and little or no interest in research, most do increase their enthusiasm some after exposure to research courses during their education (Gelso, 2006).

Conversely, academic psychologists spend only about 12% of their time in the clinic, and nearly 50% of nonpracticing psychologists report no interest in clinical work at all, perhaps indicating that those attracted to academic positions may be more scientifically minded (Larson & Larson, 2003). These disparities create substantial limitations for the field in that clinicians may be underinformed about scientific evidences and advancement, ultimately leading to ineffective and sometimes unethical practice, and researchers may be wasting their resources conducting research detached from clinical insight and application. Although it is not reasonable to assume that we can or should force individuals into a dualistic role, empirical findings should be made more assessable to clinicians and the clinic should be included in our studies. Innovations by clinicians are the impetus for advances in knowledge, and the practice of psychology adjusts with these advances in scientific findings (Belar & Aten, 2000). Thus, the scientific–practitioner model may be most effectively realized by developing collaborative relationships between clinicians and researchers, promoting a scientist–practitioner relationship rather than a scientist–practitioner individual.

The psychology of religion and spirituality may be in a prime position to model this relationship as it explores some of the most fundamental and existential aspects of human functioning. Many would argue that elements of experience, such as meaning, identity, and forgiveness, represent the very anatomy of the human psyche and are inherently intertwined with spirituality such that they cannot be understood without reference to religion and spirituality for many clients (see Slattery & Park, Chapter 8, this volume; Wink, Adler, & Dillon, Chapter 2, this volume; Worthington et al., Chapter 11, this volume). Additionally, others have suggested that the current social and political climate elevates discussion of religious and spiritual issues as one of the most important topics for psychologists to study in the 21st century (Paloutzian & Park, 2005), particularly given the heightened conflict in the world and global efforts regarding religiously motivated violence that surround religious identity.

With this in mind, we intentionally selected authors or collaborations with both clinical and research backgrounds. Each of the contributing authors provided a preview of the psychology of religion and spirituality research on their topic and intertwined this research with its clinical applicability, approaches for clinical assessment, spiritual and religious intervention strategies, and case studies. We hope you have found these helpful and informative.

These chapters represent only a select handful of potential psychology of religion and spirituality topics that could have been addressed. In our view, however, the topics selected cover some of the most fundamental concerns manifesting in psychotherapy. We also hope that the chapters we organized will provide a framework for other efforts at integrating research and practice within the psychology of religion and spirituality domain.

### Invitation for Collaboration

We encourage researchers involved in the psychology of religion and spirituality to collaborate with clinicians to explore the therapeutic utility of specific treatment orientations relative to spiritual and religious concerns. We also encourage the development of evidence-based interventions and approaches to develop new interventions that address specific religious and spiritual topics like those covered in this volume, along with the establishment of evidence-based spiritually oriented therapies. The establishment of such evidence-based approaches may best be obtained through the systematic employment of spiritual and religious assessment and outcome measures in practice. A number of promising spiritual and religious measures may be adapted for the clinic, as well as a few validated measures designed specifically for clinical practice (see Hill & Hood, 1999).

When adapting research assessment and outcome measures for clinical use, researchers and clinicians should combine their expertise and experiences to create psychometrically sound adaptations, as well as to collect data to support the advancement of evidence-based treatment across the psychology of religion and spirituality field. Along with addressing various topics of religion and spirituality, we encourage researchers and clinicians to consider religion and spirituality as an outcome variable. Likewise, we invite psychologists of religion and spirituality to integrate research and practice in the treatment of specific disorders and the understanding of particular psychological strengths. We also encourage psychologists of religion and spirituality interested in studying diverse populations to employ collaborative relationship as they explore (a) the role of spirituality and religion in these populations, and (b) the implications of these findings for the general body of psychology and for the psychological constructs of spirituality and religion.

We also invite researchers and clinicians to team up in an effort to provide research-driven clinical assessment measures and treatment strategies for populations from diverse religious backgrounds currently underrepresented in the literature (e.g., Eastern spirituality and religion).

We recommend that those interested in the psychology of spirituality and religion create interdisciplinary relationships in which researchers from various professional fields investigate psychology of religion and spirituality topics through their respective lenses and integrate their findings in a collaborative fashion. Relationships of this nature likely will provide fresh insights and multidimensional understandings about the psychology of religion and spirituality.

### Training Considerations

The academy does seem to be warming up to the notion of addressing spirituality in psychology and counselor training programs. Research shows that the majority of psychologists and counselors agree that spirituality and religion should be addressed in training, although they have difficulty articulating how that training should take place (Crook-Lyon, O'Grady, & Smith, 2005). Although many psychologists agree that spiritual and religious issues need to be addressed in training, research indicates that, in recent years, less than a third of clinical training programs offered training in spiritual and religious issues in counseling and psychotherapy (Schulte, Skinner, & Claiborn, 2002). A gap between the interests of those training and those who are being trained seems to persist. For instance, among marriage and family therapists, marriage and family therapy faculty are less supportive of including training in spiritual and religious issues than marriage and family therapists not involved in academia (Grams, Carlson, & McGeorge, 2007). Similarly, according to one study, half of the training directors indicated that they were aware of at least one student who had a major interest in spiritual and religious issues but only 23% reported awareness of a faculty member with these interests (Schulte et al., 2002).

We encourage psychologists of religion and spirituality to continue to close this gap by presenting themselves to students and faculty as people who are interested in spirituality and religion in psychotherapy, and by encouraging programs to actively incorporate training in religion and spirituality into coursework and supervision. This may be achieved by designing courses that specifically address spiritual and religious issues in counseling and psychotherapy, and by encouraging this topic to be included as subject matter in other courses.

This approach could be patterned after the movement of psychologists interested in multicultural issues who have been urging training programs to develop multicultural consideration and competency across courses along with designating specific courses to address this topic (e.g., considering issues of diversity in a supervision course as well as having a course on diversity issues in counseling).

Thus, rather than putting on a pair of lenses for multicultural issues, students would be trained to view all issues through a multicultural lens (Smith, 2004). Students could be trained to be multiculturally aware and competent counselor and psychotherapists, with spirituality and religiosity being an integral component of diversity (Crook-Lyon et al., 2005). Just as counselors' self-awareness about other multicultural issues affects their sensitivity to issues of diversity in counseling, research indicates that clinical training and the counselor's own spirituality have an impact on whether or not counselors and psychotherapists attended to spiritual themes in psychotherapy (van Asselt & Baldo Senstock, 2009). Additionally, we recommend that faculty invite clinicians who focus on spirituality and religious issues in their practice to guest lecture on the topic for faculty and students.

## CONCLUSION

The psychology of religion and spirituality is an exciting field that has gained momentum and reputation in recent years. Efforts of hundreds of courageous and ambitious researchers and clinicians have created fertile soil for future advancements in the psychology of religion and spirituality. We commend them and hope to add to their efforts. We especially express our gratitude and admiration for the contributors to this volume. We appreciate their demonstrations of research-based clinical practice that contributes to the general field of psychology in unique and important ways. Their works have enriched the soil, and we believe they have soundly responded to Hill and Bruce's (1999) call. And now we end by reissuing our own call and challenge posed throughout this book to readers—clinicians, researchers, and clinicians and researchers collaborating—to play a proactive part in further bridging the psychology of religion and spirituality gap between research and practice.

## REFERENCES

Aten, J. D., & Worthington, E. L., Jr. (2009). Next steps for clinicians in religious and spiritual therapy: An endpiece. *Journal of Clinical Psychology: In Session, 65*(2), 224–229.

Belar, C., & Aten, J. D. (2000). Scientist-practitioner not equal to science + practice: Boulder is bolder. *American Psychologist, 2,* 249–250.

Belzen, J. A., & Hood, R. W. (2006). Methodological issues in the psychology of religion: Toward another paradigm. *Journal of Psychology: Interdisciplinary and Applied, 140*(1), 5–28.

Brown, K. (2005). Does psychology of religion exist? *European Psychologist, 10,* 71–73.

Crook-Lyon, R. E., O'Grady, K. A., & Smith, T. B. (2005, August 20). *Spirituality in multicultural training: Psychologists' attitudes.* Paper presented at the annual convention of the American Psychological Association, Washington, DC.

Emmons, R. A., & Paloutzian, R. F. (2003). The psychology of religion. *Annual Review of Psychology, 54,* 377–402.

Gelso, C. J. (2006). On the making of a scientist-practitioner: A theory of research training in professional psychology. *Training and Education in Professional Psychology 1,* 3–16.

Grams, W., Carlson, T., & McGeorge, C. (2007). Integrating spirituality into family therapy training: An exploration of faculty members' beliefs. *Contemporary Family Therapy: An International Journal, 2,* 147–161.

Harari, H. & Peters, J. M. (1987). The fragmentation of psychology: Are APA divisions symptomatic? *American Psychologist, 42*(8), 822–824.

Hill, P. C., & Bruce, S. (1999). Giving religion away: What the psychology of religion has to offers psychology. *International Journal for the Psychology of Religion, 9,* 229–249.
Hill, P. C., & Hood, R. W. (1999). *Measures of religiosity.* Birmingham, AL: Religious Education Press.
Hood, R. W., Hill, P. C., & Spilka, B. (2009). *The psychology of religion: An empirical approach* (4th ed.). New York, NY: Guilford Press.
Larson, D. B., & Larson, S. B. (2003). Spirituality's potential relevance to physical and emotional health: A brief review of quantitative research. *Journal of Psychology and Theology, 31*(1), 37–51.
O'Grady, K. A., & Richards, P. S. (2010). The role of inspiration in the helping professions. *Psychology of Religion and Spirituality, 2,* 57–66.
Paloutzian, R. F., & Park, C. L. (Eds.). (2005). *Handbook of the psychology of religion and spirituality.* New York, NY: Guilford Press.
Richards, P. S., & Bergin, A. E. (2005). *Spiritual strategies for counseling and psychotherapy* (2nd ed.). Washington, DC: American Psychological Association.
Shafranske, E. P. (2003). The psychology of religion in clinical and counseling psychology. In R. A. Paloutzian & C. L. Park (Eds.), *Handbook of the psychology of religion and spirituality* (pp. 496–514). New York, NY: Guilford Press.
Shulte, D. L., Skinner, T. A., & Claiborn, C. D. (2002). Religious and spiritual issues in counseling psychology training. *Counseling Psychologist, 30,* 118–134.
Slife, B. D., & Reber, J. S. (2009). Is there a pervasive implicit bias against theism in psychology? *Journal of Theoretical & Philosophical Psychology, 2,* 63–79.
Smith, T. B. (Ed.). (2004). *Practicing multiculturalism.* Boston, MA: Pearson Education.
Tan, S.-Y. (2003). Integrating spiritual direction into psychotherapy. Ethical issues and guidelines. *Journal of Psychology and Theology, 31,* 14–23.
van Asselt, K. W., & Baldo Senstock, T. C. (2009). Influence of counselor spirituality and training on treatment focus and self-perceived competence. *Journal of Counseling and Development, 4,* 412–419.
Wuff, D. M. (1997). *Psychology of religion: Classic and contemporary* (2nd ed.). New York, NY: Wiley.

# Index

## D

## S